COMIC BOOK
ARTIST™
COLLECTION VOLUME 3

CELEBRATING THE LIVES & WORK OF THE GREAT CARTOONISTS, WRITERS, & EDITORS

WAK!
WALKING CABBAGES!!
ZOMBIES!! MORONS IN
TIGHTS!! SHEESH!! WHEN ARE
YOU @#?!%#! FANBOYS GONNA
GROW UP!!?

COMIC
ART
"For the Ce
of Con

EDITED BY JON B. COOKE • TWOMORROWS PUBLISHING • RALEIGH, NORTH CAROLINA

Dedicated to a true friend who has always believed

John Michael Crowley

COMIC BOOK ARTIST Collection, Volume Three
Compiling *Comic Book Artist* Vol. 1, #7-8, plus new material
©2005 Jon B. Cooke & TwoMorrows Publishing

TwoMorrows Publishing, 10407 Bedfordtown Drive, Raleigh, NC 27614
(919) 449-0344 • FAX: (919) 449-0327
E-Mail: twomorrow@aol.com • Web: www.twomorrows.com

ISBN 1-893905-42-X

April 2005
First Printing • Printed in Canada

"Woody" mascot illustration by J.D. King
Cover art by Michael T. Gilbert • Logo design by Arlen Schumer

Trapped In a World He Never Made

Why 1970s mainstream creators sought an '80s alternative

By its very nature, the creation of art is typically not a periodic event. It is that "certain something" which can rarely be produced on demand, under a timetable and, as in the case of comic books, it's a rarity to see it emerge from behind the trappings of genre. The bane of mainstream American funnybook publishing has always been the constraints of formula, as often talented writers and artists have been perennially forced by editorial dictums to shoehorn work into too-often palatable, pre-digested tripe served up for "safe" mass consumption. More usually, the good stuff, those comics that transcend notions of circulation and audience, come as a result of freedom, whether intended by the powers-that-be (Harvey Kurtzman at EC Comics, for instance) or by slipping it under some inattentive editor's radarscope.

But American comics, the newsstand variety of the last century, were not about producing art, but rather about the business of making money. The odds inherent in any enterprise tell us good money is on the tried 'n' true and less often with the innovative 'n' daring. But real success, both financial and critical, very often arises because something new and different invigorates an audience suddenly blissfully aware they are witnessing a fresh and clever approach that shines in comparison. Such was the case when Marvel Comics entered the 1960s.

Certainly that decade of tumult and change was dominated in U.S. comics by the success and innovation of Stan Lee's comic book company. While "Batmania" — that is, the "camp craze" fermented by the '65-67 runaway cultural hit, the *Batman* (Pow! Bam! Zap!) television series — had a significant if shortlived effect on numerous publishers getting in on the super-hero game, that boom would go bust mighty quick. Yes, the corny TV show made industry stalwart DC Comics (then called National Periodical Publications) attractive enough on a corporate level to be snatched up by media-hungry Kinney National Services (which, by also purchasing Warner Brothers Studios, would become the largest media conglomerate in world history, called until recently AOL/Time-Warner), its once-dominant comic book sales were losing ground quickly to the House of Ideas.

What would take years for staid, conservative DC to understand and finally react to (probably years too late) was that Stan, Jack Kirby, Steve Ditko, and the other Marvel Bullpenners were creating magazines that exuded… well, the essence of cool, were in tune with the changing times (both relevant and irreverent) and, most importantly, the comics of Spider-Man and company were explosively fun and spoke to the readers, not down at them. By melding the soap opera with the culture of youth by way of the storytelling and artistic geniuses of Kirby and Ditko, Stan's titles began appealing to an older, hipper crowd, which even included college kids, and for readers who had so faithfully picked up issue after issue of Mort Weisinger's *Superman* family comics, the Marvel appeal was just too irresistible.

Unfortunately, overall readership for the entire industry was dropping as the field would increasingly marginalize itself into a one-genre medium: super-heroes. The mainstream, those boys & girls — *and* men & women — once enthralled by romance, war, horror and humor comics, drifted away as those other genres passed on, and only dyed-in-the-wool fanboys stuck around for the clobberfests. Sadly, the devoted who remained were too often oblivious to the only real innovation and excitement gaining headway within sequential art: the uninhibited and drug-saturated underground comix spewing forth from the West Coast.

Sold to Cadence Industries itself in the same late '60s merger spree, Marvel was suddenly freed from the distribution shackles imposed by the Distinguished Competition, and the imprint's output simply exploded, with spin-offs and reprint titles choking the market, squeezing out all rivals and by the mid-'70s giving even Warren Publications a run for its money by flooding the black-&-white magazine field with an excess of horror and barbarian comics.

Becoming stymied by its endless attempts to replicate the Stan Lee approach in producing comics with pizzazz — only this time without essential collaborators Kirby and Ditko, and all too often without The Man himself (whose presence in the office was less and less and whose name in the books became regulated to the "Stan Lee Presents" masthead and the Soapbox column) — Marvel itself began suffering from lethargy and, yep, a creeping dullness. But the sheer volume of material necessary to fill all these new pages of all these new titles would usher in a creative renaissance of sorts.

Sure, lots of the Marvel line-up by the mid-'70s was drek, but diamonds in the rough would emerge. So much new material was needed to feed the company's coveted newsstand space and, with an understaffed Bullpen and revolving-door editors-in-chief overburdened beyond imagining, it was through benign neglect that a few genuinely innovative storytellers made it to the surface, nurturing their own idiosyncratic perspectives and infusing their odd, overlooked titles with a sincere concern for their characters. These writers, notable among them Don McGregor, and most prominently, a sleep-deprived, bespectacled former fanboy named Steve Gerber, may have been instructed to present it like Stan, but instead they courageously blazed their own trails, writing comics like no one in America — outside of San Francisco — had ever done before. Steve took the ludicrously named Man-Thing assignment, a third-rate Heap-wannabe (one speechless and imbecilic pretender to boot! How's *that* for a scripting challenge?), and polished the series to a glorious sparkle by ignoring the lead character, focusing instead on the supporting cast to examine the human condition.

And then came Steve Gerber's Howard the Duck. In appearance the alien fowl was a Carl Barks knock-off, but in substance the surprise superstar helmed an astonishingly fresh and honest comic book, one that was mature, engrossing, terribly funny and utterly human. But the character was too good to be cast as a perennial stock player in the Marvel Universe and still remain true, and his creator knew it. A new regime, under the guise of a pathologically meddling editor-in-chief, clamped shut the revolving door, imposed narrow modes of storytelling which stifled innovation, and neglect, benign or otherwise, was gone from the House of Ideas. Only a few truly talented storytellers (chiefly, Frank Miller and Walter Simonson) would transcend the crushingly dull banality of the Jim Shooter years, but Steve Gerber would not be among them. He was too busy fighting Marvel in court for ownership of his beloved feathered creation. Anyway, the writer had long since earned his wings and opted to leave the nest, and was beginning to explore the uncharted realm of the direct-sales marketplace (albeit settling in TV animation for a long spell). But Steve had set a righteous course for an artist intent on expressing himself without restraint in the early 1980s. There was but one viable destination: the freedom of independent comics.

— *Jon B. Cooke, CBA editor*

Above: *Courtesy of John Castiglia, cover of the Dec. 13, 1976 edition of the New York City alternative newspaper, The Village Voice, which contained a feature article on Howard the Duck and his creator, then-Marvel scribe Steve Gerber. Howard the Duck ©2005 Marvel Characters, Inc. The Village Voice ©2005 the respective copyright holder.*

COMIC BOOK ARTIST
COLLECTION VOLUME 3

CBA Staff

Editor/Designer
Jon B. Cooke

Publisher
TwoMorrows
John & Pam Morrow

Contributing Editors
Roy Thomas
John Morrow

Associate Editors
Chris Knowles
David A. Roach

Transcribers
Jon B. Knutson
Sam Gafford

Proofreading
Richard Howell
John Morrow
Eric Nolen-Weathington

Logo Design, Title Originator
Arlen Schumer

Cover Art & Color
Michael T. Gilbert

Book Theme Song
"Mr. Brightside"
The Killers

CBA Mascot
WOODY
by J.D. King

Contributors

Neal Adams • Dan Adkins
Jack Adler • Rob Anderson
Tim Barnes • Mike Baron
Mike W. Barr • Al Bigley
Jerry K. Boyd • Frank Brunner
Ken Bruzenak • Rich Buckler
Kurt Busiek • John Byrne
Marc Cawiezel • Howard Chaykin
Gene Colan • Andy Cooke
Steve Englehart • Steve Gerber
Keith Giffen • Janet Gilbert
Michael T. Gilbert • Mike Grell
Paul Gulacy • Dave Hamilton
Russ Heath • Fred Hembeck
Mark Hanerfeld • Klaus Janson
Gil Kane • J.D. King
Rob Kirby • Denis Kitchen
Chris Knowles • Alan Kupperberg
Richard Kyle • Dave Lemieux
Victor Lim • Jay Lynch
Sam Maronie • Scott McCloud
Don McGregor • Doug Moench

Jim Mooney • Albert Moy
Jerry Ordway • George Pérez
Mike Ploog • David A. Roach
John Romita Sr. • Allan Rosenberg
Steve Rude • P. Craig Russell
Seanbaby • Marie Severin
Arlen Schumer • Don Simpson
art spiegelman • Frank Springer
Jim Starlin • Jim Steranko
Tom Sutton • Mike Thibodeaux
Roy Thomas • Ron Tiner
Herb Trimpe • Tom Sutton
Alex Wald • Len Wein
Dylan Williams • Barry Windsor-Smith
Tom Ziuko & all other contributors
to *CBA* volume one!

Special Thanks
Bob Beerbohm • Arnold Drake
Clay Geerdes • Charles Hatfield
Adam McGovern • George Roussos
Alex Toth • Herb Trimpe

In Appreciation
TO ALL OF YE ED'S FRIENDS AND FAMILY
WHOSE SUPPORT MAKES *CBA* POSSIBLE:
Beth Ann (Whaley) Cooke
Ben, Josh & Danny Cooke
Ina Cooke & Nick Mook
Andrew D. Cooke & Patty Willett
John & Pam Morrow
Eric Nolen-Weathington
Chris Staros & Brett Warnock
George Khoury • Chris Knowles
Chris Irving • Joe McCabe
Fred Hembeck • Don McGregor
Steven Tice • Ray Kelly
Glenn Southwick • Theresa Nobile
Jim Titus & Dave Bissell
Barbara Lien-Cooper • Tom Ziuko
Michelle Nolan • Gelb & Surratt

**Original Issues
Dedicated to:**
**Jon B. Knutson
Eden Faith Schumer
Emily Elizabeth Leslie
Phillipa Frances
Cairns**

and in Memory of:
**Gil Kane
Don Martin
Mark Hanerfeld
Pat Boyette
George Roussos
Charles Schulz**

COVER ART: *It's Mr. Monster taking on the '70s Marvel guys 'n' ghouls of the House of Idea's unforgettable horror mags line-up! Art & colors by Michael T. Gilbert, who produced this masterwork in record time! Thanks, MTG! Mr. Monster ©2005 MTG. Others ©2005 Marvel Characters, Inc.*

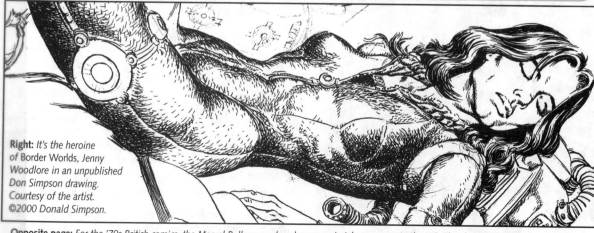

Right: *It's the heroine of Border Worlds, Jenny Woodlore in an unpublished Don Simpson drawing. Courtesy of the artist. ©2000 Donald Simpson.*

Opposite page: *For the '70s British comics, the Marvel Bullpen produced some material never seen in the U.S. The above Mike Nasser-penciled and Neal Adams-inked Vision was featured as a centerspread for the oblong weekly, The Titans. Courtesy of Tim Barnes. ©2000 Marvel Characters, Inc.*

Everybody Was *Kung Fu Watchin'*!

The Not-So-Secret Origin of Shang-Chi, Kung Fu Master!

by Jon B. Cooke

Marvel Comics, as any savvy publisher, always had an eye out for marketing trends that swept the nation and the martial arts craze of the early '70s proved no exception as it was quickly targeted by the House of Ideas. With Bruce Lee's opus *Enter the Dragon* playing to ever-widening audiences in the theatres, and David Carradine's Kwai Chang Caine character waxing philosophically before a growing TV viewership in the series *Kung Fu*, the comics publisher knew a good idea to exploit when it sniffed one. And, oddly enough, this high concept—of Shang-Chi, Master of Kung Fu—didn't emerge from Stan Lee or the suits upstairs but from two up-and-coming freelancers working in trenches of the Marvel Bullpen; and, even more surprisingly, the title, launched to cash in on what proved to be a typically short-lived craze, lasted nearly ten years with over 100 issues; but in typical *CBA* fashion, let's have the participants tell the story behind the creation of *Master of Kung Fu*, and first up is then Marvel Editor-in-Chief, Roy Thomas:

Below: *Neal Adams painting of Bruce Lee in action graces the cover of The Deadly Hands of Kung Fu #1 (June '74), Marvel's black-&-white martial arts comic book. ©2004 Marvel Characters, Inc.*

NO MAN CAN STAND AGAINST...
THE DEADLY HANDS OF KUNG FU™
ACTION STRIPS! PHOTOS! FEATURES!
BRUCE LEE
KING OF THE MARTIAL-ARTS MOVIES
SECRETS OF KUNG FU REVEALED
PIN-UP OF THE MASTER OF KUNG FU!

Comic Book Artist: *You once told me an amusing story about the genesis of* Master of Kung Fu.
Roy Thomas: Jim Starlin and Steve Englehart came to me with this idea for a book and except for suggesting that they lose a little mustache they had on the main character, I had very little to do with the concept. In the meantime, I was aware that Englehart and these guys were fans of the *Kung Fu* TV show. I saw it occasionally myself, even if I wasn't a big fan. It was an interesting show that had the youth market, but because it was a Warner show, we knew that we weren't going to get it as a comic book. We thought about it but decided that all we would do is give DC the idea to do it. DC didn't need that because Denny O'Neil and somebody else wanted to do *Kung Fu* as a comic book and I heard that they went to Carmine and told him, "Let's do *Kung Fu*. It's a Warner show, it'll be good, the kids love it, it isn't big in the ratings but it brings in the right audience." I heard that Carmine said, "We're not interested in that." So one of the guys said, "But if we don't do it, maybe Marvel will." Carmine is reputed to have said, "Don't worry. If Marvel does *Kung Fu*, we'll do *Fu Manchu*." [*laughter*] I heard this story a day or two after it allegedly took place and I didn't even care if it was true or not, because it was kind of funny. So a little later, when Starlin and Englehart came to pitch the book, my only real creative contribution was that I said, "Hey, guess who we can make Shang-Chi's father?" I thought that it would be fun to tie in another top literary character with Marvel, so we ended up securing the rights to Fu Manchu. So actually DC ended up with neither *Kung Fu* nor *Fu Manchu*.

Next, the artist/co-creator, Jim Starlin:

CBA: *Were you involved in the creation of* Master of Kung Fu?
Jim Starlin: [*laughs*] Yeah. In retrospect, that was a real mess. They had the rights to Fu Manchu, and that was added on to it at the last moment. We had been inspired by the TV series *Kung Fu*, and we were trying to talk Marvel into getting the rights to it, but Warner had it. We had Shang-Chi pretty well in development when they came along and said, "You have to add Fu Manchu." I had never read any *Fu Manchu*; I had no idea what it was about. We had to get the book out; I don't think I read it until I was most of the way through the first issue, and then I was horrified by what I had gotten connected up with! [*laughter*] The Sax Rohmer novels were the most racist things you ever wanted to read! They're *terrible*! [*laughter*]

I liked the first book; I really liked the storytelling and the layouts I did. When we were working on it, I mixed up the two British characters, and the wrong one ended up getting killed off in my notes. [*laughs*] Englehart saw this, and thought I had definitely wanted to switch the killings, so we went on with it with the wrong one being killed. This went on for years until the widow of Sax Rohmer came back at us saying, "You've got to change this" (This was long after I'd been off the book). There'd been some story where Fu Manchu had promised not to kill the one guy. So he ended up getting brought back later on. It was kind of a strange thing. I enjoyed the first issue, and I just did layouts after that, and got off it after three issues.

And, finally writer/co-creator Steve Englehart weighs in:

CBA: *What's the story behind the creation of* Master of Kung Fu?
Steve Englehart: There were a bunch of us—primarily Jim Starlin, Al Weiss, Mary Skrenes, Steve Harper, Steve Gerber, and me—who were young comic book people in Manhattan, all at

Marvel during the early '70s and we hung out together. But I was the only one who didn't live in New York City. I tried and I just didn't like it. I had grown up in the Midwest and had gone to school up in Connecticut and I really didn't want to live in a concrete city. So I moved out first to Milford, Connecticut, and then Stamford, and a lot of weekends, a bunch of people from New York would get out of the city and come to my place to party. One Saturday, Steve Harper came with the group, and after dinner we were all going to head out and go someplace; but Harper said, "Well, I'm going to stay here and watch this new TV show called *Kung Fu*," which none of us had seen. He seemed to think it was worth staying for so, hell, we stayed and watched. Starlin and I both fell in love with it immediately; we just really liked the philosophy, the action, the whole thing. At that time, they broadcast the show only every three weeks or so, so the next month I was in the city and Starlin and I wanted to watch it and we asked Roy, "Can we come up to your place and watch this show?" Roy had never heard about it and we came up and watched it mesmerized. I remember Roy walking in and watching for a while but saying, "This is pretentious nonsense," and walking out again. Roy was not a fan.

Somewhere in all of this, Starlin and I decided we wanted to do *Kung Fu* as a series but I can't remember if we asked to do an adaptation of the TV series (though it's quite probable we did) but I have half a memory of saying, "Let's just do something *like* the TV show." I don't recall getting involved in a discussion about getting the rights to the show. It certainly was Roy who said, "Let's tie in Fu Manchu; let's make Shang-Chi the son of Fu Manchu."

Roy and I have very similar reading backgrounds and we were both big Fu Manchu fans, as we were both big Doc Savage and big Robert E. Howard fans—we were very much on the same wavelength. I was very happy to do Fu Manchu, and I liked the idea of marrying the two concepts.

Jim and I were *into* this book. I remember a night before the first issue (which I colored, by the way; I had learned a little bit of coloring by working with Neal Adams and I'm actually pretty proud how the color came out in that issue), when us guys—Al Milgrom, Al Weiss, Jim Starlin and myself—went wandering around Manhattan. My favorite area of the island was always the streets below Greenwich Village because there were a bunch of 1940s warehouses—the way I liked New York to look—and, on that night, we wandered all the way down from the Village to the end of the island. We passed the AT&T Building where there were a couple of street repairmen working in a manhole. They were using welding torches which were throwing shadows five stories tall on the AT&T Building, and that's where we got the idea for Fu Manchu to be operating out of that building. On that same night we passed a big construction area where they had a big hole in the ground and a big crane, and we sat there and visualized the entire fight scene for the second issue.

Fairly quickly, we got letters from people saying, "Fu Manchu is an evil racist stereotype and what the hell is he doing in a Marvel comic?" I have personally never bought that argument. My feeling is that Dr. Doom is an evil Latverian stereotype, but with no Latverians protesting *his* depiction. Fu Manchu is just a villain; he's not evil because he's Chinese; he's evil *and* he's Chinese. But it was interesting to start getting letters like that with people saying this was terrible.

A long time after I had left the series, I've seen an interesting change in the perception of the strip. People still say that Fu Manchu is a racist stereotype but this professor at the University of California in Santa Barbara did a dissertation on the Asian hero in America and he noted Shang-Chi as being a wonderful, positive role model—this complex guy living in a different culture—and he resonated with a lot of people, and the character has become an icon.

I loved the philosophy behind the book; that's where I was coming from. I was already doing *Dr. Strange,* which represented the Western mystical philosophy, at least under my tenure. I really took it into the Western occult tradition of cabala, astrology, devil—all that kind of stuff—and I really saw Shang-Chi as a chance to do the *Eastern* mystical philosophy, albeit with a more action-oriented hero than Dr. Strange. They were different books and, because I never wanted to do the same thing twice, I saw this as a way to do two

different things and they'll make nice bookends without repeating myself; but *Dr. Strange* had gone monthly and I wanted to do Shang-Chi as a bi-monthly book, which is how it started out. It started in *Special Marvel Edition*—they just killed some reprint title and stuck our first issue in #15—and *bam* it took off! A lot of people liked this kung fu thing because, in addition to the show, martial arts were making big inroads at that time.

The story I heard was that Stan was riding in an elevator one day and he overheard people talking about this kung fu thing becoming really, really big. So he got off the elevator, walked into the Marvel offices, and said, "We gotta do this book more often." So they came to me and said, "We're going to start a second black-&-white book with separate continuity," which was something I really hated; and I didn't want to do *more* Shang-Chi than I was already doing. Inadvertently, Starlin and I came up with a concept that became bigger than either one of us. Jim had dropped off fairly early because he couldn't keep up with it as a regular book, but I had no intention of dropping off; but they wanted the b-&-w book and they wanted the color book monthly so I ended up doing only five color issues and maybe two b-&-ws. I don't recall it being adversarial but I said, "Look, I really want to do this book but I can't do it under these circumstances, so I'll drop out of the book." I didn't—and don't—have any animosity about that because, hey, we created something that had worked.

I remember going with Starlin to, I think, Roy and we said, "Look, we would like to have our names on *Master of Kung Fu* as 'Created by Englehart and Starlin'" but we were told, "No, we can't put your names on it because that could lead to ownership issues." These were early times and this concept was new in those days. In any event, I left and Doug Moench took over and (after a rocky first year, in my opinion) his run ever after was just a wonderful series. I take credit and pride for being the co-creator but what Doug and his various artists did with the book after that was just a wonderful run.

Above: *Neal Adams pencil illustration of David Carradine in his role as Kwai Chang Caine from the cult favorite TV series* Kung Fu. *Courtesy of Mike Thibodeaux.* Kung Fu ©2000 the respective copyright holder.

Below: *This cover art—by the "Gemini" team of Jim Starlin and Al Milgrom, debuted at the 1973 July 4th Comic Art Convention.* ©2000 Marvel Characters, Inc.

A Master of Comics Art
Artist Paul Gulacy and His Early Days at Marvel

Conducted by Jon B. Cooke
Transcribed by Jon B. Knutson

Paul Gulacy's star rose quickly after arriving at Marvel Comics in the early '70s, especially after teaming with writer Doug Moench on what was to become their trademark series, Master of Kung Fu. Paul's photorealistic style, aided by heavy inks, and an ongoing appreciation for Jim Steranko's sequential approach to comics story-telling, led Steranko to once state, "[Paul's art] was like seeing my own work, without having gone through the pain of creating it." A down-to-earth guy with a streetwise sensibility, Paul consented to the following phone interview on Sept. 13, 1999, and he also graced us with an all-new Gulacy cover for this issue, to which we are indebted. Paul also copy-edited the transcript. Thanks to #1 Gulacy fan Dave Lemieux for his help.

Comic Book Artist: *Where and when were you born?*
Paul Gulacy: Youngstown, Ohio. I was born in 1953.
CBA: *What kind of upbringing did you have?*

Below: Portrait of the artist. A recent studio photo of Paul Gulacy, courtesy of the artist.

Paul: A very diverse one, it was a very ethnic area. It's a blue-collar steel town, and it's all part of what they call the "Rust Belt"—which is Cleveland, Erie, Pittsburgh, Youngstown—and I had a great childhood. I had a lot of fun, great friends, good high school.
CBA: *Were you into art early?*
Paul: Yeah, when I was in first grade, I was drawing.
CBA: *What were you primarily interested in, what genre material?*
Paul: Cowboys and Indians. Army men.
CBA: *You have a very cinematic style. Did you get clued in to film when you were young?*
Paul: Not really, no. I was

definitely locked into cartoons, the Warner Brothers cartoons and a little bit of Disney. Probably my first hero, going way, way back, would be Bugs Bunny. [laughter] That's true!
CBA: *When did you get into comics?*
Paul: Probably when I was about ten, and how I got exposed to comics was because our family had one car, and my mother used to work late hours as an assistant to a pharmacist in a drugstore. My dad and I would go pick her up, sometimes with my sister, and I would hone in on the magazine rack, with the comics stand which was adjacent. I remember the "men's sweat" army magazines with all the great covers on them, done by guys like Frank McCarthy and James Bama. Then, as far as the comics, Marvel turned me off, but I liked DC's "Sgt. Rock." Army comics ran hand-in-hand with the Dell Comics and the Gold Key Comics, and Turok in particular. Mad magazine was another biggie.
CBA: *Did you clue in to anyone in particular—Joe Kubert?*
Paul: Joe Kubert was the Man. He just had this gutsy style that just expressed that World War II genre material. I can't think of anybody else who could get that across and get the feeling of war more than Joe. Even when he switched over to "Enemy Ace," I still felt that no one could outdo that either. I think he handled Von Hammer equally well. As far as I was concerned, "Sgt. Rock" was the guy. Easy Company.
CBA: *Did you begin to collect comic books, or did you just read them?*
Paul: I'd just read them periodically. I mean, I'd save these books, but I wasn't a hard-core collector. Let's just get right into it: We're talking about mid-1960s, and I'm getting a little bit older, and the James Bond movies exploded on the scene. All of a sudden, this was my new kind of interest—the spy thing. The only outlet for that in comic book form was Steranko and his "Nick Fury." That's how I got hooked into Steranko, because I couldn't find anybody handling the spy angle. At the same time, I wasn't ready for Marvel—the big foreshortening, Jack Kirby hands coming out at me on the covers, the whole bullpen thing, Stan Lee's manner of writing—the whole persona, the whole thing seemed foreign at the beginning.
CBA: *Did you start considering a career in art at any particular time?*
Paul: Yeah, I knew I was going to be an artist early on, I knew that's what I was going to do, which was draw. What I was going to do specifically with my talent was really up in the air; but I drew everything growing up. I used to enter the local home and garden shows, I won awards, and my first job was for the newspaper in Youngstown. Actually, the first time I'd gone professional was doing fashion illustrations for the department stores in their newspaper ads when I was a senior in high school.
CBA: *Did you have a flair for it?*
Paul: I just adapted to it immediately. I was told what to do, and I didn't even think about it—I wasn't conscious of it, I was just nervous as all get-out that first day. They had to put me in a little cubicle and told me what they wanted, showed some styles for me to adjust to, and I just went for it. I just did it and it came to me.
CBA: *You grew up, like you said, in the "Rust Belt," in a very working-class environment. Did you see art was a way to get out of the area, and not work in the steel mills?*
Paul: Absolutely. I mean, my dad was a truck driver, and I saw him get up at four in the morning and come home at three in the afternoon, and hang out for a couple of hours, and go back to bed. He did this for 35 years, and I looked at that and said, "This isn't

going to be my scene at all." So, I took this God-given talent and just was determined to cultivate the seed and get out. Everybody wanted to get out, *everybody*. Otherwise, it would be the steel mills, or working for a big automaker.

CBA: *Was the steel industry starting to see the end of its days, or was it still going strong at the time?*

Paul: They were in full-speed-ahead mode. Then it collapsed in the late '70s.

CBA: *Did your family support your artistic aspirations?*

Paul: Everyone in my family came from old-fashioned European roots, and my family structure was Numero Uno, and to break off was taboo, a no-no, in those days. If you broke away from your roots, it was considered going against the grain.

CBA: *So you were a wild one?*

Paul: I broke the mold.

CBA: *So, when you saw Steranko's comics, did you immediately recognize his approach? You were seeking out his work?*

Paul: Yeah, and the way I found them was in a grocery store down the street, a little mom-and-pop grocery store, and they'd have these three comics in a cellophane bag, and I saw the first *Nick Fury* with the cover gone, a great splash page that Jim had done, and I bought it. That's how I got all my *Nick Fury*s and pretty soon I collected all of them. When I saw what he was doing, it was just I never had seen anything like that before—it just flipped me out. This was the '60s, and these were experimental times.

CBA: *Were you an avid moviegoer into your teens?*

Paul: No. The whole take of my style looking cinematic with some kind of film background or whatever, is just coincidental. When I got my first script from Roy Thomas at Marvel, I started drawing, and my approach was just the way it came out. Now, I was weaned on television, and a lot of the contrasts, the imagery that comes across in my art—a lot of use of blacks and so forth—is probably from watching a black-&-white television. [*laughs*]

CBA: *There was this book I remember vividly as a kid, it came out in the '70s, and it was called* Rock Dreams. *It had images of, say,* Ray Charles *driving, the Rolling Stones just hanging out in a diner, and that approach reminds me of your work. You had movie and musician icons doing real cool stuff. You were able to see James Coburn involved with Shang-Chi, and Jimi Hendrix alive again as a hero in* Sabre, *and you took these icons and put them into your stories, and that was an interesting approach.*

Paul: And *Master of Kung Fu* is where that really was most prevalent. Doug Moench and I did not know how far we were going

to go with this thing—how long the series would last—and we just basically had fun with it. The books were a tribute and salute to a lot of people in films, you know, guys like Marlon Brando and Sean Connery, and others. I did *MOKF* right on the tail end of graduating from art school, so I had a lot of graphic influence, and I was just throwing that into the stories. It was fun, and was just a real shot in the dark. We never anticipated this thing becoming a cult collectible or a classic later on.

CBA: *Who would've thunk it?*

Paul: Nobody would've thunk it! [*laughs*] Just two guys having a ball—and that was the whole charm. We had unchallenged creative freedom.

CBA: *That's one of the real ironies of that, in that kung fu was yet*

Above: Shang-Chi has at it in this promotional picture featuring the Master of Kung Fu. Courtesy of the artist. ©2000 Marvel Characters, Inc.

Comic Strip Is Called "Morbius"—
Gulacy Draws Cartoon Hero

By JOHN A. LENCYK

Comic book heroes Superman, Batman, Robin and Captain America are destined to have another companion if Paul Gulacy, a Coitsville resident and graduate of North High School, continues his artistic success.

Paul, the 20-year-old son of Paul and Virginia Gulacy of 5999 McCartney Road, is a free-lance cartoonist who has just received his first check from Marvel Comics for his presentation of Morbius, a once dormant comic book character.

Marvel's acceptance of Paul's work acknowledges an artistic career spanning a love of comics to works presently hanging in the Pittsburgh Art Gallery.

Mother Is No. 1 Fan

Though the soft-spoken Pittsburgh Art Institute student is unawed by his earlier work, his mother avidly relates his artistic beginnings. "He began drawing when he was about 6 years old," she says. "He would always sketch scenes he saw or read about in comic books. He knew all the characters."

Later in high school, his prowess and imagination progressed. "If we were away," recalls his mother, "and someone telephoned, Paul would draw the caller's picture and place it beside the phone. When we returned we'd recognize immediately who had called."

Without formal instruction, Paul began to show his diversity. He did various pencil sketches, employed washes for Strouss fashion ads and worked on characters and dialogue for comic book cartoons.

Cartoons Convey Message

"Art for comics is basically a caricature," opines Paul. "In the way that a camera tries to convey a message, an artist, by changing shapes or elongating figures, conveys a feeling or emotion."

ACTION PACKED—Paul Gulacy, 20-year-old Coitsville resident, demonstrates how cartoonists draw vibrant characters to create a feeling of action and drama. Paul, now working for Marvel Comics, notes that cartoonists have wide latitude in design of characters.

the cultural treasures of Europe.

"I did a few sketchbooks in pen and ink," he relates, but it was exposure to different cultures he likes to remember.

In Rome he saw the sites of ancient Latin glory.

Inspired by Louvre

The Louvre in Paris evoked from his talented hand and incisive imagination a drawing which the Gulacy family considers one of the most intriguing in their collection. In the center of the 18-inch square work is a copy of the Mona Lisa, replete with laborious detail. In the foreground are two people, one in modern garb with stylish long hair, facing both the Mona Lisa and a gentleman to the right. The latter, arrayed in Tuscan robes and sandals, is gesturing in an instructive manner.

Paul drew the quasi-smiling lady after his first visit to the Louvre. The young man in this sketch is Paul Himself. The anachronisitic teacher on the right is, says Paul, the depiction of Leonardo da Vinci beside his chef d'oeuvre. The portrayal is a favorite of Paul's because it shows art transcending barriers of time.

Shortly after returning from his voyage, the prodding of Niles cartoonist Val Mayerik and Dan Adkins, from East Liverpool, prompted Paul to submit some of his work to Marvel Comics. Excited by the challenge of producing an enticing item for the comic magazine editors, he worked for weeks, often into the early morning hours. Finally this spring he finished.

Features Vampire

After preliminary groundwork, Marvel approved his ideas and asked Paul to turn out an issue featuring a protagonist called Morbius, the Vampire. In Marvel's older Spider-man series, Morbius had been an arch-villain. Management obviously felt he deserved an audition for a leading role, with Paul to be the guiding force.

With a two-page plot synopsis seent from California by writer Mike Friedrich, Paul had to expand and credibly fill 15 pages (the length of a comic feature) with his drawings. Lulls in narrative action had to be covered by dynamic sketching to ins

Youngstown Vindicator A-15
Sunday, July 8, 1973

continuity and interest. Paul hopes his ability in this first trial issue will be the stepping stone for a continuing series.

Exceedingly happy and proud of his position, he is not oblivious to pressure facing aspiring free-lancers. "Comic artists lead a tough life. They have to search out their assignments and when they get a contract they usually have to make deadlines. Your mind and hands have to work fast."

In New York this week Paul attended the 1973 Annual New York Comic Art Convention.

CBA: *Your hands are your life.*
Paul: You bet.
CBA: *When did you meet Val Mayerik?*
Paul: I met him when I was going to the Art Institute in Pittsburgh, and I sat next to this girl on the bus and started rapping about careers and so forth. She said her boyfriend drew comics for Marvel, lived in my hometown, and she said I should look him up. I gave Val a call, met with him, and two weeks later I met with Dan Adkins, another fellow Ohioan. Craig Russell was another local guy within a 40 mile radius. Adkins was the one who really groomed me towards presenting samples and so forth to give to Marvel.
CBA: *Before you had met Val Mayerik's girlfriend on the bus, did you want to do comics?*
Paul: Yeah. At that point, when I was in art school, I was daydreaming and waiting to get out—I graduated early. I was hired by Marvel with about eight months to go before I graduated from art school. The president of the school, John Johns, was a cartoonist (and had done freelance work for *Mad* magazine years ago) and he was very supportive. He cut me loose, and I still got my certificate and so forth, a citation of merit and achievement and all that stuff.
CBA: *I read in an interview that you worked on a comics-related project in art school. You said, "I came up with this crazy character one night in the middle of some kind of drunken stupor." What was the character?*
Paul: [*laughs*] I can't remember. I remember Duffy Vohland inked it, and I think Duffy wrote it, but it was something! Yeah, there was a party in my apartment, but it was my roommate's get-together. He was a year ahead of me, and his class came over, and I cut out, got tired and went to sleep. I just started hopping in and out of bed, writing notes down, and by the time morning rolled around, I had this six-page story. I didn't have the script for it, which didn't come around until later.
CBA: *Do you remember what it was, what genre it was?*
Paul: It was very mystical, it was this Chinese guy with a magic box and it was just crazy, wacky stuff, stuff you would dream up if you were high; but it made sense. Later, that was my sample work I gave to Adkins, and Dan sent it to Roy Thomas. I was hired from that whole six-page thing.
CBA: *You originally scripted it, and Adkins said, "No, go back and take all the words out"?*
Paul: No. On one of the meetings early on, before I did this story, he recommended that I should submit at least six pages with no dialogue whatsoever. Marvel was just interested in how you drew and told stories sequentially.
CBA: *So the writers can just fill in the balloons.*
Paul: Yeah, and they used it later on, it rolled around later on in one of the black-&-white magazines.
CBA: *What was Dan Adkins like?*
Paul: Adkins was one of the most eccentric little men I've ever met in my life, but a sweetheart. He has a crazy background, and you know, he knows *everything*. He knows about *you*, Jon—somehow,

Above: *Courtesy of his mentor, Dan Adkins, this* Youngstown Vindicator *newspaper article from July 8, 1973, profiles neophyte comic book artist Paul Gulacy.* **Below:** *Morbius, The Living Vampire. From Paul's splash page of his first Marvel job in* Fear *#20. ©20000 Marvel Characters, Inc.*

out of that. I think that's the shock, surprise and delight upon reading them. MOKF had an unexpected quality. One really had to almost hammer super-hero readers and say, "No, read it! It's really good!" [*laughs*] And it was great that it lasted as long as it did.
Paul: When I was given that book, I didn't know anything about kung fu, let alone Bruce Lee. When I started that first issue, I don't think I'd even seen *Enter the Dragon*, and it wasn't until I went to see this movie—almost a year after he'd died—when I really got hooked into it. I also have a good friend from the same hometown, Val Mayerik, another fellow comic book artist, and he was a second-degree black belt when I knew him, and we would go to tournaments. I would see Val teach at the *dojo*, and go to these tournaments and so forth, and that's where I got a real taste for it. I knew there was an artistry behind the whole…
CBA: *Philosophy?*
Paul: There was a philosophy and a commitment. I didn't want to portray it haphazard; I wanted to give some respect to the people who were into the martial arts. It was a fine line: You had to balance between what Marvel wanted—the thing being a comic book, and the visuals expected from that—with the treatment of having respect for the martial arts as well.
CBA: *Did you actually study martial arts yourself?*
Paul: No, I didn't study it, because I would see an artist buddy coming into my apartment always, like every other week, with a broken something or other. [*laughter*] It would postpone his ability to make a buck, and I knew right away that would happen to me. I remember one time he came over and he had a cast on one finger, and I asked, "What happened?" And he said he got it caught on another guy's *gi*—the guy's outfit—just sparring around. I thought he'd got hit, or punched somebody in the jaw, and it didn't happen like that.

another trend that Marvel was so apt to jump on in the early '70s, and you guys were able to mold something really interesting and lasting he would know your personal life. He'd call somebody, network around, "I want to know about Jon Cooke," and I could call him tomorrow or tonight and he'd tell me everything he'd learned about Jon Cooke. He could find that information; he's one of those kind of guys. He would just call people out of the blue—he'd call Frazetta in the middle of the night and say, "Hey, what did you make on that last job?" [laughter] "What's Berkeley Medallion paying right now?" [laughter] Or he could just call Frazetta in the middle of the night and talk about a hangnail on his toe!

CBA: [laughs] I heard you describe being Dan's assistant was more like being a glorified chauffeur, taking him to Elvis movies at the drive-in. What was his thing with Elvis movies?

Paul: [laughter] First off, he's terrified of cars. I was third in line in Dan's Elvis movie escort service, driving Dan to Elvis marathon movies at the local drive-in in East Liverpool, Ohio. [laughter] Now Craig was first, he got it set up, and then he dumped it on Mayerik, Mayerik wised up, and then I was the third guy in line for this nonsense. Dan would take a big quart of Pepsi and crunch on Chee-Tos, and that was his dinner. I've never seen Dan Adkins eat anything else but Chee-Tos and drink Pepsi! [laughter]

CBA: So you had to suffer through Viva Las Vegas and Charro! on the big screen [laughs]—with this eccentric artist in your car while everyone else had steamed-up windows? [laughter]

Paul: Exactly. Here's a funny one: Craig Russell was leaving Adkins' house one evening and started his car, and a cat was sleeping inside Craig's motor, and a fanbelt sliced into this cat's dome, okay? Craig had to take off, but Adkins got stuck with this cat, and he weaned this cat to health on Pepsi and Chee-Tos [laughter] and brought this cat back to health, it was in terrific shape! [laughter] It took off down the street into the sunset.

CBA: Adkins takes care of cats and art students.

Paul: Adkins takes care of a lot of people, if you know Dan… He knew everybody, he knew the guys way back when, he knew Wally Wood, Roy Krenkel, Al Williamson, all the early guys.

CBA: Right; and he obviously had a whole posse, with you guys. What was his influence on you? What lessons did you learn from Dan—besides the Elvis movies? [laughter] Did he teach you technique?

Paul: Yeah, he did. He knew about technique, he was very knowledgeable. He was the guy to go to for critique, he was the guy who would tell you what was wrong. There's another great story about Adkins: You know, he was notoriously late on everything, and when he was working with Steranko on *SHIELD*, he called Steranko one day and said, "Look, Jim, I can't finish this thing. It's just too damn much work," and I think it was the one with Nick Fury in the haunted castle, the "Hell Hound" story. So, Steranko panicked and decides to drive from Reading, way the hell over across Pennsylvania to Adkins' house in Ohio, and according to Adkins, Steranko hadn't been to sleep in three days. So, all this talk that Steranko is this nightowl and doesn't require rest, according to Adkins, is a true fact. He's one of these guys who can get by with very little sleep—and he got this thing done.

CBA: That's Steranko for you.

Paul: It just goes to show how he wanted things done his way. Even way back then, it had to be done, it had to have a look, it had to be quality, even if it took him to drive over and get it done, and that's the way it went.

CBA: When did you first meet Jim?

Paul: I met Steranko through Adkins and the posse at a Phil Seuling convention at the Commodore Hotel in the early '70s. Steranko came up with some babe on his arm. We had a big room, it was kind of like the Grand Central Station for partygoers. Phil turned it into this drop-off point, and Steranko shot in. That's when I first met him, briefly.

CBA: Would Adkins agonize over his work? Because sometimes it was so meticulously detailed, like "Dr. Strange," and some of his "Sub-Mariner" stories he did were just so lush.

Paul: He made Smith look like Smith.

CBA: Oh, he was a great inker on Windsor-Smith. He was a great inker on everybody, actually.

Paul: He had an eye for adjusting to one's style, because he was so very talented. Adkins is a very underrated artist. He could paint, and he could draw but he just couldn't get motivated. He was never one inclined to get motivated.

CBA: Was it the money?

Paul: He lost his burning desire early on, and God knows why. It could've been money. I mean, it just takes a lot of work! Most people don't realize how much work goes into these comics. When you go to a comics shop today, you can criticize it on the mediocrity, everything looks the same, and it's overworked, or whatever, but still, even in the worst comic, there's still a helluva lot of work, and people just don't get that. It's a tremendous effort.

CBA: So many artists consider Adkins their favorite inker, it's fascinating. Gil Kane loves Dan's work. He did some superb work on Barry Windsor-Smith. He'd always seemed somewhat unrealized, almost like the shadow of Wally Wood was on him, or something.

Paul: Absolutely.

CBA: A mystery. So, you saw the limelight in New York, you had to get out of the "Rust Belt," so to speak?

Paul: No, New York came after *MOKF*. I was freelancing from Ohio when I was doing that book.

CBA: Oh, really? You did that through the mail. Did you visit first in New York?

Paul: Yeah, I made a couple of excursions to New York, got a feel for the city.

CBA: And your first professional job in comics was…?

Paul: "Morbius, the Living Vampire." [Fear #20] It was my first color job. Before that, I did miscellaneous stuff for *Dracula Lives* and *Deadly Hands of Kung Fu*, the b-&-w magazines Marvel was pumping out back in those days.

CBA: Could you conceive of making a living in comics?

Paul: No, I was starry-eyed like any kid today. You know, Marvel's whole policy and philosophy is if the artist isn't happy, "Tough, we can always find another schmuck out there in the Midwest or Nebraska. They'd be more than glad to be the next star at Marvel." So, I felt at that young age, I was just rolling with whatever came my way. I mean, I was starting with the fact that I didn't think I was going to be able to break into professional comics—I wanted to, but I wasn't sure it was going to happen—so when I got a call from Roy Thomas one day, when I'm mowing the lawn, I flipped out! It was very cool. But I didn't anticipate staying in it that long. I knew I had other callings artwise, and there were other directions I wanted to go—even in the midst of *MOKF*—and that's what happened. I sent a message to Marvel that I was leaving, and I got a call from Stan Lee! He wanted me to stay, he offered me a little more money—it wasn't enough—and I told him I wanted to start pursuing other endeavors. I wanted to be a paperback book illustrator, because I thought painting was next in line for me. What happened was that one day I went to the drawing board, looked at a blank sheet of paper there, and I thought I was going to vomit—it was just too much, and I got burnt out. It was time to just back off and get away from comics.

CBA: *You were pretty young, too, right?*

Paul: Yeah.

CBA: *Getting into it, initially, you really developed very, very rapidly. I recall your "Morbius" [in* Fear *#20] and I remember my eyebrows being raised and saying, "This is interesting," but then you evolved. In a matter of a year, you really developed your chops.*

Paul: Yeah, and one reason for that was that John Verpoorten, who was head of production, let me sneak in a couple of inks on my own work. That helped a great deal, and it got to show another side of my style that the audience didn't get to see at the beginning.

CBA: *At the very beginning, Jack Abel was your initial inker?*

Paul: He and Pablo Marcos shared the bill on inking jobs, I think.

CBA: *What did you think of their work?*

Paul: I thought it was different, but it was appropriate. I thought Marcos caught the style a little closer than Jack did—and that's not to say that Jack did a lesser job—and I respect both of those guys.

CBA: *Ideally, did you want to do your own inks?*

Paul: Ideally, but there was a time factor there, a tremendous amount of pressure. That's why I never got to do covers when I did *MOKF*. That was all due to the fact that there was a deadline pressure scenario. I just lost the urge to even want to try to do covers after a while.

CBA: *You immediately started to get into a real (I continuously go back into this word) cinematic approach. Were you where you wanted to be at that moment when your work really started to shine? Did you always have your eye towards commercial art, or paperback book covers?*

Paul: No. I discovered I had this strong graphic sense when I was in high school. Prior to that, I did just a variety of all kind of art. I worked in pastels, a little watercolor—I experimented. I was looking at being able to do this stuff early on and get a taste. But you know, you're restricted when you get into a world that's pencils and inkpens and brushes and so forth, and you can only take that so far. Even though my comics work could've been more graphic, I could have probably expounded more, but I was confined to what it was—and that was comics. What Steranko did was also inspired by the fact that he worked in an advertising agency, and he had all these little studio tricks he'd incorporate into each issue.

CBA: *He had a much wider experience than the average comic artist.*

Paul: Exactly. I think a lot of comic book artists aren't exploring other directions to go in. You look at the new guys today, and it seems that a lot of them consider Image as Ground Zero for inspiration. They seem to have no knowledge whatsoever of the scope of artistic possibilities. On the other hand, even the guys in the '60s, '70s and '80s were weaned on the earlier comic book guys, and just didn't go outside comics to look for ideas. It still takes an eye and a gift to experiment and take chances. I mean, either you have that or you don't. That's why when people compare me with Steranko, it boils down to the fact that we both have a tremendous graphic sensibility, which makes us look very parallel and very similar. Now, if I hadn't seen Steranko's work ever—if Steranko never existed—my stuff would still look very strongly the way it has

through the years. I really don't think it would look any different.

CBA: *So, you were looking at other fields for inspiration. You mentioned, for instance, James Bama. Were you looking beyond what we were just lamenting about young artists today that don't seem to look beyond their particular chosen field… were you always looking around, getting* Print *magazine or* Graphis, *for instance, to keep an eye on what was happening in other fields?*

Paul: Absolutely. You know, Adkins had a tremendous library of clippings and swipes. He was known as a swipe guy. Steranko is another big clip artist, so was Howard Chaykin, and I was, too. I was getting into artists that neither one of these guys were into. I used to love all these guys that did the *TV Guide* covers…

CBA: *Bob Peake and Amsel.*

Paul: Amsel, and artists who worked on *The Ladies' Home Journal* and *Redbook*—the kind of illustration that was very prominent, very strong in the '70s, and you don't see that at all today. In fact, you could talk to people who don't even know who those great illustrators are—the Mark Englishs, or the Bob McGinnises.

I know this comic art dealer who a couple of years ago totally walked away from handling comic book art, and went solely into selling illustrator's artwork. He even opened a gallery in Greenwich Village that just failed. Nobody wanted to come in, and he ended up going back into the comic artists again. But back in the '70s, there was a tremendous interest in illustrators, especially from art students; they all knew who these artists were, and I remember just sitting around and talking about Peak and English for hours when I was younger! I just can't believe that illustration is so dead, it's too bad. Of course, you've got the advent of the computer, you know, which isn't helping things out—but it's too bad that the whole thing has gone by the wayside.

The bottom line is I don't think most of these kids are very good artists nowadays. They can adjust to some "flavor-of-the-month" style, but I don't think they're technically very well-trained artists—they could be, but they're not. I hate to say this—because I sound like I'm biased—but the guys of my era, Mike Kaluta and Walt Simonson and Howie Chaykin and Barry Windsor-Smith, we were all *inspired*, we were all influenced greatly by illustrators and great art in general. Today, it's really too bad that kids don't see that. When was the last time you saw a cover on *TV Guide* that was done by an artist? Even inside *TV Guide*, you had marvelous b-&-w artwork.

CBA: *Getting into the chronology, do you recall being offered "Master of Kung Fu"? Do you remember how that came about?*

Paul: I did the first issue of "Morbius," and then immediately after that first book was done, I got a call from Roy, who, as much as I can recall, felt that Starlin, who'd done one or two issues, was better suited for *Captain Marvel*, and felt that I would be better on the kung fu strip. That's how it came about. Now, Starlin might have a different story.

CBA: *So, you saw this as your first regular gig, right? Were you ever considered to be the continuing artist on "Morbius"?*

Paul: I would've taken it at that time. I wouldn't have passed that up. I would've grabbed anything, like anybody when they first started.

CBA: *If you'd been offered a super-hero strip, would you have taken it?*

Paul: Yeah, back then.

CBA: *Would you have had any interest in doing it?*

Paul: I could've made a lot of money with Doug Moench through the years—had we taken up offers to do super-heroes—and I always turned it down, I just don't feel inclined to do that genre. You have to have passion for that, and I never had that and never got into it. There are other people more qualified than me.

CBA: *Were you starting to use photo reference from the word "go"? You said that Dan had a huge swipe file. Did you start developing your own swipe file then?*

Paul: Not really. If I wanted to use Marlon Brando as a character, and didn't have any reference on him, I'd buy a book on Brando, or whoever.

CBA: *You were constantly looking for reference?*

Paul: Not constantly, if I felt inclined. No matter who it was, if I had to go seek it out, I'd go look for it. I didn't have piles of stuff laying around my studio. I wasn't clipping and saving in that sense.

Adkins suggested that we all do that, and it's the best bit of advice you can give to an artist starting out or an artist that's been at it for a long time. I ran into Bob McGuinness in London by accident, and I didn't know who he was at the time, and one of the things he said to me was—and I always remembered this, because I wrote it down, and I never forgot it—he said, "An artist is only as good as his reference." And he said Rob Liefeld told him that. Just kidding. [*laughs*]

CBA: *Do you think that's what's lacking, is that in the present field, kids are just using old comic books as reference?*

Paul: That wouldn't hurt; but on the other hand, they want to establish their own identity. Some are using reference, but they'll put a wacky spin on it, and it doesn't matter anyhow. I don't know if they care about the accuracy of a .45, and how to draw correctly and so forth. I don't think that's a priority for a lot of guys out there. It's more "flavor-of-the-month" technique. J. Scott Campbell has a cartoony style. Joe Madureira seems to be a big Disney enthusiast. I really like their work, by the way—and I really enjoy Scott McDaniel's *Nightwing*.

CBA: *Doing live model nude classes is probably…*

Paul: Getting anatomy down is one thing I wish they'd begin with. For me, I'd like to see more diversity when I look at comics today. I hate this clone woman that seems to permeate the whole industry. You walk into a comic book store, and it's the same chick on every magazine, it's the same eyes, the same lips, same nose, same breasts, same ass!

CBA: *It's real tiresome, the "bad girl" and "good girl" comics—it's overwhelming when you go into the shops. I've almost no interest to go into the shops except to get the weird, fun stuff and clear out as fast as I can.*

Paul: There's so much color when you walk into a comic book shop that it looks like Walt Disney threw up on the wall! [*laughter*] 90 books with the same skanks on the cover.

CBA: *Did you get into photography?*

Paul: Yeah, here and there. I would use some friends as models, but not as much as I'd do later; but let's go back to how I got Bruce Lee down. Back in those days, there wasn't videotape, no video rental places, so a friend of mine and I rented *Enter the Dragon* from a film distribution house and took it to Youngstown University, got a room there, set up a screen, and I set up a 35mm camera on a tripod, and we froze-frame the entire movie. We froze-frame every shot of that movie, and I snapped about 300 pictures! That's how I finally got Bruce Lee down. You didn't have books on the guy—*The Life of Bruce Lee*—around back in those days.

CBA: *Wasn't it an expensive proposition?*

Paul: Yeah, it cost a lot of money to do that.

CBA: *So you had to do it all in one night?*

Paul: We did it all in one long evening, yeah. We wouldn't shoot the boring parts—the talking heads—we just photographed the action scenes.

CBA: *Didn't Steve Englehart write the first couple of stories that you did?*

Paul: Yeah, I worked with Steve in the beginning, we did two or three issues.

CBA: *Do you recall meeting Doug face-to-face?*

Paul: Yep. Somebody introduced me when I went up to Marvel on one of my trips to New York. This long-haired freak came up to me, we shook hands, and we hit it off right away. He was a great guy.

CBA: *You guys obviously hit it off. What is it about your personalities that's maintained a collaborative relationship over 25 years?*

Paul: Same interests, same zeal for life, and he's just a great guy. I've known him for so long, that he's like my brother, and he's my favorite collaborator.

CBA: *You mentioned in one of the interviews that while Doug was interested in pursuing the philosophical aspects of Shang-Chi, that you were more interested maybe in the action.*

Paul: That's right.

CBA: *Do you think that was part of your burn-out?*

Paul: I think the philosophical

aspects just slowed the book down. I didn't want to get into that material. I didn't think it was necessary. I think there was room for it, but it shouldn't overwhelm the series. I thought it was too heady for Shang-Chi. I wanted him maturing, becoming more worldly.

CBA: *Less of an innocent?*

Paul: Doug saw him more in the temple, I saw him driving a jeep. That was the division.

CBA: *Were you like real brothers, in that you'd have really interesting and lively sessions, getting into arguments and stuff?*

Paul: Oh, yeah. You had two minds, two young egos who were searching for a limelight—and there's no two ways about it: We competed with each other, that's what made this thing unique. We were like Lennon and McCartney. I was really, really pushing my end, and he was countering with his, and as a result, we got this product. In retrospect, I was disappointed in the last story arc we did together. I still cringe over that six-part saga. I felt that last issue should've had more action, to this day—I'm *still* telling Doug that. All these years gone by, I'll still bring it up. He had the last jab in, so to speak.

CBA: *When did you realize you were getting noticed? Was it at shows, was it through the mail?*

Paul: Yeah, I got a tremendous amount of fan mail, from a very

Previous page: The Rook at the Alamo. Paul's painting was substantially altered when used as the cover of Warren Presents #2, with only the two main characters silhouetted and the epic background discarded. Courtesy of Albert Moy. Art ©2000 Paul Gulacy. The Rook ©2000 William DuBay.

Below: Never-before-published private collection drawing. Courtesy of the artist. ©2000 Paul Gulacy.

diverse audience. Attorneys, kids, martial artists, movie fans… and I received awards from overseas early on. That's why I knew there was a global interest.

CBA: *Were you getting better rates after a particular period of time? The book went monthly when you started, right?*

Paul: I think it was monthly.

CBA: *So you were pumping out how many pages a day?*

Paul: I had to get out at least two. I wasn't one of these guys like John Byrne, who could crank out five pages.

CBA: *Well, you had a lot of heavy blacks…*

Paul: Yeah, I was drawing in blue colored pencil, because I'd put so many darks down it would smudge by the time the inker got it. By the time the letterer was done with it, it was a blur. So, Verpoorten was the one who suggested I go to a hard blue pencil; and that even takes longer, because you've got to keep that point going.

CBA: *Right. Did you hit it off with Verpoorten?*

Paul: Oh, he was a wonderful man. It was really tragic what happened to him. I believe he had a heart attack while he was at his drawing table at home. He had a perforated ulcer is what happened there, and he bled to death internally. He was a huge guy. He was very compliant and helpful, courteous, always polite. He had a sense of humor, and was prompt; John had all the qualities of a guy you wanted to work for, all within an atmosphere of chaos. He had a very high-stress position, you know, and at the end, it took its toll on him. He and John Romita made me feel most comfortable when I first started out.

CBA: *At the same time, Marvel's corporate star was rising like nothing before; they were the number one comics publisher, they were getting TV shows made of their stuff, and they really looked hot to investors. I guess the suits took over.*

Paul: You've got to remember, I got out of there by that time, I was drawing *Sabre* in the late '70s, and was going in some other directions. I really don't know what was happening in the late '70s and almost all of the '80s there, for that matter.

CBA: *When you were freelancing for Marvel, were you into the experimentation? Did you feel in essence that were you a slave to the work, or were you really enjoying stretching your limbs, so to speak, and trying these things? Sometimes your layouts were so sequential, they were almost down to depicting a nanosecond of movement. Did you have a very rough plot from Doug?*

Paul: No, his plots were always… everything was there. Even the dialogue.

CBA: *But you had some freedom to move within that framework and use your storytelling approach?*

Paul: He would recommend things, but I rarely listen to any suggestions writers give me, particularly when it comes to action scenes. I like to choreograph all that on my own. If they want a truck in there, I'll put in a motorcycle. [*laughter*] If they want a motorcycle, I'll have it on top of a bridge; if they want it on a building, I'll put it in a subway. I attribute that more to instinct than rebellion.

CBA: *But that's what you do!*

Paul: Let me put it this way: When I did *MOKF*, I

—GULACY—

was very spontaneous. I never labored over the script and wondered and pondered how I'm going to play a scene. It was what I call "first flash": You read it, and you spontaneously get it in your mind visually how to play it. Your brain tells you automatically how to play this thing. I never liked to waste a lot of time on any other kind of approach to it. You had to get it done, you always had in the back of your mind that you had a deadline on this thing.

CBA: *It's a job, you've got to get the job done!*

Paul: That's right; but you've got to remember, it was also an era when the kung fu movies and Bruce Lee were very popular. What I tried to do at that time was bring Bruce Lee back in a sense. When Bruce died, I felt that *MOKF* was the only outlet for a Bruce Lee-type guy—that's how I saw Shang-Chi. It was a continuation of all that fun stuff. We had the spy motif, martial arts, actors, and parody. It was a big stew of all kinds of stuff that made that book. We had Fu Manchu in there… I mean, it was crazy, it was just a mish-mash! And the readers picked up on that.

CBA: *But I think you really clued in to the appeal of the strip—that it was the continuation of Bruce Lee, it was the chance to see Bruce Lee "alive."*

Paul: Right. In fact, there was a rumor around that Bruce Lee's wife had called Stan Lee and said "Knock it off."

CBA: *Did you ever get to the truth of that?*

Paul: That was told to me by someone at Marvel.

CBA: *Did you ever get any other flak? Nowadays, I don't think you could get away with it, because you had Sean Connery, for instance, for a period of time. There were a lot of recognizable characters, James Coburn, and people like that…*

Paul: Marlene Dietrich…

CBA: *Yeah, right. [laughs] You were grabbing them from all over!*

Paul: Don't forget David Niven [*laughter*]—who the hell cares about David Niven?—but we found a place for him in there.

CBA: *Casual readers—those were not comics fans—seemed to get into the book. Sales of the book indicated that guys who were into martial arts, or who were into spy stuff, were picking up the comic, who might not pick up other comics (except* Conan, *maybe). They specifically focused on MOKF. When did you first get an inkling that the book was selling as well as it was?*

Paul: I got it from Roy Thomas who mentioned it was up there in sales with *Conan* and *Spider-Man*. I encountered the most diverse crowd I ever saw in my life—and the most people I ever signed for—when I attended a convention at The Shrine in Los Angeles. I definitely heard from the down home folks who really enjoyed our series and that's really cool. We appealed to a crowd that perhaps didn't follow regular comics. These were readers who wanted to tune into something other than super-heroes. Shang-Chi brought that by being an ethnic character. Back then, mainstream comics usually featured blond guys with big muscles, and that was about it. So early on, we had a diverse character and an equally diverse audience—and that's one of the things that Doug and I are proud of.

CBA: *By your own description, you burned out on MOKF. Did you maintain a relationship with Doug immediately after your run on MOKF, or did you have a falling out—or did you say, "Hey, we'll work together again someday."?*

Paul: Yeah, it's always been like that, that's a line we always use. I mean, in the 25 years I've known him, it's always been, "We'll work again, we'll do something." And we do go our separate ways. He's worked with a score of artists and sold a lot of books with these guys, and I did different things. It was kind of sad at the end of *MOKF*. It was like a rock 'n' roll group that all of a sudden splits up or like a comedy team where the guys go their separate ways. It was melodramatic like that.

CBA: *Did you feel you were leaving comics for good at the time?*

Paul: Yeah, absolutely. I couldn't wait to get out of the industry. I just wanted to explore and try some other things.

CBA: *So it wasn't particularly negatives of the industry itself, it was that you just wanted to express yourself in other ways?*

Paul: Not being a big comics collector, I felt kind of a funny sense of isolation. I never really joined any kind of comic book professional cliques—I knew a few people—but I was never close friends with anybody in the business, outside of Doug, Mayerik, and Adkins. I was just separate from that whole scene. I didn't go to Marvel and hang out and have lunch with everybody—that wasn't my thing.

CBA: *So it's kind of a "been there, done that" kind of thing, in that the cliques just don't have anything to offer you? I mean, you didn't see comics as the end-all and be-all, but rather as another step in a direction of your self-discovery?*

Paul: If you're going to go back to those days, and Adkins was the guy who told me this, early on he said, "If you want to make a great deal of money, you're not going to find it in comics." And that was true back then. You do comics when you're young for the love of it, and you'll take whatever you can get—you'll take a low wage, or whatever—and the thrill of seeing your name on a book and having your work published nationally becomes very appealing and exciting; but after a while, you've got to look at the reality, and at that point, there was something stirring inside of me. I was being tugged at by some other natural inclination. I needed some kind of environment that was with other people, and I eventually made my way into advertising. It got me out of the house.

CBA: *Did you find any satisfaction working in advertising?*

Paul: Yeah, it was exciting—I worked for some of the biggest agencies in New York; but you know, once again, you're freelancing, you're once again like a mercenary. You're hired, you're there temporarily, and then you're shuttled off somewhere else…

CBA: *And you're expendable.*

Paul: Right. The longest period of time I ever worked at one agency was two weeks, on one particular job… one product we were working on.

CBA: *Along the way, you spent some time working at Warren.*

Paul: That was a kick. Louise Simonson was my editor. She was really easy to get along with, she was great.

CBA: *She really got good work out of a lot of great people.*

Paul: Oh, she sure did. Jim was a bizarre guy, he'd be in and out. He stayed behind closed doors most of the time, I'd met him in his office one time. He told me I looked like a wolfman, I had long hair and a beard. [*laughter*] I looked like a werewolf.

CBA: *How would you assess your time at Marvel in the '70s, overall? Was it a positive experience?*

Paul: Yeah, for the most part, it was positive. I realized how important comics are—they fall in the category of jazz, baseball, Chevrolets, apple pie… it's an American idiom; and that's what I took with me in those early days, spending time at Marvel. That's probably the most important thing I grasped. There are people who love this medium, and respect it—and it should be respected. Comics and sequential storytelling go back to the days of the Egyptians, and even further back to the Sumerians, and it's just a tremendous artform. If it made its way into the Louvre, there must be something good about it.

CBA: *Do you enjoy constantly coming back to it?*

Paul: Oh, it's in my blood.

CBA: *You'll never really leave it?*

Paul: No, I don't think so. I'll never really leave it. I'm not done! I'm still trying to figure it out! [*laughs*] I mean, I always have a story in the back of my mind I have to get out, and the way I get it out is

visually. I'm not going to write it out, I'm not a writer. I'll put it down on paper with a pencil for somebody, even if it's only for myself.

CBA: *And you've got more stories coming from you, right?*

Paul: Oh, yeah, there's a *ton*! I haven't done a gladiator story, I haven't done a World War II story, I haven't done a great western… I want to do some sword-and-sorcery, some more sci-fi. In fact, Moench and I are going to do a big sci-fi story for Dark Horse in the future.

CBA: *So are you more into creator-owned stuff now?*

Paul: I was into it 20 years ago with *Sabre*. Right now, Doug and I feel compelled to do something that's creator-owned. We have something that we feel is very special and when we get excited about something… look out.

Above: *Evocative Gulacy page from the graphic novel* Sabre, *written by Don McGregor. ©2000 Don McGregor & Paul Gulacy. Sabre is a ™ of Don McGregor. (Good enuff, DM?)*

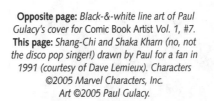

Opposite page: Black-&-white line art of Paul Gulacy's cover for Comic Book Artist Vol. 1, #7.
This page: Shang-Chi and Shaka Kharn (no, not the disco pop singer!) drawn by Paul for a fan in 1991 (courtesy of Dave Lemieux). Characters ©2005 Marvel Characters, Inc. Art ©2005 Paul Gulacy.

portfolio

-GULACY-

This page: Various depictions of Shang-Chi by Paul Gulacy from various stages of the artist's career. All courtesy of Number One Gulacy Fan, Dave Lemieux. Shang-Chi ©2005 Marvel Characters, Inc. Art ©2005 Paul Gulacy.

GULACY

Doug Moench's Memories
Chatting with Chicago Son and Prolific Marvel Scripter

Conducted by Jon B. Cooke
Transcribed by Sam Gafford

Yeesh! What Marvel book hasn't Doug Moench written?

Comic Book Artist: *Where are you from?*
Doug Moench: Born in Chicago. Lived there until I was 23, when I moved to Manhattan for two years and before buying a house here in Pennsylvania where I've been ever since. Although I have lived briefly, off and on, in Hollywood when I've been writing TV and movie stuff.

CBA: *When did you develop an interest in comic books?*
Doug: As far back as I can remember. The earliest stuff I'd ever read would have been *Uncle Scrooge* by Carl Barks, which I loved. As a matter of fact, when later I did the Marvel *Doc Savage* b-&-w magazine, I modeled it on the Carl Barks' *Uncle Scrooge* stuff with Doc as Scrooge and his five back-up guys were like Donald, Huey, Dewey and Louie.

CBA: *It sets an homage feel to that comic book.*
Doug: Those stories just stuck with me! I didn't even know it doing it but they were such great adventure stories. The structure of them was that Scrooge would somehow get mixed up in some big adventure and he'd rope the others into it and they would be his helpers; and one of them would be a screw-up and that would be Donald and the other three (Huey, Dewey and Louie) with their Junior Woodchuck knowledge would be pretty competent fellows. That worked out. I think Monk was the goof-up in the *Doc Savage* stories and everyone else was pretty competent. The structure seemed to work. I don't know at what point I realized I was thinking of it in that way but there was a point where I went, "You know, this is *Uncle Scrooge!*" And it was working.

Below: *The perpetually young Doug Moench in a recent photo. Courtesy of the writer.*

CBA: *Did you get into adventure comics or horror comics at all?*
Doug: Yeah, I think the earliest adventure comics that I remember were Joe Kubert's "Viking Prince" stories in *The Brave and the Bold*. I just loved those. Russ Heath—who later became a very good friend of mine and still is—was doing "The Golden Gladiator." Those two, Viking Prince and Golden Gladiator, were my favorites. I also liked "The Shining Knight." The horror comics...I have a dim memory of stumbling across some ECs but I can't really finger that as well as the memories of *Uncle Scrooge* and the *B&B* stuff. Also, I enjoyed war comics; and then eventually, the first super-hero things I got into were *Superman* and *Batman*.

I actually quit reading comics for a while—I grew up! I was too old for them. For about three months. Then I went into the corner place where they sold Coke and french fries and comic books, and I looked over at the comics rack and I saw *Fantastic Four* #1 and the logo was so goofy that I just had to pick it up and look through it—and I bought the thing—and then I was more into comics than ever before. Then *Spider-Man* appeared and the whole Marvel thing took off.

CBA: *Were you particularly clued into the storytelling or was it the art?*
Doug: I don't know. I just liked to read and comics were one of the first things I read and I just loved them! There's just something about the combination of words and pictures that, as a kid, I enjoyed more than just words. (Although now I love reading just words, of course!) Thing is, comics just couldn't be beat back then, in the days when there was no *Batman* or *Conan* movies and comics were the only place you could get that kind of thing. Would it that were still so!

CBA: *I talked to Bruce Jones about the influence of television drama on him that was very strong in storytelling. Was TV and film important to you?*
Doug: Yeah. My father at the time was a TV repairman for RCA (when he retired he was a real big deal in RCA, the head of the Midwest region training centers), we were really big TV people. Yeah, I watched endless amounts of TV as a kid. I went cold turkey when I became a long-hair (this was before hippies!). I remember walking down the street one day and the construction workers yelling, "Hippie!" and I didn't know what they were talking about. Yesterday it was, "Are you a boy or a girl?" and today it was "Hey, Hippie!" And I didn't know what was going on. But when I moved out of home at age 18 and started living with a girl, there was no TV so I just stopped watching. I'm one of the few people on Earth who's never seen a *Star Trek* all the way through! [*laughs*] But up until that point, yeah, I was totally immersed in television. All those westerns, *Twilight Zone, Outer Limits*, yeah, sure; and the comedies. I still love George Burns and Gracie Allen, Jack Benny.

CBA: *How about film?*
Doug: Yeah, oh yeah! This is how old I am. At the time you needed a quarter to get into the movies and I would just go into the alley on Saturday morning and pick up pop bottles. You could take them to the store and get two cents each, right? So, fifteen or twenty bottles and you've got enough to get in and buy popcorn and soda. I'd just ride my bike to the movie theater every week. They would show double features, triple features, with a half hour of cartoons in between, it was *fantastic!*

CBA: *Any particular genre?*
Doug: Horror movies were my favorite.
CBA: *The Universal films?*
Doug: No, I'm not that old. Those I could only see on Saturday night on *Shock Theatre* and it was very, very frustrating because I

Above: *1980 montage of images from* Master of Kung Fu *by Paul Gulacy. Courtesy of Albert Moy. Art ©2000 Paul Gulacy. Characters ©2000 Marvel Characters, Inc.*

...was still in school, you know? And I'd get all set for *Shock Theatre* at 10:30 at night and the structure of the Universal films is that the monster doesn't show up until near the end. That's not true with *Frankenstein* but with some of them the big-deal stuff only happens at the end (as opposed to today when you get slapped with it right in the face at the beginning) and I would always fall asleep right before the good part! *Aw, man!* So that was very frustrating; but I got to see the '50s horror/s-f films, you know, the giant bug thing and then Hammer came along and, "Wow! *Red blood!*" That was a very big deal. Hammer was very large in my life for a while. I get the laser discs and DVDs of them now and I can't for the life of me figure out why I thought they were so great. I think it was mostly the color and the gorgeous sets and they seemed to be fast-paced. Now, they're like snail's pace; slow movies.

CBA: *Lush, though.*

Doug: Oh yeah. Full color. Beautiful sets. Good-looking Dracula. Christopher Lee—you can't beat him. Lot of good things about them. Beautiful women. That heaving cleavage all the time. I can see where an adolescent kid who hadn't seen an MTV-edited fast-paced thing would have loved that stuff. It's just a shame that it's not as good as I remember it.

CBA: *So, did you draw as a child? Did you try to emulate comics?*

Doug: Yeah, I did—but I can't draw at all. Although I did write and draw my own comic strip for the grade school newspaper.

CBA: *What was it called?*

Doug: It was called "My Dog Sandy." Great school memories. I had a real dog named Sandy and this was kind of a continued adventure strip. I was constantly getting into jeopardy and Sandy was constantly rescuing me, helping me out a fix. It seems to me that I did a lot of them but the truth was probably seven or eight of them. That was my first published stuff, I guess.

CBA: *Did you do creative writing?*

Doug: Yeah, without knowing. Every once in a while I would feel possessed to write down something. In high school I wrote something that was just a shameless rip-off of an EC story, the one that Joe Orlando drew about the blue robots and the orange robots and a human goes to the planet to settle a dispute between the blue and orange robots. The shock at the end is that the human takes off his bubble helmet and he's got a black face. It's just a real powerful statement about racism. Well, I just totally ripped it off without really consciously knowing it! I showed it to my English teacher in high school and she was so impressed with it that she sent me to the high school literary magazine. They published it and it became this big sensation in the high school. This was, at that time, the only integrated high school in Chicago which had a very segregated school system—and all of a sudden, whenever any of the black guys in the school found out, "You wrote that!", I was a big hero to them. It really did have a big effect in the halls of the school and it was a big school too. 8,000 kids, all guys.

And, speaking of Chicago, I later wrote feature articles for the *Chicago Sun-Times.* Roger Ebert claimed to have discovered me and wanted a finder's fee! [*laughs*] I got this job at the *Sun-Times* just as a way to avoid starving, you know? I guess I'd lived off girls long enough! I better get some kind of job; that kind of thing—and it was just this schlump job in the communications room in the time when they had teletype machines before computers? It was actually shared by the *Chicago Sun-Times* and the *Chicago Daily News.* They were both in the same building at the time. I think maybe they still are.

CBA: *One was a morning paper and other was night?*

Doug: Right. I just worked in this loud clackety-clack communications room and I got the graveyard shift from 1:00 a.m. to 9 a.m. My job was nothing but to rip the stories from the AP and UPI teletype machines, and distribute them to the proper editors and the city desk; but the graveyard shift, there was just me and one guy who would sleep out at the city desk in case something big broke. So all I had to do at the beginning of my shift was to make sure the machines had enough paper and I could write all night long! I was writing for Warren and Skywald, writing these b-&-w stories and getting paid twice. Paid for what I was writing and by the hour from *Sun-Times*. Then in the morning I would clear off everything real quick and distribute it and then go home. Anyway, one day, Roger Ebert was not only the film critic but he was also writing the occasional article, and he wrote this article about b-&-w horror comic books. So near the end of my shift, I'm getting ready to leave at 9 A.M. while everyone's coming in, and I'm going to have a cup of coffee to go. I've just read this article and I'm walking to the coffee machine when waddling down the hall, coming the other way, is Roger Ebert and I stopped him. He didn't know who I was—I was just some long-haired freak who worked in the communications department—and I stopped him. I said, "That article on the b-&-w horror comics?" And he said, "Yes?" And I said, "It's full of sh*t!" And he says, "Really! And who are you?" I said, "I'm the guy who writes those b-&-w horror comics." And he wouldn't believe it! But I finally convinced him. I described some of the stories to him. I said, "Man, you didn't do your research well. You read a couple of issues of this and one issue of that and you got everything wrong." And he goes, "Come with me!" And he takes me way in the back to the editor of the Sunday supplement magazine which was called *MidWest* magazine. "This is the guy who writes those b-&-w horror comics," Roger told him. "You should have him write an article about what it's like to write those horror comics." So this guy says "Well, I used to like comics. Did you ever hear of *The Spirit*?" And I say, "Will Eisner is my god!" He says, "Yeah, Will Eisner. You know, we used to publish those little pamphlet inserts in the *Chicago Sun-Times* every Sunday." I said, "I know! I've got a bunch of them at home." So he says, "All right, write the article." I came up with this idea about accompanying the article with this one page comic strip about a guy who writes horror comic books and he brings a date home and she wants to know where he gets all those scary ideas from. Then the final panel is the punch line and the writer turns into a werewolf and attacks her and that's where he gets all his ideas from, from real life. Just a silly little Warren/Skywald type piece; and I got Russ Heath, who was living in Chicago at the time and was a friend of mine, to do this thing and he hand-watercolored it, and it was gorgeous. So that's a real collector's item now.

CBA: *Do you have any copies of that?*

Doug: I have one copy left. Because, about a year and a half ago, Russ came to my house and stayed and he didn't have any left and I had two so I gave him one. Anyway, that was received well and the editor, Richard Takeuchi, said, "Write something else." He was looking for something edgy. He didn't say it, but that's what he wanted. I said, "How about something stream-of-consciousness, something from personal experience, violence on the midnight subway system?" Which I knew about because I was riding the subway to get to my job at one in the morning. So I wrote this real, hyper, stream-of-consciousness type thing and it got nominated for a Chicago Newspaper Guild award, the whole thing.

CBA: *Were you into new journalism and Tom Wolfe?*

Doug: Oh, Hunter S. Thompson! I don't know if I'd read him at that point yet but this was somewhat similar. Even if I hadn't read him, I was thinking along the same lines and now, of course, I love Hunter Thompson and all those guys.

CBA: *What got you started working professionally as a writer?*

Doug: Well, it was that whole high school literary magazine thing.

Then I was involved…I was at the world's first comic book convention which was in Chicago. It was based in, I think, Eddy Navarett's basement. It was me, Don Glut, Roy Thomas, Don and Maggie Thompson… (I'm not sure if Jerry Bails was at that first one or not) Bob Butts, and a couple of other early fans who came all the way from Indiana! This was like the first fan gathering although they'd been doing it for science-fiction, and that was what ours was modeled on. That's where I met Roy although he claims he didn't remember me when we met again. He was already a big deal guy because of his fanzine, *Alter Ego*. He was a Big Name Fan, although I don't know if we called them that at the time. Anyway, I also went to some of the science-fiction meetings where Fred Saberhagen would show up, people like that. I became friends with some science-fiction fans, some comics fans. Don Glut became a really good friend. He married the twin of one of my girlfriends that I introduced him to. Anyway, every once in a while I would just have a fellow fan come over to my house and for some reason we'd just both sit down and write something. Usually a sword-&-sorcery type thing and then we'd read what each other wrote and there was never any plan of submitting it or anything. It was just a game, like playing checkers or something. So I guess I'd always liked to write but never dreamed that I could do it professionally. The thing that got me was that my friend Don Glut sold a story to Warren for *Creepy*—and I thought, "Jeez, if he can do it, I can do it! I can write better than him!" [*laughs*] You know, that's the way I felt from reading what each other had written. So I sat down and wrote five stories in a row in five days. A story a day; and I sent them off to Warren and promptly forgot about them. If I'd never heard anything, I'm sure I probably never would have written another one, just would have gone back to my crazy life at that time; but then one day there was a check in the mail from Warren Publishing for $125 which was big deal money in 1967 or whatever it was.

CBA: *He bought them all?*

Doug: [*laughs*] That's the thing. I thought, "Man! He bought one of my stories for $125? I've got to do more!" And there was no note, no phone call, nothing. Just a check for $125 and I found out that Archie Goodwin had bought all five of them for $25 each. "Well, it's not quite as good as I thought but, hey!" $25 went a lot farther in those days. So I started writing more and just kept at it and then I got the job at the *Sun-Times* and then I started writing prose fiction and that was much, much better than Warren or Skywald or any of the comics things at the time. I wrote these mens' magazine things. They were hippie-humor, sex stories, you know? And they were all true, or mostly true, embellished for fiction; and these guys at *Adam, Knight, Man to Man*, all of those, $500 for 2,000 word story! Whoa! My God! All of a sudden I felt like a rich man. Between that and the weekly check from the *Sun-Times*… Then I started writing articles for the *Sun-Times*, that paid really well too. In the meantime I had submitted a proposal and an outline to a hardcover, coffee-table book publisher called A.S. Barnes (which is now Barnes & Noble) to be called *The Encyclopedia of Horror*. From A-Z: Literature, movies, books, comics, radio shows; everything you could think of in horror. It was going to be this colossal project. One day, I got an acceptance with a contract. I'd get this advance for, maybe $500 or $1000, for just signing the contract; and literally the day I got that, the phone rang and it was Roy Thomas and he said, "Why don't you come to New York and work for Marvel?" Marv Wolfman had recommended me, so I had to make this big decision. Do I sign the contract, stay in Chicago and write the book or do I go to Marvel? So I told Roy, "Well, I'll come to New York for two weeks and try you out." [Laughs] Instead of them trying *me* out, I was going to go and see if I could handle living in New York City which I wasn't sure I wanted to do. Anyway, I went there and after the two weeks… to finance me getting there, they said, "Just voucher as many b-&-w stories—6 pages, 7 pages, 8 pages, for *Monsters Unleashed, Dracula Lives*, to get enough money to make the move to New York. Of course, later you're going to have to write all those stories!" It's like just make up a bunch of titles, voucher them, and we'll pay you and then you can write the stories later; and that's what I did. I make the big move to New York. I was on staff for probably the shortest time than anybody! [*laughs*] I was there maybe a month and half, six weeks or so, and Roy called me into his office

and he said, "We need more writing from you." I said, "Roy, I'm already writing more than any of your other writers and I'm doing his eight hours a day here in the office. If you want any more out of me I'll have to stay home." So he said, "Yeah, I figured you'd say hat. Okay, just stay long enough to train Dave Kraft, we're going to ring him in, then you can stay home. And by the way, here's *Werewolf by Night* and *Master of Kung Fu*." He eventually gave me

like six or seven books to write. Those were the days, man!
CBA: *What were you doing on staff?*
Doug: It was called either Assistant Editor or Associate Editor. I don't recall what it was called but it was basically proofreading, which wasn't just making sure that the lettering was correct, it was also, "Are there the correct amount of stripes on Captain America's outfit? Did they leave off the star anywhere?" Proofreading the

Above: *This Doug Moench-written and Russ Heath-illustrated page was shown in full gory color accompanying Doug's article mentioned in the caption opposite. ©2000 Doug Moench & Russ Heath.*

This page and next: *Courtesy of Dave "Hambone" Hamilton, here's two pages of Paul's pencils from* Master of Kung Fu *#45. Art ©2000 Paul Gulacy. Shang-Chi ©2000 Marvel Characters, Inc.*

artwork as well as the balloons which they don't seem to do much anymore. Proofreading the color and so on. You know, proofreading is a very weird thing. I went from one week sitting at home in Chicago, reading the latest issue of *Spider-Man* and thinking that Gerry Conway was great and the next week I'm in the Marvel office proofing the next issue and thinking Gerry Conway stinks. You get so involved in the minutiae. You did it with an X-acto blade and a pen;

you'd do a lot of the lettering correction yourself. I'd just scrape off the wrong letter and add the correct one. I'd do it right at my desk. Anything really involved would have to go to production, but we did a lot of the things on the fly; and you'd get involved in a lot of little things so that, by the end of the book, you couldn't remember what happened on page one. And I remember going, "What the hell happened to Gerry Conway? He stinks!" [*laughs*] Proofreading is a very hard way to tell if the thing's any good. You've got to read it another time.

CBA: *Backing up a little: You said you did some work for Skywald. Was that by mail?*

Doug: Yeah, that was all by mail.

CBA: *How did you know Skywald was looking for stories?*

Doug: Oh, I just saw them on the newsstand. When Warren would reject a story, there was a while there in which they bought every story I wrote, but then they started getting other writers and they would no longer buy everything anyone wrote, and I'd say, "Why are you rejecting this one? I could name nine that you did buy and this one's better than all of those." And they'd just say, "Well, you know, you've got five stories in the next *Creepy* as it is." So I saw Skywald on the stand and it was very different. I sent a story and got a call from Sol Brodsky and it's like, "Boy, do we want you! How about coming to New York and working for us?" And I said, "Ah, no." He said, "We're bringing out a new book called *Hellrider*. Why don't you write that?" And for some reason I turned that down. It sounded really stupid to me. That's probably why I didn't do it. I had submitted the first one that Warren rejected and then sent anything else they rejected. Then it got to the point where I started sending some things to Skywald first. Like, "Well, I've just sent three to Warren and I've got two more, so I'd better send these two to Skywald." And, man, did Warren pitch a fit! He was a very weird guy, as you know, since you did the Warren issue. Left me out of it, you son of a bitch! [*laughs*]

CBA: *I couldn't find you! I didn't know where you were, for one thing. I certainly have enough material coming up for another issue pretty soon so we can talk at more length about that.*

Doug: Well, when Warren found out I was selling stuff to Skywald, he… I actually went to New York once, before Roy called with the job offer, and it was such a crazy place. It stunk! Chicago's a clean city compared to New York. Anyway, while I was in New York, I went to the Warren office to do business when John Cochran was the editor. So I'm talking to John and he says, "Well, Jim wants to meet you." And I was like, "Okay." Cochran had already, in letters and a few phone calls, intimated that Jim Warren was not your normal, everyday duck, but I didn't really know how weird Warren could be until I was there. Cochran takes me into the outer office and he goes in and tells the secretary to tell Warren that I'm there. So I'm sitting there waiting and the door bangs open and this guy comes walking out real fast and I'm getting up to shake his hand and he stops three inches from my nose, looking up at me, because he's short, but being real belligerent and I'm thinking, "What the hell is going on here?" And he says, "So you're this Doug Moench guy?" I said, "Yeah?" He said, "You're one of our very best writers and I want to punch you in the nose!" I said, "What?" Then he goes into this tirade about working for the enemy and betraying him, you know, subverting the Warren Empire; and I'm thinking, "What the hell *is* this guy? Is this a joke?" I could not figure it out but he got really heated and I got pissed off and I started yelling, "Hey, back off, motherf*cker!" [*laughs*] And that one really shocked him! I guess nobody ever talked back to him before. And I went, "Look, if you want me to write only for you then I want you to buy only from me. And if you want everything I write to be only for you then you have to buy everything I write!" It was this real weird thing! It ended up being inconclusive. I went back to Chicago and everything was normal for a while and I kept sending things to Skywald and Warren. Then I got this series of letters from Warren about, again, me betraying him and working for the enemy and subverting the Warren

Characters ©2000 Marvel Characters, Inc.

Publishing Empire, all these weird phrasings he had; and I answered the first few, three I think, trying to reason with him and explain, saying, "Hey, I've got to eat! I can't just throw away a story because you don't want it and your editor keeps saying, 'Hey, you've got six stories in the next *Eerie* and I can't buy any more from you this month.' If that's true and I know it's true because you bought the six and you can't handle any more or I'm going to send them some-

where else." Finally he just sent this one really, really weird letter and I just couldn't handle it anymore so I sent him a letter saying, "Dear Jim, F*ck you! Sincerely, Doug!" [*laughs*] Now, a couple of days later, this was at the time when the post office really did have special delivery. I don't know if you're old enough to remember but this was when they actually sent a special postal delivery guy to your house at night or whatever time it was. So 10:30 or 11:00 at night, my door-

REVENGE WON'T SOLVE A THING, JASON! IF THIS DANGEROUS AND GROWING NOTION OF APE SUPREM-ACY IS TO BE HALTED, THEN BRUTUS MUST BE TAKEN BACK TO THE CITY --AND EXPOSED FOR THE HATE-MONGER HE IS--!

AND WHO'LL BELIEVE IT-- HIS APE FOLLOWERS--?

NO, LAWGIVER-- THE TIME FOR MERCY PASSED WHEN BRUTUS BURNED MY PARENTS TO DEATH!

BESIDES, LAW-GIVER, WOULD YOU PROTEST SO MUCH IF THE ROLES WERE RE-VERSED-- AND BRUTUS WAS A HUMAN, TRYING TO ANNIHILATE APE--?

I'M HUMAN, JASON-- AND I'M ASKING YOU TO RESTORE THE MERCY YOU SAY HAS BEEN LOST. PLEASE, JASON...NO MATTER WHO THE VICTIM IS, A MURDERER COULD NEVER RECEIVE MY LOVE...

LOVE. THE WORD. SPOKEN BY THIS GIRL HE BARELY KNOWS, SEEMING TO IMPRESS ITSELF IN HIS MIND... ASSUAGING THE FEVER OF HATE. AND THOUGH STILL SCOWLING AND DISGRUNTLED, JASON RELEASES THE MURDERER OF HIS PARENTS...

ALL RIGHT. HE'LL LIVE...

...BUT ONLY TO BE EXECUTED BY THE TRIBUNAL.

THAT'S THE BOY, JASON. LAWS SOMETIMES GIVE ME A BELLY-ACHE WITH THEIR ALL-FIRED FOOLISHNESS... BUT I'VE KNOWED ONE OR TWO OF 'EM TUH MAKE SENSE...

BESIDES, I GOT ME A BETTER IDEA FER TEACHIN' THIS BRUTUS A LESSON.

HE RISES, FISTS CLENCHED AT SIDES...

I FIGGERED THAT'D GET YUH ON YORE FEET... CUZ Y'SEE, I BEEN ITCHIN' TUH SEE IF A BULLY AS BIG AS YOU--

THAT'S RIGHT, MR. BRUTUS-- I BEEN HEARIN' AN AWFUL DANGED LOT ABOUT YOU... AND IF ONLY HALF O' WHAT I BEEN HEARIN' IS TRUE--

THEN YOU'RE THE LOWEST SLIME-SLITHERIN' SON OF A SCARY SEA-SNAKE THAT EVER DIRTIED THE GROUND WITH ITS SNEAKY BELLY-CRAWLIN'...!

SPARKS GLINT FROM BRUTUS' SHADOWED EYES, THEN MESH AND HARDEN INTO A FIERY GLARE...

Above: *Exquisite Mike Ploog pencilwork from* Planet of the Apes #8. *See CBA #6 for Chris Knowles' celebration of Doug Moench's quirky POTA stories.* ©2000 Marvel Characters, Inc. Planet of the Apes ©2000 the respective copyright holder.

bell rings. "What the hell? I'm not expecting anybody!" So it's the postman with this big box. I open it up and it's all these presents from Jim Warren! And the presents, of course, were all these six-foot tall Vampirella posters and Captain Company model kits. All this Captain Company sh*t he didn't have to pay for! [*laughs*] But it was all these gifts and a little note, something to the effect of "All is forgiven. Love, Jim." And this was in response to my letter and I'd thought I'd quit! Then everything was fine after that! [*laughs*] All of a sudden, I'm getting raises and he's saying, "Don't tell the other writers we're paying you more." An actual page rate instead of a flat $25 a story no matter how many pages it was. The last thing with Jim Warren...when I moved to New York and pretty much began writing exclusively for Marvel (although I did write a few things for Joe Orlando and Archie Goodwin at DC in between), Warren just fell by the wayside, you know? There was this thing called ACBA—the Academy of Comic Book Arts—which I became Vice President of, when Neal Adams was President. We had one of these meetings and

there's a cocktail party afterwards. After it, Jim Warren is sitting at the bar with a drink and I said, "Wait a minute, that looks like the guy who said he wanted to punch me in the nose; I think that's Jim Warren." So I went over to say hello to him and he says, "So, you're a big hot-shot now, eh?" And I said, "Well, I don't know what you mean?" He said, "I hear you're writing everything that Marvel's putting out!" I said "Yeah, I'm doing a lot of stuff for them. Not everything they're putting out but a lot of stuff and they're paying me a lot compared to you!" So he says, "Well, I just want you to know that the door to Warren Publishing is always open… for you to *crawl back through!*" [*laughs*]

CBA: [*laughs*] *Good old Jim!*

Doug: Great guy! I don't know. I kind of liked him, you know? I hated him and liked him at the same time. It was a strange sort of thing.

CBA: *Now you walked away. That seems to me the overwhelming attitude of people at that time. Maybe, contemporaneously, people hated his guts but over time, they find a charm to him that they liked.*

Doug: Yeah! Yeah, looking back, it was almost like a Bergman movie or something. There were *characters* in those days. It wasn't all bland. It was larger than life and yet, the Bullpen really was one big, happy family, believe it or not. What a tragedy, what happened there, *whoa…!*

CBA: *What did happen there?*

Doug: Well… I don't know if it was inevitable with growth. I attribute it all, perhaps rightly, perhaps wrongly, to the coming of Jim Shooter. That's when it really started going sour for me. The thing was, there was no real editor. Roy was the editor of the whole company but not a micro-manager of individual titles. You could make a deal on second base at the Marvel softball game with Roy, you know? You hit a double and Roy's playing second place and Roy'd say, "Hey, Doug, you wanna write 'Shang-Chi'?" I'd say, "Yeah, I'd love to write that." He'd say, "Okay, first one's due next week." And that was it! Nobody was looking over your shoulder. Becoming friends with my collaborators and working closely with them was what I preferred. Even if they never contributed any actual story ideas, just talking with the artist and finding out what they liked and didn't like, what they wanted to draw and you could stick that in the story and get great art from them because it was something they wanted to do. We controlled the destiny of our own books. There were times when Roy would take the last five make-readys, the last five issues of *Master of Kung Fu*, take them home and read them all at once. Then he'd tell you what he thought the next day—but it wasn't the way it is now. My God, it's smothering, it's *stifling!* You've got editors who want to know every little thing. And, "Oh, no, you can't do that." Well, how does an editor know until he sees it? How can you tell if it's going to be any good? "Well, it just doesn't sound like it'll be any good." Well, that's only because you couldn't write it that way and make it good. Too many of the editors are writers themselves and that's not the way that they would do it. Whereas Roy was willing to say, "Well, I think you're good, I think the artist is good, let's see what you can do together." And then he would see what you did, and if it was good, he'd let you keep going and that was great! If it was a disaster, well, okay, we'd better get someone else to do these things. To me, that's the perfect editor. There was a spontaneity, a freedom, an enthusi-asm, a joy to doing Marvel comics that I think is totally lacking today.

CBA: *You came to New York and became an associate editor for,* like six weeks, then you went freelance. Where were you living in New York?

Doug: Riverside Drive. It was beautiful. It was a tiny apartment but the area was beautiful. There was a park across the street and then the Hudson River.

CBA: *Were you solo then?*

Doug: No, no. I had just met a new girl in Chicago and that was another reason I didn't know if I wanted to go to New York, assuming I'd never know how this was going to turn out; but then the girl in question, who is now my wife Debra said, "Look, no strings attached. I'll go with you, we'll try it out, if it works out, fine, if it doesn't, I'll just come back to Chicago and no hard feelings." I said, "Well, if you really want to take that chance, we hardly know each other, you know?" But she did and it did work out.

CBA: *What was the first book you got on freelance? Monster of Frankenstein?*

Doug: Well, remember, financing the move, I had to voucher all these b-&-w stories. The first color comic I did during the first two weeks I was there, was *Ghost Rider,* the flaming skull-guy on the motorcycle. Then I think the next one was "Man-Wolf," which I didn't write for too long—I think six or seven issues. That was a nightmare! It was one of the times when you couldn't have freedom because of the bizarre structuring of the book. Man-Wolf was, of course, J. Jonah Jameson's son, and JJJ was important in *Spider-Man,* and if you're writing "Man-Wolf," well, the father's got to be pretty upset that his son's turning into a werewolf all the time but you couldn't have him upset because he was doing something else in *Spider-Man.* It wasn't that anybody was looking over my shoulder when I was doing that book; it was just that I was told up front that JJJ can't get upset. How can you write this stuff?! So I was glad to get out of that one. Then, I think, yeah, *Monster of Frankenstein, Werewolf by Night, Master of Kung Fu.* Somewhere I got the *Planet of the Apes* b-&-w, *Doc Savage, Deadly Hands of Kung Fu, The Inhumans, Ka-Zar, Iron Fist....*

CBA: *You did Iron Fist, too? Man, you were prolific!*

Doug: Oh, yeah! I was this phenomenon. John Verpoorten, one of my best friends at Marvel, he was just awed! He was the traffic guy; he was the guy you brought the work to and he just couldn't believe the volume of my stuff—and delivering all this writing, I would add,

"And, by the way, here's that 35-page 'Dracula' story for the b-&-w Dracula mag Marv wanted."

CBA: *That you owed for the move?*

Doug: Oh, no, no. That was after I actually got there. Oh, yeah, "Deathlok" in *Astonishing Tales* with Rich Buckler, "Morbius the Living Vampire," *Tales of the Zombie,* "Gabriel the Devil Hunter" in *Haunt of Horror,* and eventually *Fantastic Four, Thor,* and the

Above: *Recent promotional piece for Master of Kung Fu. Courtesy of Paul Gulacy. Art ©2000 Paul Gulacy. Shang-Chi ©2000 Marvel Characters, Inc.*

THE KRYLORIAN CONSPIRACY

HULK IS TIRED OF FIGHTING! HULK WILL END FIGHTING! HULK WILL SMASH YOU-- SMASH YOU ALL!!

FEATURING:

RICK JONES: THE JALOPY-CRUISING TEENAGER WHO IS THE HULK'S ONLY FRIEND!

BETTY ROSS: THE WOMAN WHO LOVES BRUCE BANNER, NEVER SUSPECTING THE DREAD SECRET LOCKED WITHIN HIS SOUL!

THUNDER-BOLT ROSS: THE IRON-WILLED AIR-FORCE GENERAL WHO HAS VOWED TO CRUSH A MON-STER!

Above: *Great mix of Walt Simonson pencils and Alfredo Alcala inks (plus Doug's dead-on early-'60s approach) make for a great start for the b-&-w mag, The Rampaging Hulk. This splash is from issue #1. ©2000 Marvel Characters, Inc.*

Rampaging Hulk magazine—you remember that color magazine? It just went on and on.

CBA: *Oh, yeah! You did a great job with the Hulk magazine! Was that with Walt Simonson?*

Doug: Yeah. I think it was me and Walt, it was still a b-&-w, then it went into a full-color process thing. Then with Moon Knight, I created him as a villain in *Werewolf by Night,* and he got a shot in *Marvel Spotlight.* He got his own book eventually; but before that, he was a backup in the *Hulk* magazine. That's where Bill Sienkiewicz got his start. He was just this kid coming in and we were like, "Oh, we'll get this kid who draws like Neal Adams, he's perfect for *Moon Knight.*" Who knew? And *Weirdworld* with Mike Ploog—we did the world's first three-page fold-out in comics. Then the "Warriors of the Shadow Realm" thing; but *Weirdworld* started out in b-&-w, too, then had a few regular-sized color comic issues, then that big full-size magazine, airbrushed… *man,* that thing was overdone to the nth degree!

CBA: *Was that work-for-hire?*

Doug: Yeah. I'm in contact with Mike Ploog now. We're supposed to be doing some big deal creator-owned project together—we'll see if it ever happens—but the last time I talked to him, "We've got to do this!" [*laughter*] I love Mike!

Oh, here's a little behind the scenes thing: When we were doing the *Planet of the Apes* magazine, I created these characters called

Gunpowder Julius and Steely Dan who were these riverboat guys—larger-than-life guys. They were always slapping each other on the back hard enough to knock their rib cages out, roaring with laughter. Gunpowder Julius was based on Mike. I created the character and he's drawing it telling me how much he loves these characters especially Gunpowder Julius and I'm saying, "Well, Mike, that's because he's *you!*" And he's, "What?! What?! *What?!* Oh, that's right! I didn't even notice but that *is* me!" [*laughter*] He did a great job on *Planet of the Apes*!

CBA: *That was beautiful! Was that taken directly from his pencils?*

Doug: The riverboat one, yeah. I remember that was the same meeting where Jim Warren told me I could crawl back through the doors. When Mike showed up with his portfolio and he had the first twelve pages of that and he did it in that special process and sprayed nail polish or something on it, I don't know…that's when I first saw these pages and I was like, "Oh, my God! If this prints right…", and it didn't. Those pages are much more gorgeous than the way they printed and you can tell even from the published pages how gorgeous they are. You should have seen the originals.

CBA: *When did you start working closely with artists? Were you submitting full scripts to Marvel?*

Doug: I was submitting full scripts for all the Warren and Skywald stuff but when I moved to Marvel, I was encouraged to use the Marvel Method—the Stan Lee Method—but I never could; so I developed this bastardized version of my own. What it amounted to was instead of three paragraphs that Jack Kirby could turn into a story (because I wasn't working with Jack Kirby, you know?), I just wasn't confident that somebody else could do it and if they did, didn't that make them the writer of the story? I mean, I was doing the word balloons, but still! Because I had done so many full scripts, I decided to try for the best of both worlds. I'll do it real tight, a real long detailed plot, but it won't be 'panel one,' 'panel two,' 'panel three'; I'll do it in paragraphs and each paragraph can be a single panel or the artist can break each paragraph into two or three panels or combine two paragraphs into one panel. That way, the artist can still have the freedom of storytelling if he chooses to take it—or, if they felt more comfortable following exactly the way it was written, the artists could do that, too. In either case, I still had the luxury of all the strengths of the Marvel method—which is getting to play off the artwork when the artwork sparks ideas. The facial expression could change the tone of the dialogue—and I could break the balloons up. See, you get to place your own balloons and that facilitates a certain rhythm, a punctuation. Instead of one big balloon per panel, you can have three or four or five of them. It brings a loose, collaborative feeling to the stuff which I thought was much better than a full script and yet I still felt, legitimately, that I was the actual writer of this stuff because I did put it all in.

CBA: *Did you experience much deviation?*

Doug: It depended on the artist! For example, one of my favorite, all-time collaborators, with whom I'm still working, by the way, Paul Gulacy, was as enamored of Steranko as I was and Paul came up with his own unique version of the Steranko/Eisner/Kurtzman kind of storytelling. He would take, say, one paragraph and break it into five sliver panels with just a little bit of difference between each panel; but it went the other way, as well. I got so confident with Paul's ability—he's one of the best storytellers ever—that sometime I would get to a fight scene for example and I'd say, "Pages 12-15, big fight." I'd set it up for him, what the situation was, setting, and so on. And I'd say, "Big fight breakdowns are up to you, it's on the dock so maybe a villain grabs a crate and Shang-Chi breaks it, but I'm leaving it up to you." And that worked great! But also, because I catered to his storytelling, it would sometimes work the opposite way. I would do a detailed, patented Paul Gulacy riff, and sometimes he would do what I wrote and sometimes he'd condense it in a Herb Trimpe style, and I'd say, "What the hell? That was perfect Gulacy storytelling!" And he'd say he just didn't feel like doing it in that sequence; aut either way he did it, it always worked and I always felt we were a real great combination and understood each other and still do and just play off each other very well. Synthesis and synergy.

CBA: *Looking at the list of books that you worked on early during your time at Marvel, they're all second-tier books.*

Doug: Yeah. Well, that's what I wanted.

CBA: *Really? Was that so that no one was necessarily looking over your shoulder? So you could have freedom without interference?*

Doug: Well, I eventually got *Fantastic Four, Hulk* and *Thor,* but I never had as much fun on those, you know? Because they were so established. When you say second-tier books, that also means they were *new* books and didn't have this history. So they don't have to fit into this mold and you can take chances and do all of these really great things at Marvel—truly, truly good things. Like you look at Gerber's *Man-Thing* and *Howard the Duck,* or at McGregor's "War of the Worlds" and "Black Panther," or Jim Starlin's *Captain Marvel* and *Warlock*—all of them were second-tier. They were freedom-giving books! So I preferred those and so did the other guys. Well, Englehart…I don't know. He might have preferred the bigger books.

CBA: *Did you have any interest in doing super-hero books or did you shy away from them?*

Doug: They were my favorite as a reader for a while but they've never been my favorite as a writer although I've enjoyed some of them. I enjoyed *The Inhumans* with George Pérez and Gil Kane which I thought came out pretty good. Certain ones at certain times. I loved working with Don Perlin and Bill Sienkiewicz on *Moon Knight* but when Bill and I did *Fantastic Four* together, it was kind of weird. I was writing these Jack Kirby-type stories and I was getting Bill's Neal Adams-influenced art and it was never what I expected. That's why I always preferred Bill on *Moon Knight* and I think he also preferred me as a writer on *Moon Knight.* On the other hand, people still come up to me and say they really like that run of *Fantastic Four,* so I don't know.

CBA: *You were really pushing the envelope with* Planet of the Apes, *too, with "The Future History Chronicles."*

Doug: I really thought Tom Sutton had a rebirth when he turned in the first "Future History Chronicles." That was another example of being really tight and becoming friends with the artist. He didn't have to contribute any ideas at all but just talking with him and hearing which aspects he got enthused about. "Oh, yeah! A city-ship! My God, yeah! I could draw that! I can do that!" So I knew to focus on that, the city-ship, because that's what he was excited about. It really seemed to wake him up and make him do what I thought was some of the best work he'd ever done. He's a good guy.

CBA: *What is Tom Sutton like?*

Doug: Garrulous. Very enthused about anything that he liked. I love people who get really enthused over the things that they like and he was like that; and he was very much into H.P. Lovecraft. He loved that kind of stuff. So much so that he even lived up there in Lovecraft country and one of my unrealized dreams was doing a Lovecraft magnum opus with Sutton that we had started to do

for some upstart new publisher who went kablooey on us. The same thing happened to me and Bill although the thing we did was for *Adventure Illustrated.* One issue came out, the first part of what was supposed to be this epic. We got paid and published, then they went kablooey and we never finished the thing.

Anyway, Tom's a great guy. He's very knowledgeable about Lovecraft, of course, and other things. Whatever his interests were. He marched to a different drummer which was fine with me. I found that I preferred working with artists like that. The ones who were different from all the rest. That's another thing that seems to have changed. Now it seems that if an artist is too different, it's a drawback rather than an asset.

CBA: *You really started hitting your stride with Shang-Chi. How do you recall that book?*

Doug: I worked with more than three artists but three main ones. They were Paul Gulacy, Mike Zeck, and Gene Day. All three, in my opinion, did great stuff in different ways. For some reason, charm, good luck, the fates smiled or whatever, I thought all three versions worked very well. All three had very long runs—comparatively, anyway. Not as long as mine, of course, 'cause I did it for ten years. I liked all three guys very much.

CBA: *Arguably, all three started off crude, early in their career, then they really shined.*

Doug: Yeah, that was another similarity. All three started on the book. Gene was the one exception in that he had been established as an inker—but as a penciler, he got his start on *Master of Kung Fu.* He might have done a couple of short stories he penciled on his own but as far as a major, ongoing book, it was *MOKF* and he really came into his own—as Mike Zeck did and Paul Gulacy did.

CBA: *What happened to Gene Day?*

Doug: Well, I don't really know. I talked to his widow quite a bit after he died. I never met Gene face to face but we became great friends. Endless hours on the phone and I loved talking to Gene just like I still enjoy talking to Mike Zeck and Paul. I can only speculate that he lived on coffee and cigarettes and didn't exercise enough… I don't know. I know that he was really under tremendous stress at the end because of what had happened with Jim Shooter trying to force him to draw a certain way. Again, it's like the style was too different and it's all got to be like this issue of *Captain America* drawn by Jack Kirby with six equal-sized panels and full-size figures in every panel on each page…what kind of nonsense was that? And Gene was so eccentric in his layouts—his greatest strength—and now he's being told, you know, not to do that. He's got to do this book and not that book. I know my last conversations with him, this was really, really stressing him out and getting him down. He didn't know if he could go on as a comic book artist under those terms. I know that his widow said that was what killed him—but I'm sure living on coffee and not exercising certainly contributed…if that's true! As I said, I can only speculate. I wasn't there.

CBA: *What was your working relationship with Mike Zeck?*

Doug: Mike was this little kid. This cool, little surfer dude with long, blond hair. I remember the day I met him. I was in Central Park, playing in a Marvel softball game and this kid with long blond hair came up and said, "Are you Doug?" I said yeah, and he said, "I'm Mike Zeck. Roy Thomas told me to come to you." I said, "Okay, why did he tell you to come to me?" And he said, "I've got these samples and Roy said maybe you'd be interested in writing a story for me." And he showed me this five-page "Solomon Kane" story with no words. You could tell that there were things happening but without the balloons, you couldn't tell *exactly* what was happening; but they were consecutive coherent pages rather than isolated sample drawings. It was a narrative with Solomon Kane fighting werewolves, I think, and I said, "Hey, these are really cool!" They were nowhere near as good as he later became but I thought they were very good and I thought the storytelling was fine so I said, "Tell you what, I'm really going to help you, buddy!" And he said, "What do you mean?" And I said, "I'm going to find a way to see that you get paid for your samples. I'm going to write a story to go with these pages and you'll get paid for these!" And he was really excited, couldn't believe it. I went home and made up a story to go with his pages and he got paid for that. Then, I can't remember the sequence, if right after that he did anything else with another writer or if he went right on to *MOKF*, I really don't remember. I know that after Paul left, we had Jim Craig and one or two other fill-in artists and it just wasn't feeling right. Then Zeck got the job and stayed with it for a really long run and became great, I thought!

CBA: *When did you first realize that MOKF was outliving the trend? That was a hot thing in America for a period of time,*

Below: Not to be overlooked is the fine work by Gene Day and Mike Zeck, two artists who ably followed up Paul Gulacy on Master of Kung Fu. *Here's a combination of the two—Mike on pencils with Gene's inks— from a MOKF splash. ©2000 Marvel Characters, Inc.*

martial arts/kung fu, but this persevered long after the craze waned.

Doug: Yeah, but it never was a big thing with me. I mean, I like Jackie Chan now and I later became a big fan of Bruce Lee but when I started *MOKF* and almost to the end, I couldn't have cared less about martial arts movies. It's only now that I enjoy them, especially Jackie Chan. I don't know, I never watched the *Kung Fu* TV show either. What I liked about *MOKF* was this *Stranger in a Strange Land* aspect. This naive guy trying to make sense of the Western world. He had been raised in seclusion. To me, that was the most interesting thing and also the pulp flavor by having Fu Manchu in there, I enjoyed that. Plus the freedom to introduce all these supporting characters and do an ongoing soap opera subplot jamboree and create all these wacky villains. That was one of the best things about the martial arts thing. I could create RazorFist and Shockwave and some weird guy swinging his head with maces in the top knot of his hair. It was really kind of goofball but, on the other hand, it wasn't quite as goofy as a cosmic super-villain who could knock out a sun, you know what I mean? It's still more down-to-earth, which I preferred. As flamboyant as they were, they were still within the realms of possibility. I mean, a guy actually could have his arms torn off and replaced with blades. I don't know how he'd wipe his butt when he went to the toilet! [*laughs*] He'd need some help I suppose!

CBA: *Right! When did you realize that it was transcending the genre?*

Doug: I don't know. I was such a recluse. I was writing so much. Sometimes like 18 hours a day. It was just gushing out. I didn't really have the time to be aware of it. I didn't even have time to read everything I wrote! To this day, I haven't read most of the *MOKF*s. I haven't even watched all the *Mighty Mouse* cartoons I wrote for CBS. That's a different situation. It wasn't that I didn't have enough time, it was because I couldn't bear to see what happened to those cartoons. Although a lot of people seemed to really like that show, I knew what it could have been and it was just painfully disappointing to me. I guess, because I was doing the *MOKF* letters pages, I knew… I was getting these letters from people saying that *MOKF* was their life, had saved their lives, they were about to commit suicide and then they read *MOKF* #89 and decided not to kill themselves. I never really took it seriously but I could tell that something was going on, that this was really affecting people more than the usual comic book.

CBA: *What was it?*

Doug: I don't know. I have no idea. Some emotional connection, I guess.

CBA: *It seemed to be, in many ways, because you and Paul, especially in the early days, were a perfect team.*

Doug: Oh, yeah! I was aware of that. I was aware of the work. I was aware that when I worked with Mike Ploog, it came out special. When I worked with Val Mayerik on *Ka-Zar*, it came out special. With John Bolton on *Kull*. John Buscema on *King Conan*, and later, Mark Silvestri. Definitely, when I worked with Paul Gulacy, there was magic. There was magic when I worked with Ploog too, but it was a different kind of magic. With Paul, I was able to…I don't know. I guess because *MOKF* was such an eccentric premise that it was able to go in so many different directions, the spy stuff, the pulp stuff, the soap opera stuff, the martial arts stuff, the fish-out-of-water stuff, you know? The Doomed Love kind of stuff. There was all kinds of stuff that wove in and out. I even got so cocky on that thing that… don't know if you ever saw any of the Rufus T. Hackstabber issues?

CBA: *I can't recall them.*

Doug: Oh, man, where I did Groucho Marx as a crazed cab driver who gets mixed up with Shang-Chi? [*laughs*] And he really *was* Groucho Marx! He looked like Groucho, he talked like Groucho, and for some reason I felt that even those issues—I don't think I did any of those with Paul, I think they were with Keith Pollard—but I thought that even those were kind of cool. I guess I didn't realize what I had at the time. That I had been blessed with this magic book to work on.

CBA: *You were working on it and it went monthly?*

Doug: It was always monthly. That, plus the *Deadly Hands of Kung Fu* b-&-w was monthly too. Then there was *Giant-Size MOKF* and *MOKF* annuals, and then it was weekly in Britain and, for a while, I had to write them in eight-page segments when Britain got ahead of America. It was *nuts!* I had *MOKF* coming out of my ears! The same thing with *Planet of the Apes*. I had to do all of the movie adaptations at the same time I was doing the new series because that was also coming out weekly in Britain. Oh, *man!*

CBA: *So were you living well?*

Doug: Oh, yeah. Verpoorten was the one handing out the checks every Friday and he'd just look at mine and shake his head.

CBA: *Did you have dealings with Stan as a boss?*

Doug: Not many, because Roy was already in the chair when I moved to New York and Stan was kind of upstairs—but every once in a while, Stan would have a meeting and get all the writers together and then Stan…it always seemed like it was his way of letting me know he knew who I was. He'd pass me in the hall and go, "There's Doug Moench!" [*laughs*] Okay, Stan, I know you know my name, that you remember who I am. Stan had these rules, but didn't clamp down on them except in a general sense. He'd have these meetings and say things like, "Some of you are trying too hard to be me! I don't want you to be me; but don't go so far the other way that it's not Marvel!" And he'd read the make-readies once in a while, including *MOKF.*

My best Stan Lee story, which I treasure the most—because there *were* a few bad ones—was where he had a make-ready of an issue of *MOKF* in which Paul and I had gone especially far in experimental storytelling techniques and Stan called me in. (He would've called Paul in too but Paul was in Ohio or somewhere.) So he calls me in and says, "You're breaking all the rules." And I'm like, "Yeah, well, Stan, you know…" He goes, "And I *love* it!" [*laughs*] "But don't tell anybody else I said that! Because not everybody else can break the rules like that and make it work; but I love it!" Stan was a big Steranko fan, too, so it figures that he would like what Paul and I were doing.

Then there was the time Stan was really pissed at me. I would get these calls from either Steranko or Ken Bruzenak (who worked for Steranko when he was putting out *Comicscene* magazine) and they'd ask, "Okay, what's the news?" If it was Ken, I'd give him all the news on what was coming up in the comics I was writing and in 15 minutes and then we'd talk for another three hours. As far as I knew, the other three hours were just me and him talking. This was a good lesson in what's on the record and what's off the record. Well, one time he asked me about Stan and I said, "Well, Stan's not really involved anymore. He's upstairs and doesn't always read the books these days." And *Comicscene* printed: "Doug Moench says that Stan Lee's really out of it and doesn't know what's going on any more." And Stan got really *pissed!* I said, "Stan, I didn't mean it in a bad way! I didn't even know it was going to be printed!" And it was like, "Well, if that's the way you feel maybe you should leave." I said, "Are you firing me?" Then there was silence. "No, I'm not firing you but…" [*laughs*] "All right, all right!" Jeez, I didn't know he could get like that.

But, on the other hand, Stan was really great when I wanted to buy a house. I was writing so much and making more money than I ever dreamed I would, and Verpoorten says, "You've got to get an accountant to do your taxes!" And I'm going, "What!?" I never thought I would need an accountant. So I got Verpoorten's accountant and this guy looks at this radical jump in income from one year to the next and says, "Well, you've got to do three things: You've got to get married, take a lot of business trips, and buy a house or else they're going to take all this money you made." I wasn't ready to get married and there was no reason to take business trips so I decided to buy a house. I had no plans to leave Manhattan until I had my taxes done, but if I have to buy a house, it's going to be out in the country, so I went looking for a house. Then when I applied for a mortgage they asked me what I did and I said I was a writer. "Oh, a freelance writer?" And they didn't want to give me a loan because writers are notoriously bad risks. So I had to go to Stan and I told him that they didn't want to give me a loan and Stan says, "Well, write a letter and I'll sign it!" I didn't want to do that and asked him if he could just write the letter for me; and he was like, "Oh, all right!" The way Stan goes, you know? And it was just this great letter for me, "Doug Moench is one of our very best writers and as long as there's Marvel Comics he'll be making enough money

to pay any mortgage you can come up with!" Of course that wasn't true! [*laughs*] But it was this terrific letter and *bam!* The mortgage went right through! Basically, I think Stan is a great guy, except for that one very nasty run-in I had with him.

CBA: *What did you do with Steranko?*

Doug: Steranko is responsible for my various forays into Hollywood Hell in a weird and roundabout way. Ralph Bakshi loved comic books and he got this deal with Dino DeLaurentiis to direct this live-action, non-animation, real-live actors movie called *Red Sonja*—and this was weird—and just by coincidence, I had written Red Sonja's origin in the comics because Roy didn't have time to do it and he said, "Here, you write it. Here's Howie Chaykin's pages." Anyway, without knowing this, Bakshi called Steranko and asked him, "Who's the best writer in comics?" And Steranko gave him my name. Bakshi goes to a couple of comic book shop owners and asks them, "Is this Moench guy any good?" I guess the comics shop owners said yes, at least that's what Bakshi told me later; but anyway, Bakshi calls me and says, "Come on out here and write this feature motion picture for me and DeLaurentiis." That's how I got mixed up in Hollywood Hell. It's all Steranko's fault!

CBA: *Did Steranko express anything about your strip,* Master of Kung Fu?

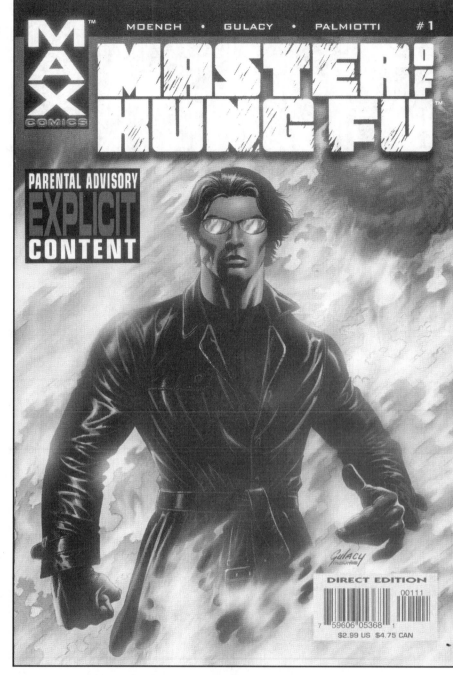

MOENCH • GULACY • PALMIOTTI #1

MAX COMICS

MASTER OF KUNG FU

PARENTAL ADVISORY EXPLICIT CONTENT

Gulacy

DIRECT EDITION

$2.99 US $4.75 CAN

Above: *Doug and Paul did recently get the opportunity to return to Shang-Chi in the Max mini-series of 2002-03. Here's the cover for #1 (Nov. '02).* ©2005 Marvel Characters, Inc.

Doug: Oh, Steranko told me several times that he loved it. Yeah. He said looking at Paul's work was like looking at his own without having to do it. He's a big fan of pulps, I guess the spy stuff. He really got into it. Steranko is like me. He loves super-heroes as a reader but I don't think he really likes doing them as much as things like *SHIELD*. Not that *SHIELD* is really down-to-earth, but it's more so than a cosmic super-hero.

CBA: *I read an interview with Paul that said that Steranko inked a couple of panels. How did that come about?*

Doug: Yeah. Well, Steranko and Dan Adkins (another good friend of mine) are very tight. I don't know if they were both living in Reading, Pennsylvania (where they're both at now) or if Steranko was just visiting Dan when he was in Ohio. I don't know how that came about but Steranko was around when Dan was inking an issue of *MOKF* and Steranko inked a few panels, just for fun.

CBA: *How did you find out about it?*

Doug: I guess Adkins told Paul—and then Paul, I guess, confirmed it later with Steranko. Paul was thrilled to hear it because Steranko was his idol—still is.

CBA: *And he remembers the panels to this day?*

Doug: Yeah, yeah!

CBA: *Did you ever have any problems with the likenesses of the*

many characters being based on real people like Sean Connery?

Doug: No, there wasn't a problem. There had been an earlier problem when Paul drew David Carradine and they actually had to go over Paul's artwork and put a mustache on the David Carradine character; but for some reason, when we were doing it, it all slipped by and there was never any problem. No one sued and we never heard anything. Although, later on, there were problems. Paul had done… I don't know, James Coburn or someone, in another book after *MOKF* and the lawyers said he had to change it; but for some reason, that window in between, we did all kinds of things and got away with them all.

CBA: *There seemed to be an atmosphere at Marvel just after Roy left where a lot of editors and writers were jockeying to get the position.*

Doug: Hey, I'm the only one to ever turn down the offer to edit the b-&-w magazines which, in every other case, led to the Editor-in-Chief position. I said, "No, no, no," and they asked me several times and I said no every time. "I'm a writer and I just want to write. Who wants to sit there shuffling papers all day?"

CBA: *You didn't seem to have the aspiration to be a star editor.*

Doug: No.

CBA: *That separated you from a number of personalities who were there at the time. You really enjoyed working with artists, it seemed.*

Doug: Yeah, yeah. It really was, in my case, the work and not a career. I wasn't going for any long-term goal or looking for fame or anything. It was just having fun, doing the work.

CBA: *Were you there when they started returning artwork?*

Doug: Oh, yeah.

CBA: *Did you start receiving artwork?*

Doug: Yeah, for…I don't know how long it was, maybe a year or so, but every writer started getting pages; but they were always the worst two pages because the penciler and inker got first picks.

CBA: *Did you think that was an odd policy?*

Doug: You know, when the artists started complaining, I was kind of a turncoat. I was saying, "Yeah, you know, they've got a point; we didn't draw these things." I don't remember who the editor was then, if it was Roy or not, but I sided with the artists against my fellow writers. I'm not saying I was the only one.

CBA: *Don McGregor was one. I interviewed P. Craig Russell and he said that Don personally gave him all the art.*

Doug: Well, that's because if anybody, it would have been Don. There might have been others but I just don't know. I do know that some of the writers were really pissed at me for going this way.

CBA: *Do you remember what the rationale was? Why the writers should receive any of the artwork?*

Doug: Well, I guess because comics are words and pictures, the combination of both. The writers, in a way, not all of them, but ones like me, were the "authors" of the pictures because they described the pictures. Some of the writers did *very* loose plots and couldn't really say they were the authors of the pictures at all because the artists had to break down and write the story in visual terms; but I was never consulted. All of a sudden these pages of artwork started showing up in the mail; and I said, "What's this?" And they told me that all the writers were getting pages now and I thought that was pretty cool even though they were always the two worst pages in the books. It was kind of cool to be getting original art, but when I found out that some of the artists were upset, that's when I said they had a point.

CBA: *Did things really start to change once Roy left the office?*

Doug: Yeah, that was a bad day. I spent that night with Roy when he quit and he was really filled with a strange combination of depression and euphoria. He was utterly relieved, on the one hand, and on the other hand, "Wow, that was really a big, momentous thing to do." I had been as close as anyone was to Roy at that time, I guess. We'd visit each other's apartments and go out to movies together. In the weeks leading up to his resignation, when we were hanging out together, I could see how much this was affecting Roy. He was going through severe stress and it was really starting to affect him. When he quit, my reaction was, "Oh, no, Roy! But, on the other hand, I may not like this, but it's probably the right thing for you. You were probably right to do this." It was really, really getting under his skin.

CBA: *The subsequent editors-in-chief. Was it a smooth transition or rocky?*

Doug: It was both. It was extremely chaotic and rocky but, on the other hand, I didn't even notice.

CBA: *So you were out in Pennsylvania?*

Doug: Was I? No, I don't think so. I think I was still in New York at that time. I'm not sure. I moved out here in October of 1975. When did Roy quit?

CBA: *That was in 1974.*

Doug: Yeah, so I was still in New York City at that time, and I remember Len Wein, when he was editor, calling me at my apartment in Manhattan and that was after Roy. I didn't really notice much of a difference at all although, in retrospect, I should have noticed. It wasn't as loose, it wasn't as much fun, it wasn't stable…

CBA: *What was it? Can you put your finger on it?*

Doug: Well, the thing that made Roy quit was obviously applied to all subsequent editors and they weren't able to win the battles either. What made Roy quit was that he couldn't win! If he hadn't quit, he would've had to give in, I guess.

CBA: *So it was just a growing corporate influence?*

Doug: I guess so. I know I remember talking with Roy about it but this long afterwards I don't remember the details. I just remember that Roy seemed to be the shining knight in armor fighting upstairs on behalf of us freelancers and he could never win anything; but what he was fighting for, I don't have a clue now.

CBA: *With the arrival of Shooter, did things drastically change?*

Doug: What a nightmare.

CBA: *You stuck around for a couple of years after that, right?*

Doug: Yeah, yeah. Shooter came after I moved out to Pennsylvania. My first meeting with Jim Shooter set the tone, let me tell you. It was one of those very infrequent things where Stan would call a meeting with all the writers and the editors. I came in from Pennsylvania to attend this meeting and here was this big guy I'd never seen before. I have no idea who this guy is, I hadn't heard that there was this proofreader named Jim Shooter. Nobody bothered to tell me. So he's sitting there and Stan's going off on whatever Stan was going off on and in the middle of this thing, Shooter literally interrupted Stan Lee in the middle of a sentence, pointed at me, and said, "I'm taking him out of here now." And this shocked me. Somebody said, "Yeah, we're just about done; you can go." So I go with this guy and he takes me to this proofreading desk where he's looking over an issue of *Godzilla* I wrote. Archie Goodwin had suggested using Dum-Dum Dugan and a couple of the other SHIELD agents in the book. Dum-Dum was a supporting character from *Sgt. Fury* and *SHIELD*, and he was created by Stan and Jack. He talked in slang which had been established way back in the early issues of *Sgt. Fury and His Howling Commandos* and had been consistent all the way through *Nick Fury, Agent of SHIELD*. And that's the way I wrote him in *Godzilla*. But now, Shooter says that I have to rewrite all of these word balloons into "proper English." I said, "What? This is a joke, right?" He said, "No. I want this in proper English—like this:" And he shows me an example of one balloon that he rewrote (which was *not* proper English, by the way). I said, "I don't think you understand. This character—*who* are you?!!" He said, "I'm Jim Shooter and I'm a new editor here." I said, "Oh, you mean you're a proofreader." He said, "Yeah." And I said, "Obviously, you haven't read many Marvel Comics yet. You better take a whole bunch of Marvel Comics home with you tonight and read them, because I didn't create this character for this one issue. And, even if I did, so what if I wrote him speaking this way?" He didn't know what I was talking about. I said, "Look! This is *Dum-Dum Dugan!* You don't know who Dum-Dum Dugan is?" And he had no idea. I said, "Have you heard of *Sgt. Fury and his Howling Commandos*?" And he didn't say anything! That book came out in *1964!* This character was established and this was the way he was supposed to talk! Shooter said, "I don't care. I want it rewritten in proper English." I said, "*No! This* is right! *This* is the way it's supposed to be!" I just couldn't believe it! I felt like Alice going into the looking glass! I finally got really pissed at him and I said, "Look, you son of a bitch, I'm not rewriting this; this is correct. If you want it rewritten, take it in to Stan Lee and ask *him* if it should be rewritten! He created the character with Jack Kirby, so he'll tell you." Then Shooter just went stone cold silent and glared at

me. I walked away. That really set the tone for my relationship with Jim Shooter. I had endless shouting matches with that "fellow."

CBA: *[laughs] How much longer did you work for Marvel?*

Doug: All the way through 1982. All the while, Dick Giordano had tried to get me over to DC Comics, and I just kept saying, "Maybe someday, but I'm doing *Moon Knight, Master of Kung Fu, King Conan, Weirdworld…*" I just started *Six from Sirius* for Archie Goodwin and Epic—I think the only book I wasn't happy with was *Thor*, because Shooter was interfering. He said, "No more Asgard. Thor is Superman and Donald Blake is Clark Kent, and it all takes place on Earth." I said, "Well, that kills all the coolest stuff in *Thor*!" But he was adamant and I wasn't allowed to do anything that I really wanted to do in that book. With the rest of the stuff, I was able to do what I wanted. The editors were thrilled with *Moon Knight* and *Master of Kung Fu*, but there was this real Jekyll/Hyde thing with Shooter. An editor would call me and say, "Y'know, Shooter takes the make-readies home and he writes notes in the margins, and here's what he said about the latest *Master of Kung Fu*," and I'd go, "Oh, boy!"—because I knew that Shooter was screaming about "breaking the rules," and all this other stuff. But then he would write things on the make-ready like, "Best book of the month!" And I said to the editor, "*Shooter* wrote that? I thought you said he was coming to you complaining." He said, "He was!" I said, "It makes no sense!" He said, "Nope, it doesn't—but let's not make anything of it. Let it go." I said, "Okay," but it was like this real schizoid thing. The editors would take all of this heat but Shooter would only confront me when I went into the office. It would always turn into a big shouting match. I could look past his shoulder and I could see all of the Bullpen giving me the thumbs-up, grinning, mouthing the words, "Get 'im, Doug!" But if Shooter would turn around, they would all act like they were working and not even hearing any of this. It was a very, very bizarre thing—and the reason I finally called Dick Giordano and said, "Okay, let's go to lunch," was the Shooter idea that became the last straw for me. He called it, "The Shooter Theory of the Big Bang of the Marvel Universe"—and, to this day, I can't understand why this isn't a bigger deal in the history of comics. All of the editors who were there at the time were fully aware of this but nobody seems to talk about it. Shooter had this plan where he was going to end the Stan Lee era of Marvel Comics and usher in the so-called Jim Shooter era. To do this, he was going to kill off all of the characters but not really; he was just going to kill Tony Stark and some new guy would become Iron Man, for instance. Well, to kill off the Stan Lee era, you have to kill Iron Man, not Tony Stark! Donald Blake would die and someone else would find the walking stick, and Joe Blow would now be Thor! Steve Rogers would die and (this is literally true!) an investment banker was going to be the new Captain America! How's that? *[laughter]*

CBA: *[laughs] The embodiment of Reagan's go-go '80s!*

Doug: That's Captain America in the '80s all right! Shooter was going to do this across the board! Peter Parker and the Fantastic Four were all going to die! Mark Gruenwald and Ralph Macchio and Denny O'Neil would call me and say, "You gotta stop Shooter!" I said, "How am *I* going to stop him?" They said, "Well, you're the

Above: Courtesy of Albert Moy, here's a sweet Mark Texiera drawing of Doug's creation Moon Knight. ©2000 Marvel Characters, Inc.

only one who yells at him." [*laughter*] I said, "I can't be the one; all you guys have got to get together and go upstairs to Jim Galton and say, 'Mr. Galton, this guy down there is trying to force us to do this!'" Stan didn't know about it because he was out on the West Coast at this point. The editors said, "This *can't* happen!" I said, "Well, it's *going* to happen if you don't do anything about it; I can't stop it." And the last straw came when Shooter called me and said, "In the next issues of all of your books, I want all the characters dead." He started discussing *Master of Kung Fu,* and he said, "I want every character killed and I want to see their blood so there's no way they can come back." I said, "These are *comic books!* Characters can always…" He said, "No! I want them dead in a way they can never, ever come back." I said, "That's crazy! Why do you want to do that?" He said, "Because I want it. I want Shang-Chi dead and a new master of kung fu—like a ninja." I said, "Well, I got news for you: Kung fu is Chinese and ninja is Japanese. A ninja would never be a master of kung fu. If you hate *Master of Kung Fu,* kill the book and start *Master of Ninja* #1, but don't tell me to kill off characters because I'm not going to do it—and, by the way, even if I wanted to, I couldn't kill Fu Manchu." He said, "Why not?" I said, "Because I didn't create Fu Manchu!" He got quiet and I said, "You don't know that Fu Manchu is a character from the pulps? We pay Sax Rohmer's widow a licensing fee every month whether Fu Manchu is in the book or not! And, even if we could, why kill Fu Manchu? It'd be like killing Tarzan or Doc Savage! Why would you want to do that? It's just insulting. Plus we'll get sued." And he said, "I'm willing to take the chance; I want Fu Manchu and everyone dead." I said, "I'm not going to do this." And he said, "In the next issue of *Thor,* I want Donald Blake killed." So after that phone call I decide I had to quit—there was no way I could do what he wanted. Shooter's bottom line was, "If you won't do it, I'll get someone else who will." I thought, "Either I do what he says, or I'm going to be fired. So I gotta quit." That's when I called Dick Giordano and Dick said, "What do you want? You want *Batman?* You want this or that?" I said, "Wow. This is nice. Too bad I have to leave *Weirdworld, Moon Knight* and *Master of Kung Fu*—all these things I love—but there's insanity over at Marvel."

But after I quit, I was determined not to do the big *Comics Journal* interview and dump on Shooter as everybody else who had already left had done; but I wasn't going to lie either. So when the magazines called me and asked, "Is it true you quit Marvel Comics? Will you give an interview?" I said, "Yeah, I quit, but no interview." They asked, "Well, will you tell us why you quit?" I said, "I'm quitting because Jim Shooter ordered me to kill off all the characters in all the books I was writing. I refused to do it and I had to quit. End of story." And they printed that. At this time, Marvel had these press conferences where the *Comics Reader, Comics Journal* and whoever went up to get the news. Someone asked Shooter, "Doug Moench said he quit because you ordered his characters to be killed. Is that true?" Shooter said, "That is not true. That is an allegation by a disgruntled former employee." And the editors who were sitting next to Shooter—and I'll never forgive them—just let Shooter get away with that; they let him lie through his teeth. But that's what in effect stopped the whole kill-off-the-characters scheme.

CBA: *Did you get the feeling that you were set up?*

Doug: No, because I later found out from some of the editors that before he made the call, Shooter said, "Doug Moench will never quit because he's got a mortgage and he's just had a kid. There's no way he will quit." Shooter thought he had me in his hip pocket, holding my mortgage and my son over my head. Now, there are spies who call back

Above: *Doug is still busy working in comics—albeit real books. The writer has scribed a number of "Big Books" for DC/Paradox, including* The Big Book of the Unexplained. *Here's Our Man taking a break on his porch in Pennsylvania. Courtesy of Doug Moench.*

and forth between DC and Marvel, and maybe five minutes after I set foot into DC and was getting ready to go out to lunch with Dick Giordano, the phones were already ringing at Marvel. [*whispering*] "Doug Moench is coming over to DC!" And Shooter, I was told later, was genuinely shocked and said, "He can't quit, he won't quit!" And he wouldn't believe it until I officially did so.

CBA: *Have you worked for Marvel since?*

Doug: Oh, yeah. I've done a bunch of stories. At the time, I agreed to script everything I had already plotted and ride it out. Plus I rationalized that Archie Goodwin at Epic was independent of Shooter, so I felt I could honorably do *Six from Sirius* with Paul Gulacy. Archie said, "I promise Shooter won't bother you at all on this." So I said okay; but, after that, I did nothing further until Shooter left. Then I got a call from someone at Marvel who literally said, "Ding-dong, the witch is dead! Jim Shooter's been fired, so come on home." But since I was committed to DC, I didn't just run back to Marvel; but every now and then, I'd do a *Savage Sword of Conan*—and I created "Coldblood-7"—and other material for *Marvel Comics Presents.* Just recently, I did two *Moon Knight* mini-series and a *Wolverine* prestige book, all within the last year or two.

CBA: *What was your high point working at Marvel?*

Doug: It always comes down to my favorite collaborators, Paul Gulacy and Mike Ploog, although there are many, many others I enjoyed working with. I loved working with Herb Trimpe; he's a great guy. *Master of Kung Fu, Moon Knight,* "Deathlok," *Weirdworld. Master of Kung Fu* was probably a once-in-a-lifetime book, although I didn't know it at the time. I thought I would go on forever doing books like that. *Moon Knight* and *Weirdworld* because I created them and they're special to me.

CBA: *What was the basis for Moon Knight? Was it doing Batman at Marvel Comics?*

Doug: Y'know, everybody thinks that, but not at all. The proof is that he was created originally as a villain in *Werewolf by Night.* When you're writing *Werewolf,* your hero is actually a bad guy who might kill people; so when you create a villain, he's actually a hero! But even though stopping a werewolf is a good thing to do, you still have to make the hero trying to stop him somewhat of a villain. So I made Moon Knight this really crass mercenary who would take on any assignment for money. Because he was going up against a werewolf, he had a night-and-moon theme, all of this silver stuff—like the silver crescent he would throw, or the silver studs he had on his gloves. Silver hurts werewolves. It was only later when people said, "I really love Moon Knight," that we tried him out in *Marvel Spotlight* as a genuine hero. I softened the crass mercenary aspect and made him change identities into someone who actually wants to atone for being a mercenary. So he worked hard to become a good guy and that's were the split personalities came from.

I think that because Bill Sienkiewicz was drawing like Neal Adams (who was associated with Batman), it looked like the "Marvel Batman." But it really wasn't like that at all, as far as I was concerned; there are far more differences than similarities. Batman never entered my mind when I created Moon Knight. Don Perlin created the visual look of Moon Knight; I described the costume but he was the one who made it work, and I know he wasn't thinking "Batman" either.

Don's a real Brooklyn guy! He *always* had story ideas. He'd say, "Hey, Doug! I have an idea for *Werewolf!* How about we do a haunted house story?" I'd say, "Okay, let's do a haunted house! Why not, if it makes you happy, Don!" He was very, very enthused on the *Werewolf by Night* book.

CBA: *Anything to add for this Marvel issue?*

Doug: Marvel feels like my first home although I wish it was more like it once was. You probably hear this from Roy and everybody who was there back then; maybe it happens everywhere. When things change, the ones who were there before the change just don't like the changes. I try to be objective, but it honestly seems to me that the books back then were better than they are now. I don't know if I'm right, but there just seemed to be more creativity and excitement in those days. It's not that there are no good comics now; obviously there are. It's just that, overall, it seems less adventurous and less spontaneous these days—a shame.

DATELINE:@!!?☆ BY FRED HEMBECK

I AM THE MERCI-LESS CONQUEROR OF GALAXIES, THANOS!

DERIVED FROM THE GREEK WORD, "THANATOS", IN *ANY* LANGUAGE MY NAME MEANS *DEATH!*

PAY NO HEED TO THE IMPU-DENT FOOLS WHO WHISPER THAT "THANOS" IS SIMPLY MARVEL-SPEAK FOR *"DARKSEID"!*

CRETINS! STARLIN WOULD BE THE *FIRST* TO ACKNOWLEDGE THE INFLUENCE JACK KIRBY'S BRILLIANCE HAD UPON HIS *OWN* CREATIVITY!

SHOULD YOU *INSIST* THAT I AM BUT A *SHADOW* OF THE FOURTH WORLD'S MALEVOLENT MASTER OF APOKOLIPS, I COUNTER WITH THE NOTION THAT STARLIN WAS THE *KIRBY* OF *HIS* GENERATION.

CONSIDER THAT OF *ALL* WHO ENTERED THE FIELD FROM 1967 THROUGH 1975, JIM WAS THE ONE WHOSE THINKING *MOST* SEEMED TO MIRROR JACK'S OWN.

NOT SOME HALF-BAKED HOMAGE--*THOSE* WOULD COME FROM OTHERS, LATER, INTERMINABLY--BUT THE *MAJESTY*, THE *POWER*, AND, *YES*, THE *COSMIC SCOPE* OF THE KING, FRESHLY FILTERED THOUGH A TALENTED YOUNG CARTOONIST'S EYES.

HAVING COME OF AGE DURING THE TUMULTUOUS *SIXTIES*, STARLIN USED ALL THAT *THAT* IMPLIED TO INFUSE MY EVER SHIFTING SAGA WITH A SENSIBILITY THAT, WHILE OWING A DEBT TO KIRBY--WHO DOESN'T?--WAS NONETHELESS UNIQUELY HIS OWN! GROOVY!

SO, YOU PITIFUL INSIGNIFICANT SWINE, WHEN I *INSIST* TO YOU THAT THIS WAS INDEED PRIMO MATERIAL, I *ASSURE* YOU I AM *NOT* LYING. *THIS TIME.*

INEVITABLY, IN MY *UNSTOPPABLE* QUEST TO PROCURE AN EVENING OF *DINNER AND DANCING* WITH THE VERY EMBODIMENT OF DEATH HERSELF, THE MULTI-SERIES-SPANNING CHAPTER-PLAY *ENDED* AS IT WAS ALWAYS *DESTINED* TO.

PIP THE INSUFFERABLE TROLL *DIED.* MY TURNCOAT HIRED ASSASSIN GAMORA *DIED.* ADAM WARLOCK--ORIGINALLY THE CLUNKILY CHRIS-TENED LEE-KIRBY CHARACTER "HIM"--*HIM* DIED, TOO!

AND *THEN*--oh JOY!--*I DIED!* OR AT LEAST MY BODY WAS TRANS-FORMED INTO AN IMMOBILE STATUE OF *STONE,* BRINGING MY DISCO-ERA INCARNATION TO A FITTING CONCLUSION.

BECAUSE--YES--THIS BEING COMICS, EVENTUALLY EACH OF MY ANTAGONISTS AND I WERE *REVIVED.* AT LEAST MARVEL HAD THE GOOD SENSE TO a.) *WAIT* A DECENT INTERVAL OF TIME, AND TO b.) *INVOLVE* STARLIN IN EFFECTING MY REBIRTH.

STILL, THE MANY LONG YEARS I SPENT AS A MOTIONLESS SLAB OF ROCK LEFT ME HAUNTED BY *ONE* OVERRIDING THOUGHT:

IS *THIS* WHAT DARKSEID'S COMPLEXION FEELS LIKE ALL THE TIME?

I GUARANTEE YOU, IN THE TIME SINCE LIFE ONCE AGAIN BEGAN COURSING THROUGH MY VEINS I HAVE *NEVER* TAKEN MY *DELICATE,* HIDE-LIKE GREY SKIN FOR *GRANITE!!*

Dan Adkins' Strange Tales

The artist on his visits to the World of Wood and the House of Ideas

Conducted by Jon B. Cooke
Transcribed by Jon B. Knutson

Last September, after I had already spoken to Dan Adkins proteges P. Craig Russell and Paul Gulacy, I thought it might be cool to include interviews with Val Mayerik (another Adkins alumni) and hopefully Big Dan himself, and make a "Adkins School" section for CBA #6. Well, subsequently learning that Val had zero interest in talking with us—and dividing the issue into a two-parter—put an end to that concept; but I did get a riotous interview with a true comics original and penciler/inker/art director extraordinaire, Mr. Adkins himself. I can only hope this is the first of many interviews cuz Dan is a hoot to encounter! This interview took place via phone on September 19, 1999, and was copy-edited by the artist.

Comic Book Artist: *Where and when were you born, Dan?*
Dan Adkins: West Virginia in 1937. I was born in the basement of an unfinished house. I was 33 years old before I found out my mother's maiden name was the same as her married name. They tried to keep marriage in the family back in West Virginia [*laughs*], but she was probably 17th cousin or something—but yeah, my dad was named Adkins and my mother was named Adkins before they were married, as well as after. They really had big families: there were 19 kids in dad's family, and 23 in my mother's family. Two sets of twins, and the last kid was born when Grandma was 55.
CBA: *Holy Moley!*
Dan: I have three aunts younger than me—and I only have one child!
CBA: *Did you grow up in West Virginia?*
Dan: Not very long... I left when I was about seven, and went to Pennsylvania. I've been from one end of the country to the other, living in Reno, Phoenix, New York, Ohio, Pennsylvania, New Jersey...
CBA: *When did you first remember seeing comics?*
Dan: I don't know when I first saw them, but I was drawing copies of Donald Duck and Tarzan and things like that on the blackboard when I was in the first grade, so I definitely knew about them early. I really got interested in comics in my teens, when I saw Wally Wood, Al Williamson, Jack Davis, George Evans —all those guys in the EC Comics.
CBA: *Did you start thinking about a career in comics at that time?*
Dan: I never had any idea of becoming a comic book artist until I went to Wally Wood's apartment. I met him through Bill Pearson, and I was working on a fanzine I was going to put out. This would be my second fanzine; I'd done the first one in the late '50s.
CBA: *What was the name of it?*
Dan: *Sata.* It doesn't mean anything. [*laughter*] I went through a lot of combinations of lettering to see what looked good, and that's what I used. It doesn't mean Satan, it doesn't mean Saturn.
CBA: *Was it an EC fanzine?*
Dan: It was a science-fiction fanzine. I discovered s-f fandom in probably '54, '55... very early. Joe Noel had put out a fanzine called *Vega.* I went on to discover the fanzines *Dimensions* by Harlan Ellison and Robert Silverberg's *Spaceship* (or something like that). I got into all kinds of s-f fanzines...
CBA: *So you were a voracious reader of s-f?*
Dan: Yeah, and I had letters printed in letter columns. I met Bill Pearson, who had a letter printed in *Amazing Stories,* and I happened to be stationed with the Air Force in Phoenix when I was 19. I saw his letter and noticed he lived near the base, so I gave him a call and said I wanted to meet him. Of course, we had similar interests (and he had no interest in meeting anybody!). [*laughs*] I went out there that night, and we met. Later on, we put out *Sata* together. I started it when I was in the service using a lot of their equipment. Pearson took it over with #6. Later in New York, after I got married, I wanted to put together a better fanzine—because by then I'd met Archie Goodwin, Al Williamson, Frazetta, and Steve Ditko, and I was working for the s-f magazines—the professional ones—in my spare time (I had a steady job). I was also working for the fanzines like crazy then—I was art editor of *Amra,* which George Scithers put out, and it had Krenkel and George Barr artwork. So I went up to Wally Wood's studio. I was working in advertising at the time, and like I said, freelancing for professional s-f magazines, and doing art for the regular fanzines. I had no idea of becoming a comic book artist—I was going to be a studio man; but I took out nine pages that I had done for a magazine, and I took up a story Jack Gaughan had given me, and I took up a story Archie Goodwin had given me, called "The Sinner" (that was reprinted in the *Comic Book Profiles* devoted to Archie—it was originally given to me to print way back in the beginning of the '60s, for my fanzine). So, when Wally saw all this stuff, he was impressed, and he said he'd do something for me, but he was busy. He said the sooner I helped him out, the sooner he'd work for my fanzine! [*laughter*]

So, I started helping Wally, and later on my planned fanzine became Wally's and it was called *witzend.* In his book *The Golden Age of Fandom,* Bill Schelly was almost correct in writing I was too busy doing other things to do *witzend;* but when it came out, I hadn't worked for Marvel yet, so I wasn't too busy working for *Marvel,* as it says in his book, I was too busy working for *Wally!* [*laughter*] Wally, by then, had gotten contributions from Al Williamson, Frazetta, and Reed Crandall, so he and *his* people were contributing more than *my* people to the first issue. But the main reason he published it, I think, was money. I had enough to publish 500 copies, and Wally had enough to publish 3000 copies—and we already had orders for like 1500—so that's how come it became Wally's fanzine.

Below: Dan Adkins at his art table as a Marvel art director in the late '70s. Courtesy of Dan Adkins.

CBA: *Was that your title?*

Dan: No, Wally came up with "*witzend*." It was originally to be called *Et Cetera*. For a time, we hadn't really come up with a title, so we just called it *Adkins' Outlet* (we didn't want to use that name for the fanzine, of course, because people would confuse it with the name of a store) [*laughs*] but we just called it *Outlet* as a going title and we were using the name in some of the promotions and stuff.

That's how I ended up doing comics; I was working for Wally by 1964, and after working for him three months, I quit my studio job, because I was making about the same amount of money—about $135 a week at my studio job, and I was making about $200 or so a week from Wally. Of course, I was doing three times the amount of work! But it was more fun, and I was able to work at home or go over to Wally's. I started with my first story in the back of *T.H.U.N.D.E.R. Agents*. I penciled that "Iron Maiden" story, and Wally and I inked it. He didn't like my inking, so he took me off that and I didn't go back to inking for about six months.

CBA: *You were ghosting and doing layouts for Wally?*

Dan: Well, I got about 60 jobs from Wally in a period of 16 months, and they were a lot of different things. I would pencil. Most of the time, Wally would do breakdowns and then I'd tight-pencil it—and, on occasion, I would do the job from scratch, from just a plot, like the Marvel way; but both of us almost always ended up inking it. Wally very seldom inked a whole job by himself. Either I or Ralph Reese (who was there at the time when he was only 15 or 16) did the inking.

After that, I did "Overworked" for *Creepy*. That was the first job I got credit on, as Wally put my name on it. The only reason I got credit, I'm sure, was due to the fact that Jim Steranko had come up to Wally's apartment while I was there, coming in with a blonde on one arm and samples under the other arm—and Wally said, "Leave the blonde, take the samples!" [*laughter*] Anyway, Jim came up there looking for work, coming over from Harvey, I think. Sooner or later, he ended up working at Marvel, and I'd seen this "Nick Fury" job he did, inking Kirby, and I pointed it out to Wally and said, "Here's that kid that came up here with the samples and had that blonde with him!" [*laughs*] Wally could tell I was a little envious, because the guy was working now, and the next thing I knew— maybe even the same day—my name ended up on that job we were working on, "Overworked," but I'd already done a lot of the jobs for Wally.

Tony Coleman from England—actually he came down from Canada—was working as Wally's assistant for six months while I was there. So we had Ralph, me and Wally's wife, Tatjana—she also did some inking and coloring and stuff. We had all of us in a little room there.

CBA: *Was this in New York?*

Dan: Yeah, I think West 76th Street.

CBA: *What was Wally like?*

Dan: I don't know what he was like! [*laughter*] I'm not sure what *I'm* like after all these years, and I'm very close to me! [*laughter*] He was always telling me I should go to a shrink, and everybody else, too! [*laughs*] His main problem was that he was an alcoholic. I never knew it at the time, and he never drank except for two weeks during the whole 16 months that I was on the job. He was on the wagon, you know? Which means he was pretty happy with the way things were going in his life. He went back to the bottle for that two weeks, and first thing, Tony and I came in and we found these nudes pasted all over the studio—this was an old building, and we were on the fifth floor, and it had 17-foot ceilings, real high. He had cut up issues of *Sunshine* and all these nudie books, and he'd taken these girls and pasted them up while Tony and I were out—and we were only out about 12 hours or so, away at home to rest up, and when we returned, there were a thousand or two thousand nudes pasted up! On the third day, the nudes had been taken down. So, that was the weirdest thing, during those two weeks… Wally came to me and told me that he was an alcoholic, and he'd tried to drink again on rare social occasions, but he couldn't stop drinking! During these two weeks, I had more of a workload, we were doing these six record album covers—I don't know who they were for, but they advertised them…

CBA: *Was it those* Journey to the Center of the Earth *and* The Invisible Man *album covers?*

Dan: Yeah, and Warren was pitching them. I got $60 each for penciling them, which was above my comic book rate (which started out as $4 a page, and then going up to $18 a page). So, I received more than the page rate and it was for just one drawing—except in the case of *The Invisible Man*, which we broke down to three panels. I came up with the whole idea, laid them out, then I helped ink them, and that's why I got paid better. This was during a period when we also did an ad for some kind of book club in *Argosy* that involved all the fictional detectives, like Perry Mason and James Bond… I'd taken a lot of swipes from Mort Drucker, who worked for *Mad*. Wally was good at certain stuff, but I wasn't very good at caricatures, so I used mostly Drucker swipes. So, I did all these high-paying ads when Wally couldn't during his drunk period—but I didn't notice he was drunk… he didn't go throwing things around the building like I heard he did later, when he took an axe to a studio! He did a lot of those things up in Connecticut, when he was living in Derby, at the end.

CBA: *Was he moody?*

Dan: No, he wasn't moody but when he got angry, you were afraid. Wally had a stare that could scare the Hell out of you! [*laughs*] But I guess he was pretty tough, though he wasn't a big guy. He was a paratrooper in the 82nd Airborne. I was in the Air Force, so I know what it was like to go through that training. They'll let you drown… I couldn't swim very well, and I practically drowned on this maneuver we went out on—and they shoot live bullets, too! They're supposed to shoot high, you know? But you had to stay down! [*laughter*] So, if you jump up, it's your own fault.

Wally ran away from home at an early age, I understand. The only thing was, he used to say, he took his mother with him! [*laughter*] His mother did come over once to the studio while I was there, and she would make this noise by cracking her fingers, and Wally said she did it on purpose to drive us crazy, and she *did* drive us crazy! [*laughs*] Al Williamson came around, and I talked to Reed Crandall on the telephone, things like that. Otherwise, it was mostly

work, work, work all the time.

CBA: *Did Wally package all the Tower books there?*

Dan: Yeah, it was his job, his responsibility.

CBA: *So, were Mike Sekowsky and the contributors dealing with Woody or Samm Schwartz on the Tower material?*

Dan: Well, I don't think he came over. People didn't go to Wally's much; they went to the editorial offices, which was in the middle of Manhattan. Wally was up on 76th Street on the other side of town. So, it was easier for Wally to send things down there, like scripts, plots. Len Brown and Bill Pearson were writers. Len was working for Topps, and probably still is!

CBA: *Yeah, he still is!*

Dan: Len was a young guy back then. So, most of these people like Mike, and Gil Kane… Gil must've actually went down to Samm's to pick up jobs and scripts, and Samm would also send this stuff up to our studio. Everybody came up with plots, not just Wally. I did plots and scripts, and even Ralph Reese did some plots. Ralph also did these trading cards—we were doing things for Topps Bubble Gum, too—and he would come up with a lot of the ideas, because he was smart, but he was one of these early beatniks, I guess. [*laughs*] He had a gross sense of humor, so he did a lot of things that we had to reject, but he would come up with things that we wouldn't imagine, and I would tighten them up, and on most of them, Wally put on the finishing touches, drawing the heads for them…

CBA: *Do you know what the series was?*

Dan: Well, we did the *Mars Attacks* set, and we did another set with these weird characters made in the shape of the alphabet. We did some that must've been called *The Uglies* or *Monsters*—they were just creepy monsters—and you know how Wally could do those creatures we used to call "organic plasmatic aliens." Ralph did things like that, and he'd go rule the borders and use the opaque projector—or "swipe-o-graph," as we used to call it—and Wally had this room the opaque projector was in, and the rest of the room was nothing but filing cabinets, six feet high. When I stayed over (which was practically *all* the time), I would sleep in there, surrounded by filing cabinets, on the floor in a sleeping bag. Other times, I'd sleep in the living room on the couch, and I'd be down for a couple of hours after being up probably 16 hours or something, and Wally would come in and say, "Daaaan…" and I'd immediately jump up! I think Krenkel did the description of Wally coming to the door not saying anything for two minutes before he'd let you in, because Wally was always tired-looking, like he was in a daze. He was only 38 in '64, or around that age. I was 28.

CBA: *You plotted some Tower stories, right?*

Dan: Yeah, I plotted a couple of Towers and I plotted Douglas Bauder's story… Douglas was a one-legged pilot in the British Air Force, Wally made me read this 300-page book so I could write this three page story! On "The Death of Menthor," Steve Ditko did the pencils, but those were from Wally Wood's breakdowns. When I killed Menthor off, I was writing that story right up there in the chair while Wally was drawing, and I'd hand Wally a page, and he'd say, "How are you going to get him out of this?" And I'd say, "I don't know." [*laughs*] And I didn't know, so I decided not to get him out of it, and killed him off! Wally had to call Samm Schwartz and talk him into killing Menthor. It took us a couple of hours. So some kids came up to Samm's office to protest killing Menthor, begging him to bring him back. Wally had Ralph come up with the idea of Weed and the peanut butter factory, or something…

CBA: *What was the story? Weed was based on Woody, right?*

Dan: Yeah. So was Dollar Bill Cash, the Flying Tiger pilot in the Harvey series. Actually, Weed could've been based on Ralph, too.

CBA: *Did you follow his method of working late into the night at the start of your career?*

Dan: Well, I've always been nocturnal. I think we're both best nocturnally. So are most of the artists I know. Steranko will be up till 5 A.M. I was nocturnal before I met Wally, but Wally was not only nocturnal, he'd just hardly ever sleep. He'd go 20, 40 hours without sleeping. It was just amazing…!

CBA: *Did you perceive him as a tragic figure at the time?*

Dan: No, I thought he was a very busy guy. That might be tragic, but I always had this saying, "In motion, so you don't feel emotion." So Wally was in a daze all the time, and just worked. He did love comics, but he just hated editors. I don't reckon you've heard the bitter things he's said about editors. He rated them pretty low, and always had this cynical approach to drawing, you know. There was a saying, "You copy it, if you can't copy it, you trace it, if you can't trace it, you cut it out and paste it up!" [*laughter*] Whatever value there was about originality, it didn't particularly matter—but the funny thing is, of the loads and loads of stuff Wally swiped, the moment he inked it, it became Wally Wood, you know?

I swiped. One thing I don't have is a style like Wally Wood, and I avoided developing a distinct style. I tried not to get a specific style, because I'd seen Wally trapped in that style, like Kirby was in his own. You get to this style so you can work fast, but it's basically a way of thinking that has little room for any other deviations after a while. So, I found that non-creative; and Wally wasn't that original, except in his cartoons—everything else was derivative from Foster or Raymond. His lighting was a helluva lot like Raymond's *Flash Gordon,* but Wally took it and did it more—double-lighting and everything.

So it was kind of weird. I was a big EC fan, and Wally was my favorite artist. So I was a fan who ended up working for Wally, which was a wish come true, so I had one of my most creative periods that time working for Wally, and working for *Creepy.* The stuff I did for Wally was my best work! [*laughter*] I didn't get credit for the most part, so it was just a strange thing. I think it was because I *wasn't* getting credit that I could afford to do whatever I wanted and take chances.

CBA: *Did you work with Wally when he was doing* Daredevil?

Dan: No. There's a graceful figure on a building or something looking down in the story where there's a cat-girl or something, and Craig Russell keeps talking about that all the time! He must've asked me on five different occasions if I penciled that cover for Wally! Because it's a long, lean figure, a little unusual for Wally, you know? I didn't do it, I don't know who did! [*laughs*] But no, I never inked on it. He was just finishing up *Daredevil* when I came in.

Wally didn't like working for Marvel, because he wanted a bigger cut of the money. He had some wrong idea that Kirby was getting a percentage. Kirby *was* getting bonuses, but a *lot* of us were getting bonuses! Jim Steranko and I got bonuses when we were sharing *Strange Tales* with our "Nick Fury" and "Dr. Strange." The book went up in sales when we came on, so I got a $400 bonus, and Jim got a bonus. I know Kirby used to get like $10,000 a year bonuses, and Wally wanted some of that, but he wasn't getting any.

CBA: *He was only on* Daredevil *for what, seven issues?*

Dan: Yeah. He's the one who made the suit into that dark red suit, you know.

CBA: *When did you go off on your own? When you were working for Warren?*

Dan: Yeah, and I did it in a cowardly way, according to Wally. [*laughs*] I went down to Archie, and had to beg him for about six months to let me do a story for him, which turned out to be "The Doorway." I was still working for Wally, until my third Warren story,

DYNAMO

"The Day After Doomsday." When that came out, I took my samples—I'd had my name on three jobs for Wally, and I had three jobs published on my own, including a one-page filler for *Blazing Combat,* plus my science-fiction stuff for years—and I went to Marvel. I saw Sol Brodsky, and went in to see Stan, and they gave me a Bill Everett "Sub-Mariner" job to ink. So I inked that, brought that back in, and they gave me my first pencil job, which Stan wrote. He gave me a plot written out on index cards. It was "It Walks Like a Man," or something like that. A thing from radiation. So, I did that story with Stan, and the second half I did with Roy Thomas, and those were my first stories.

When I started working for Marvel, I stopped doing stuff for Wally and Tower. Tower was up to about the 16th or 17th issue of *T.H.U.N.D.E.R. Agents* by then, and I don't think there was any sign of trouble, so I wasn't quitting because the books weren't selling. I was just out of there because I wanted to draw bigger panels. I always had arguments with Wally about the way to pencil the jobs, because I wanted it bigger, and I wanted to turn torsos, and Wally

Above: Dan notes this image of Tower's great hero, Dynamo, is "another re-creation done for Roger Hill. On the original, I did everything but ink the running spaceman (which Wally [Wood] inked. Wally also lettered the logo). On the re-creation, I did everything." Courtesy of the artist. Art ©2000 Dan Adkins. Dynamo ©2000 the respective copyright holder. **Opposite page, top:** *Two cover paintings done for Jim Warren. Originally ©Warren Entertainment, Inc.* **Bottom:** *Dan himself, around the time P. Craig Russell, Val Mayerik, and Paul Gulacy were working as his assistants. Courtesy of Dan Adkins.*

"ALONG CAME A SPIDER!"

Above: "Re-creation done for John Harrison," Dan writes. "On original I used Ditko Spider-Man swipe and the other figures are swiped from Kirby." Below: Roy Thomas and Dan created Starhawk, intended for Marvel Super-Heroes, but nixed by publisher Martin Goodman. Art ©2000 Dan Adkins. Starhawk ©2000 Marvel Characters, Inc.

cover anyway, "The Wanderer" or something, this guy floating down from space. Frank Frazetta said something to the effect of he'd never thought about using brown for the sky or something… I don't even remember what the sky looked like now, but I remember the quote from Frank! [laughter]

CBA: What did you learn from Wally?

Dan: He taught me about 90% of everything that's incorrect about my work. The other 10% I learned myself! [laughter] But again, Wally taught me to burn brushes—we'd burn the tips with a match (never a lighter) and you wet it a little bit, and you get a very good tip to a #3 Windsor-Newton Series 7! You've just got to bring it up to the match with your right hand, and jerk it away the moment you see it coming into contact. This gives you what they call a "bedeviled edge,"—it's long one way and thin the other way, and we had a way of inking and twisting that brush automatically so that it just gives you almost perfect control instead of the stringy little thing that comes with it. It's a very small part you'd burn, but this gave us a very good, controlled line for our outlining and we only use the sharp brushes for the feathering of hair.

CBA: When you were illustrating and inking your own work, was the first regular strip "Dr. Strange"?

Dan: No, I did the first two issues of "Sub-Mariner" with Stan Lee. These were the 11-pagers in Tales to Astonish. After that, I did 11 issues of "Dr. Strange" in Strange Tales starting with around #160. I started doing the covers first. I've seen an interview with Marie Severin in which she said I did a nice job inking her "Dr. Strange," but I've never inked Marie's "Dr. Strange"! But I did ink some Marie Severin covers. I used to call her up and tell her masturbation jokes. [laughter]

CBA: You shared Strange Tales with…

Dan: …Steranko, which is why I'm now living in Reading, Pennsylvania. As Steranko and I tell it, it was love at first sight when I first saw him in that white suit. He'd wear this white or light blue suit all the time to conventions. [laughs] So I live over here because of Steranko. I came over here for two days, he showed me the town.

CBA: For an inker who can be described as very chameleon, I distinctly recall your "Doctor Strange" work as being very lush and very Adkins, very you.

Dan: They started out as looking like Ditko, because I was told to draw like Ditko. I was never told to draw like Kirby—but I was told to draw like Ditko. I was actually told to swipe Ditko, and this was by Stan, up front. So, I did; but then I started going towards my own style, which is realistic and just a different style.

CBA: Did you kind of draw yourself into a corner by putting in that much detail? I really recall a lot of cross-hatching…

Dan: No, I met the deadlines of the first three when I penciled and inked the whole book, 22 pages a month, but it may be that one of the reasons I switched to inking is because it was hard to do a monthly book, pencils and inks. I was still very young at the time, and had a lot of energy. I didn't have much of a problem with that, but I always went up there and turn in these jobs, and I'd see these gorgeous jobs by Buscema and Kirby and Gene Colan back in those days. So I just wanted to ink these guys. John Severin, in his Comics Journal interview said he hated to do the inking, but I loved the inking, the finishing off. I think the inker makes the final statement, even when he's inking a guy that's tight, like Neal Adams.

CBA: You had a reputation for swiping.

Dan: When I started out, Wally had loads of reference to work with that went way back; but I would swipe from something that came out a couple of months ago when I was first starting, and I still hadn't made up my mind whether it was bad to swipe or not. It's bad to swipe the way I did, and it's certainly bad to swipe the way Rich Buckler did, but somehow, when Esteban Maroto swipes from Gil Kane, he gets away from it. I adored Marie Severin who used to kid me about my swiping.

CBA: So, if you could do it again, you'd do it differently?

Dan: I just did it to meet the deadlines, it was so hard, without swiping.

CBA: Many artists have historically swiped from Foster or Lou Fine, or instance…

Dan: Wally did it, but of course, when Wally and I were through with it, it looked like Wally!

didn't like to turn figures too much—he had this sort of stock way of drawing everything. Most people assume when I was working for Wally, I was just an inker—because I became an inker most of my career—but actually I was mostly a penciler with Wally. It just happened that I did inking. So, I was wanting to create my way, and that's the reason I left, nothing to do with our relationship or anything.

But once I quit [laughs], I didn't tell Wally I was going to quit, I just said, "I can't do a job for you this week, Wally, I've got to do some other stuff!" So, my wife took the last job I did for Wally up to him, and figured she'd get a check, and Wally said, "Dan was too scared to come up, right?" [laughter] So I knew he was really mad at me. We didn't speak for a couple of years. (We finally met at a convention and we talked and had dinner together.) So I went out and started painting covers. Actually, I think I painted a cover for Creepy or Eerie before I left Wally. At the time, only Frazetta, Jack Davis and Gray Morrow had done covers for Warren, so Wally said, "Too much competition!" [laughs] But I went up and sold a

CBA: *But your swipes were from pretty current material.*

Dan: They were current, and there wasn't much changing; but a lot of it was like when you take Tarzan and you'd put Dr. Strange's costume on him. I was actually redrawing it, and just stealing the pose. That's mostly what I swiped for—so I didn't have to think up the poses and I didn't have to repeat myself so much, using the same poses. It's hard for me to draw.

CBA: *So you pretty much gave up penciling?*

Dan: Well, I only penciled something in the neighborhood of 25 to 30 stories (and of course that doesn't count the 16 or 30 I did for Wally). Yeah, I went to inking for a long time, and then your mind changes; the actual *physical* work doesn't change, but your mind changes, and times where if you're inking Dick Ayers when you're young and starting out, it's like "Oh, God! They gave me Dick Ayers! This is just going to make me look bad and hurt my reputation!" But when you're older, it's, "Oh, *man*, they gave me Dick Ayers; what a break! I can do this in a day!" [*laughter*] So, there are different ways of looking at all these things. After a while, you run out of good artists and so they started giving you a lot of "fix-up" art. That was basically after Don Newton died. I did 49 stories with Don Newton, I lived down the street from him in Phoenix. That's why we ended up working so much together. You know, we did a lot of *Batman* stories.

CBA: *You could really adapt to styles. If I recall, you inked some Captain America stories by Kirby?*

Dan: Yeah, I inked Kirby on #104 and #105.

CBA: *They were just beautiful jobs. I think Gil said that…*

Dan: Yeah, Gil likes my inking.

CBA: *You did beautiful work on Gil, like in* Warlock.

Dan: Gil is less and less the academic artist I used to think he was, but yeah, again, I met the deadlines on Gil.

CBA: *But you could really adapt, you didn't necessarily have a…*

Dan: I didn't like the idea that Wally had a stamped style, you know? So, I can usually adapt to other people and the direction they were going in with the pencils, because my ego doesn't want to get in the way. I basically tried to go the way they were going. I'd try to fix little things. I just inked the Kirby cover for your friend there…

CBA: *Yeah, the Captain America cover [for* The Jack Kirby Collector *#25]*

Dan: If you look, you'll see I've added shadows to the ear, I've added little highlights to the eye. So, I do not follow these people exactly, but it still looks authentic. If you compare Kirby's pencils with my inks, you can see that I *do* change things.

CBA: *But it's a faithful adaptation…*

Dan: Yeah, what I call, "Going in the same direction they drag you into." I do add Wally Wood eyes.

CBA: *And you inked Bill Everett. How was he to ink?*

Dan: I found absolutely nobody hard to ink. The only person where I got a little nervous about inking, is when I inked a "Challengers of the Unknown" story by Alex Toth. I felt inhibited inking Toth, mainly because I didn't want to get killed! [*laughter*]

CBA: *You worked closely with Wally in a studio environment. Have you always sought out camaraderie with other creative types to work with them?*

Dan: I wasn't like Wally, no. He always had people around, but I hate assistants!

CBA: *Have you had any?*

Dan: Well, Craig Russell, Val Mayerik, and Paul Gulacy, we worked together on things, but I never really thought of them as assistants. Bruce Miller helped me on a few jobs.

CBA: *But pretty much you're solitary?*

Dan: Yeah, yeah. Although I get very bored with myself, you know? I just don't like assistants. I don't think it's a problem with delegating authority, either. I used to be a control freak. I don't know why; it would be smart to have a good person to help with some of the work, but I want to do it all. I like to do all the work.

Getting to Craig Russell, and how that started: There was an article in the local paper about me, and his father saw it, and wanted me to do a drawing for him, and that's where I learned about Craig and his collection of comics. His father asked could Craig drop by and see me. He did, and I ended up helping him get work.

These guys really weren't my assistants or anything, I was just helping them get into comics. Val was next after that, and Val—his

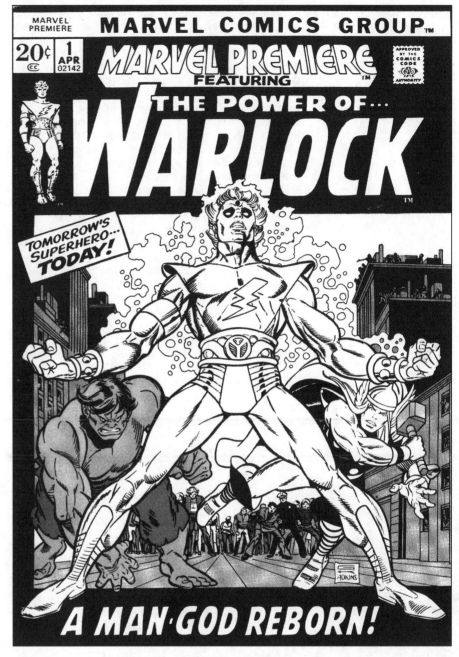

Above: *Great Adkins ink job on Gil Kane for the cover of Marvel Premiere #1.* **Below:** *Dan writes, "My favorite job—inking Big John's Silver Surfer. Head done of Surfer for John Harrison." ©2000 Marvel Characters, Inc.*

art teacher in Youngstown knew me, so he came around because the art teacher sent him, and I laid out a job for him, and without even asking Marvel or anything! I just thought of this story, laid it out, and said, "Go on, I'll make you a star!" [*laughs*] He brought it in, and we had it written by John Jakes and inked by Joe Sinnott. It was "Spell of the Dragon" with John Jakes' Brak the Barbarian.

I broke down these stories Craig worked on, one called "Thirst," where Steve Gerber did the script; but I did all the plotting, and laid them out.

Anyway, after Val came along, he had a girlfriend who was going up to Pittsburgh on the bus and she met Gulacy on the bus. They got to talking about comics, and she said her boyfriend was drawing comics, and Gulacy gave me a call in the A.M.! [*laughs*] That's how Gulacy got started, anyway. Then we had all three of them there, you see; and then we had the one that's not mentioned, Mark Kersey, who looked like Al Capp's Li'l Abner, had these brogans on—these great big shoes—and he used to walk three or four miles to come out to the studio. Anyway, he only worked one job, "Ant-Man," that Craig worked on, too. Anyway, Mark didn't like the idea of TV dinners and sleeping in his day clothes, and went home to momma! [*laughter*] Not that it's a hard life!

CBA: *What became of him?*

Dan: Well, for one thing, he was a serious artist, and he had some really great samples for a guy who was only 19. He was going to become to the comic book and art world what the Beatles were to the music world… but he didn't. We gave him credit in that "Ant-Man" book that Craig was drawing. So I helped most of those guys get started.

CBA: *You just did layouts and plotting* gratis, *just to help them out?*

Dan: Yeah. Actually, we went through a lot of dumb things together, and one of the things Barry Smith loves to recall… Barry Storyteller-Smith [*laughs*] took the name "Windsor" from the Windsor-Newton brush [*laughter*]… honest! That's a tribute to that brush, which was the Queen's brush. (Windsor came up with the Series 7 just for the Queen of England.) Anyway, we all worked on this horrible job we did for *Conan* that Barry laid out.

CBA: *You know, I remember as a kid opening that up and thinking, "Something went terribly wrong." [laughter]*

Dan: A lot went wrong there! For one thing, it was a bad deal, because John Verpoorten, who made the money arrangements, thought it was a good idea to give Barry Smith something like $30-40 a page, and then give us $7 a page to finish it off! It should've been the other way around, from the layouts we had. So, we were all working on it, and Barry can't lay out—he's like Joe Kubert (Hi, Joe!) [*laughter*]. Kubert is impossible to ink, and Howie Chaykin ain't too easy, either. I turned back a whole job by Kubert, because I thought his layouts were so vague. Who was the German guy, or the good guy? I couldn't tell… he just doesn't put down any information there. I'm talking about layouts, not tight pencils.

CBA: *What job was that? Kubert almost always inks his own work.*

Dan: This was just one of those jobs when I was working for DC and he was an editor there. They gave me a job that was laid out by Kubert, and I said, "I can't get anything from this thing. I don't even know what's going on here!" So I gave it back. Joe probably knew what the hell was going on there. Wally could almost ink with no information, a lot of times, and just turn it into Wally inks.
The thing about Barry is that he has to take his time, and has to really overwork it. So when he does layouts, it's just not right, he's just not a guy who can do layouts like John Buscema. John's a natural artist, he knows how to draw by redrawing and redrawing. Barry only knows how to draw by redrawing and redrawing, so there was just no way we could get this done on the time schedule they had. This was when Barry was very young.

CBA: *It was tight already?*

Dan: Yeah, it was always tight. See, I was late with a number of jobs, you know? I cannot ink real fast. I've inked nine pages during an 18-hour session, a page every two hours. That was a Marie Severin story, Sub-Mariner vs. the Hulk, for *Tales to Astonish* #100.
So, I inked a page in an hour, and I've penciled 11 pages in one 18-20 hour sitting; but basically, I can do a page-and-a-half a day. So, when you get Barry and what you call the slow pencilers… and he's slow. I don't know how fast he is now, because if you look at *Barry Windsor-Smith: Storyteller*, he's a fast penciler in there, and a fast inker, and a fast artist! [*laughter*]
The first issue of *Conan*, I inked and there were no problems, probably

Below: Dan notes that this is a "tone pencil of Conan (published in b-&-w Conan). From photo. Head and hair made-up." Courtesy of the artist. Art ©2000 Dan Adkins. Conan ©2000 Conan Enterprises, Inc.

because it had been sitting around forever (I think Barry had gotten #4 started before I even started on #1). But when I got to #7, I think I only did about seven pages before Frank Giacoia, I think, came in and helped finish it off. But Barry's slow, and if you give me his job, it's usually already late before I start; but if you give me John Buscema or Jack Kirby, who are both fast… I did eight John Buscema *Silver Surfer* issues with no problem, you know? And it was no problem for two reasons: 1) These guys don't put in as much detail as Smith, and 2) What they *do* put in, they put in quickly, therefore they've got some kind of system. So, you can handle problems with deadlines; but you take a guy that's meticulous like me, and a guy who's meticulous like Barry, and you're asking for trouble!

CBA: *What brought you out to Ohio?*

Dan: Running away from crime. In the Summer of '68, I got mugged coming from Wally's. I used to work up there until two or three A.M., and would come home by taking the subway, then a bus home. The bus was very late, so I started walking home—about a mile walk—and I wasn't quite sure of the direction to get home anyway. These guys followed me from the subway stop and they mugged me, cut me underneath the armpits where the guy (who was holding me) put a knife under my arm from the back. So I got home, I called Wally up, and I said I got mugged. So, that was one incident. Then, a couple weeks later, I was working real late and guys broke into my damn kitchen while I was working! I was able to get rid of them, and the cops got there real quick and they were chasing the burglars over the back of my yard! So, I decided, "This is enough of the Big City, I'm going home to good old safe Ohio." [*laughs*] So, I gave my parents a call. I have two brothers and a sister, and my two brothers came up in a big truck, and helped me load up. Those guys broke in on Friday night, and by Sunday I was living in Ohio.

CBA: *You'd had enough.*

Dan: My mother and dad, they had 11 rooms in their house, and three acres, so they had plenty of room for me and Jeanette… I had one kid, and he was only about six then. So, I was there at my parents for about three months, and then I bought a house, and I stayed there for six years. My dad ended up dying, and after my dad died—when you see someone die, it makes you think about your life, and I decided, "That's enough of Ohio!"

CBA: *You served at art editor of the Marvel b-&-w line?*

Dan: I was art editor up at Marvel on the b-&-w books, which I did for two years. Marvel had about 16 titles, I think. When they put out whatever they put out—*Monsters Unleashed, Vampire Tales*…

CBA: *You were in New York at the time?*

Dan: I lived in New Jersey, in Edgewater. I went to New York not exactly for that staff job, but for a steady job. I'd been in Phoenix—that's where I went after I left Don Newton's area—and I moved to New Jersey. I was up there probably only about two months before I started working for Marvel. Marv Wolfman is the one who got me that job. They were putting out titles, and needed somebody to talk to artists on the phone, and make sure the production stuff went through (although we had a production man of our own—besides John Verpoorten—Lenny Grow). Anything that needed fixing up, I would do; any talks with the artists about how to correct something, I'd do; and I'd help with designing. After two years, these books stopped selling and they started bringing work from upstairs—on the ninth floor, they put out the men's magazines, the gossip magazines, and so forth. They started bringing down advertisements that would appear for Simon & Schuster for their books. They were always making changes, and were always so critical about things. That wasn't a thing I wanted to do; I'd been spoiled by all the drawing! [*laughs*] This is the stuff I used to do in the studios, what they'd call paste-ups. I wasn't an illustrator so much as I was a mechanicals man. So, I'd been spoiled, and when Marvel started doing that, I went over to DC and they put me on *Superman* or something. *Return of the New Gods* was the first thing I started doing, with Don Newton, somewhere around 1976, 1977. I did a lot of Curt Swan. I did *Warlord* for a long time, with Dan Jurgens, one of the artists I had to fix up.
Let me tell you a Dan Jurgens story: I was down to six teeth (they said I had no teeth in a Wally Wood article in *Comic Book Marketplace*—I had teeth, guys!) [*laughter*], and I went down and had them pulled at 11 A.M., and the surgeon gave me Novocaine. But the night before, I'd been up all night inking a Dan Jurgens story,

and—I forget who the hell the editor was of *Warlord* at the time… anyway—maybe it's better if we don't mention his name [*laughs*]—the editors got $500 bonuses if their books were put out on time that month. [*laughter*].

CBA: *If they came in on time?*

Dan: Yeah, the editors would get bonuses! So, you see why they would go after people. So, this guy was always telling me to add more texture to Dan Jurgens—which means "Add more work." So, after a three-hour trip to New York, I went in and there was still gauze in my mouth because I was still bleeding from having the teeth pulled. I was standing there with no sleep, up all night, and the guy looks at the job and says, "Adkins, this needs more texture!" I took out the gauze and started wiping blood on the paper. "*Here's* your texture!" [*laughter*] That's the way it is sometimes; it's rough. And unappreciated!

CBA: *What was the highpoint of your career?*

Dan: Well, my Warren work was probably the peak of my creativity. What was *not* so creative was the swiping. You get a reputation and it's too bad you can't erase it, I guess, because you do get to be a better artist later on, and overcome most of that. Those guys wrote the articles about me and swiping in the fanzines—there was one called "Dan Adkins and the Amazing Tracing Machine" by Jim Vadeboncoeur—I'd be glad to sit down and draw to make it up… I could back then, too, but I don't think I particularly cared to. I guess I've always felt guilty about swiping. I don't think I'd do anything like that nowadays. I've learned how to draw, and how to meet deadlines! If you try, you can avoid situations where you have to do things too fast, and can take your time.

CBA: *What was the highpoint working for Marvel in the '70s?*

Dan: It was inking those guys, and not the penciling. I loved those Buscema *Silver Surfer* issues. I did three *Sub-Mariner* issues he did, and that was when he was doing his tight penciling.

CBA: *Russell and Gulacy told me you were a big Elvis fan.*

Dan: I was an illustrator while in the Air Force at Luke Field. I did the calendar for the base, library signs, what's at the movies this week sign, and basically kept the base filled with information. I got $90 to buy supplies with every month, and I had to go down to the art store and keep track of it with slips, but what I did—because the guy wanted me to spend all the money, or we wouldn't get that much all the time, the guy said, "Be sure you spend at least $90," so I printed out my fanzine with the $90! [*laughter*] I bought the paper with it, and everything. We actually had an article in the fourth issue of *Sata* on Elvis Presley—this was '56. Elvis was out there on one of the baseball fields performing on the stage at the pitcher's mound. He'd come up in a station wagon, and they got out there, and the mike wasn't working or something… so he got another mike, and said, "If this motherf*ckin' mike don't start workin', I'm going to leave!" [*laughter*] Elvis was only about 23. This thing was four or five feet off the ground, this stage, but he got clear off that stage and was singing from the ground. So, I became a big Elvis fan.

CBA: *From that moment on?*

Dan: Yeah. I was crazy about Elvis, and I could do a pretty good imitation of Elvis when I was younger. He had this way of moving that he stole from strippers, in the way that he moved across the stage, wiggling. We sent that issue of *Sata* to Memphis, and we got a letter from Elvis' mother!

CBA: *Get out!*

Dan: Yeah! [*laughter*] I wish I'd saved the letter! It was on lined paper, and it said, "Elvis isn't home now, but I'll show him your magazine. He's never home much anymore." [*laughter*] It was just great.

CBA: *Paul and Craig mentioned taking you to the drive-in…*

Dan: Gulacy took me to see *Charro!*, and that was one of Elvis' worst movies. We saw that practically in the rain at the drive-in. [*laughs*] So God couldn't have picked a better movie! [*laughter*]

CBA: *You're still working pretty steadily, right?*

Dan: Well, I don't like to work too much, but then again, doing nothing is even worse than working. I hate what people call a "good time," because getting drunk is a total "no-good time" for me. I can't see why kids are out there drinking booze and everything. I never drank booze; it upsets my stomach or makes me drowsy.

I certainly wouldn't want to be a workaholic like Wally. I used to work harder, where I didn't get much sleep. It's very strange, because the only thing that happens when you slow down working is you *think* more. I don't know what else there is to do! I still work, and I think I draw better than I ever did before, and I've certainly got over that swiping thing they used to kill me for! [*laughs*]

Above: A shining example of a great penciler/inker team, Barry Smith and Dan Adkins, from Conan the Barbarian *#20. BWS Studio notes that Barry composed the title logo himself. Courtesy of Barry Windsor-Smith.* ©2000 *Marvel Characters, Inc. Conan* ©2000 *Conan Properties, Inc.*

Jim Mooney Over Marvel

From *Terrytoons* to *Omega the Unknown*, Jim talks Comics

Conducted by Chris Knowles
Transcribed by Jon B. Knutson

Though renowned for his work on DC's "Supergirl" and "Tommy Tomorrow," you may be surprised to learn Jim Mooney's work for Marvel Comics began as far back as the early '40s, where he first met lifelong friend Stan Lee. And it may also come as a shock that the veteran artist's favorite work was for Marvel during the '70s, particularly on Steve Gerber's books. Let's have Jim tell it. The artist was interview by phone on July 26, 1999, and he copy-edited the transcript.

Right inset: From Jim Mooney's letterhead. Some of Jim's most memorable characters. Courtesy of the artist. Superman, Batman, Supergirl, Tommy Tomorrow ©2000 DC Comics, Inc. Spider-Man ©2000 Marvel Characters, Inc.

Below: Old buddies Jim Mooney and Stan Lee, hanging out at Stan's Beverly Hills place in 1990. Courtesy of Jim Mooney.

Comic Book Artist: *When did you start working for Stan Lee and Timely?*

Jim Mooney: We worked together doing *Terrytoons*, the animated-type comic, in probably 1943.

CBA: *So this was during the war.*

Jim: Yes, Stan and I worked together until he was drafted. Later we worked together when he was stationed in Duke University, North Carolina. I came down there to work with him on a *Terrytoons* project. We were on a tight deadline, so Stan found a place for me to work in a pathology lab. I was surrounded by jars of pickled eyeballs and various body parts. The incentive was for getting out of there fast. That speeded me up tremendously.

CBA: *You and Stan had a friendship?*

Jim: We were friends. I met Stan the first time when I was looking for work at Timely. Stan tells this story better than I do—I came in, being somewhat young and cocky at the time, and Stan asked me what I did. I said I penciled; he said, "What else?" I said I inked. He said, "What else?" I said color. "Do anything else?" I said, "Yeah, I letter, too." He said, "Do you print the damn books, too?" I guess he was about two or three years my junior at that point. I think I was about 21 or 22.

CBA: *Then you did a lot of work for a lot of people, did you ever work exclusively for Timely/Atlas?*

Jim: I never worked exclusively for anyone except for a very short period of time early on when I worked for Eisner and Iger in their shop. I freelanced except for a very brief period of time later on, and I worked for about seven or eight months in the Fiction House Bullpen.

CBA: *When was the "crash," when everyone was suddenly out of work?*

Jim: There were a couple of them in the industry. The one I remember well, I mentioned earlier on that I'd done funny animal strips, so-called "animated stuff" for *Terrytoons*, Stan and I worked on that. I'd say about '46 through there, the funny animal stuff was no longer in demand, and an awful lot of us were scurrying around looking for work, and I was one of those guys, and I heard on the grapevine that they were looking for an artist to do *Batman*. So I buzzed up there to DC, talked to them and showed them my stuff, and even though they weren't so sure because of my funny animal background, they gave me a shot at it. I brought the work in, and Whitney Ellsworth said, "Okay, you're on."

CBA: *Drawing in Bob Kane's style?*

Jim: This was actually, it was ghosting. Dick Sprang was one of their better production artists, and he'd taken off and wanted to do something else. So Dick took off for Arizona, and DC was looking for someone to fill in. So, that's where I fit in, and I stayed on *Batman* for quite a few years, and then I did "Robin, the Boy Wonder" in *Star-Spangled Comics*, and, let's see, I worked for some of their *House of Secrets* and *House of Mystery*, "Tommy Tomorrow," almost everything came along, and I handled it for DC. I was with DC on a freelance basis for almost 20 years.

CBA: *And were you working for Timely/Atlas in the '50s, as well?*

Jim: I may have done some stuff for them, but it was probably minimal, because I would've been working for DC.

CBA: *What brought you from DC to Marvel in the late '60s? What precipitated that?*

Jim: At that time, I imagine you're pretty well aware that they were trying to establish more or less of a style, the Neal Adams type of approach, and a lot of us who were drawing in the earlier, more simplistic style, well, let's just say it was myself, George Papp, Wayne Boring, Al Plastino. Our style was pretty much what they wanted to be for Superman, and the Superman characters; but it wasn't the illustrative style that Neal Adams established, and that was the direction they decided to go. Carmine Infantino was in the driver's seat at that time, and he wanted us to work more illustratively. We tried, and I did do a few "Supergirl" strips at that time that were beginning to get a little bit more on the illustrative side, but finally, it came to my attention that I didn't think my services were going to be needed there very much longer. They had let George Papp and Wayne Boring go...

CBA: *And they let a lot of writers go...*

Jim: That was a big turnover. They were wanting to try a new approach, so I went over to Marvel. Of course, I'd known Stan—we knew each other socially before that and I would have liked to have worked for Marvel before '69, but their rates were too low at that time—they didn't come up to DC's rates—they weren't equal. So, I approached Marvel and I said, "Is there anything in the offering?" And Stan said, "You picked a good time: We'd like somebody to do a little finalized penciling with John Romita, and inking." And Stan asked me if I'd give it a shot, and that lasted for quite a while.

CBA: *On Amazing Spider-Man, John Romita would do break-downs, and you'd tighten up the pencils and ink them?*

Jim: That's exactly it, yeah. Same thing with Buscema, too, on *Amazing Spider-Man.*

CBA: *Spidey was pretty much your bread-and-butter for your first two years at Marvel?*

Jim: I was also working later on with Sol Brodsky doing the coloring books, that type of thing, and I did a feature for the *Electric Company* magazine, a very simplistic Spider-Man type of thing, and I also did the same kind of tales for *Spidey Super Stories.* And in the early '70s, I did work for Goodman's men's magazines, a strip called "Pussycat." Stan wrote the first one I did, and then his brother Larry wrote the ones that came later.

CBA: *This was during the early '70s?*

Jim: Yeah.

CBA: *Were you mostly working at home, or was there a bullpen you'd work at, or...?*

Jim: No, I never was in a bullpen situation there. I used to visit the bullpen, you know. I had fun talking to the guys who were the bullpen regulars, but except for maybe doing a little touch-up or something like that, I never worked there.

CBA: *Who was at the Marvel bullpen at that time? I know Jack Abel worked there for a long time—was he still there?*

Jim: I don't recall Jack Abel being there at the time... not talking to him, at any rate. Herb Trimpe was there, and of course Larry Lieber,

and John Romita; those are the three that stand out in my mind, as the guys that I usually talked to when I did come in to the bullpen.

CBA: *So you'd come and drop off work, and socialize. Were you still seeing Stan on a social basis at this point in time? Would you guys go out for drinks after work?*

Jim: Stan was not a drinking guy. I enjoyed a draught now and then, but Stan was more of a malted milk person. Yeah, we'd go out to lunch together, of course at that time, a little bit later on the early '70s, just a little bit later, my wife had an antiques business, and I worked in the business, and Stan's wife, Joan, had the same thing in Long Island, so we used to get together and exchange views on what to buy, and what not to buy—this was a bore to Stan. We did get together quite a bit.

CBA: *You then went from mostly doing* Spider-Man *to doing a number of strips. Of course,* Man-Thing, *you worked with Steve Gerber on that...*

Jim: That was one of my favorite strips, by the way. In fact, my all-time favorite.

CBA: *Okay, let's talk a little about that. You penciled and inked that strip, and took over for Mike Ploog, who originally did it?*

Jim: I think Ploog had done it early on, and then John Buscema, and I took over after John's last issue.

CBA: *I think that John did it on a fill-in basis, just a few issues.*

Jim: He didn't do too many of them.

CBA: *And then you took that book over, and were working with Steve Gerber. Now, would you guys have a phone conversation?*

Jim: Yeah, we almost always worked on the phone. I had never met Steve in the early days, when we were working on it. We'd talk on the phone, and the opportunity I had to meet him was way, way later at the San Diego con, and that was about two years ago.

CBA: *So, you'd never met him face-to-face?*

Jim: So typical of the business. I mean, so many of the guys, like John Buscema, Sal Buscema, any of the guys who were promi-nent at Marvel at that time, we were just not in the office at the same time. Maybe they were trying to avoid me, I don't know... I'm kidding... really!

CBA: *Well, it seems it's the nature of the beast that most of these guys would work at home, presumably have their own social circles, there'd be very little chance for interaction aside from chance encounters outside of the office.*

Jim: Well, that's quite in contrast to early on, because in the early days at Timely, when we were working, we'd all get together when we had a deadline, and we'd work all through the night in the offices in the old McGraw-Hill building. We all knew each other, and we socialized to a great extent, with [*editor*] Don Rico, and quite a few of the others who were working at the time.

CBA: *Well, presumably you were younger then...*

Jim: A little!

CBA: *...yeah, but it seems to me from things I've read that back in the early days, there were a lot more bullpens, and people did a lot more work in-house. It just seemed to be a lot more conducive to the social kind of atmosphere, and a lot of the older cartoonists have those great memories from that time. It seems to just stop sometime, maybe in the late '40s, or the early '50s, when every-body was just working at home, and starting their families.*

Jim: Well, when you stop and think, most of them at the time (I'm speaking now of the early '40s, we were in our twenties, and Stan was in his teens; Stan was 19, I was 21, something like that, Don Rico was probably the "old man" of the group, he was some-thing like 25 or 26), we were just really young guys, and it was a whole different field, a new field, and it was a lot of fun. We were enjoying something that later on became kind of pretty much a staid business.

CBA: *Let's backtrack to the '70s: You were doing work on a number of books, and all this time, there were some things going on in the business. There was a whole new generation of artists, there was a period—probably the early to the late '60s, where there was no new talent really coming into the business outside of Neal. Suddenly there was a whole new generation of artists—Jim Starlin, Bernie Wrightson, Walt Simonson, and people like that. Now, as an older cartoonist—a more experienced and seasoned veteran—how did you feel about this invasion of young new blood?*

Above, upper left: *From left: Fritz (Jim's nephew), Joan Lee, Stan the Man, and Jim's wife Ann, in the early '70s.* **Upper right:** *l-to-r: Stan Lee, Jim Mooney and Fritz.* **Above:** Jim notes, *"The Great One composing the Merry Marvel Marching Society opus."* **Left inset:** *From left to right: Graham Ingels, Jim's first wife, and Mooney the artist, clubbing it in the early '40s.* **Below:** *(And we're crossing our fingers that this pic will print okay) It's Stan and Joan Lee, and Jim Mooney, posing in this 1940s pic-ture. All photos courtesy of Jim Mooney.*

Above: *When Jim Mooney came on board at Marvel in the late '60s to work on* Amazing Spider-Man, *Johnny Romita brought his fellow artist up to speed with illustrated instructions. Courtesy of Jim Mooney. Art ©2000 John Romita Sr. Gwen and Mary Jane ©2000 Marvel Characters, Inc.* **Below:** *Jim's favorite comic assignment was drawing Steve Gerber's Man-Thing. Here's a panel detail. ©2000 Marvel Characters, Inc.*

Jim: It didn't bother me too much. I was very much impressed by Mike Ploog, for example, whom I thought was excellent. Of course, Bernie Wrightson was great. I really didn't feel terribly threatened, because I'd always been able to make a living in cartooning, and I just accepted the fact that new blood was probably necessary—our blood was getting a little old. No, I'm kidding on that, but no, it didn't bother me at all. I mean, I really didn't know any of these guys, it was just...

CBA: *You just saw their work.*

Jim: Yeah, I just knew their work, that's all.

CBA: *At the same time, there was a great deal of editorial chaos at Marvel. There was a revolving editorship—Roy Thomas, then Len Wein, Marv Wolfman, and Gerry Conway—with people just coming and going. Did that affect your job all?*

Jim: It didn't really. I got to know Roy probably better than most, because I worked with him more. I got to know Len, I didn't get to talk much to Gerry Conway; but no, it really didn't. Not that I felt overly secure, it's just I thought the work was there. About this time, say about 1975, I decided that I wanted to move to Florida. So I approached the management to see what could be done, and I suggested a contract, which they went along with. I moved to Florida in 1975 with a contract, and that lasted from 1975 to 1985, about 10 years, that was just like working in the office—it was a good deal. The money wasn't too great, but I was paid every couple of weeks, I had insurance, and I had a lot of security that most freelancers never had.

CBA: *So you were basically a contractor.*

Jim: The only problem with it was I had to take pretty much whatever came down the pike. Some of it I didn't care too much for, but being under contract, I accepted whatever was sent to me. Some of the stuff I would've preferred not to have done; there are other things I would've liked to have handled, but I just felt that I was obligated under contract.

CBA: *So at this point, you moved to Florida, and you're on a contractual basis with Marvel. Was the only contact with the comic book world just the work you were doing at the time? Did you go to any conventions in Florida?*

Jim: I went to only one, a Miami convention. Later on, I went to a few: A cartoonists' convention in Orlando, and a couple of conventions in Tampa/St. Petersburg; but I wasn't really very active in the convention circles at all. In fact, the first real contact I had with conventions outside of this area was Mike Whorley invited me to the Kansas City convention, and that was fun and different. It opened my eyes to an area I was not familiar with to that extent. Then I got my first invite to the San Diego Con, about three years ago.

CBA: *Oh, that recent?*

Jim: Then I started doing a few more, and it was quite enlightening to me. I didn't realize all this stuff was going on, and I didn't realize there was that much of a market for my original pages, etc. That was kind of a revelation.

CBA: *Was the attitude of guys in your generation that this was just a job that you were doing?*

Jim: I don't know, I can only speak for myself and some of the other guys I did know. I think most of us accepted it as a way to make a buck, it was something we could do pretty well. We had the experience, but I would say except for a few strips that I did, I was

never terribly enthusiastic about it. Certainly I wasn't terribly enthusiastic about the nine years I spent on "Supergirl."

CBA: *That wasn't your favorite assignment.*

Jim: It wasn't for many reasons. First of all, it was a strip that wasn't terribly challenging. After a while, you were pretty much doing the same thing over and over. The other thing I didn't like about it was, before that I was doing some stuff for DC, *House of Mystery* and so on, in a much more sophisticated style. When I started on "Supergirl," Mort Weisinger insisted it had to be what he considered the "house style." It had to look the way he wanted it, which was much simpler than the way I'd been drawing previously. So, I was pretty much fenced in by that particular requirement that Mort had. If I changed my style at all, he'd call me into his office and say, "What are you trying to do, make a million bucks? Do you have somebody ghosting for you?" I said, "No, I was just trying something a little different." He said, "Well, don't! Draw it the way you were drawing it before."

CBA: *So by contrast, Marvel was much more "hands-off."*

Jim: Oh, yeah, Marvel was a joy. I always liked working with Stan anyway, but there was a nice feeling of freedom and cooperation; people were nice and DC—my God, you felt like you were entering a penal institution sometimes! I'm speaking of those old days.

CBA: *Very button-down?*

Jim: Yeah.

CBA: *And this would be when Jack Liebowitz and Harry Donenfeld were still in charge, before they sold out to Kinney?*

Jim: Yeah.

CBA: *Did it change? You weren't there too long for the Carmine days, but did it change at all? Did he ask you to change, or was it still very conservative?*

Jim: It was not just necessarily conservative, it was just very uncomfortable. I'll give you an incident, as an example. I had been doing "Supergirl" for a long, long while, and I used to come in and bring my work to Mort (this would be about '65, '66, through there), and I walked into the office—the door was open—and Mort was busy with a writer, and he waved me out, like "I'm busy." So I walked out to the bullpen, and I was talking to Jack Schiff whom I'd also worked with, and I think George Kashdan, Boltinoff, and so on, and shoot the breeze, and Mort came storming in, absolutely *storming in,* and said, "You're supposed to bring that 'Supergirl' to me *first!*" His voice was cracking with anger; and I was flabbergasted, and everybody was shocked in the writers' bullpen; and he kept at it, saying, "You know, you keep at this, and you won't be drawing 'Supergirl'", and I said, "I've got news for you, Mort, I'm not going to be drawing 'Supergirl' anymore."

CBA: *And what was the reaction?*

Jim: He looked at me, totally stunned, and he stormed out of the office. Then, of course, there was a buzz in there, Jack and Murray saying, "Don't worry, Jim, we'll get you some work; it's okay." And I said, "It's okay, you can only take so much of this." And I came in two weeks later to see Jack, and Mort comes down the hall with a script, and says, "Here's your 'Supergirl' script." Like nothing had ever happened! And I thought for a minute, "Well, don't be a damned fool; it is an income," and although I realized it would be as difficult as it ever was to work with the guy, I thought. "I'll try it for a little while longer."

CBA: *From what I gather, in contrast to Marvel, which seemed much more creator-friendly, everything I've read is that the brass at DC just had utter contempt for the creators.*

Jim: They did. I got some pages, "Supergirl" pages, back from a guy by the name of Sal Amendola. Sal was a heck of a nice guy, and he said, "Jim, I felt bad about this. These are your pages." When I was working at DC, they were using "Supergirl" pages to back-up reprints, and they'd just throw them away! Well, I knew they were shredding them, throwing them away, and I knew they didn't care much about it. In fact, there was a story he told me that when they had a troop of Boy Scouts come into the office, they'd give them souvenirs, and they decided that a Curt Swan page would be ideal, but they didn't want to part with an entire page, so they cut out panels from it to give to each boy! And Sal was just incensed at this kind of desecration. (I recall this type of thing was typical of Sol Harrison.)

CBA: *Were you worried about getting your originals back at that point in time?*

Jim: I just thought, I had the same attitude, this is ephemeral stuff, it's just a throwaway type of thing, so don't worry about it. Once in a while, I'd ask for something to give to somebody that wanted it. I said, "This stuff is just going down to the cellar," and I assumed it was going to the shredder (although I didn't say that), and I said, "Is it okay if I take a couple of 'Supergirl' pages here, because I've got somebody that wants them." That was about it.

CBA: *Wow. So, let's get back to Marvel, then. You were working at Marvel in '75, you were freelancing, working with Sal Buscema a lot on The Defenders.*

Jim: I really liked working with Sal as an inker—he was great. I don't think he drew as well as John did, but it was all there, very pleasant to ink, very concise, and very well done.

CBA: *And you returned intermittently to* Amazing Spider-Man, *particularly towards the late '70s, and basically did whatever they threw at you. You were still penciling as well?*

Jim: Yeah, I referred to it as trying to make my deadlines, and fulfill the terms of my contract. I gravitated more and more to finalizing other peoples' work and inking, because I could do it faster, and I could fulfill the terms of my contract that way. I did like to pencil, and I did do a little bit of it, but I didn't do that much during those later years.

CBA: *Yeah, it seemed as the '70s wore on, you did less and less penciling. The books that really stand out in my mind that you had penciled were* Man-Thing *and* Omega the Unknown. *You did a* Ms. Marvel *and a number of issues of* Peter Parker, the Spectacular Spider-Man *as well.*

Jim: Yes, I did.

CBA: *Then it became more and more finished art. Stan Lee, as the '70s wore on, was almost completely out of the picture?*

Jim: Yes. I went out to Hollywood in the late '70s or very early '80s.

CBA: *Marvel Productions days?*

Jim: Yes, when he was there, and I spent a little time with Stan. I had to go out there to visit my father, who was in a rest home, and that was about the only contact I had with Stan except for a phone call every now and then at that period of time.

CBA: *What about with people at Marvel? Would you basically just deal with editors, and you wouldn't deal with people like Jim Shooter, Archie Goodwin...*

Jim: Oh, I dealt with Jim, yes. I had to.

CBA: *Let's talk a little bit about that. What would your dealings with Shooter be—as an editor on books you were working on, or when he became Editor-in-Chief?*

Jim: I always got along with Shooter early on. Toward the last, the relationship deteriorated pretty badly. I got the feeling that Shooter was getting a little bit too dictatorial. He'd harp on small things, production things. The fact that I was using blue pencil, which a lot of other guys had done, and the fact that I was using dry ink pens. Anyway, he resented that, and I said it's just a matter of speed. I think an awful lot of other guys are doing that, too. He was kind of curt about that, "Well, you don't have to," etc. Anyway, I'm not going into a lot of details about the relationship, except that unfortunately it wasn't terribly pleasant to deal with Jim in those later years.

CBA: *This would be into the '80s?*

Jim: Yes.

CBA: *We'd discussed that you were somewhat unhappy with the quality of the pencils you were being given to ink, and this would*

presumably be towards the early '80s when there was yet another turnover of new people entering the business. Did you spend a lot of your time doing redrawing, and things like that?

Jim: That was one of the things they wanted me to do, was to re-establish rather loose drawing and sketchy drawing. Of course, some of the stuff I'd have to designate as being pretty poor drawing. A lot of it was okay. You take somebody like John Romita or John Buscema sketches, it was all there, even if the lines weren't all there, the gesture or the pose, the feeling, the action, everything was there. Even in a few lines, and it wasn't really too difficult to take that a few steps further and make the drawing a little bit more complete, and then go on from there and ink it.

CBA: *Did you resent that, or did you just accept that as part of your contract?*

Jim: I resented it, yes, but I had to accept that as part of my contract. After all, I was here in Florida, I'd bought a house, the whole bit. In retrospect, in many ways I'd have been better off staying in Connecticut, and commuting to New York. I would've had much choicer assignments, not taking a contract to begin with; but, it did give me a great feeling of security, and a good many reasons for wanting it at the time. The beach, the climate, etc.

CBA: *It's pretty well known among freelancers that the real money-paying jobs that artists would get would be the commercial work, for licensing and advertisements, things like that. By being in Florida, were you denied access to those kind of jobs, or were you still able to do that kind of work?*

Jim: I didn't have too much of the so-called "advertising material." I did work with Sol Brodsky on things like coloring books and special assignments, like designing of lunch boxes, and that type of thing. That was quite lucrative, and I took as much of that as I could handle and still fulfill my contractual obligations to Marvel on the other stuff. Now,

Above: *Jim's double-page spread from Spectacular Spider-Man #25, inked by Frank Springer (who was scheduled to be featured in this issue but, due to space limitations, we've had to postpone his interview until the upcoming National Lampoon/Heavy Metal ish coming later this year).*
©2000 Marvel Characters, Inc.

this was still Marvel, this was still Sol Brodsky, but this was not considered part of my contract. In other words, it was not considered the material I needed to fulfill my contract obligations.

CBA: *So you billed separately on these obligations?*

Jim: Right.

CBA: *Let's forward to the '80s. The comics industry changed quite a bit, you saw fewer and fewer comics on the newsstand, and you saw the explosion of the direct market, and you also saw changes in tastes; more stylized cartoonists are coming to the fore. People like Sal Buscema were tailoring their drawing styles to fit this better. Did you feel the pressure in those days?*

Jim: I was aware of that, but of course, most of the stuff I was doing at that time was primarily inking. I was inking John Romita, Jr. at that time, and it was finalized, true, but John also had the talent his father had; if he did give you a sketch, it wasn't too difficult to finish it in preparation for inking.

CBA: *Do you remember what books you would be working on in the early '80s before your contract was up?*

Jim: I think I was primarily working on *Spider-Man*.

CBA: *Spectacular Spider-Man, mostly? There was Web of Spider-Man that came along.*

Jim: *Web of Spider-Man*, yes, I did a lot of that. I did *Web #10* with my full pencils.

CBA: *There were probably scattered assignments here and there.*

Jim: I think it was a little later on, it may have been even after my contract was up, that I worked with Mike Carlin on *Thundercats*.

CBA: *That's something I do remember you working on.*

Jim: That was into my retirement years. I was doing that in '88, '89, through there, and then right after that, I thought I was going to totally retire, and the *Superboy* TV series came my way. That was

1990, and I was five years into retirement by then!

CBA: *Busy retirement!*

Jim: It was, it still is! I'm still working!

CBA: *I've read you were working for Claypool Comics?*

Jim: I'm inking *Soulsearchers & Co.*, penciling and inking *Elvira*.

CBA: *Wow. You seem to be the most active of your generation at this point.*

Jim: I'm hungry most of the time.

CBA: *Oh, is that what it is?*

Jim: I've got to keep feeding myself, my family, and my eight cats.

CBA: *Eight cats? I only have five.*

Jim: They seem like eight sometimes, don't they?

CBA: *Are there any anecdotes, anything interesting with different personalities you'd like to go into?*

Jim: Well, I think I mentioned earlier on it was such a pleasure to go into that. I used to dread going into the offices at DC, but I looked forward to going into Marvel, and I think one of the real nice pleasant things, and a lot of the guys who have great memories say the same thing. You'd come in, and Flo Steinberg would be there, and she would say (in her marvelous enthusiastic voice), "Stan, Jim Mooney's here," and that would just make me feel great, as if I were very important. Then I realized everybody else got that same treatment, which was darn nice. I'd occasionally hang out in the bullpen and shoot the breeze, but I don't have too many bullpen anecdotes, because I really wasn't there all that much. The one thing I really liked, and I haven't had that experience before with Stan when we collaborated on the funny animal stuff, we'd get together for a story conference in the early '70s, and Stan would act these things out, and I'd think, "This is amazing, I've known this guy for years, I've never seen anything like this!" He'd jump up on the desk, nd go through the motions, the actions that he expected either from the Green Goblin or whatever the heck it was we were doing, nd he was having such a great time with it, it was contagious. I'd egin to think, "Hey, this is kind of fun, I'm enjoying this."

CBA: *When Stan became Editor-in-Chief/Publisher, your contacts with him outside of the social arrangements you'd mentioned before ould be pretty minimal?*

Jim: Yeah, I'd just say "Hi!" when I came in to the office, or maybe we'd chat a little bit in the hall, or maybe go out to lunch occasionally, but the contact wasn't as often as the early days when e was scripting *The Amazing Spider-Man.*

CBA: *You enjoyed being able to draw however you wanted for Marvel, and there was never any pressure to draw in the "house tyle," the way Mort Weisinger wanted you to...*

Jim: I wouldn't say there'd be a "house style" so much, but at that oint I was working with John Romita. I learned a great deal working with him, and I think it certainly improved my drawing of girls, articularly; but John had a very nice way about him. If something wasn't right, he'd tell you, and he'd just say, "Hey, maybe you can do it a little bit more this way," or "You notice with Gwen you draw er face a little more like this, maybe this angle is better, try to keep he head up if you can." All very pertinent, and very acceptable criticisms. I never took offense in any way; there was no reason to. I wouldn't even call that "house style," it was because I was trying to do something that I could make look as much like John's work as possible.

CBA: *Keep up the continuity.*

Jim: Yeah.

CBA: *I was born in '66, and when I was reading those comics, it seemed like Marvel was this constant party, when you read the editorial pages—Stan's Soapbox—and everything. It just seemed like everyone hung out together, and was just one big party, and the comic books would come out as a result of that; and later I learned everybody just basically came into the office once a week and dropped off their work!*

Jim: You're speaking of freelancers now, not the bullpen. I won't say there was a lot of partying, but everybody seemed to get along, and I enjoyed going in, I enjoyed talking to them. It was always pleasant. I think everybody had pretty much that same attitude; it was a fun place to work.

CBA: *Did you get the feeling when you were working for Marvel you were part of something that was new in comics, and exciting, and something that was much different than what had come before, did you get the feeling that there was just a whole different sense of mission with the books?*

Jim: Oh, yeah. I actually became quite enthusiastic about a lot of things I was doing there, and that had never occurred when I was working at DC. I kind of enjoyed getting a good *House of Mystery* script or something like that, and some of the "Tommy Tomorrow" scripts were pleasant to do, but I always had the feeling like "This is a job, accept it as a job, do the best you can, get your paycheck, and go home." At Marvel, I had a feeling of being *involved,* and being a part of it, particularly when I was penciling and worked with the outline script Stan provided and some of the others, because you did contribute something. You broke it down the way you wanted to. You could use any number of panels per page, as long as you still told the story.

CBA: *I wonder if there'd be comics today if it wasn't for Stan.*

Jim: I would be embarrassed to say that in front of him, but I feel the guy certainly provided movement for the whole industry—we all know that—that's no revelation. Stan and I, through the years we've always had a good relationship, and I've enjoyed that. We've had fun together, and I still consider Stan a very good friend. I'm sometimes in awe of how much he's accomplished.

CBA: *At the end of your contractual days, what precipitated you leaving Marvel, although not fully? What brought that about?*

Jim: You mean in '85? I was 65 years old.

CBA: *You were ready to retire.*

Jim: I was not necessarily ready to retire, but when I queried Jim Shooter about it, I got a very short note: "Retire." I'm paraphrasing that a little bit. It wasn't quite that abbreviated, but it was damn close. Real friendly. "So long, we hate to see you go—bye!" I was

ready to retire anyway (although I really didn't). It didn't bother me too much, because there was a lot of other things I wanted to do anyway. At the time, I was painting, working with ceramics, and I thought, "Well, I'm going to enjoy my retirement doing a lot of the things I didn't necessarily have the time to do when I was under deadline pressure."

CBA: *And you probably got the feeling Marvel had become a much different company under Shooter.*

Jim: Oh, God, under Jim it was... well, I don't think I was the only one who sensed that... there was a certain tension there that had never existed before.

CBA: *So, you leave Marvel, but you eventually continued to do some freelancing for them.*

Jim: Yeah, I did "Sub-Mariner" for their weekly comic, *Marvel Comics Presents.* During that so-called retirement period, I worked with Millennium Publishing, doing layouts for *Anne Rice's The Mummy.* That was with Mark Ellis, the editor. It just seems like when I kept thinking I was going to stop, I never did.

CBA: *Do you still enjoy it?*

Jim: Yeah, I enjoy it to some extent. I've slowed down a lot. You're bound to slow down a little bit, it's part of the life-cycle; but I guess it makes me feel that I'm still capable of doing it; that's rather a pleasant feeling as you get older.

CBA: *You seem a lot more youthful than most of your contemporaries, that's for sure.*

Jim: Well, thank you. If you see them, you just tell them that!

Above: *Jim Mooney pencils and inks from Marvel Spotlight #27, featuring Prince Namor, the Sub-Mariner. ©2000 Marvel Characters, Inc.*

CLASH OF

Comic Book Artist *was shocked, I tell you, shocked to find piles of evidence depicting the very-public feud between lovely Marie Severin and loathsome Don McGregor that sullied the Marvel Bullpen during Don's reign of terror as a staff editor back in the 1970s. On these pages we present Marie's artistic rendition of the conflict, as she tried to defend herself against Don's senseless, vile editorial attacks in issues of* Planet of the Apes *and* Deadly Hands of Kung Fu. *Most of the drawings on this spread appeared in various issues of POTA and DHOKF. The photo of Marie diligently working is by and courtesy of Sam Maronie.*

THE TITANS!

THE WARMUP

The photo at right, of Dauntless Don slacking at work (as usual) is by Richard Burton, and appears courtesy of the malevolent McGregor (who also loaned us virtually every Severin drawing appearing here). Marie was kind enough to grant CBA an interview regarding her side of the Battle of the Bullpen, but alas, we've just not enough space. Our thanks to both combatants and Sam Maronie for their contributions. All art ©2000 Marvel Characters, Inc. The Sinful Dwarf ©2000 the respective copyright holder. (Okay, Don, I'm done teasing you now, so holster that genuine Hopalong Cassidy six-shooter now, boy!)—**JBC**

Nice Person Award — MARIE SEVERIN

GOODNESS

BADNESS

LIMELIGHT

PLINK!

PLUNK!

IN A TYPICAL ACT OF KINDNESS MARIE SEVERIN PREPARES AN EXPERIMENTAL GROWING FLUID FOR ASST. EDITOR McGREGOR

How the feud was resolved: It may be fuzzy, but you should be able to see in this picture, snapped a nano-second before the final resolution, of how Mirthful Marie finally ended her war with McGregor. On bended knee, Don sputters, "Now, let's not be too hasty, Severin!" as the artist supreme takes a swing of her samurai sword (with open-mouth glee) and… *THWACK!* And you thought Don quit Marvel because of the work-for-hire contract, ehh?

Steve Gerber's Crazy Days

The writer discusses his days in the House of Ideas

Conducted by Jon B. Cooke
Transcribed by Jon B. Knutson

In the days before superstar writers, Steve Gerber was The Comic Book Superstar Writer. While his Howard the Duck *solidified Steve's position as a true comic book original, his* Defenders, Man-Thing, Omega the Unknown, *and (yes) even his* Kiss *comic all exhibited quirky and hilarious material that made Steve a creative power to be reckoned with in the '70s. Today still scribing the occasional Vertigo comic, Steve was interviewed via phone on Dec. 12, 1999, and he copy-edited the final transcript.*

Above: *Vote the Duck! In 1976, Steve Gerber ran the Howard the Duck for President campaign out of his New York apartment, selling the above Bernie-Wrightson-drawn buttons to devotees across the nation. Howard the Duck ©2000 Marvel Characters, Inc.*

Above: *Steve Gerber circa 1976 in the Marvel offices. Photo by and courtesy of Sam Maronie.*

CBA: *Are you from St. Louis?*
Steve: Yes, born in St. Louis, Missouri on September 20, 1947.
CBA: *When did you first get interested in comic books?*
Steve: September 21, 1947. [*laughter*] Probably… oh, God, I must've been four or five years old. An aunt and uncle used to pick up comics for themselves—I guess they must've read them when they were teenagers, and may have been in their twenties at the time—and they'd just pick them up at the newsstand. The first one I ever recall seeing is an issue of *Batman*, in the very early '50s, with art by Dick Sprang. I also remember having seen what must have been some of the last issues of *Plastic Man* and *Captain Marvel*.
CBA: *Were you attracted to the comics format immediately?*
Steve: Well, yeah, I must've been, even as a child. There was something interesting about them that wasn't like movies, and wasn't like television or whatever. Yeah, I found them interesting and attractive from the beginning.
CBA: *What was your upbringing like? Were you a voracious reader, or were you an active kid?*
Steve: I think I had a very active fantasy life. [*laughs*] I was not the voracious reader I should've been, unfortunately. We had a television in the house from the time I was born. That mitigated my reading habits in ways that I now wish it hadn't.
CBA: *Did TV influence you creatively?*
Steve: Early TV? Probably, in some way or another. I can't really point to any direct influences from television except the *Superman* TV show, old science-fiction series like *Tom Corbett* and *Space Patrol*, and I must have

unconsciously picked up a lot about writing humor from watching *I Love Lucy*, Phil Silvers, and Steve Allen. Later, of course, there were shows like *The Prisoner* that I looked at very carefully. I also remember, during what must have been my early teens, paying close attention to some of the issue-oriented dramas like *The Defenders* and *East Side/West Side*. Certainly, TV isn't any kind of influence on my work today, but I absorbed all that stuff, just like any other kid.
CBA: *I know you would've been awfully young, but do you recall seeing* Mad *comics and the other ECs?*
Steve: I never saw one of the *Mad* comic books, and I don't know if I ever saw any EC comics. There's a story I remember reading when I was very, very young—a really grim old science-fiction story about everybody in the world dying of a disease that manifested itself in bulbous purple pustules—that may have been in one of the EC books. I have absolutely no memory of what the title of the book or the story was, but it's the kind of story that could've come from EC.
CBA: *You were reported to have started your own fanzine while in junior high school.*
Steve: Yeah, I was about 13, 14 years old.
CBA: *So you were really getting into it by then?*
Steve: Oh, yes! Well, that was about the time the comic books started running letter columns, or at least the Marvel and DC books… well, no, there were no Marvel books at that time! [*laughs*] The DC books began running letter columns, and Julie Schwartz began printing his correspondents' addresses, so I started writing to Roy Thomas and Jerry Bails, and the two of them were kind enough to actually read my letters, and answer a lot of questions I had, and even loaned me a couple of comics from the really early days. If you can believe this, about 40 years ago, one fan, Douglas Marden, actually loaned me his copy of *Flash Comics* #1 through the mail! He trusted me with that.
CBA: *And you sent it back, right?*
Steve: Of course, I sent it back, yeah! [*laughter*] Roy used to loan me issues of *All-Star Comics*.
CBA: *Were you into super-heroes, or into other genres?*
Steve: By that time, I was primarily into super-heroes. That's where fandom was pretty much at that time; but I certainly grew up reading everything. You know, for most of my childhood, Superman, Batman and Wonder Woman were really the only super-heroes on the stands, so I also grew up reading *Uncle Scrooge, Archie, Li'l Archie, Little Lulu, Peanuts*, the whole plethora of Disney books, and the other kinds of comics. Also *Mad* magazine.
CBA: *Were you exposed to horror or war comics?*
Steve: I never had much interest in war comics, and there really weren't many horror comics left by the time I had learned to read. The few that were around in my formative years were things like the ACG publications, *Adventures into the Unknown, Forbidden Worlds*, and things like that. I did read some of those and liked them quite a bit, actually, but the really early horror comics were all gone. I was seven years old in 1954 when the Code was enacted, so I saw almost nothing of the old ECs, or the really horrific horror comics, which I would've dug. [*laughs*] I wish they hadn't gone away. [*laughter*] They might've changed my life!
CBA: *So you started a fanzine when you were about 13 years old. Did you get the first issue of* Alter-Ego, *for instance?*
Steve: Yes, I did.
CBA: *Did that spark you right there?*
Steve: Oh, sure, sure. That, and the letters I was exchanging with Roy, Jerry and with God knows how many other fans at that point,

ome closer to my age.

CBA: *Did you have an inkling that you wanted o write or draw?*

Steve: I knew that I wanted to write from the me I was very young. I didn't start seriously hinking about comics, writing comics, until my eens.

CBA: *As far as writing, did you write essays, or keep a diary?*

Steve: No, I didn't.

CBA: *Did you write fantasy stories?*

Steve: A few, and I used to—and I use the erm extremely loosely—"draw" my own comics. *laughs*] I can't draw my way out of a paper bag. *laughter*] I did, like, little stick figures, basically, ut yeah, I think I learned a lot about visual story-elling just by drawing comics on paper napkins!

CBA: *They had running narratives, with a beginning, a middle, and an end?*

Steve: Yeah!

CBA: *What was "The Little Giant"?*

Steve: That was the strip that, I believe, Ron oss drew and I wrote for the first issue of the anzine I did, called *Headline*.

CBA: *What was the premise behind it?*

Steve: Oh, it was a rip-off of The Atom. *laughs*] The original Atom. The character was horter and smaller than everybody else, and got ushed around a lot, but then somehow acquired uper-powers.

CBA: *Was it straight super-hero, or humor?*

Steve: No, it was very straight super-hero.

CBA: *"The Little Giant."* [laughs] *Cool name.*

Steve: I don't know… [*laughs*] It's not like a eally good name, like "Cable." [*laughter*]

CBA: *You know, I naturally assumed it was atirical because it was written by you, and the trip was also mentioned in Bill Schelly's* Golden Age of Fandom *as having an impact on fandom…*

Steve: It did?!? [*laughter*] Now we know where fandom went wrong! [*laughter*]

CBA: *Did you do it for any length of time?*

Steve: No, it was just for one or two episodes.

CBA: *Was* Headline *a straight fanzine, too? Did t have text in it?*

Steve: Yeah, we had text, and a few articles. We did some illustrated stories of other people's original super-heroes, and a couple of mine, and one or two other strips also. Some humor, as well.

CBA: *How long did the fanzine last?*

Steve: Oh, just three or four issues, I think.

CBA: *When Roy got a job at Marvel, did you tart considering that, "Hey, maybe I can get work n the comics"?*

Steve: Yeah, I was taking it very, very seriously by then, but I was going to go to college first. Although, right after I graduated from high school, Roy let me spend a week or so with him in New York. I stayed at the apartment he shared with Len Brown down on Avenue A. That trip was actually the first time I met Stan Lee, went to the Marvel offices and all that stuff.

CBA: *How old were you?*

Steve: 17, I guess… I'd just graduated from high school.

CBA: *Where did you go to college?*

Steve: Well, I spent two years at the University of Missouri-St. Louis, one semester at the University of Missouri-Columbia, and then finished and did a little bit of graduate work at St. Louis University.

CBA: *So pretty much all in the St. Louis area.*

Steve: Yeah, in Missouri.

CBA: *When you started getting into fandom, was Roy far away from you? Did you go and visit him?*

Steve: Roy came up on occasion—I couldn't drive yet! [*laughs*]—

Roy was in college at the time, and I was still in junior high school. He would occasionally come up—he had a girlfriend in St. Louis—so he would visit St. Louis, and every now and then, he and I would get together, just to talk and look at old comics and stuff. I look back on that now, and it's remarkable to me that someone his age could have been so gracious to an obnoxious 13-year-old [*laughter*]. I'm amazed by it.

CBA: *When you started to consider a professional career, were there super-heroes that you wanted to do? Was it that kind of thing, where the characters were important to you, or was it just generally you had stories within you that you wanted to get out?*

Steve: Probably both. There was no one particular character—except Superman—that I wanted to write, and if I was going to work for Marvel, that seemed pretty unlikely. [*laughter*] My favorite Marvel character at the time was Spider-Man, which was still being written by Stan back then, so that also seemed unlikely as an assignment. I think I just wanted to try my hand at the medium in general.

CBA: *Did you have prose aspirations, too?*

Steve: Oh, somewhat. I never really thought of myself as somebody who would write a novel, you know, or a short story. I always thought my inclination would be more toward film or comics.

CBA: *There wasn't much of a market, right? Was that a consideration, too—was the marketplace a consideration?*

Steve: Oh, no, I was far too stupid to think about the marketplace. [*laughter*] I really had no idea, you know. Yes, I knew it was very difficult to break into writing science-fiction for the prose market, and that very few people were successful in doing it. Besides, I didn't have a scientific background, you know. My major in college, actually, was communications—TV and film—and that's really where I thought I was going to go.

CBA: *To L.A. and become a screenwriter, or go into TV?*

Steve: Something like that, yeah.

CBA: *Did you have any writer heroes, like Rod Serling or Paddy Chayefsky?*

Steve: I took a couple of film courses in college, and there were a few people—directors mainly, writers secondarily (because they never talked about the writers)—yeah, I mean I can't point to anybody like that. Honestly, it was more like being interested in the medium and the stories than being interested in making money or any creator's particular work.

CBA: *Were your parents supportive of your creative aspirations?*

Steve: Yes, they were. Well, they were until they found out I was taking them seriously. [*laughter*] They were very supportive until they found out that I really wasn't going to go to law school first, or something. Then they got very worried. Fortunately, I was able to find this job or that job, and sort of allayed their fears.

CBA: *You were able to work pretty steadily, then.*

Steve: Yeah, pretty much. I've supported myself as a writer, basically, since 1970.

CBA: *You started working for Marvel in 1972?*

Steve: Yeah.

CBA: *How did that all happen?*

Steve: I had been working at an advertising agency in St. Louis as a copywriter. The advertising stuff was just making me crazy, just absolutely nuts. I wrote a letter to Roy Thomas saying, "I don't suppose…" [*laughter*] As it turned out, my letter arrived just at the time that Marvel had been acquired by Cadence Industries, and had found a new distributor, and was about to expand its line significantly for the first time in decades, so there actually were some positions available. Roy sent me what was called then a "writer's test"—six pages of artwork with no dialogue.

CBA: *Was it pages from Jack Kirby's Fantastic Four?*

Steve: No, it was a Gene Colan *Daredevil* story that had been scripted by Gerry Conway, and it was a very difficult sequence, actually. It was a car chase—something that's not simple to do. It was a real test, because all you had was the artwork—the whole point was to see if you could make a story out of these pictures, without knowing what the original plot was. I sent the script back to Roy, and apparently, I did okay. They offered me a job as an associate editor and writer.

CBA: *Did you agonize over it, or did you just say "whoof!" and got it over with?*

Steve: There was no question I was going to take the job. I had always wanted to live in New York, for one thing…

CBA: *Oh, I mean the test itself.*

Steve: I probably just sat down and wrote it. I didn't know it was difficult! [*laughter*] Ignorance can sometimes be a big advantage, you know? I looked at it, and, "Okay, it's a car chase, here comes Daredevil swinging over the street, blah blah blah," whatever it was, and I could sort of make sense of what was going on. I have no memory whatsoever what I wrote.

CBA: *But they liked it?*

Steve: Roy liked it, I guess.

CBA: *Remember roughly when that was?*

Steve: I started during the Summer of 1972, so the whole process with the writer's test probably took place a few months earlier, in late Winter or Spring.

CBA: *Recall what you were getting paid?*

Steve: Oh, yes, I do. [*laughs*] You know, in order to take the job I had to take a $25 pay cut from what I was getting at the advertising agency! [*laughs*] I would get $125 a week as an associate editor/proofreader at Marvel, and I think my starting rate for writing was $13 a page.

CBA: *And you were making $150 St. Louis dollars at the agency! The standard of living in New York was obviously much higher.*

Steve: It was a lot more expensive; but I was young, and youth can be as big an advantage as ignorance.

CBA: *This was* The Stuff!

Steve: "Oh, man, I get to hold these? You're going to let me touch them?" [*laughter*]

CBA: *Did you get your first opportunity to write pretty quickly?*

Steve: Oh, immediately. They understood that I was not going to be able to live on $125 a week [*laughs*] in New York. The first thing I actually wrote… well, it depends on how you look at things. The very first thing I did for Marvel was a "Man-Thing" plot that I wrote while I was still in St. Louis, immediately prior to coming to New York. The first story I dialogued was an issue of *The Incredible Hulk* that Roy Thomas had plotted.

CBA: *Did you find writing easy?*

Steve: I don't know if I would use the word "easy." It was fun. The two are not necessarily the same… I mean, I agonized over it.

CBA: *But it was worthwhile?*

Steve: Oh, yeah.

CBA: *What were the offices like when you were coming in as a nine-to-fiver?*

Steve: Tiny, very tiny. They had what amounted to three or four large rooms on the sixth floor at 625 Madison Avenue. There was the bullpen—the bullpen being all of the production artists, myself, and the receptionist. Stan had an office of his own. Roy and John Verpoorten shared an office along with Holly Resnick, who was John's assistant, and that was it. Stu Schwartzberg worked in the photostat room, but as I recall, the stat machine wasn't actually in the office; it was one or two doors down the hall.

CBA: *Where the men's magazines were done? Was that across the hall, or upstairs?*

Steve: The men's magazines were upstairs.

CBA: *In the bullpen itself, there was Marie, there was Herb…*

Steve: Herb Trimpe was there, I believe Mike Esposito, Frank Giacoia… I'm trying to run down the cubbyholes now…

CBA: *Was Don McGregor there the same time as you?*

Steve: Don came aboard a little later. In fact, I think I had already gone freelance by the time Don started.

CBA: *They listed you and Don both as assistant editors, I remember, in one bullpen page. It must've just been on the cusp.*

Steve: It could've been, yeah. We had moved to 575 Madison, I think, by that time, and had a lot more room, and Don started in that office along with Marv Wolfman. I believe that's right.

CBA: *Was Steve Englehart around a lot?*

Steve: Englehart had already gone free-lance by the time I was starting—in fact, I think I was Steve's replacement on staff—but yeah, he was in and out of the office a couple of times a week.

CBA: *Did you have anybody that you started at the same time with at Marvel?*

Steve: I was the only newcomer in the bullpen at the time I started—which, now that I think about it, should have terrified the sh*t out of me, but didn't; the arrogance of youth again, I guess. There were any number of people who started within a few months either way of when I did, though. Englehart had started about six months earlier. Marv and Don started a few months later. Doug Moench began working at Marvel within, oh, a year of when I started, something like that.

CBA: *Was it a fun place to be?*

Steve: In those days, yes it was.

CBA: *Was Stan there a lot, or was he there two days a week by that point?*

Steve: Stan was there almost every day, but he was functioning as publisher, rather than as an editor or writer at that time.

CBA: *So he wasn't exactly Creative*

CBA: *Did you hook up with other comics fans to find a place?*

Steve: No, because I didn't know anybody there. My brother lived in Brooklyn at the time, which was fortunate. I was married then, so my wife went to New York, stayed with him, and found us a place. Once we had an address, a friend of mine and I brought all our stuff from St. Louis to New York in a U-Haul.

CBA: *And you stayed in New York for a period?*

Steve: I was in New York for four or five years. I lived in Brooklyn for a while, then my wife and I split up, and I moved to Manhattan.

CBA: *What were your duties as associate editor at Marvel?*

Steve: "Associate Editor" was mainly a title. I was a glorified proofreader. I read over the stuff; Roy taught me how to make proofreading marks and the terminology to use in notes for the production department. I looked for errors on the artwork, and occasionally took a razor blade or Liquid Paper to it myself and cleaned up little spots of ink that were in places they didn't belong. Spatters in word balloons, tips of run-together letters, that sort of thing.

CBA: *Was it pretty mundane work, or were you excited to be in the field?*

Steve: It was pretty mundane work—the work itself—although it's kind of hard to think that when you're sitting there holding a bunch of original Bill Everett pages in your hand, you know? [*laughs*] Or a Frank Brunner "Dr. Strange" written by Gardner Fox, or whatever.

Below: *Gerber's writing also appeared in a run of Daredevil. Here's Bob Brown's cover to DD #105. Courtesy of Al Bigley. ©2000 Marvel Characters, Inc.*

WELL WE'RE HERE, WHERE EVER THIS IS! WE LANDED IN
SOME SORT OF NEST REMINDES ME OF WHEN I WAS FIRST LAID!...

Above: *Courtesy of David "Hambone" Hamilton, here's Frank Brunner's pencils from* Howard the Duck #1. *Note Frank's margin note on the bottom featuring Howard's classic double entendre, "Reminds [sic] me of when I was first laid!" Art ©2000 Frank Brunner.* Howard the Duck *©2000 Marvel Characters, Inc.*

Director at that time?
Steve: He was, but he worked mainly with Roy.
CBA: *You didn't pitch ideas directly to Stan?*
Steve: On occasion, but not very often.
CBA: *Were you seeking out particular strips yourself? You'd have liked to have done Spider-Man, but as a newcomer…?*
Steve: Well, "Man-Thing" was the first thing they actually gave me, and it was interesting because I had never even thought about writing horror or fantasy prior to that time. I found I had a knack for it, and after a few months there, and starting to get a little bit of a notion of how the office worked, and how the politics of the office worked. I discovered that working on books like "Man-Thing" could be very advantageous, because they weren't the assignments everybody else was after. Nobody else really cared about them! [laughs] It allowed me to work in my own little corner of both the office and the Marvel Universe, and be pretty much left alone.
CBA: *You know, Don has always mentioned that everyone was ignoring his books, nobody was really looking at his books too much, and he was able to really experiment with what he wanted to do. What were the problems with the headliner books?*
Steve: Those books got a lot more scrutiny.

CBA: *So there was a lot more editorial futzing with those?*
Steve: In those days, futzing was different. [laughs] You made mistakes, and then you corrected them in the next issue. [laughter] Everything was on such a tight schedule, and everything was such a rush, that there was really almost no time to correct a mistake at the time it was made. Fortunately, to the best of my recollection, there was never a really terrible mistake or creative misstep, where we would've had to pull a book and substitute another story. No one ever did a story where, say, Spider-Man went berserk and strangled Aunt May with his webbing, or Iron Man peed his pants and rusted out his crotch, or Doc Ock held an issue of *Hustler* with two hands while fondling himself with the other four. The writers functioned pretty much as *de facto* editors of their own books in those days, and we all knew what our responsibilities were. I don't even recall very many instances when we had pages rejected by the Code. There was one case where I, personally, inadvertently went 'way over the line: The original Wundarr story in *Man-Thing,* about the baby who was rocketed to Earth from a doomed planet by his scientist father, but whose rocket landed in the Florida swamp and was never found. The baby grew up in the spaceship and emerged a super-powered innocent when Man-Thing tipped the ship over. We later elaborated on the story and explained that, in fact, the supposedly "doomed" planet had never blown up. That was something I'd planned all along, assuming we ever brought the character back. What I didn't know until some time later, though, is that DC actually threatened to sue over the original story. I saw it as satire. They viewed it as plagiarism. After we did the later story, and changed Wundarr's costume, DC apparently decided it wasn't worth pursuing the matter.
CBA: *I don't know if you remember this, but I remember there was a page that Val Mayerik had drawn in "Man-Thing" where a bulldozer ran over Man-Thing, and then Man-Thing rose up again, and the antagonist was dispatched by the bulldozer, and it all happened off-camera, and it all looks like it was drawn by John Romita. It all looked like it was very futzed-with, and it's the only sequence that I could ascertain that seemed to be changed.*
Steve: I do remember that. It was probably changed because Val's storytelling, for one reason or another, didn't work in that sequence. I don't recall there being any arguments over that story—anything about its being too violent, or too graphic, or anything like that. Every so often, a page would come in that just didn't work, and because some of the artists didn't live in the New York area—Val, at the time, was living in Ohio; still does, I think—there wasn't time to mail a page back and forth for changes. So some unfortunate revisions were sometimes done in the office. John, being the art director, would've been the one to fix that. His style and Val's have almost nothing in common, so in this case the changes were glaring and far too obvious.
CBA: *Generally, did some of those changes incense you? Did you ever get really bothered by changes?*
Steve: There were a few changes that were made in copy—not so much in artwork, but in copy—that bothered me. Somebody thought such-and-such line of dialogue was a little too strong, or this had to be changed, or that had to be changed, and yeah, I would argue it and sometimes win, sometimes lose.
CBA: *Did you look at it like you were occasionally being subversive, and you were sneaking things in? I noticed some hilarious references, double-entendres, especially in* Howard the Duck #1, *when he falls into a nest, and he says, "This nest reminds me when I was first laid!" [laughs]*
Steve: Did that go out that way? I thought it was changed to "hatched."
CBA: *Then there's a sequence with a really rich guy, a country-western singer—I forgot his name, the guy with the Rolls-Royce—picked up Beverly and Howard who were hitch-hiking, and the guy looks down Bev's cleavage and is talking about a "great pair."*
Steve: Oh, right. I think everybody at Marvel knew what those things meant. We all sort of held our breaths and hoped it got past the Code! [laughter] I don't think anybody at the office was deceived by that stuff.
CBA: *But it was fun to get it through?*
Steve: Sure!
CBA: *Did you have many sequences changed by the Code that*

you recall? Were they a hassle?

Steve: No, not really. I seem to recall one or two things the Code objected to, but I really don't recall what they were. I mean, all of this was so long ago. Anyway, there was nothing we could do about it... it was either make the changes, or not publish the book. You just have to shrug and go on.

CBA: *Did you pretty quickly develop a following? Did fans start noticing your work?*

Steve: I think so, yeah. I think the letter columns helped, they brought attention to the credit box on the books.

CBA: *You edited your own letters pages?*

Steve: I did all my own letter columns. For a while, I was also handling the letter columns for more than half of the Marvel books. Some writers just didn't want to deal with them, and it was optional, so Marvel gave me those as a freelance assignment.

CBA: *You included in a Man-Thing story, Fear #19, almost a throwaway character tossed in who has subsequently had an impact on your career: Howard the Duck. The character became a phenomenon. As a pretty green writer in comics, did you have any realization or recognition of the treatment of creators within the field?*

Steve: I really didn't, no.

CBA: *As compared to book publishing (where there have been royalties since time immemorial, and there's the Writers' Guild, and there's a lot of protection for creators, comparatively to comic books, at least), the comics industry often discards writers and artists easily and creators' work is exploited without any remuneration…*

Steve: In the beginning, I had no clue that was the situation, I really didn't. My understanding, at that time, of copyright and trademarks, the whole subject of what we now call "creator's rights," was little more than nil.

CBA: *When did you first realize this maybe wasn't the deal you wanted?*

Steve: You know, I think my first realization of it came when I heard the Siegel and Shuster story in full for the first time.

CBA: *That was in '75 or '76.*

Steve: Around then, yeah. Although I'd heard it mentioned by other people in the industry, of course, but the whole thing really came to light in very public form in '76, the year before the *Superman* movie came out.

CBA: *But the Academy of Comic Book Arts started ostensibly as a real professional, promotional organization. Stan likes to say how it's the "Academy Awards for Comic Books," but almost immediately from its initiation, Neal Adams, Archie Goodwin and a number of other people were involved and they said, "No, this is more than that. This is about professionals working together, creating equitable standards." Were you involved in ACBA at all?*

Steve: No, I wasn't. ACBA started before I came to New York and had pretty much devolved into little more than a social club by the time I was working in comics. I do remember going to one meeting of ACBA, and there was a whole discussion about rights and royalties and all of this stuff, and I said something, and people looked at me as if I were nuts. I had suggested donating original art that ACBA

could sell to build up a strike fund or something. They all looked at me like I was crazy! "I have to give up something in order to do this?" That was the kind of look I was getting, and at that point, I just walked out and never went back.

CBA: *Did you perceive in your fellow professionals there was a naiveté about the future, about what kind of protection can be had?*

Steve: There was extreme short-sightedness and in some people a level of greed that matched the publishers'—on a much smaller scale of course. It was all nickel-&-dime stuff. I hate to say this, but as a creative community, I'd never seen so many people who were so backward in their thinking and so terrified of their employers.

CBA: *In a* Comics Journal *interview you tell a story of an artist or writer going in to Stan's office….*

Steve: I know the story you're talking about. Bringing in a lawyer, right? And Stan refusing to speak to him while the lawyer was there. That happened. The writer was trying to work out a contract with Marvel, Stan was the publisher at that time. The writer came in with his lawyer to talk about the terms of the contract, and Stan would not hold the discussion. Looking back on it, I think I understand what happened, and why. At the time, Marvel and DC didn't have business affairs people who dealt with talent on a routine basis. All the business arrangements were essentially the same: "Here's the assignment, here's your page rate, take it or leave it." Nobody really negotiated anything. Stan wasn't a lawyer; his expertise was in creative matters, not business; but he would have been held accountable by own bosses at Cadence for any promises he might have made in that meeting. So, probably, he just decided not to hold the meeting at all, rather than agree to something he'd regret later. I don't think Stan handled it very adroitly, but the problem, like most

Above: *Wonderful Steranko artwork for the cover of* Shanna the She-Devil #2. *Courtesy of the artist. Shanna ©2000 Marvel Characters, Inc.*

Above: *If ever there was an artist born to draw Man-Thing (and The Glob, for that matter!) it was Mike Ploog. Here is Mike's cover art to Giant-Size Man-Thing #1. Courtesy of the artist. Man-Thing, Glob ©2000 Marvel Characters, Inc.*

animals was one of the dimensions in the multiverse, so I guess I unconsciously retrieved that, and just yanked the duck out!

CBA: *What contributions—besides, obviously, the visuals—did Va. Mayerik bring? Did you work closely with him on plotting?*

Steve: No, not really.

CBA: *It feels like your stories were fully written.*

Steve: Well, Val was in Ohio, and I was in New York, and they didn't have 5¢-a-minute long distance in those days. I would send him very detailed plots for the stories. I believe he added the cigar to the character, actually. [*laughter*] I don't recall, but I think he told me once that he did, and I have no reason to disbelieve him. [*laughs*] He also put spats on the feet, which we later removed. [*laughter*] And the costuming, the hat, all that… I believe my instructions to him were, "Whatever you do, don't put this thing in a sailor suit!" [*laughter*] That was the extent of my instructions as to what the duck should look like. Val put Howard in the rumpled coat, and the porkpie hat, and that became the look of the character.

CBA: *A smart-ass, sarcastic character as you dialogued him?*

Steve: Oh, yeah, as I recall, the dialogue was actually in the plot. The barbarian's saying, "My life has become an absurdity," and the duck's next line is "Pal, you don't know the meaning of absurdity!" [*laughs*] Something like that; and yes, from the very beginning, that's how he was written.

CBA: *What was the difference between the final piece and your plots? Was there much? Did you always include a lot of dialogue within your detailed plots?*

Steve: Not always, but very often.

CBA: *So it's pretty much finished when the artist received it?*

Steve: Well, it wasn't quite finished, but when I knew what the dialogue was going to be—both for my benefit and for the artist's—I'd include it in the plot, because… first of all, if I had a good line of dialogue, I didn't want to forget it. I always kept the plot close at hand when I dialogued a story; and also because it would give the artist a better sense of the scene, of the characters' attitudes, a way of approaching the scene.

CBA: *What was Val like?*

Steve: He's the polar opposite of me. Completely physical, karate expert… [*laughter*] Really! He was like a black belt in karate, very confident and very… he's a complete opposite of what I am, not tormented at all. [*laughter*]

CBA: *What did you think of Val's storytelling?*

Steve: He was very new at the time he was doing stuff on "Howard" and on "Man-Thing," and the work had all the problems of a new artist, and, of course, all the enthusiasm of a new artist.

CBA: *Do you remember requesting any number of changes? Like you said, you had pretty much finished stories delivered to him?*

Steve: If there were changes, I would've taken the page to somebody in the production department and said something like, "You really can't see what's supposed to be happening in this panel."

CBA: *There was no time to send it back to Ohio?*

Steve: We didn't have Federal Express in those days, either, don't forget. Not that Marvel would've paid for it, if we had.

CBA: *Were you happy with the inkers Val got on the books?*

Steve: No, I think Val got really terrible inking on "Man-Thing." I think John Tartaglione inked a lot of them, and his style was so far removed from what Val was trying to do that it really hurt some of Val's stuff.

CBA: *There were some work by Sal Trapani…*

Steve: Both he and Tartaglione tended to lay on the ink with a trowel. Somebody—I think it was Sal—tried to ink Val with a really wide brush stroke, very bold and direct, but Val was trying to do, essentially, the same kind of detailed work that Craig Russell was doing at the time. Val's pencils had a very delicate feel. The combination didn't work at all; I think Val was very poorly served by the inkers assigned to his work.

CBA: *Almost immediately after leaving Man-Thing, Val was drawing and inking "The Living Mummy" [in Supernatural Thrillers]. Did he have any interest in inking Man-Thing?*

Steve: Val definitely wanted to ink himself—but he never got the chance, I guess, until "The Living Mummy." And you can see the difference in the artwork immediately. It has a completely different feel.

CBA: *Actually, I thought some of the strongest Mayerik art was*

problems in the industry at that time, was systemic, not personal. Today, that incident could never happen.

CBA: *What was the genesis of Howard the Duck? Was he a throwaway character?*

Steve: I've talked about this before: I was doing the story about the collision of multiple realities, right, the whole multiverse caving in on itself. I needed a visual to top that of a barbarian leaping out of a jar of peanut butter, you know? [*laughs*] Okay, what do I do next? So help me, this is true—it sounds like one of those too-cleverly-concocted stories about how a character is created, but it is true—my home office faced out on a row of backyards in Brooklyn, up and down the street. Somebody in one of the brownstones along that row had apparently just gotten himself a new stereo, and it must have been the most expensive stereo in the world, because he could only afford one record! [*laughter*] A salsa record, that he played over and over and over! [*laughter*] I sat at my desk, going into some kind of a trance, and the next thing I knew, I was typing something about a duck walking out from behind a shrub in the swamp! [*laughs*] That's all there was to the creation, there was no conscious process at all, it all happened in the back of my mind!

CBA: *Was it a funny-animal duck you had in your mind, or was it just a duck?*

Steve: Oh, no, no! It was a talking duck! We'd done one panel earlier in the story where we had postulated that the world of funny the first couple of stories you guys did together. Val really focused on the face, for instance, on the grandfather character, and things like that. His emphasis wasn't diluted by the inker's line.

Steve: I've found that most readers—and today, even a lot of editors—really don't understand how much the inker contributes to the look of the final product. They think of an inker as someone who essentially traces the pencil art to make it reproducible. They don't seem to realize that an inker is an artist, that his or her style overlays that of the penciler. When the two are compatible, the results can be gorgeous: Colan & Palmer, Miller & Janson, for example. When they're diametrically opposed, you get something like Mayerik & Trapani, which does a massive disservice to both artists' work.

CBA: *Then you were able to team up with Mike Ploog on Man-Thing. It seems obvious that Mike had an influence in some of the stories. There's a credit he received as a co-plotter, or even plotted, I believe, in the second part of the "Dawg" story, with the old lady and the old guy in the swamp and the hound dog. Did Mike also plot the first part, but just wasn't listed in the credits?*

Steve: No. I don't recall that credit, but there are probably some things, some changes he made in the story as he was drawing it, and I felt he should have the co-plotting credit, or he asked for it and I certainly didn't object, something like that.

CBA: *Did you feel challenged by Man-Thing? One would see it on the surface as being a rather thankless job. I mean, he's not a vegetable, but you know, he ain't talkin' much! [laughter]*

Steve: It was a very difficult book to write. Again, I think my inexperience served me well in the beginning on that book, because I didn't know until halfway into my run on the series how hard it really was. As I grew in sophistication and tried to write more ambitious stories, I came to understand how and why the series and the character worked, which, if anything, made it more difficult to write. I couldn't settle for a sort of energetic primitivism anymore.

CBA: *Did you have an interest in sneaking your political point of view in there? For instance, you had the guy who was trying to drain the swamp, the acronym of his name was "fascist." [laughter] Then Ted Sallis, the Man-Thing character, had his hand in creating this chemical which would enable people to breathe pollutants. You obviously were promoting an environmentalist message.*

Steve: I saw those aspects as themes. I didn't view that kind of thing as sneaking anything by. They were just subjects I wanted to write about.

CBA: *There was a great story with the characters all trapped in the swamp, and one of them was an ex-P.O.W., one of them was an apathetic radical....*

Steve: You thought that was a great story? [laughs]

CBA: *It was in the run for me! [laughter] I liked it because it was focusing on characterization and it didn't seem to be something that was typical of what was going on in regular comics. There were still interesting dynamics going on in that story. Sure, it was cliché, but you were pushing storytelling devices within that formula.*

Steve: Well, I was trying to, yeah, but I regard it as an experiment that failed. Reading it now, it comes off like one of those *Airplane!* pictures. [laughter]

CBA: *The lefty (whose motivations I still can't fully understand) is just kicking back, after this huge bus crash, corpses all around, and he's spouting that non-involvement is a political act! It was interesting. Did you have any inkling that Howard the Duck would be a popular character? What was the reaction to his first appearance? You killed him off in the first issue of Man-Thing (Howard's second appearance). Was he killed, or did he just trip and fall into oblivion?*

Steve: He wasn't killed, we just nudged him out of the story. [laughter] This is true, so help me! I really didn't think about it at the time I plotted the story, I just sent the plot out, and then the pages came back from Val, and I came into the office to get them so I could dialogue them, and I was looking at them, and I got this weird little grin on my face, and walked in to Don McGregor and Marv Wolfman's office, and I said, "Roy is going to kill me!" [laughs] They said, "Why?" I said, "I put a duck in the 'Man-Thing' book!" They said, "So what? It takes place in a swamp!" [laughs] I said, "It's not that kind of duck!" and I showed them the pages. [laughs] They looked at them, and they said to me, "You're right, Roy is going to kill you!" [laughter] So, I figured I had better head off the problem,

and I took the pages to Roy right away, and I said, "Look, I did this story with the multiple dimensions and reality... and this." And he said, "Okay, get it out of there as fast as you can." [laughter] And so, we did! Roy never actually said, "Kill the duck," but he made it absolutely clear to me that he didn't want him around by the middle of the next issue.

CBA: *The duck or you? [laughter]*

Steve: If the duck had still been there by the middle of the next book, he wouldn't have wanted to see me, either! [laughter] I complied, and we sent the duck spinning off into limbo. I never figured we'd bring him back. It would just be some interesting little comic book curiosity that people would remember fondly or vituperatively, and that would be that; but then the mail started coming in... "Murderers! You killed my duck!" [laughs] That kind of thing. We even got a package—I was out of town at the time, so I didn't see it—but somebody sent us the carcass of a duck they had eaten for Christmas dinner. [laughter] With a little note attached to it, saying, "Murderers!" with 12 exclamation points. We figured maybe we had stumbled onto something.

CBA: *Wow. How quickly did you turn around and do the first short story, "Hell-Cow"? Neal Adams was initially slated to draw Howard's first solo story, right?*

Steve: Right, Neal was going to draw it, and for some reason or another, he just never got around to it, and it wound up with Frank Brunner; and we did it in, what was it, the third or fourth issue of *Giant-Size Man-Thing*?

CBA: *#4. It was planned for #3, but it made it into the fourth.*

Above: *The female Red Guardian was but one of the second bananas Steve Gerber brought to the fore in his delightful run on* The Defenders. *Art by Johnny Romita Sr. ©2000 Marvel Characters, Inc.* **Below:** *From* The Brunner Mystique, *depicting Frank's as-drawn and revised* Howard the Duck *panels, changed due to Code objections.* ©2000 Marvel Characters, Inc.

Steve: Right. So, I guess it was almost a full year, maybe more, before we got around to actually doing that story.

CBA: *That issue was enormously popular, right?*

Steve: Yeah. It did very well.

CBA: *The buzz immediately went out in fandom. It was a full year after that before the* Howard the Duck *book came out, correct?*

Steve: More like six months. Or six months after the second story, because *Giant-Size* was a quarterly, so yeah, it would've been six to nine months.

CBA: *When you were doing the short stories, did you say, "Hey, I could do things with this character?"*

Steve: By that time I wanted to do Howard as a book, no question about it. Marvel was not convinced it would work, but the reception to the short stories was persuasive to them, I think.

CBA: *So, was Frank Brunner involved in the development of the characterization at all?*

Steve: No, not really. I had dinner with Frank when he decided to come aboard and do the book. I hadn't met him in person at the time we were doing the short stories, both of which were written as full scripts, by the way, not "Marvel style." We had a really nice dinner, we talked out some ideas, I told him I wanted to do a sword-&-sorcery story, and he liked that. We played around with various different things, and some of those… a couple of the lines in the book, the one about "This reminds me where I first got laid," were from Frank's notes in the margins of the artwork. Mary Skrenes was at that dinner, also, and she came up with the name "Beverly." Bev's last name, Switzler, was the name of a building on the University of Missouri campus in Columbia.

CBA: *You were a prolific writer at the time, doing a number of books,* Daredevil *and a lot of b-&-w stuff.*

Steve: Compared to Doug Moench, I looked like J.D. Salinger. Compared to my own output now, I was fairly prolific in those days, yeah. I was writing *Tales of the Zombie* for *Dracula Lives!* and an occasional b-&-w story for *Vampire Tales*, I was doing *Marvel Two-in-One, Defenders, Omega*… actually, *Omega* started the same time as *Howard the Duck*.

CBA: *Rich Buckler told me he was allowed to do "Deathlok" pretty much to placate him so he would remain on* Fantastic Four. *Was* Omega *something you wanted to do as a pet project?*

Steve: Actually, I proposed that and the *Howard the Duck* book to Stan at the same time. Mary Skrenes and I went up to his office, I told him I had two ideas I wanted to do: One of them was *Howard*, and he said, "Great, do it." (By that time, he really liked the character and was very much in favor of it.) The other one was a harder sell because of the kid hero aspect, even though the kid wasn't the one in the costume. You have to remember, this was before the era of Marv's *Teen Titans* and the *New X-Men*, back when fans still had an aversion to teenage super-heroes; but when we explained it to him, he liked that idea too, and said, "Yeah, go ahead, try it." In fact, I think Stan came up with "Omega the Unknown" as the title.

CBA: *In a nutshell, can you give me the concept behind* Omega?

Steve: [*sighs*] In a nutshell?

CBA: *Or in a bathtub, I don't care.* [*laughter*] *Or an 80-foot pool.*

Steve: What Mary and I wanted to do originally was a kid hero—James Michael without the guy in spandex. I didn't think that would work as a Marvel book, so we wound up compromising, doing a series about the kid that involved a super-hero and some mysterious connection between the two of them. For us, the important part of the book was the story of this strange, distant kid who'd been raised to function more on intellect than emotion, being thrust into the environment of Hell's Kitchen, where intellect is in somewhat short supply. The super-hero aspect of it, I felt, needed to be equally as grounded in reality. The super-hero wasn't terribly super. He couldn't do everything.

CBA: *He wouldn't talk.*

Steve: He finally did speak, but not much. A few words here and there, toward the end of the series.

CBA: *I remember as a young reader, being really intrigued with the book, and I think by the ninth issue, I walked away, being perplexed by the book, not really knowing what were your intentions. Then you made some statements within the* Comics Journal *interview that people didn't get it. Was it metaphor, simile, analogy? What were you trying to achieve? There was obviously some kind of psychic connection between the kid, James Michael, and Sam, the "super-hero."*

Steve: What most people didn't get was the book was about the kid, not about the super-hero. It had to be disguised as a super-hero book, or Marvel would never even have considered publishing it.

CBA: *A lot of your work seems to me to be an investigation into the nature of violence. The stories depicted the day-to-day violence that actually takes place within urban settings—is as true today, if not truer, than it was then.*

Steve: The violence has moved to the suburbs, too.

CBA: *Right. With Columbine High School… just outrageous. But I noticed that you didn't really seem to exploit gratuitous violence, but violence was always a part of the story. If I can put forth a criticism about it, maybe a problem with the book was that James Michael was highly uncharismatic because he had a very stilted emotional range to begin with.*

Steve: That's possible, although I found James Michael a very compelling character, and the book was about his emotional growth and the tension between intellect and emotion in general. When the book was cancelled, we had barely begun to explore those areas.

CBA: *You announced plans to finish the story in* The Defenders *book. Did that ever happen?*

Steve: No. Steven Grant wrote an ending that appeared in *Defenders*, but it had nothing to do with what Mary and I had planned.

CBA: *Because you had a falling out with Marvel before that happened? Do you recall what you intended to do with the book, where you generally wanted to go?*

Steve: Yes. Among other things, it would have explained what those metal guys were, why they were after James Michael, and what the relationship was between James Michael and Sam/Omega. I've promised Mary, though, that I would never reveal what our ending was. I never have, and I never will! [*laughs*]

CBA: *Now I've got to get it out of Mary!* [*laughter*]

Steve: It would be easier to get it out of me, I'll tell you that! [*laughter*]

CBA: *Did you enjoy doing a pure super-hero book like* The Defenders?

Steve: Oh, sure, yeah. I used to tell people that *Howard* was my serious book, and *The Defenders* was my humor book. [*laughter*]

CBA: *I just made a misnomer there… I meant* Daredevil *because obviously, I know* Defenders *was satirical. Did you have a good time with* Daredevil?

Steve: *Daredevil* was always frustrating to me. I don't think I ever had a really solid handle on that book; and most of the artists I worked with on *Daredevil* weren't right for the series.

CBA: *You were working with Bob Brown, for instance.*

Steve: The work I did with Bob was the only *Daredevil* stuff of mine that I really liked. I was very unhappy when they took Bob off the book. I did a number of issues with Don Heck, but he was completely wrong for *Daredevil*. Earlier, there was… what was his name? I don't recall.

CBA: *You started with Gene Colan.*

Above: Howard the Duck Sunday strip (from July 10, 1977) written by Steve Gerber and drawn by Gene Colan. Arguments over the syndicated strip instigated Gerber's break-up with Marvel. ©2000 Marvel Characters, Inc.

Steve: Gene did the first issue I dialogued, but that was from a plot by Gerry Conway, so I don't think of it as "my" start on the book. Gene came back to do the 100th issue with me, and I believe he did the Mandrill stories, but that was all. We only did a handful of DD stories together.

CBA: *Do you recall any artist who would add to those stories?*

Steve: You know, that didn't happen very much.

CBA: *You didn't really work "Marvel-style" per se, then?*

Steve: No, I did. The artists still had quite a bit of freedom with the pacing, the layout of the pages. What I would do is block the story out, usually in groups of pages—say, pages 13 through 15—and describe what should happen on those pages. I pretty much let the artist handle the pacing and the layouts, unless something very specific was called for. In those cases, I might break down a certain page panel-by-panel, then go back to the looser form. So, my plots were a little tighter than some writers', but not so constricting that the artist didn't have freedom to be creative.

CBA: *Gil Kane, for instance, has expressed frustration with the Marvel style, of getting a single paragraph as plot for a complete story, and saying the artist would end up doing the job of the writer. Yet, artists working with you indicate the opposite. You seem to have strong relationships with your artists and you and the artist had clearly defined tasks. Jim Mooney recalls working on Omega and Man-Thing as being highlights of his career. He was saying they were some of the best work he did, while everyone wants to talk to him about Supergirl, and he disliked working on that! [laughter] But he loved working on Omega.*

Steve: I know he did. Jim and I spoke a few times on the phone during the course of that book. He had some suggestions for it that I may have incorporated. I really don't remember. I know he really liked the stuff, and I know he really liked *Man-Thing*.

CBA: *Do you agree that a lot of that pleasure might've been due to the fact that you delivered strong stories?*

Steve: I think it had to do with the kind of stories we were telling.

And the fact that when I knew who was going to be drawing a book, I would try my best to play to that artist's strengths. So whether it was Gene Colan, who did incredibly interesting faces on his human characters, or Jack Kirby, who did incredibly interesting everything, [laughs] but whose strongest suit was the action stuff, I would try to slant the story towards what I knew that artist did well.

CBA: *Before you delivered a story, you knew who was going to draw the material?*

Steve: Most of the time, but not always.

CBA: *Did you have an interest in working with headliner talents, like Barry Smith or Neal Adams? You seemed to work with a lot of veterans, established and true professionals, but they weren't superstars, per se.*

Steve: I'm going to say something that's probably going to make people mad. I got spoiled by working with people like Sal Buscema and Jim Mooney and Don Heck, and later Kirby—although Kirby certainly wasn't just a superstar, he's a Comics God!—[laughter] but I got spoiled by working with people who were more interested in telling a story than in showing off.

CBA: *I was amazed looking at the detail of Gene Colan's work in* Howard the Duck, *and the wonderful inks Steve Leialoha gave.*

Steve: That's fabulous work!

CBA: *It really is underrated. I didn't notice it as a kid so much, but I look at it now, and I'm simply in awe of Gene Colan.*

Steve: Well, my own philosophy—and I think Gene would agree with this, too—is that you're not supposed to notice the detail in the artwork or the mechanics of the storytelling when you read a story the first time. If they're that close to the surface, that obvious, the story has failed at its primary task, which is to make you believe it. The art and the story should be so much of a piece—so unified—that you just read it first and ask questions later. If you look at it a second time, then it's fine to notice the craft in both the writing and the art. The whole point of a comic book is to tell a story that engages the reader. The art and the writing should both serve that end. I tire easily of writers whose main interest is showing off, too.

CBA: *Frank Brunner did the two short stories, and the first two issues. Was that a pretty quick falling-out?*

Steve: He left for reasons I still don't understand. He never told me why he was leaving. Frank discussed it with Roy, not with me.

CBA: *He was a star artist by that time.*

Steve: At the time, yeah.

CBA: *Jim Mooney at the time, for instance, I looked at his art at the time and went, "Eh!" but it was the story that sucked me in, and now I look at it differently. I really like Jim's style now, especially when he inked his own work.*

Steve: Again, Jim's art was working so much in service to the story—note, I don't mean subservient to the writer, I mean the story itself—that's probably why you were indifferent to it at the time. I hope you didn't notice the writing as writing at the time, either.

CBA: *Well, I did know that reading a Steve Gerber story was going to be fun.*

Steve: That's different. If a writer produces work that you like…

CBA: *I especially enjoyed your Defenders work. There was something about it that was really different.*

Steve: It was psychotic, yeah. That had to be the craziest super-hero book that Marvel ever published. [*laughter*]

CBA: *Did you seek out the assignment?*

Steve: I probably asked for the book when it became available, yeah. I was tired of doing *Daredevil,* and wanted to do something else. *The Defenders* book appealed to me. I think I asked for it, but there was no campaign or anything—everybody else had done it already! [*laughs*] "Okay, give it to Gerber." [*laughter*]

CBA: *Did you start stripping the main characters away? I recall, for instance, second- and third-tier characters like Nighthawk and the Red Guardian coming to the fore.*

Steve: And the Valkyrie, yeah. I did that very deliberately, because Dr. Strange and the Hulk had continuity going on in their own books. It was much simpler to use the first-tier characters in more minor roles than it was to try and deal with the outside continuity. My other reason for downplaying those characters was that I couldn't develop them at all in the context of *The Defenders.* That was, properly, the purview of their own series. So, if there was going to be

any character development of any kind in *The Defenders,* it had to be focused on the supposedly secondary characters.

Sal Buscema drew almost all the Defenders stories I wrote, except for the *Giant-Size* books, which were done by several other artists, including Don Heck and Jim Starlin.

CBA: *You did that book for about two or three years?*

Steve: Something like that, yeah.

CBA: *After* Howard the Duck *started, what was the reaction? The first issue, do you recall the sales situation? I lived in the Northeast, and any store up here we went to, we couldn't find it.*

Steve: *Howard* #1 was hijacked at the distributors. You know about that, right? It was assumed, as with the first issue of *Shazam!,* that *Howard* #1 was going to be some big collector's item, so comic book dealers bought the books off the distributors' tables before the got to the newsstands. Far fewer copies reached the stands than should have. Readers who should've been able to see that first issue never got to, which is why it was reprinted in the *Treasury Edition* so soon after its initial publication.

CBA: *There was actually a plea within the letter column not to deal with gougers. I recall almost immediately it was a $5 back-issue item, and I still don't have it in my collection because I didn't go ou and pay that high price for it.*

Steve: I don't blame you.

CBA: *What was your reaction to it at the time?*

Steve: I was angry as hell. I felt as if the book had been sabotaged by the very people who supposedly liked the character.

CBA: *Then, #2 came out. How were the sales?*

Steve: The sales on #2 were respectable. I don't recall exactly what the sales figures were, but I think it would've done a lot better—I think the whole series would've done a lot better—had that first issue reached the stands.

CBA: *Was it pretty much from the word "go" a respectable series? Was it selling well? Was it rising in sales? It seemed to me there was a mainstream interest with the book that transcended virtually any other title that was coming out.*

Steve: It was getting a lot of publicity. It was doing okay in sales. It was certainly not one of Marvel's top sellers, but it did well, and the publicity on the book alone made it very valuable to Marvel. It was being written up in *The New Yorker,* and *New York* magazine, *The Washington Post,* all over the place.

CBA: *Were those magazines calling you?*

Steve: They were calling me, they were calling Marvel. Occasionally, they'd just write stories based on the book itself.

CBA: *Generally speaking, throughout your earlier career, you were working on "b-level" books. You weren't writing* The Avengers *or* Fantastic Four *or* Amazing Spider-Man. *You were working on books you were developing yourself. When the popularity of* Howard the Duck *was happening, did you see a commensurate raise in your page rate? Was there any relationship between sales of a book—that you could perceive—and what you were getting paid?*

Steve: By time, I was getting what was Marvel's top rate, I think. You would laugh if I told you what it was: $26.50 a page—but on the other hand, my page rate had doubled in three years. [*laughter*] It depends on how you look at it. [*laughter*]

CBA: *Did you ever ask to see the sales figures?*

Steve: Well, they weren't kept secret at Marvel the way I've heard they were at DC. At Marvel, we were at least generally told the percentages of the sales, because that's how they gauged the sales, by percentage of print run.

CBA: *Yeah, but that's still being somewhat duplicitous, too, isn't it? It's a percentage… "Ooh, I sold 60% of the press run," but it's hard numbers that count, right?*

Steve: No, not entirely. Any book that sold over 33% of its press run in those days was doing really well.

CBA: *But if they're printing out 750,000 copies of a book…*

Steve: That didn't matter in those days, because we weren't receiving any royalties. People used to brag

Above: *Lest we forget: Steve Gerber was also the creative force behind the highly successful* Marvel Comics Super Special #1 *featuring those monster rockers, Kiss! Below is a detail from Alan Weiss and Gray Morrow's cover. We're still awaiting the follow-up Abba ish, Steve! Kiss ©the respective copyright holder.*

about their percentage rates, not the number of copies sold. We could find out the number of copies printed if we wanted to, but a book's survival was generally determined by the percentage of print run sold.

CBA: *Comparatively, I would assume that* Omega the Unknown *was not doing as well.*

Steve: No, *Omega* never did big numbers.

CBA: *Was it told you by editorial, even though the Editor-in-Chief's office was a revolving door by that time, that the next one could be it?*

Steve: I think Archie Goodwin was the editor at the time. He called to let me know that #9 or 10—I forget exactly how many issues the series ran—would be the final one.

CBA: *Why didn't you and Mary write two issues of the book?*

Steve: Scheduling problems, probably. It had to do with the schedule on *Howard the Duck* and on other things. I just got too busy at some point or another. The book wasn't taken away from us for those two issues. There were just other things I had to do—it may have been the *Kiss* book, now that I think about it—that interfered with the schedule on *Omega*.

CBA: *It's historically known that Marvel, moving into the late '70s, was turning into a very politicized office. For a number of creators, it was not a fun place to be at any more. The climate had changed. The suits had moved in, and corporate changes were taking place. You had said in one of your interviews that you had been perceived in the office as someone who was wild, unstable and a bit volatile. People within the organization were saying things about your behavior that may possibly not have been true. Did you feel like you were beginning to be ostracized from the company? Did you perceive that climate change?*

Steve: There was a change in attitude, yeah. And yeah, there were stories being told about me, strange theories being posited about me.

CBA: *Why? Were you a "troublemaker"?*

Steve: I'm not sure what you mean by "troublemaker." I wasn't the kind of personality that comics were accustomed to, at least in those days. I took the work more seriously than some people did. I didn't let every political bump, nudge, or gouge to the eyes roll off my back the way comics people were supposed to. I never felt grateful to be working in comics, or for any particular company, in the way that used to be expected—which doesn't mean that I didn't enjoy it, by the way. I did. I just wasn't a proper supplicant to the companies or the industry; and I didn't live in the suburbs, or in Queens, or on the Upper East or West Side of Manhattan. Mary and I lived in Hell's Kitchen, which, I'm told, some people thought was a perverse psychological tactic to keep myself miserable. (In fact, it was just cheaper. Mary and I were planning to move out of New York and wanted to keep our expenses down.) There were also rumors that I was violent. When I confronted somebody about this, and asked them what I ever did in front of them that was violent, they said, "Well, you once picked up a poster and smacked it against a file cabinet when you were making a point in a discussion."

CBA: *Oooo! [laughter]*

Steve: Really!

CBA: *"Watch out for Steve! He's waving that poster!"*

Steve: Yeah! It's *Taxi Driver* all over again! [*laughter*] I mean, that's violence?!?

CBA: *That's anger.*

Steve: Yeah, anger or frustration, and I showed it, and I suppose someone considered it to be a sign of instability or something. I don't know. Certain people played it that way. What their motives were, I can't tell you. Some of it may have been jealously, or it may have just been a need to gossip about something. Or maybe somebody just wanted to get hold of the books I was writing and thought that attacking my mental state would get him the assignments—I truly don't know. I didn't even learn until years later that some of these things were being said.

CBA: *I come from an advertising background, and to me, advertising—wacky as it is—is much more "real world" than comic books, and throwing down a poster on a table is actually being very nice! [laughter] Anger is anger, and it's part of the creative process, and getting your way is a very important part of establishing parameters,*

and achieving creative goals. Was it just a very unprofessional, unreal world atmosphere in the Bullpen? Was it just very fanboyish?

Steve: I think it may have been less fannish then than it is now. There were still some first-generation people involved at that time—artists and writers who hadn't grown up on comic books—and those people tended to approach the work very differently from my generation or those that followed; but again, I even have to wonder about the definition of "professional," because at that time... well, there seems to be now, today, a new kind of corporate definition of "professional." It used to mean that people in their twenties dressed respectably on the weekdays and freaked out on the weekends. Now, they all dress like freaks, with the long hair and tattoos and piercings, and think like middle-management drones all week long! [*laughter*] This is about to veer off into a really strange discussion. [*laughter*] What was the question again? [*laughter*]

CBA: *Professionalism. I love the interview you did with Gary Groth in* The Comics Journal *back in the late '70s, because it said a lot of things that I'd been thinking for a long time. The problems with comic books in many ways is that the creators—especially writers—seem much more interested in playing with their favorite characters rather than telling stories of substance. It's very fannish, with an obsession with continuity that, I think, has been ultimately destructive to the field, and making super-heroes so dominate that storytelling has lost. It seems to have started around '75, when it stopped being fun for these creators, and the books just plain reflected that. They weren't fun anymore.*

Above: *And remember this, too, Frantic Ones: Steve was also editor of Marvel's* Mad *rip-off,* Crazy, *in those swell '70s. Steve tells us we can find a pic of the Gerbster in drag in one of his issues. First reader to send ye editor a photocopy of Steve in a dress gets a complimentary copy of CBA Special Edition #1! Photo by and courtesy of Sam Maronie.*

Below: *Readers would repeatedly recall the showgirl and ostrich in this Tom Palmer-drawn spread (from the mostly-text issue of* Howard the Duck, *#16), so Steve eventually developed the odd duo as bona fide characters in his 1998 mini-series for Vertigo,* Nevada. *Cool, huh? ©2000 Marvel Characters, Inc.*

Steve: It did for a while, then… you know. Here we are again. The business right now is almost entirely nostalgia-driven. This began happening in the '70s, and yet, it was a little different back then. For some reason, the whole mood was more experimental then. Everybody had begun to see the potential of comics, and what they could be, and while we all came to the medium with a fondness for the comics we had read as children, we all wanted to try to do something new, whether it was based on the older stuff or not. Sometime around 1980, about the time Shooter took over Marvel as Editor-in-Chief, the experimentation came to a crashing halt. Nobody wanted to look at anything different anymore. Nobody wanted to look at anything except what had gone before. Now, it's reached the point where, because of the preferences of fans and those of the retailers, you can't sell anything except something that's already been done. The business right now is in its death throes. It's in a downward spiral that's going to end when the remaining 4,000 comic book stores close up and blow away with the wind. We're looking at the end of the comic book business.

CBA: *Is it suicide?*

Steve: Yeah. I don't know if it's willing or intentional, but suicide —yeah, of course it is.

CBA: *Would you have any suggestions on survival?*

Steve: The same suggestion I've always had: *do something new!* It's a given that publishers will resist any attempt to change, but now it's become just as big a challenge to move the writers and artists in that direction. There are some very talented people working in comics right now, but their work, while some of it may be well-crafted, is frighteningly unambitious. They've learned how to make serious money in comics—on which I congratulate them, by the way—by catering to the stunted tastes of a certain limited market, but they seem completely uninterested in expanding the readership of comics, or the medium's artistic horizons. You have some artists

and writers whose whole careers are based on reworking stories that were first published forty years ago—not just working on the same characters, which would be boring enough, but actually rewriting and redrawing the same damn stories, with a couple of continuity fixes tossed in! And they seem largely oblivious to the fact that the current market for comics is dropping dead right at their feet. If the publishers don't get comic books out of that tiny dead-end market of the comic book stores, and back into places where real people actually go to buy things, and if the artists and writers can't produce material that interests people whose main concern isn't super-hero nostalgia, the business is finished.

CBA: *What happened between you and Marvel?*

Steve: We had some problems with the *Howard* newspaper strip, which led to problems with the Howard book, which ultimately led to the lawsuit.

CBA: *What were the problems with the newspaper strip?*

Steve: Marvel wouldn't pay the artist to draw it.

CBA: *Who was the artist assigned to do it?*

Steve: Gene Colan. Gene and I were supposed to get a percentage of the syndicate's take for the strip. The problem was, the money came in 90 days, 120 days, six months—I don't remember how long, exactly—after the strips were published. So, essentially, the artist was working for nothing up until that time, and no artist can afford to do that. Particularly on a strip he doesn't own.

CBA: *Was this the same policy that was taking place with the* Amazing Spider-Man *and* Conan *strips at the same time?*

Steve: As far as I know, except that Stan, as publisher of Marvel, had a regular salary coming in, and John Romita, I believe, was also on staff at the time. They didn't have quite the same problem.

CBA: *John Buscema and Roy Thomas…?*

Steve: Again, as far as I know, John and Roy did the *Conan* strip under the same terms that Gene and I did *Howard*. I had a huge fight with Marvel about getting Gene an advance for his work. I wasn't even asking them to pay Gene, as such—just advance him regular comic book rates against the income from the syndication.

CBA: *Because of the six-month delay?*

Steve: Yes; and they wouldn't hear of it.

CBA: *Did you feel this was political?*

Steve: No, I felt that it was stupid. It wasn't an attempt to kill the strip. They just didn't want to spend the money, it was that simple.

CBA: *Was it ignorance of the realities of what syndicated life is like?*

Steve: Well, ignorance of what a freelancer's life is like.

CBA: *I've been told syndicated strip work can be surprisingly grueling work. It's really tough, because you've got to put out six strips a week—without fail—and if you've got a Sunday, you've got to put out a Sunday within that time frame, too. So the artist is just pumping the work out. To expect an artist to wait six months to get paid for that full-time work…*

Steve: The more so, because it meant Gene had to give up at least one comic book assignment while we were getting the strip up to speed. Marvel simply didn't want to understand that. That's how the problems started. It only got nastier after that.

CBA: *Did you start perceiving there that you were losing—that you never had your character to begin with, so to speak?*

Steve: That, ultimately, was the feeling, sure.

CBA: *It became antagonistic very quickly?*

Steve: Once the arguments started, they escalated very quickly, yes.

CBA: *Could it have been easily resolved?*

Steve: Of course. They could've advanced Gene standard comic book rates to do the *Howard* newspaper strip. The whole problem would've gone away.

CBA: *Did you receive a settlement with Marvel over ownership of* Howard the Duck?

Steve: We negotiated a settlement, yeah. I can't disclose the exact terms, because Marvel insisted that they be kept confidential. Interestingly, I'm told that Marvel recently breached the confidentiality clause in open court, in Marv Wolfman's bid for ownership of Blade. They apparently used the Duck settlement agreement to bolster part of their case. I'm not sure what that means legally. [*laughs*]

III. obligatory comic book fight scene

CBA: *Well, find out, and give us the exclusive!* [laughter]

Steve: I may end up owning the duck again, I don't know. [laughter] I'm sorry, the question about the settlement was…?

CBA: *Well, just that, was a settlement reached?*

Steve: A settlement was reached. As I've said elsewhere, I gave up more than I wanted to, and I know that Marvel conceded more than it wanted to, so the settlement was probably fair. As part of the settlement, I agreed that Marvel owned the character. That was necessary in order to reach a settlement. Did I really believe Marvel had established ownership of Howard from the character's inception? No.

CBA: *It was an agreement. Were you involved at all in the movie?*

Steve: Very little. Basically, they handed me the script they were going to shoot, and said, "If you have any comments, let us know." I looked at it, I made a couple of suggestions—one of which I know they took, and others they didn't pay much attention to—and that was the extent of my involvement.

CBA: *Did you have a financial stake in that picture?*

Steve: Not any huge amount, but yes.

CBA: *What did you think of that movie?*

Steve: What did everybody think of that movie? [laughter] It was a very bad movie. Although, I have to say that I have seen so many worse pictures since then… [laughter] that it starts to look good. I just wish the duck suit had been better.

CBA: *How would you assess, overall, your time at Marvel?*

Steve: In the beginning, it was a terrific, creative time. I enjoyed most of the work I did there, I enjoyed most of the people that I met there, I enjoyed working with the artists. I made some good friends among the writers. It was a lot of fun, and then it became not a lot of fun.

CBA: *Can you put your finger on why it became not a lot of fun? Was it the corporate changes that were taking place? Was it the editorial revolving door?*

Steve: It's attributable to all of that; and I still resent the fact that I never got to go through that revolving door. [laughs]

CBA: *Oh, did you want to be Editor-in-Chief?*

Steve: Nobody ever suggested it, it never even got to the conceptual stage, okay? [laughter] I would've been glad to try my hand at it, yeah. I figure I would either have put the company out of business in six months, or pushed it into a much more interesting creative direction than it ultimately took. I visited the Marvel offices sometime in the mid- to late-'80s, probably around the time I was doing *Void Indigo*, and I was shocked at how the atmosphere had changed: It had gone from Toonerville to Jonestown! [laughter] Toonerville was better! [laughter]

CBA: *That water cooler was full of Kool-Aid, eh?* [laughter]

Steve: I had never seen so many people wearing the same, strange smile. [laughter] It looked like a Hare Krishna convention. Honest to God, everybody looked sort of glassy-eyed and hypnotized, and very frightened. It was not the Marvel I had known and loved.

CBA: *Destroyer Duck was obviously a reaction to your later Marvel experiences, right?*

Steve: In part, but it wasn't just Marvel I was parodying. The story was a metaphor for the lawsuit—and not a very subtle metaphor, at that—but by the time I did *Destroyer Duck*, I was living in Los Angeles, and the story was sniping at the so-called entertainment industry in general, as well as at Marvel.

CBA: *What was it like working with Jack Kirby? Did you work closely with him?*

Steve: I worked more closely with Jack than I had with most artists. For one thing, he was local. We got to see each other frequently. He was working for Ruby-Spears Productions at the same time I was, and that's when we did those books. Jack would come in a couple of times a week, and we'd sit and talk about the stuff. Occasionally, I'd drive out to his house, and see him and Roz. The experience of working with Jack was just… well, it was more personal than artistic. We became good friends. In retrospect, the book pales in comparison to the importance of the friendship.

CBA: *Did you ever really have a long hiatus from comic books? You worked in animation a lot.*

Steve: For about half of the 1980s, I did very little in comics.

CBA: *But you occasionally did an Epic project. You were willing to work with Archie Goodwin.*

Steve: I did *Void Indigo*, yeah; and there was the *Phantom Zone* miniseries that I did for DC during that time, also. I always kind of kept my hand in it, but most of the '80s I spent doing stuff other than comics, primarily in animation.

CBA: *You know, the weirdest thing happened when I was looking through that text issue of* Howard the Duck. *The Tom Palmer spread had an ostrich and a showgirl—two characters featured prominently in a recent Vertigo series of yours,* Nevada.

Steve: That was the inspiration for *Nevada*, yeah, although the character in the *Howard* story looked completely different and never had a name at all. Actually, from the time that I did that double-page spread, I started getting letters about the ostrich and the chorus girl… it's the same thing that happened with the duck! [laughter]

CBA: *You continue to keep a hand in comics here and there?*

Steve: Yeah. I'm finishing up an Elseworlds book right not for Andy Helfer, but mainly, my work right now is in Internet media. I'm working with Stan Lee's new company in L.A., and we're doing material for the net, which may prove to be the salvation of comics.

CBA: *I felt a twinge of irony when I found out you were at Stan Lee Media.*

Steve: Twinge?!? [laughter] Try "convulsion"! The last year of my life has been so bizarre… in December of '98, I left Los Angeles to live in Las Vegas again for a while. I needed a change of scene, and I'd lived in Vegas briefly before and enjoyed the town and the desert air, so I decided to try it again. In April, I left Vegas to start up an Internet comics venture in Amarillo, Texas, of all places. That fell apart in July for various reasons, and, in August, after another short stay in Vegas, just a couple of weeks this time, I came back to L.A. to take this current job. It's as if somebody threw a jigsaw puzzle of my life up in the air, and it landed with all the same pieces, but wildly rearranged. I'm working for Stan again. Jim Salicrup, who started as a gofer at Marvel the same Summer I went to work there, had the office across the hall from me—Jim still has that office; I'm working from home now—and home, for the moment, is in a condo complex in the Hollywood Hills where one of my ex-girlfriends used to live. I still see my most recent ex from time to time—it was an amicable split—and one of my two dogs lives with her, in the building in Burbank where I also used to live. If parts of this interview seem a bit incoherent, you now know why. Half the time, I can't even remember what city I'm in anymore.

CBA: *And are you 25 years old again?* [laughter]

Steve: Unfortunately, no. As I said in one of the *Nevada* letter columns, I've gone from being a Young Turk to an Old Latvian, and nothing seems likely to change that.

CBA: *Are you dealing with Stan more than you ever have?*

Steve: Until a couple of weeks ago, when I started telecommuting from home, yes. Even now, we still see more of each other now than we did 28 years ago. I'm not sure Stan's thrilled with that, [laughter] but it's true. The strange thing is, Stan and I—for all those problems, the lawsuit and everything—have always gotten along very well. I've always liked him, he's always liked me. There have been difficulties, professional matters, along the way, but when we ran into each other at conventions, it was always very cordial. In some ways, convulsions notwithstanding, it's less a surprise to me that I'm working for Stan again than it might be to a lot of fans.

Above: Omega the Unknown *is a very fondly-recalled 1970s Marvel comic which focused on the life of a prepubescent boy caught in the violence of New York's Hell's Kitchen (where creators Mary Skrenes and Steve Gerber were living at the time). We had hoped to interview Mary for this issue, but, alas… Jim Mooney, who penciled and inked the above detail from Omega #1, is interviewed elsewhere in this issue. ©2000 Marvel Characters, Inc.*

Below: *Marie Severin's sequential (and succinct) portrait of Steve Gerber, drawn for Steve's heading in the editor section of FOOM magazine. ©2000 Marvel Characters, Inc.*

Rich Buckler Breaks Out!
The artist on Deathlok, T'Challa and Other Marvel Tales

Conducted by Jon B. Cooke
Transcribed by Jon B. Knutson

Rich Buckler emerged from the Detroit fan scene in the early '70s and made an immediate impression on fans with his work on The Avengers and numerous appearances in DC, Marvel and Warren books. A confessed "chameleon," Rich has worked in a number of distinct styles derived from artists as diverse as Jack Kirby and Neal Adams. The artist is probably best known for his creation of Deathlok, the warrior cyborg. Rich was interviewed via telephone on December 15, 1999 and he copy-edited the transcript.

Right: *From October 1969: "Neal Adams ('Hey!') and me (I was 20, but I look like a 15-year-old geek)," Rich commented. Courtesy of the artist.*

CBA: *You're from Detroit?*

Rich: Actually, originally I'm from my mother's womb. [*laughter*] But, yes, originally I'm from Detroit.

CBA: *When did you first get into comics as a reader?*

Rich: I loved comics from about nine, ten years old. When I found out there were other people I could write to, from the letters' pages—actually, that's how comics fandom got started; one person got ahold of another person, and it got organized eventually.

CBA: *What books were you particularly interested in?*

Rich: At first, I was interested in DC Comics, I was captivated by Superman's universe, and then I found out about their other characters, and it became fun. I don't think I was really into it as a fan yet. I think people forget that fan is short for "fanatical"—I didn't get fanatical about it until I ran across what turned out to be a new title; I simply misread it at first, and I thought it was another Superman title, but it was *Spider-Man*. I wondered, "What was this spider web thing?" I picked that up, and that's when I found out all about Marvel Comics, and then Stan and Jack just broadened my universe, and I got carried away from there.

CBA: *Were you exposed to Jack Kirby's work beforehand?*

Rich: My favorite artist was Curt Swan, and at first I wasn't all that aware of different artists even when I started collecting. I did see there was this one artist that drew better than the rest: Curt Swan; but when I discovered Marvel Comics, I found there were different artists on different stories, because Marvel more frequently gave credit! That's when I discovered Jack Kirby, and that led to lots of favorites: Steve Ditko, Dick Ayers,

Below: *Rich noted on this 1994 picture he shared: "Me being smart (or trying to be—guess I should have tried harder!) with unidentified friend." Courtesy of the artist. Spider-Man ©2000 Marvel Characters, Inc.*

Gene Colan, Wally Wood, Bill Everett, Joe Sinnott... it's a long list..

CBA: *Were you always drawing?*

Rich: I guess I've always been drawing since I was a kid. I realized I was an artist shortly before I came across comics. I wondered what to do with it, and when I discovered comics, I thought, "This is it, this is what I'm going to do."

CBA: *It was through the letter pages in Marvel comics you discovered other fans?*

Rich: Yes, I made friends with all kinds of people from the early days—Larry Herndon, Roy Thomas, Jerry Bails. Jerry gave me my very first cover assignment (and paid me, too—I think it was around $30, which was a lot of money to a teenager then).

CBA: *Did you start ordering fanzines?*

Rich: Yes! I subscribed to practically everything I could find. *Rocket's Blast/Comicollector, Alter Ego*. I was involved early on with fanzines. I contributed to other people's fanzines, and wrote lots of letters. I drew awful-looking covers, and my own brand of strangeness, which was always new super-hero comics work. Very crude, very amateur, but totally sincere. That was my beginning as a comic book artist.

CBA: *Did you want to do comics as a career?*

Rich: Absolutely. Once I started drawing them for the fanzines, I thought, "This is really cool, let me publish something." So I started publishing fanzines before I got published in the mainstream comics. I published two fanzines and contributed regularly to dozens.

CBA: *What were the names of your fanzines?*

Rich: My fanzines were *Intrigue* and *Super-Hero*—actually, I didn't originate *Super-Hero* magazine, it was started by Mike Touhey. I became friends with him and he turned it over to me because he was going off to college full-time.

CBA: *Do you remember the characters you drew?*

Rich: I had a character named Excalibur, one named The Ghost, which was co-created by another friend of mine... I can't remember them all. They were mostly take-offs on popular characters

CBA: *Were they all different genres, or pretty much super-heroes?*

Rich: They were strictly super-heroes. I was an avid Edgar Rice Burroughs fan and a sci-fi addict, but I stuck to the fun stuff. See, I saw comics as very immature—even though I was immature at the time, so of course I didn't understand that was my point of view—but that's how I related to them. They were for kids, and I loved that. Later, comics grew up, and became serious, perhaps too serious. When I was young, they were lots of fun, and what I did for a living probably kept me immature for much too long! [*laughter*] You need to grow intellectually to mature, and try to be not too retarded. It's kept my thinking young and fresh, though, and I still love all the comics of my youth.

CBA: *In the late 1960s and early '70s, Detroit really started coming into fandom very strongly, what with the Detroit Triple Fan-Fair.*

Rich: Yes, it started to grow really fast. In fact, I was involved with that convention early on. I think I went to the first one as a fan, and after that, I joined the organizing committee. At one point, I ended up running things. Robert Brosch was the co-chairman of that one—I forget which year that was. I think he did one or two after that on his own, and then new people took it over who turned it into the Motor City Con. They've sort of forgotten that I was involved. I don't know how, but they've left me out completely. By the time I left it, there were all kinds of politics and clashes of the will. It was on its way to becoming a profit-making venture, and entirely too businesslike.

CBA: *Was Greg Theakston involved in the Triple Fan-Fair?*

Rich: Greg was involved early on, too, yes. I became friends with Greg. He started out wanting to do comics, and I remember meeting him and he had this huge collection that made mine look ridiculous! He seemed to be into all kinds of things I wasn't. We had a lot of artistic exchanges, and then he became involved with the convention.

CBA: *During this time, were you sending out samples to the big publishers? Did you think you could do comics through the mail?*

Rich: Oh, I was absolutely certain I was capable of drawing comics (even though I wasn't ready at that time), and that I could do it through the mail. Unfortunately, I had to deal with reality—as everybody does eventually. I was told even at one point to just give it up, and go away! "Stop trying, stop bothering us! Stop coming to New York, stop doing this to yourself, stop doing this to us!" [*laughter*] And I didn't know better, and it's not like I was totally unflappable, because I was just a kid. Well, actually, I was in my 20s, but emotionally I was a kid, and it was hard for me to handle the disappointment, but I just kept on trying. I couldn't give up believing it could be done. At one point, Julius Schwartz asked me, "You actually think you can draw comics at the level of an artist who has been doing this for 20 years?" This was a serious question, and I answered very seriously, very solemnly, "Yes, I do, and if I can't now, I will soon."

CBA: *So you obviously went to the DC offices. Did you go to all of the New York comics publishers?*

Rich: Not just any company, but every company that I could find! Where only months earlier they all turned me down, now I got work at every company! First, I got work at DC Comics. My big break was with Neal Adams and Dick Giordano. They believed in me and backed me up, and guaranteed that I would grow up (which I didn't) and they are the reason that I got into DC at that point. It was a big boost for me, and very encouraging. It's all their fault! [*laughs*] You know, it's funny: Any profession, or any field, that you try to break into, you have to meet someone who believes in you and gives you a chance, someone who just says, "I'm going to operate on his or her behalf, and vouch for them, and give them that jump start." That's what Dick and Neal did for me.

CBA: *When you went to the DC offices, was it when Neal had that little office with the Art-O-Graph machine?*

Rich: Yes. Actually, that was before I got regular work in the comics. I only got one assignment, a six-page mystery story by Marv Wolfman entitled "The Symbionts." I went home to Detroit and drew it, and I was just thrilled! I did everything right, sent it in, everything was fine… and I waited. Nothing happened. So, I kept bothering Dick and finally, he told me frankly, I probably wouldn't get another assignment while I was living in Detroit. So, of course, I asked him, "Well, if I moved to New York, would I get more work?" To which he replied: "I can't guarantee you'll get work. I don't want

to be responsible for you moving here—I can't take that upon myself." I understood that he was choosing his words very carefully. Finally, he said: "Yes, your chances would be greatly improved if you came here." So, I made up my mind to do it, and a few months later, I took a trip to New York specifically to become a professional comic book artist. Prior to that, I was going to New York every time there was a comic book convention.

CBA: *You were going to the Phil Seuling cons?*

Rich: Exactly. I knew Phil and I loved the whole comic book fan thing; but I was willing to give up my amateur status in a moment to become a professional (whatever that was). I left for New York with just enough money to live on for about two weeks, and it was borrowed money (from my sister, no less—thanks again, Peggy!). I stayed at the YMCA and hit all the companies, and because I told them I lived in New York, it seems to have made some difference; but I also had by this time prepared huge amounts of sample comic

Right: *Probably Rich Buckler's most memorable Marvel creation, Deathlok (who was originally named "Deadlock," Rich tells us). The above drawing is offered by Rich when he exhibits at comic cons. Courtesy of the artist. Deathlok ©2000 Marvel Characters, Inc.*

Sword of Dragonus

In the distance stood the castle of the wizard Talvuras! It was built on a rocky crag, and its spires and towers thrust upwards into the clouds. This was truly an evil, forbidding structure! Dragonus spurred his frightened mount onward!

A few days earlier, Dragonus had been in the chamber of Balthus, the albino prince of one of Stygia's colonies.

Story: CHUCK ROBINSON II   Art: RICHARD BUCKLER

Above: *Rich worked with fan writer Chuck Robinson II to produce a sample story for the fledgling* Web of Horror *magazine, edited by noted-sf author Terry Bisson. The story was rejected but subsequently redone for publication by Frank Brunner. Art courtesy of and ©2000 Rich Buckler.*

pages. But before going to a single publisher, I made my pilgrimage to Frank Frazetta's house. He was living in Brooklyn at the time, and I was accompanied by Marv Wolfman and Len Wein. We got to see just about every painting Frank did up to that point. He was so generous with his time, and he just held everything out and showed it. "So, guys… what do you think?" We were awestruck. After we saw everything that he had, I showed him my samples, and I was really nervous about his reaction. He looked them over carefully—there were about twenty pages with 11 or 12 different styles. He studied each page silently, then handed them all back to me. "So, Mr. Frazetta: Can I have your opinion or critique… or, uh, whatever?" He didn't answer right away. (It's interesting, the parallels between this and what happened with Salvador Dali meeting Picasso, and Picasso not commenting after seeing Dali's work.) [*laughter*] Frank said to me, "Well…"—he was also careful at choosing his words [*laughter*]—"I've seen a lot of samples from a lot of different guys, but never from someone with so many different styles." That was his only comment; but I had impressed him, and I took that to be so much encouragement. That, coupled with something that happened to me just prior to my leaving for my big trip to New York to get all this work from all the different companies: I'd spoken to Jack Kirby on the telephone after sending him samples of my inking. He turned me down, but Jack said that I was very good—I'd also sent penciling samples—and that I should go to Stan Lee and tell

Stan that Jack said to give me a job! I never did—I did go to Stan, but I didn't tell him that Jack said to give me a job. But I have a feeling Jack called him, because that appointment was way too easy! [*laughter*] I got an assignment right on the spot—Stan just made up a lot on the spot, and nothing was written down, and he said, "Go draw this."

CBA: *Wow. So, Jack was in California and you just called him up?*

Rich: Yes. Well, I didn't initiate things. This was all arranged by Shel Dorf (of San Diego Comic Con fame—and Shel created the Detroit Con, by the way).

CBA: *This was obviously prior to Jack's leaving Marvel.*

Rich: Right. I'm dropping big names here, but my point, again, is it doesn't matter who you are and how much talent you have, you have to connect with people who are willing to take a chance and help make something happen. I'm very grateful that these people were involved in my life!

CBA: *I was looking through* The Golden Age of Comics Fandom *and there's a couple of illustrations done by you in the mid- to later-'60s, and they seemed to exude a really strong Kirby influence. You went to Frazetta with all this material in different styles…*

Rich: I had a Frank Frazetta style, too! I had Ditko, Kirby, Toth, Alex Raymond, Wally Wood, Gil Kane, John Buscema, Jim Steranko, Al Williamson, Angelo Torres, Burne Hogarth—whew!—and, of course, a Neal Adams style. Neal and Frank Frazetta were my idea of the highest level of draftsmanship in comics (along with Hal Foster, Burne Hogarth, and Alex Raymond). I always considered myself a real artist (not only a cartoonist), so I set my goals very high.

CBA: *Do you have a style you could point to and say, "This is me; this is as close to my style as I can get"?*

Rich: Well, actually, you know what? It's funny… well, it's not funny, you don't hear me laughing, right? [*laughter*] This is not funny… this was actually a source of frustration and it was strange: You see, I never did quite find a style I was comfortable with. I loved Jack Kirby's storytelling, I've tried to combine it with the good drawing that Neal Adams has, and the dynamics of Joe Kubert and Gil Kane and a few others… Oh, yeah, I went to work for Gil Kane as his assistant, also. I just got carried away, I'm telling this out of sequence, but around the same time I got assignments from everybody, and of course I couldn't do all of them at once (I got into all kinds of deadline trouble, as you can imagine). I had an assistants' job for Gil Kane that lasted something like three days! [*laughter*] Howard Chaykin was working for him at the same time. Gil was very polite when he fired me, saying, "I really don't think you need this job."

CBA: *Gil was living in Manhattan?*

Rich: Yes. Gil was a complete gentleman about the situation, and I felt awful that I'd done that; but I was like a kid in a candy store, I guess. I thought I could do everything, and of course, you can't. So I finally got down to work on these assignments and got them in on time (how, I don't know—I think I didn't sleep for three or four days straight). That was real tough.

CBA: *Again, is there anything in your work…?*

Rich: The style, getting back to that. Sorry, we took that sudden detour. What I finally arrived on was something that combined the draftsmanship of—or at least trying for the draftsmanship level—of John Buscema and Neal Adams, combined with Jack Kirby's and Gil Kane's dynamics; but really, it's hard to tell, because so many artists thrilled me. Like Joe Kubert's work, and there was a long period where I studied Alex Raymond's work. Every guy seemed to be The One.

CBA: *Were you influenced by Steranko's storytelling?*

Rich: I would say I wanted to do the types of things Steranko was doing—the daring and experimental graphics. What I ended up doing was an imitation of Bernie Kriegstein.

CBA: *"Master Race"?*

Rich: Exactly. Well, remember again, I was very naive [*laughs*] but also fearless! (If my work sucked today, hey, tomorrow it'll suck a little less—who cares if thousands of copies are printed and everyone knows I'm a madman?)

CBA: *To what do you attribute your perseverance?*

Rich: Oh, I have a tremendous ego. I was born to greatness, and am absolutely totally convinced that I am a creative genius.

[laughter] I'm still convinced of this, although I hope I'm a little less annoying about it. [laughter] Hey, I'm not the only genius in the world, but I don't have a problem with that. Just because you're a genius doesn't mean you actually know everything.

CBA: *The first DC work I recall of yours was a short science-fiction story in the back of a Dick Giordano mystery book, which was actually partially inked by Neal Adams, wasn't it?*

Rich: *House of Secrets.* Yes. Actually, Neal was supposed to ink it, and then I ended up working on it at one point to finish it, because I was anxious to be finally published.

CBA: *Neal did some of the faces on it, though, didn't he?*

Rich: No, he did most of the inking. I just finished things up. Neal did all the fun stuff. [laughter] He did all the stuff that made the job look good. I had some photocopies of some of the pencil work so I could prove how I really drew it, but after I saw it inked, I just somehow… err… lost them. [laughter]

CBA: *That story was an impressive debut, wasn't it?*

Rich: Yes, it was! It certainly helped get things going. It got published about a year, maybe a year-and-a-half after I'd done it. I had been published by Marvel and at DC with other work before that came out. Sometimes things get mixed up that way, so your first work is not necessarily the first that gets published. The first assignment I got from Stan Lee was a Man-Wolf story, which was a character he wanted to do something with, and he made up a story on the spot. I drew it, and it never was published. I believe later George Pérez did something with the Man-Wolf character…

CBA: *Oh, this was before the start of the Man-Wolf series in* Creatures on the Loose?

Rich: Yeah. I think Stan liked my pages where I'd handled the Black Panther, and he thought, "Wow, let's have Buckler try an animal-like character—he seems to be good at this."

CBA: *Didn't you get work from Warren early on? I recall a werewolf serial in* Eerie.

Rich: The first story I did was something I wrote and illustrated, entitled "The Demon Within." Jim gave me the assignment when he immediately recognized my genius (just kidding). So, yeah, I think Warren was one of the first to try me, even though Jim was pretty tough on me critically. It was funny, because I remember talking to him recently about this, but when I first came to him—I didn't know he was an artist, that he's coming from an artist's point of view. I just thought he was a guy with eccentric behavior who was just very tough on everyone. That's how people sum him up, but there's actually much more to his character than being critical. He was pretty tough on me, but he gave me some of my first couple of assignments. Jim was very encouraging. After I had my appointment to see Jim Warren again to hand in my pages, I told Alan Weiss (who was my roommate at the time) and he warned me just how tough Warren could be on artists. I don't know if Alan

remembers now, but he told me a story about how he went to see Warren, and it went something like this:

Alan handed in his finished pages (which looked really great—he had shown them to me earlier), and Warren perused them carefully, taking his time, making Alan squirm. Finally Warren spoke up and asked, "Is this honestly the very best that you are capable of?" Alan was very proud of the art on that assignment, and began to say so, when Warren reached into his desk and pulled out a rubber stamp and pad. Before Alan could react, Jim stamped each of his pages with the word "Crap!" Just like that: Whump!

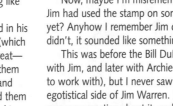

Crap, crap, crap, crap, crap!

Well, the story did more than a little to undermine my confidence, and I remember saying to Alan, "Gee, he never did anything like that to me…" But I was thinking, "Yet!"

Now, maybe I'm misremembering and Alan was telling me how Jim had used the stamp on somebody else, and did he do that to me yet? Anyhow I remember Jim did do it to somebody! And even if he didn't, it sounded like something he would do!

This was before the Bill DuBay days, and I was dealing directly with Jim, and later with Archie Goodwin (who was always a pleasure to work with), but I never saw this supposed twisted, monstrous and egotistical side of Jim Warren. I think he just knew how to have fun, was very creative about it, and sometimes used intimidation to get what he wanted.

Oh, and speaking of Bill DuBay, I knew Bill before he was an editor for Warren (and before I did assignments for Bill). DuBay was a fan trying to go professional with his art, but he was having a lot of problems. When I first met him, it was at one of the big companies—DC Comics, I think—and Alan Weiss and I met up with him. My first impression wasn't a very positive one; Bill seemed to be self-enamored, and really good at getting on people's nerves—maybe it was just youthful exuberance, nervousness or insecurity, or all of the above.

Anyway, Bill called me up the next day and asked if Alan and I

Above: *Ever the stylistic mimic, Rich produced (with writer Doug Moench) this "Filipino" approach to Warren horror storytelling but, the artist explains, "I lost interest because I needed to use too much photo reference." Courtesy of and ©2000 Rich Buckler.*

Left inset: *Photo of "Me with Jim Warren—What a swell guy!" taken at a 1999 N.Y. comic convention. Courtesy of the artist.*

could pitch in and help him meet a deadline. We agreed, with some reservations, but figured, "What the hell, we'll help him. He's a fellow freelance artist. How can we say no?" Besides, he sounded gravely serious on the phone about the whole thing—and his employer was none other than… Jim Warren!

We got to Bill's place (somewhere way out on the tip of Long Island), only to find out that the job was due the very next day, so it meant staying up all night to finish it; but that's not all.

Seems this particular assignment, and its timely delivery, would determine Bill's future with Jim Warren. The assignment was a test. If Bill passed the test, Jim would hire him as assistant to the publisher.

So, Bill's first work for Jim Warren was actually a collaboration (mine and Alan's participation had to be kept secret, so we didn't get any credit). As I recall, we penciled, inked and lettered at least half of the assignment in one night—it was totally nuts, and of course, the styles clashed, and overall the art was a mess. But next day, Bill handed it in, and Warren gave him the job—and the rest, as they say, is history.

CBA: *Did you go to Skywald?*

Rich: Yes. Skywald was started by former vice-president of Marvel Comics, Sol Brodsky. I recall the visits there, because I tried to date the publisher's daughter. That was probably my first wrong move! [laughter]

CBA: *Sol's daughter?*

Rich: No, his partner Israel Waldman's daughter. Anyway, I was told I was not Jewish enough—understandable since I'm not Jewish.

(I'm a mixture of German, Irish and French—but I look mostly German.) Anyway, I'm married to a Jewish girl now, so it's like things have come full circle. Now I have a whole Jewish family (and I have a Jewish heart). At Skywald, along with Chuck McNaughton and Jack Katz, we put together a magazine for them called *Science-Fiction Odyssey* (I think one or two issues came out). So, in addition to doing freelance art and writing, we created a new title for them. Unfortunately, they didn't know what they had, or what to do with it… too bad. I worked on their first black super-hero. First of all, black characters weren't taking off at the time. They put this feature in the back of *Hell-Rider* (and I don't know where they got the idea that motorcycle characters were going to be hot).

CBA: Hell-Rider: *One heck of a book.* [chuckles]

Rich: Not only that, but female characters at the time were not real big. So, here they've got this female black character. It was very dull and uninteresting the way they were handling it, and when I came on, I was told to do what I want. Okay, great. So the first thing I did was make her more sexy, more female, more black! They had a problem with that, because when I brought in the artwork, they felt that she looked too black! [laughter] You know, people, what's the point? Why don't you just turn her into a white woman? One way or another, make up your mind! [laughter] The long and short of it, is I refused to change the character, and they had Bill Everett do touch-ups on her and her boyfriend, who also looked too black, I guess (or maybe not Jewish enough?). Nobody at Skywald knew what they were doing, except for Sol.

CBA: *Was that your singular piece for Skywald?*

Rich: No, that was the main thing. I did a horror story Gerry Conway wrote, and… oh, yes! I did, for two issues—I can't remember if it was *Psycho* or *Nightmare*—an epic written by Marv Wolfman, and it had to do with a huge war between heaven and Hell. I can't even remember the title, but it was sort of an epic, which appealed to me a lot—and I thought I was going to get out all of my Leonardo DaVinci/Michelangelo reference, and prove what a phenomenal genius I really was! It was comics, but it had all the epic stuff I saw in Jack Kirby's *Thor* and "Tales of Asgard." I got to do my version of that, in terms of storytelling and layout.

CBA: *Did you continue to read comics? Did you read Jack's "Fourth World" stuff?*

Rich: Oh, absolutely, I loved it, I thought it was great. In fact, about two or three years ago, I did a comic book Roy Thomas co-wrote with me called *Forever Warriors*, which I self-published. That was a sort of take-off and a tribute to Jack Kirby's Fourth World. In fact, I dedicated it to Jack and to Stan Lee. It was kind of a fan project. In fact, I've always been a fan, it's one of the reasons I don't have a specific style, or maybe I do, but I'm not aware of it, and I just keep doing fannish things like that. Roy is a lot like that, too—even bigger fanboy than me. We think a lot alike, which is why we teamed up at DC to create *All-Star Squadron*.

CBA: *How deeply involved were you with* Science-Fiction Odyssey?

Rich: I did a story for it. Initially, it was my inspiration, I came up with the idea to get real s-f authors, or at least to contact them and pay for the rights to adapt their stories. So, we had some pretty big authors… if Harlan Ellison wasn't in there, he was meant to be. I remember I did an adaptation with Roy Thomas for a Harlan Ellison story, that became an issue of *The Avengers* for Marvel. As I mentioned before, I was a big s-f fan—not in the sense of going to the s-f conventions and knowing all the s-f people; I hardly knew any of them—but there was a little bit of a crossover into comics. Initially the committee on the Detroit Triple Fan-Fair were all s-f fans.

CBA: *They were "The Misfits"—the Michigan Science Fiction Society?*

Rich: Right. I was their youngest member (and they probably thought of me as their mascot). The comic cons were modeled on the s-f cons. That was pretty much the map they used. I do go off on tangents, don't I?

CBA: *That's okay. This is fine. Together, we'll rearrange the transcript into a more chronological order.*

Rich: There's probably no need, as I think very much like this. [laughter] Maybe the reader should just go along with it. What I'm currently doing is a series of surrealistic paintings, and really, I've discovered I've been a surrealist all along, and it's pretty much how I think. I'm going to be exhibiting the paintings at the New York Art Expo this March, and it's completely unlike anything I've done in the comics. In fact, I feel like the comics were sort of a training ground for me so I could reach this point.

CBA: *So you're devoting a lot of time to it?*

Rich: However long it takes to paint each painting. Some of them take months. I just started about seven months ago, and I'd never painted prior to that. It's totally bugged stuff. You'll get used to how I think, and my strange sense of humor, not that it's all that strange to me! [*laughter*]

CBA: *You started to get a lot of work, and suddenly, roughly '71, '72, you really hit it, right? Were you beginning to receive fan recognition at that time?*

Rich: I had fans actually, when I was doing the fanzines! And I was a fan of a lot of the guys who were drawing in the fanzines. I wanted to do the kind of stuff Biljo White and Ronn Foss were doing. I thought for sure they were going to make it big. I remember *Star-Studded Comics* Larry Herndon did. That's what I wanted to do. Steve Fritz I thought was really, really good; and I always wanted to be able to draw as well as Alan Weiss.

CBA: *And here you were, one of the few who made it into professional comics.*

Rich: See, when I started meeting professionals who I knew previously in the fan days, I realized, "Whether I try to make it happen or not, something seems to be coming together here that's bigger than all of us!" Here's Roy Thomas, who I knew from the comics fandom, and Marv Wolfman, Len Wein, a lot of people… Alan Weiss. So, [*laughs*] you think, "Gee, something special is going on here." There was a renaissance going on in the comics (though none of us knew this at the time it was happening). It was the arrival of a new generation of artists and writers. Prior to that time, there weren't many people breaking into the business.

CBA: *Was your hope to get a regular series, or did you like doing the short stories?*

Rich: I've never even figured out my thinking, okay, so I don't know how anybody else is going to figure this out. Probably there are people out there who like my work, but they like specific work. I hear a lot of people say, "*Fantastic Four*: That's Rich Buckler's best stuff." But that was just one thing. When I did *The Avengers*, I had a John Buscema-like style; and then, I was probably thinking, "Gee, if I do *Fantastic Four*, I can do a Jack Kirby-type style." That's what I did, I changed to a Kirby-type style. At first, it had a little bit of a John Buscema feel, I just went more and more into it; and then, I got off into my own thing. Around the time of the end of my run on *The Fantastic Four* (though I never had a long run on anything, really), I created Deathlok. I saw that as an actual next step, creating a character for a series.

Now, I'm sorry I created anything in the comics, because I didn't get anything out of it. A lot of imitations came about, and I had bad feelings about it, but I went through all that, forget about it. I knew it was a mistake; but anyway, every time I would go to a different company, I would have a different style. For example, at DC Comics, I did a DC style. Then, I'd go to Marvel if an opportunity came up, and then I'd have a Marvel style. Sometimes, I'd mix it up. I think on *Detective Comics*, I did Robin back-up stories where I used a Jack Kirby style. I remember Vinnie Colletta hated it. He was the art director at the time, and he got me to change it around. It's funny, he said it wasn't my style, it doesn't work, don't do this. Well, what's my style? And he said, "Well, I don't know, but I'd know it if I see it." [*laughter*] I said, "Okay," so I went home, I got out all my Neal Adams art books, and I just swiped everything from Neal Adams, and I brought it in the next day, and he said, "Now, that's your style!" [*laughter*] I said, "Thank you, okay. At least we know what you expect, and I'll continue to do that." But I got bored with Adams swiping.

CBA: *So you were a chameleon.*

Rich: That's because I'm a genius. It's just one of the things I'm good at. I study, practice, figure something out, use it; but I'm also very eclectic, I'd never know what I was going to be interested in next.

CBA: *You started off doing very Neal Adams-like work, and next a*

John Buscema style—full figures, big panels—and then you move into more and more Kirby stuff. But with Deathlok, you seemed to be pushing a more individual approach.

Rich: I figured out the comics were a great training ground for me, and I was afforded the opportunity of training and learning, and getting paid as I learned; but I love the comics medium. I wanted to draw these incredible comics, with all this great draftsmanship that I wasn't capable of yet, but I was always studying. Now, I finally got it down, and I found as my drawing improved, my comics following would shrink! The better-drawn comics material people just didn't like as much! Probably, some of the excitement disappeared, too. It's a trade-off. To have the same style for 20, 30 years would drive me nuts! Actually, it couldn't make me crazy, because you can't go somewhere when you're already there! [*laughs*] But I would never allow myself to get bored.

CBA: *Can we talk about your collaborators? Roy Thomas…*

Rich: Probably my favorite writer. My second favorite is Gerry Conway.

CBA: *Why was Roy your favorite writer?*

Rich: A number of reasons. Roy is like this incredible reservoir of energy and enthusiasm and dynamic ideas. He never had a problem coming up with some interesting slant, some look, some new way of doing something. And yet, when he writes it, it's like it always was there, it's like it always existed. Everything, the dialogue, the way he tied up the narrative, he worked so naturally, like nothing was work. I'm sure he was sitting there swearing over my pages at times. "How does he expect me to connect this with that?" I remember talking to him on the telephone, him complaining a few times about strange transitions, but… or maybe I didn't leave enough room for dialogue, but writers always complain about that! [*laughter*] Letterers would complain when there was too much to fit in, and the writers have too much power.

CBA: *And Gerry Conway, as a writer?*

Rich: Gerry was very much at the same level as Roy. Both of them are really very smart people. I like smart people, because I consider myself a smart person. Not that I have anything against dumb people, I just don't hang out with them.

CBA: *And you worked with Gerry on Thor?*

Rich: Yes, and that was really a lot of fun. Gerry was very good to work with. Another one was Doug Moench on "Deathlok." Doug is a very smart guy, and a pleasure to work with. I'm usually considered the creator of Deathlok, but Doug was very heavily involved from the beginning. He came up with the name, and really co-created the character.

Below: *Rich's Atlas/Seaboard character Demon-Hunter was resurrected after the company's demise over at Marvel as Demon-Slayer. Courtesy of the artist. ©2000 the respective copyright holder.*

Below: *"This is a sample I did for Joe Kubert in the late '70s," Rich noted. "He was looking for a replacement on Tarzan, so I 'aped' (pardon the pun) his style as closely as possible." Courtesy of the artist. Tarzan ©2000 ERB, Inc.*

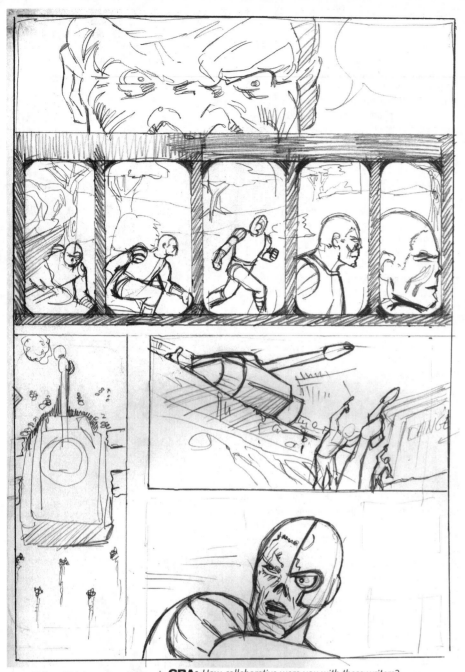

CBA: *How collaborative were you with these writers?*

Rich: I like to be as interactive as possible. I've always felt the comics were like rock 'n' roll, okay? So it's like a rock band, only the rock band in this case is not making music, they're making comics, and it's the people that put together the comics. You've got the letterer, the colorist, the writer, the artist, and everybody shares in the creation. It's hard to figure out, you know, you've got these job descriptions, but everybody does a little bit of something else, too, and it all comes together. It's sort of like making a movie.

CBA: *A very collaborative effort.*

Rich: Very collaborative. Another reason I loved working with Roy and with Gerry, their plots were so easy to work with.

CBA: *They were visual?*

Rich: They were totally visual, like movies. Their plots were written out, like a conversation to the artist describing a film treatment. It allowed me to pretend I was the writer and interpret, because they'd allow for that interpretation, too, to make the scene play. Then I'd give that back to them, and they'd maybe have to rethink the writing here and there, but for the most part, they could pretend to be the artist, look at the pages and think, "Well, I don't know what I think of this, but I'll make the magic work. This is what I want the story to be." The dialogue would start to come, because there would be life and movement in the art and characters.

I'll just throw in again the comment about my thinking being surrealistic, because you have to understand something about the comics—this is true for me, anyway. When I drew them, they were totally real, so things that happened—in my imagination—were real. These were movies, the characters were alive, and they were all people that I knew.

CBA: *So you obviously got involved.*

Rich: Yes, totally, I hallucinated on a regular basis. I've been told by more than a few people that, "Gee, your work looks like you take drugs," but I've never taken drugs.

CBA: *Never had to? [laughs]*

Rich: Never needed to! [laughter] I'd probably go somewhere and never get back if I took drugs.

CBA: *You bring up the collaborative point, because I look through the "Deathlok"s and I see a real team there: You, Doug Moench, Klaus Janson, and Annette Kawecki.*

Rich: They all got involved, very much.

CBA: *Annette was a great letterer on "Deathlok." Do you recall her?*

Rich: She had the thankless job of coming up with this new type of lettering. You can look at it now and say, "Gee, it wasn't all that innovative," but there wasn't anything like it before, she had to do all those computer boxes and create totally new typefaces. And it was tough, and she wasn't paid enough, she put in extra hours, and she didn't really complain about it. Annette just got into it. She just tried to make it happen, no matter what the challenge.

CBA: *The complex nature of the captions within "Deathlok"—you had the computer talking, then you had Manning talking, and then you had both of them talking!*

Rich: Doug, I think, was a little bit into his own thing, regular visits to "The Zone," so he and I would sort of go to the same places [laughs] where you pull in everything, and crazy things would happen, and crazy ideas would happen that at first didn't seem to work; but then they did. So, you'd have a narration with three different voices, and I found it perfectly easy to follow. A lot of people found it very difficult.

CBA: *Well, the captions were color-coded!*

Rich: And it was fun! Roy Thomas at one point said, "I have no idea of what's going on with Deathlok, but I like it." [laughter] He pretty much just let me do what I wanted to do on it. It was pretty cool.

CBA: *Was that Roy's editorial style, to really let the creators be themselves?*

Rich: Roy is so easy-going! If he were any more easy-going, he'd be dead! [laughter] Well, that's a strange way to put it, but he's just so easy to get along with, and he lets people do their thing, yes, and he loves to collaborate, too. I can't imagine anybody having a complaint about him, in terms of working with him. He is very logical, too. I like logic, too, even though I get all crazy with the imaginative stuff. I like logic, too… I like for things to fall into place, and make some kind of sense. Occasionally, I have an anchor in reality.

CBA: *You also worked with a real character, Don McGregor.*

Rich: Don McGregor is total nuts. [laughter] Yes, again, he's just one of those smart people, no limits, and plus I liked him a lot—I still do—and his thinking is incredible. I don't think he's ever been really appreciated.

CBA: *He's got very complex plots and he's a very intense writer…*

Rich: And God bless him, that's exactly what I loved about his work, and I still do.

CBA: *Did you have any input into the "Black Panther" stories?*

Rich: Absolutely. Don didn't have a problem with it. He would pretty much do what he wanted to do, yeah. Understand that with Don—as much as things were real to me—they were even more real to Don. He would take characters away from me! [laughter] "No, that's not going to happen! I know, because they told me!" [laughter] Real involved. We had that going, that kind of depth in collaboration, and we were also excited about doing something new. He's had lots of headaches and lots of problems and lots of resistance from people because he tried too many new things. Hey, somebody has to! I guess you might say I'm guilty of encouraging him. [laughter]

CBA: *So, you worked very closely with him on "Black Panther." And then you…*

Rich: He would say, "Is that too much dialogue here, Rich?" I would say, "Don, there's space here you missed!" [laughter] I would never ask him to cut anything, I'd say, "No, we'll make room, we'll make it work somehow." Letterers always complained.

CBA: *Were you interested in making political statements in your work about racism, for instance?*

Rich: I don't know if that's political. Racism is just stupid!

CBA: *Nonetheless, it was a political issue in the '70s.*

Rich: I mean, it's stupid, being against women because they're female, that's stupid! There are things that are probably just anti-intellectual.

CBA: *But with the situation at Skywald, where they requested you make black characters "less black"…*

Rich: The companies did not want to deal with issues like racism. Absolutely, they were sensitive issues. Don and I would seek out opportunities to piss off people by doing things with these subjects. Coincidentally, there was a point where *The Comics Journal* actually in a review, someone attacked me as a racist! Obviously, that was totally ridiculous. Or attempted to, but it was completely off the mark. It turned out it was someone who was pissed off at me.

CBA: *Are you just full of boundless energy? I recall that you were involved in martial arts, too, right? And you also conceived of Deathlok as a novel…*

Rich: The novel didn't happen, although I had written about a third of it. I had actually figured out that I wasn't going to be that good of a writer. I'm better at collaborating, so it was ego that said, "Hey, do a novel." It was good sense that made me pull back.

CBA: *Is it that positive, competitive edge that helps, in the collaborative process?*

Rich: See, there's the downside to being a genius: You think you can do everything, but you can't. I would try things, just to do them, but I would lose interest, or just not take it far enough. I learned photography, I learned to play music… these things I didn't take anywhere, but filmmaking I got involved with initially through photography, and I always really saw comics as being film, and I always dreamed of being a film director. I went for five years, really trying to break into the film business. After five or six years, if you haven't broken in, you can pretty much figure you're on the wrong road, and it's not going to happen. I wasn't connecting with the right people. I was financing myself, and I was ruining my comics career in the meantime—or at least putting my comics career in jeopardy—so it was a mistake. But experience-wise, I have no regrets, it was absolutely great. I started a martial arts actors' repertory group, which I felt obligated to continue as long as possible. It was a great source of inspiration for me.

CBA: *"A martial arts actors' repertory group"?*

Rich: Yes, actors in training who were real martial artists. I even hired a professional acting tutor. We were working on a documentary film about the group, we did several performances of a stage show, which I wrote and directed. We did a performance at one of Phil Seuling's conventions, and it was a big hit.

CBA: *What kind of martial arts?*

Rich: Well, all the different forms: Karate, kung fu, taekwondo, you name it.

CBA: *Was it a daily aspect of your life?*

Rich: For quite a few years. It's definitely a part of my life. I'm probably more into the philosophical side of it, in the fact that I consider it an art, and probably I'm more… how do I put this? I'm closer to the philosophy side of it than I am to the actual physical, where we're all beating people up, and working out regularly.

CBA: *Was a part of your delving into certain fields and different things you were doing and later dropped, was that a need for recognition that you didn't get? Did you want recognition for what you were trying to achieve, or was it economic necessity?*

Rich: Well, happiness is getting your own way; everybody doesn't want to get somebody else's way, they want to get their own way. Certainly, I wanted to get things on my terms, my way. I don't think there was a desire to get rich from it so much as make some money, so I could continue to do it. Then, indulge my every creative whim, which I found out is pretty much what Salvador Dali did constantly… Oh, that's what I was doing! Not too smart, actually, because I'm not independently wealthy, right now. I do okay, but I'm not financially set. I could've been smarter at it, I could've actually run my career, but I wasn't thinking of it as a career. I was just thinking, "Now I can be Joe Kubert, now I can be Jack Kirby." Deadlines were always met, and I always made enough to pay the rent and living expenses.

CBA: *When did you start a family? Because your son Rick has been professional for some time, right?*

Rich: He started his professional career when I was working for Neal Adams at Continuity Graphics as a commercial artist. That was about nine or ten years ago. Neal started Rick as an apprentice—he was basically a messenger—but he was taken on as sort of an apprentice. That's actually when Rick realized he was serious about being an artist. Initially, he just needed a job.

CBA: *So his exposure to Neal's Continuity Studio….*

Rich: …Helped him make up his mind. I have to admit there was probably another reason Rick got the job: Neal is Rick's godfather. So it was natural, you know, "My son needs a favor, I can't hire him, but my boss happens to be his godfather, maybe if I go to him, just maybe, nepotism, it might work." I guess it did.

Above: *Last issue we featured a bunch of Rich's pencil breakdown pages for Jungle Action #24 and, as promised, here are a few more. Courtesy of Don McGregor. Art ©2000 Rich Buckler. Black Panther ©2000 Marvel Characters, Inc.*

Above and next page: *A couple of Rich's penciled pages to the 1996* Captain America: The Medusa Legacy *one-shot. Art courtesy of and ©2000 Rich Buckler.* Captain America & Bucky *©2000 Marvel Characters, Inc.*

CBA: *Well, Neal's a big believer in family. Have you always maintained a relationship with Neal?*

Rich: Yes. It's had its ups and downs, but yes. Neal is a complicated person. He's probably also my favorite artist on the continent. To me, he's the Leonardo of comics. One of the smartest people I know, and he's smarter than me (I do know people who are smarter than me). I think he's smarter than a lot of people, good at conceptualizing and problem-solving.

CBA: *When did you work at Continuity in the '80s, post-Archie?*

Rich: Oh, late '80s, early '90s. The last days of Continuity Comics, the last wave, with *The Rise of Magic* and all that. Prior to that, I did two or three books for them. Lots of commercial work. I was really there to sort of go back to school. I called up Neal, and he said, "I think we've got some work for you." I showed up and tried something, and he said, "This is working," and then I didn't leave! I just came in there every day. I couldn't stay away from the place, and I looked at it as training. It took my drawing to a whole other level.

CBA: *Were you also developing a studio situation in the mid-'70s? There were a bunch of Detroit artists who entered the field and worked on your material: Keith Pollard, Arvell Jones…*

Rich: Well, that's another part of my character that's probably hard for people to figure out. I've always been into helping people. Since the last time I worked with Neal Adams at Continuity, I started my own studio again and took on a lot of artists. Most of them didn't work out, but I've always been helping people. They would help me by doing assistant work, I would pay them, most of the time they

were very damaging to my work, but I'd somehow figure out how to minimize the damage. They learned and trained and were encouraged, and would go on and get work in the comics (well, some of them, anyway).

CBA: *Some Detroit compatriots followed you into the business.*

Rich: Those were friends from before I got into the comics… no! Actually, I met them after I broke into the comics. Around the period of that run on *Astonishing Tales* with Deathlok, I moved back to Detroit for a while, that's when we got together.

CBA: *That's when you met Keith, and Arvell?*

Rich: Yes. Then, I moved back to New York, and they just came into the comics. A couple of other guys, friends of theirs, Albert Bradford and a couple of other people. I remember at one point, John Verpoorten asked me, "Rich, have you got any friends who aren't black?" [*laughter*] I said, "Well, Don McGregor, he's still friends with me! [*laughter*] I haven't spoken to him recently, so I might've said something that pissed him off, I don't know." I do tend to be opinionated and outspoken. I remember years ago I said or did something that pissed off Klaus Janson. He never forgave me, even though I apologized.

CBA: *Were you getting stretched too thin? You were working on* Jungle Action *but Billy Graham took over from you pretty quickly…*

Rich: I was always challenging myself; but I always worked 12-14 hour days, I just totally stretched too thin… I guess I still do it.

CBA: *Did you get Klaus Janson to work with you? You two hooked up together for a while.*

Rich: Yeah, Klaus came and showed me his work, and said he wanted to be an inker, and I said, "Why do you want to be an inker? Why don't you want to be an artist?" I can't remember what his answer was, but he could draw! His inking was okay, but there were some things that I liked in there, that were imitative of Dick Giordano, and I thought, "Gee, if I get a new guy to do my work, maybe he'll stick closer to the drawing!" So I had him try a couple of things, and I liked him, and then went to John Verpoorten and asked, "John, can Klaus ink this book?" And John said, "No." I said, "Why? You got an inker slated?" He said, "No." I said, "Well, I want Klaus on it!" He said, "No!" Okay, the next day I came and asked… "No!" And I kept asking him… "No!" Then, I finished penciling on the first issue, and I said, "John, I'm taking the pages, and Klaus is going to ink them." He said, "No, he's not!" I said, "I'm taking the pages, I'm leaving the office now. I'm going to get Klaus to ink these." "No, you're not!" [*laughs*] But he didn't stop me. I think by not stopping me, he made me responsible for how it came out, and I got Klaus to work on it; but initially, he didn't officially get the assignment. He did the first three pages, and they saw them, they liked them, they saw everything was working, so they didn't object. Klaus put in his vouchers and everything was fine, and suddenly, he was a professional.

CBA: *And then he followed you over to "Deathlok" in* Astonishing Tales, *working with you regularly.*

Rich: And then I lost him. He got good really fast. Then, he did some work on a few other pencilers, and he became in demand. You take what you can get, you know? He developed later into quite a comic book artist.

CBA: *I recall reading in a text piece in the first issue of the* Deathlok *series in* Astonishing Tales *that you had first conceived of—I think he was called "Deadlock" at the time—as a novel?*

Rich: Deadlock was the original name I had for this character. It seemed to be descriptive; but I wasn't married to it. Doug Moench and I worked on the proposal, and he brought it in the next day, and it was 10 minutes before the appointment to see Roy, and I looked it over, and I almost died. Doug changed the name to "Deathlok"! It sounded so strange to me! [*laughter*] I looked at him, and I said, "I can't believe you did this!" He said, "Well, what difference does it make? Deathlok, Deadlock, whatever. Our meeting's in ten minutes." Roy preferred Doug's choice, so I just got used to it.

CBA: *Broadsided, eh?* [*laughs*]

Rich: Yeah, and I think he was right, it just sounds better.

CBA: *Had you previous experience working with Doug before that?*

Rich: No, I met Doug, and he was very strange. There were very few people stranger than me—I thought—but here was a guy that was really out there, and I started talking to him, and he was getting started doing some writing at Marvel, so I can't remember if I went to visit him, or if we went out to lunch, or whatever, we hit it off right away. I wanted to work with somebody new. I just kept this thing about "new." That's why George Pérez came along, or any number of people that I've worked with that went on their own paths and developed… most of them became bigger stars than me. I never was out to be a comic book star.

CBA: *What did you want to achieve?*

Rich: For me, it was the art, and it always has been.

CBA: *George showed his portfolio to you?*

Rich: Yeah, he was a friend of a friend of my wife. Because of that, he was invited to come over to my house, and I took a look at his work. He seemed likable, and I needed an assistant, and I can't remember taking him all that seriously. At one point, I was probably even abusive. That's how he got his break, though knowing somebody who knew my wife, who coincidentally knew me [laughs], she twisted my arm, and that was it.

CBA: *Did you have a literal studio set up in your house, where you had a couple of drawing tables, where another person could come in?*

Rich: No, no. Everybody did everything at their own homes. I never had any kind of a workshop. Although, at one point, when Klaus got started, I had an office at Marvel Comics. I was the only artist at the time there (other than their regular staff people) who had their own office. That developed sort of accidentally. One side of the building was being worked on—at least that floor—and it was all empty, and they hadn't figured out what to do with it. There was an empty space that had been there for months, and so I asked John Verpoorten if I could set up some kind of a drawing situation over there, and he said, "Sure." A couple of artists followed me afterward, but that's how I got my own office.

CBA: *You just took it? Squatter rights? [laughs]*

Rich: Right, I just got it there. Eventually, they moved Tony Isabella back there, and once they let the editor-writers in, that was it, it went to Hell. [laughter] That's the only time I ever had a studio situation, but it never really was set up where assistants could work next to me. More often than not, the assistant work, I would take the pages after they did it, and I would just get out the eraser and redo stuff, and cursed them out. "Why did I do this?!?"

CBA: *With the original Deadlock concept, did you see it as a science-fiction novel?*

Rich: Yeah, I wanted it as a s-f novel, and as a movie, and of course, I was mistaken in that my agreement with Marvel Comics was not really all that good. I was supposed to share in the percentage. I had a percentage of participation of profits from a novel or movie version of this; but not ownership of any kind in the actual property.

CBA: *Not even acknowledgment?*

Rich: Not even anything that stipulated that I should get credit, they wouldn't even give me that, although unofficially, they told me I could put credit in there wherever I wanted, which was altered whenever they felt like it, too.

CBA: *When it was reprinted?*

Rich: Right, either reprinted or when other people worked on the character, there was never any mention that Doug or I had worked on it, or that I created the character, or anything!

CBA: *What was Doug's contribution to the character?*

Rich: It was more than just writer and dialogue, he helped to develop the character, as I said earlier. Probably it should've been "Co-created by Doug Moench and Rich Buckler." That's probably how it should've read, but me being such an egomaniac, I took all the credit; but I was trying to get that novel/movie thing going, and I was determined to use my "star" status to get something I really wanted.

CBA: *Those are very prominent credits for mid-'70s books.*

Rich: It was actually unprecedented. I went nuts, I put my name on there "A Rich Buckler Production," just like the movies, I wanted to be Cecil B. DeMille. I thought, "If nothing else, this'll get other artists started to do this stuff, and they'll grab credit." The more credit you can grab, the better. The only thing that helps you with credit, at least that I've discovered, is that first of all, it makes you

look important. It helps you get your next assignment, and there's no question what you worked on. It wasn't more than a few years before I got into the business where most guys didn't even sign their work or were even allowed to! You'd get a lot of anonymous stuff that way. Hey, you want to work anonymously, get into commercial art!

CBA: *Was that the mistake? Do you think in hindsight, that you could've pushed for a piece of the comic pie?*

Rich: Marvel didn't want to make any kind of a decent deal, and I just wanted to create a new character, I wanted it to happen. So I went for the crappy contract they gave me, and I was naive and a bad business person.

CBA: *Are you sympathetic with Marv Wolfman's plight with Blade?*

Rich: With the movie? Absolutely.

CBA: *It sounds totally parallel.*

Rich: And Steve Gerber, and anybody else who's created something and feels they should get something afterwards.

CBA: *Did you, through litigation, try to…?*

Rich: I sued them. I didn't win, I lost, but then I appealed, and they made a settlement, and that's about all I can say about it.

CBA: *Oh, I see. This was connected with the revival of the character in the early '90s?*

Rich: Yes. There's no one person for me to get mad at, so it's not like I can say, "Those bastards!" There wasn't any specific individual

Above: Page to the '90s unfinished "Death Machine" story drawn by Rich. The artist intended to have Roy Thomas dialogue, and the character was, "a version of Deathlok—an updating. But I lost interest after unsuccessfully shopping the concept around." Art courtesy of and ©2000 Rich Buckler.

Panel text: VIRTUAL REALITY INTERFACE COMPLETE.

Panel text: TARGET LOCKED IN?

Panel text: GENTLEMEN... ...YOU ARE NOW WITNESSING CYBERNETIC TECHNOLOGY IN ITS MOST DYNAMIC EXPRESSION.

Panel text: MAN AND MACHINE ARE NOW ONE!

acting against me, nothing like that.

CBA: *It was the corporation?*

Rich: Right. Stan Lee, at one point, took it personally. He was so upset, he wouldn't even get on the phone with me. He had Roy Thomas call me on his behalf. I remember Roy calling me, saying, "Stan is really upset." I said, "Well, tough, I don't have anything against Stan. I just want what is fair."

CBA: *Was this in the beginning of this decade?*

Rich: That was in the '80s. I wasn't out to piss off Roy or Stan, or anybody. I don't treat people personally that way, I was just trying to defend myself, and get my character back, you know? But it didn't work; and I grew up by going through that experience, having some people pissed at me, and putting it through the legal machine.

CBA: *Were you surprised when it happened, or did you kind of know, looking at Siegel and Shuster's plight.*

Rich: No, I wasn't surprised at that point, I was pretty much grown up, knowing how things work, and how it would happen. I knew my lawyer was telling me what he should tell me, "Oh, the case looks great." Of course, it was doomed from the beginning!

CBA: *There's a very cinematic style to the issues of "Deathlok." Was it, literally, a storyboard for the potential movie?*

Rich: For me, it was as if it was already a movie, so it was very

much like storyboards.

CBA: *You were just visualizing the movie.*

Rich: Since I was the editor on the book, even though I wasn't paid to be editor, I pretty much did whatever I wanted to do.

CBA: *Do you see other properties that were developed that you see as incredibly similar to Deathlok?*

Rich: What do you mean? Since Deathlok?

CBA: *Yeah.*

Rich: Things that were influenced by it? In comics, or otherwise? Deathlok (as far as looks go) seems to be *the* prototype for *Cyborg*. I see it everywhere. Of course! It's as if nobody has any of their own ideas about it, but no one wonders who created it in the first place.

CBA: *Did you achieve what you wanted with Deathlok?*

Rich: Oh, absolutely. Except it didn't sell well, and I didn't understand that. I thought if I put everything into something new, and it has incredible energy, and it's fresh and innovative, it'll fly. But it won't, necessarily. It had a comeback there in the '80s, but didn't benefit me at all. They didn't even invite me to work on it! That sucks, but that kinda goes with the territory, too. You expect that.

CBA: *Did you read the character when it was resurrected?*

Rich: No, I never much paid attention to it. I did find out that they turned him into somebody non-violent, and it was a different person, and I thought, "Gee, what was the point in doing that? Doesn't it negate the concept and undermine the character?" So, I just ignored the whole thing; but I was probably at the time so much into what I was doing with whatever that was, that's why I wasn't paying attention to it. I tend to be pretty self-absorbed most of the time in whatever project or work that I'm doing.

CBA: *Did you ever feel any reason to be suspect of the sales reports that you were receiving? Was it just a* fait accompli?

Rich: They never shared sales figures with me, and they never felt obligated to. I don't think the contract stipulated that, even. It just wasn't done. Heck, there was no precedent for my deal with them! I don't even know why they gave me the deal!

CBA: *Well, you were a popular artist, right?*

Rich: What it was is, I was working on their most popular book, *Fantastic Four.* I was a comic book superstar at the time, which I didn't know. Because I was working on their top books, they gave me a side project to do whatever I wanted; but I started to edge off on the best-seller that I was working on, and put more time onto this, and of course, you do that and pretty soon you lose your status, and the whole thing kind of falls apart.

CBA: *So when Peter Gillis wrote a letter to* The Comics Journal *that said that you were told… it said you were told to draw like Kirby. Was that so?*

Rich: I never heard that. With my attitude, no one could tell me to do anything. [*laughter*] So, forget about it, I did whatever I wanted. Also, they got used to my attitude, and that's how I got away with the outrageous things I did, like getting George Pérez into the system, and Klaus Janson; and after a while, just about anybody I worked with got right in! They just went along, they said, "Well, if he's working with Rich, he must be something," and he was just right through the door! I got spoiled, but no one told me I had to do this, or I had to do that.

CBA: *I recall in* The Fantastic Four *you started out pretty much in what I say would be your style, then there was an almost complete Kirby pastiche.*

Rich: There were people who said I had no style, or people that would think I had no drawing ability—which is ridiculous, because I could do so many different styles—it would bother me when I heard that, but it was obviously from ignorance. So it bothered me for a few minutes, and that's it.

CBA: *You were really trying to recapture the Kirby…*

Rich: Oh, I went totally into it, to try to do a Kirby-like style that captured more of the vitality of Kirby than anyone else did. It was an ego thing, definitely. It was a "Hey, look at me!" kind of thing. I can do this! But I did it, and I had fun with it, and then I dropped it.

CBA: *Did Jack ever mention it when you were doing it?*

Rich: Oh, I got in trouble at one point. I took some pages that Jack had done on *The Double Life of Private Strong,* the Shield for Archie Comics, and I reworked his pages, like a six- or eight-page story, and a few other pages from another story, and I boiled it all down to like two pages. I signed it as my work, and somebody gave me some flak about that, because it was all Kirby lifts, very, very close. Which was a strictly fan thing for me, and I probably shouldn't have signed my name to it. That time, I got in trouble; but I didn't mean to piss off Jack about it, or steal anything from him. In fact, someone pointed it out, and I remember contacting Jack about it, and no, he wasn't upset. If anything, he was complimented.

CBA: *Was that a knee-jerk reaction for you to sue* The Comics Journal *when they accused you of plagiarizing?*

Rich: Oh, I sued *The Journal* because they called me a racist and a plagiarist, and it was mainly the racism thing that bugged me.

CBA: *But you dismissed the suit.*

Rich: But to call me a plagiarist, too, is to accuse me of not loving the comics, not loving the art, not having any respect for it, and that is just not the case.

CBA: *So you regret now that you signed your name to* The Shield *work that was virtually a complete lift from* Private Strong?

Rich: But that wasn't part of their case.

CBA: *Well, you were the one who was suing, right?*

Rich: Right. I mean, that wasn't part of their defense or whatever; actually they did some really dirty moves in order to discourage me, and I just dismissed the case. Then they ended up apologizing on Page 412 or whatever. That was a sorry experience. However, if anybody attacks me, I'm going to defend myself. I feel a person should be the best person they can be, but when it comes to my art, I feel absolutely my integrity should be defended… with my last breath, I would defend it! I love being an artist, and everything that I do is probably for artistic reasons first, and damn the business side, which has been a little bit of my undoing.

CBA: *How do you, overall, look at your comics career? Like you said, it's a training ground for what you're presently doing.*

Rich: You know what? Recently I went to a comics shop, and there was this *Comic Book Index,* and I looked at the John Buscema entry and the listing was huge. Then, I looked at my section, which was fairly near it, and it was almost as large! I couldn't understand that! That bugged me out! [*laughter*] I did all that? All I can say is I take the blame or the credit, if you liked it or if you didn't like it, whatever. I was totally into it, I was obsessed, and totally into it, and that's why I did it. I don't regret anything.

CBA: *Were you discouraged with Marvel? Did you move on from Marvel in the mid-'70s? Were you out of business opportunities?*

Rich: Well, there were power things going on over there, from different people. I think at one point, depending on which week you came in, there was a different person who was Editor-in-Chief, and that was ridiculous.

CBA: *Right, the revolving door.*

Rich: So I just couldn't deal with it anymore. My best days there were when Roy Thomas was the editor, and the Editor-in-Chief. Then, for a brief period of time there, when Gerry Conway was Editor-in-Chief. I don't think Gerry was ever comfortable with the job, but he was cool. After that, it was just a lot of people…

CBA: *Were you creator or co-creator of Devil-Slayer or Demon-Slayer? Wasn't Demon-Hunter based on Devil-Slayer?*

Rich: Based on what?

CBA: *There was a character over at Atlas/Seaboard called Demon-Hunter.*

Rich: Yeah. There was Demon-Hunter who I created at Atlas.

CBA: *It seemed very much like Devil-Slayer that was over…*

Rich: Right. It was the same character. I went over to Marvel, then, and since Atlas wasn't going to do anything with the character, I put it in the "Deathlok" continuity.

CBA: *Were you a Blue Öyster Cult fan?*

Rich: Big time.

CBA: *Did you get to meet the band?*

Rich: No, I never did.

CBA: *They're comics fans, aren't they?*

Rich: I never got to meet them. In fact, I met few rock personalities when they came up to Marvel. Each time I'd miss them. I know David Bowie's been there. I know there are a few comics fans in rock 'n' roll… I'm a big rock enthusiast, I love rock 'n' roll, I'm practically an encyclopedia when it comes to the music, the knowledge about the music, and I didn't get to meet any of the personalities. There was one point where Roy Thomas had an opportunity to do a project with John Lennon, and he was trying to set up a meeting, and it looked like that was going to happen. At the last minute, that fell through, and shortly after that, two months after that, John Lennon was killed. I didn't get to meet anybody.

John Byrne's Early Marvel Years
Marvel's Superstar Artist on his Humble Beginnings

Conducted by Jon B. Cooke

After a notable stint at Charlton Comics in the mid-'70s, artist John Byrne blasted onto the Marvel scene like a bombshell, and he became a true superstar artist in short order, developing a devoted fan following with his memorable work on The X-Men. Regarded for his revampings of Superman, Wonder Woman, and more recently, Spider-Man, John remains an enormously popular—and often controversial—creator. This interview was conducted through electronic mail in June, 1998.

Comic Book Artist: *After attending a Fine Arts program in college, previous interviews have revealed that you showed work around to the major publishers in New York in the mid-'70s. Do you recall your trip to Marvel? Any anecdotes to share?*

John Byrne: I was at Marvel the first time in 1971. It was part of a trip to New York my parents bought me for my 21st birthday. (Wait! Surely, that must have been my *11th* birthday!) I remember being very turned off by the Marvel offices. Compared to DC, which I visited earlier the same day, they were small, crowded, and seemed not altogether clean. The whole bullpen, which was pretty much the whole office, was not much bigger than my front hall is now, and Stan Lee (who was not there) and Roy Thomas had tiny little shoebox offices just off that area. The bullpen was cheek-by-jowl with artists at drawing boards, doing paste-ups and art corrections. When I was introduced to Roy he gave me a distributor's bundle of the new *Savage Tales* black-&-white, which had not come out in Canada at the time. I took it home and promptly passed out all but a single copy to my friends.

CBA: *What kind of samples did you show around?*

John: I had a homemade portfolio full of stuff I had clipped out of my sketchbooks, plus the original art for some humor strips I'd done while at the College—bits and pieces of everything, basically, with no real super-hero continuity stuff for anyone to get a fix on.

CBA: *You also mentioned that you were a "lapsed" fan after turning 15. Was it easy getting back into the habit? Any comments on the post-Kirby Marvel books of the '70s?*

John: In those days you could walk away from comics for years, as I did, and still be able to come back and, within the space of a couple of issues, figure out what was going on. Storytelling was important, more important than splashy pictures, and almost every writer followed the standard rules of the time, letting us know all the who, what, where, when, and most especially why of every tale, every issue. I remember the only thing that had me scratching my head for a little while was the question, "Who the heck is Galactus??"

CBA: *Were you specifically a super-hero fan or did you also have an interest in the other genre books—war, mystery/horror, humor?*

John: I used to read westerns and some of the "kid" books. I read *Casper* and *Spooky* up until I was about 14—and I read *Archie* stuff—but, mostly, it was super-heroes. All DC first, then a gradual shift over to Marvel once I discovered them around 1962.

CBA: *You've mentioned that while DC had the strength of great characters/archetypes, Marvel dominated because of the strength of its stories. Can you elaborate on that?*

John: It's pretty much that simple: DC had the best characters, Marvel had the best stories. DC stories were very much "gimmick" oriented in those days. They were not really stories, so much as they were devices by which something odd could be done to the characters. Marvel, on the other had, had characters who were deliberately less iconic than their DC counterparts, but the effort invested in the stories more than balanced any lack—small as that was—in "oomph" in the characters themselves.

CBA: *As you were doing increasing work for fanzines, were you becoming more attuned to the industry? Did you perceive non-ownership of characters you would potentially create as a problem?*

John: Never occurred to me. Personally, I think it's a bit of a paper tiger. I guess it would have been nice and good if people like Stan Lee and Jack Kirby and Steve Ditko could have had a "piece of the action," but at the time it never seemed to bother them. Maybe they learned the lesson of Bob Kane, who *did* keep a piece of Batman, and was generally reviled for being a money-grubber. A definite lose-lose situation, if ever there was one.

Above: Probably John Byrne's trademark character (after Rog 2000, natch!), Wolverine. John's inked drawings in this section are all from photocopies (received anonymously by CBA) taken from a stolen Byrne sketchbook, pilfered the artist said, in the early '80s. Art ©2000 John Byrne. Wolverine ©2000 Marvel Characters, Inc.

Right: Sam Maronie's photo of the increasingly popular artist John Byrne—taken, actually, just before his sojourn over to Marvel. Here the then-Charlton artist is signing program books at the 1975 Seuling con. Courtesy of the photographer.

CBA: *Did you retain any ownership of your Charlton work?*

John: I didn't create any of the characters I worked on at Charlton, so, no.

CBA: *Did you think of your stay at Charlton as a training period until you broke into Marvel?*

John: Very much. Charlton was a good place to be, in those days. It's a great pity there are not more places like that today, where artists can develop their craft and their own "voice." Today the sausage factory seems to rule the industry more than it ever did in the past.

CBA: *Did you visit the other publishers on your second go-around? DC? Warren?*

John: Not sure I understand the "second go-around" reference. I visited Marvel, DC and Warren all on that first New York trip, in '71.

CBA: *How did you break into Marvel? Were you and Duffy trying to break in as a team?*

John: Duffy was certainly trying to sell us as a team. I was not so sure, but figured as long as he was there, in the Marvel offices, if it got my work attention, if it lead to my getting assigned to something, having Duffy along would not be so bad. I was not all that thrilled with his inking over my pencils, but I could certainly imagine worse fates—like not getting work at all!

CBA: *If memory serves, your first break came with "Iron Fist" in* Marvel Premiere. *Did you have an affinity for the character?*

John: I had been reading "Iron Fist" since it first came out, though I had not paid much attention to the few issues immediately preceding my getting the assignment. Of course, "Iron Fist" was my break at Marvel. I'd been with Charlton about a year when it happened.

CBA: *How would you characterize your early years at Marvel? Did you feel that you were making an impact with the fans right off the bat? Was fan reaction a concern with you?*

John: Then, as now, the first ones who react, by writing fan letters say, are the ones who *hate* the work, whatever it is. It was always disturbing to me that the first dozen letters would come in and the universal reaction would be "This sucks!" (or whatever it was we said in the '70s!). A few days later the *good* letters would start to trickle in, and they would inevitably come to outnumber the bad manifold, but I always used to wish there was some way I could get the ones who *like* the stuff to voice their opinions as fast as the ones who *didn't*.

CBA: *In interviews, you seemed to look at comics publishing as a growing field when, as a matter of fact, the readership was shrinking dramatically and mass-market distribution was significantly reduced over the decade. How do you assess the '70s in retrospect? Was the direct sales market a lifeboat for an otherwise "dying" industry or might have decisions for different methods of mass distribution been more wisely chosen?*

John: I think the growth I saw was more creative than commercial. In the mid-'70s, for the first time in a while, there was an explosion of creativity in the industry. Things were really happening in a big way, and there was a genuine enthusiasm for the work. Had to be. We were all getting pretty much slave wages in those days, so the only satisfaction we got was from a job well done. (Another one of those things which have been lost, mostly, and to the detriment of the art form.)

CBA: *What is your memory of the "creation" of the New X-Men?*

John: I remember hearing bits and pieces. I remember Duffy getting me to do some pinups to "audition" for the book. I think the only thing that came about as a result of that was Len Wein deciding to put Banshee in the group, 'cause Duffy was pushing for him. Certainly, I had no real input on the "creation," since I was 3,000 miles away and pretty much an unknown.

CBA: *How did you receive the assignment?*

John: Dave Cockrum left, I threatened people with death and/or dismemberment if the book did not come to me.

CBA: *How much did you develop the characters? Was it an equal collaboration with Claremont?*

John: Hard to say. I ultimately left the book because I did not like the way Chris was taking some of the characterizations. I sort of woke up one morning, realizing that I did not like what Chris was doing, and since what Chris was doing was what was seeing print, that meant I did not like the characters. So I left.

CBA: *Overall, how would you now assess the Claremont/Byrne/Austin team?*

John: An amazing synergy. The *whole* was very much greater than the *sum* of the *parts*. Chris and Terry, in their separate crafts, come from very different places than I do—I don't write like Chris, I don't ink like Terry. Yet when we were all added together there was an undeniable magic. Perhaps not *quite* so much as the *legend* which has grown around that time, but definitely something special!

CBA: *Did you do most of your work through the mail? When did you move to the States?*

John: All my *X-Men* work was done long distance. I quit the book in September of 1980, and moved to the States in November.

Above: *The First Family of Mutants: The X-Men by John Byrne (circa 1978). Art ©2000 John Byrne. X-Men ©2000 Marvel Characters, Inc.*

CBA: *On your visits to the Bullpen, what was the atmosphere?*

John: Variable. Then as now, there were many factors at work, and sometimes it would seem like the gates had come off an asylum somewhere, others it would seem like the gates had slammed shut on a prison. And just about every increment in-between!

CBA: *Marvel went through a number of Editors-in-Chief. Was it disheartening to see such a revolving door of editors coming and going?*

John: It seemed like Marvel had come unstuck, in those days. That it was on the verge of becoming a stumbling giant. The one thing that can be said about the Jim Shooter who became Editor-in-Chief (as distinct from the Jim Shooter who was fired) is that he brought order out of chaos, gave the whole company a form and a direction.

CBA: *Did you deal with Stan Lee or Roy Thomas at all? Any memories?*

John: I had no editorial contact with Roy, and only one "audience" with Stan, back then. That latter was a hoot. I was— and am—in awe of Stan. I remember him looking over my work—I think it was an issue of *Iron Fist*— pointing out some things he felt I should do differently, calling in John Romita to add his own comments. It was exhilarating and debilitating, at the same time!

CBA: *Do you recall the opinion held of Jack Kirby's later-'70s work by Marvel staffers?*

John: I remember Jack being called "Jack the Hack." I remember pages of his stuff being posted on various office doors with all the funky phrasing and misplaced *bold words* indicated, derisively. There was very much a "Sure, but what have you done for me *lately*" attitude then. That's not surprising, since the industry is notorious for not taking care of its own. We eat our young and abandon our old. Still, I'm glad Kirby lived long enough to see his work recognized for what it really was, to see his contribution to the industry celebrated in his lifetime.

CBA: *On your first stay at Marvel, are you satisfied with your body of work? Did you accomplish what you set out to do?*

John: I've always said—still say— that there is not a single piece of work out there of which I am ashamed in any real way. Everything I have done was and is the best work of which I was capable under the

circumstances. I can look back at the Marvel work from those days and think "Sure am glad I've learned to *draw* since then!" but I don't feel embarrassed by any of it. People still come up to me at conventions with ancient work, expecting me to cringe, and I normally don't. A body of work, after all, is more important that the individual parts, and I'm pretty proud of the stuff I've done at Marvel down through the years. Proud to have been a part of the whole thing. Proud to have my name more or less permanently associated with characters like the Fantastic Four and Captain America.

CBA: *Was it fun to work for Marvel? Do you have any favorite memories?*

John: It was mostly fun. During the darkest days of the Shooter reign there were still moments of intense exhilaration—a sense of accomplishment when we were able to do it *right,* not just do it Shooter's way. Erase the frustration and anger over the creative hammerlock he put on everything he could, and you might say the whole period becomes a "favorite memory." Certainly, working on *FF* shines above all as a dream come true.

Above: *John's version of The Black Widow. ©2000 Marvel Characters, Inc.* **Right inset:** *Self-portrait of the artist. ©2000 John Byrne.*

Right inset: *Unused and unfinished X-Men cover by John Byrne. Courtesy of the artist. X-Men ©2005 Marvel Characters, Inc. Art ©2005 John Byrne.*

Mark Hanerfeld: Abel with Cane
The late Assistant Editor on his DC days in a 1998 interview

Conducted by Jon B. Cooke

[On January 4, former DC assistant editor and longtime comics fan Mark Hanerfeld passed away. Mark was instrumental in helping to prepare the first issue of Comic Book Artist *and he granted us an interview on February 15, 1998, which appears below. The talk reveals a comics fan who delighted in small (and often unheralded) achievements and one who truly loved the form. This phone interview was copy-edited by Mark.]*

Comic Book Artist: *Did you write letters to DC?*
Mark Hanerfeld: I wrote one in 1961 to Julie Schwartz, which was printed in *Justice League of America* (for which he sent me the art to a previous issue), and I started sending in letters that were illustrated because I thought I might become a cartoonist. So he asked me to come in and we looked over my art, which I agreed was not up to snuff. I then started sending in cover ideas to Julie, and the first one he used was the cover to *Green Lantern #29* featuring Blackhand.

I also started going in the office with other fans. I met Len Wein, Marv Wolfman and a few other fans at the 1965 Comic Con, Dave Kaler's show. We used to go up together into the DC office every Thursday when they would have a tour and within a couple of weeks, I started hosting the tour myself and got very used to being with the people around there. I almost forgot about it, but Robert Greenberger (who later became an editor at DC) reminded me that I'm the guy who showed him around the library and showed the bound copies of *The Brave and the Bold* with the first JLA stories. He was floored, but to me it was normal stuff at that point.

I also wrote a letter to Julie's *Strange Adventures,* but that was when he had a rare issue with not enough letters for the lettercol. I used the pseudonym "Charles Nussbaum" for that issue, but by that time I was at the office every week.
CBA: *Was it formal? Did you dress up in a jacket and suit?*
Mark: Oh, yeah! Always in a suit and I wore it to the office until Carmine began as editorial director. He took off his jacket when he was among the creative staff. It was an Emancipation Day!
CBA: *Were you looking to work in comics?*
Mark: Well, Julie said my stuff wasn't up to snuff and I agreed. I sent two Batman scripts, for which he sent me a edited, old Batman script by Gardner Fox to show the proper form for writing comics. I tried selling, unsuccessfully, a few scripts to Tower and, in the meantime, I picked up writing the regular assignment "On the Drawing Board" for Bob Schoenfeld's fanzine, *Comic Reader*. The problem was that he would cut down on all of the DC news, especially information on the Superman titles. I went to every company to get news; Marvel, Archie, Tower, Gold Key, and even Milson, but he didn't particularly like DC. So, on my own, I started doing "On the Drawing Board" as its own fanzine and ended up getting *The Comic Reader*. I kept that going for about a year or so but then I got involved in the tour at DC and was asked to write a couple of columns that were floaters (appearing in every magazine), "The Wonderful World of DC Comics" and "Fact Files." Those columns were eventually cancelled and Joe Orlando asked me to become his assistant editor. That's about when I sold *The Comic Reader* to Paul Levitz. I stayed with Joe for some years and also helped other editors here and there.

E. Nelson Bridwell and I shared an intimate knowledge of the DC Library—heck, going through the bound copies was like a vacation in

WRIGHTSON

DC Historyland!—and I was asked to do emergency jobs when they went up to the 25¢ larger size… Julie Schwartz needed back-up features, and I picked out the Golden Age Sandman and Starman reprints in *JLA #94*. I immediately recommended the cross-adventure tale of Aquaman-Green Arrow story from *Adventure Comics* for the first 25¢ *World's Finest* for Murray… I chose a lot of initial material for the *DC Special*s and the *100-Page Super Spectaculars*. Nelson did most of those books, but I did Orlando's that featured weird material. I really enjoyed picking out the contents of the first *100-Page Super Spectacular Weird Mystery*. With the four new frontis pages by Bernie Wrightson in that issue, I think it showed some of the wide range of different angles that can be done with that field. With the *DC Special* title, the third issue was originally slated to be

Above: The late Mark Hanerfeld served as the model for House of Secrets *host, Abel. Here is a Bernie Wrightson cover depicting the character from* House of Secrets *#103. ©2000 DC Comics, Inc.*

the Joe Kubert issue, but it was really late. I had gone home Friday for the weekend, when I got a phone call from Joe Orlando and Carmine. (Normally, I'd be at the office by 7:00 in the morning, and drive home around 7:00 in the evening—a personal choice; I hated bucking traffic!) So Joe and Carmine told me that Kubert couldn't do his issue on time and they came up with this cover to *DC Special* #3 with 13 mystery weird tales and a bunch of kids on the cover by Neal Adams. Could I do the lineup for the issue by Monday? I said, "13 stories?" Yeah! "In an 80-page package?" Yeah!! Well, thank the collector in me, as I went through my own collection at home, ferreting out 13 tales of varying lengths of two-, three-, four-, and six- and eight-page stories, added all the then-existing weird-book hosts from the DC weird mystery magazines, added a group of youngsters, and fabricated a yarn tying all together, and delivered the finished job Monday morning! It was under the gun, but I really enjoyed doing that job.

I vaguely remember helping Dick Giordano pick out the "Love: 1970" stories in that *Super DC Special*. Also, I think I helped on the *100-Page Super Spectacular Young Romance* issue; and the premise of the "Cowboys and Aliens" issue of *DC Special* #6 was mine.

I remember helping Murray Boltinoff put together the guts of *Stop! In the Name of the Law*. Murray used to work on the source magazines (*Gang Busters*, *Big Town*, etc.), but I brought in such unconventional choices as Fireman Farrell from *Showcase* #1. I think that of all the stories and alternatives I suggested, he replaced only one tale that he liked. I knew the material and what would be appropriate.

CBA: *You chose the reprints from DC's negative file?*

Mark: They had film negatives from about 1951 and on, occasionally missing a page here and there. For instance, when they reprinted a Martian Manhunter story they were missing a page from that issue of *Detective Comics* and so borrowed my own personal copy (in the process which they ruined, though they eventually replaced my copy).

CBA: *So you predominately worked for Joe Orlando until the early 1970s?*

Mark: Yeah, we had a very diverse line of books. At one point, we had six to eight books a month. We started doing *Korak, Son of Tarzan* as a 25¢ volume using "Carson of Venus" and "Pellucidar" as backup features. We used no reprints in the issues; it was all-new.

In the 48-page *Adventure Comics*, Joe and I put out about eight or more straight issues with a lot of reprints, but we were gearing up to use new stories written by Len, Marv, and a couple of other people and drawn by the Filipinos. Under my assistant editorship, we were able to do two issues with five stories per in that run, which is a really good package for a quarter. Unfortunately, I had to leave DC for a time just before those stories were to be assigned, (because my father had some personal troubles). Marv Wolfman took over the assistant editing and he had to change the contents that I had decided to put in the following issues, because they had to trim the contents when the line reverted to the old 32-page package.

In my plan, we settled on a 14-page Supergirl as the lead, followed with 10 pages for the second feature, and that followed

by two eight-pagers (replacing the 16 pages of reprints). We'd feature Vigilante, Black Canary and Animal Man, all rotated from one month having the second 10-page lead, and the next two months getting an eight-pager in the next two issues. It was a four-feature magazine and we discussed Zatanna as an alternate. We almost fudged the budget (using the Filipinos doing the replacement material) to try to make it so that if there was any good feature, we would try them out like in *Showcase*. It was a great idea, but it didn't work; they had to go back to the 32-pages for 20¢. I still believe in anthology comic books.

CBA: *Joe got Alex Toth to do the Black Canary two-parter.*

Mark: When the second part of that story came in the office, Neal Adams was right behind me when I opened the package and he ripped the pages out of my hands! Neal is a strange kind of guy with art—he absorbs art. I remember his comment about Toth did the impossible—he'd managed a black figure, standing in front of a black van, in a dark alley (on page one of that story).

CBA: *Joe did all the weird books. Even the super-hero books had a weird element creep in for a time. They obviously sold pretty well.*

Mark: Very well. That's why Marvel did *Tomb of Dracula* and other horror books. Carmine knew that super-heroes alone will not survive and that you have to do other things.

CBA: *Where did Carmine get the idea that Joe Orlando would make a good editor?*

Mark: Don't forget that Shelly Mayer knew that artists have certain types of talent and writers have different talents. Carmine, in the back of his head, knew that he had to balance the literary types and artists together. The idea of using artists as editors was very plain, very logical; half should be literary people and the other half artists, if only because otherwise you would have the same product. The idea was to use the best talent of your people. The idea was to make sure that the books are not static and not the same old material as before.

CBA: *Whose idea was it to start the EC-type mystery books?*

Mark: It was Carmine's idea and one of the reasons he brought Joe along. Actually *House of Mystery* was a super-hero title with "Dial H for Hero" and *House of Secrets* had been cancelled. Giordano started *Witching Hour* and Murray Boltinoff took over *The Unexpected* and started *Ghosts*. (Murray occasionally outsold Joe's books.) He knew what to do. Joe came back from the EC days and brought his thinking processes (the use of the hosts), while Murray was always looking for something different. Murray was, in many ways, the most modern editor, as he'd look at a book and realize what sold it in the past and considered what can be done now. The diverse editorial styles at DC helped the line; whereas most of the comics today seem all alike. *Witching Hour* had terrific art but sales were the weakest of all the books. We even tried the gothic romances, *Dark Mansion of Forbidden Love* (they started out as 48-page comics), and they were very interesting. The first issue we did a novel-length story for 36 pages plus two or three pages of text. We actually finished off the story in prose. The second or third one—by Alex Toth—was a terrific art job, but overall gothic romances didn't fare very well.

CBA: *So was the plan to interest a women audience?*

Mark: Yes. The romance line was faltering and Carmine tried everything. I'm surprised he didn't resurrect Detective Chimp! (Maybe as the *Weird Science-Fiction Romance Adventures of Detective Chimp?*)

CBA: *Did you work on Adventure Comics when it took on the weird format?*

Mark: No. I'd left the position because of my father's troubles. For a while, I used to go up to the office once or twice a week, just to keep in touch.

As far as Joe's books go, what he used to have is a heckuva lot of stories in inventory in preparation of his mystery books going from the bi-monthly to monthly status. Carmine decided to push the weird books because he didn't have the faith in super-heroes as the only comic books. Joe's attitude with the mystery books were that they had been done well by EC before.

Now Gold Key/Dell used to have their books in the drawer a year in advance as a normal, everyday practice, and in the '40s DC had a heavy inventory of their lead characters—Superman, Batman, The Flash/Hawkman, Green Lantern—that was pretty much a year ahead too. (Julie Schwartz once told me that his first assignment for Shelly Mayer was to "Put together an issue of *Flash Comics* by choosing the art out of the drawer!" Get a good balance of the magazine characters and put together a cover for that issue.) The best way to publish is to have at least three or four complete issues in the drawer. Joe worked that way on the mystery books. One time he said, "Let's do an issue about snow," and we did the cover, "Sno' Fun" for *House of Mystery; and* we went through the drawers looking for any material with a snow-oriented story as Joe kept an awful lot of inventory. A lot of the stories in *House of Mystery* were changed with stats of Cain replacing Abel—sometimes the opposite.

CBA: *Is there a resemblance with a certain mystery host and you?*

Mark: Yeah! Abel in *House of Secrets* is based on me and I have Joe's original sketch. He took two rolls of film just shooting me with every expression that I could come up with. I became a vaudevillian, mugging all the emotions and nuances of facial language. The strange thing is that I could never portray fear! I was still wearing a suit to the office when Joe did the sketch, but then Carmine decided that only he had to wear suits, because he had to deal with the executives from "above," so I complied.

CBA: *When did you first meet Carmine?*

Mark: Initially when I went on the DC tour. Marv and Len—who wanted to be artists and had just done "The Conjurer" for *Castle of Frankenstein*—asked Carmine, who was at his drawing board, for advice, particularly in his use of hands in captions to direct the reader to something that is happening. He started telling them how to do the art and turned the page he was working on over, and started drawing all over the back. He has a habit of warming up by sketching stuff on anything just to get the feeling in his arm to get ready. He does it sometimes with pencil or pen and even sometimes colors it himself. Sometimes just for the heck of it!

CBA: *Did you receive much credit for your work?*

Mark: No. I never wanted credit. Carmine turned out books because he liked them, not for credit, and I followed his example. Nowadays, it seems that you have to run a regime, but back then there was free-flowing thought in the office and it was relaxed. Once in the coffee room, we took our break and we were goofing off. There was catered deli meat (I can't remember why) and Neal Adams asked for a piece of salami or bologna, so I grabbed one and threw it at him, which flew like a frisbee. We started laughing and throwing the frisbee food around, and Sol Harrison came in and said, "What are you *doing*?!?!" That was a fun day.

CBA: *Do you remember an incident with a $200,000 check of Mort Weisinger?*

Mark: I tried hard to be the only person at the office to *not* see that check and thought he put it in the bank months before. One day, he asked me for some help with scheduling or reprints in books, and closed his office door. So we sat down, and suddenly, midst business, he said, "By the way, have you seen my $200,000 check?" And I knew he had me! Ambushed! I was probably the last person in the office he got! As best as I could, I'd tried not to talk about it and it must have been six or eight or ten weeks since he got the check! *Ohh!* I was caught totally unaware.

CBA: *Mort really wanted out of comics?*

Mark: Well, he wrote that $200,000 book (which was entitled *The Contest,* about beauty competitions. I don't think it was ever published.) And he wrote that *1001 Things You Can Get for Free* book, which had something like 25 printings at that time, and I'm not sure why he retired but evidently the books had something to do with it.

CBA: *Do you remember an incident when Len and Marv were*

accused of stealing?

Mark: No. Maybe you're thinking of Sol Harrison who had two pages from *Danger Trail* #3 on his wall, a terrific art job by Alex Toth. I think this was back at 575 Lexington Avenue and one day he came in and they were gone. Len, myself, and Marv plus other fans were in the office at the time (we were still fans taking the tour). Now, Sol used to destroy the art—literally—and he'd take pages to the cutter and cut right across everything. He asked us to help. I said we would do it, only if we did it the proper way. We could cut it between the panels without actually destroying the art—we did an awful lot of that—and Marv and Len (and fans Stan Landman and Eliot Wagner) as well as myself, got a lot of pieces of unprinted Golden Age material that way. So it might have been suggested that they were stealing art but that's not so, I can guarantee you. I've known them more than thirty years. That's not their way!

We all got into the industry because we loved the comics. It used to be a challenging and fun place to be.

Above: *In collaboration with artist supreme Neal Adams, Mark Hanerfeld script the Tarzan comic booklet that accompanied the Aurora model kit in the mid-'70s. Tarzan ©2005 ERB, Inc.*

The Blue-Jean Generation

Inker Steve Mitchell talks about his '70s ups & downs

Conducted by Jon B. Cooke
Transcribed by Jon B. Knutson

There's a chance you might not have heard of Steve Mitchell—but he was there, in the thick of it, hanging with the Young Turks during the '70s: Working at Neal Adams' Continuity Studios, serving as a "Crusty Bunker," and he even had a job in DC's production department for a few years there. In 1972 he got his shot at the Big Time with an inking assignment on Gil Kane's pencils for Marvel Team-Up #4 *and… well… let's have the artist tell the story. Steve edited the transcript (conducted via phone on Sept. 20, 1999).*

Comic Book Artist: *When did you first get involved in comics?*
Steve Mitchell: It was probably about 30 years ago, believe it or not. I was a New York City fan, and I was one of the DC Comics' "Thursday after-lunch Mafia," with Len Wein and Marv Wolfman and a bunch of those other guys. I wasn't a crony of theirs, it was just that we kind of got to know each other because we kept bumping into each other on that DC Thursday after-lunch tour. I started going into town to try and meet these people who produced these books. They were my heroes, so I said, "Well, I live in New York, they're in New York, I want to go to the comic book factory and see how comic books are made." I think, like most guys, I was disappointed that the artists weren't actually working in the offices. Although there were always a couple of guys...
CBA: *Was Murphy Anderson there?*
Steve: Murphy was there a lot, I think, once I started to work at DC professionally; but when I was a kid, when they were over on 575 Lexington Avenue, the offices were not really artist-friendly. I think there were one or two places in the production department—which was a dark, dreary, windowless, foreboding environment. I mean, it kind of had a real Bat-Cave quality about it, [*laughs*] because there wasn't much daylight in there. I met Neal Adams in there. Jack Sparling was inking a *Strange Adventures* cover. I think Mike Sekowsky was actually working in the bullpen, but it might've been one of those things where he was doing a little work there on a delivery day. Curt Swan I think I bumped into as well, but there were no guys who really worked on staff. Carmine had his own office, it was his studio—I think they had it set up with him when he was art director. My first memories were that he was doing art-related stuff only at first, and then he got into larger areas which you have documented so perfectly and wonderfully later on. Anyway, I just

basically started going to those offices, and then I went to high school at a place called The High School of Art and Design, which a lot of comic book guys attended. At one time it was called the High School of Industrial Arts, before it was the High School of Art and Design. It was only a couple of blocks away from the 909 Third Avenue offices, so all during the 575 days, I was just a fanboy, and then at 909, I was still a fanboy, but I was a high school-aged fanboy who wanted to do comics. I remember—I think I was about 16—and I was up there bothering somebody, probably Dick Giordano, who's a good friend of mine and an influence, a mentor, and just a life-long friend... Sol Harrison, who was the Production Manager, came up to me and said, "If you're going to hang around, you might as well make some money." So, this was an Easter vacation. I think I was there on a Wednesday, so I came in for Thursday and Friday of that week. I was erasing pages, and delivering things, and Xeroxing stuff, and just doing art touch-ups. It was all grunt work. I was the happiest 16-year-old on the planet, I was actually where they were making comic books, and I wasn't a visitor. I was actually working there and getting paid, and it was the greatest thing in the world! I guess I didn't piss anybody off, because Sol Harrison asked me back the following Summer to work up there in a Summer job.
CBA: *What year was that?*
Steve: That was probably about 1970, or 1971.
CBA: *So Neal Adams was still there?*
Steve: Yeah, Neal was still there. In fact, Neal had that famous office across the hall from Julie Schwartz's office, the famous Murphy Anderson/Neal Adams Art-O-Graph clubhouse. Murphy and Neal went to work there every day, and it was their mid-town Manhattan studio. A lot of people would just stop by and hang out with those guys.
CBA: *Was Murphy in the same room as Neal?*
Steve: Yeah, they shared the room.
CBA: *Were they facing opposite walls?*
Steve: No, they were right next to one another, they were both facing one wall, Murphy had the drawing table in the inner part of the office, and Neal had the drawing table in the part of the office closest to the door, and that's where the famous Art-O-Graph was, where Neal would blow up his thumbnails and make such beautiful pencils.

I spent a lot of hours in that room, it was a good room to hang out in. It was just sort of magic being a kid and being around people whose comics I was still reading. I was getting to know these guys, and actually because of that relationship, and getting to know Neal in particular, it's my understanding that Neal lobbied for me to get my first ink job, which was *Marvel Team-Up* #4. I had done some background work for guys like Rich Buckler, who kept me very busy. I would work for him after school and on weekends.
CBA: *Do you remember what the work was for?*
Steve: That was DC stuff, it was just sort of general stuff... mystery stuff. I wanted like mad to be an inker. I'd worked towards that. In fact, when I was in the production department, I had done a number of samples over a number of guys, and apparently *World's Finest* was going to be penciled by Dick Dillin, and I heard they did not have an inker for that, so I said, "Okay, here's my chance." I'd done a number of samples, and I thought I'd done a nice job—I probably would look at them today and think they were terrible. But at the time, I felt pretty good about it.
CBA: *Who did you ink over?*
Steve: I got some Dick Dillin Xeroxes. The one thing that was

Above: Steve's debut as an inker was featured in Marvel Team-Up #4. ©2000 Marvel Characters, Inc.

great about being in the production department was I had access to everybody, and those pages had to get lettered before they could get inked, so I was able to get Xeroxes, and I think Julie Schwartz had Xeroxes in hand. Julie was so organized, he always had copies of everything. So, I managed to get some Dillin stuff, and did some inking samples over some Xeroxes of his pages, showed them to Murray, and Murray didn't want to have anything to do with me, because a) I was a kid, b) I was unproven, c) somebody else hadn't given me my first job…

CBA: *I don't think Murray ever gave anybody their first job! [laughter] He's legendary for that! "Has anyone else used you before?" he always asked.*

Steve: Yeah. I mean, it made sense! As a kid, I was a wanna-be, and I didn't understand it, but as an adult now, it makes a certain amount of sense. You have to understand something about Murray: Murray is probably every bit as professional as Julie Schwartz ever was, and Julie had this tremendous reputation for being a professional editor. So was Murray. Murray's attitude was, "Well, part of my job is to make sure I have other professionals working for me," and I think that meant, "Well, I don't know if the guy's professional unless I see published work, or I have some idea as to whether or not these guys can make a deadline." As far as I can remember, of all the various times I worked at DC in the production department, I don't think that a Murray Boltinoff book was ever late. Murray was a consummate, professional comic book editor. I don't always agree with his choices creatively, but in terms of how he did his job, Murray was a very, very professional guy.

CBA: *Right, and it's been pointed out he was DC's best-selling editor. They weren't enormously critically popular books, but they sold! Ghosts was, for a long time, one of their biggest books.*

Steve: Murray is one of the best-kept secrets in comics. I mean, he was never a show-bizzy kind of editor; I don't think he was really that interested in fans *per se*, but he was a very professional guy, he always did his work. He was so good at his work, nobody really knew he did it, in a sense, it was just always there! It was always here, it was always solid. I think his one shortcoming was his books were kind of colorless.

Anyway, getting back to my Murray Boltinoff inking story: They gave the job to Henry Scarpelli. Well, at the time, being a teenager full of hot air—and most people who know me think of me as an adult full of hot air—I said, "Henry Scarpelli?!? He's not a super-hero inker! He doesn't know anything about super-heroes! He's the *Binky* guy!" But, Henry Scarpelli was a grown-up, and a professional, and that's what Murray liked. I'm going to take a little sidebar to just get on the record with this, and say I was a member of what I call the "blue-jean generation." All the guys that preceded us were the "suit-and-tie generation." I mean, Murphy Anderson, to this day I think, still wears a suit and tie wherever he goes, and all those guys were commercial artists—they weren't comic book guys—they used to wear sports jackets, and ties and suits, and they looked like grown-ups. Then, all of us guys came in, and we were wearing blue jeans, and striped shirts, and we had long hair, and we were fans. We were really the polar opposite of what the expected professional in that business had been for 20-30 years. I think that if nothing else

gets in print, I just want to see the phrase "blue-jean generation," because we were the first generation to wear blue jeans to work. We were fans. That's the other thing: We were really devoted to the form, and wanted to be a part of it. It wasn't just a job.

CBA: *So, there was Scarpelli.*

Steve: Scarpelli did one issue, nobody liked it, and they gave it to somebody else, I don't even remember who it was.

CBA: *Frank McLaughlin?*

Steve: It might've been. Again, Frank had been working for Julie, but I'm not sure; but I do know Scarpelli did one issue. In a weird sort of way, I felt somewhat vindicated; but I never could get a job while I was working at DC in my first stint in production, as an inker. Then, after that Summer was over and I was going to college, Neal had lobbied for me with Roy Thomas to start working at Marvel. So I got a phone call—I believe it was from Roy—asking me if I would like to ink this *Marvel Team-Up #4*, which was going to be Spider-Man and the X-Men, and it was penciled by Gil Kane. Well, this is a major job in my life, not only because it was my first one, but because of all the repercussions of this job. I did the job, it took me probably about four weeks working at night… I mean, it was Gil Kane! I was so intimidated by this stuff, and I was very slow, because I didn't want to screw it up; but at one point, I think Holly Resnick called me up for John Verpoorten, said, "How's it going? We haven't heard from you in three weeks." I didn't understand how things worked. I didn't know that communicating with the office was part of the job. I think they thought I had vanished from the planet. I should have kept them up to speed with my progress. It was my first mistake. I should have let them know how I was doing, and whether they would receive the job on time. So, I inked the job, turned it in, and it met with very, very negative results. The job didn't go over. It didn't go over for John Romita, Sr., who gave me a critique of the job, and said, "Stan wouldn't like this, and Stan wouldn't like that," and there were a number of places where either Romita or Frank Giacoia had done some corrections. It's still fundamentally my job, but I think that on some of the big heads, they might've done some redos.

CBA: *Like the fat lady at the top of the stairs [on pg. 5]?*

Above: *Steve Mitchell self-portrait for "my Milestone trading card, circa early '90s,"* notes the artist. ©2000 DC Comics, Inc.

Steve: Exactly.

CBA: *That looks like Romita.*

Steve: That one in particular. It's either Romita or Giacoia, because Frank used to work on the Bullpen staff. I don't remember if he was there five days a week, however. Frank had a drawing table that he could always sit down and work at; but that was my last job at Marvel... actually, that's not true, I inked a *Sgt. Fury* cover over Dick Ayers, but I didn't get any more work from Marvel after that. They didn't like either job very much. My inking career was, as far as I was concerned, one of the great flame-outs of the 1970s. I had one job, they didn't like it...

CBA: *Were they specific about why they didn't like it?*

Steve: Well, the most specific response I got was, "Stan wouldn't like this," which I always believed to be something of a cop-out on Romita's part. Now, I'll say this: I really like John Romita, Sr., I think he's a great guy, a nice guy, and he's always been nice to me... but when it came to criticizing my work in that particular instance, he never said, "I don't think it works," or "This doesn't work for me because of such-and-such." It was just "Stan wouldn't like this," which even at the time, I felt was... "Why don't you just tell me you don't like it?" or "If it doesn't work for you, tell me what I can do." This is a job that has haunted me my entire life! [laughs]

CBA: *But looking at this job, I wonder if one of the criticisms was the fine line you used on the work. It's always been an outstanding splash to me.*

Steve: I worked like mad to try and do the best job I could. At the time, I learned from looking at other guys who I admired, and Tom Palmer was a guy whose stuff I really admired—I don't think I understood it, but I admired it. (When I say I didn't understand it, it's not because it was bad, or it was vague, it's that I wasn't sophisticated enough to know how good it was; but I tried to learn from it as much as possible.) My drawing table was littered with guys' stuff that I admired at the time. I just did the best job I knew how—I was scared to death! I was the youngest inker in comics in those days! At one time, I was the youngest kid in the comic book business. I was also probably one of the tallest guys in the business, but I was the baby of the litter; but the job didn't work out, and here's the ironic part: Jim Shooter, who gave me work later on in my career, always said, "I always liked that job." [laughter] Okay? He remembered it! You've just said, "I like that job." I find that astonishing! Everybody liked that job except, I guess, "Stan Lee" and John Romita, Sr.

Above and right: *In an issue otherwise penciled by George Tuska and inked by Vince Colletta, Neal Adams inked a likeness of his Continuity employee Steve Mitchell (regardless of the name tag) in a couple of panels from* Iron Man #72. ©2000 Marvel Characters, Inc.

Maybe Roy didn't like it, I don't know; but my career as an inker wa[s] over for years.

CBA: *The Giacoia stuff in there is jarring!*

Steve: It's that big, juicy, twice-up comic book ink line, which he was so fantastic at; but I was working on a contemporary-sized job, and a lot of guys I liked worked in pen. Now at the time, I was tryin[g] to use a brush, because Sinnott used a brush, Giacoia used a brush, George Klein used a brush—a lot of the guys who were really the best guys in the business were all very handy with a brush. Dick Giordano, of course, could make magic with a brush. So I said, "That's how I have to ink." Now, when I ink, most of the time I'll us[e] a dipping pen, I use a #170 or a #290, or anything that seems to strike my fancy at the time, and I can usually make a pen line look like a brush line; but at the time, I was making a brush look like a pen, and that's why that line was finer and thinner. Also, I was timid[.] I'd look at that stuff, and there's no confidence, no boldness, and I just look at that job... it has got so much baggage for me, but it's ironic that all these years later, people are saying, "Oh, yeah, that's [a] regarded job!"

CBA: *And then, by the turn of the decade into the '80s, I noticed in* The Comic Book Index, *you did a lot of comics work, right?*

Steve: I started working as a full-time freelancer at 26. I inked some Herb Trimpe stuff, *The Defenders*—which I think Al Milgrom was instrumental in giving me—and then, once I started working at Marvel, I would still hang around both offices, because it helped to get work. I don't know if you've talked with other guys, but both comic book companies were sort of the unofficial club houses for wayward freelance boys. [laughter] And that's ultimately what Continuity Associates became. After I couldn't have a career on my own as a freelancer, I went to work for Neal and Dick at Continuity. [I] was Giordano's first assistant (the first of many), and I was around for all of the Continuity stuff. I was a "Crusty Bunker"! I was one of the in-house Crusty Bunkers; we would have guys who would come to the studio, and Neal would ask, "Do you want to ink a panel?" to guys like Bernie or Kaluta or Jeff Jones or Ralph Reese... all kinds of guys. The Crusty Bunkers were the in-house guys—which were usually me and Alan Kupperberg—and then whoever... Alan Weiss... anybody who would come into the studio, Neal would say, "Do something!" That was the thing that was really fun. We used to do all of these jams. It was a very musician-like thing. God, I inked some spots of a Berni Wrightson job, I'm trying to remember if it was the first *Swamp Thing* job or not, I can't remember... I wish I had that book in front of me, because if I saw it, I would know; but anyway, it's not relevant. All of the young guys, the blue-jean generation, would share their work with one another at the DC coffee room at 909 Third Avenue on Friday. We would hang out with one another socially, and we would occasionally work at one another's houses, usually through the night, and jam or help guys out with stuff; sometimes for fun, sometimes for necessity! It was this really fraternal, communal environment, which was tremendous fun. My greatest frustration was that I wasn't freelancing, and being a freelancer with all these other guys when they were doing it!

I was the production manager at Atlas Comics for the first six or seven months of that year or so they were in business. I was hired b[y] Jeff Rovin. Prior to Atlas, I was Jack Adler's assistant at the DC production department, and Jeff—who I had known when he was a[n] assistant editor at DC—called me up and offered me this opportunity, and of course, I was young and full of myself, and I said, "Oh, yeah, I know how to do this job." In point of fact, I did— just probably wasn't as good at it as guys like Jack Adler and Sol Harrison; again, very unsung heroes of the DC Comics business. Jack was an amazing colorist.

CBA: *When you handed in the* Marvel Team-Up *job, they didn't give you any specifics about what you did wrong?*

Steve: Not a lot. I think generally speaking, everybody up there was disappointed by the job.

CBA: *So were you just crestfallen?*

Steve: *Crestfallen?* Crestfallen *squared!* You've got to understand something, this is all I ever wanted out of my life, was to be able to work in comics and to ink. I loved the brush, I loved the pen, I loved[ ]what the possibilities of what you could do with a line were. This wa[s] a pretty major blow for me, I'm surprised I wasn't staggering around[.]

the streets walking into taxicabs after it happened... I really don't remember what things were like after I sort of got this little critique from Romita. You know something? I have to tell you, I've looked at a lot of portfolios, and it's interesting: I can tell whether or not somebody's got the goods, literally, in five seconds. If you know your business, you can look at a piece of artwork and know whether or not somebody's got it. I guess Romita felt I didn't have it, and I guess he didn't want to spend as much time as he might've thought critiquing me! He might've said, "Well, this doesn't work, and that doesn't work, and this doesn't work, and that doesn't work," and he just basically went through the job fairly casually, and basically said, "Stan wouldn't like this, and Stan wouldn't like that." I don't think his heart was in it, and in point of fact, I think that—at that time—Marvel was less youth-friendly than DC was, and I think (and maybe I'm patting myself on the back) every time a young guy was shown not to have the goods, I think the older guys might've felt a little more secure. I don't know if that was the case with me in particular or generally, all I know is I didn't make the grade with that job, and I didn't get any more work from Marvel for many years to come.

CBA: *Did you try to get more work?*

Steve: Constantly! You know, I didn't give up, partly because I was still working for Neal at Continuity, I had jobs on- and off-staff at DC in their production department. I mean, had I not always wanted to be a freelancer, I probably could've worked at the DC production department forever. Bob Rozakis, who used to be in charge of the production department at DC, came into comics around the same time I did, maybe a couple of years later. Bob was the proofreader at DC Comics, and he wound up staying there for 25 years before he left. Had I really wanted a career in production, I could've had the same thing, but I really wanted to be a freelancer, because all my buddies were freelancers.

CBA: *The glamour.*

Steve: Such as it was. You know what I think it was, Jon? I think you could do something you wanted, get paid for it, and not have to be a grown-up. It was very appealing! Back in those days, we made enough money to get by. Nowadays, it's a little tougher than that, but in those days, everybody managed to get by. It was a fun way to live your life! It was the '70s, and life had fewer restrictions than it does today. We were doing things we were passionate about. Man, everybody loved doing comics in those days, and a lot of people would go and show their stuff to Neal because Neal was God, okay? If Neal would say, "Wow, this is good stuff"—if you got a "this is good stuff" from Neal—it's like smoking dope all day long! You'd be so high from that compliment because it was coming from God! [laughter] It was coming from the guy who we all wanted to be as good as!

But... Neal could be a ball-breaker. I've seen Neal savage guys' stuff and break hearts and bust backs; but, I guess Neal also knew you had to really have it to be in this business and make a living. In a sense, he was doing you a favor if you didn't have it. You might want to try some other line of work.

CBA: *Did you show the job to Neal, and ask his opinion of it?*

Steve: You know, I think I did. He probably said something like, "It's not as good as you'd like it to be, but it's probably not as bad as they think it is."

CBA: *Did you feel a little defensive? Did you feel that you did a good job?*

Steve: Let me put it to you this way: I was very intimidated, I worked very hard, I thought I did the best job I knew how at the time, being so green. Man, I was green—as green as an apple—but it wasn't like I was nonchalant about it! It wasn't like I was just knocking it out while hanging out with my buddies. I did the best job I could at the time. At the time, it wasn't good enough.

CBA: *Did you have a difficult time opening up that book after a period of time?*

Steve: Well, actually, when it was published and I looked at it, I didn't really have much of a problem at the time! I was actually so jazzed—I mean, there was my name! That was exciting to me! But it was just the fact that not long after I was so jazzed by that, that I wasn't getting any work, so I had to do assistant work, and background work, and work at Continuity. I tried my hand as a writer for a while—I don't know if you know this or not, but I wrote a handful

of war stories for Archie Goodwin, backup stories. Ken Barr drew two of them, and Dan Spiegle drew one. They were good stories. Archie Goodwin was the single greatest person I ever met in comics. As a human being, as an editor, as a guy who was fun to hang out with at parties. I used to bother Archie as a 12-year-old, and go visit him at the Warren offices, and Archie showed me nothing but warmth and courtesy. He would say, "If this kid thought it was important enough to come into the city to bother me to look at stuff, I'll show it to him." Archie always was great about sharing stuff. He was always in touch with that kid inside of him, and he showed me all that Warren stuff before it came out... I loved it! Archie was nice to me then, he was nice to me as an adult. I've never had a moment with Archie Goodwin that I didn't feel great about. Like everybody else, I miss him tremendously. Archie knew I was into war books and into movies, and he gave me a couple of chances. I wrote a couple of stories for him, and they turned out okay! He rewrote a number of things in those stories, but it was also an educational experience, because when I saw what he did with them, I said, "Oh, that's how you can make it better." But I lost interest in writing, though I don't really know why. I guess maybe I was busy making a living in production. I really wanted to make a living as a freelancer, every way I possibly could, and I couldn't. At one point when I was in my early 20s, I said, "Well, I guess I'm going to be on staff, I guess I'm going to work for Neal, I'm going to work some place in comics, I'm just not going to be one of those guys who gets his name in the book."

Above: *The splash page to Gil Kane and Steve Mitchell's art job on Marvel Team-Up #4.* ©2000 Marvel Characters, Inc.
Below: Steve notes: "Dedicated young production dept. 'professional' circa early '70s. The suit and tie were unusual… probably for one of DC's famous (at the time) Christmas parties." *Photo by Jack Adler. Courtesy of Steve Mitchell.*

Actually, I was on staff at DC, and I had done a few oddball ink jobs for Joe Orlando—I inked a couple of Bill Draut jobs and a couple of romance stories. I had done this one romance job which Orlando didn't like, and Vinnie Colletta was the art director at the time, and Joe said, "Well, have Vinnie give you some pointers, because Vinnie was a very good romance comic book inker." Vinnie was completely useless. In fact, when I asked him for some pointers, he acted like I was a mosquito buzzing him. I don't have a lot of great stuff to say about Vinnie, other than I liked the way he inked Jack Kirby on *Thor*.

Working in comics in the 1970s was a magical time, because there was a willingness on the part of both companies to experiment a bit—DC more than Marvel, but even Marvel was willing to try. They were willing to throw stuff against the wall to see if it would stick! They were always looking to try and do stuff that was going to find an audience, because they were in the entertainment business! That's one of the things that I don't think anybody ever talks about: People forget that comics were created to be a cheap form of entertainment, and I think somewhere along the way the cheap part and the entertainment part kind of got lost a little bit; but in the '70s, there was an opportunity for a lot of guys to break into the business with their areas of interest, and their enthusiasms, from movies and literature, pulps, and even television to some degree!

CBA: *By the late '70s, there was a void of quality, innovative stuff.*

Steve: Well, you know what happened? In the late '70s, I was already working pretty steadily then, everybody was starting to make a living, we were already starting to become grown-ups. In the '70s it was tremendous to be in the Bullpen, it was tremendous to be at DC. Every time I go back to New York—and I go back to New York with some frequency—if I walk past those 909 Third Avenue offices, I always smile. Those were fun offices. I know you've talked to people about the famous coffee room that was shared by Independent News and DC Comics; but there were more exchanges of fun ideas in that room than in maybe any other place in comics at that time. Maybe ever! You had a whole bunch of guys who were so hungry and so enthusiastic and we were all going, "Oh, let me see your stuff! What are you up to? Oh, great stuff! Oh, man, fantastic stuff!" (If I had a buck for every time I heard the word "stuff," I could go out and buy a very, very expensive dinner.)

But the thing is, there was a lot of enthusiasm, because as a freelancer, if you work at home, you're essentially working in a vacuum. The opportunity to go to DC and hang out with Neal, go to the coffee room and hang out with your peers, it was a chance to get out of the vacuum and have an exchange of ideas and thoughts. A lot of these guys were basically like musicians, they were riffing off one another. Somebody would be doing something interesting, and the other guys might bring that home with them, and that might be planted in their subconscious. We were really into learning from one another, and learning together! I mean, Sol Harrison created the Wednesday night life-drawing class. DC used to pay for a model, and in that coffee room, everybody would sit down and draw. It was fun and occasionally competitive, especially between guys like Neal and Joe Kubert. Sol felt that everybody would benefit from life-drawing classes, and it would help everyone with fundamental drawing. I don't think anybody's given Sol credit for that, but that was his idea!

I was also a Junior Woodchuck, I worked on *The Amazing World of DC Comics* fanzine. Again, that was a Sol Harrison idea. What happened was, Sol was getting requests for all kinds of stuff from a number of fanzines, and Sol (being Mr. DC, you know—he probably

had underwear that had the DC logo on it! [*laughter*]) was so devoted to the company and said, "Well, why don't we do a fanzine because we've got all these fanboys working on staff, and then we'll do a better fanzine than anybody else, because we have the professional production talent to really make these fanzines look great!" We got Joe Kubert to do covers, for crying out loud, amongst all the other great guys. So, for a while, the *Amazing World* fanzine was quite the definitive outlet for things about DC, because it was coming from the source! It wasn't second-hand, but was coming from New York City, from within the DC offices; but strangely enough, for a guy I thought hated fans when I first met him, he realized that the fans were also the future, professionally and in terms of the sales of the book. Sol, in his own strange sort of way, did these things to embrace the fan marketplace.

CBA: *The cover of* Marvel Team-Up: *Was that inked by Giacoia?*

Steve: Yeah, that was. I think if I'd inked the cover first, they wouldn't have given me the job.

CBA: *Was Giacoia the art director there at the time?*

Steve: You know, I don't really remember. I seem to recall he was kind of on staff at Marvel, and I think the reason was that Frank was one of the nicest, warmest, sweetest, friendliest guys I ever met. He was very nice to me, he was nice to everybody, he was the definition of easy-going; but I think Frank was a very slow inker, and I think that Marvel was very devoted to him personally, and I think they tried to find ways to help Frank continue to make a living, because I don't think he was fast enough to make it as a freelancer. Frank was there, but I don't know exactly what his function was at the time. I had some sort of vague notion that Frank was on staff, rather than being a freelancer sitting behind a drawing table up there.

You have to understand something: This *Marvel Team-Up* story brings back a lot of bad memories for me. One of the things I'd like you to understand is that this rejection crushed me! The non-acceptance of my work in the comic book business at that time was a crushing blow to everything I lived for. I don't mean to be melodramatic, but this was Major League Baseball for me, and I wanted to play the game! I wanted to go up there and I wanted to swing the bat every single day! But they took the bat out of my hands.

CBA: *Looking at it now, do you think you were ready?*

Steve: No, I wasn't. In all honesty, I wasn't. I probably needed to continue to work with other guys, I think I probably became ready once I had worked for Giordano at Continuity and had been around so much penciling and inking. Again, I learned how to do it in a vacuum. When I worked at Continuity and I was inking backgrounds and filling in blacks, and really working on pages, that's when I really started to learn how to do this stuff. You don't learn how to ink comics by inking Xeroxes with vellum tracing paper overlays, that's not working on the pencils! That's working on something that was a representation of the pencils. There's nothing like having a piece of Bristol board with carbon on it and you're taking a brush or a pen and actually working on it. There's no substitute for that. I really didn't have any experience like that. I had done some jams, I helped Alan Weiss and Bernie Wrightson. When I was trying to break in, I had very little experience, and very little opportunity to work on pencils. If I want to be really honest: No I wasn't ready. What I didn't have in terms of ability, I think I had in terms of enthusiasm and a sense of work ethic; but I just don't know if I had the chops then. It's very nice that people look favorably on that job, I just look at that as my first failure. It was a big failure, the repercussions of which I suffered from for years.

CBA: *Why are you talking about it now?*

Steve: Well, a lot of time has elapsed. I guess it's maybe like a little closure for me, although I got the closure years ago. I've been a working comic book inker for a long time. I'm actually sort of good at it now, and I guess maybe there are a couple of reasons to talk about it: 1) Because it's an interesting time, 2) There aren't a lot of stories about guys who got in and then sort of failed the way I sort of failed and then managed to get in later. I was still part of something interesting at the time, and I like to talk about that. But I think, for the most part, it's that I was down, but I wasn't out, and I managed to somehow get that fire that I possessed for comics in me, to somehow get a chance—using the baseball metaphor again—to get back at the plate, and to take some pitches.

The Twinkie Age of Comics
David A. Roach on the Hostess super-hero ad campaign

by David A. Roach

Editor's note: *CBA takes pride in presenting a new column which will "chart the unknown" in comics by new CBA associate editor David A. Roach, Welsh artist/historian extraordinaire (who penned the exhaustive and ground-breaking survey of the Spanish artists in our Warren ish, #4). First up: Investigative journalism at its finest—the real sense-shattering story behind those super-hero Twinkies ads and the shocking truth on why (gasp!) you never saw our heroes actually eat a Hostess pastry. Sit tight and prepare for our mind-bending examination of Hostess, the bakery with the mostest bizarre comic universe!—JBC]*

Everything you know is wrong: The Hulk's arch-foe was Cousin Betsy the Plant Lady. Gold Key was having intercompany crossovers with Marvel and Harvey comics in the '70s. Neal Adams' last Green Lantern strip appeared in 1977; and Mera and The Penguin had their own strips. Not a hoax! Not an imaginary story! This is comics history courtesy of that well-known publishing house, the Hostess Company. From the Spring of 1975 until well into the '80s, the pastry manufacturer ran a series of ads in Marvel, DC, Harvey, and Gold Key titles advertising the dubious culinary delights of Twinkies, cup cakes and fruit pies; but as any reader of '70s comics will know, what elevated these ads from the depths of crass commercialism to the heights of genuine trash culture icons was the fact they were comic strips.

Of course, comic strip ads were nothing new and had been appearing in comics, magazines, and newspapers for decades before Hostess initiated their campaign. Cartooning masters Milton Caniff and Noel Sickles had provided a number of "Mr. Coffee Nerves" ads for wartime Sunday supplements under the name "Paul Arthurs." The ad agency Johnstone and Cushing specialized in comic strip ads, and Neal Adams, one of their graduates, went on to do the same with his own Continuity Studio. In the comics themselves, all sorts of companies used strips to advertise their wares, most memorably the Tootsie Roll, personified as Captain Tootsie by the great C.C. Beck; but while Tootsie looked like Captain Marvel's long-lost brother, Hostess' masterstroke was to use the comic companies' own heroes in their ads, and for about eight years that's just what they did.

Of the four comic groups that ran the ads (Charlton being deemed too small presumably), DC was by far the most prolific and the longest-lasting, creating at least 60 different strips. The first ad, "Batman vs. The Mummy," appeared in issues dated April and May 1975 and it pretty much set the template for the whole campaign: the evil mummy has captured the professor and his beautiful daughter who had inadvertently violated his tomb. So it's up to Batman and Robin to save the day. Tragically Robin's special Mummy Ray Gun barely fazes the Monster of the Nile, but just in the nick of time, Batman lures him away with an offer he can't resist: A succulent box of Hostess Twinkies. "M-m-m! I've been around for 2000 years and I've never tasted anything so good!" testifies the recalcitrant Egyptian. There's a wonderfully generic quality to the whole thing—the Mummy is there simply to be villainous, the victims don't have names—they don't need names—they're just the professor and his beautiful daughter (aren't professors' daughters always beautiful?), and the strip seems to take place in some nondescript cave in who-knows-wheresville. Throughout the series' run this pattern of hero meets villain, hero frees innocent bystanders and villain succumbs to beckoning pastry was repeated almost without change, creating an almost zen-like effect.

That particular ad was drawn with some aplomb by Dick Giordano while the next installment, "Superman and The Spy," was by Curt Swan and Tex Blaisdell. Swan would go on to draw all but one of the entire run, occasionally blessed with Giordano inks, but more frequently cursed by the dread hand of Vince Colletta at his most minimalist. The sole exception to Swan's reign was a surprising guest appearance by Neal Adams, drawing his old favorite Green Lantern (that was in the June and July 1977 titles for you Adams completists out there). What makes Adams' ad all the more noteworthy was that he actually drew with some conviction which is unfortunately more than can be said of Swan. The principal writer was longtime DC editor, writer and historian E. Nelson Bridwell, with the occasional fill-in by Bob "Answer Man" Rozakis, under the editorship of Sol Harrison.

According to Rozakis, Harrison imposed several restrictions on his writers: Primarily that the hero of the ad should never appear in a comic he or she was starring in and that DC characters—no matter the irresistible temptation—must never be seen to actually eat a

Above: *Neal Adams thumbnail of his single entry to the Hostess ad campaign featuring a bisected Hal Jordan. The finished ad appeared in DC Comics cover dated June and July 1977. Art ©2000 Neal Adams. Green Lantern ©2000 DC Comics, Inc. Hostess is a registered trademark of ITT Continental Baking Co.*

Twinkie. Rozakis was sure this last stipulation came from Hostess themselves, their objections being they didn't want DC characters to be seen endorsing their products (though, since these sundry super-heroes were featured in strips expressly designed to promote Hostess items, surely they were endorsing the products anyway?). Since DC characters couldn't be seen stuffing their faces with sponge cake with creamy filling, some other protagonists had to be dreamt up, and therein lies much of the ad series' bizarre appeal. So, roll up Aunt Minerva, Jet Set Jessie, Topsy Turvy Man, Mr. Fox, Cooky Ca Moo, Spindly Klutz, Pigeon Person, Slud-Jak, the Three Svengali Brothers, and the decidedly un-P.C. Fat Lady. It could be argued that since DC had already given us the likes of Ding Dong Daddy, the Mad Mod, Egg Fu (with his living mustache), Bwana Beast, and the Killer Moth, this motley band of grade-Z losers were quite at home.

Sadly, later installments tended towards the rather more pedestrian—hero helping to avert a catastrophe (or rescue a space-man, or stop a bobsled, or rescue a skydiver, etc.) category, sacrificing the inspired and clueless "go-go check DC" for the "all-American, mom's apple pie, respectable and dull DC." This latter approach was emphasized by their choice of hero with Superman, Batman and Wonder Woman predominating. However, since both Hostess and DC wanted to avoid confusing the ad with a regular

story page, they occasionally resorted to giving more obscure characters an outing (according to Rozakis, this was particularly helpful with the Justice League book which invariably starred all of DC's top-flight super-heroes). Sadly we never got to see Kong the Untamed, Jonah Hex, Ultra the Multi-Alien, or The Dingbats of Danger Street chowing down on a Twinkie but we did get second-stringers like Mera, Plastic Man, Batgirl, and The Penguin.

A month after DC's inaugural ad, Marvel joined the frat with a Ross Andru and Mike Esposito Spider-Man strip, the first of at least 50 entries in a campaign that ran until 1982. Unlike DC, Marvel utilized a wider variety of artists, particularly in the early days, and often with impressive results. The underrated Andru contributed several more nice Spider-Mans and an incongruous Captain Marvel (which featured perennial children's favorite Nitro—the villain who blows himself up!) as the pastry-scoffing miscreant. Another great Spider-Man artist, John Romita, drew several typically impressive installments as did Dave Cockrum, George Tuska, Don Heck (nicely inked by Frank Giacoia), and Gene Colan who teamed up with Jack Abel on a rare outing with Thor. By the second year, the bulk of the artistic chores were handed over to the ever-reliable Sal Buscema who was teamed with a succession of Marvel's best inkers, from Joe Sinnott and Frank Giacoia to young turks like Bob McLeod and Klaus Janson. In the '80s, Buscema did notably fewer ads, allowing Alan Kupperberg, Herb Trimpe, and plucky newcomer Frank Miller (in January 1980, drawing the Human Torch of all characters) their chance at comics immortality.

To date I've yet to find anyone to admit to having written any of the strips, though Marv Wolfman admitted he might have but couldn't be certain. What is known is that they were commissioned by the head of licensing at the time, Sol Brodsky, and would almost certainly have been written by Marvel staffers. Clearly Hostess' reservations about endorsements applied as much to Marvel as they did to DC, since none of the heroes are ever seen actually eating their products and, again like DC, this led to as bizarre a menagerie of villains as ever graced a page. Who among us can ever forget Cousin Betsy the Plant Lady, McBrain, The Phoonie Goonies, June Jitsu, Professor Sneer, The Roller Disco Devils, Home Wrecker, or Impercepto The Malevolent Alien. A particular favorite of mine is the Buscema/Sinnott ad which pitted Thor with Sif, Odin, and Falstaff against those forgotten Norse gods, The Ding-A-Ling family, who were nothing less than an all-fighting, all-cussing hillbilly family—in space!

But surely the most bizarre strip appeared in Marvel's July '77 issues, Iron Man's "City Crisis," drawn by either Keith Pollard or Arvell Jones, and inked by Pablo Marcos. As the first caption explains, "Kwirkegard, a philosophically sinister villain, aims his existential depression ray at New York City's water supply." "Puny humans are about to learn the sad truth about life," gloats the wild-maned wrong-doer. These being pre-Prozac days, Iron Man finds the city gripped in despair and tracks down the villain to give him a good walloping. On discovering that the laughter of cake-eating young-sters weakens the effects of Kwirkegard's ray, Shellhead hands out depression-defying Twinkies to the island's entire population and—hooray!—saves the day. I had always assumed that the unique juxtaposition of Twinkies and existentialism could only be the work of the legendary Steve Gerber, but he denies writing it (though, he adds, he wishes he had!). So for now the author of this classic episode shall remain a tantalizing mystery.

Again, like DC, Marvel's ads generally featured their most popular characters with Spider-Man alone appearing in almost a third of the strips, followed by The Hulk, Captain America, and Daredevil. Surprisingly, Captain Marvel, never one of Marvel's biggest sellers, cropped up five times; but perhaps the biggest surprise, as far as both companies were concerned, was the general lack of teams; no Avengers, X-Men, or JLA. It might be argued that the one-page format made team appearances rather impractical, but in the early '80s, Marvel ran a Herb Trimpe-drawn ad starring The Fantastic Four which rather destroys that theory. Around the same period, they also ran a number of strips featuring The Thing, The Torch, and even a solitary Mr. Fantastic outing, so it's possible in this case they were reacting to the screening off the *FF* cartoon show.

Of course, Invisible Girl didn't get her own strip; no Marvel super-heroines did—and it's a shame Marvel wasn't willing to use some of their more outré characters. Imagine Hostess' reaction to twinkie ads featuring Man-Thing, Brother Voodoo, Tigra, Howard the Duck, or—gulp!—Daimon Hellstrom, The Son of Satan (how *did* Marvel get away with that character?). It would have been equally entertaining to see Magnus Robot Fighter, The Owl, Mighty Samson, or Dagar the Invincible save the world with the aid of a cup cake but sadly Gold Key chose a more conservative approach to their ad series.

Initially Gold Key ran a number of strips featuring Warner Brothers' favorites like Bugs Bunny or The Road Runner, but by 1976 they were running Marvel ads, seemingly oblivious to the possible conflict of interest in promoting their competitors' comics. To make matters even stranger, these were different ads to ones appearing in Marvel's own comics, but created by the same Bullpen regulars (and including another early Frank Miller appearance, this time starring Spider-Man in an ad which appeared in January 1980). Gold Key also printed Twinkies strips starring Harvey's top attractions, Richie Rich and Casper; and Harvey in turn printed yet more Marvel ads. Quite how many advertisements were drawn altogether is hard to guess without having both every comic printed between 1975 and '82 and the patience to look through them all, but the number could be as high as 200!

Of course it's easy to get swept along in a mad, sugar-induced rush of excitement over the sheer scale and bizarreness of the whole campaign. It is still crass commercialism when all's said and done. However, maybe if we allow ourselves a slight indulgence of romanticism, we can perhaps see it as something more. As a child growing up in Britain, what appealed most to me about American comics was their strangeness, their exoticism, their sheer otherness. The strips, and almost equally their ads, were a glimpse into another culture—a culture partly like my own but also innumerably different. It was a culture of Sea Monkeys, Grit, Evel Knievel, X-ray specs, Charles Atlas, and American Seeds; a world away from the mid-'70s Britain of strikes, The Bay City Rollers, power cuts, and three TV channels.

The Twinkies strips were absolutely central to that strange beguiling world; they weren't just ads hawking pastry products, they were a bizarre slice of pure Americana. Maybe it's a British thing. We couldn't buy Twinkies, or any other Hostess product, so we could only imagine how amazing they must have tasted—because, of course, if actual super-heroes were endorsing them, they *had* to be great! I think it's telling that as recently as last year, a comic lampooned the ads, some two decades after they last appeared, and that it should be Alan Moore—a Brit—who wrote it. In *Tomorrow Stories* #4, First American stands trial for the heinous crime of advertising Mistress Fruit Pies in his own comic—a charge he only escapes by the cunning distraction of declaring war on the Middle East, the Balkans, China and Russia. Alan Moore understands the evocative power of the Twinkies ad!

As a postscript to this, in 1980 I visited the U.S. for the first time and one of the first things I did upon arrival was head for the nearest deli and buy myself some Twinkies. If I was going to immerse myself in this strange country's culture, where better to start than with the Prince of Foods: the Twinkie? If I had wanted a car tire filled with polystyrene I'm sure I would have turned with the "Hostess experience," but since I was expecting something edible, I was crushingly disappointed. It was a salient lesson to learn and I never trusted an advert again… though, if anyone knows where I can buy some sea monkeys….

Solving the Hostess Mystery with Bob Rozakis

While you're reading Hostess ads, I'm sure you wonder, "What person wrote these f*cking things?" And then you probably wonder, "Who gave that person a sharpened pencil?" Or, if you're the warden of an institution for the criminally insane, you might be thinking, "How can I capture and restrain this person to help my business grow?" I had an e-mail conversation with Bob Rozakis, who wrote hundreds of comics, was the executive director of production at DC Comics, and scripted six of the Hostess ads that tempt your tummy and stalk and kill you in your nightmares. Specifically, Bob wrote "Pirates' Gold," "Fruit Pies for Magpies," "Lights… Camera… Crime," "The K-9 Caper," "Concerts and Cupcakes," and "Wonder Woman vs. the Robot Master." After you see them you'll know why for my own safety and sense of style, I wore a helmet during the interview.— Seanbaby

Seanbaby: *Your ads covered so many types of enemies... robot clones, pirates, movie directors, people at a concert, man in a dog-suit. What are some of the types of villains you would use today if you were still writing these? And, of course, if you weren't allowed to use man in dog-suit again.*

Bob Rozakis: I suspect the villains would still be pretty much the same, basically goofy, lame characters who could be stopped with the enticement of a sweet dessert food.

Seanbaby: *I don't think you're being fair to the non-lame, non-goofy characters who could be stopped with delicious snacks, like any villain from Ethiopia. And speaking of places God rejected, do you remember any ideas for Hostess ads that were rejected? And if so, what in the holy sh*t could they have been?*

Bob: I don't recall any that were rejected, though my file contains only rewritten versions of "The K-9 Caper" and "Fruit Pies for Magpies," so I guess there was something in them that they didn't like. The heroes were chosen in advance, usually to fit a schedule that somebody (probably Sol Harrison and the [advertising] agency) had set up. We were instructed that the heroes could never eat the cupcakes, Twinkies or fruit pies, because that could be interpreted as an endorsement of the product. So, we were always pressed to come up with some interesting way to stop a crime or a riot or something else using a dessert.

Seanbaby: *Behind the closed doors of insane asylums, past the hallways of feces jars, then past the room where patients carefully catalog those jars of feces, then still past the underground pit where the restless bodies of the insane rise to kill, I like to think there's a breakroom where orderlies vote on who their favorite mental crazies*

are. I also like to think that even further past that, there's a room filled only with crazy people dressed like Napolean. What I'm trying to ask is, did you have any favorite Hostess ads?

Bob: I liked the ones that used some tongue-in-cheek humor. Of the ones I wrote, I'd say "Lights, Camera, Crime" was my favorite, especially the last line in which the Crime Director sets up the slogan and package picture as he's being taken away by Batman.

Seanbaby: *When I ask most people what the best part of Hostess ads are, and I do, they all say the same thing — FASHION! How much were you involved in fashion choices of the villains? Particularly, in "The Robot Master," did you just give a vague description to the artist and leave, or did you stand over their shoulder and say, "No. Uglier jacket. My grandma could draw a bigger afro than that, and she's in a dog-suit! And you didn't even make his sweater a turtlene — AGHHH! Just give me the pencil!"*

Bob: All it says in my script for "The Robot Master" is that he is a "mad scientist type." The actual design of the villain was left up to the artist. I never got to see the art until it was completed.

Seanbaby: *Everyone knows about how Disney's panty-sniffing animators have been sneaking pictures of penises into their movies for years. In* The Lion King, *the word "SEX" is spelled out in the sky;* Little Mermaid *grew a hard-on during the scene where she married the lobster (or whatever)… It's the classic counter-cultural technique of shaking society up by subtly implying that it might have genitals. The Hostess titles "That Dirty Beach," "Spider-Man Spoils a Snatch!", and "Big Black Ball Banging!" are pretty suspicious regarding subliminal vulgarity. Was it intentional?*

Bob: I can't speak for what the guys writing the Marvel ones were trying to do. My approach to these was to try to use the characters in a way that was as close to the way they appeared in the books without turning them into pitchmen. It's probably debatable whether I was successful in that.

Seanbaby: *Most people have their own ideas of how these ads came about — maybe a magical troll tricked a marketing executive. Or maybe someone else tricked a marketing executive while the magical troll hit him on the head. We may never know since history is recorded by the victors, not magic trolls. Could you tell us what the first thing out of your mouth was when you heard that someone wanted you to write comics about super-heroes fighting crime with pie?*

Bob: I'm sure my first words were "Hey, that's great!" And my second line was, "What are you paying?" From what I can tell of the scripts I have, Aquaman in "Pirate's Gold" seems to be the first one I wrote.

Marvel Value Stamps
Or how to destroy your Bronze Age comics collection

by Rob Anderson

Let me paint you a horrifying picture: it's 1974 and I'm eight years old, sitting in the floor of my bedroom. I've just flipped to the letters page of a comic. I'm smiling because I've discovered that this particular issue contains a strange little thing called a Marvel Value Stamp—specifically, #54, Shanna the She-Devil.

Carefully, scissors in hand, I cut around the edges of the stamp, so as not to mess up the border. Satisfied with my work, I toss my copy of *Incredible Hulk* #181 back onto the stack. It has some funny character in it called Wolverine—his first full issue appearance.

I bought the comic for the stamp.

To this day, if you take a quick flip through any issue I owned between 1974 and '76, you're likely to find a mutilated letters page that flaps in the breeze. I wasn't the only one taken in by this insanity. A search on eBay will reveal countless "reading copies" of Bronze Age comics available in great condition… except for that missing stamp.

In the strictest sense, Marvel Value Stamps weren't really "stamps" at all. Basically, they were color portraits of Marvel characters, less than two inches on each side, which generally appeared on the letters page of selected issues. They had a little pseudo-perforated border running around the edge, but that was as close as they came to being stamp-like. Really, they were just square pieces of paper, and they certainly weren't sticky, unless you added your own glue.

Each stamp also had a number on it, ranging from 1 to 100, and I suspect that was the beginning of the end for obsessive collector-types like me. Add numbers to something that looks like a stamp, provide a book to put them in, and offer ill-defined but fabulous rewards, and a certain part of the population will find themselves compelled to collect them all. Not surprisingly, that portion of the population overlapped pretty well with those of us who were obsessively collecting comics in the mid-'70s.

Why stamps?

So where did this wacky comic book stamp idea come from in the first place? From the 1950s to the '70s, stamp programs outside of the comics world were huge. Businesses from gas stations to grocery

stores offered stamps to their loyal customers, and completed stamp books could be redeemed for all sorts of things, from toasters to silverware. The most popular stamp loyalty program, run by Sperry & Hutchinson (S&H), penetrated 60 percent of U.S. households at its peak, according to *The New York Times* (Nov. 26, 2001). S&H claimed that in 1964 it printed three times as many stamps as the U.S. Postal Service!

So stamp collecting was still a common promotion in the '70s, but then-Marvel editor-in-chief Roy Thomas recalls that there was also a specific precedent for stamps in comics. "There had been stamps in comics before," Roy said. "Fawcett had them for several years back in the early '50s, late '40s, whatever it was—very similar to Marvel's in the '70s… It was a sales gimmick, I suppose." Although Roy's memories of the origins of the Marvel program were vague, he seemed to recall getting the directive from Stan.

"Now whether somebody else suggested it to him or not, I don't know," Roy said. "But I have this feeling that it was Stan's idea."

The quest for stamp artwork

Once the decision had been made to launch a stamp program, the next step was selecting characters and creating the artwork. Characters chosen for the stamps ran the gamut from Spider-Man to Galactus, with everyone from Brother Voodoo to the Super-Skrull in between. The artwork for the stamps was lifted from covers, interior pages, and even house ads.

"It would have been too expensive and time-consuming to have drawn new art for these things," Roy said, "and sometimes it took a long time to find just the right picture—and then you had to white out some of the art and maybe… get rid of a balloon that might overlap, or something like that."

According to the April '74 Marvel Bullpen Bonus page, "Jazzy Johnny Romita, [Sr.], Mirthful Marie Severin, and Titanic Tony Mortellaro" were the parties responsible for digging up "the spiffiest bunch of super-hero drawings since George Washington first said 'Cheese!'"

The stamps featured artwork by a wide array of artists, from Mike Ploog and Gil Kane, to Barry Windsor Smith and Steve Ditko. Jack Kirby's work made up the most stamps—18 of Series A, followed by John Buscema and John Romita, Sr. with more than 10 apiece. Marie Severin, a huge Kirby fan, felt that Jack truly "represented Marvel," and she admitted that the large number of Kirby stamps was likely her doing.

Kirby, Buscema, and Romita were also favored in the selection process because, according to Marie, "Their artwork was clean and clear, and they did the major characters, and that's what we were after—something that fit nice that wouldn't need too much touching-up."

"We sort of had to have a production eye doing it," Marie continued. "A lot of stuff I did, I chose for reproduction—what would show up best. You can't choose a mural and bring it down to an inch. So when you found a head, you would maybe cut off part of it, maybe do something like we did with [stamp #100] Galactus." Lifted from the cover of *Fantastic Four* #49 by Jack Kirby, Marie remembered adding the "crackle" around his head on the stamp. "A lot of stuff had to be touched-up and backgrounds knocked out," she said.

Gil Kane's Man-Wolf stamp was another example of this. Lifted from an interior page of *Giant-Size Super-Heroes* #1, Man-Wolf needed a right foot, a left leg, and a right elbow added in order to

Above: *The actual Cooke Brothers' Mighty Marvel Value Stamp Book purchased in the mid-'70 from the House of Ideas. Courtesy of Andrew D. Cooke.* **Below:** *Just for kicks, Ye Ed made up this faux MVS of Mirthful Marie. Art ©'05 M.S.*

A PERSONAL MESSAGE FROM YOUR BENEFICENT BULLPEN

We promised it to you—and here it is!

By the time you receive this colorful Marvel Value Stampbook in the mail, chances are you've either amassed a complete series of 100 Marvel Value Stamps—or else you're within web-spinning distance of it, right?

So now, here's what you do, effendi:

Simply clip the stamps out of the comic mags themselves, paste each one into its proper, numbered slot in this catalog—and, when all 100 spaces are properly filled, take this treasured tome around to any of the star-studded Comic Book Conventions, comic art dealers, or other centers of contemporary culture which you've seen enumerated in recent issues of Marvel mags. There you'll collect your MVS discount, free gift, or other goodies. The conventioneer, dealer, or whoever will then mark this book in the proper place on the back page—so that you can hang on to the Stampbook itself, which is sure to increase in value as years, months, even weeks go by!

Don't lose it, hear? 'Cause we've got other plans for it as well—which concern the special number on the cover of this Stampbook!

Oh yes—and if you want to get set for the next lettered series of MVS mini-posters to paste and ponder over, just send 50¢ to cover postage and manhandling to:

MARVEL VALUE STAMPBOOK
c/o Marvel Comics Group
575 Madison Ave.
New York, N.Y. 10022

We've got a million of 'em—and you know how the Thing's dear Aunt Petunia hates those cluttered-up old warehouses!

MIGHTY MARVEL VALUE STAMPS NO.'s 1 THRU 8

...ear complete within the confines of the stamp. Others, such as ...y's Enchantress from the cover of *The Avengers* #7, were already ...fect.

Where covers or famous splash pages were used, the stamp ...ork is instantly recognizable—such as the headshot of Mary Jane ...tson from the last page of *Amazing Spider-Man* #42. ("Face it ...r—you just hit the jackpot!") Other stamp artwork is maddening-...bscure—like the Volstaag stamp, which originally appeared on an ...ublished cover to *Thor* #170.

"Some of the subjects were hard to find," Marie recalled. ...olstagg] was hard to find because he wasn't on that many covers. ...wouldn't be like [Doc] Octopus… where he appeared all over the ...ce. Volstagg was [generally] on interior shots only."

Although she was one of the people tracking down the art-...rk, Marie was not the person choosing which characters were to ...featured—and she couldn't remember who had done so. But she ...s central to much of the production, from touch-up to coloring. "I ...s doing other things," Marie said, "but if they had a letters page, ...y might have thrown it at me one month and said, 'Hey, get a ...mp in here of such-and-such.'"

From the sidelines, Roy remembered the effort as "a fair ...ount of trouble. It wasn't the easiest thing in the world, especially ...get it going."

...ow Marvel convinced ...s to cut up our comics

...how did Marvel whip so many of us into a destructive frenzy? ...e hype-fest began in issues cover-dated February of 1974. An ...umbered Hulk stamp appeared on the Marvel Bullpen Bulletins

page, soliciting guesses from fans as to what the stamp-like thing could be. The comics outfit was tight-lipped about the program, but promised "a zingier bargain than you ever saw on *Let's Make a Deal!*" The following month, the Bullpen was still light on details, though heavy on hype, using fully half of the new Bullpen Bonus page to promote the program. Whatever the stamps were, we were told to "keep 'em safe and secure, like the family jewels."

To an eight-year-old mind, these stamps were clearly going to be something spectacular. Why risk leaving them in the comics? Many of us went to work on our collections immediately. I know from talking to other fans that many of us also immediately went about "protecting" them—by pasting them into photo albums, taping them into notebooks, and undertaking other equally logical activities.

Two months after the initial teaser, a surprise followed for those of us who had been diligent. A stamp album would soon be available for purchase. I had already committed to the notebook and tape approach. It didn't occur to me until much later that the stamps would need to be in a stamp book to provide any benefits.

The Mighty Marvel Stamp Book

The Series A stamp book was first offered for sale via a mail-in coupon in issues cover-dated July, '74. For a mere 50¢, the cost of two Marvel Comics at the time, it would be "winging its way" to you, along with a special bonus poster.

Above: Opening spread of the first Mighty Marvel Value Stamp Book. Look for the other 91 stamps on pages 98-99. All characters ©2005 their respective copyright holders.
Below: The book also came with a photo-realistic Spider-Man (produced in England, so ya gotta wonder if the supply was overstock from a weekly comics premium). Courtesy of Rob Anderson. ©2005 Marvel Characters, Inc.

The stamp book arrived in a plain brown envelope, with a non-descript "Marvel Comics Group" return address. Folded inside was an unusual Spider-Man poster with a seemingly live-action photo, which pre-dated the 1977 television show. The bottom of the poster read that it was "Printed in England by H.B. Dorey & Company Limited," and carried a trademark notice for Magazine Management (London) Ltd.

While the poster might have been disappointing, the stamp book itself was not. The 5$\frac{1}{2}$" x 8$\frac{1}{2}$" book carried portraits of Conan, Spidey, and the Hulk on the cover. Each book also had a serial number stamped above a pre-printed line.

The real draw of the stamp book was the interior. Inside, against a red background, all 100 stamps (other than the mysterious Stamp #100) were reproduced in black-&-white glory. It was almost like having a completed stamp book before you pasted anything inside. More than one collector, faced with the stamp book, decided not to fill it—even if the stamps had already been clipped.

The fabulous rewards

Reading the Bullpen Bulletins with the benefit of hindsight, it seems pretty clear Marvel hadn't figured out what the rewards would be when the program was launched. It wasn't until July '74, five months into the promotion, that the benefits were unveiled. After such a long wait, many of us had grand visions of our reward. An all-expense-paid tour of the Marvel office, perhaps? A bag of unique goodies in the mail? At least a free subscription maybe?

Not exactly. It turned out that we could get discounts on admission to two comic conventions, the New York Comic Art Convention, hosted by Phil Seuling, and the San Diego Comic Convention, Shel Dorf's show. The stamp book

had squares on the back where the discount could be stamped at the door.

At some later point—never mentioned in the Bullpen Bulletins–Marvel decided to hold a special event for MVS collectors at the San Diego convention. The 1975 Mighty Marvel Comic Convention program book contained a picture from the previous year's San Diego con showcasing the "hardy souls who managed to clip and paste all 100 Marvel Value Stamps." Of the thousands who had ordered a stamp book, the picture showed about a dozen kids.

According to Roy Thomas, the special program held for these stalwarts treated the group of young fans to a chat with Roy, Frank Brunner, and Mike Friedrich, among others.

"They were mostly younger kids, who by pasting that whole book full of stamps got admission to that little meeting," Roy recalled. "I just talked to them for half an hour, an hour, I don't know if they felt it was silly, but I tried to make it seem like it was a big deal. If there was anything other than the talk itself, I don't remember it and didn't have anything to do with it. Maybe Marvel gave some free comics. I can't recall after nearly 30 years."

For the hardy souls who made it to the session, it might have seemed worth the effort. To an eight-year-old, living hundreds or thousands of miles away from the convention, a more disappointing benefit would have been hard to imagine.

However, all hope was not lost. The Bullpen stated they still had "a bunch of surprises up [their] sleeves." Perhaps it should have been a warning sign that they admitted they were "racking [their] brains, every day, to dream up even more sensational surprises," and then ended with a plea to send them suggestions on how the books could be used.

Months later, Marvel explained they were now "in the final stages" of preparing a list of comic-book stores and conventions where the filled-up stamp book would provide "free Marvel mags at a special MVS Discount!" For some reason, that list was never published.

The next mention of rewards didn't appear until five months later, in April '75. To read between the lines of the hype, the fans were restless. The "batty Bullpen" was now being "constantly deluged with letters wondering just what sort'a goodies" were available

In an apparent surrender, the stamp book now would entitle users to a 10% discount on Marvel mail-order merchandise. To receive this huge discount, we would only have to mail our stamp book to New York, which would (hopefully) be returned to us along with a 10% discount coupon.

The upside was that each time you risked your stamp book to the vagaries of the U.S. Postal Service, it would be returned with yet another 10% discount coupon. "In other words," Marvel wrote, "all holders of completed Marvel Value Stamp Books are eligible for a perpetual ten percent discount."

Based on that language, the discount should still be honored. Perhaps someone should try sending in their stamp book and see what happens. It's your best shot at getting "value" out of the program, because that was the last reward ever offered in print in exchange for all that comic book clipping.

And then they did it again

In December '75, the same month that the last few trailing Series A stamps appeared, Marvel began releasing the second set of stamps known as "Series B." This set featured "puzzle-piece" stamps which could be placed together to form larger images. In a later Bulletin, Bullpenner Paty Greer [Cockrum], a merchandising aide, was given credit for "conceiving the idea for [the] second stupendous set of stamps."

For Series B, there were 100 stamps, making up 10 images, with 10 stamps per image. Many featured stellar artwork such as Barry Windsor Smith's cover to *Conan King-Size Annual* #1, Frank Brunner's *Doctor Strange* #1 (1974), and a Kirby Silver Surfer splash page from *Fantastic Four* #72. The last of the ten puzzles was touted as containing a "special secret super-stamp of a shocking Marvel star" which turned out to be none other than Stan "The Man" Lee, as drawn by Marie Severin. Unlike the Series A Stamp #100 (Galactus), which eventually appeared three times, the Series B #100, which completed the Stan Lee puzzle, really did appear only once, in the rather obscure *Omega* #3.

Despite some great stamp artwork, everything about Series B seemed to indicate waning support for the program within Marvel. There was much less hype about the program in the Bullpen Bulletins—only four separate single-paragraph items, with a three-month gap between the first announcement and the second. The series lasted a much shorter period of time—less than a year between approximately December 1975 and August 1976—and each stamp appeared only once or twice.

Even the stamp book itself seemed less complete. Unlike the Series A books, no stamped serial numbers appeared on the B albums, and instead of black-and-white versions of the stamps, the B book contained only blanks for the stamps (presumably to keep the completed picture a "secret"). No mention was ever made in the Bullpen Bulletins of the benefits received for a completed Series B book. The program just seemed to fade away.

If Series B received a lesser reaction from fans, perhaps part of the problem was that the individual B stamps simply didn't stand on their own. You could get a single Series A stamp—and you immediately had a useless, but fun "mini-poster" (as the Marvel hype-masters referred to it). With a single Series B, you had one-tenth of a poster—maybe just somebody's foot or an elbow—and even when assembled (if you could get the dang things to line up) you had a bunch of lines running through your "masterpiece."

Still, the generation of fans who first caught the collecting bug around 1976 remember Series B fondly. Like most things nostalgic, it's all about when you entered the game.

Letters pages that flap in the breeze

So how bad was the destruction? Series A was the worst offender. Of the 850+ regular sized-comics printed between March 1974 and November 1975, more than one out of three contained a stamp. In contrast, Series B only put around 125 issues total at risk.

To add to the pain, the stamps generally did not appear in reprint titles. So, whereas all the copies of *Marvel Tales* were safe, a run of *Amazing Spider-Man* (beginning with #130) could easily be missing 14 Series A stamps and four Series B stamps.

There's no way to estimate how many stamps were actually cut out, but no matter how you slice it, both programs left their fair share of gaping holes in Bronze Age comics.

Still chasing the stamps

Marvel's hype in 1974 indicated that all the clipping would be worth it in the long run. The completed stamp album was "bound to become a real collector's item in the years to come," they said. In fact, the Bullpen rather breathlessly pointed out that, at the time, *Fantastic Four* #1 was selling for up to $50 in comic stores, and that the first issue of *Amazing Spider-Man* wasn't far behind. Of course, they didn't mention how much less *FF* #1 would have been worth if someone had taken the scissors to it back in 1961.

So how rare are the stamp books now, and what are they worth 30 years later? As for scarcity, if the serial numbers are any indication, the print run on the Series A stamp book was probably at least 8,000. The lowest serial number I've seen is 100,043, with the highest being 107,116. It seems unlikely that the print run exceeded 10,000. The print run of the Series B stamp book, which contained no serial numbers, is unknown.

And as for value? Believe it or not, the stamp books are the subject of some fairly fierce bidding on eBay. Apparently, there are still many of us who never quite got over our compulsion to have a completed set. In the latter half of 2003, stamp books with some number of stamps intact were selling for between $100 and $180, with an average over the last few years of around $130. Not bad for a stamp book, filled with pieces of paper, that gained the owner almost nothing in the mid-1970s.

On the other hand, if you compare the value of the comics destroyed to the value of the book created, the equation doesn't quite balance. To use the worst example, if you cut the Shanna the She-Devil stamp out of *Incredible Hulk* #181, you probably decreased the value of your collection by at least $500. With just the difference in value on *Incredible Hulk* #181, you could currently buy yourself several complete *Marvel Value Stamp Books* on eBay. And by going the online auction route, you could enjoy the *Stamp Book* without the trauma of using the scissors yourself.

Maybe the people still seeking the stamp books never got to complete their set when they were kids. Or maybe it was something they had and lost in the past. Regardless of the motivation, you can bet you'll see people trying to track them down for years to come. A nostalgia buzz is the main "value" the stamp books provide—but that's enough for some of us. *Excelsior!*

A PERSONAL MESSAGE FROM YOUR BENEFICENT BULLPEN

Betcha thought you'd never see it, didn't ya?

Well, you were wrong! Here it is. The Second Marvel Value Stamp-book has finally arrived— and, boy, is it ever worth the wait! We've gone all out to make this the weirdest, wackiest, and most way-out little item you've ever laid your baby-blues on! (We don't care what color your eyes are.)

This time, though, we aren't letting you off as easy as we did in the first Stampbook. This time, not only do you have to cut the little buggers out of our Mighty Marvel Magazines and paste them up in this booklet, but you also have to figure out what each group of ten stamps forms a picture of. (We'll tell you this much: Each one of the first nine groups forms a memorable scene featuring the character talked about on each particular page.) And just wait till you see who the last group depicts! (No, effendi, it's not Galactus!)

Now, just what can you do with this little book? Well, after all 100 spaces are filled take this titanic tome around to any of the star-studded Comic Book Conventions, comic art dealers, or such which you should have seen mentioned in recent Marvel Mags; and you'll be able to collect the appropriate discount or goodie!

Keep this around—— it's sure to become a valuable collectors' item in years to come, just as the first one already has!

That's it for this time, group; keep your eyes glued to our terrific titles to collect the whole set. Enjoy!

Above: *Inside front cover of the Mighty Marvel Value Stamp Book, Series B. Courtesy of Rob Anderson. The Vision ©2005 Marvel Characters, Inc.*

Below: *Photo of the "hardy souls" who earned entry (by having filled up their Stamp Books) to an exclusive meeting with Roy Thomas & company at the 1975 San Diego Comic-Con. This pic appeared in the 1976 Mighty Marvel Comic Convention souvenir book.*

FOR MORE INFO *on Marvel Value Stamps, including complete checklists and sources for all stamp artwork, visit my* Unofficial Marvel Value Stamp Index *at <http://www.mvstamps.com/> Marie Severin was interviewed on Jan. 29, 2004, and Roy Thomas on Dec.17, 2003, for this article. Thanks to Marie, Roy, and the many contributors to my Web site for their participation here.—R.A.*

CAPTAIN MARVEL 9

POWER MAN 10

BLACK BOLT 17

18

THE TORCH 25

MEPHISTO 26

DEATHLOK 11

DAREDEVIL 12

HOGUN FANDRAL BALDER 19

BROTHER VOODOO 20

THE BLACK WIDOW 27

HAWKEYE 28

DR. STRANGE 13

THE LIVING MUMMY 14

KULL 21

MAN-THING 22

BARON MORDO 29

THE GREY GARGOYLE 30

IRON MAN 15

SHANG-CHI, MASTER OF KUNG FU 16

SGT. FURY 23

THE FALCON 24

MODOK 31

THE RED SKULL 32

THE VULTURE 57

THE MANDARIN 58

ICEMAN 65

GENERAL ROSS 66

KINGPIN 73

THE STRANGER 74

THE GOLEM 59

KA-ZAR 60

CYCLOPS 67

SON OF SATAN 68

MORBIUS 75

DORMAMMU 76

THE RED GHOST 61

THE PLUNDERER 62

MARVEL GIRL 69

SUPER SKRULL 70

THE SWORDSMAN 77

THE OWL 78

THE SUB-MARINER 63

SIF 64

THE VISION 71

THE LIZARD 72

KANG 79

THE GHOST RIDER 80

SERIES A — SUE RICHARDS, INVISIBLE GIRL — 33

34 — MR. FANTASTIC

SERIES A — THE GLADIATOR — 41

42 — MAN-WOLF

SERIES A — 49 — ODIN

BLACK PANTHER — 50

SERIES A — KILLRAVEN — 35

ANCIENT ONE — 36

THE ENCHANTRESS — SERIES A — 43

SERIES A — THE ABSORBING MAN — 44

SERIES A — 51

SERIES A — 52 — QUICKSILVER

37 — THE WATCHER

SERIES A — RED SONJA — 38

SERIES A — MANTIS — 45

MYSTERIO — SERIES A — 46

THE GRIM REAPER — 53

SHANNA THE SHE-DEVIL — 54 — SERIES A

39 — IRON FIST — SERIES A

SERIES A — LOKI — 40

SERIES A — THE GREEN GOBLIN — 47

SERIES A — 48 — KRAVEN

SERIES A — 55 — MEDUSA

SERIES A — 56 — THE RAWHIDE KID

SERIES A — 81 — RHINO

SERIES A — MARY JANE WATSON — 82

SERIES A — HAMMERHEAD — 89

HERCULES — 90

SERIES A — BLACK KNIGHT — 97

98 — THE PUPPET MASTER

83 — DRAGON MAN

DR. DOOM — 84

HELA, THE GODDESS OF DEATH — 91 — SERIES A

SERIES A — BYRRAH — 92

SERIES A — SANDMAN — 99

O.K, that takes care of the first 99 . . .

LILITH, DRACULA'S DAUGHTER — SERIES A — 85

SERIES A — ZEMO — 86

SILVER SURFER — 93

SERIES A — 94 — DR. STRANGE

This space reserved for the rarest Marvel Value Stamp of all!

SERIES A — GALACTUS — 100

Who'd you think we were gonna feature?

Millie The Model?

SERIES A — J. JONAH JAMESON — 87

SERIES A — 88 — THE LEADER

SERIES A — MOLE MAN — 95

DR. OCTOPUS — SERIES A — 96

CBA Interview

Comix Book: A Marvel Oddity

Denis Kitchen talks about Stan's short strange trip

Conducted by Jon B. Cooke
Transcribed by Jon B. Knutson

For over 25 years Denis Kitchen was the publishing mogul behind Kitchen Sink Press, the lamented comic book company which transcended its underground comix origins to become a premier direct market power in the industry. While KSP has since closed its doors, Denis—a talented cartoonist in his own right—continues to be involved in the industry as a consultant and he kindly consented to an interview during International Comic Con: San Diego in August, 1999. Denis copy-edited the transcript.

Above: *1974 photo of struggling underground comix publisher/cartoonist Denis Kitchen teaming up with Marvel's head honcho Stan Lee. Photo taken at Marvel's New York office. Courtesy of Denis Kitchen.*

Comic Book Artist: *When did you first get into comics?*
Denis Kitchen: As far back as I can remember. It was one of those childhood "addictions," like all of us in the field.
CBA: *Were you into the Dells…?*
Denis: I had a lot of Dells, *Superman, Li'l Abner,* the early horror comics—like Atlas, I really dug those—just about everything. I enjoyed *Uncle Scrooge, Donald Duck, Humbug* and *Mad* when I could find them; it was a pretty eclectic diet. All the kids in my neighborhood collected and we traded, so all kinds of tastes would get mixed up, because you'd just swap your stack for someone else's. It was great.
CBA: *When did you recognize something was happening with Marvel Comics?*
Denis: Well, I was at the right age, I was about 14 or 15 when Stan's Marvel Revolution took place. I was just starting to earn money part-time, so I was buying the comics; I was there when the first "Spider-Man," and the first *X-Men* hit the stands. I think I discovered *Fantastic Four* with #4. I became very hooked on these things and—I hate to admit it—I was what you would have to call a "Marvel Zombie" as a teenager. They were a genuine phenomenon back then. I continued reading and ardently collecting them through

college. The smartest thing I ever did, in the '60s, was I used to buy five copies each of those earliest Marvels, put four away and keep one to read, long before I was even aware of an active fandom. I ended up selling most—not for nearly what they're going for now, but at many, many times over what I paid for them, and they helped me start my publishing company. So in an ironic way, Marvel helped capitalize me, and in the '70s, they subsidized me. So, they unintentionally supported underground comix.
CBA: *Did you recognize Kirby as being special?*
Denis: I did. I certainly admired Kirby, and Ditko I liked a lot. Like everyone, I had some strong tastes, but I most enjoyed the Kirby/Sinnott *Fantastic Four* and the Ditko *Spider-Man,* the flagship titles.
CBA: *Did you recognize the editorial voice of Stan Lee being a hip kind of thing?*
Denis: You know, I did, and when I self-published my first comic, *Mom's Homemade Comics* #1 in 1969, I sent copies to a handful of professionals—not thinking I'd ever get a reply back—and one of them was Stan. Well, he sent a very sweet letter back, encouraging me. That began a correspondence I never anticipated, because he was a pretty busy guy, and I was just some kid in Wisconsin; but I guess he saw a spark and I appreciated his commentary. (That's not to say we were weekly correspondents, but we sent letters back and forth every few months.) He actually started calling me, offering me jobs, which flattered me, but at that point I was very much into the underground comix scene. I really didn't want to move to New York and work for Marvel; but I was flattered that Stan was periodically calling and writing me.
CBA: *Do you remember the initial call?*
Denis: I can tell you it would've been in the early '70s, probably 1971 or '72—because our deal finally happened in 1973, so it had to be the year or two preceding that.
CBA: *Were you surprised Stan the Man was reaching out to you?*
Denis: Very surprised; but, you know, there were little things I did that he seemed to appreciate. For example, I used to change stationery all the time, as I enjoyed having a variety of letterheads. Early on, for Krupp's corporate symbol, I created an octopus, and each tentacle held a different division, and each division had its own letterhead. [*Krupp was the "umbrella" company that eventually became Kitchen Sink Press*] I'd just get tired of writing letters on the same letterhead. It'd be like, "Okay, it's Tuesday, I'm going to use this one." We had a studio we called "The Cartoon Factory," and there were two artists and myself, and we did a jam drawing at the top. It was a literal cartoon assembly line (which maybe Stan related to) but at the bottom, the address read "Studio at 1530-something North Street, Located above the prestigious Polly Prim Dry Cleaners," or something like that; it was very tongue-in-cheek. [*laughter*] Stan told me it made him laugh out loud, and he said, "We need clever guys here, come over to Marvel and we'll put you to work." So on one hand, it was very flattering because he'd been a childhood hero, but I really didn't relish the idea of going to New York. That was a large part of it—I just liked being where I was; and also, I didn't know how I'd fit in at Marvel. I really didn't want to write his kind of comics, I couldn't draw his kind of comics, so he saw me in an editorial role, but I didn't want to edit Marvel comics, even though I had enjoyed reading them during my formative years. The kinds of comics I wanted to do increasingly made Stan's hair stand on end, but then finally, a couple of coincidences changed things.

I started Krupp/Kitchen Sink in 1969. The underground comix industry—which had been burgeoning, mushrooming in size—ran into a couple of serious hurdles in 1973. First, the Supreme Court came up with a new definition of obscenity that basically threw the definition back to local communities to define. That sent a chill through all of the head shops that were the base of our distribution. These retailers were already paranoid because they were selling drug paraphernalia and the authorities were looking for a reason to bust them. So they figured underground comix were where they were the most vulnerable. Overnight, a lot of our head shop accounts literally stopped buying underground comix, and that cut out a good part of our mainstay. (You've got to remember, this is well before the direct market.)

CBA: *So, it wasn't necessarily tied to declining interest in the books?*

Denis: Well, actually, when I said there were two things, the other thing was a glut in the underground market. They had been so successful in the late '60s and early '70s, that a lot of what I called "wannabe" publishers and artists jumped in. These were often more amateurish and more derivative guys who would just be copying Crumb, instead of being inspired to do their own work. Just like today, the problem is a lot of retailers weren't paying close attention to the product. They would carry anything, and put any comix on the shelf just because they thought everything was selling; and it wasn't. The consumers began to say, "Some of this stuff is sh*t, and I'm not going to buy it," and it started clogging up the racks. And these retailers—who by and large were not comics fans (remember, they were primarily selling tie-dyed shirts and bongs and beads, so they didn't necessarily know a great underground comic from a horrible underground comic), so that combination put a lot of us on the ropes. We all stopped in our tracks. About that time, good ol' Stan called—I'd also just married, and had at that point an infant daughter, and another on the way—and suddenly his offer sounded intriguing! It also sounded like a lifesaver.

CBA: *To go to New York and work at Marvel….*

Denis: It was not specific. So basically I said, "Stan, tell me exactly what you have in mind, because maybe now circumstances are different." So he said, "Fly out here, and let's talk!" So I went out there and met with him in New York. I've even got a terrible picture somewhere with me—hair well past my shoulders—with my arm around Stan or something. Sol Brodsky was there—Sol was his production manager, as I recall. The three of us sat down at Stan's desk and he said, "I really admire the energy that's going on in underground comix, and I'd love for Marvel to capture a piece of that energy. Do you think you can put together some kind of hybrid magazine for us and bring some of that talent to Marvel?" There were a lot of reasons why much of that talent would not want to work for Marvel, but on the other hand I said, "A lot of these artists are very eager to expand their distribution and audience, and you've got distribution clout. Right now our distribution system is in real disarray. Maybe there's enough each side can give the other and we can make it happen." So, we worked up the terms, but it was conditioned on my not moving to New York. I insisted I stay in Wisconsin, and Stan said, "Well, we just don't work that way." They had the bullpen in New York, and everyone worked there, but I said, "Why spend New York rent on me when you can pay Wisconsin rent? I'll send stuff to you promptly, I'll be in constant touch with you or Sol or whoever you designate; I'll meet my deadlines. So does it matter where I am?" It was basically the equivalent of a "flex-time," and surprisingly, he relented. If he hadn't, I would've just nixed it, even though I needed the work—I would've done something else.

CBA: *Stan was very anxious to work with you?*

Denis: Yes, surprisingly. Honestly, I really didn't get it. I still don't completely get it. I guess he was trying to prove that he was hip—or Marvel was hip. Anyway, when he met that condition, I thought, "Wow!" And he offered me a salary of $15,000 a year—gold in 1973 compared with the pittance I was making in underground comix. It was suddenly like… I couldn't believe it!

CBA: *Yeah, working through the mail….*

Denis: The other nice thing was I didn't have to stop my own publishing company! Basically, I moonlighted for Marvel, and I continued to do what I did before. I just didn't have to draw any money out of my company. So, that's how Marvel subsidized Kitchen Sink!

CBA: *Were you basically, after living expenses, pouring money*

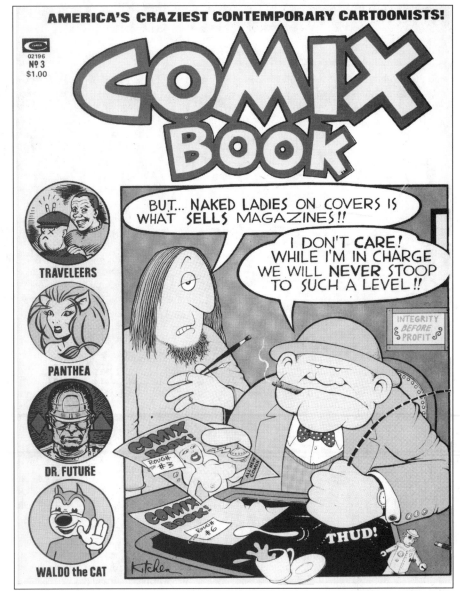

AMERICA'S CRAZIEST CONTEMPORARY CARTOONISTS!

02196
Nº 3
$1.00

COMIX BOOK

TRAVELEERS

PANTHEA

DR. FUTURE

WALDO the CAT

BUT… NAKED LADIES ON COVERS IS WHAT **SELLS** MAGAZINES!!

I DON'T **CARE!** WHILE I'M IN CHARGE WE WILL **NEVER** STOOP TO SUCH A LEVEL!!

INTEGRITY *BEFORE* PROFIT

Kitchen

back into KSP?

Denis: Yeah, absolutely. Especially at that time. Because the margins were even thinner, with fewer shops willing to carry them, we had to basically work harder on our mail-order business and to find other kinds of shops and bookstores to carry our books. At that point, there were just a handful of what you could call comics shops. Bud Plant was doing mail order back then, Phil Seuling had his conventions and was doing a bit of distribution—they were our first real alternatives to the head shop system. We couldn't have anticipated how the direct market would grow and turn into thousands of shops. At the time, it was just a curiosity that a few guys could actually just mostly sell comics. I didn't see it as the next big industry trend. Getting back to Stan, what appealed to me was that Marvel, through Curtis Distribution, could get our magazine to newsstands—that was our dream: Instead of printing maybe 10,000 underground comix, getting them to our readers through this rickety head shop distribution system, with *Comix Book* we could have a couple hundred thousand printed and out in front of a much wider audience. So, I signed the bottom line, and we were in business.

CBA: *So, when did the issue arise of returning original art?*

Denis: At the very beginning, I tried to explain that I could not, in good faith, invite the artists I knew to work for Marvel if they had to give up the artwork and copyright and freedom they were accustomed to. And Stan kept saying, "Well, this is a hybrid. They've got to learn how to compromise, and we'll learn to compromise, and we just have to find a place we can compromise on."

Basically, the point we won the quickest was the original art, because I just said that was non-negotiable. We simply would not give Marvel the art. If they insisted on it, there would be no deal.

Above: *Denis Kitchen cover art for Comix Book #3, tweaking Stan's request for more racy material in the magazine. Courtesy of Denis Kitchen. ©2000 Marvel Characters, Inc.*

Below: *Skip Williamson's work was featured in every issue of Comix Book.*

COMIX BOOK

©2000 Marvel Characters, Inc.

Missives to Stan the Man

Living far afield of Marvel's New York base, Denis Kitchen retained a correspondence with Stan Lee regarding the progress of Comix Book. With the help of Stacey Kitchen, Denis was kind enough to share carbon copies of his letters to Stan the Man. Below is the actual letterhead Denis used.

February 13, 1975

Dear Stan—

Send your lovely secretaries out of the room for a while and tell them to hold your calls… this report may take a bit of your time. But I think it's important to fill you in on the state of the West Coast artists I've visited.

As you are probably aware from many different sources (a proliferation of scholarly "histories," attention in *Playboy* and other top magazines, product spin-offs, etc.), the underground cartoonists are an important development in comics. They are too numerous and influential to ignore. And they are too independent and irascible to submit to a traditional assembly-line role. *Comix Book* was the first attempt to bring this talent into a regular newsstand publication. The mail I've been getting is overwhelmingly favorable, and the new direction we have taken has been applauded by most artists. The mere fact that we are facing a number of new imitators should prove that a market does indeed exist, and you can take pride in being the first to crack it.

But let me break down some of the key subjects. I'll try to be succinct. If you want to discuss any of them further, just give me a call.

DISTRIBUTION. Every artist I talked to said *Comix Book* was difficult to find in the Bay area. The few places that carry it sell out quickly, but it is just not readily available. This is a particular shame because the Bay area could be the single best sales area in the country for this publication. It has always been the backbone of the underground comix industry because an underground comix publisher could sell tens of thousands of comix in his own back yard, using the most primitive means of distributions. So by all means have your road men check out the problems there.

Artists and friends in Chicago and Milwaukee report a similar situation: They cannot find the magazine. I talked to a distributor in Michigan named Donahoe who said he had sold 100% of his shipment of *Comix Book* (some 1700 copies) but he also relayed the story of another distributor who never even opened his boxes. He allegedly reported a small sale and returned the rest unopened. I shudder to think that this is happening on a large scale. It's frustrating to hear these stories, because there is an obvious demand for the book, but [there are] widespread reports of bad distribution. I just hope the road men you now have can educate and prod the local jobbers.

COMPETITION. There are basically four competing publications available or in the works:

Funny Papers. This may not be in direct competition because of its tabloid format. But it has the advantage of being colorful, it allegedly is being promoted by a series of national radio spots, and it is allowing artists to retain the copyright to their work. The first two issues contain cameo Crumb pieces because Crumb's lawyer is one of the co-publishers, and the lawyer owns some of Crumb's stuff. But Crumb himself is not involved in the publication. A couple of *Funny Papers* regulars (Trina and Ted Richards) are also *Comix Book* regulars. The last time I spoke to you, you

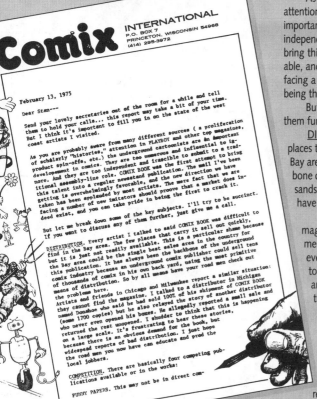

Above: Denis Kitchen used a number of different letterheads and envelopes for his fledgling companies. The above and envelope on next page are collaborations of Denis and Peter Poplaski. Courtesy and ©2000 Denis Kitchen. Next page: Denis' "sort-of" introduction page from Comix Book #1, featuring a very J. Jonah Jameson-like Stan Lee. ©2000 Denis Kitchen.

Below: Named for the German "Merchant of Death" munitions manufacturer, Krupp Comics Works was the umbrella corporation for Kitchen's various entrepreneurial "schemes and plots." ©2000 Denis Kitchen.

So he said, "All right, fine, fine; but we've got to own the copyright." And we just argued and argued about it. So the first compromise was they agreed that any pre-existing characters—like Skip Williamson's "Snappy Sammy Smoot," or any character like that—the artist would continue to own the trademark, and Marvel couldn't make any claim on any material, ancillary products, foreign or otherwise. Once I won that point, I just kept hammering away on the copyrights, and initially, as I recall, we compromised to the extent that Marvel would own the first publishing rights, and they had certain limited and defined rights. It didn't make either side enthusiastic, but it was a compromise. Then ultimately I think I just wore Stan down, to be honest. Since this was not a typical Marvel property, Stan saw it as an experiment, and he finally in exasperation just said, "All right, fine." As soon as he said that, I immediately sent out a letter to all the artists, because I knew that would make a lot of difference to artists who would never contribute if they had to give up the copyright. So, that automatically expanded the number of potential contributors.

CBA: *Were you frank with Stan about what was happening in the marketplace, or did you just feel it was a distribution problem at that time not worth mentioning?*

Denis: I think I didn't want to give away too much. I didn't want to say, "Stan, my business is on the verge of collapse." I think what I said was that it was changing and we were adjusting, but distribution was the core of the problem, and that they had something we needed, and vice-versa, we had something he needed, which was fresh blood, fresh perspective. I think he already saw that during his career he'd seen super-heroes flourish, and then die, and be reborn, and other genres he'd been involved in—like *Patsy Walker* and those kind of teenage comics, romance comics—he'd seen all these genres go; it was cyclical, and here was a new generation, doing these new-fangled underground comix, and he wanted a piece of it. Stan wanted to be the guy who brought them in before the competition. I don't think he realized how intrinsically incompatible they were philosophically. To be honest, I don't think he read very many of them, he just spotted a trend. I kept trying to explain to him that guys like Crumb and S. Clay Wilson and so on were going to be doing things that might be shocking, and he said, "No, no, we can't be too shocking, the newsstand distributors won't carry it." He gave guidelines, and we pushed and shoved, and basically, we ended up with typical kinds of compromises, it didn't make either party happy. For example, we were allowed limited nudity—which was another first for Marvel—but we were not allowed frontal nudity (I even made fun of it on my cover); we were allowed swear words, but not the "ultimate" swear words…

CBA: *So what were you allowed to say?*

Denis: I think we could even say "f*ck," but you couldn't say "motherf*cker." Things like that. I just remember Stan was very uncomfortable when we tried to push it too far, but he kept saying it wasn't him, it was the distributors who would never allow that sort of language. Curtis would not allow frontal nudity. We even got around frontal nudity, because in the very first issue, John Pound had a centerfold on the wall with pubic hair, but it was a centerfold, not a character. So, we were always trying to figure out ways to break the

eported that *Funny Papers* was having difficulty with its distributors… that an over-whelming number of the first issue were returned. But, according to the artists I spoke to, the project is still going strong and artists are being paid for work in forthcoming issues.

Comix International. As you are probably aware, Jim Warren fully intends to develop this title along the lines of *Comix Book*. Warren gave Keith Green an expense account and authorized him to put together an underground-format magazine. I can safely predict that this venture will fall flat on its face. Nearly every artist I spoke to had nothing good to say about this project. There are three primary objections to it: 1.) Warren (deservedly or not) had a bad reputation among the artists. 2.) Keith Green displays a reckless arrogance that offends many artists, and he has a history of being personally unreliable. 3.) The artists don't like the idea of sharing a book with dozens of pages of monster type ads, which are essential to Warren's operation.

Green apparently gave up hope of getting any new material, so he has begun solic-iting permission for reprints, but he is running into considerable resistance here too. So I strongly suspect that Warren will be able to offer no competition to *Comix Book*, certainly not with Keith Green at the helm.

Arcade. This book has yet to appear. Its initial deadlines have already been stretched, but, from the information I gathered, it will apparently be strong in content. It is also weak in terms of organization and distribution. The biggest thing going for *Arcade* is that it allows artists to retain their copyright. This has allowed them to obtain the loyalty of certain of the more militant artists. Robert Crumb has designed the front cover, but has little inside. Bill Griffith and art spiegelman share the role of editor. They also share personality flaws: extreme arrogance and intolerance. This stance has created a cliquish atmosphere around *Arcade*. It is being published by The Print Mint, the largest of the remaining underground publishing houses, in an initial press run of 25,000. They hope to do well enough on this small run to attract a national distributor through contact with Woody Gelman in New York. Their current rates are only $50/page, but the copyright policy has attracted some top talent.

Apple Pie. I mention this as a fourth competitor only because it is beginning to solicit work from more and more underground artists. The publisher, Dennis Lopez, is paying $100/page, which equals the *Comix Book* rate, but he has begun to promise the artists a compro-mise on the copyright policy. I did not see this new policy in writing, but according to one artist (Kim Deitch) Lopez is allowing the artist to retain the copyright on his work in return for which Lopez gets exclusive use of the material for something like 18 months and has a special option for reprints. If this is true, it sets a precedent that will attract many artists.

rules, because part of it was that the whole generation of young cartoonists was part of this anti-establishment, revolutionary fervor, and the last thing we wanted to be told was, "You can't do some-thing." Marvel was paying us very good money—at that time, it was $100 a page, which was well above the underground rates—and I think there were enough hungry and pragmatic cartoonists, and I was among them, to be willing to do *Comix Book.* My feeling was the worst that could happen was we'd increase our exposure and get through this tough time in our core market; the best that could happen is it would be very successful and a much larger audience would find us.

CBA: *What was KSP's best-selling book before the crash?*
Denis: Well, in 1971 I published *Home-Grown Funnies,* which was a perennial. We just kept reprinting it. R. Crumb did the whole thing. That cumulatively reached, I think, 180,000, but not by '73. That was just one where every year we'd reprint it once or twice, and it just kept adding up. It was hardly ever out of print.
CBA: *What was the typical print run?*
Denis: Typical was 10,000. We never did anything less than 10,000. It depended on the artist. When Crumb did *XYZ Comics* for us, our initial printing was 50,000, and that wasn't something that came from a purchase order from Diamond. It just came from the gut. For 20 years, I picked numbers from the "gut system."
CBA: *Ulcers in that gut! [laughs]*
Denis: But you know, it was relatively easy to sell 10 or 20,000 copies of *any* underground comic.
CBA: *What was the distributing cut?*
Denis: Pretty much the same: We sold at 60% off, we paid the creators 10% of cover royalty, and we lived on what was left after paying the printer and covering overhead.
CBA: *Was the average cover price 50¢?*
Denis: In the beginning it was 50¢, and there was a period when there was rampant inflation, and comics rapidly went to 75¢, a buck,

The copyright question is the most volatile issue concern-ing underground artists. It is, in fact, of grave concern to many older, more expe-rienced artists as well. Like the women's liberation movement, it is a ground-swell which shows no signs of abating. The artists generally concede that where house characters are involved and where traditional assembly-line techniques are used, the publisher has a valid claim to copyright. But where an artist is the sole creator (writer, penciler, inker, letterer, etc.) and sees his creation as a work of art, he sees no reason why the copyright should not be retained by him. Authors of novels retain the copyright to their creations. Comic book artists are beginning to feel the self-respect that questions the old practice. Obviously, the publisher has concerns too. As you have pointed out, profits are ultimately made in many cases only by reprinting, selling to overseas markets, etc. But some compromise must be possible. If you examine *National Lampoon, Funny Papers, Apple Pie,* existing undergrounds, and other publications in this genre, you'll see that each artist retains the copyright. As the list of publications allowing this grows, my ability to recruit top talent becomes more inhibited.

I'm not saying that I cannot put together a package under the current arrangement, but Marvel will find itself in an uncompetitive situation if the current trend continues.

If all other factors are equal, I can put together the best damn comix magazine anywhere. I can recruit Crumb, Shelton, Kurtzman, anybody—you name him—if we can resolve this copyright dilemma. But I feel like I have an editorial leg-iron. Do you see the point? Can you think of an arrangement that can protect the interests of Cadence/Marvel and still give the artist ultimate control over his creation??? I think some sort of compromise will need to be worked out if we are to attract the top talent. And we need to attract the top talent in order to reach the high circulation figures we both believe are possible.

You personally have a lot of respect from the artists I know. They realize that you have stuck your neck out to publish *Comix Book*. They see you as an innovator. Most grew up on the early pure-Stan Lee Marvels of a decade or so ago… and they see *Comix Book* as the beginning of a whole new wave. But you must also know that today's young cartoonists have an acute awareness of comic book history. They know all the stories. They see a Will Eisner who kept the rights to his work and they see a relationship between his being a great artist and his retention of copyrights. They hear about the contemporary French cartoonists who retain rights to their work—and the French publishers still flourish. And there is a whole group of underground artists who own their work and who are reluctant to compromise on this key issue. There are a good number of second-level talents who will opt for the quick money, but the best artists will produce their best work only when the proper incentive is there… and that will mean a book which (if your editor does his job right) will sell better and be even more profitable for the publisher.

If I seem to dwell on this subject it is because I was bombarded with it during my four-day visit to the coast. Excitement is in the air. New titles. Lots of activity. But I wanted to convey the general mood to you in hopes that we can continue to maintain our vanguard position in what is proving to be a large new market.

I'd like to hear your attitudes and ideas along these lines sometime soon.

Best regards,

Denis

[*As the next Kitchen letter indicates, apparently Denis and Stan have a phone conversation in the interim, hashing out a revised copyright policy, and Stan makes a suggestion for "spicier material." The following was edited for pertinence.*]

February 28, 1975

Dear Stan—

…[N]ow that your feelings toward spicier material is clear, I will point artists in that direction more. I think you'll agree that each issue has gotten progressively better. You'll love the cover for the fifth issue, and, as I indicated earlier, Richard Corben has left Warren and will be doing the sixth cover for *Comix Book* (probably a combination of the two things he draws best: Monsters and women). I also have a promise from Ron Cobb for a cover. Cobb, as you may recall, is an excellent political cartoonist who appears in virtually every underground newspaper.

From the mail I'm getting, and phone calls, I can sense a growing surge in favor of the magazine. The mail I get is 95% favorable. I have to work hard to fit in a derogatory letter to balance the letters pages. People like Kurtzman, Eisner, [*Michael*] O'Donoghue, and other respected professionals have had high praise for the magazine. The recent trip I took to San Francisco indicated support from artists I previously considered unapproachable, like Gilbert Shelton. And the new copyright policy will undoubtedly result in better work from the current staff and new contributions from the top artists around. I just hope you and [*then-Marvel president*] Al Landau are aware of the unique position of *Comix Book*. You told me over the phone that you expect all your books to make money right from the start. But in our very first conversations you told me you wanted a magazine with a European flavor; one that commanded respect, and one that had a high growth potential… one that could ultimately reach the circulation of something like [*National*] *Lampoon*. I firmly believe I can meet those initial goals, but I'm also worried that I have a very short rope around my neck. You apparently are unable (or at least Cadence is unable to) give the magazine too many issues to establish itself in the black. I can understand that from the publisher's viewpoint, but I think there are other factors to consider. *Lampoon* was allowed to lose money for eight issues, but then it grew into one of the hottest magazines on the market, with sales in the area of 1,000,000/month. *Comix Book* is probably one of the few books Marvel/Cadence has with the *potential* to reach that kind of circulation level.

In terms of sheer respect, I think you personally have received and deserve a lot of it for getting *Comix Book* off the ground. I think you will be rewarded financially as well, when the magazine establishes itself.

I realize you have far more experience in marketing magazines than I do, so I am steering future covers in the direction you've indicated: Blurbs, sexy girls, and a more blatant "underground" image. I'll also intend to make greater use of text pieces to break up the cartoons, and to avoid juxtaposing styles that are too similar.

I have prepared a form letter to send to contributors and potential contributors outlining the new policy on copyrights, based on our recent phone conversation. I have

---

$1.25, etc., until they got where they are today. When we started, it cost only about a nickel to print a comic, so they could usually retail for fifty cents.

CBA: *Did you get on the phone to R. Crumb and S. Clay Wilson?*

Denis: Yeah, Wilson was willing to contribute, but Crumb was not. Crumb had a very strong prejudice against Marvel, and I knew that—I knew he was not going to be on the list.

CBA: *Was it because Marvel was the "establishment"?*

Denis: Exactly. I think he saw it would've been some kind of sell-out, and I respected that. I didn't expect him to at least initially do anything. My feeling was if we broke enough rules and we were able to impress him with the content, he would eventually contribute something, but if he didn't that was fine. The truth is, I expected him to do stuff for Kitchen Sink Press, and I didn't count on him for *Comix Book*. To me, using Marvel terms, these were parallel universes, and the overlap was fairly minimal. I knew there were certain artists more appropriate for the Marvel product—with exceptions, the hungry, more pragmatic, less political, and those capable of doing more mainstream work. I also wanted to mix it up editorially. Again, it's hard in retrospect when I look at those magazines; it would've been done a lot differently now, but at the time, I was trying for a real mix, and I thought the feedback we got from the letters column and distributors and so forth would start to help us know what was most successful. The truth is, aside from the hard-core "hippie audience" we were reaching with our Kitchen Sink comics, I wasn't sure who would pick this up off the newsstands, and neither was Stan. That's why we called it an experiment, and a hybrid. One of Stan's biggest concerns was how closely he'd be associated with it. He was very concerned that we'd embarrass him and Marvel, so he wanted to distance himself from *Comix Book*. At the same time, he desperately wanted to get credit if it were a trend-setter and successful. That quandary lasted right up until the moment the first issue went to press. As I was fine-tuning the contents page, I had

basically everything in place except whether Stan was on the masthead or not, and if so what his title was. He'd already made it clear he didn't want Marvel's name on it. I think the only clue was Curtis was on the cover. So, basically, I remember on the last day, I had to get this thing in Marvel's production all pasted-up. I called him and said, "Stan, you've *got* to tell me: Are you the publisher, or are you off the masthead altogether?" And he said, "I'll tell you what: Why don't you list me as 'instigator,' because if you guys really embarrass me and get me in trouble, I can just wave my hand and say, 'Look, I just instigated the thing.' But if it's very successful, I can get credit and say, 'Hey, I *instigated* that!'" That was the ambiguous term he thought would fit both scenarios, so that's how he was listed.

CBA: *The "sort-of" introduction page you drew—featured Stan pretty prominently, looking a lot like J. Jonah Jameson.*

Denis: Yes, I drew Stan as Jameson. What I wanted to make sure Marvel understood was that they were not going to be immune to satire, and I wanted to set the tone early on by kind of poking fun at Stan! So it was very tongue-in-cheek; it was basically my way of saying, "We kind of, sort of, sold out… but don't worry, we're still feisty and we're still going to be throwing punches, and no one's going to stop us, not even the hand that feeds us. So stick with us."

CBA: *How do you think* Comix Book *did? Was it successful?*

Denis: Measured by sales, it was apparently unsuccessful. That was the official word.

CBA: *How privy to sales reports were you?*

Denis: They did not reveal it to me. I know they printed between 200,000 and 250,000 copies of each issue, and whatever the break-even was (which I think was somewhere in the 30% range) we'd obviously all hoped it would sell half the copies and be profitable based on comments Sol Brodsky made to me. I think it was selling somewhere in the 30% range, and it was looking to break even or not quite. So, early on, I remember saying to Stan that I wasn't an expert in the magazine field, but I knew from what I had read that a

Below: *When Marvel bailed out from publishing the magazine, Kitchen already had two issues of* Comix Book *ready to print. #4 (below) and #5 (next page) were published under the Kitchen Sink imprint. Courtesy of Denis Kitchen.*

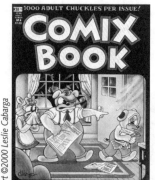

1000 ADULT CHUCKLES PER ISSUE!

COMIX BOOK

"YOUTH'S COMPANION"

explained that Marvel/Cadence will allow artists to retain the copyright to the work, with the clear understanding that Cadence/Marvel can reprint the stories at any future date without further compensation. I'd appreciate it if you'd send me an official note confirming that position....

Best regards,

Denis

Your favorite Wisconsin editor

[Our last missive is the form letter sent out to Comix Book *contributors regarding the revised copyright policy.]*

March 5, 1975

Dear Artist—

Working for a large publisher like Cadence/Marvel has its advantages, such as large circulation and high page rates (paid promptly). Cadence has also altered some of its traditional policies to the benefit of *Comix Book* contributors. It now returns all original artwork to the artists, and it has ceded trademark rights to characters in *Comix Book* to the artists.

But there has been one area that has continued to disturb most artists… *copyrights.* Cadence/Marvel has been paying contributors to *Comix Book* $100 per page for new material. For that they have been buying permanent rights to the material (except trademark rights to the characters).

Those of us who have worked for the various underground presses have been accustomed to retaining the rights to our work or have been assured of receiving future residuals from the copyright owner. But large publishers of comic books have traditionally owned copyrights outright. In cases where house characters are produced by a changing line-up of writers, pencilers, inkers, letterers, etc., it is understandable that the publisher owns the material. It has also been the publishers' claim that the only way they can make a profit off their comics is by reprinting them later. But underground artists in most cases work on a solo basis, creating their own characters, consider their comix as Art, and feel a basic moral right to own the material.

I am happy to announce a major policy change with regard to future contributions to *Comix Book* (beginning with issue #5). Henceforth each artist will retain the copyright to his/her own work, with the understanding that Cadence/Marvel may reprint the work without further compensation. But the artists are now free to arrange their own reprints

in anthologies or elsewhere. This compromise allows each side, I think, to operate with maximum flexibility and protection. It should be remembered that if we want the rates and exposure a large publisher offers, we cannot expect to also retain *total* control over our work, although that should be our ultimate goal.

Sincerely,

Denis Kitchen, editor

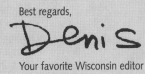

COMIX BOOK

P.O. BOX 7
PRINCETON, WISCONSIN 54968
(414) 295-3972

March 5, 1975

Dear Artist---

Working for a large publisher like Cadence/Marvel has its advantages, such as large circulation and high page rates (paid promptly.) Cadence has also altered some of its traditional policies to the benefit of COMIX BOOK contributors. It now returns all original artwork to the artists, and it has ceded trademark rights to characters in COMIX BOOK to the artists.

But there has been one area that has continued to disturb most artists... COPYRIGHTS. Cadence/Marvel has been paying contributors to COMIX BOOK $100 per page for new material. For that they have been buying permanent rights to the material (except trademark rights to the characters.)

Those of us who have worked for the various underground presses have been accustomed to retaining the rights to our work or have been assured of receiving future residuals from the copyright owner. But large publishers of comic books have traditionally owned copyrights outright. In cases where house characters are produced by a changing line-up of writers, pencillers, inkers, letterers, etc., it is understandable that the publisher owns the material. It has also been the publishers' claim that the only way they can make a profit off their comics is by reprinting them later. But underground artists in most cases work on a solo basis, creating their own characters, consider their comix an Art, and feel a basic moral right to own the material.

I am happy to announce a major policy change with regard to future contributions to COMIX BOOK (beginning with issue No.5.) Henceforth each artist will retain the copyright to his/her own work, with the understanding that Cadence/Marvel may reprint the work without further compensation. But the artists are now free to arrange their own reprints in anthologies or elsewhere. This compromise allows each side, I think, to operate with maximum flexibility and protection. It should be remembered that if we want the rates and exposure a large publisher offers, we cannot expect to also retain TOTAL control over our work, although that should be our ultimate goal.

Sincerely,

Denis

Denis Kitchen, editor

lot of magazines start out unprofitably, and they require the publisher to have some patience. I used to say to Stan, "Give me some rope on this. It doesn't look to be immediately profitable, but let us flex our muscle. Give it a year, at least."

CBA: *You had Skip Williamson, Howard Cruse, Kim Deitch, Justin Green, Trina Robbins—just in that first issue. And of course, you had art spiegelman's first version of "Maus."*

Denis: *Comix Book* gave the first real national exposure to all of them, including *Maus.*

CBA: *How long did the magazine last?*

Denis: Basically, I was working on #5 when Stan pulled the plug on it, and they had published three. My cover was on #3, the last one Marvel did. There were two in the can when he cancelled it, and so I negotiated the right to publish them under the Kitchen Sink imprint. So, #4 and 5 are the ones we did ourselves.

CBA: *So you were just committed to using up the inventory?*

Denis: Well, sure. It deserved publication. What was happening at that point at Marvel was what I call the "Pandora's Box Effect." When Stan made these concessions—letting us have our art back, letting us keep copyrights and trademarks, and pushing the envelope with nudity and all of these things—all the other people who worked for Marvel (in the bullpen and the freelancers) all started giving him a lot of sh*t about it, because they resented that these newcomers had a different deal than they did. I think it was Lee Marrs who told me she was in the office and heard a lot of grousing about, "How come the hippies get special considerations; what's the deal?" It seemed that Stan had to either broaden those rights to include the other artists or just stop. And that's why I still don't know exactly if *Comix Book* was killed because of sales alone, or whether the political issues raised were causing so much trouble that he just had to cut it and then say to people, "Well, look, it was just an experiment, one-time only, never gonna do it again, stop asking for it, just get out of my face." But I know there were some disgruntled voices—and I'm not

surprised. I'm glad, because the truth is,
all of us were part of what we thought was a generation
that was making change, and the comic book industry certainly, desperately, needed a change. The way artists were treated was just plain wrong. I certainly understand even today that a house-owned property like Spider-Man, for example, has to be work-for-hire, but what we were
championing wasn't house-owned properties. We wanted to do creator-owned properties, and autobiographies, and illustrated histories—all kinds of things that various artists were excited about doing that were not part of mainstream comics. So, when I heard inklings of discontent, I thought, "Great, even if the magazine fails, we let a few demons out of the box, and they'll never quite be able to put them back." The truth is, gradually, grudgingly, all these things came to pass in terms of returning original art and treating artists more fairly. Obviously, the big houses still can't give the same broad rights to creators working on company titles, but they are, for example, paying royalties based on re-use, foreign editions, all kinds of things that, when we were started *Comix Book,* were unheard of. You got a flat rate, and that was it—it didn't matter if they sold 100,000 or a million. It didn't matter if there was a German edition or a Brazilian edition, it was like, "Here's your check; go away." So, in a lot of ways, the underground comix forced economic changes in the industry, as well as obviously opening up the kinds of topics comic books tackled. They broke the formula in many ways, positive ways.

CBA: *It's also interesting that* Comix Book *seems to be a precursor of some sorts—at least maybe the catalyst—for* Arcade.

Denis: Yeah, in fact, it was—in an interesting way—perceived as a too-cautious and limited experiment to a handful of artists like spiegelman and Bill Griffith. When it started, I inadvertently forgot to send an invitation to Bill Griffith, and he was pretty miffed by that. He sent me a nasty note. He thought the snub was deliberate—it was not. Spiegelman consented to being in the first two issues, but

Art ©2000 Justin Green

MAUS

he was not happy with some of the other contributors. For example, he detested Howard Cruse's work. He detested a squirt gun piece that Mike Baron wrote that art thought was infantile. Art just went off on what he saw as flaws in the first issue or two, and basically, he and Bill decided they'd go to Print Mint, and they'd do their own magazine as kind of an answer to this. Ultimately, they did a great magazine series in the traditional underground format of no rules, no restrictions. As a result they were able to get Crumb to do covers and contributions, and it was a marvelous series. In fact, I actually contributed to it myself—I made up with Bill, and art. We always got along personally. What it really boiled down to was I was in a position where I, personally and professionally, had to do something pragmatic, and I was willing to do something pragmatic, weighing all the possible consequences. My wife abandoned me with two baby girls. She never came back. I was feeling desperate. I think art and Bill saw it as some kind of betrayal to what underground comix were all about, in that you couldn't compromise. So they put out *Arcade* as a more "pure" underground comix magazine. The downside with *Arcade*, of course, was that Print Mint could not get the kind of national distribution that Marvel could, and so it ended up being distributed no differently than any other underground comic, except it was a magazine which made it tougher to sell. Its circulation was relatively modest.

CBA: *How was that distributed? To music stores?*

Denis: They probably tried, but no, I don't think they had much penetration there. I think it was just like the other three or four "major" underground publishers, which were Rip-Off Press, Last Gasp and Kitchen Sink, along with Print Mint—all relied initially on the head shops as the primary outlets, and then it was whatever you could find retailers willing to carrying 'em—the independent bookstores, college bookstores, used record stores… and then the Bud Plants, the Phil Seulings. I think they knocked themselves out and did a great magazine, but it was also not commercially successful. So, you had two magazines failing for different reasons, and each having—I think—a positive impact on the medium.

CBA: *I believe you said, if you could, you'd do some things differently with* Comix Book?

Denis: I think the cover choices and color could've been better. I would've lobbied hard for a color section, and I think when I saw Stan making the concessions that he did, I should've tried to get a firmer commitment for a longer rope. I think we had it yanked out from under us before we really got a feel for it. I thought *Comix Book* was building momentum, growing.

CBA: *How long was it? Nine months?*

Denis: I think it was a little over a year I actually worked for Marvel. I know it was '73, '74, but I can't offhand remember the months. I think it was over a year, and even at the end, when he killed it, I think he gave me a few weeks as kind of a bonus so that I wasn't suddenly cut off. Stan was very decent to me on an economic level, and I think he honestly was trying to do a good thing in making the compromises he did. I think he just probably caught political flak from other people in the organization who….

CBA: *From below and above….*

Denis: Yes… below and above, who found it intolerable that these concessions had far-flung ramifications. Stan must've given it some thought, I think in his mind he could segregate this from Marvel Comics, that the twain would never meet, and he could somehow pull it off. He was politically naive in that regard.

CBA: Comix Book *is quite the oddity in comics history.*

Denis: That it is. I'm glad you're doing this, because a lot of people, you know, the younger fans, don't have a clue this existed, that Marvel ever could or would do such a thing. Even Stan, when I occasionally see him at one of these shows, he always jokes about it in a way that gives me the impression he has fond memories of it. I think he likes the fact he gets some credit for experimenting and doing something rather unconventional. He doesn't seem to have any regrets about it; and neither do I.

CBA: *Did it really help pull you through that year?*

Denis: Absolutely.

CBA: *Were you able to get back on your feet?*

Denis: Yes, the timing was just about perfect. About the time Stan said, "Look, we're going to kill this," the industry was rebounding, principally because the glut I described took care of itself, because the newcomers couldn't sustain themselves. They dropped out. They were weeded out. The "Big Four," if I can call them that, were able to survive the scare, and even the Supreme Court decision which sent that chill didn't have the effect people feared it would; cops didn't start busting shops for carrying comics. Basically, the shops just got bolder again, and I think what happened is a lot of the customers missed the comics rack—you've got to remember, it was hard to find these things anywhere, so if you normally found them in "The Electric Eyeball" on Main Street, and you said, "Hey, where's the comics?"—if enough people ask that—the retailer finally would say, "Let's bring back the comics; the cops don't seem to be hassling us about it."

CBA: *Did the mail order start to pick up then?*

Denis: That's about the time we created what we called "Krupp Mail Order." My partner Tyler ultimately spun that off, and moved to Boulder, Colorado, and kept it going for a long time. We were in geographically separate areas though still partners; and mail order proved to be integral to our survival and growth. Comix Book was an interesting piece of underground comix history and Marvel history. I think the changes we "instigated" would have happened inevitably but we sped them up. I enjoyed being a saboteur, of sorts, at Marvel.

Jay Lynch & Comix Book
The underground comix cartoonist on not working for Marvel

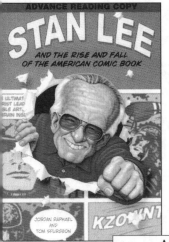

Stan Lee and the Rise and Fall of the American Comic Book ©'03 Jordan Raphael & Tom Spurgeon

[Ye Ed recently received this e-mail from Jay Lynch, creator of "Nard 'n' Pat," Bijou Funnies, *and* Garbage Pail Kids *for Topps. His comments and the check are reprinted here with Jay's permission.*]

I was in Barnes and Noble the other day… and I was looking through the [Jordan Raphael and] Tom Spurgeon bio of Stan Lee [*Stan Lee and the Rise and Fall of the American Comic Book*, Chicago Review Press, 2003]. And it sez in there that I wouldn't work for *Comix Book* (the Marvel imitation of *Arcade*) and implies it was for some idealistic reason on my part. But in fact, I did do some stuff for the first issue, but when I got the check, there was a contract on the back of it where I would be assigning trademarks to my characters to Marvel… so I told them no deal and pulled my stuff because of that. So it wasn't because I liked or disliked Marvel; it was just a practical move on my part. I was just protecting my own properties.

I like Stan Lee. I think his public relations value and his gregarious personality is the greatest asset Marvel ever had… And I think Stan understood and respected my position on the *Comix Book* thing.

I still have the check, that I never cashed, with the contract on the back, which I never signed. Not that there was anything intrinsicallly wrong with the contract, which was pretty standard for comic publishers then… It just wasn't for me, since we were dealing with my trademarks there.

Inset left & below: *Cover & page 138 in* Stan Lee and the Rise and Fall of the American Comic Book.

Almost immediately, there were problems. Some cartoonists, including Crumb and Jay Lynch, refused to work for Marvel.

Above: Front and back of Marvel's unendorsed and uncashed $40 check made out to Jay Lynch in 1974. From a facsimile transmitted by Jay Lynch. It appears here with J.L.'s permission.

By endorsement of this check, I, the payee, acknowledge full payment for my employment by Magazine Management Co. and for my assignment to it of any copyright, trademark and any other rights in or related to the material, and including my assignment of any rights to renewal copyright.

Above: *Self-caricature by Jay Lynch.*
Below left & right: *Jay's comix team, "Nard 'n' Pat." Both from* The Apex Treasury of Underground Comics *(1974). ©2005 Jay Lynch.*

When a fan sent Marie Severin some comics to autograph, the Mirthful One mailed back a delightful bonus. The splash page of Sub-Mariner #19 featured a plethora of beachcombers carrying the likenesses of Bullpenners and friends, so Marie drew up a key on a tracing paper overlay as a gift for our faithful fan. (CBA has unfortunately mislaid the name of our generous contributor so, if that be you, be sure to contact us and we'll make sure you get a freebie ish of the next CBA.)

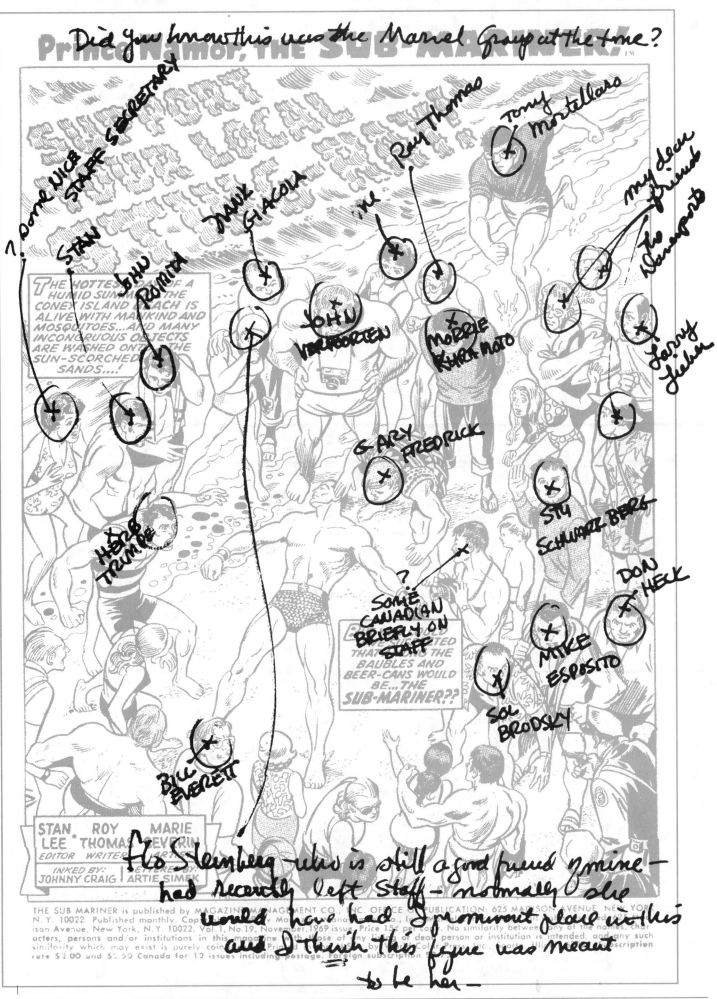

The Great Marvel Exodus

Creators explain that breakin' up ain't so hard to do

By Chris Knowles
Transcribed by Jon B. Knutson

Below: *Courtesy of art collector Victor Lim is this unaltered Mike Ploog cover for Kull the Destroyer #12. The printed version featured a pasted-up John Romita Sr. face on our hero king. ©2000 Marvel Characters, Inc. Kull ©2000 The Estate of Robert E. Howard.*

All good things must come to an end, and so it was for the halcyon days of the '70s Marvel Bullpen. One by one, many of the great names who had become so familiar to fans began to vanish from Marvel credits by 1978. All had different reasons and motivations for leaving, so here are some of Marvel's most notable comics creators to explain in their own words their reasons for moving on. All were contacted via phone in January, 2000.

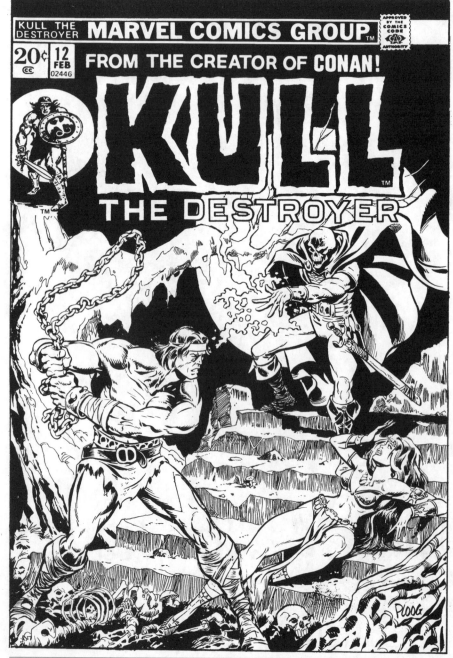

LEN WEIN

Marvel's top writer in the late '70's, Len had previously served as Editor-in-Chief of the House of Ideas.

Len: It was a combination of factors, actually. At the time, I was writing *Fantastic Four, Amazing Spider-Man, Mighty Thor,* and *Incredible Hulk,* all at the same time, and I was getting too obsessed about the little day-to-day details of the job, and going crazy. At that point, DC was wooing me like crazy to come back and work for them, and Jenette Kahn made me incredible offers of all kinds of things that I could have if I came back. I was sort of resistant for a while, and then they finally offered me Batman—*Detective Comics*—right after Steve Englehart left. Marshall Rogers was continuing with the book, but they needed a new writer, and they offered me Batman, my all-time favorite character. I thought about it, and said, "Yeah, I'd like to do that," and so I gave them a tentative yes on the gig, and went to tell Stan that I was taking over a book at DC as well. Stan didn't think it was right or fair, but I kind of explained that I just needed to do a little distancing if I was going to keep myself sane, and finally, with great reluctance, he said, "All right, fine. If you have to write Batman, then write Batman, but we don't want you to use your name on the book, because you're top writer on our four top titles. Use a pseudonym, and do what you've got to do, and we'll live with it." But he was clearly not happy. I called DC back, and said, "Okay, here's the deal: I can do the book, but Stan doesn't want me to use my name on the title, I have to use a pseudonym." Of course, DC was not happy, because what they wanted to do was promote me writing the Batman book. So, I now had pretty much what I wanted—the four top books at Marvel, and Batman at DC—and nobody was very happy.

Rather than having everybody unhappy with me, (I thought) that maybe it was simply time to take a clean break, take the deal DC was offering, and use my own name, and give myself a chance to sort of refresh my batteries and take on other projects! So, I finally said that was the thing to do, I had gotten too obsessively involved in my Marvel books, and I came back that Monday and basically sat there with Stan and said, "Look, I want to use my name on the Batman books, and if that means I've got to go, then I will leave." It took Stan so many years to understand my feelings, it was like, "I gave you what you wanted, I said you could write Batman! Why are you leaving?" I just felt I needed it for my own mental sanity at the time.

JIM STARLIN

Marvel's psychedelic superstar was artist/writer of such cosmic comic series as Captain Marvel *and* Warlock.

Jim: Basically, I did *Captain Marvel* and *Warlock* during that time, and when I left finally—the permanent time—was to go and work in animation in California. I worked for Ralph Bakshi for a while. Eventually, I ended up coming back and doing some more work for Marvel after a while, because the animation wasn't where I wanted to be. I came back and did the end of the Warlock series, which was inside those two annuals. I left for some reason after that again, I guess just to go off and work for different companies. I did some work for Warren for a bit, some commercial art and things like that, and finally Jim Shooter approached me on *The Death of Captain Marvel,* and I was working for *Epic Magazine,* too—I stopped working for the Marvel comics and I was doing work for *Epic.*

I had very fond memories of working on all those characters. It was a time when you'd get in and play with their characters—which you can't do much of right now, because they're corporate entities.

STEVE ENGLEHART

One of the true visionaries of comic book writing, Steve's work for titles like Captain America, Defenders, *and* Dr. Strange *rank with Marvel's best.*

Steve: There had been a series of editors at Marvel—Len Wein, Marv Wolfman, Archie Goodwin—and a new editor came in and decided that since he was the Editor-in-Chief, he should be able to write whatever he wanted to write, and so he told me he was taking *The Avengers*, and he told Steve Gerber he was taking *The Defenders*. Neither of us... I mean, we didn't like it, and that's basically why I left.

I went over to DC straight from there and did the *Batman* stuff, and then left the country for a year, and when I came back, I did a few things for Warren and stuff, but mostly I was writing a novel and getting off into computer games and stuff.

All I ever really wanted to do when I started was be a Marvel Comics writer. I really liked Marvel comics, it felt very good to do it, I got immediate positive feedback on the stuff I did, and immediately made people take notice both inside and outside of Marvel. So, I had started my career, and had pretty much worked entirely at Marvel—I had done a few things for Warren—*Vampirella* and stuff like that—but basically, I was what I wanted to be, which was a Marvel Comics writer.

GEORGE PÉREZ

One of Marvel's hottest young talents in the '70s, George is best remembered for his work on Fantastic Four *and* The Avengers.

George: In my case, actually, the initial departure wasn't because of anything I had against Marvel, but because of the fact that I was offered by Marv Wolfman—who had gone over to DC—a new series of *The Teen Titans*, and my goal—since I was doing *The Avengers*—was to get a crack at doing *Justice League of America*, which at that time was really the book I was interested in doing, when unfortunately Dick Dillin passed away. I ended up having the chance of taking over *JLA* as well as doing the *Titans* book I promised for Marv. So, after a while, it became obvious that I couldn't maintain a schedule of three monthly team books, so I dropped *The Avengers*—which happened to be the only thing I was doing for Marvel at that point, not because of any political reasons,

but because I had already been doing that one. The other two were new, and in retrospect, I probably thought that I'd eventually be returning to *The Avengers*, because I didn't think *Titans* would be a successful book anyway, and obviously I wanted *JLA*. As we all know, the *Titans* did succeed, and ended up being a book that occupied most of my time, so it wasn't until the big political football of the *JLA/Avengers* book that I actually stopped working for Marvel in any capacity, because I'd been ticked

Above: *Ye Ed's Dr. Strange collection is woefully incomplete so I'm not sure if this is an unpublished Colan/Palmer cover. Regardless, ain't it a beaut? Courtesy of Roy Thomas.* ©2000 Marvel Characters, Inc.

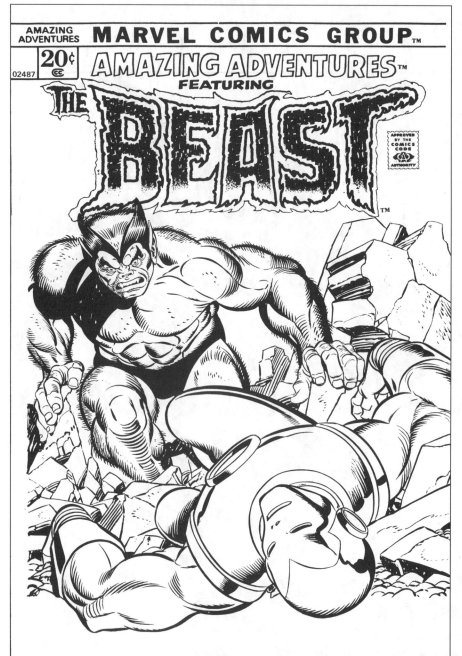

 is positioned in the left column top area.

MARVEL COMICS GROUP™

AMAZING ADVENTURES™
FEATURING
THE BEAST™

AMAZING ADVENTURES

20¢ 02487 CC

APPROVED BY THE COMICS CODE AUTHORITY

Above: *Glorious Gil Kane cover for Amazing Adventures #12. Ye Ed has a soft spot for this odd "Beast" series, probably because of Gil's superb cover work. Anyone have the line art for AA #11's cover? Please send us a copy as the Kane/Bill Everett team rules eternal! Courtesy of Albert Moy. ©2000 Marvel Characters, Inc.*

off at the politics of that, and I did not do any more work for Marvel for the next—God—close to ten years, I guess. So, my actual departure from Marvel was later than some of the others were. I had already started doing most of my work for DC, but I was doing occasional things for Marvel at the time. I signed an exclusive contract with DC Comics after the *JLA/Avengers* debacle.

GIL KANE
One of the true living legends of the comic book field, Gil was Marvel's top cover artist in the '70s

Gil: It was the end of a natural period. I'd been with them since the '60s, and all through the '70s, and by the late '70s, I had landed a newspaper strip called *Star Hawks*, and so I left comics to do a daily two-tier science-fiction strip. The big thing was it offered greater possibilities. I would still occasionally do work [for Marvel], it was just that I was no longer part of the day-to-day crew that did all the "heavy lifting."

Every company goes through a period of evolution, and by the 1970s, they had become another company. I think Shooter had come into the situation as being totally in charge, and a new set of editors, and it wasn't quite… Roy was gone, and the thing was that it wasn't the sort of loose outfit that you found during the mid and late '60s, and early '70s, where in effect, there weren't many restrictions on what you did, the biggest problem was to get you to do it! By that

time, I think Jack had gone and come back, and so their whole identity was undergoing another transformation, and it was the identity that Shooter forged that would last for another 10, 12 years. It was a different sort of company, and as I said, opportunities abounding and besides, DC made an effort to recall some of their earlier people, and they were also going through a process of re-establishing themselves with new identities and new artists, and I believe it was John Byrne took over Superman, so it was a very competitive period, and you looked for a situation of your own that was not where, in effect, you weren't such a cipher in the works. When you were a cipher—at least at Marvel, in the early days—nobody bothered you. That is, you were allowed your idiosyncrasies, provided they liked the work. Later on, it became a more rigid sort of place, it headed over here to certain situations, there was a political situation in the office that became stronger, the management team became a real force—as opposed to the creative.

GENE COLAN
A master craftsman whose skill for realism and dramatic storytelling is unmatched, Gene drew nearly every major character for Marvel during his tenure there.

Gene: I'm trying to remember why [*he left Marvel*], at the end of the '70s. Was Shooter in charge at that time?
CBA: *Yeah.*
Gene: That was the reason.
CBA: *Okay. Is that all you'd like to say?*
Gene: It's enough. I think you can fill in the spaces yourself. He was difficult and threatening, and he doesn't have a good reputation. This was after Stan left. I thought Stan might have left somewhere in the early or mid-'80s for California, so I'm not sure of my dates, but when Shooter came aboard, it was downhill. I could see the handwriting on the wall, and I didn't want to continue with him at the helm. He was making life too difficult for me. He made it too difficult for a lot of other people as well.

DON McGREGOR
Don brought a new kind of socially relevant storytelling to Marvel on titles like Jungle Action *and* Power Man. *His work bridged the gap between comics' old guard and the then-burgeoning counter-culture.*

Don: It's not so much that I left Marvel, as Marvel left me. You know, the work-for-hire contracts had come in, and if I'd been willing to sign them, and furthermore, been willing to let anybody change my material in any shape or form that they wanted to, that perhaps I could've stayed in the hallowed halls a little longer. When I refused to sign the work-for-hire contracts, about three weeks before my son was born, I was told never to darken the hallowed halls again.

ROY THOMAS
Roy was, if not one of Marvel's founding fathers, then certainly one of the major figures in the company's evolution.

Roy: Of course, now it's all kind of water under the bridge, because I'm back doing a little work. In fact, I did quite a bit of work in the late '80s on through, and I sort of made my peace with Jim Shooter and so forth as it is, and it was Tom DeFalco who kind of brought me back in; but at the time, in 1980 I guess it was, it was kind of an unpleasant situation. The basic thing is that, while I didn't really know Shooter, or know that much about him—I had met him a few times when he was on staff for a few weeks, we said a couple of words and so forth, then the next thing I knew he was gone. Once I got in there, I didn't have much to do with him one way or the other, but what happened is I had a situation after I'd left being Editor-in-Chief in 1974 where to keep me from leaving and going to work for DC or somewhere—which I was thinking about doing at the time, just for a change in scenery—I'd gotten a contract to be writer and editor of my own material, just so I could handle it myself. I remembered that I called Stan in late 1977, or dropped him a line, and told him that if Archie Goodwin left being Editor-in-Chief, that I really hoped that Jim Shooter didn't become Editor-in-Chief. While I had respect for his talent, and I barely knew him personally, I just had a feeling that we wouldn't work together, and I felt there were a lot of other people who might feel the same way, although I couldn't speak for anybody but myself. Of course, I'm sure Shooter saw the letter, (laughs) so that didn't do any good. Anyway, somehow or another, we went off on the wrong foot, but we never really had very much to do with each other. We talked on the phone a handful of times, but then when 1980 rolled around, as the second of my three-year contract as writer and editor was about to come up.

The books I were doing, a lot of them were doing pretty well, but *Conan* had been one of Marvel's better sellers by the middle to late '70s, and if *Invaders* wasn't a huge hit, then some other things I was doing were. I just had this feeling that things might not work out, so I said (to Stan), "Look, I know that there might have been a bit of bad blood between me and Shooter simply because he knows that I wasn't wild about the idea of his becoming Editor-in-Chief, but he's become Editor-in-Chief, he's Editor-in-Chief, and I've got no problem with that. If you don't want to give me a writer/editor contract, I understand, if the policy's changed or whatever, that's okay, just let me know, and I will spend my time, and I'll spend a few dollars talking to a lawyer about the contract, we'll just part company and that's it." You know, I felt I could be as up front as I possibly could. If they didn't want it, they didn't want it, and that was their business. All I ask is that you not negotiate with me if it's not going to be a writer/editor contract, because that's all I'm interested in having with Marvel. Shooter said, "You go ahead, and you make up the contract, however you think it should be, and then send it to me." So I did, and I think it was almost the same contract, except that I made it so now I reported to him; I just had a few changes made to it—it wasn't anything to my advantage at this stage—and I sent it in, and I suddenly get back this letter from Shooter that says, "We cannot guarantee you in writing for you to be a writer/editor. Naturally, we would want to use your editorial expertise, but I can't guarantee you anything like that in writing." I just mentally blew up, because I thought, "This guy has wasted my time, he's wasted a little bit of my money, because all I said was just be honest with me, don't lie to me." So, that was it, that was the end of it.

I don't have a vendetta against Jim Shooter anymore at all, or anything like that; but, it was one of those things where I felt, this is a matter of history, to the extent that why did Marv Wolfman, why did Roy Thomas, why did a number of people at that time leave—it's just the honest truth. That doesn't mean that I was right, there is no necessary right and wrong, as far as whether they should or should not have given me a writer/editor contract—maybe there's some circuitous reasoning that somebody can figure that they dealt fairly with me.

JIM MOONEY

Jim Mooney, one of Marvel's most reliable draftsmen, actually left the firm in the mid-'80s.

Jim: I was not necessarily ready to retire, but when I queried Jim Shooter about it, I got a very short note: "Retire." I was ready to retire anyway, although I really didn't. It didn't bother me too much, because there was a lot of other things I wanted to do anyway. At the time, I was painting, and working with ceramics, and I thought, "Well, I'm going to enjoy my retirement doing a lot of the things I didn't necessarily have the time to do when I was under deadline pressure."

KLAUS JANSON

Klaus Janson was a one-man inking army for Marvel in the '70s and early '80s. He left the company shortly after his acclaimed run on Daredevil.

Klaus: When I left *Daredevil*, I went to DC and I signed a one-year contract with them, and that was, again, to try something... I wanted to see what it would be like being an exclusive person to a company... I'd never done that before. I wanted to pencil more, but I thought that penciling and inking a monthly book, which was 20-22 pages, was too much for me to develop an individual voice, and I wanted to go somewhere else with my work, in terms of approach, or a point of view... if you do that amount of work for a month, it's very hard to give yourself the time needed to be creative, and push a little bit, and DC at that point had a whole spectrum of books that had short stories in them.... Marvel had nothing. There was no place you could do a 10-page story. For that reason, and for a couple of other reasons, but that reason primarily, I went to DC. At least for that year, exclusively.

Above: Back in the glory days of the Marvel Bullpen, Rolling Stone featured a look behind the scenes at the House of Ideas, with candid talks with Stan, Flo Steinberg, Jim Steranko, Roy Thomas, Marie Severin, Herb Trimpe, and others. The September 16, 1972 article (entitled "Face Front! Clap Your Hands! We're on the Winning Team!") was written by onetime Marvel secretary Robin Green and also included dynamite pictures of the Bullpen staff. Cover art by Herb Trimpe. Seek and ye shall find, True Believer! Courtesy of Allan Rosenberg.©2000 Straight Arrow Publishers. Hulk ©2000 Marvel Characters, Inc.

Killraven of the Apes!

Brit Marvel's weird melding of "War of the Worlds" & POTA

Insert right: *Vignette of John Romita Sr.'s Killraven taken from the cover of* Amazing Adventures #18 (May '73). ©2005 Marvel Characters, Inc.

Below: *The strange and wonderful morphing of "Killraven" with* Planet of the Apes *began in this issue, #23 (Mar. 29, '75), of the U.K. edition. Cover art looks to be by Ron Wilson (pencils) and Mike Esposito (inks). Courtesy of Rob Kirby. POTA ©2005 20th Century Fox. Apeslayer ©2005 Marvel Characters, Inc.*

by Rob Kirby

By 1974, the *Planet of the Apes* franchise was viewed as a somewhat spent commodity, and we certainly didn't foresee that the next Big Thing was only three years away (or so it seemed in youthful times), coming from some galaxy... "far, far away." In all probability you probably think that nothing came in between these two cinematic giants, at least as far as comic adaptations are concerned, but you couldn't be more wrong. There *was* something else, you just didn't see it... unless you lived in Britain during the mid-'70s. It's name? *Planet of the Apes!*

After becoming publisher at Marvel Comics, Stan Lee started to take a look at the company's various worldwide operations, and "The Man" quickly realized that his outfit's *other* biggest English-speaking market was getting a pretty raw deal from the very limited imports that did reach the United Kingdom's shores — usually as ship ballast (just to rub salt into the wound!). By Autumn 1972 Stan had solved that problem by creating a new Bullpen within the heart of the old one, and so was born the "British" Marvel Bullpen, a group of Yanks charged with producing weekly comics for the U.K. news-agent trade, and aided and abetted by some of the latest rising stars in the American comics firmament, such as Jim Starlin, Allen Milgrom, Marshall Rogers, Michael Nasser (a.k.a. Netzer), and Tony Isabella.

The long-lived *Mighty World of Marvel* comics weekly debuted on the British Isles in Oct. '72, and in the two years that followed the line-up began a slow expansion that would accelerate to a full-scale explosion by 1975. In Feb. '73, Spider-Man spun out of *MWOM* (as it understandably soon became known in the letter pages) into his own title, *Spider-Man Comics Weekly*, the first in a long line of changing titles for that periodical, as it would be later known as *Super Spider-Man With the Super-heroes, Super Spider-Man and the Titans, Super Spider-Man and Captain Britain,* and then merely *Super Spider-Man,* to name but a few of the later merger titles). The Avengers started out in *MWOM* before receiving their only U.K. book in Autumn '73, to be followed a year later by a double-release, one of which was the U.K. range's first media crossover title, and so *Planet of the Apes* joined with *Dracula Lives* at the newsagents, the debut cover-dated Oct. 26, '74.

With the new *Planet of the Apes* TV series due to air soon in Britain, Marvel obviously felt that now was the best time to promote the *Apes* material to their new weekly audience, and it was this swift launch that caused the "scheduling" problems which prompted the discussion in this article. POTA (the letter pages positively buzzed with these abbreviations back then) notched up a very respectable 123 issues before merging into *MWOM*, in the latter's #231 (cover-dated Mar. 2, '77) and concluded in #246 (June 15, '77). Thereafter, *Dracula Lives* took over the *Apes* feature slot (though the blood-thirsty Count had merged as a co-feature in POTA way back in #88, creating a bizarre delayed double-merger. By the time the *Apes* exited the United Kingdom for good, every American strip had been reprinted at least once, and many of the cut-down color format American reprints had been used up too, probably simply because they were readily available for immediate use.

Planet of the Apes began its life in the same way that most of the early U.K. Marvel books did: reprinting the earliest adventures of whichever characters that respective comic featured. This voracious appetite by British kids for Marvel material created several headaches over the years. Only the gradual expansion of Spider-Man's stateside titles saved the U.K. books from catching up completely (although the occasional jump back in time between a run of *Amazing S-M,* and then *Spectacular S-M* stories were kinda fun!)—even with most strips being divided over periods of anything from two to five weeks at a time. Having only been launched some two months after the American magazine, POTA took just 22 issues—one every seven days, mind you—to run out of material (a lesson soon taken to heart when Marvel prepared *Star Wars* for U.K. publication, which lead to adopting the task of producing two months of U.S. material on a monthly to grant enough slack for weekly serialization).

Even though the British Bullpen had first-use of each newly completed strip (which technically then makes some of the later American issues the *reprint* edition), still the crunch came and a desperate plan was hatched. The production team was handed stats from an entirely different American series and instructed to redraw most of the characters as apes, re-dialogue where necessary, and

rename many of the characters. So commencing in *POTA* #23, noneother than Killraven, star of the "War of the Worlds" series in the stateside bi-monthly, *Amazing Adventures,* made his first U.K. appearance… as Apeslayer! The American serial co-stars were rechristened for the British hybrid: Old Skull became Socrates, Hawk is called Arrow, and everyone sprouted previously-unseen black hair. I know it sounds too outrageous to be true, but this was a desperate editorial decision, proving the truth behind the saying, "Sometimes you can't make this stuff up!"

After eight weeks of frantic redrawing and recycling, the *Apes* weekly resumed its usual rotation of one film adaptation interspersed with new material by writer Doug Moench and artists Tom Sutton and Mike Ploog, backed up by a selection of science-fiction material sourced from *Unknown Worlds of Science Fiction, Captain Marvel,* as well as the *Warlock* counter-Earth stories, to name but a few. And yet… still the comic devoured stories at a pace that even Seymour, the ravenous plant, would have been hard pressed to beat. I can almost see the British Bullpen crew eagerly awaiting couriers coming down the corridor outside their little den, deftly redirecting the latest package of *Apes* artwork into the hungry maw of the overworked production team. This, then, is where it gets really interesting.

For the past decade I have become embroiled in my own personal Mission: Impossible, in an attempt to compile, as near as is practical, a complete index to absolutely everything published by Marvel U.K., as it became known from the early '80s (later to be joined by Marvel France and so forth from the continent). When my work is eventually released onto an unsuspecting comics fandom, (and those British readers of this esteemed journal reading this, and who know me, will now be rolling about in fits of surely uncontrollable laughter), it will include listings for almost every teenage to adult reprint and U.K.-only strip (including several annuals that predate *MWOM* in 1972, but continued throughout the next two decades as official British Marvel products, even though initially released by other publishers). I can feel my pockets emptying of cash already!

The *Apes* strips turned out to be the most surprising source of previously-unseen material, at least since those six American-produced *Star Wars* strips came to light many years ago; having only ever been published in continuity within the pages of *Star Wars Weekly,* because they made way for an earlier start to *The Empire Strikes Back* adaptation in the color comic (the stories later made a brief appearance in two American paperbacks), the three Archie Goodwin and three Chris Claremont stories at least prove that Marvel had learned something from the "Apeslayer" debacle. Mind you, if I hadn't been buying up cheap copies of any series I didn't have an index for, in order to list and compare the material, then I might never have come across what follows at all! My collection would have been smaller though… well, *slightly* smaller anyway.

It was several summers ago when I finally got my hands on a good condition set of all 29 American magazines, and I swiftly listed out their contents in order to identify the source issue for every reprint and to check the page counts in case a story had lost any pages, making note of those tales which were incompletely reprinted (not many). This process had actually provided the impetus to thoroughly index all the U.K. comics in the first place, with a simple wish to compile a personal wants list of those issues that never appeared (or only ever incompletely appeared) in the British books.

I was convinced that I must have made a mistake when adding up the page counts for each story, several chapters from some of the movie adaptations seemed to have more pages in the U.K. comic, which surely couldn't be right… could it? There was no alternative but to sit down with both versions of each offending story, matching up every corresponding story page-by-page. My initial disbelief quickly turned to delight as I discovered several pages removed prior to U.S. publication, and several more double-page sequences condensed down into just single pages by the time they had reached their American audience. A bit more than a *minor* discovery, I think!

It now seems reasonably safe to presume that once the UK books had made use of the newly-completed stories, artwork was then passed to the American magazine's production team, which was when these pages were cut and alterations made in order to keep within the very strict format they used. At this point, the odd mistake was also corrected before the pages were then grey-washed and many captions were re-photographed from white to black just for good measure, matching the look across the rest of the b-&-w magazine range.

Okay, so we're not talking about unseen Steranko pages from *S.H.I.E.L.D.* #1 (we can only wish) or even U.K.-only Paul Gulacy *Shang-Chi* pages (although Grant Morrison *did* write a short British Master of Kung Fu story as part of the U.K. produced *G.I. Joe/Action Force* series), but if you are *any* kind of *Apes* fan—and specifically of Marvel's sterling work across all five of the film adaptations—you really do owe it to yourself to check these strips out. After all, this is Alfredo Alcala, uncut and at his best, hitherto unseen artistry surely worth tracking down. Good hunting!

This page: Before the War of the Worlds took over the Planet of the Apes: The original panels as penciled by Neal Adams and inked by Frank Chiaramonte from Killraven's debut tale in Amazing Adventures #18 (May '73). Panels below courtesy of Rob Kirby. ©2005 Marvel Characters, Inc.

This page: After the Planet invaded the Worlds' war, Marvel's production team in charge of U.K. Marvel weeklies futz with the art, changing panels to include apes rather than the human Quislings of the Killraven serial. The hero was renamed Apeslayer and… voilá! Panels from the U.K. edition of Planet of the Apes #23 (Mar. 29, '76). Courtesy of Rob Kirby. ©2005 Marvel Characters, Inc.

This page: Chaykin & Chiaramonte's *Amazing Adventures* #18 (May '73) panels before the U.K. alterations. ©2005 Marvel Characters, Inc.

Changed!

"THEY TAUGHT US ALL THE ANCIENT ARTS-- SWORD-PLAY, KARATE, SAVATE, WRESTLING-- AT FIRST, WE THOUGHT IT A GAME--"

"--A GAME WITH DEADLY RESULTS--"

"THEN THEY PITTED US AGAINST THEIR OWN CHAMPIONS..."

"--AND I TOOK PLEASURE IN BATTLING THEM."

"I WAS GIVEN A NAME-- AT FIRST IT WAS SAID MOCKINGLY. BUT I CHERISHED IT--"

APE-SLAYER!

"WE PUT THE FEAR OF APESLAYER IN HIM, OLD MAN-- AND THAT'S WHEN I GAINED MY FIRST TRUE RECOGNITION-- LARGE ENOUGH TO HELP ME ADD TO MY BAND OF MEN, SOON AFTER THE APES ATTACKED ME ON THE PUBLIC MONITORS!"

LISTEN TO HIM, DAGGER. "A CUT-THROAT AND THIEF"!

I THINK HE MISSED THE POINT.

"ALL THAT TRAINING-- FINALLY I HAD TO PUT IT TO USE."

SKREEE! ATTEMPTED ESCAPE IN BLOCK 4-D... TRAINEE J. DOZER ATTACKING... SKREEEEEE!

SPK!

QUIET, MONKEYS. THEY CAN PATCH YOU BACK TOGETHER--

I'M A LITTLE MORE DIFFICULT.

I WANT REVENGE, NOT MONEY.

THAT'S ENOUGH, APE! IF THE WOMAN DOESN'T WANT YOU TOUCHING HER--

-- THEN YOU DON'T TOUCH!

PLAK!

This page: The revised British panels from the U.K. edition of Planet of the Apes #24 (Apr. 5, '76). Courtesy of Rob Kirby. ©2005 Marvel Characters, Inc.

AS SOON AS WE GET ENOUGH MEN TOGETHER--

-- THERE'S A MAN I WANT TO SEE: THE GENERAL.

APESLAYER

--HIS TRAINED MUSCLES JUMP IN REFLEX--

-- HE SWINGS LIKE A JUNGLE BEAST--

-- AND BEFORE TWO SECONDS HAVE PASSED--

KILLRAVEN

Below: *Trimpe & inker Frank Giacoia's panels from Amazing Adventures #20 (Sept. '73). ©2005 Marvel Characters, Inc.*

Above: *The revised panels from the U.K. edition of Planet of the Apes #28 (May 3, '76). ©2005 Marvel Characters, Inc.*

Checklist of the Planet of the Apes

Planet of the Apes [U.S. Marvel edition]

#1 "Planet of the Apes" [r: POTA (UK) #1]
"Terror on the Planet of the Apes" chapter 1
[r: POTA (UK) #12], chapter 2 [r: POTA #12]

#2 "Planet of the Apes" chapter 2 [r: POTA (UK) #2-3]
"The Forbidden Zone of Forgotten Horrors"
[r: POTA (UK) #14]
Chapter 2: "Lick the Sky Crimson"
[r: POTA (UK) #14]

#3 "Planet of the Apes" chapter 3 [r: POTA (UK) #4-5]
"Spawn of the Mutant Pits" [r: POTA (UK) #16-17]
Chapter 2: "The Abomination Arena"
[r: POTA (UK) #17]

#4 "Planet of the Apes" chapter 4 [r: POTA (UK) #6-7]
"A Riverboat Named Simian"
[incomplete r: POTA (UK) # 18]
Chapter 2: "Gunpowder Julius"
[r: POTA (UK) #19]

#5 "Planet of the Apes" chapter 5 [r: POTA (UK) #8-9]
"Evolution's Nightmare"
[incomplete r: POTA (UK) # 20-22 and in
Marvel Superheroes #384 some years later]

#6 "Planet of the Apes" chapter 6
[incomplete r: POTA (UK) #10-11]
"Maiaguefia Beyond a Zone Forbidden"
[r: POTA (UK) #75-76]

#7 "Beneath the Planet of the Apes"
[r: POTA (UK) #35-36]
"Beneath…" part 2 [r: POTA (UK) #37-38]

#8 "Beneath the Planet of the Apes" part 3
[r: POTA (UK) #39-40]
"Planet Inheritors"
[incompletely r: POTA (UK) #77,78]

#9 "Beneath the Planet of the Apes" part 4
[r: POTA (UK) #41-42]
"Kingdom on an Island of the Apes"
[r: POTA (UK) #31]

#10 "Beneath the Planet of the Apes" part 5
[r: POTA (UK) #43-44]
"Kingdom on an Island of the Apes" part 2
[r: POTA (UK) #32-34]

#11 "Beneath the Planet of the Apes" part 6
[r: POTA (UK) #45-46]
"When the Law-Giver Returns"
[r: POTA (UK) #79-80]

#12 "Escape from the Planet of the Apes" part 1
[r: POTA (UK) 50-52]
"Future History Chronicles I"
[r: POTA (UK) #47-49]

#13 "Escape from the Planet of the Apes" part 2
[r: POTA (UK) #53-54]
"Terror on the Planet of the Apes: Phase 2"
[r: POTA (UK) #87,
POTA & Dracula Lives (UK) 88-89]

#14 "Escape from the Planet of the Apes" part 3
[r: POTA (UK) #55-56]
"Terror on the Planet of the Apes: Phase 2"
[r: POTA & DL (UK) #90-92]

#15 "Escape from the Planet of the Apes" part 4
[r: POTA (UK) #57-58]
Future History Chronicles II
[r: POTA (UK) #81-82]

#16 "Escape from the Planet of the Apes" part 5
[r: POTA (UK) #59-60]
"Escape from…" part 6 [r: POTA (UK) #61-62]

#17 "Conquest of the Planet of the Apes" part 1
[incomplete r: POTA (UK) #63-64]
Future History Chronicles III [r: POTA (UK) #83-84]

#18 "Conquest of the Planet of the Apes" part 2
[incomplete r: POTA (UK) #65-66]
"Conquest of…" part 3
[r: POTA (UK) #67 (1/31/76)-#68 (2/7/76)]
[**NOTE:** *Part 3 (U.K.) includes two additional pages
of story not found in U.S. edition (which is cover
dated Mar. '76).*]

#19 "Conquest of the Planet of the Apes" part 4
[r: POTA (UK) #69-70]
"Terror on the Planet of the Apes: Phase 2"
[r: POTA & DL (UK) #93-95]

#20 "Conquest of the Planet of the Apes" part 5
[r: POTA (UK) #71-72]
"Terror on the Planet of the Apes: Phase 2"
[r: POTA & DL (UK) #96-98]

#21 "Conquest of the Planet of the Apes" part 5
[r: POTA (UK) #73 (3/13/76)-#74 (3/20/76)]
"Beast on the Planet of the Apes"
[r: POTA (UK) #85-86 & POTA & DL #99-101]
[**NOTE:** *Part 5 (U.K.) includes one additional page
of story not found in U.S. edition (which is cover
dated June '76).*]

#22 "Quest for the Planet of the Apes" part 1
[r: POTA & DL #102-104]
"Quest…" part 2 [r: POTA & DL #105-107]

#23 "Battle for the Planet of the Apes" part 1
[r: POTA & DL #108-111]
"Terror on the Planet of the Apes"
[r: Mighty World of Marvel #235-236]

#24 "Battle for the Planet of the Apes" part 2
[r: POTA & DL (UK) #112-114]
"Future History Chronicles IV"
[r: MWOM (UK) #237-238]

#25 "Battle for the Planet of the Apes" part 3
[r: POTA & DL #115 (12/29/76)-
#117 (1/12/77)
"Battle for the Planet of the Apes" part 4
[incomplete r: POTA & DL #118-120]
[**NOTE:** *Part 3 (U.K.) includes several additional
pages, including the original two-page introduction
replaced by a solitary page drawn by Marshall
Rogers in the U.S. edition (cover dated Oct. '76).*]

#26 "Battle for the Planet of the Apes" part 5
[incomplete r: POTA & DL #121-123]
"Northlands" [r: MWOM #239-240]

#27 "Battle for the Planet of the Apes" part 6
[incomplete r: MWOM #231-232]
"Terror on the Planet of the Apes"
[incomplete r: MWOM (UK) #241, 242]

Above: *Herb Trimpe's cover art for
Amazing Adventures #20 was adapted
for Planet of the Apes (U.K.) #28.
Courtesy of Rob Kirby. ©2005 Marvel
Characters, Inc. The accompanying
checklist was compiled by and is
©2005 Rob Kirby.*

#28 "Battle for the Planet of the Apes" part 7
[r: MWOM #233-234]
"Revolt of the Gorilloids" [r: MWOM #243- 244]

#29 "Future History Chronicles V"
[incomplete r: MWOM #245-246]

Adventures on the Planet of the Apes [U.S. edition]

#1 "Planet of the Apes" [r: POTA & DL #93-96]

#2 "World of Captive Humans" [r: POTA&DL #97-99]

#3 "Manhunt" [r: POTA & DL #100-102]

#4 "Trial" [r: POTA & DL #103-105]

#5 "Into the Forbidden Zone" [r: POTA&DL # 106-108]

#6 "The Secret" [r: POTA & DL #109-111]

#7 "Beneath the Planet …" [r: POTA & DL #112-114]

#8 "Enslaved" [r: POTA & DL #115-117]

#9 "The Warhead Messiah" [r: POTA & DL #118-120]

#11 "Children of the Bomb" [r: POTA & DL #121-122]

#12 "The Hell of the Holocaust" [r: POTA & DL #123]

Amazing Adventures [U.S. '70s edition]

#18 "Prologue: Future Imperfect" (U.K. edition title)
[r: POTA (UK) #23-24

#19 "The Sirens of 7th Avenue" [r: POTA (UK) #25-26]

#20 "The Museum of Terror" (U.K. edition title)
[r: POTA (UK) #27-28]

#21 "The Mutant Slayers" [r: POTA (UK) #29-30]

[**NOTE:** *As detailed in the proceeding article, parts of the
U.S. edition — the War of the Worlds/"Killraven" series
— were modified as "Apeslayer" for the U.K. edition.*]

Hey, kids: Look! POTA "Conquest" pages never before seen in the U.S.!

Planet of the Apes #18 (Marvel U.S. edition), "Conquest of the Planet of the Apes," part 3, page 17. This page, drawn by the incomparable Alfredo Alcala (whose work is reproduced throughout this feature) was pasted together from panels in the two pages originally drawn by the artist, as seen below. Courtesy of Rob Kirby.

Planet of the Apes #68 (Marvel U.K. edition), "Conquest of the Planet of the Apes," part 3, pgs. 17-18

Planet of the Apes #21 (Marvel U.S. edition), "Conquest of the Planet of the Apes," part 5, pgs. 9-10

Planet of the Apes #73 (Marvel U.K. edition), "Conquest of the Planet of the Apes," part 5 page. This page, which comes between the two seen above, was omitted from the U.S. edition. Note the U.K. POTA did not feature the grey wash effect used in the American version.

24

ZOT! NEXUS! CONCRETE! MS. TREE! SKATEMAN! WHO CAN EVER FORGET THESE PRIME EXAMPLES OF THE EARLY EIGHTIES BURGEONING MOVEMENT TOWARDS ARTISTIC INDEPENDENCE IN THE COMICS FIELD? WELL, EXCEPT FOR MAYBE SKATEMAN. BECAUSE FOR EVERY AMERICAN FLAGG, EVERY ROCKETEER, THERE WAS A SKATEMAN, LONG SINCE FORGOTTEN, SOMETIMES JUSTIFIABLY SO, SOMETIMES NOT. SORTA LIKE THE FOLKS BELOW...

WHEN HEIRESS SERENA NEIMAN FEELS AN ATTACK OF LIBERAL GUILT COMING ON, SHE DONS A FRIGHT WIG AND APPLIES HER AEROBIC DEFENSE LESSONS TOWARDS STOPPING CRIME ON THE OTHER SIDE OF THE TRACKS AS NIGHTINGALE, COURTESY OF MARK EVANIER, AL GORDON, AND LEGENDARY PENCILLER, MIKE SEKOWSKY, RUNNING A MERE TWO EPISODES IN 1984'S ECLIPSE MONTHLY -- PUBLISHED BY ECLIPSE, NATCH-- NUMBERS 6 AND 7.

THE VILLAINOUS DJINN APPEARED IN THE ONE AND ONLY ISSUE OF NMP'S FANTASY ILLUSTRATED (1982), BUT, OH, WHAT A MEMORABLE PEDIGREE! STEVE ENGLEHART, STEVE DITKO AND STEVE LEIALOHA! Y'KNOW, HAD THE FEATURE SOMEHOW GAINED MASSIVE POPULARITY AND BEEN TRANSFORMED INTO A BROADWAY MUSICAL, IS THERE ANY WAY STEVE SONDHEIM COULD NOT HAVE BEEN INVOLVED??

AFTER RICHARD BENJAMIN BUT BEFORE ARMIN SHIMERMAN, THERE WAS MIKE BARON AND RICK BURCHETT'S QUARK, A TELEKINETIC TEEN WHO BRIEFLY ENTERED OUR CONCIOUSNESS VIA PACIFIC COMICS' VANGUARD ILLUSTRATED #4 AND 5 (1984).

SPINNING OFF FROM A FEATURE CO-CREATED WITH STEVE ENGLEHART, MARSHALL ROGERS GUIDED HIS IDIOSYNCRAT-IC CHARACTERS, CAP'N QUICK AND A FOOZLE (SPECIFICALLY, KLONS-BON) THROUGH SEVERAL ISSUES OF ECLIPSE MONTHLY, EVENTUALLY WINDING UP IN A SHORT RUN TITLE OF THEIR VERY OWN, CIRCA 1984. WHAT EXACTLY WAS IT ALL ABOUT? HEY, YOU'LL HAVE TO ASK MARSHALL-- HE WROTE 'EM! ME, I ONLY READ 'EM!!..

TAKE THE TITLE, "LAD, A DOG", THROW IT UP IN THE AIR, AND -- IF YOU'RE LUCKY-- WHEN IT LANDS YOU'LL HAVE JAN STRNAD AND DENNIS FUJITAKE'S DALGODA, PROBABLY THE GREATEST ORIGINAL ADVENTURE SERIES FANTAGRAPHICS EVER PUBLISHED (AN ADMITTEDLY SMALL POOL TO FISH FROM, BUT...). COMMENCING IN 1984, THIS TAIL (heh) OF A CANIDAN (NO, NOT CANADIAN) ASTRONAUT ARRIVING ON EARTH SEEKING SALVATION FOR HIS DOOMED WORLD LASTED A FAR TOO SHORT EIGHT ISSUES, AND JUST LIKE OLD YELLER, IS STILL MISSED. snif...

EVANGELINE, THE NUN WITH THE GUN, FOUGHT RELIGIOUS PERSECUTION IN THE 22ND CENTURY...AND SHE DID IT HEAVILY ARMED!! DEBUTING IN 1984 AT COMICO, AND AFTER A SPECIAL FROM LODESTONE IN '86, SHE FINISHED UP BY PREACHING HER GOSPEL FROM THE FIRST COMICS PULPIT WITH A 12 ISSUE RUN THAT CONCLUDED IN 1988. ORIGINALLY DRAWN BY JUDITH HUNT, MY MAIN RECOLLECTION OF THE SISTER WITH THE SHELLCASINGS WAS THAT SHE WAS THE ONE WHO INTRODUCED ME TO THE NO-NONSENSE SCRIPTING OF THE PROLIFIC CHUCK DIXON.

ERST-WHILE DNAgents ARTIST, WILL MEUGNIOT, TOOK UP SCRIPT-ING TO LAUNCH HIS OWN CREATION, VANITY, A FUR BIKINI CLAD CAVE GAL WHO SOMEHOW VAULTED FROM PREHISTORIC TIMES TO THE SPACE AGE-- AND INTO AN OUTFIT ONLY AN ...IMAGINATIVE MALE CARTOONIST COULD CONCOCT! 1984 WAS THE YEAR PACIFIC COMICS UNLEASHED A PAIR OF ISSUES OF THIS, ahem, VANITY PROJECT.

RALPH ROWLF AND BART BARC, IN THEIR CRIME-FIGHTING GUISES OF THE DOG AND PUP, SAW THEIR SOLE RECORDED ESCAPADE APPEAR IN THE INITIAL ISSUE OF THE LATE RAOUL VEZINA'S SMILIN' ED COMICS (FANTACO PUBS, 1980), WRITTEN AND DRAWN BY FRED HEMBECK. YUP, THAT'S ME! BECAUSE WHILE THE EIGHTIES CERTAINLY WERE ABOUT ARTISTIC INDEPENDENCE, THEY WERE ALSO ABOUT ARTISTIC INDULGENCE!! AND IF YOU'LL KINDLY INDULGE ME, I'D LIKE TO FINALLY TELL EVERYONE WHAT HAPPENED WHEN OUR DOGGY DUO RECEIVED THE SHOCK OF THEIR LIVES AS THEIR FEMALE ARCH-NEMESIS CONFRONTED THEM WITH EVIDENCE THAT IS WAS SHE WHO GAVE BIRTH TO THE HERETOFORE THOUGHT TO BE ORPHANED YOUNG BART IN A TAIL (heh heh) THAT HAD TO BE CALLED "PUP--SON OF THE BITCH?" OOPS! LOOKS LIKE I'M OUTTA ROOM. WELL, CHECK BACK WITH ME IN 2020 FOR MORE, I GUESS...

Dateline: 0!!!
BY FRED HEMBECK

Rude's Awakening

"The Dude" on the Importance of Art Over Commerce

Conducted by Chris Knowles
Transcribed by Jon B. Knutson

Steve "The Dude" Rude immediately came to the attention of comics art fans with the arrival of his (and writer Mike Baron's) Nexus in 1981. The artist's work is confident, the storytelling compelling, and the style reminiscent of Russ Manning's art, and the artist's contribution to the series has made Nexus one of the more successful independent projects to survive the '80s. Currently working for Marvel Comics, the artist has also recently completed work on the cover of this issue of CBA, to which we are thankful. Steve was interviewed by telephone in January 2000, and he copyedited the transcript.

Comic Book Artist: *Let's start at the beginning. You were born in 1960, I believe, in Madison, Wisconsin.*
Steve Rude: No, I was born on December 31, 1956.
CBA: *Were you a big Kirby fan back in the day?*
Steve: I became a Kirby fan around the year 1966. That seemed to be the year everything happened for me. But I wasn't buying them myself, but reading my friends' copies. I had this cool friend who was the same age, and he was a single child, and he got everything he wanted, so I'd always be over at his house.
CBA: *One thing I've noticed with your work is that there's a strong Dr. Seuss element floating around, so you were probably a fan of a lot of children's books before you started to read comics.*
Steve: Well, I remember Dr. Seuss being the first thing I read when I was in kindergarten. I had a friend of mine that, when the teacher would read these Dr. Seuss books, we'd just start laughing among ourselves, and nobody knew what we were laughing at. *[laughter]* That's because we had this bizarre sense of humor where certain things would just make us start break out laughing, like the way Dr. Seuss would have certain characters running their toes; we thought that was funny.
CBA: *[laughs] Now, were there other people besides Dr. Seuss you were aware you were a fan of, or were you just a general reader, and took things as they came?*
Steve: I took things as they came, but I wasn't much of a reader as a kid. I didn't read any of the classic books at all. I think I got that from the old man. To

Below: "The Dude," at home. Courtesy of the artist.

this day, he's a World War II freak, and you can give him a video or movie on World War II, and he'll look at it in a second, but if you give him a book, he still won't read it.
CBA: *So what other comic artists did you like at the time?*
Steve: I loved Gene Colan's "Iron Man." When Iron Man would fight the Mandarin, those were just the greatest stories. These were the things, the forms like this sketch in my head, that would eventually form what I think about life. It's a good thing it happens in adolescence, because the lessons that those comic books were teaching us were of… there were good guys and there were bad guys, and if a bad guy had done something to anyone—yourself, your girlfriend, your friend, anyone—you'd go after them.
CBA: *Justice.*
Steve: Yeah, justice, and I think to this day that's a very powerful way that I view life. You have to stand up to bad guys. I'm taking karate lessons now for that reason.
CBA: *You had been taking them before, hadn't you?*
Steve: I had, on and off. I was never a guy who really loved doing martial arts.
CBA: *So, comic books helped color your view of the world, gave you a sense of morality?*
Steve: In fact, right now, I'm reading the story I talked about so much in my *Jack Kirby Collector* interview, the Thor/Hercules battle. It works on so many levels that it basically brought me to the conclusion one day that comic books are the Greek myths of 20th Century society. These are the timeless stories that mankind has put in print, or written about, or orated for as long as there've been human beings on the planet, and it makes you wonder where this comes from. Why all these cultures have these things in common with themselves about right and wrong, or how the world began, and who controlled it—basically, our view of ourselves in the larger picture of what everything is supposed to mean. Knowing the foundation of right and wrong. Building not destroying.
CBA: *Did you ever read Joseph Campbell?*
Steve: I tried, but he's too damn academic for me. He just talks in such a college professor way that it wasn't talking to me in a language that was accessible to my brain. Comic books were always accessible to me. That's the beauty of them, and of course, everything is dependent on the creative team that's doing the book. That would make all the difference to me.
CBA: *Well, I think also it's that you were very fortunate, as an individual, to be born at a time where there were still very high standards for naturalistic drawing, to be reading comics at a time when there were very high standards of narrative. The '60s Marvel comics had a very high standard of moralistic storytelling that I don't think has been equaled on a consistent basis since. It was just high quality material coming out all the time. You were very fortunate in that regard.*
Steve: I always say I would never want to be born a minute earlier or a minute later than I was.
CBA: *Yeah, I understand that. Were there any other people you admired besides Colan, Kirby, and Romita? I know that you were a big fan of Russ Manning.*
Steve: That's right. When you were a kid, you'd go over to your friend's house, and there's these comic books floating around the floor or the couch or whatever. Even though I wasn't a collector of *Famous Monsters of Filmland*, I had friends who were really into that stuff, and that was the culture of ten-year-old boys then, that's what was coming out, so that's what we read, and that was always cool to

us: Comics and monster magazines. Rarely did we see any paperback books lying around, it was always comic books.

CBA: *It was always visual.*

Steve: It was always visual, yeah, that could grab a child's mind like nothing else. Then, of course, there were the cartoons at the time, and the TV shows, like *Star Trek* was just coming out in '66. This was the perfect time for a kid to grow up!

CBA: *Were you a fan of* The Outer Limits, *as well?*

Steve: Yeah. It's funny, because I've since reviewed every episode of *The Outer Limits,* and bizarrely, I actually remember reading in the books about how the networks would complain to Joseph Stefano and Leslie Stevens about the illegibility of what the hell they were trying to do. [*laughter*] The funny thing is, I agree with them! There were some episodes that were so padded; it was just like, "How could I have remembered this show as being so good?"

CBA: *Well, it had great mood.*

Steve: Well, that must've been it, the power of the mood must've been so strong, the scary music and of course, the monsters, warped my mind [*laughter*], they were so scary to me. It must've just been the feeling of the show that came across. I also remember there were big lapses in what I remember about the shows of that age later on, because it was all during the parts where they sat there being redundant with dialogue, or just over-dialogue—there was no reason for this slow scene to be going on so long like this, that kind of stuff.

CBA: *Let's talk about when you first started drawing. When was that, when did you first start taking drawing seriously, and when do you first think you wanted to become a professional cartoonist? You wanted to do what people like Gene Colan and Jack Kirby were doing.*

Steve: I decided in high school, around 1974. When I graduated in '75, that was the year I was just so hardcore into Kirby and the Fourth World books, actually having to get all the issues that I'd missed, because there was a period when I was just not reading comics.

CBA: *The traditional period, the adolescent period.*

Steve: That was the thing I'd go through, and when I became aware that I'd missed all this history, I was curious about it. I actually thought back then there's no way this Jack Kirby guy I remembered from the '60s could still be drawing comics. When you're a kid, four years is like a lifetime! Now, you can do that over a cup of coffee, four years.

CBA: *It seems time has definitely accelerated.*

Steve: Yeah, it's a pretty funny thing. So, that's when I decided comic books would be my path in life. Paul Gulacy was doing *Master of Kung Fu,* the greatest work he's ever done, and it's just an evolutionary path of seeing the great things people were doing, getting so excited, and having an aptitude for drawing to begin with, and nothing could've ever excited me in life more than comic books.

CBA: *When you were in school, or even when you were younger, did you ever do any of the traditional homemade comics?*

Steve: No, I wanted to be a cartoonist like Charles Schulz. When I was a kid, I'd do these little one-panel cartoons called "Last-Minute Humor," and they were about people who were about to be executed and what they would say before they died. [*laughter*]

CBA: *Did you do any serious drawing in high school?*

Steve: High school is when the serious drawing started, I kind of went from this cartoony big-nose kind of character you see in comic strips to trying to draw like the guys in comic books. Like the realism of Paul Gulacy and the great impressionistic style of Jack Kirby.

CBA: *Which were two polar opposites, it seems.*

Steve: Yeah, they are polar opposites, and that's why I give my famous quote, "There's no accounting for taste."

CBA: *At the same time, you could also draw a line where Kirby begat Steranko, and Steranko begat Gulacy.*

Steve: Sure.

CBA: *So you get out of high school, and presumably go to college and start taking art classes?*

Steve: Yeah, I took a year off from high school, which I've always told people was the smartest thing I ever did. I was very backwards in high school, I didn't have much of a peer group, which is detrimental to a kid. You need a peer group to talk about things, figure stuff out, talk about girls and maybe go to a party or two, learn how to drink beer and be cool, and I never had that.

CBA: *Were you very shy in high school?*

Steve: I was very introverted, and yet, I felt this weird energy about me. This very strange emotional energy that developed from reading comic books. I would read these stories, and the show *Kung Fu* was on at the time, in 1972 and '73, and when these things would come on—always seemingly at just the right time in my life—they would propel me into this fanatic emotional maelstrom of inspiration and excitement, and these were the things that kept me going in life. High school is traditionally a very confusing stage for people, and God knows it was for me, because I had all these powerful emotions, and I just remember feeling things very strongly. I was always like that as a kid. I was very sensitive when I saw animals getting hurt, and would cry my eyes out for weeks sometimes, and so I would look to the culture I was living in—comic books, movies, TV shows—to supply me with answers that wouldn't come from friends who were much more stupid than I was. [*laughter*] Their thing was getting drunk and stuff, and that was never something I ever felt compelled to want to do with my life. I never went through a phase like that, with drinking or drugs or anything like that—but I needed other things in my life, like when Bruce Lee came along in '72, I can't tell you what he did to my life, he was a real-life superhero to me. I continued my incredible admiration relationship with Bruce Lee to this day. I find a kindred spirit in the guy, a guy who wanted to risk anything in life to pursue his dream.

CBA: *So that was a good model for you to have, taking off into the* terra incognito *of being a cartoonist and certainly something you weren't going to get a lot of validation for from your peer group, or teachers.*

Steve: I never thought about that aspect of it. I know other people who've gone to art school have complained about that, all that stuff, but geez, I never had that goofy stigma attached to thinking about comic books as this medium for children. For me, they were just the greatest, and how anyone could not see this was beyond me. I used to pass comics out on the bus on the way home

Above: A Steve Rude commission job featuring his trademark character, Nexus. ©2000 Mike Baron and Steve Rude.

Above: *One of Steve's favorite characters growing up was Alex Toth's animated hero, Space Ghost. In 1987, Steve drew the Comico one-shot,* Space Ghost, *written by Mark Evanier. Space Ghost ©2000 Hanna-Barbera.*

Below and opposite page: *Steve and Mike Baron have been pitching Nexus to animation studios over the years. Here's some recent presentations drawn by The Dude. Courtesy of the artist. All characters ©2000 Mike Baron and Steve Rude.*

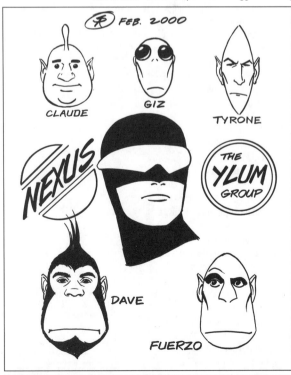

from high school, and say, "Look at this guy! Look at this Jack Kirby guy! Can you believe this stuff?" And they'd all be looking at his stuff in awe, like I was.

CBA: *But they didn't have your sensitivity.*

Steve: No, most people don't. Most people are incredibly callous, insensitive, and boorish, I've learned in life.

CBA: *[laughs] I concur. It seems to me that so much of the culture today is callous, boorish, and insensitive as well.*

Steve: It is, and it actually always has been, and always will be, but I think it's the character you're born with, you're born with a certain aspect to your person that is imprinted in you for your entire life. I used to wonder where this sensitivity came from, and when it started to really interfere with my life sometimes… get me very depressed and I used to think, "Well, where did this come from? When did this start? Can I think back far enough to find the answer?" And as far back as I could think, it was always there, so I think it's something you're born with.

CBA: *So, how did it go for you when you were in school? You're in higher education now, and you're pursing your studies, did you feel that the environment in school was positive for you? Did you feel that the ideas and the values that you had were being validated then?*

Steve: Yeah. I didn't need validation from other people, I was so set that this was "the path" that I never needed that. Basically, my first art school, which was the Milwaukee School of Arts that I began in 1976 through '78—I lasted two years there and I got bored out of my mind and left—but it was a moment of figuring out where you were in comparison to other people who were there in art college for the same reasons you were, and that was very, very good.

CBA: *So that was an exciting time, you had a new peer group, and new challenges. Is this when you started getting into the illustrators?*

Steve: I got into Loomis when I was in the sixth grade, actually, maybe even the fifth grade, I discovered him at the library. I was always looking for art books to look at, and draw from, because a kid's got to have something to do at all times, and I would find his books at the library, and I fell in love with him right away.

CBA: *Did you go from Andrew Loomis to some of his contemporaries? Flagg and Henry Pitz and people like that?*

Steve: Yeah, all those people came later on as I started to research the whole history of illustration and things like that.

CBA: *I had actually become aware of his work through you.*

Steve: Loomis?

CBA: *Yeah, because like I said, it's very difficult to find his work, it's been out of print for a number of years.*

Steve: That's why I say I was the guy responsible for the books not being around anymore. [laughter] I think I was the first guy to ever mention him in the whole world, in the comic book circles.

CBA: *He's actually really popular. The problem is that when tastes changed, you didn't have a built-in fan base back then for these people, because a lot of times, these guys were anonymous and I think that maybe his work fell through the cracks, despite its incredible quality, just*

because there wasn't an apparatus set up that would keep the work alive.

Steve: Oh, no, the books were the thing that immortalized him, unlike Dean Cornwell, who thought his immortality would come from murals, people remember him much more for his illustrations. So, the joke's on him.

CBA: *When did you start painting?*

Steve: I never did a single painting until I actually got into college, and I was frustrated. I wanted to learn how to do it, and Frazetta was really big at the time, and we all wanted to paint like him. I never touched paint until I got into college, and the teachers were terrible there, they didn't know anything about how to teach anybody to paint. I remembered a classic moment where this one teacher in charge of the painting department came up to me and said—I was in the middle of an oil painting—and he said, "How does it feel, Steve?" I said, "Okay, I guess." He said, "Well, keep going." That was the extent of my entire so-called "art school teachers" who were teaching how to paint at that particular school.

CBA: *The recruiters you spoke to were contemptuous about illustration?*

Steve: I must bring this up, that's one of the things I'm most proud of my own character. I never give a rat's ass what those people would say to me. I just looked at them with contempt, "You're clueless, Jack."

CBA: *Well, when you follow a fad…*

Steve: Oh, fads… that's another thing that drives me nuts. Fads drive me out of my mind, unless they had any real content, part of the universal greatness of the human condition, then they're empty, they're fads, that's what fads are. Our whole capitalistic culture's been based on that, and I know some people that have complained their whole life about what they've learned from these fads, and what they've had to unlearn, but I was always my own man so much that I never paid any attention to those fools. If I liked Jack Kirby, by God, that was it, you know? [laughs]

CBA: *So, you're in college, you're starting to paint, and then where do you go to? What's the next school you end up at?*

Steve: I dumped the art school after two years, I couldn't see myself going through another year of that grind, and moved down to Madison, Wisconsin, and I then starved for about two, three, four more years.

CBA: *Was it true you were living at the YMCA?*

Steve: Yeah, I was over at the Y, and I had a couple of other places I was living at in the first year I'd moved down there, but I remember one of the lowest points of my life. I was walking around barefoot on campus with my sketchbook, and I stepped on this piece of glass, and my foot got infected. I started getting this incredible pain in my foot, and the campus hospitals wouldn't take me because I wasn't a student, and I thought I was going to die of gangrene or something, and all I could do is sit there with my foot in this tub with Epsom Salts, with my sketchbook, drawing from comic books, and for the first time in my life, I thought, "Am I ever going to make it? Is my dream ever going to really happen? It's going to take me forever to get as good as these guys!" I just thought, "I don't know if I can do this or not." There's always these moments, to make the story good, where you don't know if you can pull it off or not. Bruce Lee went through that; God, the guy hurt his back so bad it messed him up for his whole life. A guy with his emotional temperament spending six months in the hospital? I mean, it's unthinkable! It's like trying to tell a bird not to fly for six months.

CBA: *When did you hit your breakthrough? When did you really start to come into your own?*

Steve: Probably about now. [laughter] Actually, the funniest thing is, I get so bored out of my mind talking about this historical crap, because everybody does that in interviews and all, but I'm so excited since I'm now 43 years old and I can't help but recall that Kirby was in his mid-40s when, in 1966, he was doing his greatest of all work. He was always doing great work. That I kind of timed it to that career point where you either forge ahead, and become truly your own man in charge of your art, or you falter and just give up and go back to some worthless day job.

CBA: *Mike Baron says when he met you on the steps of the Madison Area Technical College….*

Steve: Actually, it was the student campus, the steps of the Memorial Union, in Madison, Wisconsin.

CBA: *Okay—but he said when he saw your work, it made him give up!* [laughs]

Steve: That's been the joke with me and Baron all these years, I actually talked him into giving me some of his art books when I first met him, and one of them was the Loomis book, and it said… [laughs] here, I'll read it for you, I'll give you the exact quote, this made me laugh… First of all, Baron's name is on the top of the book here, because he owned it, and when I asked him to inscribe it to me, he continued it from the name "Mike Baron," and it says, "Mike Baron bought this book at the Harvard Co-Op in 1975 in the mistaken belief that he could turn himself into an artist through hard work and practice, however…"—this is classic Baron—"…in 1979, he met Steve Rude, and discovered a mundane, but profound truth: If God had wanted me to draw, he would not have introduced me to Steve Rude." [laughter] "Merry Christmas, 1981."

CBA: *That's fantastic. He said you guys started working on the Encyclopedia set stories, and then you started talking to John Davis.*

Steve: Baron did all the talking, I just sat in the Y and drew.

CBA: *You're still living in the Y at this point?*

Steve: Oh, yeah.

CBA: *You really suffered for your art, Steve!* [laughs]

Steve: Oh, I went through it all. I was on food stamps for a long time, the whole Summer.

CBA: *But you were dedicated.*

Steve: Frankly, I didn't know what else to do with my life! I had this mission that I had to do, and even though 90% of the time I was compelled to work at it all the time, it still doesn't stop a guy who's only moderately talented—I was certainly no prodigy, like I think Alex Ross is—from having doubts about, "How can I do this?" I'd go to Marvel, I would fly there, spend every cent I made in my day jobs moving baskets of paper from one end of the room to the other, and I'd go there to New York, and I'd get my critiques from people… I remember Jim Shooter gave me a great critique on my work one time, he told me to go back to basics—but I wasn't interested in basics, I was interested in flash. Basics are something you learn retroactively.

CBA: *Shooter was always really strong on the fundamentals with his artists, which I think Marvel misses now. I think he was very strong on storytelling, structure, construction…*

Steve: Yeah, almost obsessively, I've heard.

CBA: *Yeah. That's the lore. But I think that was good advice. So Nexus debuts, your work is not quite developed in the black-&-white stuff, but you're doing all the work yourself, inking, and doing a lot of work with shading film.*

Steve: Yeah, I did the lettering on the first issue, everything, painted the front and back covers, and all that.

CBA: *Did you feel like you'd arrived at that point?*

Steve: Did I feel like I arrived? No. But I can tell you I was extremely grateful I was actually being published in a real comic book. I didn't know what meeting Mike Baron would do for my life, because what we created with *Nexus* was all the timeless things that were inside of me, my image for nature, and not realizing the extent of where it would take me at the time. I had no idea where this thing was going to lead to, and what it would do to my life.

CBA: *I don't know if this is a function of your artwork, but I first started reading* Nexus *in the very early color issues; it seemed to me like there always was a Nexus* [laughs]. *It seemed to be something that just seemed so, well, "instant classic" is a horrible cliché.*

Steve: Those are high words of praise to me.

CBA: *I saw so many echoes of Russ Manning, and there were those kind of touches you picked up from Seuss. I mean, synthesis is kind of like a derogatory term…*

Steve: No, not at all, I've never known anything that worked except as a synthesis. That's just a fact of life for all artists, for all creative people. No man is an island, you know.

CBA: *Every good artist has a large group of influences that are sometimes at odds with each other, and a synthesist is somebody who can put it all together, and that's the way I felt when I was reading that book, and it wasn't just the art, it was also the writing and the beautiful production values, as well. It seemed like such a classic book when it first hit the stands. It was just this incredible leap from the last issue of the black-&-white book to the first issue of the color book. Was that just a function of consistently putting the work down? That, to me, would be the first of your breakthroughs.*

Above: *Part of a Nexus presentation pitch to an animation studio, it's our hero in defensive stance. ©2000 Mike Baron and Steve Rude.*

All characters ©2000 Mike Baron and Steve Rude.

Above: *Example of Steve's pencils from his recent* X-Men: Children of the Atom *mini-series. Courtesy of the artist.* X-Men ©2000 Marvel Characters, Inc.

because that meant I was becoming the artist I wanted to be, but couldn't, because I simply didn't possess the aptitude at that time to be that good. I was always drawing in my sketchbooks, and I think the sketchbooks looked a lot better than the stuff I was actually drawing in my comics, which was mostly out of my head, and then I sort of developed into this… "Well, let's start taking photo reference for certain things and see what happens."

CBA: *Were you taking photos for a certain shot you wanted to use in the book, or was it more general than that?*

Steve: Well, it was more general in the beginning. Then I started taking Polaroids of my friends, and I think the reason I did that is I was reading those Famous Artist course books, and I would read, "This is what you have to do to become an illustrator, you do these roughs in small, and then do a color rough, and then call in your models and do your photography session, and that's what you work from." So, being a guy that wanted to learn from anyone he could, this was the method I adopted. It really helped me understand things much better, to work from photos, and ultimately, the bridge between the photo reference and the sheer skill level of learning basic drawing better that evolved from constant practice became indecipherable.

CBA: *I remember when I was struggling with lettering when I was at the Kubert school, and there was this great guy named Hy Eisman who did a lot of ghosting for Albert Andriola on* Kerry Drake. *Fantastic artist. I was just struggling and struggling, I had terrible handwriting, and I just could not do lettering, and he told me, "You just keep at it, and what happens is that a template is formed in your mind, and it will sink in." Did you feel that's what happened with your artwork, that all that struggling, the lessons just finally sunk in?*

Steve: I think the answer is yes, and it's simply inevitable. I mean, the idea of a guy working all the time with something, and getting worse…

CBA: *That just seems paradoxical.*

Steve: Yeah, it does, and I do see it happening to people once they've lost their zest for the excitement of learning new things. I see that later on in life, like when the hotshots of the '80s were getting into their 40s and 50s and stuff, then they'd simply… something would be lost in their motivation to want to do superior work. Their new work clearly showed it, and I'm so fearful of that happening to me. It was like the worst thing that could ever happen. The ultimate disgrace in life was getting like these guys that were gods to me, and then suddenly, I don't understand what happened to them, they're not exciting me like they used to.

CBA: *It becomes a question of diminishing returns.*

Steve: Yeah, and it wasn't me that was changing, it was them! Great artwork is great artwork, and when it's not, a person senses that.

CBA: *Alex Toth told a real interesting story: When he was a kid, and starting to show his work around, he was waiting in the lobby of some publisher, and there was an older artist there who said, "Hey, kid, look at my work, what do you think?" and he showed Alex the portfolio, and Alex didn't think much of it, and he said, "Oh, it's good." And the artist said, "Wrong. I used to be able to draw circles around myself. I don't know what happened, I just can't do it anymore." At that point, Toth realized he constantly had to challenge himself, to improve, or he'd end up like that guy.*

Steve: Wow, that's the damnedest thing I've ever heard. That's a great story.

CBA: *That story made a big impression on me as well. I think there's a tendency for a lot of guys to get locked into a certain style, and then ride it, and I think their work just diminishes, because there's a sense of freshness that gets lost.*

Steve: Yeah, I agree, and I think what a good artist needs is a good, healthy dose of paranoia.

CBA: *That's easy to come by these days! [laughs]*

Steve: A healthy dose of insecurity and non-arrogance.

CBA: *Yeah. Well, arrogance to me is when you begin to congratulate yourself, you lose that sense of self-criticism.*

Steve: I still feel I'm hardly an ounce different from the 17-year-old Steve Rude, or even the ten-year-old Steve Rude about that stuff.

CBA: *Enthusiasm and a lust for new learning experiences?*

Steve: Well, I've asked myself because people have asked me that so often. I think it's really exciting to see an artist who starts out being pretty mediocre in many ways, and then suddenly, there's this, "Oh my God, what happened to this guy? He's learning at this accelerated, exponentially high rate," and I think it's because I started to learn how to use photographic reference a little bit better; that made my work look more real. I used to get out these *Star Trek* photo-novels and try to figure out how lighting would work. I really had no clue, I was not one of these guys… I was born with a talent, but….

CBA: *You were not a prodigy.*

Steve: Nothing close to that, nothing at all. I was just a guy who was determined to get somewhere in life. It was a slow process and it's easy to confirm that by simply looking at the first b-&-w *Nexus*. I remember George Freeman did that with *Captain Canuck*, starting out semi-amateurishly, and he suddenly took this huge leap forward. Gulacy the same thing, but he always had this great energy about his work. I don't think there's anything more exciting than to see a guy develop in print like that.

CBA: *Did you see it in yourself? Were you just so thrilled you were really putting the things you saw in your head down on the page? Was it just more routine than that?*

Steve: No, it felt good to know I was somehow getting better,

Steve: It's wanting to be as good as your masters, but never being as good. Therefore, you have to keep trying to be as good as them. Like, I'm looking at this Kirby *Thor* story as we're doing this interview, Chris, and I'm just humbled to the ground with this stuff! I mean, it's the apex of everything that I've ever felt life was about! You know, stories that are timelessly ingenious, artwork that has a dramatic impact that goes beyond anything a literal artist could ever achieve.

CBA: *What's so humbling about Kirby, too, is that when you look at his work in pencil, you don't see the construction lines, it just seems like it just suddenly appeared!*

Steve: That's something else that really frustrates me, because no matter how many times art teachers discourage you to be like this, I'm always comparing myself to people who are 1000 times better than I am. That's probably what keeps me so damn humble, you know?

CBA: *I think for any artist in this day and age, it's tough to be impressed with yourself when you look at the work of people like Rockwell, Leyendecker, James Montgomery Flagg, Windsor McCay and Maxfield Parrish… never mind the great masters! There's always much better work than your own available if you care to look at it, if you care to learn from it.*

Steve: Well, I'm always looking at it.

CBA: *So, you did* Nexus *for quite some time with different publishers. Why didn't you do any outside illustration work?*

Steve: Because comics encompassed everything that I wanted to do with myself, artistically. I could paint my covers, and I consider that my art of learning illustration with tone and color and anything that was done linear. So I was doing everything I wanted to do through comics. My covers were painted, because I wanted to learn the things I learned from my illustrators, and the comics were drawn because I love comics and all my great comic book heroes who were artists and writers.

CBA: *You also had a greater level of autonomy. Let's back it up a bit: When you first started doing* Nexus, *all of a sudden, there's this explosion of new concepts and new artists and new approaches to doing comics. Did that fuel you at all? Is that something you really felt a kinship towards? Were there other artists you really felt you were almost compatriots with?*

Steve: No, I never felt like that. To me, my idols were my idols, and they stayed my idols.

CBA: *You didn't feel any connection to people like Jaime Hernandez, or some of the work Bill Sienkiewicz was doing?*

Steve: Yeah, I guess I did with people like Hernandez, because he came out at the same time I did, but he was much more developed than I was. I remember I felt a kinship toward guys like Matt Wagner, people like that, because we were all in the same boat. There were these new companies developing, and we were all part of that new thing that was coming about with comics in the '80s.

CBA: *Was that exciting for you? You being in your studio in Madison, Wisconsin, did you feel like you were part of a movement, did you feel like you were part of something beyond just doing the book, as far as the things going on in comics outside?*

Steve: I remember being very excited because I was someone who was now published, so I could approach my idols at the time, feeling less intimidated by them, actually. I was still intimidated, and I was still in awe of them, because they were working for Marvel or DC and I was working for these guys in Madison, it wasn't the same kind of yardstick to me. I remember loving to talk to people about their art, and what they learned, and I liked shop talk. I hardly ever engage in it any more these days. I'm simply at a point where, unless it's something of substance to me, I don't like discussing it. The most boring thing in the world is to argue about the merits of one artist versus another. Somewhere along my late 20s, I just completely dis-engaged myself from those ridiculous, pointless arguments, and I would remove myself from any kind of conversations about those kind of things. My excitement about shop talk didn't last long with people, because most of these people didn't have anything to say, they had nothing really solid to teach me, and I wanted to learn some things that could really help me. Unless you were there to give me that, if you want to sit there and talk about the color of your underwear that day, [*laughter*] I was just going to get bored and

walk away. I wanted to learn. I mean, there were great secrets to be uncovered, and to me, the only people fitting to teach me those were masters, like Alex Toth.

I remember when I met Alex for the first time, I believe in '86 in San Diego, and that was the only time I ever saw him there. So thank God I went! I made him look through my sketchbook and asked for some advice before he went on to the next guy, and he gave me some superb advice, all based on the most basic fundamen-tals imaginable, and that's probably when I started to reconsider what fundamentals meant, and what it really means to break down a figure into its most simplistic terms, and get something seemingly complex and accurate out of simple basics. Alex was the guy that imparted things like that to me.

CBA: *A couple of years earlier, I recall seeing a picture of you and Jack Kirby when you'd won the Russ Manning Award.*

Steve: You know, I've got to tell you, my relationship with Kirby was always one of… I know people say this all the time, but it's almost a sense of non-reality to it. It just wasn't *real*, there was something *Twilight Zone*-ish about standing next to the guy, or being in his company, or listening to his voice. He was more than human to me.

CBA: *It's funny, because you towered over him, physically!* [*laughs*]

Above: *Rare example of a non-painted* Nexus *cover by The Dude. Courtesy of Alex Wald. ©2000 Mike Baron and Steve Rude.*

Steve: Yeah, I towered over poor little Jack Kirby—but he was, by far, the taller guy on the inside. He was always a giant to me.

CBA: *In 1984, you were probably about 28, right?*

Steve: When that picture was taken? I was 28.

CBA: *Plus, it must've been meaningful to win the Russ Manning Award.*

Steve: That was my first award, and I must tell you, the convention guys pulled that off without flaw, I mean, they really had me going for a moment there. I had no clue there was any nomination of any sort for me. I remember sitting in this crowded banquet with these geniuses around me, and I remember they dimmed the lights—the award was just being introduced for the first time, Dave Stevens had won it the first year, and I think someone else won it the second—and we're all sitting in this banquet room, the light got dark, and they threw these slides up on this big screen, and one of them was my work! I remember being there with my girlfriend at the time, and I just kind of went into this state of shock!

CBA: *[laughs] The room started to spin.*

Steve: Kind of, yeah. I got this feeling that it's almost impossible to actually put into a sentence or words, but I could tell you my heartbeat was racing like it never felt before, you know? I had a feeling that was something that could not be described, and when they announced my name, I went into a deeper sort of shock, where I barely had the presence of mind to stagger up to the podium! And I wasn't really a newcomer, either. I mean, I'd been doing *Nexus* for five or six years by then, but it meant that in the minds of my peers, I had arrived in some way. That was extremely flattering.

CBA: *You had the biggest grin on your face in that* CBG *picture. [laughs]*

Steve: Well, it was *insane!* I was with Kirby afterwards, and all I can say is, whoever invented the word surreal, it was invented for a reason, because there are some things you simply can't explain, it just became more than a sense of normal reality, and you went into a literal *Twilight Zone* state of shock, where your mind seldom goes in everyday life.

CBA: *That begs the question, did you ever feel that experience since?*

Steve: Yeah, I have. As the San Diego convention got larger, and I started winning these "best artist" and "best penciler" awards for *Nexus*, I remember one time I got up there, and I won the Will Eisner award, and I remember Will himself being the saving presence of my mind at the time. I was feeling pretty close to the way I felt when I won that Russ Manning award, and Will Eisner was just this tower of quiet strength to me. Because he was so down-to-earth, and so real, he just looked at me with this grin on his face—he probably saw the predicament I was in mentally—and just said, "Say what you feel, Steve. Say what you feel." And I did! If I stuttered, that was because it was part of the way I was feeling. I stutter anyway, [*laughter*] I never got over that. Me and my brother are terrible stutterers, but the only thing that was ever important in my life—and this goes down to almost everything I do, even on a day-to-day basis—was to be true to what I was, to be true to what I was born as. Even though it's hard to put that into words, and when people try to describe it, it sounds like it's indications of ego, but it's actually nothing like that, it's a feeling that certain things were passed on to me; I see that

Above and opposite page: Steve works out the design for the cover painting of the prestige-format one shot, The Incredible Hulk vs. Superman *(above) in this collage of four pages from his sketchbook (opposite). Courtesy of Steve Rude. The Hulk ©2000 Marvel Characters, Inc. Superman ©2000 DC Comics. Art ©2000 Steve Rude.*

much more clearly now in my 40s, that literally dictates my path in life. That is, I've got to be worthy of the people who've been influencing me since my childhood.

CBA: *Well, you certainly almost came close at that one point, it sounds like. [laughs]*

Steve: I did, yeah. I since learned from those moments of calamity that the only thing that matters to me is how good the work is. Nothing else matters.

CBA: *I think there's so much nonsense that affects all of us as a society, particularly in the comic book business, there are all these secondary considerations that cloud the quality of the work itself.*

Steve: Well, I have a comment about that, Chris, that simply must be put in words. If your thinking evolves to that point—assuming you didn't start out thinking that way—and suddenly your thinking becomes one of strict commercial considerations, you have literally lost your soul.

CBA: *You did so many issues of Nexus—16 years all told—and you did very little work outside of that, and the book certainly was never a cash cow. I think that what you're saying is borne out by your actions.*

Steve: Thank you.

CBA: *But what is it about Nexus that kept you so dedicated to it, despite the fact it was never a big seller? It was almost on the periphery of the market, as the market became more and more commercialized. What kept you on that, what connection did you have—maybe not to the character, but to the book, or to your relationship with Mike Baron—that kept you dedicated to Nexus?*

Steve: Because personal considerations aside—things which I've never been concerned about—the book was literally a diary of my evolution as a human being, and I believe it was that for Baron, too, even though we tend to have very different ways of thinking about our lives and philosophies. I would say that everything I ever wanted to say or do in life was within that book, and as I evolved as a person, I became aware that I had things I wanted to say about society. It was because of what I was reading in the newspapers, and that in turn made me think about historical context of humanity since there' been the written word, and it led me to various philosophies, one of which prompted the "God Con" issues. So, since the only things that were of true value to me were things that were tales that were based on the timelessness of the human condition, where could I get that, except in doing *Nexus?*

CBA: *You weren't going to get that in the run-of-the-mill superhero bang-'em-up kind of comic.*

Steve: Well, had I done those kind of comics, Chris; I still would've made sure that quality came through, because of my personality.

CBA: *So obviously, you had a real deep synergy with Mike Baron, connecting on a very deep level.*

Steve: Well, I'll say this, and I'll say it until the day I die: Mike Baron is the greatest writer I've ever worked with. I can't believe, sometimes, that we could work so well together, knowing that we're literally from different planets about some things—but when he gave me those scripts, I mean, it was like reading Marvel comics from 1966… the greatest stories and morality tales that I've ever read.

CBA: *That harkens back to the kind of timelessness that I was talking about that I experienced when I first read that title.*

Steve: Yeah, so you've said. That's a great compliment.

CBA: *I just remember the feeling when I was a kid reading Nexus that the whole tableau just seemed set in stone, it seemed timeless. could fumble for words, trying to pin this down, and it's not a fawning kind of thing.*

Steve: Well, those would be exactly the same words I would say about my Jack Kirby/Stan Lee comics, and later on, the Fourth World books, and it also led me to a personal philosophy that—I think I've never quite heard anyone give people permission to think like this— there are many things in life that can't be inscribed into words. For example, I was asked so many times, "Why *Space Ghost?* Why did this 'kids' cartoon appeal to you?" It just did. I had no answer for why. I would listen to songs that would make me feel things, and someone would ask me to describe why a certain singer sends me to this emotional epiphany. I realized it couldn't be done, and I didn't even try. I thought some things were simply relegated to the reality

Above: *Steve emulating the styles of some of the great magazine illustrators of yesteryear. Courtesy of the artist. Art ©2000 Steve Rude.*

of non-verbal feelings, and you should just leave it at that.

CBA: *So, let's talk about how you feel about your work today, and about your place in the business, how you feel in relationship to the standing in your environment. First, let's talk about the work: You mentioned you really feel like you're really starting to progress onto a new level, and how would you explain that?*

Steve: Well, first of all, it certainly hasn't made me any faster. [*laughs*] Like everyone told me I'd get when I was younger, that's the first thing I have to debunk. It actually gets slower in some ways.

CBA: *Like Dan Clowes says, "The more you know, the longer it takes, because there are more things in play that you have to address."*

Steve: Well, I would agree with that. When I went to this new art school in Calabassas, California, my painting time slowed down considerably because I had more knowledge that I had to apply to my work, and if I was going to keep it in my memory, it would be something you'd have to put into practice. So, even though my paintings got better [*laughs*], I slowed down quite a bit, too.

Could I mention some thoughts about the new things I'm working on now and the current state of our business?

CBA: *Please, talk about what you like.*

Steve: Well, for starters, and for the first time in my career, I've begun to work for Marvel.

CBA: *Which you were dead-set against doing for some time because of what they did to Jack Kirby.*

Steve: Yeah. I simply saw them as people who were devoting themselves to everything that I thought was the antithesis of what Marvel started out to be, which is "Anything goes, comics are dying, let's try anything and everything, and let ourselves go creatively." Then they became this gigantic commercial entity. Commercial was first and artistic was second. There also came a time in this business when people—some deserving, some not deserving—became millionaires, and I watched this with great interest. I sat back on my little lotus leaf and watched this extremely bizarre turning of events take place, and the one thing I knew at the time was that things usually start out one way, and they may end up another. What it ended up doing was basically being an incredibly corrupting factor to most people who achieved that incredible wealth in a short amount of time. A guy like Todd McFarlane seemed to be born more a businessman than an artist. He seems to have found his calling in life.

I couldn't be farther from the way a business guy thinks. It simply does not compute to me. I just remember watching the Image explosion from a vantage point of, "I want to see how this all turns out," because only fools rush into things like this. It was very much a warning sign to me, personally, something that could be incredibly corrupting—something I'm extremely fearful of, maybe unduly, about making incredible amounts of money. If I had been sucked into that greed factor, I believe everything in my life would be lost. I would be completely without purpose. It's funny, Chris, I've been paging through this *Thor* issue where he fights Hercules the whole time we've been talking, which is great, you can look and talk at the same time.

CBA: *Yeah, multi-tasking. [laughs]*

Steve: This is another case where words have no place, it goes

beyond the ability to translate feelings into the greatness of these stories here. They're felt in a way that's so powerful that it transcends language to me. Anyway, getting back to the point, I watched this period in time take place where all these kids—literally, kids—were making *millions* of dollars, and I remember talking about it with a few friends of mine that had some insights into this, and they told me how many times in history these things have occurred, where everybody wanted to be in on the gold rush bandwagon, and almost always, inevitably, the final result was one of negative consequence.

CBA: *Total collapse.*

Steve: Yeah, collapse. Somehow, thank God, I just had the wherewithal not to be sucked in by this, you know? I wanted to get my worth for the work I did, but it was never going to be something that would corrupt me, because it's human to be corrupted by the things in life that unseat your purity of intent.

CBA: *Let me put it this way, Steve, and see if you agree with this: I put myself in your position, and I see all this stuff taking place, what I would regard as substandard work is making people enormous amounts of money, it's kind of like selling your soul. For somebody who's already oriented to do that kind of work, the kind of work that was very popular then, it's not that big a leap, it's perfectly natural to cash in on that—but for you, you would be sacrificing something innate in your personality and in your character, that once the gold rush was over, you'd be left with nothing. That what was more important to you was your standards and your ethics and your artistic values, and if you sacrificed them, which had brought you that far along, when the gold rush was over, you'd be left with nothing.*

Steve: Yeah, well said. There's all these historical examples that you can parallel with this thing. There's nothing new about the tricks humanity pulls on itself. They're cyclical, and they're never ending. This is the first time it ever happened in comic books, unless you want to consider the time when millions of people were reading them in the World War II days. There's nothing new under the sun as far as human nature goes. There never will be. I could recite a *Star Trek* line from the episode about Khan—is that, yes, technology has brought mankind this far, but mankind himself, how little he has changed. I don't know, maybe it's just hearing things like that and having some sort of sixth sense about learning these lessons that always kept me on the straight and narrow. And also, I never cared about money! I mean, all I wanted to do was be a better artist! I wanted to learn how to paint and draw better, Chris, that's what I wanted! There is nothing I needed money for, really.

CBA: *Let's get back to your working for Marvel.*

Steve: And why I'm doing it?

CBA: *Yeah. Haven't you done some of the in-house licensing work for them?*

Steve: I have, that was my original first start with Marvel. They'd call me up and want these renditions of classic characters done in a Kirby style, and everybody knew I idolized Kirby, and I would try to draw them in his style. It was fun and it was a great challenge for me, and it made me feel like I was becoming part of that world of comics that I remembered by trying to draw like him; but I'd never work for their editorial department, for the political reasons.

But one day, as destiny would have it, I was in Spain for a convention, and I had these extremely heart-felt fans come up to me and start asking me in their broken English, bless their hearts, because I could speak no Spanish except *"hola"* and *"intiendo," "no intiendo Español,"* you know? They asked me why I didn't work for Marvel, and I told them. And they said to me, "Well, do you realize what impact you might have on comics if you worked for them?" I'd say, "Well, what do you mean?" My stupid American friends would always say, "Think of the money you could make, Steve," and I would always instantly turn my brain off to those idiotic comments, because they were so offensive to me, even people I thought knew me real well, after all these years, would still make those stupid comments about all the money I could be making. But in Spain, they said, "Steve, don't you realize you could influence an entire new generation of kids that like the current vogue style that everybody does nowadays that appeals to so many people, but there's a lot of people who look at that style and associate it with the lowest common denominator of artist." [*laughter*] I actually had to think about that.

They gave me an original thought, which, I must say, is the most exciting thing I ever experience in life, is an original thought. Most people spew pablum their whole lives without an ounce of originality to it. I crave original thoughts about human beings and why they do what they do, because *people* are the secret of life. No matter how isolated you want to remove yourself from people, as I do sometimes, I realized a long time ago the secret to life is *people* and how you affect them, what you can do to affect them. When the guys from Spain mentioned that to me, it kind of seemed to mesh with a growing personal philosophy of mine: "If you believe you've inherited some skill that was passed on to you from former greats, you must in turn pass it on to the generation after you."

CBA: *An obligation.*

Steve: An obligation, yeah, in the best sense of the word. Kirby, my God, if anyone should've been a billionaire, it was him. He died making probably a barely above-average sort of living, and because he is my role-model for everything—not just as a comic book artist, he became my role model for a human being, as well.

CBA: *I didn't know him personally, but I actually called him up at his house one time, just on a whim, just to talk to him, and he took the time to talk to me, and he actually was quite gracious, even though I interrupted him in the middle of dinner! There's just so many testimonials as to how gracious he was, and that he was a dignified human being. Money comes and money goes, but…*

Steve: Money comes and money goes. Well said.

CBA: *…but his legacy—I mean, how many people in the world have a magazine devoted to them?*

Steve: Well, you've hit on the exact right point which is: What do you want to leave behind? Now that I'm literally at the half-way point in my life, the concern of what I leave behind is important to me.

CBA: *Your legacy.*

Steve: Yeah, and the fact that so many comics are without context of meaning to anything beyond the newsprint or slick paper they're printed on is very disturbing to me. So, I feel even more responsible to deliver the things that the greats gave to me. That's

why I'm working for Marvel, the place it all began for me, and the place where I seem to be finally ending up. I am devoting myself, my career, and everything I believe in to returning Marvel to that sense of wonder through a non-vogue style of art—which mine is not—to the glory days that made that company so great from the beginning. That's my statement about why I'm working for Marvel.

CBA: *I think those are noble aims. I would say only that—and I know you know you are—swimming against the tide. Is that part of the appeal for you?*

Steve: Actually, it is, yeah. I like impossible odds.

CBA: *Do you have anything lined up after* Children of the Atom?

Steve: Yeah, I promised the editor of *Spider-Man* that I would do his project next. And coincidentally, it was funny how all the Marvel editors seem to call at once when word got out that *Nexus* was no longer being published by Dark Horse, I just got this sense from Marvel that I'd never gotten before, that they wanted me to come in for very specific reasons: Their editors grew up reading *Nexus,* they knew my work, so that's what I'm most thankful for.

CBA: *You know, for some reason, a phrase that is becoming popular these days is "first principles," the theory of getting back to the basics of what makes something work, and what made Marvel comics work was exactly what you said, that sense of wonder. Have you read any of Alan Moore's material he's been doing at DC, the* Tomorrow Stories *and* Tom Strong *and things like that?*

Steve: *The League of Extraordinary Gentlemen,* does he do that?

CBA: *Yeah, that's him.*

Steve: No, I haven't read any of that stuff because I actually don't read comic books these days. I'm sure they're great, but if you could ask me to tell you how great they are, I have no doubt they're superb, even though I'm not a reader.

CBA: *I think what he's trying to do with those books is very much what you said that you're interested in.*

Steve: I think I'm seated strictly in traditional '60s Marvel ethics, I think he comes at it from a much broader, literary perspective than I.

Above: *Courtesy of Jerry Boyd, Steve Rude's depiction of Joe Simon & Jack Kirby's The Fly. The Dude is one of the few artists who "gets" Jack Kirby, emulating the King's dynamic approach without simply swiping. The Fly ©2000 the respective copyright holder. Art ©2000 Steve Rude.*

CBA: *Tom Strong reminds me a lot of Silver Age DC. People like Mike Sekowsky, and that whole classic style. Have you ever really responded to that work as much…*

Steve: No, not at all. I was strictly into Jack Kirby and the Marvel artists.

CBA: *Not even later?*

Steve: Not even later.

CBA: *Not even now? [laughs] Let's talk about who's in the pantheon of work that you liked, aside from Kirby, if you were held at gunpoint and told that you had to tell someone your top ten.*

Steve: My top ten? I couldn't even go to ten.

CBA: *Okay, your top five. [laughs]*

Steve: My top five? Well, number one would be Kirby, the second would probably be John Romita, the third probably would be Russ Manning…

CBA: *Toth?*

Steve: Actually, that's another weird thing, I'm more affected by Toth in his animation work than his comic book work.

CBA: *He spent a lot of prime years in animation.*

Steve: He sure did, and his art was translated into my favorite cartoon shows. I've never been affected by his comic book work in the same way I did with his designs and layouts for the cartoon shows. Again, no accounting for taste, so nobody should take any offense to my personal opinions. Later on, I discovered people like Alex Raymond and Hal Foster…

CBA: *How about Wally Wood?*

Steve: Wally Wood was not one of them, I never grew up reading the guy. Paul Gulacy was my hugest high school influence.

CBA: *And you later became friendly with him.*

Steve: Yeah.

CBA: *Did you know him before you went professional?*

Steve: No, not at all. I called him out of the blue one day and told him I thought he was the greatest artist I'd never seen.

CBA: *[laughs] That's a great way to introduce yourself.*

Steve: Yeah, I was not shy about it. It's just a moral directive for me to tell people that I thought were great, to tell them they're great.

CBA: *Artists tend to work in isolation. I remember I'd written Gene Colan a letter when I was about 18, because I was just really enamored of his work back then—and I still admire it—but I was spending so much of my time absorbed in his work, and I wrote him a letter, and I got a letter back about four or five days after I sent it! [laughs] He must've written me back the day he got the letter! I really enjoy talking to guys like that, because they just have that sense of graciousness.*

Steve: Graciousness is the perfect word to describe those guys. Of course, there's a sense of this basic appreciation, graciousness, good manners in things that we find so often today, right?

CBA: *Well, you know, I think it's become very fashionable to be coarse. My only hope in that is that fashions change, and this year's fashion is next year's leftovers, so maybe that whole mentality will shift. So much of what you listen to on the radio, particularly, is just so coarse and vulgar.*

Steve: Yeah, it's unbelievable what they can get away with saying on TV nowadays. The greatest movies and TV shows I ever saw, there never had to be a single curse word or anything degrading or vulgar—ever!

CBA: *I think a lot of it is intellectual laziness, too. The thing I really appreciate about what you're saying is your emphasis on standards and excellence, and your emphasis on the traditional rules of drawing and storytelling, which are traditional because they've been time-tested.*

Steve: Well, I think you've hit on the essence of our whole conversation, here in the second half of our talk, Chris. The things of the moment, things of transience, that this culture will always throw in our face, but there are things that will transcend it because they're based on a basic, simple truth about the human heart. For me, that calling is the medium of comic books.

CBA: *Well, Steve, aside from admiring your work, I admire what's behind it. What I like to see in any artist is somebody bring a lot to the table, not just surface.*

Steve: Well, especially since "surface" is most visible in the new ways people are telling stories and drawing the art. We've talked about how things can only go so far before the transient things have to shift to act as a balancing act. It's critical, that somebody is out there with talent that is not based on trends.

CBA: *Well, I've got to tell you something that I believe personally, the justification for a lot of the work that's out there, for being put out there, is that, "Well, this is what the kids want, this is what sells." Except for when you look at the sales figures, that opinion isn't borne out.*

Steve: I don't think I've ever heard more offensive words to my ears than, "This is what kids want." I actually cringe when I hear those words, "What kids want." I mean, one of the things Chuck Jones always emphatically stated about the cartoons that he made, that are universally regarded as works of geniuses, is he never made them for anyone but himself! If you have a basic sense of good taste, and a talent that is based on something more than some trick you learned in art school, that's the way all art should be done, and from there it's simply a matter of the reader and what they prefer. I've never had any problem with the fact that so many kids want to read what I would consider garbage. I don't understand it, but there's always been an association with popularity and junk! It's also interesting to think that there may be some kid who is emotionally accelerated for his age to take a chance on picking up the books that Joe Casey and I have done, and actually found something that would kind of shift his way of thinking about what he thought was cool! I mean, what a great honor that would be for me and Joe!

So, with that in mind, I'll forge ahead with Marvel and see if I can make the hands of time go back a bit.

CBA: *Or forward! [laughs] Maybe they've been frozen for a while.*

Steve: That's what the funny thing is, I'm looking at 30 years in the past, but in fact, it's actually a way of moving forward and getting Marvel on the track they were before they became commercially corrupted. I like that phrase.

CBA: *I think the commercial corruption of the company is what brought them to their knees.*

Steve: Always, it's a given. It will almost always inevitably happen. It leaves me with many questions about the very compunction for greed. Why, when you're making money, does one always want to make more? That's the irony. It takes common sense to see that pattern, that consistent pattern that always plays itself out into the evolution of almost all companies.

CBA: *Well, if you're not very, very careful, and not very, very diligent, you maybe inevitably lose sight of the original mission and that's when the corruption sets in.*

Steve: The fact that we could point to so few examples of any place throughout any time, anywhere, that has gone against this commercialism growth principle, that should tell us most of what we need to know right there. It's hard to avoid for most people.

CBA: *It's like a natural inclination to degenerate, it seems to me, degenerate in the classical sense of the term, to just fall apart. [laughs]*

Steve: There is one other thing I want to add to everything I said about why I'm working for Marvel. This is the most critical of all, and that is, even though I'm doing work based on the classic characters that have affected everything about the person I am, I think it's ultra-critical that the generation of creators must be our own men or women. We must not regurgitate the past. We should acknowledge it. I don't want history looking at this generation as nothing but people that have basically done nothing but redos of what's gone on before them without any individual creativity of their own. In the 60s, they were their own men, creating their own stories. We can use all the things we got learned them, but we can't be looked at as people that are just retreading old ground from 35 years ago. We're the here and now. Let's take smarter advantage of that.

Baron of the Comics

On Nexus, Badger, The Flash and Life with the Dude

Conducted by Chris Knowles
Transcribed by Jon B. Knutson

Mike Baron has written for any number of comics publishers—DC, Marvel, First, Image, Valiant, Comico, Dark Horse, Malibu, Pacific, and even Jademan—and is probably best revered for his work on Nexus, The Punisher, *and* The Flash, *though (as you'll learn) his prose work dates further back. He was interviewed via phone in January 2000, and the writer copyedited the final transcript.*

Comic Book Artist: *Where are you originally from?*
Mike Baron: Madison, Wisconsin.
CBA: *When did you start reading comics?*
Mike: God, probably when I was around 12 years old.
CBA: *Any particular favorites?*
Mike: Yeah, *Uncle Scrooge* was definitely my earliest. Then, later, when I was in college, I got into that whole first rush of exciting new wave comics, like *Conan the Barbarian.*
CBA: *And you were a journalism student.*
Mike: No, I was a political science student at the University of Wisconsin.
CBA: *So, when you got out of school, what happened then?*
Mike: I heard you could find work as a writer in Boston, so I moved to Boston, and it was true, I found work as a writer. I wrote for *Boston After Dark, The Phoenix, The Real Paper,* and a bunch of other magazines. I bummed around, I lived with pals in apartments, eventually got my own place.
CBA: *What was your political bent at the time? Coming from a very liberal city, and then going to another very liberal city....*
Mike: Well, I grew up in South Dakota, actually, though I was born in Madison. I was pretty apolitical when I was in Boston. If anything, I had suppressed my natural conservative leanings.
CBA: *Okay, so you're doing real writing, which is unusual for somebody who found their way into comics.*
Mike: Well, I always wanted to do comics, and fiction in general, and anything I did in-between was just practicing my craft while I tried to break in.
CBA: *Did you take any stabs at prose fiction?*
Mike: Oh, yeah. I sold a couple of short stories to science-fiction magazines that are no longer around, and I'm taking another stab now, but that's another story.
CBA: *Were you a s-f fan more than a comics fan?*
Mike: Not really, kind of equal. I read everything when I was growing up. I haven't read science-fiction in a long time except for some Joan Vinge. When I grew up, I read everything: Asimov, Heinlein, Jules Verne, Clifford Simak, Larry Niven....
CBA: *So, you read a lot of hard s-f, it seems.*
Mike: Everything. I particularly liked Philip José Farmer, and I guess Larry Niven for your hard science-fiction.
CBA: *How long were you in Boston?*
Mike: 1971 to '77.
CBA: *Did you continue writing when you went back to Madison?*
Mike: Well, I'd never stopped writing, but I did get a job at an insurance company for two-and-a-half years.
CBA: *Were you a writer there?*
Mike: I designed ads and wrote copy.
CBA: *When did* Nexus *start to bubble up in your mind?*
Mike: Well, that was actually after I met Dude, and probably around '80.

CBA: *So you wanted to somehow get into the comics business?*
Mike: Well, I'd always been looking around to get into comics. I tried to draw for years and years.
CBA: *Did you ever train, or just do it on your own?*
Mike: Not really; it was all on my own. I suppose if I'd gone to school, I could be a pretty decent comic book artist.
CBA: *Where did you meet Steve?*
Mike: On the steps of the Student Union in Madison, Wisconsin. He was a student at MATC, the Madison Area Technical College.
CBA: *So how did you two hit it off? What was the connection?*
Mike: Well, he'd been shopping his art around at this newspaper in town, and I knew the editor there, and the editor said, "You should give this guy a call, he draws just like you." The editor didn't know his ahem from his elbow. [*laughter*] So I called Dude up, and we chatted a little, and he was into comics and I was into comics, so I said, "Let's meet," and I met him on the steps of the Union, he had his portfolio, and he showed me what he was doing, and I was just blown away. I stopped drawing right then and there.
CBA: *Discouraged?*
Mike: Well, discouraged about my drawing, but encouraged about the future of our comics, because he wanted to do comics but couldn't write. It was a very fortuitous meeting.
CBA: *Did you have other ideas before starting work on* Nexus?
Mike: Oh, yeah, we did this whole thing called "Encyclopedias," which was serialized by Pacific Comics.
CBA: *In* Alien Worlds, *right?*
Mike: Yeah, something like that. About a guy trying to sell encyclopedias in a war-ravaged future, door to door.
CBA: *How did* Nexus *come about?*
Mike: We were trying to interest these people that were publishing, Capitol City Distribution. It was John Davis, Milton Griepp, and Richard Bruning at the time. I showed them what we were doing, and one of them—I think it was Milton or John—said, "Oh, we don't want s-f, we want a costumed crimefighter," so I went into my costumed crimefighter huddle, and bounced ideas back and forth, and came up with *Nexus.*
CBA: *How much of this was Steve's contributions? There were a lot of whimsical elements in there that were balanced with maybe some of the more hard-boiled stuff, which I maybe credit you with.*
Mike: Who can say?
CBA: *It's totally organic, right?*
Mike: Totally. Lerner and Loewe.
CBA: *So,* Nexus *was a full collaboration, then.*
Mike: Oh, yeah. It always has been.
CBA: *So you worked* Nexus *as a costumed crime-fighter, and brought it back to Capitol, and they were presumably interested.*
Mike: Yeah, they said, "Hubba, hubba! Let's go!" First 12 pages we did, they printed them.
CBA: *There were only 12 pages of story?*
Mike: Well, initially,

Below: *A recent shot of Mike Baron. Courtesy of the writer.*

but then they said, "We need 20 more pages." So, when we put the book out, it was 32 pages of story, but what we showed them initially was just the first 12 pages.

CBA: *So, you guys hit it off, and you did the three issues of the b-&-w* Nexus. *Do you have any memories of the response to that?*

Mike: Everyone seemed to like it. [laughs]

CBA: *So there was a lot of enthusiasm for the project?*

Mike: Yes. I don't remember anybody coming up and spitting in my face or anything. [Chris laughs] You know, fans are named fans because they're fannish about new projects, and if you do halfway-decent, fans will be enthusiastic, and we were halfway-decent, and they were enthusiastic.

CBA: *Were you guys making enough money out of* Nexus *to quit your day jobs?*

Mike: Not really, no. Not for about a year and a half, and after it attracted attention, and Mike Gold came by and said, "I want you to write *Flash*," and we got this deal with First, once we went with First and they started coming out monthly, I could quit my day job.

CBA: *And you were still working on the insurance?*

Mike: No, actually, I was just freelancing at a newspaper, rolling old ladies for quarters.

CBA: *So,* Nexus *does well enough as a black-&-white title to merit a color title, and then you chimed in with The Badger. Was The Badger a character you had formulated before, in the dim past?*

Mike: *The Badger* is more uniquely mine. I had Badger in mind before I found Jeffrey. Of course, he put his indelible stamp on it, I'm speaking of Jeff Butler, the original Badger artist. But it was just a combination of things, I'd always been fascinated with multiple personalities—and around here, it's badger this and badger that, and I wanted to do a regionally-based comic.

CBA: *I've never made that connection before. So the color Capital line starts, and does pretty well, presumably?*

Mike: I have no idea. [laughs]

CBA: *You were never told, you were kept in the dark, as far as figures and royalties...*

Mike: Well, Capital wanted to publish comics, but they were much better at distributing than publishing, or they never would've sold those titles.

CBA: *They had very high production values on these titles.*

Mike: Yes, they did.

CBA: *Was this all done in Madison, or did they farm some of this out to shops outside Madison?*

Mike: Coloring was all done here by Les Dorschied.

CBA: *To me, that is the essence of the titles, I was just so blown away by those books when they came out. I just read them*

and re-read them. The coloring, and the production, there was so much going on. Unfortunately, the crash of '83 sweeps away Capital with it, and two of your titles, as well as Whisper, are homeless. Then, First comes out of Chicago, and scoops them up. Do you want to talk a little about that?

Mike: Well, we were lucky to land with First. They were always interested. Again, it was a regional appeal.

CBA: *Midwestern solidarity?*

Mike: Sort of. [laughter] They weren't the only publisher that was interested. I liked them, I was very impressed with what they'd done initially with *Warp* and *American Flagg!,* I liked the product.

CBA: American Flagg! *was a big hit at the time.*

Mike: I liked that they were closer than any other publisher, so I could drive down there and bang on their door if they owed me money. So, we had a meeting with those guys, and we ended up with First.

CBA: *How many of the stories that were printed in the early run of the first title were actually done for Capital?*

Mike: Oh, one at most.

CBA: *It was a pretty smooth transition?*

Mike: Oh, yeah. When you think about First Comics and the fact that Dude managed to turn out, I don't know, nine or ten issues a year there, I mean, he was never really quite monthly. But we whipped him into quite a gallop at one point! [laughter]

CBA: *I've heard whispers in the wind of Steve's lack of prodigious output in recent years, but I'd never had an inkling of that in the early days, because it seemed* Nexus *was pretty regular.*

Mike: Well, it was regular, and I say that not because he's slow—he's not slow—but when you look at his art, it's so beautifully designed, it takes a lot of time, and he's not one of those guys that just slaps sh*t down on the page.

CBA: *Sometime in the run where you're doing Nexus, and Badger was also picked up by First, Mike Gold called you, and you start writing The Flash. I presume this was about '86?*

Mike: Yeah.

CBA: *Was The Flash a favorite character of yours?*

Mike: I liked The Flash, I initially had this big burst of energy, and I had all these great ideas, then I ran out of ideas. [laughs] I shouldn't admit this, but that's why I stopped doing the book. I didn't know what to do next! Now, I look at guys like William Messner-Loebs who've kept it going for years and years and years... but it just wasn't my groove at that point, you know?

CBA: *You had no real affinity for the character?*

Mike: I liked the character a lot, I had tremendous affinity for the personality, but it was the powers that I got lost on. I'm probably too literal to deal with a mind-bending power like faster than light travel or anything like that, because I'm always looking for scientific principles to back it up, and if I can't find any, then I just throw my hands in the air and just say, "Oh! I don't know what I'm going to do!" and just be silly, and he'll visit the Bizarro World. [laughter]

CBA: *Was that a concern of yours with Nexus as well?*

Mike: No, not really.

CBA: Nexus *was more flights of fantasy.*

Mike: All-encompassing. I think one of the reasons is that.. not being constrained by any other version of the universe, or who should be in the book, if we just allow the Nexus Universe to kind of grow naturally, and what happened was we created so many diverse characters and situations that I'm never at a loss for story ideas.

CBA: *It's your own little universe that you can explore at will. Now, at some point, you start doing The Punisher for Carl Potts, as well. How did that come about?*

Mike: Carl asked me to.

CBA: *You teamed up with Klaus Janson for that. Do you have any reflections on your time on that?*

Mike: The first year-and-a-half when Carl was editor were great, I did it as a straight crime book, I tried to keep all the supernatural and super-hero aspects out of it completely. Then, Don Daley became editor, and Don kept coming up with story ideas of his own. The Punisher kept getting drawn more and more into the Marvel Universe, Doctor Doom and all these other clowns... [laughter] and finally we ended up with this ridiculous plot where he became a black man like Black Like Me, and it was just... humiliating.

S.RUDE '98

CBA: *The early work you did under Carl Potts, I thought you were bringing the character back to its pulp/Executioner origins.*

Mike: Yes.

CBA: *It was also very topical. The stories were very... I hate to use the word "relevant," because it brings up* Green Lantern/Green Arrow *associations, but you seem to be really plugged into a lot of things that were going on. I remember the first storyline was sort of a Contra storyline, then a neo-Nazi storyline, and one with a Jim Jones type character. So that must've been a lot of fun for you.*

Mike: Well, I was ripping those stories out of the headlines.

CBA: *All through this time, you're doing* Nexus *with different people at this point. Paul Smith becomes a semi-regular on the books. He seemed to fit in well.*

Mike: Yeah. Paul's a great artist, a great storyteller, and one of nature's gentlemen.

CBA: *So, one of the themes of this issue we're trying to deal with is sort of the spirit of independents, and the spirit of the times, the zeitgeist, I guess. Did you feel plugged in to that, or were you just doing your own work?*

Mike: What do you mean? [*laughs*] I'm writing a story that takes place in the year 2600, you know?

CBA: *What I mean is, all of a sudden, people weren't limited to the old work-for-hire system, the tightly-edited books...*

Mike: I was certainly a beneficiary of a new freedom in comics.

CBA: *Did that time feel particularly special to you, or...?*

Mike: When *Nexus* and *Badger* were coming out monthly, I was just on such a high, man. Such a high.

CBA: *You were also branching out into other publishers as well.*

Mike: I'm very proud with most of the work I've done—not all of it, as I've written my share of clinkers.

CBA: *As the '80s go on, First starts to get wobbly, and things become kind of uncertain. What was your view of that situation?*

Mike: I attributed it to high overhead, fancy offices. If they had stayed in an attic, or an apartment in Evanston, or wherever they started, they would probably still be in business today. Low overhead is the key!

CBA: *[laughs] Yeah, well, there was a rush for a lot of independent publishers at the time, to make themselves feel more legitimate and get fancier digs and spend a lot more money, keeping in the spirit of the late-'80s. Trying to maintain a Hollywood image.....*

Mike: I ain't saying nothing.

CBA: *[laughs] Your silence is deafening! Were you reading any of the material coming out in the early-'80s? Have any favorite titles?*

Mike: Oh, sure. You know, I'd have to go back and look and see what was being published then. *Grimjack* I always enjoyed.

CBA: American Flagg!, *I'd presume.*

Mike: Not so much. It was certainly a beautiful book. Fun to look at. What was going on? Geez, my feeble mind. I'd have to go back and drag the boxes out of there and see what was being published.

CBA: *But you were pretty enthusiastic about some of the other material that was going on?*

Mike: Yeah, I liked all sorts of sh*t. I like Frank Miller's stuff. He was doing *Daredevil* around then, I guess. Anything Mike Mignola drew. I liked Jim Starlin as a writer and an artist. He came back and did a series of *Captain Marvel* stuff after he quit the book that I thought was just really great. Tim Truman, when he came on the scene, had just such an aura, such power. Great talents, all. Alan Moore. I remember *Watchmen*, of course, at least that had enough impact on me I can dimly remember it.

CBA: *[laughs] Lost in the mists of time!*

Mike: Oh, I can remember it vividly, in fact. That's one of those books where I can recall these little details.

CBA: *Okay, so First starts to get wobbly, and presumably, Mike Richardson of Dark Horse comes calling.*

Mike: Yes, he did.

CBA: *And he offered you a very unique deal where he had the option to buy out the rights to* Nexus, *and he reverted them to you, which is extremely generous.*

Mike: Unheard of, unprecedented.

CBA: *When did Dark Horse start doing* Nexus?

Mike: With Dark Horse? I think it was '89.

CBA: *So,* Nexus *ran pretty smoothly, made the transition pretty well?*

Mike: Well, Dark Horse were sweethearts, but somehow, at First, they cajoled the book into a monthly, and that was the key to its success. Once we went to Dark Horse, we stumbled, we had an infinite delay between the special and the first mini-series, and we just killed any momentum we might've had.

CBA: *It was just a production issue?*

Mike: No, there were all sorts of problems: Finding a decent colorist, a decent inker, Dude getting the penciled pages done on time, it just seemed to be a real hard period in everyone's life.

CBA: *One transition too many, perhaps?*

Mike: I don't know what the problem was.

CBA: *Then the market starts to implode a few years after. What did you think of some of the work that was coming out in the early-'90s? The more garish and sensational kind of material?*

Mike: Well, it depends, I think Jim Lee as an illustrator is terrific, and I like a lot of the guys who copy him, but I don't like a lot of the guys who copy him, too.

CBA: *What did you think of the aesthetic? There wasn't a big amount of literary writing.*

Mike: It was becoming more adult, more sensational, more experimental. You got some good stuff, you got some bad stuff.

CBA: *Did you feel a part of it?*

Mike: Oh, yeah, I feel connected to what's going on right now.

CBA: *And* Nexus *is now in development as a cartoon series?*

Mike: Oh, yeah... geez, they keep pushing back the go date.

CBA: *Presumably you worked on the scripts?*

Mike: No, I haven't. They're by a screenwriter named Karen Kolus.

CBA: *So, it's still in pre-production limbo, as they say?*

Mike: Development hell is the term.

CBA: *Oh. [laughs] But I would say even at that point, it's quite a validation of what you guys were doing.*

Mike: Oh, for God's sakes, they turned *The Tick* into a TV series.

CBA: *[laughs] Well,* The Tick *was a real hit!*

Mike: Yes, it was. My hat's off to *The Tick*. Being chosen as the subject of a TV production is no validation of anything, it's just, "Give me the money, honey, and I hope it's as good as we can make it," but *Nexus* was a comic book, first and foremost. We'd like to see it become a quality TV show, but I'm not kidding myself that's necessarily going to be the case, because we're not going to have the control we had when it was a comic.

CBA: *Any plans to do* Nexus *specials and comics in the future?*

Mike: I think if the show happens, it's a certainty, we'll be back.

CBA: *You were publishing your own* Nexus *newsletter?*

Mike: I have, from time to time, but we stopped, because there's no *Nexus* news! [*laughter*] I will publish it again, as soon as I have some *Nexus* news.

CBA: *What work are you doing in comics right now, if any?*

Mike: None.

CBA: *Temporarily retired?*

Mike: Well, not by choice.

CBA: *Really? That's very surprising to me.*

Mike: Well, it doesn't surprise me, I had no real big hits that belonged to any companies, *The Punisher* notwithstanding. You've got to have a fan following, you've got to have people clamoring for your stuff, and the industry has shrunk, the audience has shrunk, so... I'm not going to stay at the party.

Above: *The character we will always associate with Mike Baron and Steve Rude: Nexus, the Executioner. ©2000 Mike Baron and Steve Rude.*

Mr. Monster's Maker

The Independent Career of Doc's Poppa, Michael T. Gilbert

Conducted by Jon B. Cooke
Transcribed by Jon B. Knutson

In the mid-'80s, when so much quality material was coming from Fantagraphics, DC, RAW, Eclipse, and others, I found that just about the only character I gave a hoot about was Michael T. Gilbert's wonderful Doc Stearn, Mr. Monster—and Doc might be the only comics character I'll continue to buy to this day. So if my prejudices reveal that I love Michael and his work, well, sue me. While I do CBA to get to the bottom of the story, I also want to showcase the guys I like! This interview was conducted by phone on January 11, 2000 and was copyedited by the artist.

Comic Book Artist: *Michael, where are you from?*
Michael T. Gilbert: I'm originally from Levittown, Long Island, New York, a veritable hotbed of cartoonists, including George Evans, who—although I didn't realize it at the time—lived a few blocks from me. I would've given my left arm to know about it at the time! [laughter]

Below: Michael T. Gilbert's first published drawing of Mr. Monster (and his first Graphitti T-shirt design!) with lettering by Ken Bruzenak. Courtesy of the artist. ©2000 Michael T. Gilbert.

I learned decades afterwards Bill Griffith lived there.
CBA: *Bill Griffith of* Zippy the Pinhead *fame?*
Michael: Yes. Len Wein also lived there, who I did meet when I was about 15. He and I and a bunch of comics fans went to a big opening of the *Batman* movie in 1966 or thereabouts. That was pretty interesting. He was still trying to break into the pros at that point.
CBA: *Did you ever go down and visit the DC offices, for instance, on that Thursday afternoon tour they used to have?*
Michael: No, not really. I know some of these guys used to do it all the time, but to me, that was just a huge trip going on the Long Island Railroad to travel down there… so I never did. It never even occurred to me I could.
CBA: *When did you decide you wanted to become a cartoonist?*
Michael: As far back as when I was a kid. I mean, I don't know if I knew there was such a thing as a cartoonist, but I was always drawing my super-heroes and this and that when I was seven, eight years old. My father was a tailor and he would have these used scratch pads, they'd write down the prices of the stuff, and I'd get the leftovers and draw on the back. As far as exactly when, I don't remember a specific time.
CBA: *Did you kind of realize that you could make a living, that there were really people doing this stuff?*
Michael: At some point I did, obviously. I'm sure that was years after I started drawing. There wasn't a great deal of fan information to be found in those days. When you're first starting very young, you don't even think about behind-the-scenes too much, you just knew there were super-heroes and monsters, and they looked very cool. You'd want to draw them. Eventually, maybe you start picking up these things bit by bit.
CBA: *Looking at the body of your work over the years, it seems you had a real appreciation of all genres. Did you grow up appreciating horror as well as funny animal and super-heroes?*
Michael: Yeah. Basically, I would read anything I could get my hands on. I didn't have an allowance, so I couldn't buy comics, but my grandmother worked at Montifiore Hospital in the Bronx, and she would swipe some of the comics they'd give to the kids and she would give them to me. Anything I could get my hands on, I would read. There were some things I liked more than others, and there were some things I would read under duress, such as *Classics Illustrated*—which was a comic book—so I wanted to read it—but boy, it was kind of a dull comic book, like school, so I tried to avoid that as much as possible; but yeah, anything I could get my hands on. There were things I liked more; I mean, I preferred super-heroes, and I would go crazy over the Stan Lee/Jack Kirby horror comics in the late '50s/early '60s.
CBA: *Did you start appreciating the different styles? Were you able to differentiate between a Ditko story and a Kirby story, for instance?*
Michael: Yeah, pretty early on. By the time I was 11 or so, I started looking at the credits, and I began to recognize styles. Jack Kirby, of course, Gil Kane, Wally Wood, people with really strong, distinctive styles.
CBA: *Were you a social kid, or pretty much a bookworm?*
Michael: Like many of us, I was kind of a loner. I spent a lot of my time in my room drawing, reading books and comics or whatever.
CBA: *When you were doing your strips, were they complete comic book stories?*
Michael: Not for the most part, no. They were just single illustrations, or covers, or things like that. I periodically tried to do a

comics strip, and I'd get really frustrated after I'd do a page or two, and just give up after a while here. When I first started doing comics, I started doing things for the school paper, and I would do illustrations for high school and junior high school, and I'd sometimes do three-panel comic strips and things like that.

CBA: *What were the subjects?*

Michael: Oh, just little gags.

CBA: *You were doing super-hero stuff when you were doing your own little things at home?*

Michael: Yeah, I would do tons of Superman and Batman and J'onn J'onzz, Manhunter from Mars… I remember one time I was about 14, I did some parody of a *Fantastic Four* cover, where I had Sue Storm pregnant with Sub-Mariner's baby, or something like that, and Reed was really horrified. [*laughter*] Shocked and stuff.

CBA: *So, you were known as an artist in school?*

Michael: Yeah, pretty much.

CBA: *Were you able to showcase your talents through that? Did kids always say, "Oh, yeah, he's a good cartoonist!"?*

Michael: Not a huge amount, but yeah. As I said, I was doing things for the school paper, and that was always a thrill to see your work printed, and it became real at that point. My identity as a cartoonist grew, it was in there fairly early on.

CBA: *So did you want to seek out larger audiences with that recognition?*

Michael: Sure. Obviously, when you're a kid, if you get in the school paper, that's immediately "a lot of people," but of course, I hoped to eventually become a real cartoonist.

CBA: *Were you involved in early fandom?*

Michael: I was involved to the extent of reading the early fanzines and such. If I'd been hooked up with somebody, I'm sure I would have been, but for one thing, it was the early days of Xerox machines, so if I drew anything, I'd be scared to send it through the mail, and was afraid it would get lost or something like that.

CBA: *So, you bought the first issues of* Alter Ego, *for instance?*

Michael: Not the first issues, but when I was trading with some of my pals, I was able to get some of the early issues. I've got quite a massive fanzine collection at this point.

CBA: *When did you first see the work of Will Eisner?*

Michael: I think I first saw his work… there was an IW reprint of *The Spirit,* and shortly after that, the one that really knocked my teeth out was when Harvey Comics came out with their two issues in 1966, and I just couldn't believe how good those comics were. I couldn't believe how diverse the subject matter, and the writing, and the artwork all together… it just knocked me out.

CBA: *It's funny: Those* Spirit *issues published by Harvey came out in '66, when I was seven, and it's one of my earliest distinct comic book memories. I recall reading it in the backyard of our house in Westchester, New York. I didn't collect comic books, until I was 12. The "Plaster of Paris" story, for some reason is very memorable… I guess because it was really sexy… I don't know!*

Michael: [*laughs*] It really made a big impact, because I remember it was a 25¢ comic book in the days when comics were 12¢, and I actually bought two copies of that (which was unheard of for me), and I bought two copies of the companion *Fighting American* book they put out, with Simon & Kirby artwork. That was spectacular stuff.

CBA: *Was Kirby becoming an influence for you?*

Michael: Kirby was, once again, one of these people that was influential early on. I loved the Kirby monsters from a couple of years earlier, and I loved the early *Fantastic Four* and whatnot, and I was crazy about the *Fighting American* stuff when I saw that. I mean, I still think that is the most visually impressive super-hero that I have ever seen.

CBA: *Were you also keyed into the humor elements in that?*

Michael: Yeah. I always liked the humor aspect quite a bit. As a matter of fact, I started getting a little less interested in Kirby in the mid-to-late-'60s, when he started getting more and more serious and "cosmic"! When I was reading the early Ditko-Lee *Spider-Man,* one of the things I loved most was that there was so much humor to it, and it just really appealed to me.

CBA: *Ditko was becoming important for you?*

Michael: Oh, I was always in love with Ditko. Again, you'd have those Jack Kirby monster comics, and then this wonderful little Ditko story that I always looked forward to, and usually enjoyed even more than the lead story— and then when *Spider-Man* came out, I went nuts over that stuff, too.

CBA: *You must've been in heaven when the all-Ditko* Amazing Adult Fantasy *came out, right?*

Michael: Yeah, it was terrific. Five or six little Ditko mini-stories, they were great fun, and I still wish someone would put out a collection of all those back-up stories, Ditko's tales… they're really worth reprinting. I actually have a couple of Ditko originals on my wall right now, from that period of those stories, and it's a constant inspiration, just because of how clean and clear the artwork is. There's not a line there that you don't need—it's perfect.

CBA: *Did you key into Eisner's storytelling? Was it overt for you?*

Michael: Yeah, it really was. I mean, at that point, I was about 14 years old, so I was mature enough to appreciate all that stuff. I would be studying how he did these long panels with the downshot, or a three-panel sequence, or this or that… just reading it over and over and over again, trying to dissect how he got the emotional effect and the movement effects in what he was doing. It was just a perfect teaching tool. He was doing everything.

CBA: *And doing it, again, with humor?*

Michael: Yeah, he would have the humor, he would have little Ebony, the Tom Sawyer character, they'd have these gorgeous, sexy women. You can just imagine how much I enjoyed reading those! [*laughter*]

CBA: *I've been working with you and Roy on* Alter Ego, *and you obviously have a full appreciation for comics history. Did you have other interests, whether it was in history… in school, were you singularly interested in art, or did you have other interests?*

Michael: I wouldn't say I had a huge interest in history. I was interested in writing. I enjoyed my art classes and English classes. Every so often, you'd get an interesting bit of history in class, but for the most part, no… which I think is really a shame, because I think if they had some good history teachers, history can be really fascinating—but you don't get too much of that in school, not when I was growing up at least.

CBA: *So, it was really a drive for self-expression?*

Michael: Yeah.

Above: *1971 pic of Scott Gilbert (age 10, left) and Michael as Green Lantern (20, at right), recreating a scene from the classic GL/GA series. Green Lantern ©2000 DC Comics.*

Below: *MTG himself in a recent photo. Note the sweater—the artist and Doc share the same tailor! Courtesy of the artist.*

Above: "The Reflection," a super-hero concocted by a 15-year-old MTG in 1965. Courtesy of the artist. ©2000 Michael T. Gilbert.

Below: Table of contents illustration for the 1978 book, Jerry Brown Illustrated. ©1978 Beauxarts.

CBA: *Did you have an appreciative audience in your family?*

Michael: Yeah, they liked my comics. I'm lucky that way. My parents liked my artwork, and they were encouraging.

CBA: *Did you seek out further art education?*

Michael: It was pretty much understood I'd be going to college. It's not something I really thought about too much, but I wanted to go to a college where I could take art classes and such. They didn't have any comic book schools at that point, so I went upstate New York to New Paltz to get an art education degree. But that primarily was to please the parents so I'd have something to fall back on if I couldn't make it as an artist. But I was taking a whole bunch of drawing courses and the like.

CBA: *In 1970 you went to college?*

Michael: Yeah, I graduated from high school in '69. I went to two years of Suffolk Community College in Long Island, and then I transferred to New Paltz to finish my last two years.

CBA: *During that time—from '67 on up into the early '70s—underground comic books really exploded. Were you exposed to that work?*

Michael: Yeah. I saw my first underground comix in my first year of college, when a cartoonist friend of mine, Gerry Mooney, had gone to New York and showed us these incredible *Zap Comix* that he'd scored. These comix had Bob Crumb, S. Clay Wilson, super-violent, sexy things, and I just went nuts over them. "Oh, what's this stuff? It's really different! It's really forbidden!" It's just the kind of stuff that someone who's starting to break away from the family and from childhood really goes for, it's like, "These are *adult* comics!"

CBA: *Did you immediately see the implications for self-expression, to tell more adult, more substantial stories?*

Michael: I suppose, on some level, although I had already been exposed to a lot of the EC comics. I was aware you didn't just have to do kids' stuff. I'd seen things like the *Shock-SuspenStories* with the social commentary, and of course, the great *Mad* comic books and such, with all the nihilism and whatnot.

CBA: *Was Kurtzman an influence to you?*

Michael: If I had to name my five big influences, he's up there, with Ditko, Eisner, and Kirby. Harvey definitely was. He was just a remarkable cartoonist and a remarkably good writer, and he always impressed me with the combination of the fact that he was able to do serious comics like *Two-Fisted Tales* and *Frontline Combat*, as well as more goofy things like *Mad* comics and *Mad* magazine.

CBA: *Did you get those as back issues, or were you exposed to them when they were coming out?*

Michael: Oh, I wish I was old enough, but no, I didn't get them until I was about 14 or so, which was about '65.

CBA: *You saw* Mad *comics in those Ballantine paperback reprints?*

Michael: Well, the *Mad*s I *did* see earlier, because I did read the *Mad* paperbacks. My mother would go shopping at the Kleins (which was a department store), and I'd be at the magazine and book racks, devouring these things. Which is kind of funny, because the first time I was exposed to things like Captain Marvel and Plastic Man was in the parodies that were done in *Mad*—and these characters were not being published in real comics; I was like, "Who *are* these characters?"

remember one of the things that kind of threw me for a loop at one point was… as I said, my grandmother would get me these old comic books, but they weren't very old; two, three years old before I got 'em, so unfortunately, I never got any Golden Age comics or anything. But one item, I got this coverless, just partial issue of *Panic*, and there was the tagline "Humor in a Varicose Vein." And I was like, "I'll bet this is an old *Mad* comic, but why does it say *Panic?*" I didn't know EC had done a rip-off of their own comic! I just couldn't figure it out… I couldn't connect the two.

CBA: *And you went into a panic!* [laughter]

Michael: I didn't know it was a parody of *Mad*.

CBA: *So, were you starting to hang around other cartoonists, or seeking out connections with other artists?*

Michael: Well, when I was in college, if you knew anybody that was into comics, you certainly wanted to hang with them a little bit. I did see a couple of cartoonists here and there, and you'd share techniques or compete with them, or do whatever it is, but yeah, there were few enough that you'd certainly gravitate towards them.

CBA: *Were you interested in going out to California, where the undergrounds were exploding? I mean, New York didn't seem to be a large market for that, right?*

Michael: Well, my thing was getting into any comics I could… whether it be underground or regular comics or whatever. I remember one company I was really hoping to get into was Warren with *Creepy* and *Eerie*. I came kind of close with that. [See MTG's sidebar in CBA #4 for an account of his near brush with Warren] I went to DC Comics a couple of times in the late '60s, early '70s, I guess.

CBA: *Was it a cold call for you?*

Michael: We called up first—me and another guy—and we were trying to show our own stuff, and I remember the first time, we were shown to Sol Harrison, who struck us as a pretty arrogant guy. I must've been about 17 or 18 at this point. He seemed to lord his position over us and I realized he wasn't a guy I wanted to work for. I remember how he showed us some Joe Kubert page and bragged, "Joe Kubert's really great, top-notch. He used to have some real bad habits, but I showed him how to draw water and things like that, and now he's good." [laughter] Yeah, Sol, *you* had to teach Joe Kubert, who was doing things like *Tor* and whatnot before he even came back to DC!

CBA: *Was the atmosphere at DC not conducive to creativity?*

Michael: Well, I don't know how it was with the creators, but it certainly didn't seem like DC was running itself ragged to hire guys like me! They probably shouldn't have. I remember going to some of the early New York comic conventions, and at one of them, they had these "Junior Woodchuck" recruitments. They were talking about how they were going to hire trainees to learn how to do work for DC. I remember thinking, "This is a corny idea." But when DC actually looked at portfolios at the convention, it seemed like there were a few hundred people in line! [laughter] It became pretty clear early on they weren't hiring much of anybody. I think they eventually hired Mike Grell, who was probably a professional at that point anyway. But they weren't hiring guys like me to train them!

CBA: *Did you stop off at Marvel?*

Michael: You know, I was down there once. The only time I tried to get to Marvel, they had just moved their building somewhere, and I called up and tried to get it, and they wouldn't give me their address. [laughter] I wasn't too encouraged.

CBA: *Oh, they knew you were Mike Gilbert, and they kept you away? [laughs] Were there specific characters you would have liked to have drawn?*

Michael: Yeah, I would've loved to have drawn *Spider-Man*. The

Ditko Spider-Man is still one of the all-time best super-heroes, as far as I'm concerned. I would've loved to taken a crack at that. Batman, Superman—who I've since worked on, I'm happy to say—but I'm sure there were a lot of others, but those were the main ones.

CBA: *The sample pages you submitted to Warren back in the early '70s—it was done in a straight narrative style, right?*

Michael: There was one in there that originally appeared as a continuing comic strip in our high school and college paper. I worked with Harvey Sobel, a friend of mine from High School, and it appeared in the school paper. It was a straight EC horror/science fiction story sort of thing. We later reprinted it in *New Paltz Comix.*

CBA: *You were pushing a straight style back then?*

Michael: Yeah. I don't think my style has changed too much from that, but yeah, pretty straightforward style.

CBA: *Well, you certainly got some elements of humor within your work subsequent to that. I mean, it seemed like certainly "The Wraith," when you started doing that, it was obviously a funny animal comic book, you went for humor, which seems to be a strong element in all your work.*

Michael: It's funny, I think cartoonists are pulled towards certain directions, and it comes up in what they're most attracted to—and again, I was most attracted to *The Spirit,* which had humor and adventure, I was attracted to *Spider-Man* because there was humor and adventure and stories about the little guy, which appealed to me…as well as Kurtzman's *Mad, Two-Fisted Tales* and the like. So, the humor element was always very important to me.

CBA: *Were you attending a lot of comic book shows, or were you basically going to the Phil Seuling cons, or…?*

Michael: Basically, the Phil Seuling cons, although I did make it to the first and only EC convention in 1972, which I really enjoyed.

CBA: *At the shows, were you basically just looking for contact with professionals, or were you looking for back issues?*

Michael: I think for the most part, I was looking for the back issues, and to see some of the creators and whatnot. I remember the first New York convention I went to, it was either in 1968 or '69, and I just remember it was this incredible rush! I'd heard about this New York convention for a couple of years before that, I finally got a chance to go down… my grandmother was living in the Bronx, so I stayed with her a few days, and took the train there. I almost didn't eat for two, three days, whatever the convention was, because I wanted to spend every penny on old comic books! So, at the last day here, I came down with this incredible case of hives, and I just had not slept and had not eaten for three days, and it's like, "Ugh.…"

CBA: *Comics can kill you! [laughter] Were there any professionals you were seeking out to show your work, or seek advice from?*

Michael: I don't think I was thinking about that in particular, in the first place. Although, in some of the later conventions, I showed some of my work to Bernie Wrightson, who was very nice and generous. He was one of the guys whose work I really loved. It was kind of funny, because I remember his being very encouraging…and I'd shown something to Ralph Reese at the same convention, and he was really dismissive—and I was thinking, "Boy, Wrightson's ten times better than this guy, and so much nicer!"

CBA: *Did you get to meet Jack Kirby?*

Michael: No, not until many years later. In San Diego, one of those things, I guess. I would've gone crazy, getting a chance to meet Jack Kirby. He was certainly one of those guys that I idolized.

CBA: *How many years did you spend in college?*

Michael: I went four years, and got my B.A. in art education. Did my student teaching, and was reassured once and for all that I was right in not wanting to be a teacher, and never did.

CBA: *So, you moved out of New Paltz in '74?*

Michael: Yeah, and went to New York, and lucked out and got my first job at NBC News, doing their graphics on the nightly news program, which I only did for about a year. I'd call my friends and say, "Look! I've got a thing that'll be appearing tonight, so watch it, it's the gun that's pointed to the narrator, the newsman."

CBA: *[laughs] Do you recall any crises or any big issues going down at the time you had to respond to quickly?*

Michael: I remember the whole Patty Hearst thing was going on here, and we would use some cut-and-paste stuff with Symbionese Liberation Army stuff, but… I can't think of anything specific, but I

do remember there was a lot of pressure, because they would tell you what the story was for the evening. And you would have to put the stuff together, and it would take them a few hours to photograph this thing, so they could make a transparency to show it. You're always real nervous. Actually, I was working for a company called Vizmo, which is right across the street from NBC, and we'd get our things finished, and then I'd have to race across the street, get on the elevator, race upstairs to give it to these guys—and sometimes it'd be like seconds before it went on the air, so it was like, "Oh, geez!" [*laughter*] It was good experience with real deadlines.

CBA: *Did you want to get out? [laughs]*

Michael: I wasn't crazy about the deadline aspect of it!

CBA: *So, you worked there for a year. During that time, did you continue your cartooning at night?*

Michael: I always did my cartooning. I'd published my first comic book while I was in college, *New Paltz Comix,* and it was the Summer after my fourth year, just before I started my student teaching. When I was in New York, I was working on issue #2.

CBA: *You were self-publishing?*

Michael: Yeah.

CBA: *Did you seek out a local printer, and have to go through all the logistics?*

Michael: Yeah, it was kind of interesting, because I'd never really thought about publishing. I became a publisher almost by accident. The way the *New Paltz Comix* thing worked, it was originally going to be put out by the school paper. I'd been doing a lot of cartooning for them, and they asked me to contribute to this underground comic book they were putting out. I later found out they'd been talking about doing this for years, but never came through—and they'd always get the stuff together, and never actually publish a comic. Anyway, I'd done the cover and a couple of stories for *New Paltz Comix,* and me and a bunch of cartoonists were waiting to see our first comic stories in print. And we waited

Above: *1971 self-portrait of MTG. "I used this in my portfolio to get into SUNY New Paltz," Michael said. Courtesy of MTG. ©2000 Michael T. Gilbert.*

Below: *Melange of New Paltz Comix covers, courtesy of the artist. ©2000 Michael T. Gilbert.*

and waited. Then, at the last minute, they decided not to publish it. This was just after a big year-end school party with bands and fireworks and so on. So when I asked them why they hadn't published the comic, they told me they'd spent all the money—$2000—on fireworks for the party!

CBA: *Oh, well… priorities.* [laughter]

Michael: I was so pissed that I grabbed the negatives and told them, "I'm going to publish this myself." So I started looking for someone to print the book. The first people I called were going to charge $1500 for a little pamphlet-sized thing here, and I thought, "Oh, man, I'll never be able to afford this, this is ridiculous." Fortunately, I took it to a second place, and they told me they'd print it full size on good paper for $500. So it became a reality.

CBA: *How many copies were printed?*

Michael: I think it was about 4,000.

CBA: *4,000? And what were you selling them for?*

Michael: 50¢.

CBA: *And how did you market them?*

Michael: I sold some to Bud Plant in 1973, I think it was. Bud was the first guy that encouraged me by buying some. Ironically, just a couple of days ago I just sold my very last copies of *New Paltz Comix* to Bud Plant. It was really funny, after all these years.

I was able to get a Long Island magazine distributor to take some copies of the thing, too. I didn't realize how unusual that was, but he took about 500.

CBA: *Was this on a returnable basis?*

Michael: Well, that's what I thought! After he'd had it for a while, he gave us a check for whatever he had sold, and I said, "That's really nice, can I have the rest of my issues back?" And he said, "Oh, no, we trashed and pulped them," and I went, *"What?!?"* [laughter] "What are you talking about, you pulped them?!?" [laughter] I was just horrified! "Oh, yeah, it's a standard thing: We remove the covers, and destroy them." Well, I wound up taking them to court, because I said, "You can't do that, I want to be paid for all the stuff that wasn't returned." I

actually wound up winning! It was the first time I'd actually gone to Small Claims Court. Of course, I was terrified, but it worked out okay.

CBA: *So, overall, at the time, what did you think of your experience as a self-publisher?*

Michael: I was just, of course, thrilled to finally see my work in a real comic book, and I thought it turned out great. What I didn't like was trying to sell the things. These are the days before there was Diamond, or whatever. Actually, one of the ways—now that I think about it—that I was selling the book was, literally, going door to door at New Paltz, knocking on doors and saying, "Would you like to buy *New Paltz Comix #1?"*

CBA: *[laughs] Now, that's direct sales!*

Michael: That's direct sales, that's it. [laughter] I could live without that *real* easily!

CBA: *Right. That's a lot of work. You had* New Paltz Comix #2 *prepared, or was it ever finished?*

Michael: Oh, yeah. We eventually wound up doing four issues. They had different titles… one was called *Amazing Adult Fantasies* (#2), *Iron Soul Stories* (#3), and *Mythos* (#4).

CBA: *How do you characterize the contents?*

Michael: The first one was more like a fanzine than an underground, but #2 and 3 were real underground comix. We had Tim Boxell, we had a painted cover by Larry Todd…

CBA: *Did you pay them for their contributions?*

Michael: Just in copies. The second issue was actually sort of a co-publishing thing with a lot of the other cartoonists, and…

CBA: *So you were obviously mailing out issues of #1 to other cartoonists, right, to get their feedback on it? Did they seek you out?*

Michael: In a lot of cases, it'd be people I bumped into, or I'd send people copies.

CBA: *So then you were involved with circles of cartoonists?*

Michael: Yeah, off and on over the years. I met some cartoonists at college, and at NBC, back in '74. Later that year I worked at a place called Hit Sales, which produced a lot of advertising things like keychains and such. Pewter letter openers with embossed company logos…gimmicks like that. I met lots of artists in their art department. I worked there for six months. Then I got tired of it, and decided it was time for a change. The work was getting to be kind of repetitious, even though I learned some valuable things about pasting and production and things like that. Anyway, I lived in New York all my life at that point. Then one of my friends from the art department moved to California, and suddenly I thought, "Why can't I do that?" I really wanted to break into comics and by now it was clear I had little or no chance at DC or Marvel, because they had a pretty closed shop. They weren't hiring a tremendous amount of new talent at that point. But underground comix were always using new talent, so moving to San Francisco sounded like a good idea. Within a couple of months I'd sold or stored everything I owned, packed some duffel bags and started off to California with about $200 in my pocket.

CBA: *Did you drive a car?*

Michael: No, it's kind of cool. This is a really quintessential California early '70s kind of story here. They had… you know the *Green Tortoise?* It's a cheap bus version of a Greyhound? Well, I had the *White Rabbit,* which was the cheaper version of that! But it was really cool, going down. It was this old bus that was going down from New York to San Francisco. It had a wood stove in it, really hippie-dippie stuff, but it was just perfect for what I wanted to do. I was starting this great adventure!

CBA: *There was a wood stove in it?*

Michael: Yeah, they had a wood stove in this thing and no seats. They would have mats on the floor so you could sleep, and it took about three or four days, whatever it was, to get down there.

CBA: *Did you become buds with your fellow passengers there?*

Michael: Yeah… [laughs] there was one gal in particular, we were enjoying ourselves a little bit. [laughter]

CBA: *Yep, quintessential.* [laughter] *What were your experiences in San Francisco? Did you have a place to live lined up?*

Michael: Sort of. Edgar Bacelis—the fellow that was working with me at Hit Sales— had moved to Santa Rosa and was staying with his cousin. So, when I got off the bus with four duffel bags of all my worldly possessions I called him, and they let me crash there for a few days. Santa Rosa is about an hour away from San Francisco and I had no transportation or anything, so I would be hitchhiking down to San Francisco, and looking for a job and a place to live. It was actually kind of funny, a few days later Edgar and I went down to Berkeley for the first time. Thirty seconds after we stepped off the train onto Berkeley proper, we were hit on by this cute girl. She starts talking to us, and asks if we'd like to have a free dinner.

CBA: *Oh, no…*

Michael: I thought, "This was great, I *love* free dinners!"

CBA: *Glory be.*

Michael: So we went to this old house they had, there's a whole bunch of people here. Well, I didn't realize until weeks later, these were Moonies! So, we're eating salad and singing songs and no one's talking about religion or anything like that…they didn't want to scare us away. Then at the end of the night they say, "Hey, you know, we're going to have this great camp out in Booneville, we're going to camp out, we've got some sleeping bags… how would you guys like to come with us?" [laughter] "Oh, okay, I don't have a place to live, sure! Let's try that." Before I know it, I'm in a Moonie camp! [laughs]

CBA: *How did you get out? Who deprogramed you?* [laughs]

Michael: Edgar left, but I stayed. The weekend turned into a week, and then two weeks. I eventually got suspicious because they didn't like comic books! I said to myself, "These guys can't be too on the level if they don't like comic books." [laughter] And eventually… yeah it was a pretty intense, interesting two weeks. Eventually, I found out who they really were, and decided to leave. I bumped into one of the other guys that had been there, a few years later. He told me that he had stayed there for a couple of years and finally broke away, but he said he was having nightmares every night, and was just totally screwed up. So I was lucky to get away with no damage.

CBA: *So you went back to San Francisco?*

Michael: Yeah, and I went to San Francisco and found an apartment to rent with three others. It was, again, a great counter-cultural experience, because I rented an apartment with three other people… this cute gal who was in her early twenties, who was living with her good-looking, friendly black boyfriend, and this other guy was this Communist. So you know, you've got the black guy, you've got the Communist, you've got the chick…!

CBA: [laughs] *You've got The Mod Squad!*

Michael: Yeah! It was actually funny, because periodically, the Communist—the only guy who didn't have a sense of humor…

CBA: *Of course!* [laughs]

Michael: …would have these parties to raise money for "The Cause," which I thought was kind of funny, because it was literally a "Communist Party!" [laughter]

CBA: *What were your cartooning experiences in San Francisco?*

Michael: Well, I knocked on a lot of doors. I didn't have a tremendous amount of luck. But I was able to get some work at the *Berkeley Barb* doing some cartoons for them. So that was my first real professional cartoon job. I got to meet a few people, and started making some phone calls, because I figured the cartoonists were more accessible at that point. I went to see Trina Robbins, way back when… I'm sure she was wondering who was this crazy guy coming down here asking all these questions. She was very friendly and she mentioned a couple of people I could call. I went to see art spiegelman, way back, who was in San Francisco at that point. Years later, in '82, I saw him again in New York.

CBA: *When you went to San Francisco, you came at a real lean time for undergrounds, right?*

Michael: Right. Naturally, my timing was impeccable. [laughter] The underground comix had peaked in '72 and '73. By '74 and '75, it had really gone down the tubes because they were busting head shops and such, and people were a lot more reluctant to buy undergrounds, so their sales were going down. Plus, they'd flooded the market, as they stupidly do every five or 10 years in comics history.

CBA: *Did you go to Last Gasp to see Ron Turner, for instance?*

Michael: Yeah, I went there, and actually was able to work out some kind of a trade deal with some back issues of *New Paltz Comix*, and whatnot. And Ron promised to keep me in mind if they needed a cartoonist for some comic book job. Eventually, I got to meet a lot of the underground cartoonists. They had periodic cartoonist parties, and I went to Rip-Off Press and got to meet Gilbert Shelton there, for instance. For the most part, it seemed like a pretty friendly, loose place. Unfortunately, they weren't producing a lot of comic books, so I didn't have a great deal of opportunity to get too much stuff in print. I did a little thing for *Dope Comix* eventually, and for *Slow Death*, and this and that—but not too much.

CBA: *A fellow who was also in the Bay Area was Mike Friedrich. When did you first hear tell of the Star*Reach?*

Michael: Early on. When it came out, it was kind of exciting. I guess that must've been about '74 or so when the first issue of *Star*Reach* came out. I felt it was pretty interesting because it had some above-ground cartoonists like Jim Starlin, and Howie Chaykin doing stuff that was slightly more underground…it was a combination of the two. It was not too far off from some of the stuff I was trying to do with *New Paltz Comix* at that point, and when I got to the Bay Area, Mike was

Left: *The Wraith, inspired by Will Eisner's The Spirit, was MTG's first bonafide comic character and was featured in the Star*Reach title, Quack! This image is from a Wraith "pin-up" page. ©2000 MTG.*

Below: *Splash page from an unfinished 1981 Wraith story. Courtesy of the artist. ©2000 Michael T. Gilbert.*

Above: MTG's redo of a Harvey Pekar story from American Splendor, 1980. ©2000 MTG and Harvey Pekar. Below: Rejected (by MTG) Elric #5 cover design. Courtesy of the artist. Elric ©2000 Michael Moorcock. Art ©2000 MTG.

one of the people that I did approach. He was reasonably friendly, liked some of the stuff in my portfolio, but he couldn't use anything at that time. About a week later, I got a call from him. Earlier he'd mentioned this new funny animal comic called *Quack* that was about to start. Well, apparently, the first issue was just close to being finished, and one of the people who had committed to doing a bunch of pages dropped out at the last minute, and he asked me if I'd ever done funny animal comics before, and I assured him I was a master of the genre. Naturally, I'd never done one in my life! [*laughter*] But they said, "Come up with an idea, and let's see what you come up with," and I batted around a number of ideas… science-fiction, this, that and the other stuff, and I finally came up with the idea of a take-off on The Spirit called "The Wraith," a funny-animal version of The Spirit. It gave me the opportunity to have a structure on short notice, and still be able to do something a little different.

CBA: *So was your feeling behind that: "Oh, I can do my take on Eisner"?*

Michael: It was certainly part of it. I'd always wanted to do *The Spirit*, when I thought about which comics I would have liked to have done, and of course, I would have given my right eye-tooth to do *The Spirit*, and here was my chance to write and draw it! And since I was doing my own version, a new character, I had freedom to play around with things, and I didn't have to get anyone's approval.

CBA: *Do you know what the genesis of Quack was? Was that tied into the popularity of Howard the Duck?*

Michael: Yeah, that was the impetus… *Howard the Duck* by Brunner was a huge runaway success at that point, and I know Mike was friends with Frank Brunner, and I'm sure Frank thought the idea of doing a version of Howard the Duck that he'd own was a good idea. Mike wanted to get on the bandwagon, so he created *Quack!* as a showcase for Brunner's duck. Then he had to have a bunch of filler to fill the rest of it. As it turned out, Brunner only did one duck story, but *Quack* gave me the opportunity to finally get my foot in the door.

CBA: *What was the frequency of Quack? They came out with a few, right?*

Michael: They came out with six issues… I think it was every two to three months.

CBA: *So you were working pretty steady by that time. Did you have a page rate, or did you have a cut of the profits?*

Michael: Well, it was a cut of the profits, but there was an advance. I think what it came down to, the first issue was the one that sold the most, and I wound up getting a grand $50 a page for writing, drawing, lettering, the works. Every issue after that, it was $25 a page for all that. So, I

wasn't getting rich. Actually, going back for a little bit: Earlier, I mentioned moving in with a few other people in San Francisco. That only lasted a few months, before the house broke up for various reasons, nothing negative, really. So I had to find another place, and I was down to about $50 at that point. I hadn't been able to find too much cartooning work, and I didn't know how I was going to come up with the dough. Then I heard at Berkeley, they had some kind of a bulletin board at the college where you could find cheap places to live. I called this professor and his wife, Everett and Lauramay Dempster, who'd periodically find graduate students who'd live there in return for doing jobs around the house. I figured, "This might be a good place to hang my hat for a couple of months until I can get some money together," and I wound up spending about four years there! It was a very nice situation, they were lovely people (they were both about 70 at that point), and they had been doing this for years. They had built their own house in Orinda—which is this really ritzy area on about 3 acres of land. So I would work about 15 hours a week, and I'd get these nice home-cooked meals, and had my own room. So it was the perfect situation for being able to draw comics while not being dependent on making a great deal of money.

CBA: *Do you think had that not happened, would you have pursued so aggressively the professional comics route, of working at either Marvel or DC?*

Michael: Well, it wasn't like I had the opportunity.

CBA: *But I mean, would you have continued to work at it to get in there? Did you see at a point in the beginning of your career where, "Gee whiz, maybe I'm not going to make it in comics, and maybe I should focus on something else," or were you single-minded, driving for that?*

Michael: I don't think I'd be doing comics today if I hadn't been single-minded. I mean, it really takes an incredible amount of stubbornness to make it, particularly if you're not born with the talent of a Neal Adams or a Frank Frazetta, you have to really want to badly.

CBA: *When you lived at the old couple's house, you were single?*

Michael: Yeah.

CBA: *So you didn't have a domestic pressure to make a paycheck?*

Michael: Right, exactly.

CBA: *So, they were, for all practical purposes, your patrons?*

Michael: Yeah, they were my patrons in a lot of ways. They eventually became sort of like family. We kept in contact for many years, the Dempsters. Everett passed away about seven years ago, and his wife passed away about two years ago, but until that point, we were keeping in touch, and visiting, and I still keep in touch with his family and such.

CBA: *Were they enthusiastic about your endeavors?*

Michael: Lauramay liked my artwork, but she always thought it was kind of wasted on comic books. [*laughter*] It's kind of funny, because they were scientists. He was in genetics, and she was in botany and such, and they had a bunch of graduate students over the years, many of whom also were in the sciences. So, I was sort of the odd man out here. Fortunately, Lauramay liked doing a little painting, she liked the arts, so I was like a breath of fresh air for her.

CBA: *On the weekends, did you go to town? Were you sociable with the other cartoonists, or…?*

Michael: Yeah, I would go down to Berkeley periodically, get my comics once a week or something like that. Once a month, we had a group of cartoonists that would meet. We called ourselves the "Ground-Under Cartoonists." [*laughter*] It was a cheaper version of the undergrounds. We had various people over a period of a few years, but Trina belonged, and Roger May, and Dot Boucher.

CBA: *Was Lee Marrs a part of it?*

Michael: I think she was down there. She may have come to a couple of meetings here and there, but I don't seem to remember her being one of the regulars.

CBA: *Was your agenda to basically be sociable and hang out?*

Michael: Hang out, share information about cartooning jobs—stuff like that. We'd do sketches and such, and pass them back and forth. It was just for fun.

CBA: *It would seem to me it was almost a perfect match for you, to be in "ground level" comics… did you feel that way?*

Michael: Yeah, I was. I thought it was fine. I never liked to use the term "ground level," I think "middle-ground comics" might've

been better. [*laughter*] I liked them, and I still do the occasional underground comix stuff. It's kind of funny… you're kind of stuck with a certain amount of expectations in mainstream comics, but it's not much different in the undergrounds. Mainstream comics have the Comics Code, and all those taboos—but the underground comix had just as strict a code in their own way… often encouraging lots of sex and drug references so they'd sell better; but that seemed contrary to the spirit of the undergrounds. I'd think, "Why are you giving us any rules? It's really stupid, the undergrounds should be just total freedom to go in any of a thousand different directions." And yet, sex and drugs are what sold to the college students, and that's what the publishers were trying to push. They didn't force you, they didn't have a gun to your head, but this is what they were encouraging. I didn't like the underground rules any better than the mainstream rules. So, in a way, the ground-levels seemed like a reasonable alternative.

CBA: *Were you cognizant of the experience of other long-time comic creators—such as Siegel & Shuster's predicament with DC—and was having the copyright to your creations an important aspect?*

Michael: Yeah, it really was, and that's one of the things I really liked about the underground comix, is that everybody keeps their own copyrights. Getting back to Will Eisner yet again, I was aware that he was smart enough to keep his copyright way back when, and I said, "That's what I want to do." Own my own character.

CBA: *So you were really making your own path, right? You weren't seeking any support, necessarily, from the mainstream publishers, but you had the opportunity to live with the Dempsters for four years, you could really stake out your own claim in the field.*

Michael: I'm sure I would've found some other way to do it, but yeah. It's one of these things where DC and Marvel weren't interested in getting me, but that turned out to be a really positive thing. God help me if I'd gotten in and they'd said, "We want you to be an

inker," and for 15 years, that's my title. I wouldn't have developed my writing abilities, my drawing and inking abilities, whatever. It made me very independent.

CBA: *So, as you were doing this strip for* Quack, *did you start developing other strips, other characters on the side, looking to do your own comic, for instance?*

Michael: Well, in addition to that, while I was working on that, I was working on science-fiction stories for *Star*Reach* and *Imagine* magazine. I did one called "A Dream of Milk and Honey," a very dense 32-page story. It was my longest ever at that point (1978), and I was really trying to do a really serious story with some real meat to it. The fact that it did or didn't have new characters was besides the point. I was trying to tell more serious stories, and I think I was reasonably successful with that one. I still think it was a terrific story, and I hope to reprint it someday. It appeared in the last two issues of *Imagine* [#4 & 5].

CBA: *What was* Strange Brew?

Michael: Originally, it was supposed to be a book collecting the best of my comic stories. I'd been contacted by Dave Sim and Deni Loubert, who were interested in doing a Wraith comic. I was worried about being able to produce a regular comic, so we did *Strange Brew* as kind of a way to dip my toes into the water. It was going to be an actual book collection, but it somehow wound up as an oversized comic book.

CBA: *With the end of* Quack, *what were your options?*

Michael: Well, at that point, I was just looking for more work, I suppose. About 1979, I married a graduate student I'd met a couple of years earlier. She was

Above: *MTG's second Elric try-out page, inked by P. Craig Russell. Elric ©2000 Michael Moorcock. Art ©2000 Michael T. Gilbert & P. Craig Russell.* **Inset:** *MTG & PCR, 1982.* **Below:** *Unpublished sketch by MTG & PCR. ©2000 the artists. All courtesy of MTG.*

A TALE OF SCREAMING TERROR FROM THE SECRET FILES OF DOC STEARN...

MR. MONSTER

DEDICATED TO THE GREAT FRED KELLY

LETTERING: KEN BRUZENAK

SCRIPT/LAYOUTS COLORS © 1984 MICHAEL T. GILBERT

PENCILS/INKS WILLIAM F. LOEBS

File number 12484:

The Case of the Reluctant Werewolf:

FROM TIME TO TIME IN THIS IMPERFECT WORLD, STRANGE CREATURES ARE BORN... TWISTED...WARPED... ABOMINATIONS FROM HELL!! MR. MONSTER HAS DEDICATED HIS LIFE TO FINDING THEM... AND DESTROYING THEM!!

"DOC STEARN...MR. MONSTER" IS © 1984 BY MICHAEL T. GILBERT

Above: First page to the first MTG Mr. Monster story, and a great example of Ken Bruzenak's lettering. Courtesy and ©2000 MTG. **Below:** A '93 strip MTG did in 1933 style. Courtesy and ©2000 MTG.

accepted into the University of Texas Anthropology Department, and so I moved down from Orinda to Austin, Texas, and started looking for more work here and there. It was kind of a lean period, I got the occasional cartooning job here and there, but I was also paying the rent by teaching a cartooning class at my house. Periodically, I'd put up flyers on the campus, and that helped pay the rent.

CBA: *Any students of note?*
Michael: Yeah, actually, although I didn't realize it at the time. A cartoonist who took one class and then dropped out was George Pratt, who did the *Enemy Ace* book. I didn't realize until years later, when we met and he mentioned that he'd dropped out of my class. There was a also a woman who took one of my classes with her eight-year old son. I later found out that boy was Shannon Wheeler, creator of Too-Much Coffee Man. Small world, eh?
CBA: *Then you got the* Elric *gig?*
Michael: Yeah, that's when Mike Friedrich contacted me. Star*Reach the company had gone under at that point, after they'd tried publishing some color comics. It turned out to be a disaster, financially, and they went under. He had to pay his debts, so he got job at Marvel Comics in the sales department. Later, he reinvented himself as an agent, and he was packaging an *Elric* series for Pacific Comics. They already hired Roy Thomas to do the writing, and they had Craig Russell to do the artwork, but Craig didn't want to spend all his time just working on a bi-monthly comic. Mike remembered me, and I had met Craig just briefly at some convention. We both liked each other's work, so they offered me the job. I did a couple of samples, which were mixed, but Mike finally said, "Let's give it a try." The tricky part [*laughs*] was about this point (1982 or thereabouts), my wife and I had split. It was just a terrible time for me, and then this offer came—which perked me up quite a bit—but the scary part was they wanted me to move to Ohio, so Craig and I could work together. I'd never been to Ohio before, so that meant packing up and moving down there and everything. If it had happened even six months earlier, this would've been a tough decision—would my wife come with me, would I go there?—but now, it was like this perfect opportunity, although scarier than Hell, because it was one of these deals again where… "Have you ever done sword-&-sorcery?" "Oh, yeah! I'm a *whiz* at sword-&-sorcery!" [*laughter*] Of course, I'd never done any. But I went down there, and it actually worked out!
CBA: *How long did the title last?*
Michael: I worked with Craig for six issues. After we finished adapting the first *Elric* novel, Craig bowed out, and George Freeman and I adapted books two and three. I worked on Elric for about 18 issues. It continued after that, but I got off it at that point.
CBA: *You and Craig had distinct styles—an interesting mix.*
Michael: It worked. I've had people say they liked the blend because I brought a little more humor to the thing, and of course Craig did most of the inking and such. He's got his elegant linework and everything, gave it this really beautiful look. I put together the letter pages and stuff, and we both did the coloring, which was incredibly difficult. This was the early days of full-color comics, so we were really just learning as we went along, trying to figure out how to make this coloring thing work.
CBA: *So, it was a great experience working with Craig?*
Michael: Yeah, I really liked it a lot. It was a strange time for me, as I said, it was right after my divorce. Living in Kent was a mixed bag for me…especially the weather. Of course, when I came to Ohio, it was a beautiful spring day, and everything was just gorgeous. Well, very quickly you learn it becomes freezing cold in the Winter! I brought my car with me from Texas, which was this 1959 Volkswagen Beetle with no heat! [*laughter*] It's like driving an ice box, so I would go to his studio, and the car would freeze. Brilliant! Sometimes if it got too bad, I'd work at my place. I'd take Craig's rough layouts, and bring back the finished pencils for him to ink.

Eventually, I got tired of the Ohio winters, and decided to move back to California. It's funny, I stayed in New York for the first 24 years of my life. Now I was really starting to feel like The Wandering Jew, going all these different places. [*laughter*]

MR. MONSTER--Dead Wrong!

GRRR! NASTY KIDS TELL POOR, POOR TURTLEBOY HE HAVE "COOTIES"! WELL, TURTLEBOY SURE FIX THEIR WAGON, HUH, OOOZ?! HO! HO!

MEANWHILE, BELOW...

AUNT KELLY! KIDS CAN'T GROW TURTLE SHELLS, CAN THEY?

ONLY DOC'S ARCH-ENEMY, TURTLE-BOY! BUT HE'S DEAD!

TEDDY ROOSEVELT ELEMENTARY SCHOOL

©1933, Gilbert Tribune Syndicate.

SSSSSSS!

TNT

LITTLE DO YOU KNOW, KELLY!

9/26

As it turned out, I wound up meeting my present wife there just before I left. When Craig and I finished our first *Elric* series, the local paper did a big story on the two of us. They had our photographs on the front of whatever section it was, and this elementary school teacher, Janet Clark, saw the thing and figured she'd sucker one of us into talking to her class and doing her work for her. She was going to call Craig, and then she kind of chickened out… she thought he looked too stern in the photograph or something. [*laughter*] So she wound up calling me up. I thought she sounded really cute on the phone, and I told her I'd talk to her class if she'd take me out to dinner afterwards. I couldn't lose. Even if she wasn't cute, at least I'd get a nice meal out of it! [*laughter*] Luckily she *was* very cute, and we hit it off. We started dating, and a couple of years later we got married!

CBA: *So, what was the genesis of Mr. Monster?*

Michael: Pacific Comics was one of the early independent publishers, and they'd gotten guys like Kirby and Ditko to do stuff for them. They had a comic called *Vanguard Illustrated,* and the premise of that was to match… it was sort of a "new talent tryout" book, where they'd get a professional and team them up with an up-and-coming talent. Well, somewhere along the way, after we finished the first *Elric* series—Craig was leaving after that one, but I was going to continue with George Freeman. But there were a few months in between, it would've been a dead time, so Mike Friedrich—who was my agent—worked out a deal where I would create a feature for *Vanguard Illustrated.* Dave Scroggy, the editor, said to come up with something, and we'd find a newcomer to work with me. I thought this was great! It was a very exciting time for comics. Everyone was coming up with new ideas. Chaykin's *American Flagg!*, Dave Steven's *The Rocketeer* and so on. There was a lot of really creative, fun stuff going on, and I wanted to be a part of it. After working on *Elric* a couple of years, I was delighted to create a character I'd own. I thought about doing The Wraith again, but I wanted to do something different. I started going through my old comic collection to see if there was any kind of neat idea I could use as the springboard for a new series. While digging through piles of comics, I found this old coverless comic book from 1947. It was an old anthology title with lots of different features…including a strange monster-fighting hero named Mr. Monster! I bought it at an old Seuling-Con for 50¢ back in the late '60s. Over the years I'd look at this weird eight-page story and think, "Someone should bring this guy back!" Turns out it was one of only two Mr. Monster stories that had ever been done. So anyway, I pitched Mr. Monster to Pacific. They were a little doubtful at first, but they approved it. And that's how he started.

CBA: *It was a '47 Fred Kelly story from* Super Duper Comics?

Michael: Yes.

CBA: *Did you think about copyright, or did you try to seek out Mr. Kelly anywhere? What was your thinking on that?*

Michael: My thinking was that copyrights last for 27 years, so there certainly didn't seem much chance of anybody renewing this character…especially since the original publishing company, F. E. Howard, went out of business in 1947. That was actually the last book and the last character that this company had put out.

CBA: *A pretty sure bet, then.*

Michael: And just to make sure, I redesigned the character and costume, and changed Jim Stern to Strongfort Stearn. I created Kelly and all the secondary characters from whole cloth—and as I said, they went for it.

CBA: *It was going to be a three-parter in* Vanguard Illustrated?

Michael: Yeah, it was going to be three eight-page chapters of a single story. They came out with the first installment, I was working with Bill Loebs on the artwork—who was not exactly a newcomer, but I was able to make them think he was! I wanted to get someone with a real Eisner feel to the inks and whatnot, he was just perfect for it. So, I had done the scripts and the rough pencils, and then he did the finishes on the thing. Bill did a tremendous job, adding lots of Eisner-esque atmosphere.

CBA: *And Ken Bruzenak worked with you from the first story?*

Michael: I've always admired really good lettering in comics, such as Abe Kanegson's wonderful work on *The Spirit,* and Artie Simek's on the Marvel horror comics in the late '50s. I wanted someone

Above: *Line art for the cover of Mr. Monster #1. ©2000 MTG.*
Below: *The artist catching up on classic literature.*

equally expressive as a letterer for Mr. Monster. When I saw some of the work Ken had been doing on *American Flagg!*, I said, "This lettering is completely different from the style I'm looking for, but this is one letterer who can really think." And I wanted someone who could think like an artist, so I contacted him to see if he'd like to give it a try. I wanted spooky *Spirit*-style lettering, which was totally different from his futuristic *American Flagg!* work he was doing for Chaykin, and Ken did a fantastic job. His lettering really helped create the gothic feel I was looking for!

CBA: *Did you hit it off with Ken as a person?*

Michael: Yeah, he's a great guy. We keep in touch, and it's fun talking to him. He's about the same age I am, 48.

CBA: *I think he's about 20 years older now, after working with Steranko, right?* [*laughter*]

Michael: Yeah, that'll do it. [*laughter*] Jim gave him a hard time!

CBA: *I believe I saw in your* Wraith *collection, a letter from Will Eisner. Did you maintain a continual contact with him?*

Michael: Yeah, we've kept a correspondence over the years, and Janet and I went down to his studio a couple of years ago in Florida. He's actually been very supportive over the years. I first got a chance to meet him in 1982 or thereabouts. I went on a short trip to New York, and he invited me to talk to his class at the School of Visual Arts. I had just finished my first full-

Unused 1990 "Origins" cover. Monsters by MTG, Mr. Monster by Fred Kelly. Courtesy of and ©2000 MTG.

Below: *Unpubbed MTG drawing made for Shannon Wheeler. Mr. Monster ©2000 MTG, TMCM ©2000 Shannon Wheeler.*

DEAR GOD!! IT'S A WORLD GONE MAD! MONSTERS EVERYWHERE! VAMPIRES! ALIENS! ZOMBIES! HACK CARTOONISTS!

WHAT'LL WE DO, TOO MUCH COFFEE MAN? WHAT WILL WE DO !?!?

H-HAVE ANOTHER C-CUP OF C-COFFEE!

ALL THE BEST FROM MR. MONSTER AND... MICHAEL Gilbert '99

color story, "The Circle Game" and he invited me to talk about it. After the class ended, he asked me what methods I used to color my story. That really impressed me! Now, I was just 30 at the time, with no big reputation… and here was Will Eisner asking me about my coloring! To think that a cartoonist of his stature— in his 60s, no less—was still trying to learn, even from even a small-timer like me! Will even took me out to lunch afterwards, which I was pretty impressed with. Eisner: Spending money on lunch! [*laughter*]

CBA: *What was the response to the first Mr. Monster story?*

Michael: Very positive. It's not like there were thousands of people writing in, but I got the feeling people did like it. Of course, it was kind of tricky, because the first issue of the three-part thing had come out in *Vanguard Illustrated*, and then the company went belly-up, it was like a continuation of the first time Mr. Monster had appeared 20 years earlier, but

at Pacific Comics this time!

CBA: [*laughs*] *Uh-oh, kiss of death! So he'd only appeared once?*

Michael: Yes. The first chapter had only appeared. So, the whole thing went under, and again, it was another one of these strange times, because at this point, I'd decided I had enough of Ohio. The first Elric series was over, and I didn't need to stay there any more. I wanted to move back to California to work on the next one, and take Janet with me. So, we packed up everything we owned into this huge, oversized U-Haul (much too dangerous for the size of our car—not that the U-Haul people cared!). The night before the big move, Mike Friedrich called to tell me Pacific Comics was dead. Suddenly, it's like, "Oh, I don't have a job anymore! How grand!" What a good time to be moving! [*laughter*] But it was too late to back out now, so a week later we arrived in Berkeley and stayed at a friend's house. Luckily, while we were gone Mike had managed to sell *Elric* to First comics and *Mr. Monster* to Eclipse. Eclipse was buying a lot of unused Pacific material, and they agreed to publish all three of the Mr. Monster stories in a single one-shot comic. So suddenly, it was like, "Oh, yes, I'm happy!"

CBA: *Did you have all the chapters finished?*

Michael: Yeah, the whole book was finished. The three chapters were done. It was even more frustrating because you kept waiting for chapter two, "Oh, boy, I can't wait to see chapter two!"

CBA: *Did you have a finished cover painting ready?*

Michael: No, we didn't have any covers, and we hadn't convinced them to give us a cover on the *Vanguard* book.

CBA: *So, from the demise of* Vanguard *to the first issue of* Mr. Monster, *do you remember roughly how long that was?*

Michael: I think the first chapter in *Vanguard* was July '84, and the other one came out in January '85.

CBA: *Did you receive letters from fans, for instance, saying this was a neat guy? Did people start sparking into it immediately?*

Michael: When the *Mr. Monster* book came out, we got some nice fan mail. However I don't think I heard that much about the *Vanguard* appearance.

CBA: *So you guys had faith in the character?*

Michael: Oh, yeah, it's just a terrific character, I was just in love with him from Day One.

CBA: *So, you had developed him, really, from the word go. He was the character at that moment that he is today, pretty much?*

Michael: Yeah. He's not much different.

CBA: *A guy who's cocky, full of himself, overly melodramatic?*

Michael: Yeah, just kind of a kid at heart, enjoying being a super-hero, and enjoying his purpose in life, which was killing monsters.

CBA: Killing! [*laughs*]

Michael: Killing *monsters*! Killing *monsters*!

CBA: *His gal Friday, Kelly, is a sea of sobriety. She's a smart one.*

Michael: Right, she is the balance to the strip. She's the readers' stand-in. Doc's an over-the-top comic book hero, but Kelly acts more like a real person. It makes a nice contrast.

CBA: *Obviously, she serves as the sexy babe for a lot of the covers, for instance, but she was also the anchor.*

Michael: You've got Mr. Monster, your big executive, taking all the photo-ops and whatnot…while she's quietly doing all the 1,001 things you need to have for an organization to run properly. She buys the bullets, gets the plane fixed, or does spin-control when he blows up the Chrysler Building fighting Godzilla. She's doing all that stuff out of the spotlight. She's willing to do without all the fame and whatnot because she's got a fantastic pension plan, and she's got a real nice deal for herself. Doc needs the ego-boost. She doesn't.

CBA: *With Mr. Monster #1, what kind of deal did you have? Was it for a percentage or a flat deal for submitting the work?*

Michael: We would get a page rate in advance of publication, but if it sold more, we'd be getting a higher percentage, so we'd get a combination of the two. Of course, whenever they're discussing the stuff in advance, they're telling us, "Well, if you sell 20,000 copies, you get X amount… Once you get to selling 100,000 or 200,000, boy will you be rich!". The "rich" part never comes, but it's nice to fantasize about it. [*laughter*]

CBA: *#1 came out in January of '85. What were the sales on it?*

Michael: I think it was something like 25,000 or thereabouts.

CBA: *Did it go to a second printing?*

Michael: Not that I recall.

CBA: *My first memory of Mr. Monster was seeing it as—probably only a couple of months later, because the second issue was on the stands at the time—I'd seen it as a back issue, and it was a highly-inflated price perhaps because of the region I was in.*

Michael: Well, Eclipse was probably doing their back-issue thing, here. They just had a few back issues, and they were jacking it to whatever they felt like asking for it.

CBA: *The price was up there. There was something about that, immediately. Alan Moore once wrote an introduction to one of your collections of Mr. Monster—I'm paraphrasing here—by saying the character was one of the five really, truly interesting super-heroes. He threw Mr. Monster in with the likes of Plastic Man, Captain Marvel and Fighting American. Are there any archetypes for Mr. Monster? He's really an amalgamation, right, of Dr. Van Helsing, and Captain America… and he had guns!*

Michael: There have always been some characters who had some connection to horror here and there, but I can't think of anyone off the top of my head who was as much a specialist as he is, mixing the horror and the super-hero genres together.

CBA: *And the humor!*

Michael: And the humor. I was really trying to… as you mentioned earlier, I really love a lot of different genres, and I was trying to put the love of all those genres into a single character.

CBA: *What was the planned frequency when you started?*

Michael: Bi-monthly.

CBA: *Did you have a set contract for a year?*

Michael: We had like six issues or something. I really had a lot of faith in the character, I still do. I think he's a wonderful character, and there was a lot of excitement when we came out here. I was able to, by showing the first issue, get Dave Stevens, for instance, to do a cover for us. He agreed to do a cover, and I wrote a story around it.

CBA: *So he was the first other professional—other than the regular team—who was working on the book, that you reached out to?*

Michael: Yeah. Shortly after that, the next issue, we were able to get Alan Moore. There was a real sense of "Wow, there's a lot of great people who'd like to work on this character!" People liked the idea of getting involved in this.

CBA: *Were they seeking you out? How did you get in contact with Alan Moore, for instance?*

Michael: I was reading his *Swamp Thing*, and I thought it was the greatest thing since cream cheese, and I sent him a little postcard to DC telling him how great I thought Alan Moore's writing was, and of course, how much I loved Bissette and Totleben's artwork on the series. Shortly after, I got a call from Alan. It turned out he had been a fan of The Wraith from years ago, and we went from there. He said he'd be interested in doing a script.

CBA: *What kind of commercial aspirations did you have for your character? Merchandising began with T-shirts pretty quick, right?*

Michael: Yeah, Graphitti came out with the T-shirt before the first issue came out.

CBA: *Well, that's confidence! [laughter]*

Michael: It was confidence on Bob Chapman's part at Graphitti! They did a very nice job, as always. I can't say enough nice things about Bob Chapman—he's a prince!

CBA: *You were almost an editor at that point, right?*

Michael: Yeah, I was editing the book.

CBA: *This was new for you, right? Other than* New Paltz Comix.

Michael: Well, that's the thing. I had been doing the *New Paltz Comix* stuff, so it wasn't as new as it could be. From the start, I'd always put together books, trying to get a nice balance of writing and artwork. I was certainly new to it professionally, but I had some practice.

CBA: *Do you look at editing fondly? Packaging the books, and doing the whole production?*

Michael: Yeah, everything. You want to make sure there are no spelling errors, you want to make sure the coloring looks good, and this story is a nice kind of balance to the story in the back of the book, 1,001 little things—like how the letter pages go. I spent a lot of time doing letter pages that would give a good, friendly and informative fan-feel to the whole book.

CBA: *I guess this is a good point to say that my one and only*

contribution to comics was a very small illustration that appeared in a *Mr. Monster* letters page.

Michael: I like to think that illustration made that issue! *[laughter]*

CBA: *I put a happy face on instead of the skull emblem for the chest, and I saw that used in a subsequent issue and said, "Oh, cool!" [laughs] Not that I'm going to take credit for the happy face!*

Michael: What issue was your sketch in?

CBA: *It must've been #6—the washing machine cover.*

Michael: Yeah, that's the one with the Ditko reprint.

CBA: *That was a lot of fun. I just made a little crack about the "ghastly disappearance of Graham Ingels"…*

Michael: Yeah!

CBA: *…and you added a little word balloon that said, "Or else!"*

Michael: Always the editor, always the editor!

CBA: *[laughs] So, you were obviously getting a good response from the title! Were you growing in circulation? Were they printing*

Above: *Unused 1992 cover rough by MTG for a Dave Dorman painting. Courtesy of MTG. ©2000 Michael T. Gilbert.*

Below: *Ye ed's single contribution to comics—from the letter pages of Mr. Monster #6. Mr. Monster ©2000 MTG. Art ©2000 Jon B. Cooke.*

THE TIME HAS COME TO SOLVE THE CASE OF THE GHASTLY DISAPPEANCE OF GRAHAM INGELS

…OR ELSE!!

more copies, for instance?

Michael: I think it was holding steady for a while there, but we always had the problems of getting the publisher to advertise the thing! It seemed like Kitchen Sink, for instance, did a lot more advertising. So, it's working with one hand tied behind your back. I think we could've done a lot better, particularly in those earlier issues, if we had a really effective advertising campaign. I'd design them, but they wouldn't appear.

CBA: *Not actually seeing print?*

Above: *Aborted Trencher/Mr. Monster comic by MTG and Keith Giffen done for Blackball Comics in 1994. Trencher ©2000 Keith Giffen. Mr. Monster ©2000 MTG.* **Below:** *Homage to Mary Marvel's first appearance in MTG's cover to Kelly #2, on sale now! ©2000 MTG.*

Michael: Right. Or seeing print in the back of some unread magazine somewhere.

CBA: *With your first run of* Mr. Monster, *how many issues did that last?*

Michael: The first series from Eclipse lasted 10 issues plus the double-sized Airboy-Mr. Monster Special.

CBA: *Was one of the joys of collaborating, that you could step back, and, for instance, Don Simpson would do finishes on the art? Jeff Bonivert would do Mr. Monster stories, for instance. Were you looking to do experimentation with the books?*

Michael: Yeah. I really was. I mean, one of the things—getting back to Kurtzman again—I always liked how he would lay out the stories for these various artists, and try to write stories to display their strengths. You'd get him doing a western story he'd give to John Severin, he would do a Civil War story and give it to Jack Davis. Al Feldstein would do the same thing, writing a science-fiction story and give it to Wally Wood, because he did the best s-f in the world. So, I was trying to find people who I thought could do this genre or that genre better than I could. I'm still controlling it, the layouts and the script and everything, to get my vision across. But hopefully, the finished product would be even better than I could do.

CBA: *During this time, you were also working with—I believe it was during this time, correct me—with Harvey Pekar on his* American Splendor. *When did you do work for Harvey?*

Michael: The first story I did was in '79, I think. It was a one- or two-pager.

CBA: *Did you contact him?*

Michael: Yeah. I liked *American Splendor* when I saw it, and it was very impressive, and I offered to do a story or two, if Harvey was interested.

CBA: *You did two stories?*

Michael: Actually, I wound up doing about five mini-stories here and there. I think it was about eight or ten pages total, I guess.

CBA: *How was it working with Harvey?*

Michael: It was a trip. [*laughter*] Harvey could have a one-page thing, and he'd just tell it to you over the phone, or he'd send these stick figure drawings of this, that and the other here. And I'd ask him, "How about sending me a photo of you, Harvey, so I can see what you actually look like?" He said, "Oh, just look at Gary Shamray, look at Dunn, and see how they do it." I said, "It would be easier if I could just see a photo of you, so I could…" "Oh, no, no!" [*laughter*] He was so worried about each page… "Make sure panel three is this, that and the other…"

CBA: *So was it a lot of hard work, say, compared to other editors?*

Michael: Well, again, I didn't do it too long. Once you got it in your hands, you're basically doing it. It wasn't that horrible.

CBA: *Right. What was the page rate, do you remember?*

Michael: I think it was $35 or $50 a page.

CBA: *Did you do it as wanting to be part of* American Splendor, *or did you see that as viable employment opportunity?*

Michael: I wanted to do it. I'm always trying to get jobs I care about. He'd worked with so many people. I think the first time I wrote to him, I was actually mentioning I didn't like a one-pager some artist had done. I thought the guy had stepped on the punch line, or hadn't effectively done what Harvey wanted. He actually had me redo it, and he printed it as a *re-do* of that thing.

CBA: *With the success of* Mr. Monster, *and your name being recognized more and more in the field, did you pitch ideas to the mainstream houses at all?*

Michael: I actually had no interest in doing that, I was doing just what I wanted to do. I loved the idea of being able to do this character with super-heroes and horror and humor and all this stuff that I liked, that I owned the character, full-color… there wasn't anything that DC had to offer me. The only exception to that was Alan Moore and I had pitched the idea of a Mr. Monster/Swamp Thing crossover, which DC had actually approved, we actually signed a contract to do it. I'm told that was actually the first contract between DC and one of the independents. Unfortunately, shortly after that, Alan had this big blow-up with them, with the merchandising of *Watchmen*, and said he wasn't going to work with them anymore. So that pretty much killed that.

CBA: *He's never worked for them again, right? [laughs] I'm just having an America's Best Comics joke. Was anything ever completed on the Mr. Monster/Swamp Thing crossover?*

Michael: Basically, Alan and I had just kicked the story idea around, so we had a pretty good idea of what we were going to do—but nothing, really.

CBA: *So no pages were drawn of that?*

Michael: No. It's kind of a shame, because I think it would've been a really exciting and interesting comic.

CBA: *It was heavily anticipated, right? I would assume you receive a lot of questions on that project.*

Michael: Some over the years, but there's not much you can say!

CBA: *Would you ever still like to have it see the light of day?*

Michael: Sure, of course! But Alan's not going to be working for DC, so I don't think that's going to happen.

CBA: *Can you give us an idea of what the story would've been like?*

Michael: As I remember it—mind you, this was 15 years ago—I seem to recall it was going to be something along the lines of there was going to be some kind of a thing where we'd have little mini-stories. There was some kind of villain, Weird-head, and we were going to have Mr. Monster and Swamp Thing chase him through these horror comic dimensions… actually pastiches of various horror comic genres through the decades. We planned to do a story in the style of the the '50s ACG *Unknown Worlds,* then another in the style of the Kirby monster comics and so forth. A big chase scene through the history of horror comics! It would have been cool. Of course, at the same time, Mr. Monster would be trying to kill Swamp Thing throughout this whole thing. [laughter] He'd blow him up, and then he'd re-grow again… so they were almost working at cross-purposes at the same time.

CBA: *Did you have great aspirations for that one-shot? Did you see it as maybe you could even double your audience?*

Michael: I don't remember thinking about that in particular. What was exciting to me was working with Alan, and giving Mr. Monster more legitimacy. Yeah, I'm sure I had thoughts that the circulation would certainly go up, I wanted that, too.

CBA: *What was the idea behind the* Mr. Monster Super-Duper Specials? *Did you initiate that with Eclipse?*

Michael: Yeah, it just goes back to my love of old comics again. I wanted to reprint some of my favorite old comics in the back of *Mr. Monster.* Each issue would have a classic Steve Ditko horror story, or a Dr. Drew horror story, or whatever. We got lots of great response from the readers, but we also got some people saying, "Well, we don't want to pay for the back-up features in *Mr. Monster.*" But I loved doing them, I loved getting the stuff back in print. So I came up with the solution of basically having one book that would be totally Mr. Monster again, and another one that would collect rare stories by Jack Cole, George Evans, Basil Wolverton…all that great stuff—and I called them my *Super-Duper Specials.* Our reprints usually looked much better than the originals! I'm really proud of those books.

CBA: *You reprinted some fine work there. Did you work with Ray Zone on the 3-D stuff?*

Michael: I worked with him to the extent of trying to come up with stories that would look good in 3-D. I would do the Mr. Monster introductions or whatever, keeping in mind what you could do with 3-D. So I tried to say, "Let's do something that will really pop up when Ray takes it," and then Ray would go there and do his thing. I try to work to the strengths of whatever medium I'm working in.

CBA: *Were you concerned about the integrity of your character when you had them do a crossover with Airboy, or did that not bother you at all?*

Michael: Well, that was a whole other story. Originally, it wasn't supposed to be a crossover with Airboy. It was supposed to be a crossover between Mr. Monster and the Heap. Airboy and the crew were going to be in there too, but the Heap was going to be the main character, and he was a monster; and I was a big fan of the Hillman version of Airboy and The Heap, and that was the version I was doing—the 1940s versions. It seemed entirely in character for Mr. Monster to be dealing with the Golden Age characters. After I wrote the story, Eclipse insisted that Airboy become the main character, since that was one of their better-selling titles. I didn't like the change, but I made it work.

CBA: *So you made the best of the project.*

Michael: No, it was a project I wanted to do. It was actually a story I felt very deeply about, and it's one of my more underrated stories. "The Cafe At The Edge Of The World" was a story about a washed-up Golden Age cartoonist and the pain he suffers when he loses control of his characters. It was a rough story to do, made rougher because I was about to leave Eclipse, and they knew it. It wasn't too much fun working with them at that point.

CBA: *Was there just a change of atmosphere working with the company?*

Michael: It hadn't been too much fun for the most part, but it was getting worse and worse. Once they know you're leaving to go to a different publisher, it's not going to be too much fun there.

CBA: *So there wasn't a stop there at that point? You had decided to go over with Michael Richardson's Dark Horse while you were still with Eclipse?*

Michael: Yes.

CBA: *And what attracted you to Dark Horse?*

Michael: Well, at that point, they were a pretty exciting company. They had Paul Chadwick's *Concrete,* and Bob Burden's *Flaming Carrot* and so on. Lots of neat creator-owned titles. They seemed like a small, quality-oriented company, and I thought *Mr. Monster* would fit in. As much as anything, I was tired of Eclipse at that point.

CBA: *There was a change of atmosphere in* Mr. Monster *with the Dark Horse series. What was your approach?*

Michael: I wanted to try a much more serious, more sustained work. That's when I started doing my "Origins" series. Our circulation had gone down somewhat…so from a practical point of view, I thought it'd be smart to do this new series as a black-&-white book. Then I thought as long as Mr. Monster was going to be b-&-w, let's really try to take advantage of the fact. Make a lemon out of lemonade. So, I started using Craftint, and taking advantage of all the neat things you can do without color. The bright, garish color was perfect for those over-the-top Mr. Monster stories I was telling at Eclipse. Now I wanted to see if we could tone the whole thing down…the color, the humor, the lightness…and come up with a much more serious, gritty Mr. Monster story. I really wanted to see if I was capable of doing a really long, sustained work. That was my goal.

CBA: *Did you just want to step away from the humorous elements and start with actual continuity?*

Michael: At that time, I had seen things like *Watchmen* and *Dark Knight.* There were a lot of serious works going on, and I wanted to try my hand at it. I've always experimented with *Mr. Monster,* each issue was a new experiment. "Let's try horror this issue. Now let's do humor. Hey, how about a story from the monster's point of view?" So this time I said "Let's do a really long, serious story and see if I can

Above: *Thumbnail MTG layout for "Mr. Monster vs. the Nazis from Mars." Courtesy of and ©2000 MTG.* Below: *Marvel commissioned MTG to do a pin-up reinventing one of their characters for Marvel Vision #22. MTG chose Molecule Man, pretending he was a 1955 Atlas Hero. Courtesy of MTG. ©2000 Marvel Characters, Inc.*

Below: *Janet Gilbert does her take on Mr. Monster. Mr. Monster ©2000 MTG, art ©2000 Janet Gilbert.* **Bottom:** *Kent-Rolvenna Record Courier, Oct. 11, 1983, news article which led to Michael and Janet's first meeting. Courtesy of MTG.*

pull that off. And let's see if this character, who has been absolutely goofy at times, can still work in this new format." I think it did.

CBA: *What is your feeling, overall, of the serious "Origin" issues?*

Michael: It was a real bitch to do, it really was. It took me years to finally finish my 200 pages of the thing. Part of it was I was doing all of the work, all the art and stories. I'd also started scripting Disney comics, to help pay the bills. So that slowed me down, too—but it was really the first time I'd done a series by myself, and it was really difficult; and as I said, it's an incredibly complex story, which I'd never attempted on this scale. So I was doing all these different things at once, so it was a slow going.

CBA: *Overall, how do you look at the series?*

Michael: I had real mixed feelings about the initial Dark Horse run. I thought there were some really good things in there… and some real weaknesses in the artwork and some writing. But, years later, when Bob Chapman approached me about collecting the book, he gave me the opportunity to correct my mistakes… God bless him! I went back and drew some new pages, got rid of excess pages and panels and colored 200 pages. I must have changed a good 25% of the story. It took months, but I'm really proud of the final product. When it was finally collected, "Origins" received two Eisner nominations.

CBA: *Like you said, the tone of the strip with the Dark Horse series became more dramatic, with less humor. Was there reaction from readers? I continued to buy the series, but it wasn't as fun.*

Michael: I have to say it was probably 50-50. We got some people that liked the new direction. We got some mail from

fans who said the earlier stuff was starting to feel like fluff, and they were happy to see this more serious version. Other people felt just the opposite.

CBA: *"Where's the fluff?"* [laughs]

Michael: I liked the fluff too, so I can certainly understand how you felt. Dark Horse actually preferred the humorous approach, but I wanted to stretch my muscles a little bit further. It was kind of interesting to see how "Origins" changed as I went along. The first two or three issues were a little too restrained. I think I was trying to be a "serious" writer, like Alan Moore or Frank Miller, and then, at a certain point, I said, "Wait a second, now! I don't have to be Alan or Frank! I can be myself!"… and I started adding more humor. I finally figured out that I could lighten the story, and still keep the overall serious tone. In those later issues, I'd have a teenage punk vampire with a skateboard sassing his granddaddy, or I'd show Mr. Monster as a kid sneaking a peek at *Tales from the Crypt*. Things like that.

CBA: *Did you feel you were supported by Dark Horse?*

Michael: Not particularly.

CBA: *Was it again, a failure in marketing?*

Michael: Yeah, that's it as much as anything. I mean, I dropped the ball by not getting issues out regularly—that hurt sales—but I think in general Dark Horse gets excited when they have a new book coming out. They'll push it for a little bit, and then it becomes an "old" book—so they find the next "new" new book and put their efforts there. Also, I was initially attracted to Dark Horse because it was a small people-friendly company, publishing a few quirky, creator-owned characters. Well, shortly after I signed on, they started getting into all their licensing things, like *Aliens* and *Godzilla* and whatnot.

CBA: *So the atmosphere of the company changed.*

Michael: Yeah, it changed dramatically, and I didn't like it nearly as much.

CBA: *So, how many issues did you last with Dark Horse?*

Michael: We were contracted to do the eight issues. I finished those as well as two or three *Dark Horse Presents* stories featuring Mr. Monster.

'Battle' rages in Kent

Comic book artists evoke pen-and-ink fantasy world

By JOHN KUEHNER

An epic battle is being fought in an apartment on Lake Street in Kent.

But the weapons in this "war" are pencils and ink.

P. Craig Russell and Michael T. Gilbert, two artists living in the Kent area, are combining their inking and penciling talents to adapt Michael Moorcock's sword and sorcery novel, "Elric of Melnibone," to the pages of a full-color comic book.

"Fantasy, which is very visual, is just perfect for comics," said Russell, in whose apartment most of the work is penciled, inked and colored.

"It's a real collaboration," said Russell, a fantasy artist comic book artist for 10 years. "We're both doing a little bit of everything."

The bi-monthly comic, which sells for $1.50 at direct-sale comic book newsstands, deals with Elric, emperor of the fantasy kingdom of Melnibone, and his struggle against his cousin. It also deals with Elric's struggle against himself as he ponders emotions awakening in him which are foreign to his race.

"It's an adult, sophisticated fantasy," said the 32-year-old Gilbert, who moved to Kent from Austin, Texas, about a year ago so he could work on the project with Russell.

"It deals with a person and his motivations, not just simple actions, such as in 'Conan the Barbarian.' Elric is someone who wants to be peaceful and compassionate

in a society that demands warriors and cruelty," said Gilbert, who resides in Twin Lakes. "There's nothing like it on the stands."

The 30-page comic, printed on high-stock paper, is slated for a six-issue run. The fourth issue is to be released this month.

Russell and Gilbert, who have been working on the project for more than a year, come from opposite ends of the comic field.

The 32-year-old Russell, a graduate of the University of Cincinnati's art school, got his first work on comics while a junior in college.

A native of Wellsville and a reader of comics since a young age, Russell met Dan Adkins, an inker at Marvel Comics, which publishes the super hero comics Spider-Man and the Incredible Hulk, among others. Adkins got Russell work on some of the firm's titles.

"I was always interested in comics, but never saw it as a career opportunity," he said.

After graduation, Russell moved to New York and penciled and inked his own Marvel comic.

In 1980, after doing freelance work for two years, Russell moved to Kent to teach a class in comic art at Kent State University.

Because of his work on a graphic novel Elric adaptation and another short adaptation he did, Russell was asked by Pacific Comics, a new comic book publisher, to do a complete adaptation of

the six-novel Elric series.

Since Russell could not do a bi-monthly series himself, he suggested Gilbert assist on the project because he thought their work would mesh well together.

Gilbert, a graduate of New Paltz State University of New York, was writing and drawing alternate comic stories because he could not get into Marvel or D.C. Comics, the two big comic book producers.

He had work published in many alternate publications and worked for a while as a cartoonist at the "Berkeley Barb," an underground newspaper.

Also a comic book reader since his grandmother gave him his first "Jimmy Olsen" comic, Gilbert agreed to join the project and moved to Kent.

Gilbert does the penciling on the Elric series and Russell the inking. However, both alternate this when there is a scene the other wants to do.

Roy Thomas, who lives in California, writes the book after he receives the pages from Kent. He then sends them to a letterer, who writes in the scripts. The pages then are returned to Gilbert and Russell for coloring.

Usually, from 8 p.m. until 4 a.m., the pair work on the exploits of Elric.

"The freedom is wonderful," Russell said. "If it's a beautiful day, you can take it off. But we still have to work as much as anyone, or more."

COMIC BOOK artists Michael T. Gilbert and P. Craig Russell display the cover of an upcoming issue of Elric of Melnibone, a fantasy hero which the Kent pair are adapting for comic books. (R-C photo by Ernie Mastroianni)

CBA: *What did you want to do with the character after that?*
Michael: At that point, I wanted to do some fun stuff again, the shorter fun stuff. The Dark Horse stuff was kind of a reaction to my Eclipse experience (where I had done all these short, funny stories with other people. That was a lot of work, dealing with this inker and that colorist…just the logistics of it). When I went to Dark Horse, I just wanted to strip things down and get back to basics. Just me and the strip. Now, I was ready to play around again…to work with other people, and do some of the short, funnier stories.

CBA: *What was the first opportunity? A-1?*
Michael: Yeah, I was doing some stuff for Dave Elliott and Gary Leach at *A-1* towards the end of my Dark Horse run. They've always been very supportive fans of *Mr. Monster* and my other work. Great guys! So, I did some short stories for them, and had a good time with it.

CBA: *Was that where the Dave Dorman painting started?*
Michael: Yeah, I came up with a story that took place in a *Mr. Monster Museum* I invented. Actually, this was just a sneaky excuse to get Dave to do some Mr. Monster paintings that I could integrate into the story. The *A-1* story was going to be printed in black-&-white, but I said, "Dave, why don't you do it in full color? Eventually, we'll print this thing in color." And we did.

CBA: *Right. And one of them did appear as a cover?*
Michael: Yeah. Eventually we printed all three as covers for Tundra's *Mr. Monster Attacks* mini-series. Gorgeous covers, too.

CBA: *Oh, beautiful stuff. For instance, I would see Mr. Monster on different magazine covers, finding the character hither and yon. I picked up a copy of the punk music zine* Black Market, *so your character obviously had across-the-board popularity in at least some sub-cultures, right?*
Michael: Yeah, it is pretty interesting. I know Glenn Danzig was a big Mr. Monster fan… he even

plugged it in one of his videos! He bought a lot of originals from me, years ago. Supposedly Metallica and Marilyn Manson were fans, too. So, you get that heavy-metal element of fan there, and at the same time you get… I've heard from parents telling me their little eight-year-old likes reading *Mr. Monster*. And one letter talked about how his little son was scared of the dark, so he put the Dave Stevens Mr. Monster poster in the room, and now he feels safe! [*laughter*] That was really nice to hear.

CBA: *Was Mr. Monster, between 1985 up to this day, your sole character, or did you have other things you wanted to do, other characters you wanted to develop?*
Michael: I kicked around a couple of things, but nothing popped. If someone came up to me and said, "Let's come

Above: Janet Clark's article on MTG, from Career World Vol. 13, #7 (March 1985) led to a relationship between writer and subject lasting (so far) 17 years! ©2000 Curriculum Innovations, Inc.

Below: Michael and Janet Gilbert. Courtesy of MTG.

up with a new character for this," I would've done something. But no, Mr. Monster is really the character that I love the most, and given half a chance, I'll continue drawing him.

CBA: *And you are right now, with a mini-series, right?*

Michael: Yeah, a three-issue *Kelly* series from Image Comics, which will probably be out by the time this interview comes out.

CBA: *Is that a relationship you have with Jim Valentino or Eric Larsen?*

Michael: We came out with a one-shot, *Mr. Monster vs. Gorzilla,* from Image about two years ago, through the auspices of Erik Larsen. This latest one is through Valentino.

CBA: *You did a three-issue mini-series with Tundra?*

Michael: Yeah, I did a three-issue *Mr. Monster Attacks,* which was a full-color super-deluxe series. The *Kelly* series was also originally done for them, too… just before they folded. We also did another series called *Crack-A-Boom.* It came out three years ago, from Caliber, but it was originally done for Tundra.

CBA: *That was an anthology book, right?*

Michael: It was a Mr. Monster lead story and a lot of other creator-owned horror and humor characters in the back of the book. We had "Wolff and Byrd" by Batton Lash, and Mark Stokes' "Zombie Boy."

CBA: *That was great!*

Michael: Zombie Boy, Monster Boy—we had all the boys in there. [*laughter*] And Mr. Monster as a boy… Li'l Doc!

CBA: *Is Mr. Monster your proudest achievement?*

Michael: Yeah, I'd say it is. I was very proud of the *Elric* work, but yeah, this is certainly the thing that I am proudest of. I think I've done a wide variety of stories, I've worked with some of the best and most interesting people in the business. I did my longest, definitive solo work on *Mr. Monster* with the "Origins" story. I'm really proud of the books, when I look at them.

CBA: *Are there more things you'd like to do with the character?*

Michael: Yeah, I'd like to try doing some more serious stories again. There's lots of stuff, I have all sorts of ideas. I even played around with a pseudo 1930-style *Mr. Monster* newspaper strip, just for fun.

CBA: *Now, Supernatural Law by Batton Lash, has been optioned for a motion*

picture. There seems to be cinematic possibilities with Mr. Monster. Has Hollywood ever courted you with a project?

Michael: Oh, yeah, we've been approached by Hollywood over the years. As a matter of fact, as we speak, Mr. Monster is optioned by Nelvana, the animation studio, and they commissioned an animated *Mr. Monster* pilot script from Jeph Loeb. He just delivered it last week, so now we're waiting to hear from the guys upstairs.

CBA: *So it's pretty much Mr. Monster's been your bread and butter for all these years?*

Michael: Yeah, but I've also done other projects. I do some stuff for DC, occasionally. I wrote and drew a Batman story (*Legends of the Dark Knight* #94) a few years back, and an issue of *Showcase 94.* Right now I'm writing and drawing a 48-page Superman graphic album called *Mann And Superman* that should be out by the end of the year. I also do a lot of work writing Disney comics for the Egmont publishing group in Denmark. My wife Janet and I have worked for them, on and off, for eight or nine years. We take turns writing Donald Duck and Mickey Mouse stories. It's fun!

CBA: *Has Janet always been a writer?*

Michael: Yeah. When I met her, she was teaching art. She tried to goof off by getting a sucker like me to talk to her class—but it backfired! [*laughter*] But she always wanted to be a writer, in fact, her first professional writing was for *Career World,* and the subject was Michael T. Gilbert and Mr. Monster… before the first issue even came out! Since then, she's written a lot. She's scripted over 1,000 pages of comics at this point, and is one of Egmont's best writers.

CBA: *But unfortunately, a lot of Americans haven't seen that work?*

Michael: Yeah, occasionally some of that stuff will get reprinted in some of the Gladstone comics, but currently, there aren't any Gladstone *Donald Duck* and *Mickey Mouse* comics, so it's real hard to do it—but she's a very talented writer.

CBA: *I notice Janet wrote much in Kelly. I enjoyed the banter in that.*

Michael: She's got a real good ear for dialogue. In fact, it's good because she's helped me get my writing better and more precise.

CBA: *Helps you write gooder.*

Michael: Yes, "gooder." [*laughter*] And I've helped make her stories more visual, so we help each other out.

The Newest, Absolutely, Positively Coolest Mr. Monster Checklist Ever!

One Darn Thorough Listing of All of Doc Stearn's Appearances to Date

Compiled by Marc H. Cawiezel & Jon B. Cooke

[EDITOR'S NOTE: *If anyone's suffered my diatribes on how I'll never devote an issue of CBA to comic book characters but only to creators and publishers—real people above fantasy folk—a definitive checklist on Michael T. Gilbert's trademark super-hero may seem oddly out of place in these pages. But you'll just have to forgive me as I think Mr. Monster is just the most fun muscle-bound palooka ever conceived (though Plastic Man is my favorite rubberized hero!). Plus a perusal of the credits reveal contributions by an eclectic bunch certainly worthy of note. Note that all referenced interviews discuss Mr. Monster. The following was derived from Marc H. Cawiezel's exhaustive list as submitted by MTG, updated and expanded by yours truly, and fact-checked and revised by MTG.* **Please note this listing has been revised and expanded by MTG and myself for its appearance here in CBA Coll., Vol. 3.—JBC.**]

A-1 Book 2, 1989. MM cover (John Bolton); "…The Absolutely, Positively Coolest Mr. Monster Story Ever," MTG, Dave Dorman, 10 pgs. Atomeka Press (British).

A1 Sketchbook 3333, 2004. Pin-ups, 3pgs., John Bolton, Rufus & Alex Horley. Atomeka.

A-1 True Life Bikini Confidential #1/A-1 Special Book Vol. 1, #1, 1990. MM cover; "Mr. Monster in the Dumps," MTG, 8 pgs. Atomeka.

Airboy #28, Aug. 18, 1987: Cover mention, back-up prologue leads into *Airboy-Mr. Monster Special*, Mark Pacella, 11 pgs. Eclipse Comics.

Airboy-Mr. Monster Special #1, Aug. 1987. MM cover (Mark Pacella); Marc Pacella/Ken Hooper, 28 pgs. Eclipse Comics.

Alter Ego Vol. 3, (45 issues to date) 1999-present. MTG's comics obscura column, "Mr. Monster's Comic Crypt" is featured in every issue of *A/E* (a magazine/fanzine about the history of comics), which usually includes new MM artwork (and often short MM narratives) by MTG. TwoMorrows.

Amazing Heroes #53, 1984. MTG interview. Fantagraphics.

Amazing Heroes #77, Aug. 15, 1985. MM cover (MTG), MTG interview. Fantagraphics.

Amazing Heroes #133, Jan. 15, 1988. MM cover (MTG); preview. Fantagraphics.

Amazing Heroes #164, May 1, '89. Swimsuit Special '89. MM pin-up, MTG, 1 pg. Fantagraphics.

Amazing Heroes #194, Sept. 1991. MM/Captain Sternn cover (MTG/Bernie Wrightson). Fantagraphics.

Amazing Heroes Preview Special #1, Summer 1985. Preview. Fantagraphics.

Amazing Heroes Preview Special #3, Summer 1986. Preview. Fantagraphics.

Amazing Heroes Preview Special #5, Summer 1987. Preview. Fantagraphics.

Amazing Heroes Preview Special #10, June 1990. Preview. Fantagraphics.

Amazing Heroes Swimsuit Special #1, June 1990. MM pin-up, MTG, 1 pg. Fantagraphics.

Amazing Heroes Swimsuit Special #3, June 1992. MM pin-up, MTG, 1 pg. Fantagraphics.

Anything Goes! #1, Oct. 1986. MM intro to non-MM MTG story, MTG, 1 pg. Comics Journal, Inc.

Best of Dark Horse Presents Vol. 1, 1989. MM back cover (MTG); reprints "His World," [*DHP* #14] 12 pgs. Dark Horse Comics.

Best of Dark Horse Presents Vol. 2, 1990. MM back cover (MTG); reprints "Inklings," [*DHP* #28] 10 pgs. Dark Horse Comics.

Blackball Comics #1, Mar. 1995. One-page ad announcing MM newspaper strips intended to run monthly in *Hero Illustrated* and *Blackball Comics*. Blackball Comics.

Black Market #13, 1994. MM cover (MTG); MTG interview. Black Market Productions.

Blast! #1, June 1991. MM cover (Simon Bisley); "Mr. Monster and the Lair of the Lizard Ladies," MTG/Simon Bisley, 7 pgs. John Brown Publishing (British).

Blast! #2, July 1991. Reprints "Mr. Monster and the Demon of Destiny Drive," MTG, 8 pgs. [*MM* #5] John Brown Publishing (British).

Blast! #3, Aug. 1991. Reprints "The Case of the Reluctant Werewolf, Part One," MTG/Bill Loebs, 8 pgs. [*Vanguard Illustrated* #7] John Brown Publishing (British).

Blast! #4, Sept. 1991. Reprints "The Case of the Reluctant Werewolf, Part Two," MTG/Bill Loebs, 8 pgs. [*MM* #1] John Brown Publishing (British).

Blast! #5, Aug. 1991. Reprints "The Case of the Reluctant Werewolf, Part Three," MTG/Bill Loebs, 10 pgs. [*MM* #1] John Brown Publishing (British).

Career World Vol. 13, #7, Mar. 1985. MTG interview. Curriculum Innovations.

Comic Book Artist Vol. 1, #4, Spring 1999. MM back cover (MTG). Actually the "front cover" for the flip-book feature, *Alter Ego*, V. 2, #4. TwoMorrows.

Comic Book Artist Vol.1, #8, May 2000. MTG interview (with MM checklist and plethora of unpublished and rarely-seen art), 19 pgs.

Comics Between the Panels, 1998. MM article. Dark Horse Comics.

Comics Buyer's Guide, Nov. 27, 1992. MM cover (MTG); article. Krause Publications.

Comics Interview #29, 1985. MM cover (MTG); MTG interview. Fictioneer Books.

Comics Interview #73, 1989. Bill Loebs interview with MM art. Fictioneer Books.

Comicscene Vol. 4, #10, Dec. 1989. MM cover (MTG); MTG interview. Starlog Communications.

The Complete Wraith, 1998. MM intro, MTG, 2 pgs. MU Press.

Dark Horse Presents #14, Jan. 1988. MM cover (MTG), inside front cover; "His World," MTG, 12 pgs. Dark Horse Comics.

Dark Horse Presents #20, Aug. 1988. MM cover vignette; "The Thing in Stiff Alley," MTG/MTG & Chuck Wacome, 5 pgs. Dark Horse Comics.

Dark Horse Presents #28, Mar. 1989. "Inklings," MTG, 10 pgs. Dark Horse Comics.

Dark Horse Presents #33, Sept. 1989. MM cover, back cover; "Mr. Monster—The Movie: Dodo Death," Brian Buniak (w/MTG intro page & dialogue assist)/Donnie Jupiter & Brian Buniak, 13 pgs. Dark Horse Comics.

Elvira #138, Oct. 2004. "Party Monster," Frank Strom/Ronn Sutton, 15 pgs. MM parody featuring Captain Creature. Claypool.

Eugene Register-Guard [Oregon], May 4, '90. Entertainment & Arts section cover story. MTG intvw.

Even More Fund Comics, Sept.2004. Six-page crossover between MM and Ronn Sutton and Janet Hetherington's kid hero, 5-Alarm Charlie. MTG/MTG & Sutton. Sky Dog Press.

Fire Sale, 1989. MM intro (partial) to non-MM MTG story, MTG, 1 pg. Rip-Off Press.

Guide to Dark Horse Comics, 1996. Listing and descriptions of MM Dark Horse appearances. Golden Marmot Press.

Heavy Metal Vol 16, #11, July 1992. Reprints "Mr. Monster and the Lair of the Lizard Ladies," MTG/Simon Bisley, 7 pgs. [*Blast!* #1]. Metal Mammoth, Inc.

Hero Illustrated #11, May 1994. MM cover (MTG). Mini-poster insert with MM "interview," MTG. Warrior Publications.

Lee's Bullshoot Bulletins #22, 1986. MM cover (MTG); MTG interview. Lee's Comic Book Shop.

Mighty Mites Vol 2, #2, Sept. 1987. MM guest appearance. Eternity Comics.

Mr. Monster #1, Jan. 1985. MM cover (MTG); "The Case of the Reluctant Werewolf, Chapters One-Three," MTG/William F. Loebs, 26 pgs. [Reprints Chapter One from *Vanguard Illustrated* #7]. Eclipse Comics.

Mr. Monster #2, Aug. 1995. MM cover (Dave Stevens); "The Hemo Horror," MTG/Bill Loebs, 26 pgs. Eclipse Comics.

Mr. Monster #3, Oct.1985. MM cover (Stephen R. Bissette); "The Riddle of the Recalcitrant Refuse," Alan Moore/MTG/W.F. Loebs, 16 pgs.; "Prologue," MTG, 1 pg.; MM subscription pitch, MTG, 1 pg.; Eclipse Comics.

Mr. Monster #4, Dec. 1985. MM cover (Jeff Bonivert); MM prologue, MTG, 5 pgs.; "No Escape from Dimension X," MTG/Jeff Bonivert, 7 pgs.; MM epilogue, MTG, 3 pgs.; "Mr. Monster's Hi-Octane Horror," MTG, 2 pgs. Eclipse Comics.

Mr. Monster #5, Feb. 1986. MM cover (MTG); "The Demon of Destiny Drive," MTG, 8 pgs.; "The Yellow Death," William Messner Loebs, 7 pgs.; MM pin-up, MTG; "The Invaders from Mars?," MTG, 6 pgs. Eclipse Comics.

Mr. Monster #6, June 1986. MM cover (Don Simpson); "Bubble Bath of the Damned," MTG/Brian Buniak/Don Simpson, 10 pgs.; MM intro, MTG, 1 pg.; "The Olde Curiosity Shoppe," MTG/Keith Giffen, 10 pgs. Eclipse Comics.

Mr. Monster #7, Dec. 1986. MM cover (MTG); "Mr. Monster's Bedtime Stories," MTG/Mark Pacella, 13 pgs.; "The One Who Lurks," Randall A. Frew/MTG/Mark Pacella, 12 pgs. Eclipse Comics.

Mr. Monster #8, Mar. 1987. MM cover (MTG); "Automatic Terror Machine," MTG/Mark Pacella, 17 pgs.; "On The Job," Scott Deschaine/MTG/Bill Wray, 8 pgs. Eclipse Comics.

Mr. Monster #9, Apr. 1987. MM cover (MTG); "Mr. Monster's Vacation," Greg Georgas/MTG/Gerald Forton, 16 pgs.; "Guilty as Hell," Batton Lash/MTG, 8 pgs. Eclipse Comics.

Mr. Monster #10, June 1987. MM cover (MTG); "Mr. Monster's Atomic Condenser," MTG/Marc Pacella, 10 pgs.; "Terror in 6-D," MTG/Don Simpson/Ray Zone, 15 pgs. Eclipse Comics.

Mr. Monster Vol. 2, #1, Feb. 1988. MTG/Dorman cover; frontispiece, MTG, 1 pg.; "Origins," 25 pgs. (includes reprint, "The New Adventures of Doc Stearne as Mr. Monster," Fred Kelly [*Triumph Comics* #31]). Dark Horse Comics.

Mr. Monster Vol. 2, #2, Apr. 1988. MM cover (MTG); frontispiece, MTG, 1 pg.; "Origins, Chapter Two," MTG, 25 pgs. (includes reprint, "The Terror of Trezma," Fred Kelly, 8 pgs. [*Super-Duper Comics* #3]); "Mr. Gilbert Has His Day in Night Court," Brian Buniak, 1 pg. Dark Horse Comics.

Mr. Monster Vol. 2, #3, June 1988. MM cover (MTG); frontispiece, MTG, 1 pg.; "Origins, Chapter Three," MTG, 17 pgs.; reprint, "Doc Stearne," Fred Kelly, 7 pgs. [*Commando Comics* #21]; "Mr. Gilbert Has His Day in Night Court," Brian Buniak, 1 pg. Dark Horse Comics.

Mr. Monster Vol. 2, #4, Nov. 1988. MM cover (MTG); "Origins, Chapter 4," 18 pgs.; prologue, Mike McCarthy, 1 pg.; "Cadavera," Janet Clark/Mike McCarthy, 8 pgs.; Kelly pin-up, Stu Hoffman, 1 pg. Dark Horse Comics.

Mr. Monster Vol. 2, #5, Mar. 1989. MM cover (MTG); frontispiece, MTG/Tom Sutton, 1 pg.; "Origins, Chapter Five," MTG, 23 pgs.; MM pin-up, Alan Moore, 1 pg. Dark Horse Comics.

Mr. Monster Vol. 2, #6, Oct. 1989. MM cover (MTG); frontispiece, MTG/Tom Sutton, 1 pg.; "Origins, Chapter Six," MTG, 22 pgs. Dark Horse Comics.

Mr. Monster Vol. 2, #7, Apr. 1990. MM cover (MTG); frontispiece, MTG, 1 pg.; "Origins, Chapter Seven," MTG, 27 pgs.; MM pin-up, Kim & Simon Deitch, 1 pg. Dark Horse Comics.

Mr. Monster Vol. 2, #8. MM Cover (MTG); "Origins, Chapter 8" MTG, 48 pgs.; MM tryout, Bill Loebs, 1 pg. Dark Horse Comics.

Mr. Monster Ashcan Comics #1, July 1994. MM cover (MTG); MM previews: Excerpts upcoming MM projects "Mr. Monster vs. The Nazis From Mars," *Crack-A-Boom!*, *Kelly*. Digest-size, 16 pgs. Yellow & black covers. Gilbert Studios.

Mr. Monster Attacks! #1, Aug. 1992. MM cover (MTG/Dave Dorman); "Black and White and Dead All Over," MTG, 9 pgs.; "Prologue," MTG, 1 pg.; "Wish You Were Here," MTG/Dave Gibbons, 9 pgs. Tundra Publishing.

Mr. Monster Attacks #2, 1992. MM cover (MTG/Dave Dorman); "Monster Boy," Bob Supina, 1 pg.; "Menace Of The Space Zombies," MTG/Sam Keith, 2 pgs.; "Monster's Night Out," Scott Deschaine/ Bob Donovan, 4 pgs.; "Mr. Monster at The Movies," Ken Bruzenak, 5 pgs.; reprints "Mr. Monster In The Dumps," MTG, 8 pgs. [*A-1 Special Book* #1]; MM pin-up, Brian Buniak, 2 pgs.; back cover MTG/Bernie Wrightson. Tundra Publishing.

Mr. Monster Attacks! #3, 1992. MM cover (MTG/Dave Dorman), back cover (John Bolton); reprints "Mr. Monster and the Lair of the Lizard Ladies," MTG/Simon Bisley, 7 pgs. [*Blast!* #1]; Kelly,"Just Desserts," Janet Gilbert/Tom Buss, 9 pgs.; MM pin-up, Lyndal Ferguson, 1 pg.; reprints "…The Absolutely, Positively Coolest Mr. Monster Story Ever," MTG/Dave Dorman, 10 pgs. [*A-1 Book* 2]; MTG/Dave Gibbons, 9 pgs. Tundra Publishing.

Mr. Monster: His Books of Forbidden Knowledge, Vol. 1, 1996. MM cover (MTG); reprints stories from *Mr. Monster* #1-5, 121 pgs. Marlowe & Company.

Mr. Monster: His Books of Forbidden Knowledge, Vol. Zero, 2001. MM cover (MTG); self-described "part scrapbook, part memoir, part who-knows-what" collection of MM unused art, a couple of new stories and other previously unpublished material, esoterica, and hard-to-find tales. Introduction by George Evans; "Never Touch a Satan Glass," MTG/MTG & Keith Giffen, 8 pgs.; "Ooook," MTG/MTG & Mark Martin, 9 pgs.; "Midnight Snack," MTG, 1pg.; MM Sunday funnies, newspaper strips & promos, MTG, 12 pgs.; MM "Creature Alphabet" by Ken Bruzenak & MTG; MM pin-ups by George Evans, Sam Glanzman, Paul Chadwick, Denis Kitchen, Paco Rodriques, & MTG. Reprints "His World," MTG, 12 pgs. [*Dark Horse Presents* #14]; "The Thing in Stiff Alley," MTG/MTG & Chuck Wacome, 5 pgs. [*DHP* #20]; "Inklings," MTG & Terry Beatty/MTG & Terry Beatty, 10 pgs. [*DHP* #28]; "Mr. Monster—The Movie: Dodo Death," Brian Buniak (w/MTG intro page & dialogue assist)/Donnie Jupiter & Brian Buniak, 13 pgs. [*DHP* #33]; "L'il Doc: Eel's Well That Ends Well," MTG, 6 pgs [*Mr. Monster Presents (Crack-A-Boom!)* #2]; "The Collector," MTG/Kerry Talbott, 12 pgs. [*MMP* #1]; "Mr. Monster in the Dumps," MTG, 8 pgs. [*A-1 True Life Bikini Confidential* #1;]; MM "interview," MTG, 2 pgs. [*Hero Illustrated* #11]; *Mr. Monster Ashcan Comics* #1 cover reprint, MTG; *Scary Monsters* #10 cover reprint, MTG; 136 pgs. TwoMorrows.

Mr. Monster Mini-Bust 2003, by Randy Bowen, designed by MTG. Bowen Designs.

Mr. Monster: Origins, 1996. MM cover (MTG/Richard Bruning); reprints *Mr. Monster* Vol. 2, #1-8, with dozens of revised/replaced pages, MTG, 210 pgs. Graphitti Designs.

Mr. Monster Presents (Crack-A-Boom!) #1, 1997. MM cover vignette, MM inside front cover; "The Collector," MTG/Kerry Talbott, 12 pgs. [other stories include MM cameos.] Caliber Comics.

Mr. Monster Presents (Crack-A-Boom!) # 2, July 1997. MM cover (MTG/Batton Lash); MM intro, MTG, 1 pg.; "Li'l Doc," MTG, 6 pgs., MM intro, MTG/Mike McCarthy, 1 pg. Caliber Comics.

Mr. Monster Presents (Crack-A-Boom!) # 3, Sept 1997. MM cover (MTG/Bob Supina); "Mr. Monster Meets Monster Boy," MTG/Bob Supina, 2pgs.; MM intro, MTG, 1 pg. Caliber Comics.

Mr. Monster Collector's Pack, 1994. Signed, numbered limited edition repackaging Eclipse's *Mr. Monster* #4-10 with original MM thumbnail sketch. Gilbert Studios.

Mr. Monster's Gal Friday… Kelly #1, Jan 2000. MM cover (MTG); frontispiece, MTG/Tom Buss; "Temporary Insanity," Janet Gilbert/MTG/Tom Buss, 10 pgs.; "Ask Doc" MTG, 1 pg.; "I Married A Monster," Janet Gilbert/MTG/Shawn McManus 18 pgs.; "Kelly's Recipe Page," Janet Gilbert/MTG/Tom Buss; back cover MTG/Trina Robbins. Image Comics.

Mr. Monster's Gal Friday… Kelly #2, March 2000. MM cover (MTG); frontispiece, MTG; Intro page MTG; "Meet Mary Monster," MTG/Tom Buss, 11 pgs.; intro, MTG/Mark Pacella, 1 pg.; "Suspicious Minds," Janet Gilbert/MTG/Shane Glines, 5 pgs.; intro, MTG/Ed Quimby, 1 pg.; "A Wolf In Wolf's Clothing," MTG/Scott Deschaine, 6 pgs.; "Kelly's Recipe Page," Janet Gilbert/MTG/Tom Buss; back cover, Trina Robbins. Image Comics.

Mr. Monster's Gal Friday… Kelly #3, May 2000. MM Cover (MTG); "Kelly's Recipe Page," Janet Gilbert/MTG/Tom Buss; intro, MTG/Ronn Sutton, 1 pg.; "It's Kelly's Boyfriend… Mr. Monster" Alan Moore/Alan Smith/Pete Williamson, 12 pgs.; intro, MTG/Mark Pacella, 1 pg.; "File 'M' For Monster," Janet Gilbert/MTG/Shane Glines, 3 pgs.; "The Sinister Slumber Party From Alpha Centauri," MTG, 11 pgs.; "The Space Chix"/"No Glory," MTG, 1 pg.; pin-up, Alex Toth; back cover, Trina Robbins. Image Comics.

Mr. Monster Special #1/Mr. Monster: Worlds Wars Two (a.k.a. "Mr. Monster vs. the Nazis from Mars"), Oct 2004. Reprints *Penthouse Max* #3, MTG/George Freeman, Ken Bruzenak & Laurie Smith, 48 pgs. Atomeka.

Mr. Monster Special #2/Mr. Monster: Who Watches the Garbagemen, March 2005. MTG/Alex Horley cover. "Babs: File M For Monster," Janet Gilbert & MTG/Shane Glines, 3 pgs.; "Revenge Of The Boneless Man," MTG, 10 pgs.; reprints "Riddle Of The Reluctant Refuse," Alan Moore/MTG & Bill Loebs (recolored), 16 pgs [*MM* #3]; "The Olde Curiosity Shoppe," Keith Giffen/MTG, 10 pgs. [*MM* #6]; "Wish You Were Here," MTG/Dave Gibbons, 9 pgs. [*MM Attacks!* #1]. Atomeka.

Mr. Monster Special #3/Mr. Monster: Swamp Zombies and Space Cases!, May 2005. MTG/Alex Horley cover. "Never Touch A Satan Glass," MTG/Keith Giffen, 8 pgs. Reprints "Menace Of The Space Zombies," MTG/Sam Kieth, 10 pgs. [*MM Attacks!* #2]; "Lair Of The Lizard Ladies," MTG/Simon Bisley, 7 pgs. [*Blast!* #1]; "The Collector," MTG/Kerry Talbott, 12 pgs. [*MM Presents* #1]; "His World," MTG, 12 pgs. [*Dark Horse Presents* #14]. Atomeka.

Mr. Monster's Super-Duper Special #1/Mr. Monster's 3-D Hi-Octane Horror #1, May 1986. MM cover (MTG); "Mr. Monster's 3-D Hi-Octane Horror," MTG/Mike Mignola, 3 pgs. epilogue, MTG/Mike Mignola, 1 pg. Eclipse Comics.

Mr. Monster's Super-Duper Special #2/Mr. Monster's Hi-Octane Horror #1, Aug. 1986. MM cover (MTG); "Mr. Monster's Hi-Octane Horror," MTG, 2 pgs.; epilogue, MTG, 1 pg. Eclipse Comics.

Mr. Monster's Super-Duper Special #3/Mr. Monster's True Crime #1, Sept. 1986. MM cover vignette (MTG); MM intro, 1 pg. Eclipse Comics.

Mr. Monster's Super-Duper Special #4/Mr. Monster's True Crime #2, Nov. 1986. MM cover vignette (MTG); MM intro, MTG, 1 pg. Eclipse Comics.

Mr. Monster's Super-Duper Special #5/Mr. Monster's Hi-Voltage Super Science #1, Jan. 1987.

MM cover vignette (MTG); "Postscript," MTG, 1 pg.; "Mr. Monster's High Shock Shlock," Fred Hembeck, 2 pgs. Eclipse Comics.

Mr. Monster's Super-Duper Special #6/Mr. Monster's Hi-Shock Schlock #1, Mar. 1987. MM cover (MTG); "Prologue," MTG, 2 pgs.; "Mr. Monster's High Shock Shlock," Fred Hembeck, 2 pgs. Eclipse Comics.

Mr. Monster's Super-Duper Special #7/Mr. Monster's Hi-Shock Schlock #2, May 1987. MM cover (MTG); "Hi-Shock Prologue," MTG, 3 pgs. Eclipse Comics.

Mr. Monster's Super-Duper Special #8/Mr. Monster's Weird Tales of the Future #1, July 1987. "Prologue," MTG/Monte Wolverton, 2 pgs. Eclipse.

Mr. Monster Triple-Threat 3-D, July, 1993. MM cover (MTG); Single-page pin ups, MTG, Tom Sutton, Fred Kelly, Bill Loebs, Terry Beatty, Alan Moore, Paul Chadwick, Paul Ollswang, Brian Buniak, Denis Kitchen, Kim & Simon Deitch, Jeff Bonivert, Dave Stevens, Mike McCarthy; "Tiny Terror Tales," MTG, 4 pgs.; back cover Lyndal Ferguson. Gilbert Studios/Ray Zone.

Mr. Monster vs. Gorzilla, July 1998. MM cover (MTG); "Mr. Monster Goes to Japan," Ken Bruzenak/MTG, 23 pgs. Image Comics.

Ms. Tree #50, July 1989. MM pin-up, MTG, 1 pg. Renegade Press.

Penthouse Max #3, 1997. MM wraparound (Dave Dorman); "Mr. Monster vs. the Nazis from Mars," MTG/George Freeman, 48 pgs. General Media.

Previews Vol. 4, #1, Jan. 1994. Blackball Comics crossover serial. MM/Trencher, Keith Giffen, 1 pg. Diamond Distribution.

Previews Vol. 4, #2, Feb. 1994. Blackball Comics crossover serial. MM/Trencher, MTG, 2 pgs. Diamond Distribution.

Scary Monsters #10, Mar. 1994. MM inside front & back cover (MTG); MTG interview [some issues include inserted trading card "Scare Card/Horror Comic Book Legend Promo Card #1" featuring MM by MTG]. Druktenis Publishing.

Scream Factory #19, Summer 1997. MM cover (MTG); MM overview by Charles Hatfield. [Cover mention of MTG interview and original art but none found inside.] Deadline Press.

Sharky #4, 1997. MM cameo, Dave Elliott/Alex Horley. Image Comics.

Silverfish Mini-Comic #1, December 1995. MM Cover (Bjob Craig/John Q. Adams); "Silverfish" Bjob Craig and John Q. Adams, 24 pgs. [Fan publication, MM cameo.] Cryin' Shark Studios.

Sin #1, Dec 1993. MM cover cameo (Jay Stephens). Black Eye Productions.

Speakeasy #114, Oct. 1990. MTG interview, 3 pgs. John Brown Publishing (British).

Super-Duper Comics #3, May 1947. "The Terror of Trezma," [Second and final appearance Fred Kelly's Golden Age MM] Fred Kelly, 8 pgs. Bell Publishing (Canadian).

Tales of the Terminal Diner, 2003. "Square Eggs," MTG, 6 pgs. (horror story narrated by MM). Sonic Comics.

1313 Magazine #3, Dec. 2004. MTG interview (discusses MM).

Thunder-Bunny #4, 1985. Panel cameo, Marty Greim/Gary Kato/Brian Buniak. Warp.

Too Much Coffee Man #9, Apr. 2000. Pin-up (MM & Too Much Coffee Man), MTG.

Total Eclipse Book Three, Dec. 1988. MM inside back cover vignette (MTG), character profile; "Mr. Monster," Marv Wolfman/Marc Pacella, 2 pgs. Eclipse Comics.

Trencher: X-Mas Bites 1994 Holiday Blow-Out Comic #1, Dec.1993. Holiday greeting/comic strip, MTG, 1 pg. Blackball Comics.

Triumph Comics #31, 1946. "The New Adventures of Doc Stearne as Mr. Monster," [First appearance Fred Kelly's Golden Age MM] Fred Kelly, 7pgs. Bell Publishing (Canadian).

USA #64, 1992. Reprints "Mr. Monster and the Lair of the Lizard Ladies," Simon Bisley, 7 pgs. [*Blast!* #1]. (French)

Vanguard Illustrated #7, July 1984. "The Case of the Reluctant Werewolf" [Chapter one, first appearance MTG's MM], MTG/William F. Loebs, 8 pgs. Pacific Comics.

Wacky Squirrel Halloween Adventure #1, October, 1987. MM Cover (Jim Bradrick); Wacky Squirrel, Jim Bradrick, with 5-page MM crossover [MM illos by MTG], 24 pgs.

Wolff & Byrd #1, Feb. 1997. MM pin-up, MTG, 1 pg. Exhibit A Press.

Worlds of Horror #1, Sept.1988. MTG interview. Eclectic Publishing.

Below: Blackball Comics promo poster. All ©2005 their respective copyright holders.

Right: *MTG's cover art for an issue of The Frying Pan, a pro-APA zine. Courtesy of & ©2005 M.T. Gilbert*

Below: *Scream Factory #19 (Summer '97) cover art by MTG. Courtesy of and ©2005 Michael T. Gilbert*

Above: *MTG's pencils for the upcoming Mr. Monster Special #3. Alex Horley will render the finished painting.*
Below: *MTG drew this for Mr. Monster fan Harlan Ellison after an earthquake hit the author's California home in '94. Both courtesy of and ©2005 M.T. Gilbert.*

This page, clockwise from left: *This Mr. Monster bookplate was drawn by MTG specially for Bud Plant's illustrated book and comic art catalog. Cover design for the never-realized Mr. Monster Annual. Look for a discussion of the aborted Mr. Monster vs. Swamp Thing — and the project it mutated into, the realized MM vs. The Heap/Airboy Special — in Ye Ed and George Khoury's forthcoming TwoMorrows book, Swampmen: Muck-Monsters of the Comics in Summer, '05! Another Bud Plant bookplate. Uncle Scrooge artist Don Rosa drew up this version of Mr. Monster. ©2005 Don Rosa. All other illos and Mr.Monster ©2005 Michael T. Gilbert.*

This page, clockwise from left: MTG tells us that the first computer-colored comic book story ever appeared in Mr. Monster #5 (Eclipse, Feb. '86), "Rot," a four-page tale drawn by Jeff Bonivert and colored by Steve Oliff. MTG called the process "Terror-Chroma" and pitched the idea of the world's first computer-colored comic with this cover rough. Eclipse passed... Mr. Monster intro page. Ramona Fradon's cool rendition of the Monster Killer(©2005 R.F.), and the unused Mr. Monster 3-D cover. All courtesy of MTG and ©2005 Michael T. Gilbert.

DOC STEARN'S
Mr.MONSTER

This spread: *From soup to nuts, the creative process behind a Michael T. Gilbert collaboration with artist Dave Gibbons, "Wish You Were Here," Mr. Monster Attacks! #1 (Aug. '92).*
Opposite page, clockwise from upper left: *The only aspect missing from this look at how a Mr. Monster page is created is the tissue-overlay which was placed over this MTG rough. Then Dave Gibbon's thumbnail was sent for approval, soon followed by Dave's pencils. (MTG's design suggestion for the story's antagonist, an alien tourist completes this page).*
This page, clockwise from right: *Dave's inked page. Dave Dorman's cover art for Mr. Monster Attacks! #1. The final page, reproduced directly from the Tundra comic book. Finally, a wee mini-self caricature of MTG. All courtesy of Michael T. Gilbert. Gilbert art and Mr. Monster ©2005 Michael T. Gilbert. Gibbons art ©2005 Dave Gibbons.*

DON'T FORGET, MR. MONSTER FANS!
Doc Stearn is coming back in a big way in 2005, courtesy of Dave Elliot's revived Atomeka Press! Look for three volumes of 48-page Mr. Monster Specials, all with boffo cover paintings by the terrifying talented Alex Horley! Tell 'em CBA sent ya! (And many thanks to Michael T. who contributed in huge fashion for the material he loaned us this time. Sure, we're monster fans of Michael's character over here at Casa CBA, but our real hero worship is for the big guy himself, MTG!)

Ken Bruzenak: Superstar!
The art of design and typography in comic books

PUBLISHER'S NOTE:
Due to editorial considerations, the following interview was edited from its original appearance in Comic Book Artist #8.

Conducted by Jon B. Cooke
Transcribed by Jon B. Knutson

While Ken Bruzenak may have gotten his start as a protegé of the legendary Jim Steranko, his star rose when readers began taking note of his lettering and logowork contributions to Howard Chaykin's American Flagg! in the 1980s. Through exposure in that title, Ken's exceptional custom logo design work—so integral to the strip's futuristic, trademark-littered ambiance—was soon to be found in Michael T. Gilbert's Mr. Monster stories and on projects throughout the industry. Sure, calling Ken a "superstar," may be slightly tongue-in-cheek, but the letterer was, for a time, the most highly-regarded in the field, with even casual readers beginning to recognize his name. This interview (surprisingly, his first) was done by phone on February 4, 2000, and was copy-edited by Ken.

Comic Book Artist: *Have you done interviews before?*
Ken Bruzenak: I've conducted them, but I've never been the subject of one.
CBA: *Where are you from?*
Ken: A little town called Finleyville, Pennsylvania.
CBA: *When were you born?*
Ken: August 30, 1952.
CBA: *Did you have an interest in comics early on?*
Ken: I'm trying to remember my first comic: I think it was an

Below: Howard Chaykin's cover to the 1983 Chicago Comicon program book with lettering by Ken Bruzenak, featuring American Flagg! ©2000 Howard Chaykin.

Opposite page, top: Bruzenak's lettering on a Mr. Monster ad.

80-Page Giant, the one with the giant Superman on the Empire State Building. Then "Sgt. Rock" in Our Army at War, the Kubert material... The flying dinosaurs and the like were powerful and I was about 10 or so.
CBA: *Did you get into fandom at all early on?*
Ken: No, I didn't know about fandom when I started reading the Marvel books. I picked up Fantastic Four around #30 or so, and probably within a year, Steranko had arrived on the scene, and then I sent to Howard Rogofsky for back issues of a couple of Jim's "Nick Fury" books.
CBA: *Were you a comics collector?*
Ken: Oh, yeah. I was collecting runs of "Sgt. Rock" and FF, Thor, Captain America. The Kirby books really intrigued me. Avengers. Al Williamson's Flash Gordon.
CBA: *Did you think about a career in comics?*
Ken: At that point, no. We're talking early teens, so I didn't know what I wanted to do.
CBA: *Did you draw?*
Ken: Badly. [laughs] Horribly. I did the usual tanks and submarines, war stuff. Airplanes; but not very well.

CBA: *Were you interested in other aspects of collectibles, like Famous Monsters?*
Ken: Pulps. Doc Savage and The Shadow. Operator #5.
CBA: *How did you get exposed to that?*
Ken: The Doc Savage paperbacks. I picked up the Doc Savage where he's shooting bats on the cover, #6. They were coming out—at one point—twice a month, and I was really getting quite a mainline of Doc Savage there for a couple of years, scouring the newsstands, getting the old ones. I was really into Doc for maybe the first 70-80 books that came out. And from that, I got into the Tarzan material—all the Burroughs' material, the Mars books, Camille Cazedessus' ERBDom, Fred Cooke's Bronze Shadows. I got letters from Walter Baumhoffer, Tom Lovell and James Bama.
CBA: *Did you get into Robert E. Howard?*
Ken: Yeah, Conan. Conan went kind of fast, because there wasn't that much material. Then Solomon Kane, Kull, Bran Mak Morn and Breckenridge Elkins—that's what I remember out of Howard... it's a small body of work.
CBA: *Did you get into horror, too, such as H.P. Lovecraft?*
Ken: Not Lovecraft. The Corinth paperbacks were coming out, with Dr. Death, though. I loved Dr. Death! I've been tracking down the two or three unpublished novels. I think I've got most of the material, but I'm missing the first few chapters of one of the unpublished novels, and it's driving me crazy, because I can't read the story yet without getting those chapters!
CBA: *What was Dr. Death?*
Ken: It was just whacked-out pulp from 1936 or '37 that lasted three issues. He was just hell-bent on overthrowing the government of the United States and taking over the world. Dr. Death was the villain of the book, and the hero just kept foiling him every month. Death did stuff like magic and the occult and zombies, resurrected millions of Egyptian mummies... I think it was written by Fred Z. Ward under the pseudonym of "Zorro." It was just really far-out pulp stuff, like poisoning postage stamps, and shrinking the Vice-President of the United States down to the size of a Ken doll, stuffing him inside a shoebox and delivering it to the Senate.
CBA: *All right!* [laughter]
Ken: It's not quite as good as The Octopus, where there are troops driving through the streets at night, throwing live people into garbage trucks and grinding them up. [laughter] Dr. Death had its naive charm. It's why I can't get real bent out of shape by anything I see in movies. "Eh, been there, read that." [laughter]
CBA: *Did you recognize the cheesiness of the pulps pretty quickly? After my fourth Doc Savage novel—I tended to collect them for Bama's covers—Robeson would use phrases like "the piano-wire chest," over and over again. It became all the same.*
Ken: I was probably in sixth grade, seventh grade when I started reading that. It was still new to me. I really bought what was being sold there as good adventure writing. Then, the sameness did start to pile up, but by then, I was out of Doc Savage and into Tarzan. By the time you finish 24 Tarzan novels you realize right around Tarzan #11 that it's like, "Okay, I know the schtick here." But it's still interesting: It's like reading Tom Clancy novels. I've read probably all the Tom Clancy I need to read, same with Stephen King, but there's still a seductive quality about their writing. When I'm done with a new Clancy or King, it's like, "Was that worth two months? Probably not, but it was a fun ride," and that's kind of the way I was into the pulps as a teenager. I look at them now—I tried to read The Shadow last year sometime, and I couldn't get into that frame of mind again, I

couldn't have as much fun with it. Pulp writing is definitely a matter of time and place in your life. If you're ready for it, man, it is fun! You know what you're getting.

CBA: *Do you think it's the same security of like when you're a little kid, and you read the same Dr. Seuss book over and over, and you always requested the same story over and over for your parents to read, there's that same security in reading pulps? I was attracted as a youngster to serial books, I started off with the* Dr. Dolittle *series and one of the main things I was into was there was always another one coming, I could always get another one after that one, and the saga was never really over.*

Ken: Definitely. I still find myself doing that. If I see a book on the newsstand, I look to see if the author has written anything before or after this one, using the same characters. It's like, "If I enjoy this, can I get more?" [*laughter*] I'll go into a used book store and buy stuff for 50¢ or 75¢ and I'll just get into this little mental dialog, "Oh, look, there's six Clive Cusslers. I can get the first five or six of the Dirk Pitt novels, and try them out," and I'll buy all five or six! I won't buy one as a test. I'll get them all, because when I'm done, I can immediately dive into the next one!

CBA: *Do you think we're ill?* [*laughs*]

Ken: Absolutely! The thing I do notice—I just got a DC freebie package today, and I was going through it, and it struck me how I don't have that feeling about comics anymore. I don't look for a book to be there every month, as something I'm anticipating.

CBA: *You're looking for something that stands up on its own?*

Ken: No, I'm just saying I can't find that comforting reliability anymore. I can't trust Batman to be Batman every month, so I don't look out for or save or collect *Batman*. The characters are now less important than the celebrity artists and writers. Batman and Superman often don't behave like Batman and Superman anymore, and that's a little disturbing. I blame Miller and his *Dark Knight* books. [*laughs*] But I'm only half joking.

Back when writers and artists were locked onto books for years, you had genuine personality investment by the talent, and a kind of integrity in how characters developed. Even the Bizarro Superman had an internal logic, because he was thought out by Binder and Siegel and Weisinger—maybe as a joke—but still, conceptually developed. When you start changing the artist every four issues, as they do today, you change the tone, the look, you change everything about the comic. And the writer and editor cannot force their vision to override those visual changes. Alan Moore and Chris Claremont are two of the few guys who can almost overcome changes in artists, but even they cannot make up for conflicting interests in panel size and selection, or emphasis on what is shown. If Alan and Chris are working with Steve Bissette or John Byrne on *Swamp Thing* or *X-Men*, you have a finite group of *Swamp Things* by Steve Bissette and *X-Men* by John Byrne—and as soon as somebody else takes over, you've broken the run, and neither book is the same anymore. Most of the intimate character development and personality definition flows from the artists' attitudes in posing, angles, shot selection, lighting… which changes from artists to artist. It's something I know that writers do not enjoy….

CBA: *What, the change of artists?*

Ken: The fact that they're always going to be subservient to the art in a comic book. It's a painful reality for the writers, but it is there. You can go back to when Roy Thomas was writing *The Avengers*, and John Buscema was drawing it, and as soon as John dropped out of that book, and Sal took over, it was a different book. Roy was writing straight through that whole period, the continuity was there, the drawing was even superficially similar. But Roy couldn't carry it alone, he couldn't bridge the transition, because the art is always the focal point of comic books. It's the same thing with everybody. When Jack Kirby left Marvel, the *FF* and *Thor* were not the same *FF* and *Thor*, even though Stan remained as writer.

CBA: *That could also be tied to that aspect of the Marvel style, that half the storytelling, if not more, was done by the artist. Gil Kane would always complain he was doing two jobs.*

Ken: Yeah, he was. But it's more than that. It's about the balance of power on the page. Even when Buscema was trying his hardest to become Kirby on those *FFs* and *Thors*, he couldn't, and Stan couldn't, either. The whole essence of material just completely

changed… you didn't have that "whacked-out, anything can happen" Kirby provided. Buscema was much more stately and poised. I have an enormous amount of respect for what John did on those books, I just think he was in a real tough spot—a terrible spot for an artist to be in. He was the best guy Marvel had, and to put him in that spot was very cruel, actually. [*laughter*] It was, "You're the best guy we've got, be somebody else."

CBA: *"Follow Kirby."*

Ken: "*Be* Kirby!" John had his own style… those *Avengers* that John did with Roy that Tom Palmer was inking were superb. I mean, he didn't deserve to be crushed down like that… and those *Silver Surfers*, John really, really put himself out there. It's like Marvel just stamped John right out of existence. He couldn't do his best John Buscema anymore. That was a real tragedy in John's career. But it is the way all those great Silver Age *Superman* and *Batman* comics maintained the look and integrity of the characters. It's a real dichotomy of cross purposes in comics… talent versus character stability… and I'm not sure runaway talent is proving to be successful or beneficial in the long run.

CBA: *Okay, you were collecting pulps, and where were you going?*

Ken: I graduated high school at 17, and that was a different problem. I couldn't get a job! I just wasn't old enough to get any kind of real job, and I didn't have anything I was trained for, either.

CBA: *What kind of real job were you looking for?*

Ken: At that point, anything! I graduated high school at 17. You had to be 18 to work, and there really wasn't

Below: *Ken included this comment with this picture of himself and his bride Kristie taken at their very recent wedding: "I know this is just too cute for words, but Chaykin will laugh his ass off. And I do love my wife."*

money for college, so I got a job busing tables at a restaurant until three in the morning, and a few weeks in road construction. I was getting Gary Groth's *Fantastic Fanzine,* and he had the Steranko interview in it, and I was really hot on Steranko's work. What Jim was doing was really taking over comics at that point in time. If you look at the fanzines, everybody was trying to be Steranko with all that feathered muscle work. I went to a Detroit Triple Fanfare, and Jim was there, and I got a chance to talk to him for just a moment, it was nothing major. What I really remember is I bought a Neal Adams double-page spread from the *X-Men,* it was the big Sauron double-page for like $35, and Neal came up to me and did a con job on me, where he really had to have that page, it was his, it was stolen art, so he'd trade me for another page. Because it was Neal Adams, I was like, "Duh!" [*laughter*] "Sure, okay!" So I gave up this really neat double for an average Sentinels page, which I can't complain too much, because many years later, I sold it for like $800. [*laughs*] But think of the Sauron, man! I could've bought a car with it! There were entire issues of Kirby's *FF* originals for sale, too.

CBA: *So was the Detroit Fanfare the first con you attended?*

Ken: It was the first one I went to, and I know Chaykin was there. At that point, Chaykin had a girl on each arm, he was in the movie room at 2:30 in the morning watching *Kelly's Heroes* from under the piano, and there was a smoke haze [*laughter*]. Howard was playing the young *artiste* to the hilt. This was pre-*Cody Starbuck.* Howard was a fanboy, like everybody else. I'm pretty sure that's where Howard and I first crossed paths. And then, a couple of months later, there was a Seuling con in New York. I went there, and Steranko was running a seminar on how to write and draw comic books. He ran it three evenings, from 8 o'clock until 2 in the morning. I still have the folder he prepared. It cost $200. There were eight of us that took this class in a hotel room. We started talking.

CBA: *$200 per participant? Jim was doing all right!*

Ken: Yeah! We're talking 1970 dollars. Jim and I talked comics, and we talked on the phone a few more times, afterward. He'd just bought a three-story row home in Reading, Pennsylvania, and he was starting up SUPERGRAPHICS. He said he was putting the final touches on *The History of Comics Volume Two* at that point, and had this big building that needed renovation. I kind of promoted myself as being able to do painting, fixing up the house, work like that.

CBA: *Were you a handyman?*

Ken: Yeah. I can handle the simple stuff. There's not a lot to patching plaster and painting. Tearing out walls and plumbing are beyond me, but changing a wall socket, changing light figures, putting up ceiling tile, that's not a problem. So I did that, and Jim had brought in Greg Theakston from Detroit.

Theakston was part of the "Detroit Mafia." Jim had brought him in basically for the same type of thing, to work on his house. But Greg had more writing and artistic ambitions, so he was the guy that was going to help Jim on the *History of Comics.* I was going to help fix the house. Unfortunately, Greg wanted a life [*laughter*]—that included girls. Working for Jim, when you're getting up at noon and working until six in the morning, you don't have much of a life. So Greg had problems just bearing down and sticking with it to the extent Jim wanted. I don't think Greg was out of line, and I don't think Greg did anything wrong. Jim demands 150%, and he expects you to produce 175%, and Greg just wasn't in for that. There were also personality conflicts between me and Greg, and I'm trying to keep that in perspective, too. Bottom line: When there's a ton

of work to get done, and you're on a deadline, it's not the time to go to sleep; you just bear down and don't go to sleep for three days. [*laughter*]

CBA: *Why did you decide to work for Steranko? Was the motive that through some osmosis, you were going to assimilate Jim's creative approach?*

Ken: I wanted to learn how to draw, and he said he would give drawing lessons. I can't say he didn't try… He was going to teach Greg and I both how to draw, but that faded into the background, because there was so much work to do on the second volume to the *History of Comics.* It took another year-and-a-half to get that book together, and Jim was really working on it, taking breaks to do paperback paintings for financing.

CBA: *So Vol. One was already completed before you went there?*

Ken: Yeah, it had already come out. Volume Two was two-thirds written. Jim was still doing interviews, still doing copy-editing. I wound up doing a lot of proofreading, and I pasted it up. Greg was not a really good proofreader, and he didn't have the patience to sit there and do paste-ups for hour after hour after stripping wallpaper all day. Jim was still taking photos of the covers… it was a long, drawn-out process. Somewhere in there, Greg sort of disappeared, because Jim wasn't doing comics, and Greg wanted to do comics. Things sort of went in another direction… *Comixscene* was becoming a germ at that point, it started to move into a different area, so Greg just moved out. I think he was there maybe two years.

CBA: *Did seeing and reading Volume One clinch the decision for you to work for Jim? You could see that you were of a like mind, as Jim was obviously very much into the pulps?*

Ken: Oh, yeah.

CBA: *Did you have an interest in the history of the pulps and comics?*

Ken: Yeah, I still have a ton of that worthless history in my skull. [*laughs*] I have all these facts and dates and details about cover painters… being able to recognize Jerome Rosen as opposed to George… that kind of stuff. I did the preliminary research, synopsizing and rough draft writing for about two-thirds of *The History of Comics* Volume Three in the mid-'70s—all the Street & Smith, MLJ, Fox, Hillman, Powell, Meskin, and Biro material. I just don't have a real use for that knowledge anymore. But it was good for me to make that connection with Jim. Even though it didn't go where I wanted it to go, it ultimately went well.

CBA: *Would you characterize it as an apprenticeship?*

Ken: It was definitely an Old World apprenticeship, where you served for so many years, and you learned the craft, you learned the skills… I worked on the first 50 issues of *Comixscene/Prevue,* *FOOM, Chandler, Outland,* posters, and the Doc Savage and Shadow Fan Clubs… Anyway, after about 12 or 13 years, I was…

CBA: *"12 or 13 years"?!?*

Ken: I was there for 12 or 13 years. Greg Theakston, Gary Groth, David McDonnell came and went. I outlasted them all… what a masochist!

CBA: *Did you have a stage of disillusionment that your aspirations weren't being met?*

Ken: Right around year eight. [*laughs*] Seven or eight, yes.

CBA: *Were you under the influence of narcotics beforehand? [laughter]*

Ken: I was a different person. I did not have the greatest of childhoods, and this plugged into it, and the work ethic was definitely in me, but it was very warped. And I was learning. I was really being pushed. I was learning production. I was learning lettering, type. I was running a stat camera, writing, editing. I had 50 jobs. I was doing stuff that, when I look on my resume now, it's like, "Holy sh*t!" [*laughs*]

CBA: *You're accomplished! [laughter]*

Ken: I have got so much background, and I remember—I'm skipping time here—but I remember when I started lettering comics, it was like, "Wow! I'm getting paid so much more money, and it's so easy! I'm not having to sit up five days straight to meet a press date!" And I did! You know, when press time was upon us, we were doing 24, 36, 48-hour days regularly. Stay up 48 hours, sleep six, stay up another 36… that was "normal."

CBA: *One of the quotes from Gary Groth's interview with Peter*

Bagge in I Like Comics *said that he remembered you living a monastic lifestyle.*

Ken: Absolutely. I was… well, there were many factors in that. I was certainly very immature and insecure. Another major issue was that I had a crushed disk in my lower back, so I had sciatic pain. That was unbearable. I didn't sleep more than four hours at a time, and I was a miserable person. I was not somebody fun to be around. I just plugged into the work. There are many reasons people do things, and that was certainly a major one.

CBA: *Right. Obviously, the production work you could do, you could do it tolerably with the back pain?*

Ken: Well, I could sit and bend over a drawing board. I couldn't walk, my leg would go numb. Sitting in a movie theater was a different kind of sitting. Sitting over a drawing table stretched my spine. Sitting back would crush into that area. That started when I was about 12, and it lasted until I was about 28, because nothing ever showed up on X-rays. I was living with a lot of pain every day, which got worse every year. Me and the TV and the record player and work were just fine for quite a while.

CBA: *You started designing, right? Were you dealing with Steranko's thumbnails, or did you feel you were starting to spread your wings as a designer?*

Ken: Jim doesn't let go. Jim would do thumbnails, sometimes tight, sometimes loose. I remember I got to lay out very few things. They weren't gems, so they weren't going to be accepted, and that was just the way it was. The only place I really got to do pretty much my own work was in the writing and the editing. I was editing everything except Jim's writing. In *Prevue*, there's me and about six other me's under other names. I was writing more than half of every issue, including ad copy, and Jim would read what I did. Jim would edit me, but it was light, and actually the last 10 or 15 issues, Jim was not grinding me completely out of existence. I was writing to meet Jim's standards at the same time, so we sort of met in the middle there.

CBA: *Were you satisfied with the product, generally?*

Ken: *Comixscene, Mediascene, Prevue…* I've been looking over them recently, and yeah, I think if I'm looking at it as a learning curve, it was a very primitive beginning, me with absolutely no skills, and Jim not really having the facilities to do things. We were operating with only a black-&-white stat camera, and having to send the type out to get galley sets, doing X-Acto paste-ups, including run-arounds, cutting up lines of type… I did that so many times. It's amazing what we did.

CBA: *That really broadened your experience, right?*

Ken: Oh, it did! When I started in the comics, I was asking for things that First Comics could not do! They just didn't have a clue what I was talking about. Same with Marvel, I would ask for stuff and, "Nope, can't do it. Just can't." I had to prep the overlays and give it to them, they just didn't want to deal with production extras. But looking at the experience, we did posters, comic boxes, all kinds of packaging, the fan clubs… the range of experience I had is something that you're not going to get today anywhere. I look at the development of the magazine and the kinds of stuff we did… right up until about *Mediascene/Prevue*, somewhere around #40 when we were doing the *Star Wars* coverage, it was a steady progression, it was always getting a little bit better…

CBA: *Was there life after Steranko?* [laughs]

Ken: Yeah, because I transitioned, I didn't leave immediately. I was still doing production for Jim. I wasn't writing as much. I was the only guy that knew how to run the stat camera. I was doing paste-ups and run-arounds and all that stuff very quickly, so I hadn't completely cut the apron strings, but I was also doing lettering samples. Dan Adkins took me up to DC, where I didn't get anything. So I went up a second time—I think again with Dan—up to Marvel, and struck out again. I kept doing lettering samples, just filling page after page with lettering. I had lettered *Outland,* and worked on *Chandler* doing backgrounds, and the basic mechanical work of SUPERGRAPHICS, so I knew I had skills. And there was something in me that still wanted to do comics work.

CBA: *Was it to be involved in comics, or was it*

specifically to do lettering? Did you see lettering could be done more accomplished?

Ken: Yeah, I did. I also knew that I would get the chance to see artwork by guys that I had always admired, I'd get to see Buscema and Kane and Kirby and all of that stuff, and I did. I guess I was arrested in the fan mentality of just being around these guys, because I didn't get to socialize with them while working for Steranko much more than a phone call here and there. That's not the same: It's not the artwork, it's not the comics. I really wanted to be involved in that, because all the big guys were still alive, and I wanted to contribute, and the lettering was something where I felt like, "I can do this, I know I can do this, I've done it. It's just a matter of getting in the door."

CBA: *Did you feel you could do comics lettering and take it to a higher level? I would assume that you did a lot of the background work on Chandler, like you said, but a lot of those were neon signs, right?*

Ken: Yeah.

CBA: *There was some beautiful stuff.*

Ken: I looked at what was out there, and I saw how they threw away the signage. Some of the sound effects I thought were great. Other stuff, I looked at it, and said, "Eh, who did this in four seconds? Boom, boom, let's just get it done." I understand now how that happened, when the deadlines are pressing, and there's no alternative, you do substandard work. But I didn't know what the realities were at

Opposite page: *From Ken's sketchbooks, variations of logowork for Howard Chaykin's 1986* First Comics Graphic Novel #9, Time² : The Epiphany. *©2000 Ken Bruzenak.*

Below: *More logo variations from Ken's sketchbooks, these for the 1988* Blackhawk *mini-series by Howard Chaykin. The fifth version was the one selected. ©2000 Ken Bruzenak.*

the time. I did realize that, "Okay, I need a pattern, I need somebody to really study to see what's good," and I kept coming back to John Costanza's stuff.

CBA: *Would you call him your favorite letterer?*

Ken: Yeah, I still like what John does. He has such a comfortable lettering style, and I still look at him as the ideal for easy readability. There are other guys who do different things that are admirable. I think what Tom Orzechowski does is certainly brilliant: He does wonderful stuff, but at that time, he wasn't stretching it as far as I did.

When I got into *Flagg!*—the story here is, I went to Marvel and there was no work there, but the editor of *Star Wars* at the time, Mary Jo Duffy, knew that Chaykin was calling around looking for a letterer. He was going to start up *Flagg!* for First Comics, and Marvel didn't want any of their letterers going there, so Mary Jo suggested I give Howard a call. Chaykin was at Upstart Studios, somewhere in the lower 40s in the garment district of New York, sharing space with Simonson and Miller. I went there that afternoon. Howard and I had been circling each other for years, like a couple alley cats. Howard's little story is he was in the Neal Adams Jets gang, and I was in the Steranko Sharks gang. So we knew each other, but not friendly, by any means. Howard looked at my samples, and he knew that working for Steranko, I had real solid training. Chaykin took a chance on me, that our differences would mesh, rather than conflict. But he wasn't ready to start on *Flagg!* just yet. So he made the phone call to First Comics and recommended me, so I really started working on the Frank Brunner book at First Comics. I was on *Warp* for two or three issues before *Flagg!* got into gear.

CBA: *But* Warp *was your first professional lettering job?*

Ken: Besides *Outland*, yeah. Brunner penciled with an incredibly heavy hand. I mean, black. I had to go in and erase just to get down to paper, because the ink was beading up on the lead. The inker didn't like that. [*laughs*] He was complaining that I was taking away essential information that he needed. [*laughter*] *Warp* didn't call for me to do anything really outstanding. I was looking at a super-hero book, just like Costanza does, just looking at regular comics and saying, "What should I do here?"

Warp got what it needed, but *Flagg!* needed more. When Howard started asking for signage—to me, a sign is a formal typeface, a sign is not just hand-lettering that says "Exit" or something, and Howard asked for a ton of signs. Honestly, Howard overwrote the first six issues, and he was surprised at how much he wrote. I was obliterating so much artwork, it was crazy. The first three issues I probably knocked out half of what Howard drew. [*laughs*] He saw that—he's not stupid. He saw that I was giving him exactly what he wanted. When he asked for a sign in the background, for it to be legible, I had to take a certain amount of space, and if there was a balloon with that, and then there was the figure work on top of that… Howard saw that

Below and next page: *Ken's logo variations on The Shadow. The version directly below is the classic version, copped from a 1970s DC Shadow comic. Background image is a spread from Howard Chaykin's mini-series. Number 12 was the version selected. The Shadow ©2000 Condé Nast. Art ©2000 DC Comics. Logos ©2000 Ken Bruzenak.*

SHADOW

SHADOW

SHADOW

SHADOW

SHADOW

THE SHADOW

SHADOW

SHADOW

SHADOW

SHADOW

SPINE

53%

EDGE OF BOOK

◁ I LIKE THESE SHADOW ONLY IDEAS — BUT MAYBE TOO SOPHISTICATED FOR A DC COMIC

NOW WE'RE GETTING DECORATIVE

60%

I DON'T REALLY KNOW IF THIS KIND OF GIMMICKY STUFF IS COMPATIBLE TO YOUR ART — DEPENDS HOW COMIC BOOKY YOU WANT TO GO

67%

10

11

A FOUR INCH CROSSBEAM

THE

RUN CONT'D ART INSIDE LETTERS

OUTLINE & SHADOW CARRY WORD IMPACT

A%

14

MODERNS

16

JUST FOOLIN' AROUND NOW — IT'S BEEN ANYONE AT ... W/ 6 HRS.

what he was asking for led to this, and subsequently, he didn't need to put as much drawing in the panel, so he started doing less and less penciling on the page before I got it. We were working on that goofy double-tone board which had to be lettered with felt tip pen. Ink would take on it, but Howard had a particular kind of felt tip pen he was using, and I got a batch of them, and was sanding them on emery board to get a point I could letter with! Technically, I was playing with tools I'd never handled before, and then I started doing all this signage. I remember around #4 or 5, he said, "We're going to have TV screens all over the place, and I need signs." Then he got sick. So, his part of the job came to a stop for a week, and in that week, I did 40 or 50 signs, TV screen-type things, "Inter-Species Romance," and "Plexus Rangers." I use them in my show-&-tell with my resume. "This is what I did for a comic book." [*laughter*] I sent that to him as a package when he was sick, and he called me up and said, "Holy sh*t!" [*laughter*] "Okay!" That's when we really started going crazy doing signage and typefaces. Setting type, having robot type, mixing formal type with balloon type for special effects, using typography as an artistic element on the page.

CBA: *Actually the lettering became a character of sorts within the book, it was integral. Did you feel you were working on a truly collaborative effort? Was it freeing for you?*

Ken: Oh, yeah. I was doing stuff that… "I don't know if this is going to work, but let's give it a try." Howard was encouraging all the way, "Go for it, try it." When I decided to use the formal type, I had to have—this was before personal computers—I had to have the local newspaper set galley type, which is really a science you know? "This is kind of what I'd like, I'd like to take this amount of space." You count characters, and spaces, and you send it out, and it comes back three days later, and it fits or it doesn't. If it doesn't fit, you're there with a razor blade slicing it up, trying to make it fit. All of a sudden, I'm handing Howard $600 bills for type! He kept saying, "Go for it!"

CBA: *Really? Wow.*

Ken: He saw the look I was after, how it was going to work. What it was going to do.

CBA: *That was going to be one of my questions: What was the percentage of any given issue of* American Flagg!—*what was the percentage of typeset copy?*

Ken: The first three, nothing. I had Presstype, that was all that was available at the time. If I could do it with Presstype, I would, but most of it was hand lettering. I guess when Howard brought in the robot Ranger, I said, "Howard, this guy ought to speak in formal type, it's got to be cold, it's got to be mechanical, and I'm going to have to send it out to get typeset for this," and certain other things, and it kind of grew. And I told him, "I've got to send you the bills for the type," and he said, "About how much?" I think that was like $250 at first, but by the time we got to *Times*[2] the bills were getting into the $600, $700… I think First picked it up, but it was still something unusual for comics. It's the kind of thing I would knock off today on the computer in an afternoon, but back then, I'd have to type it up, I'd have to spec it, I'd have to organize it. "Set this two inches wide, set the next to three inches wide, make sure it's four wide."

CBA: *Well, the computer revolution was starting in the early '80s, I think the first Mac was '85. Did you have an eye towards that at all?*

Ken: No. I still have a great ambivalence about computers. I'll use it as a tool, but I'm not comfortable with how easy it makes mediocrity acceptable, just because it looks slick.

CBA: *Right. A lack of discipline.*

Ken: It's one of the things I'm having to deal with in working up a resume; they're asking for computer skills, and I'm trying to be as honest as I can, "Yes, I can use it. Yes, I do use it. But I probably use it a lot later than you'd like." I work with a pencil for the first half of any given job, I'll puzzle it out on paper first, and go to the computer for execution, because if I

Right inset and next page: *From left to right, progressions in the production of a Mr. Monster comics page. First, the page as penciled and written by Michael T. Gilbert, next the lettering overlay by Ken Bruzenak, and finally the finished composited page as inked and finished by Bill Loebs. The page is from Mr. Monster's first modern-age appearance in Vanguard Illustrated #7. ©2000 Michael T. Gilbert.*

don't have the idea going in, I can type up something that looks okay, but it's not right.

CBA: *It's not worked out.*

Ken: Yeah, it's superficial and shiny and shallow. I find tweaking, making the changes, reworking it, reworking it, absorbs so much time that when it comes to splash page titles, things like that, often if I want something interesting, I can do it much faster by hand. The computer does not save me one second when I want to do something really good. When I just want to get a title out there—like I had an *Azrael* recently where the title was "Witness," and I knew that was a typewriter face—I can pull that up on the screen, *bang!* typewriter face, put an outline on it, make sure it's bulky enough, "Witness," that's exactly what it needs to be. But if there's something like…

CBA: *Heavily stylized?*

Ken: Yeah, it hasn't come up yet, but in *Azrael*, "Night in Baghdad," for instance. I'm going to have to sit down and letter "Night in Baghdad," because I'm going to have to have to go through a typebook, bump the letters around, stretch and twist and make it work, and I can't do that easily on a computer. I can do it, but it's such a mechanical process, it has no heart, it doesn't really interest me where I want to spend three hours staring at a monitor. I can do it in an hour by hand, with no lockups or crashes or waiting for saves to finish.

CBA: *I was the art director for an advertising agency for a number of years, until recently, and when new people would come in, they'd always immediately jump on a computer to do preliminary design, and I'd always put down the caveat that no, they had to sketch it out, they had to put the pencil to the paper, and I was amazed by the grudging resistance I got, and also by the fact that so many newcomers can't draw. My experience goes back to galley type, and I'd wax up the galleys, use an X-Acto to do hand-kerning. [laughter] I feel like I'm a veteran, you know? It's the level of tactile experience that computers can't teach.*

Ken: My wife teaches art—part of the reason we moved to New Jersey is she's teaching at a high school here, and that provided a steady job. She used to teach university-level art, and I would see her homework assignments, and I saw nobody can draw! It wasn't even a consideration! She said, "This is normal. The people teaching art can't draw, how can they teach it?" There is an Old World teacher in Allentown, Pennsylvania named Myron Barnstone, who really teaches the Old Masters' techniques of golden section, and proportion, and parallel construction… the real deal, like fine European art school training. He's got people coming in from Drexel, from the Fine Arts League, to take lessons. He's got the art professors coming in for lessons. They never learned how to draw! [laughter] It comes back to the whole issue of there being a lot of "artists" out there who can't draw, and a lot of them are teaching drawing. A lot of them are using computer clip art and filters to add special effects and polish to fundamentally terrible drawing and graphic design. I fully recognize my limitations, and am enormously frustrated by them, but I know that when I'm in a room full of art teachers, a room full of art students, I'm still head and shoulders above many of them. But that's only because the standards are so damn poor.

CBA: *When you left SUPERGRAPHICS and decided to go on your own, was your aspiration to be a letterer, or was it a case of, "That's a marketable job, that's something I can pursue."*

Ken: Probably the latter, "This is something I can do right now." I was at a point in my life where I was discovering I had more of a life than I thought. There is no question that with money comes great power. [*laughs*] I had been struggling for 12 years on a shoe-string, and all of a sudden, I went from $12,000 to over $30,000 in one year. I got a car! I hadn't had a car! My interests, my viewpoint

on life took a definite shift, and it was a good job that provided a lot of resources that I had not had for a long time.

CBA: *You were bolstering your self-esteem, with the rewards you were getting for your singular efforts.*

Ken: I needed a period of that. I started taking dancing lessons, because I realized I had spent most of my life watching TV at 2 o'clock in the morning. [*laughs*]

CBA: *You got out! [laughs]*

Ken: I got out! So, I had a couple of years where it was about, "This is good, I can letter by day, and go out and have a life." I was trying to find a balance.

CBA: *Existing in what could be termed a dysfunctional situation, were you able to reflect on that and did that help you in the future to recognize that, and that you weren't going to make the same mistakes? Did you learn from the experience?*

Ken: I learned a lot. I learned to say "No!" and to walk away from some situations early on. But something else I learned was that, in order to do good work, it does take a certain obsessive monomania. You do have to focus. I noticed now that when I'm focused on work, or whatever it is, even if I'm reading, I can tune out everything, and zero right on to what I'm doing. And I'm constantly pissing off the other people who can't. I can work with the TV on, and it's just a little chatter out there, that I don't feel compelled to interact with, because that's the way I learned how to work. The TV was on all the time, that was company. That ability to focus is something that I think is a benefit. If an editor calls up and says, "Can you do ten pages by tomorrow?" I will tell them right up front, "It's a real pain and an inconvenience, but yeah, I can do it." I know I can just plug in and do it… I'll just shut the door, put some music on and go for it all night. I find that those of us in the comics business that achieve, that can actually do work in any kind of volume, have this ability, where you just go into that isolation mode. It's not collaborative, it's

whatever I put into it. Whenever Chaykin is penciling… I've seen him, it's like there's nobody else in the room! [*laughs*] I hear stories about Neal Adams being able to pencil while having a conversation with somebody… God bless him.

So I did learn how to really bear down. I think it's an asset, but at the same time, I realize whenever I go up to the DC offices, these guys can take out and go to lunch for an hour-and-a-half, and they can take time out to talk to me… where are they getting all this time? [*laughter*]

CBA: *The luxury!*

Ken: It's like, "I want one of these jobs where I come in and then I have time to talk to other people!" It's not looking unattractive to me, but I'm spoiled by the freelance life, where if I sit down and I work for eight solid hours, I might have the next two days off to do whatever I want. I enjoy that a great deal.

CBA: *Your star started to rise working on* American Flagg!, *right? People started taking notice?*

Ken: That was it. That was the rocket that took off, yeah.

CBA: *Do you think that was a unique position you were in for letterers?*

Ken: At that point in time, yes.

CBA: *It was a real breakthrough situation.*

Ken: I was the first celebrity letterer, yes. [*laughter*] I didn't realize how big I was until I talked to Orzechowski, when I went out to California. There was a blizzard in Pennsylvania, and it was so bad—there was like three feet of snow—I just called up Chaykin and said, "Howard, it's snowing up here, I'm coming out there." [*laughter*] I asked, "Can I use your couch?" He said, "Okay." So, I went and crashed on his couch, spent a couple of days there, rented a car, and drove up to San Francisco and met Orzechowski, and stayed with Michael Gilbert. Anyway, Orzechowski told me he was getting

instructions from Chris Claremont to "do things like Bruzenak does." [*laughter*] I feel so bad about that, because Tom does stuff that I envy, where I'm like, "Wow, that's really good! I'm going to steal from him!" Nobody ever instructed me to do things like Orzechowski. [*laughter*]

The celebrity lasted about three years. I really had *carte blanche.* I was getting calls, "Want to work on *Star Wars?*" "Yeah, sure! Okay." [*laughs*] Whenever somebody started up a new book, they wanted me. It was nice! Now I'm hustling to get any work at all… I can't get phone calls returned sometimes.

CBA: *Howard has full appreciation for the illustrators of the past, and he was discussing with me his vast collection of originals of the old magazine illustrations. Did you have an appreciation for the letterers of the years gone by? Did you recognize, for instance, the work of Howard Ferguson, Artie Simek or Ben Oda?*

Ken: I knew the material. I was just bringing it forward in time. I probably didn't have that kind of appreciation for Ferguson and the early Simek and Gaspar's stuff. *The Spirit* was certainly the Holy Grail, of course. I also saw that there was a dimensional difference when they were working on 12" x 18" original art. When they went down to 10" x 15", there had to be a rethinking of how the work is handled, how it prints. I worked on a Steve Ditko job one time that was 12" x 18" and it really struck me how that changed the look of the material, even though I was trying to work with bigger pens and just scale up what I was doing. Today, on a computer, it would be identical, because you'd simply enlarge it.

CBA: *That's interesting, because when you'd see Artie Simek's smaller-sized work in the later years, it really overpowers the page, especially in* Astonishing Tales *and* Amazing Adventures *with the Inhumans and the Black Widow, not adapting to the smaller page size. He was overwhelming.*

Ken: Yeah, and Jim Novak still letters in a slightly larger size than a lot of the rest of us. I've been getting smaller and smaller and smaller…

CBA: *As small as Orzechowski?* [laughter]

Ken: Oh, my God! I worked on something two years ago where the guy was penciling same size as printed! I couldn't believe it! He said, "Well, it fits in my scanner. I'm going to color it, too," and I'm like, "Oh, give me a break!" You're not building any margin of error in here at all, but Jason Pearson doesn't need it. Jason's just that good. That's one of the things I like about comics, I've seen a lot of good work… I mean, I was just ecstatic, seeing Kirby pages, Buscema, all these guys! I loved it! The comic fan came out, and it was like, "*Ooo, yes! I'm having fun here!*"

CBA: *How did you get introduced to Michael T. Gilbert?*

Ken: Michael called me. He'd seen *Flagg!* and he gave me a call, because he wanted wild and wacky stuff! So we did some! [*laughs*]

CBA: *Did you embrace the work?*

Ken: Yeah, it was fun. Funny material was something Chaykin didn't do a lot of, though when Howard had the cat in *American Flagg!*, I loved those pages! Raoul the cat was just so… "Oh, Howard, he's so cute!" [*laughter*] Michael is like wall-to-wall humor. Even when he's blowing a werewolf's brains out with a .45, it's *funny!* [*laughter*] The flying eyeball's in there somewhere.

CBA: *So was it a liberating aspect?*

Ken: Yes.

CBA: *You seemed to hearken back to a lot of classic comic book lettering. Did you reference that, or was it intuitive?*

Ken: Well, I knew that for a horror comic, it was going to be all this drippy, gothic, Old English stuff. I didn't reference comics. I have tons of type books, the Dover typefaces. I've got two dozen of them, all on a bookshelf. "I need another drippy letter… let's drag out the books and see what's here!"

CBA: *[laughs] The drippy letter book.*

Ken: There are so many exotic typefaces, so it was really a lot of putting slime on things. And lightning bolts. Michael writes on overlays, so there'd be the penciled page, then there'd be this piece of tracing paper with all the writing on it. Michael's one of these guys, when he's writing a lot, he writes small. When he's writing one or two words, he writes big! That doesn't translate! [*laughter*] But sometimes, for a splash page, he'd have a cyclotron, and there'd be this "Mr. Monster" scribble with these scraggly lighting bolt indications, and a notation, "Like lightning!" [*laughter*] "Okay, I've got the idea, how do I make it work?"

CBA: *Did you feel you were transcending into cartooning?*

Ken: At times. It's an area I wish there was more of in comics. One of my big disappointments recently was two days after New Year's, getting a phone call, and losing the *Dexter's Lab* assignment. I had been working on *Dexter* and loving it. It was such a fun thing. When I talked to the editor, I said, "I'm really pissed off about losing *Dexter*, because this is fun! There's not too many fun books." But Wildstorm was taking over the lettering on computer. And the computer is going to be used, like it or not… not that it's better, not that it's faster, not that it's cheaper, it's just the toy that they want to use. DC and Marvel are already pushing for letterers to send in their font so the companies can make "corrections." And we all know what that means!

CBA: *Welcome to Fontographer [font-creating software]!*

Ken: It's not going to be the same comics that way. It's more about technology than art. Richard Starkings has had an enormous impact on the lettering field, both good and bad. I see books, when I go through the freebie bundle, that Starkings has worked on, or I see the name Comicraft,

and I see some things are just wonderful, like *Steampunk*. I'm like, "Wow, I wish I could make my computer sit up and dance like this!" Then, I'll open up another book, and it's the most amateurish crap… heads carved out by balloons, pointers stabbing people, thought bubble amputations… then I start wondering "What is this? How did this happen?" I don't know if some of his guys are still doing hand lettering badly, or if they are sneaking their fonts in and they're just ugly, but it's definitely the work of many hands—it is becoming erratic in quality, without real personality or individuality. It's just typing, but that is the way things are going to be.

CBA: *The thing I noticed in looking at your career, it seemed like—and tell me if I'm wrong—the two biggest collaborative efforts that you had, you really became, you seemed to become a part of the book, were Flagg! and Mr. Monster. Did you feel there were other memorable collaborative efforts you had?*

Ken: *Cyberella* was very good. It was a DC book, part of the Helix line, three or four years back, where I worked with Don Cameron. Chaykin was writing, and Don was only drawing, supposedly. But Don was plotting and doing preliminary writing, and Howard was… bending his deadline, which got us all in trouble. [*laughs*] I honestly don't know whose fault that was. But *Cyberella* was something where I went crazy with injecting typefaces and balloon shapes— every issue's credits spilled over 10 pages! Unfortunately, Don was not a strong enough draftsman to carry it off monthly, which I don't think is really any news to him. It was his very first comic work. There was friction with the editor, and the colorist just didn't know his job—I mean, putting solid red and yellow over black 12-point type is indefensible, and the editor chewed me out! Being late certainly didn't improve anyone's disposition. Maybe the time just wasn't right for *Cyberella*, which is why Don wants to try again with a different publisher.

See, that brings up something I don't understand about the current comics market—I really don't know what a "hot book" looks like anymore. I don't know that people even read the books! We've swayed so much towards flash art, I don't know if there's room for content. When I read Alan Moore, I guess it was in *Tomorrow Stories*, the short "Jack B. Quick," where Kevin Nowlan had done a nice six-page story, I was enthralled! That is one of the first things in a couple of years where I picked it up, and I was like, "It's the perfect art, it's the perfect story, everything about it is absolutely perfect, I want to see the next installment!" But it's just this little short story chapter within a regular comic. I don't see any big titles generating that kind of excitement.

Today's comics are so different from the narrative structure that I grew up with, that I don't know I would even recognize a "hot" book today. I guess Miller's *Daredevil* and the Claremont *X-Men* were the last two series that really seemed to have that magic, where you read this month's issue and you wanted to get the next issue now! I don't know that we have books coming out like that, where there's a real appeal to them, and there's sales to back up the interest. It's scary, because this is comics, it's my livelihood, I love the form, but I'm looking at disjointed picture books. I'm not looking at books that even seem to be concerned with telling a solid story. It's like blockbuster movie mentality… every movie that comes out has to be *Die Hard 3* or *Armageddon*. Hollywood is not allowed to make good, fun, small movies anymore. Meanwhile, I'm watching Miramax foreign movies, and I'm really enjoying them enormously! Like *Brassed Off*, which is nothing more than a story of a brass band in a Welsh coal mining town when the mine closes. It's like, "Wow, neat!"

CBA: *Right, it can be done!*

Ken: It's good, and it has a cute story, and it's engaging characters who actually do something that matters. I'm looking at books, including stuff I've worked on over the years, and so little of it matters. I was on *Silver Surfer* for 100 issues, and I don't think ten of them amounted to anything. I'd get the Xerox pencils on a Friday, and the writer would fax me manuscript on Sunday afternoon, and the pages had go out Monday. 22 pages! Very light writing, I think that was Ron Marz. Very light copy, so it was doable, but it was also disposable. And I loved working with the editor, Craig Anderson. That just wasn't the same caliber of *Silver Surfer* that Stan and John Buscema did for twelve issues. I'd rather work on the older stuff that had more words, that had more care, that had more time. I was just up at DC a couple of weeks ago, and we were talking about *Dexter's Lab,* and somebody—it might've been Bob Greenberger—said, "Well, it's light copy." And I said, "I'd rather work on heavy copy and have it mean something!" It's not about the volume of copy, it's what are you producing? I'm really not happy with a lot of what I see in comics, even the Vertigo stuff, which is more personal. The guys doing those Vertigo books are not doing it for the money,

granted. But so much of it's this dark and grim and nihilistic material, and that's not any more fulfilling or engaging than something that's empty and vacuous.

CBA: *So, when you were working in the mid-'80s on* Flagg! *and* Mr. Monster, *and the other work you were doing, how do you characterize them in retrospect? Was it an important time for you?*

Ken: Oh, very. It was very good work. Howard was doing good work, Michael was doing good work, I was matching them. I was really augmenting the best they could do, I supported what they were doing, and I really don't know that anybody else could have supported them as well. I look around at who else was lettering at that point, and… I don't know that somebody like Costanza would have carried *Flagg!* I think what he wouldn't have done is get in there and take charge of those areas and run with them the way I did. I mean, I just took over panels. [*laughter*] I knew there were panels that had backgrounds and people in them, and I knew the volume of copy I had, and what Howard wanted in the panel. I was going to knock out every bit of the background that he spent three hours drawing, and it was just gone. I checked with Howard in the beginning about some of this stuff, to tell him what I was doing, and he'd really say, over and over say, "Stop bothering me. I trust you to do what's right for the material." It did get to the point where I started getting general, sketchy thumbnails, and the last couple of books I worked on with Howard, there were no pencils whatsoever.

CBA: *That's an enormous level of trust that you hadn't previously experienced?*

Ken: Yeah, that was really a lot of fun to run like that. It's something I still try to do. I get books in all the time where they have spotted the balloons on the Xerox, and I'll break the balloons up, I'll move them around, I'll completely ignore what the editor wants. I've just got to know who's talking. I'll move balloons to different panels. I think it's not really noticed. [*laughter*]

I think the first 12 issues of *American Flagg!* in particular were a real turning point for a lot of things about comics, not just the lettering. It was the beginning of the break from traditional panel breakdown storytelling. It was taking stuff that Gil Kane had

developed and going another step forward. Howard knew what he was doing. Howard is a brilliant storyteller. A lot of the people that have copied Howard since are not. So, we've got a lot of books today where the page is complete chaos.

And I still think Steranko is probably the only guy who can do truly cinematic storytelling technique in comics, even if he's not working anymore! Miller pops up now and then, but it's not this ongoing cinematic approach that Jim understood so well. As I look through the bundles, I don't see anybody doing that. I don't see anyone self-consciously concerned about the two-shot followed up by the close-up for information, followed by the long-shot for geography, and the upper angle shots contrasted with the low angle shots… just doing all these things in a very cinematic way. I don't even see people doing side lighting and close-ups as a character delivers an important line. It's all MTV throwaway images that don't connect. There's a lot of storytelling technique that is being lost in the pursuit of pretty pictures, in the pursuit of pages to resell afterwards.

CBA: *Right, pin-ups.*

Ken: It's really crippled comics terribly. Where I do see good storytelling is in things like *Dexter's Lab,* and the animated *Batman* material, where the cartoon guys came in—working in their normal TV mode, cutting and everything—and they just transferred that right into comics. I'm seeing all these wonderful, gimmicky things they do that advance the story. What's missing is the illustrative drawing style—the eye candy—that keeps your attention on the page to digest more complicated story development. But the principles of storytelling can be as simple as one job I worked on, where Dexter is zapped by a ray and he grows large…and all of a sudden, we've gone from six panels on a page to three panels per page! I mean, everything grew large! I looked at that and thought, "Oh, my gosh!" [*laughs*] It's that primitive, it's that fundamental, and yet there's a lot of guys that don't get it. They really don't want to know, either. And that is scary!

The Chaykin Factor

American Flagg! Creator Howard Chaykin Talks Comics

Conducted by Jon B. Cooke
Transcribed by Jon B. Knutson

Howard Victor Chaykin came into comics along with other "newave" artists Bernie Wrightson, Mike Kaluta, Walter Simonson, etc., and quickly established himself as a fan favorite on such strips as The Scorpion, Dominic Fortune and Cody Starbuck. But it wasn't until American Flagg! did the artist become identified with a character. While currently a television producer, Howard continues to write comics, though sadly, he no longer draws. Howard was interviewed by phone on January 14, 2000, and he copyedited the final transcript. My thanks to Tim Barnes and Alex Wald for last-minute art contributions.

Below: *Courtesy of one-time First Comics production manager Alex Wald comes this Chaykin drawing of American Flagg. ©2000 Howard Chaykin.*

Comic Book Artist: *Howard, where are you from?*
Howard Chaykin: I was born in New Jersey, for a number of reasons that have only recently come to light. I was raised in Brooklyn.
CBA: *As a youngster?*
Howard: I was raised in East Flatbush, and resided in Brownsville, a slum neighborhood in Brooklyn. I moved with my family to Queens when I was 14. When I finally left New York City, I'd been living in Manhattan for quite some time. I'm a New York City kid.
CBA: *I read in an interview you did with Gary Groth for* The Comics Journal *that you grew up just a few blocks from where Gil Kane was raised?*
Howard: Yeah, I grew up at 370 Saratoga Avenue in the 1950s, and he grew up at 420 in the '30s and '40s.
CBA: *I take it that it was a rough neighborhood?*
Howard: It was rough when he was a kid, and it got rougher when I was there. I was a kid who ran away from a lot of fights. A film called *The Wanderers* is a cleaned-up version of what it was like. It was a scary way to grow up, but it was enlightening.
CBA: *Did you retreat to comics?*
Howard: Absolutely. I was raised on Welfare, my parents separated when I was very young, and my father was ultimately declared legally dead—although I found him some years back—so as a dysfunctional family, it covered all bases. I started stealing comic books from the time I was five or six years old.
CBA: *What was your routine? How did you get 'em out?*
Howard: The two-finger flip. You went in, put your thumb on the front, two fingers on the back, folded it down—again, I was not a dedicated collector, so mint condition was not a concern [*laughter*]—and stuck 'em down my pants. I had an innocent face—with my crew cut, I looked like a chubby little billiard ball. *Blackhawk* was the first comic book I ever stole. I had a real reign of terror and larceny when I was a little boy. I just made amends, in many cases.
CBA: *How did you do that?*
Howard: I try not to be the asshole I was as a kid.
CBA: *Aside from the petty larceny, were you able to avoid*

becoming a juvenile delinquent?
Howard: Yeah. I was short, fat and Jewish, and in those days, you either fought or ran, and I ran… to comics. Comic books, television and movies: They were true obsessions.
CBA: *So, you pretty much missed the ECs when they were coming out?*
Howard: I became an EC collector later on in my teens, rolling over my Golden Age collection, which I'd been accumulating since the late '50s and early '60s.
CBA: *How did you get Golden Age books?*
Howard: I was a Golden Age collector when I was a little boy. In those days, you could get pretty sizable runs of *Detective, Action* and that stuff for $2.50 a pop.
CBA: *Were you predominately attracted to the super-hero books?*
Howard: I read nothing but super-hero comics. I was a total super-hero geek, *Batman* and *Superman*. And I was always a big fan of *Blackhawk*. I liked the look of the book, especially the covers on the DCs in the mid-'50s.
CBA: *When did you get into drawing?*
Howard: Some years back I discovered that the man who I'd always thought of as my father, turned out to be my adoptive father. My actual blood father's name was Drucker. So, as a number of people put it, I'm officially a bastard, not just figuratively.

As nutty and cruel as my adoptive father was, he encouraged me to draw. He bought me sketchbooks, and I'd fill them with kid's drawings. The first things I drew were cowboys, because that was my obsession. Growing up in New York, Channel 13 in New York—now an educational station—showed nothing but cowboy movies and cartoons. I lived in front of Channel 13. It was all those sh*tty *Farmer Alfalfa*s with the f*cking mice and sh*t. [*laughter*] I loved it! I was a big fan of Johnny Mack Brown, Wild Bill Elliott and Don "Red" Barry. It was a schlock, a cut or two above WNEW. Sandy Becker, Sonny Fox, Uncle Fred Scott, Uncle Fred Hall… that was my world.
CBA: *Soupy Sales, Chuck McCann….*
Howard: Yeah, actually I had the pleasure of having lunch with Chuck McCann and Will Jordan a couple of years ago.
CBA: *Get out!*
Howard: At the Friar's Club. McCann was one of my f*cking gods.
CBA: *Do you remember when he played Little Orphan Annie, with the closet filled with millions of the same red dress?*
Howard: Oh, yeah! [*laughter*] I loved that. Chuck is intense. Meeting him was a really big, big thrill. I'm still a fanboy. And Will Jordan is one of the funniest men I've ever met.
CBA: *Did you draw amateur comic books?*
Howard: Nah. I've realized my entire career is based on two things: Playing with toy soldiers and drawing Nazi planes bombing my Hebrew school homework. [*laughter*] I was an indifferent student, and I coasted. School was easy for me up to a certain point. Then, I just checked out and didn't do sh*t. I aced through grammar school, I was one of those kids because I was smarter than anybody else in the class, but that got me into trouble because I developed no study skills whatsoever.

The one time I actually made it clear in my class that I was a comic reader I took sh*t endlessly, because comics were really shmucky things to be interested in. I taught myself to read from comics. I entered the first grade on a fourth grade reading level as a result of comics—like Tarzan teaching himself to read from his parents' books.

I was in junior high when I developed a relationship with Michael Abromowitz, Alvin Fayman and Jan Mondrus, three guys I read comics with. Michael and I were in the same class, Dan and Alvin were a year behind us, and we collected Silver Age stuff. That was our big thing. I was the first guy to lead us into Golden Age collecting. There was a hustler named Harvey King who was a couple of years older than we were, who turned me on to a lot of sh*t. Mark Skubicki was another collector. and there was another guy whose last name I don't remember named Artie the exterminator, who traveled around with his own homemade version of Mylar-snugged Golden Age stuff inside his exterminating kit. [laughter] The stuff smelled of bug spray. [laughs]

CBA: *So did things change when you moved to Queens?*

Howard: When I moved to Queens, I became a complete and total isolator. My high school graduation picture has nothing underneath my picture but my name—a complete non-entity. Ironically, when I went to my ten-year high school reunion, there was one woman there who I barely knew whose husband insisted they go so he could get his comics signed.

I kept to myself in high school—it was me being very quiet and unobtrusive. I had a couple of pals, who ultimately became much better friends later, who had read comics at one point, but we kept it to ourselves.

CBA: *Did you catch glimpses of the counter-culture during that time?*

Howard: I smoked an enormous amount of pot.

CBA: *Did it help with the drawing?*

Howard: No. I thought it did, but we were just pot-heads! I had a good time.

CBA: *So after high school, did you plan to go to art school?*

Howard: I had been talked out of becoming an artist, and went off to become a radio broadcaster. I hitchhiked around the country, just pissed around. I ended up working for Gil Kane when I was 19 as a gofer. I didn't do any drawing for him. From there I drifted to Wallace Wood, and to Gray Morrow, and to Neal Adams… I served an apprenticeship with these guys. I had no idea just how much I sucked until I'd occasionally go back and look at that stuff.

CBA: *How did you get a break with Gil? Was he the first?*

Howard: I'd heard on the grapevine that Gil's assistant had dropped dead of a heart attack at 23. I gave Gil a call, and he said, "Yeah, I can use you," so I went to work for him. I was really slovenly, as most guys of my generation were in those days, and he was ashamed to let me deliver his work for him. He didn't show up with a necktie at the drawing table in his own house, but close.

CBA: *Was Gil primarily working for Marvel at the time?*

Howard: He was doing *Blackmark,* and I did a really bad job pasting up the dialog and putting in Zips and dirtying up pages. But it was a great apprenticeship, I learned a lot from watching Gil work.

CBA: *Did you meet Harvey Kurtzman (who did the breakdowns on* Blackmark*)?*

Howard: I didn't meet Harvey until many years later. As much as I revere Harvey, on a personal level he and I never got along. I always had the impression he was kind of a bitter guy.

Harvey is one of the greatest talents comics has ever produced. Only half an hour ago I was talking to a guy I'm working with on a couple of projects. I insisted that he had to sit down and read *Two-Fisted Tales, Frontline Combat* and the *Mads.*

CBA: *How did that lead to working for Woody?*

Howard: Woody had a studio in Valley Stream, Long Island,

where Jack Abel and Syd Shores rented space. Syd was a strange guy, kind of out of it. Jack, on the other hand, was really funny. Jack Abel is one of my all-time favorite human beings. I adored him.

CBA: *As far as you know, did Syd leave comics for a while?*

Howard: I think comics left Syd. [laughter] Woody would sit in a lotus position and drink vodka and tea, and rail against women, psychiatry, Jews, and anybody else he could come up with that day, and I would sit there and pencil his Westerns. Nick Cuti was there, too. It was an education.

CBA: *Was he an assistant, too?*

Howard: Woody put his stuff together by creating a body of work with swipes. Nick would take Woody's layouts, accumulate an Alex Raymond shot here, a John Prentice shot here, and assemble pencils based on Art-O-Graphs of this stuff. Woody would ink it and make it all Woody!

CBA: *How long did that last?*

Howard: A couple of months. Gray Morrow was one of my favorite artists. He drew realistically, in an engaging style. I worked with Gray for a while, I ghosted some stuff for him.

CBA: *What, breakdowns, or…?*

Howard: No, I penciled a Man-Thing story he did, and I penciled a thing for *National Lampoon* called "Michael Rockefeller and the Jungles of New Guinea."

CBA: *Well, actually, you* did *get credit for the Man-Thing story.*

Howard: Did I?

CBA: *Yeah, and it was weird, because it was a natural assumption that you had inked the job when, in fact, you penciled the story.*

Howard: I don't remember. Frankly, I paid very little attention to my own work.

CBA: *From there, where did you go?*

Howard: I went to work for Neal Adams, and apprenticed for him. This was before Continuity, when he was in the Bronx. Neal lived in a house with a million kids and his wife, and we'd go up there in the middle of the night and pencil pages, and I did a lot of storyboard stuff for him, and I learned a lot.

CBA: *[laughs] You dealt with a lot of strong, opinionated characters in comics.*

Howard: Some might say sociopaths.

CBA: *Yeah. Gil and Woody and especially Neal are very strong, opinionated type people. You're a strong, opinionated type person yourself.*

Howard: Gil and Neal are very analytical men. Woody was too, but in a very different direction. I've learned a lot about analysis of the work from Gil. Less so from Neal, because Neal and I are from different planets.

CBA: *Did you pick up technique from these guys?*

Howard: No. Technique was totally out of my reach. I spent the first ten years of my career dumping on technique, and the second half of my career regretting the fact that I couldn't learn it. [laughter] I was learning how to think visually, and that's always been my single greatest gift: I'm a good storyteller, and I understand how to convey narrative visually. That certainly applies to what I do for a living today. I've always liked pictures with continuity, with narrative ideas. Although I don't collect original artwork from comics, I collect original magazine illustrations. There's great storytelling there.

Gil always said the best storytellers were *The New Yorker* cartoonists, because they're able to convey an enormous amount of information with the fewest images and lines possible.

CBA: *So, what was your entré into getting your own work published?*

Howard: Neal showed me to Murray Boltinoff and Julie Schwartz. Murray gave me a one-page filler. I also got some work from Dorothy Woolfolk, who edited the love comics. It was all just dreadful stuff, but you stumble along, and you learn. A problem for me was that by the time I became a professional, I lost any interest whatsoever in super-hero comics. I'm not a horror guy, and I didn't know what the hell to do! [*laughter*] What I wanted to draw is guys with guns, guys with swords, and women with big tits, and that was the extent of my interest in comics at the time.

CBA: *Were you a Crusty Bunker?*

Howard: The Crusty Bunkers came into existence because they needed an inker for *Swords of Sorcery*. I penciled the book, and Neal created the Crusty Bunkers, who ultimately inked the book. That's how that started.

CBA: *Were you involved in the plotting at all? Was it Marvel-style?*

Howard: Things were a bit more organic in those days. We all hung out a lot, and it just happened. My generation of comics guys had a whole overview of the culture, so you could have guys as disparate as Kaluta, Simonson, Wrightson, and still have a certain unity of idea that was not based on a superficial inking style, but on the approach to narrative.

CBA: *Let's say the first new generation was Bernie and Kaluta who came in '69, and you came in with Simonson in what, '72?*

Howard: '72 or '73. I had been around for a couple of years. Dick Giordano barely remembers throwing me out of his office at Charlton when I was

15. [*laughter*] We all knew each other. A lot of the guys came up through the fanzines, but I did very little fanzine work. I was only at one comic book convention before I became a professional. One of my best friends is David Armstrong, a serious Golden Age collector. There are still pictures around of Dave dressed up as Captain America when he was 13. David's my connection to collecting comics.

CBA: *You're still a collector now?*

Howard: No. I collect *American illustration*. I get a box from DC every six weeks, and throw out 95% of it.

CBA: *Oh, so you're actually collecting the original art!*

Howard: Of course.

CBA: *I was thinking about the tear sheets.*

Howard: I've got tear sheets up the ass. I'm in my office right now, and I've got 18 feet of bookshelf space with both 11" x 14" and 8 1/2" x 11" binders of… I mean, I could walk you through the shelf, I've got McCarthy, Beckhoff, McLeod, Buckham, Peters, Connor, Beall, DeMers, Ludekens, Williamson, Varady, Rockwell, Hooks, Von Schmidt, Bowler, McGinnis, Cornwell, Dohanos, Bundy, Petty…

CBA: *I get it, I get it! [laughs]*

Howard: I've been trying to find an Albert Dorne for years. The ones out there aren't quality material… mostly WWII stuff. It's difficult to find the great watercolor work. I own three Robert Fawcetts, two of which are world class. A couple of Bernie Fuchs' pieces, a couple of Bob Peaks, Cornwells….

CBA: *Bob Peak? Wow. Were you into Amsel?*

Howard: I have a nice Amsel. I also own "The Outsider" by David Grove.

CBA: *What happened to Amsel?*

Howard: He died a couple of years back.

CBA: *He seemed really hot, I've seen him around for a while, when I was a kid, I was into him.*

Howard: When he died… he was apparently spending his money to produce an animated film. I have no idea whatever happened to it.

CBA: *Well, that's something to track down.*

Howard: Illustration is a dead industry.

CBA: *Did you, back then, have an appreciation for illustration?*

Howard: I loved it, but I didn't understand it. I did not have an educated eye. Comics was all, it was everything.

CBA: *Mike Kaluta was really obviously beginning to get into iconography, and into poster images and the like with* The Shadow.

Howard: My first favorite illustrator was Robert Fawcett, who I still revere. It was 1975, and Michael and I got into a public fight about illustration. Michael's always been a nostalgist of the 1920s, which is a great way to meet chicks. In comics, when you say "illustration," you're generally talking about the so-called "Golden Age of illustration." You never think of a guy like Jack Potter, who did those great Cola-Cola ads that ran in the back of magazines.

You'd never think of Frank McCarthy, unless you were a movie poster collector. Illustration didn't die in 1935. As much as I was a fan of Leyendecker as a kid, I'm less interested now, because he never really developed an editorial sensibility—he was an advertising *artiste* unlike guys like Cornwell, who could do advertising but also had a strong narrative sensibility. Cornwell could do decorative stuff, like the Eastern Airlines mural, or the L.A. Library, but he was also a terrific book illustrator.

CBA: *Did you believe yourself as a man out of time?*

Howard: No. I was a comic book artist, I was having a good time. I made no money, but none of us did in those days. It wasn't until the early '80s that money came into it. But we had a great time. We hung together, lived together, did each others' work, and most of us assumed the comic book business would disappear by the 1980s.

CBA: *Where did you want to go?*

Howard: I had no idea. I was just coasting. Byron Preiss was publishing his books, and I ended up doing some stuff for him— which was like going to prison—but I learned a lot. I put my earning potential on hold for three years while I worked for Byron. I made no money on that job.

CBA: *Was that* Stars Be My Destination?

Howard: That and *Empire*… but I learned a sh*tload. Again, it was a time to learn technique, and I could not have done *American Flagg!* if I had not done that.

CBA: *Did you learn a lot about production, too?*

Howard: Well, yeah. A lot of the mainstream comic book work in those days was simply to pay the bills, which is why so much of it just looks totally dashed out, because I was making three times per page on the DC Comics what I was making on *Stars Be My Destination* and *Empire,* and that work was full-page color.

CBA: *Did you have a comics series for a time? I remember* Star Wars, *obviously, but was there anything before that?*

Howard: No, I did one-shots here and there, I did this and that. I did "Ironwolf," *Sword of Sorcery*. I didn't develop a physical and emotional commitment until the early '80s, when I did *American Flagg!* I did 26 issues of *American Flagg!,* and it ruined my f*cking life! [*laughter*] It was a very, very production-heavy, all-consuming project, and it just demanded a lot of me.

CBA: *You did a number of characters who resembled each other: Dominic Fortune, Cody Starbuck, The Scorpion.*

Howard: I always approached the stuff as if I was a touring company of actors, and the hero was a version of either James Garner, William Holden, Errol Flynn… actors that reflected my own sensibilities at that point. So they were all the same guy. It's like Michael Moorcock's Eternal Champion— Elric and Hawkmoon and Corum and Jerry Cornelius. I tried to create a hero with a point of view that reflected my own sensibilities. I think I succeeded first with American Flagg!

CBA: *The Scorpion and Dominic Fortune and these guys were prototypes.*

Howard: I created Dominic Fortune because the people at Atlas were f*ckheads, and after doing two issues of *The Scorpion* for them, the editor of the company f*cked me behind my back. I walked over to Marvel and asked them if they'd like to do *The Scorpion* under a different name.

CBA: *So you were just jumping around from publisher to publisher, pretty much?*

Howard: Why be loyal to them? They wouldn't be loyal to me.

CBA: *Did you do work for Warren at all?*

Howard: Yeah, but I'm not a horror guy. I'm not a big fan of horror pictures. I prefer pussy to fear.

CBA: *Were you steeped in '30s imagery?*

Howard: I knew that material very well, I liked the look and the design, and it was fun to play with. It's haunted me forever.

CBA: *Were you into pulps at all?*

Howard: No. I thought they were worse than comic book writing. I've read all the Burroughs' stuff, I've read the Robert E. Howard stuff.

CBA: *Man, try reading three* Doc Savages *in a row! Woof!*

Howard: I've barely been able to get through reading one *Doc Savage.* The spiritual descendent of Doc Savage is Robert Ludlum. I don't share my generation's enthusiasm for the pulps.

CBA: *Another aspect of the pulps was some good crime writing, like Dashiel Hammett.*

Howard: Oh, I read all of Hammett and Chandler in the '70s. I read David Goodis, Cornell Woolrich, read Rex Stout, John Carroll Daly, William Campbell Gault.

CBA: *Was the attraction that the material was based on reality?*

Howard: Crime paperbacks were just as fantastical as science-fiction, but were based on an observed reality. Crime fiction took place in a world that resembled the world I grew up in, the kind of a childhood I had. That led me to Hubert Selby, Henry Roth… and ultimately, it turned me off to science-fiction.

CBA: *When did that happen? The later '70s?*

Howard: I've done s-f for television, but I don't much read it, except for alternate world stuff. If the Golden Age of science-fiction is 12, that's what I read when I was 12, and I still occasionally dip into it.

CBA: *How did you get involved in the* Star Wars *comic adaptation?*

Howard: Apparently, George Lucas had liked the Cody Starbuck stuff, and asked me to do it. Had I known the movie was going to be as big a hit, I'd have worked harder. The fact is, that stuff was done a year-and-a-half before the royalty system came in, so I made $15 a page over my rate on those pages. I made more in royalties from the Dark Horse reprints than I ever made from Marvel. They were selling millions of copies.

CBA: *So you got off the book pretty quick, right?*

Howard: I adapted the first movie, and I did four issues after that. I respect the phenomenon, but even back then, I always felt, "Why wasn't this movie around when I was 15?" I've never seen the third picture. I know who won, because there wasn't a fourth movie for a couple of years. [*laughter*] I took my girlfriend to see *The Phantom Menace* because she wanted to see it. Oh, God. The only movie that I saw last year that was more relentless than *Phantom Menace* was *Anna and the King.* I turned to her at one point and said, "If Chow Yun Fat doesn't grab two pistols and jump across that room shooting people with a bunch of doves flying around him, I'm pissed." [*laughter*]

CBA: *Did it become a grind, for instance, with* Star Wars?

Howard: No. The '70s were a blurry, itinerant life. I partied pretty hard. Comics were ancillary to my life. I didn't really buckle down until I did the stuff for Byron and the *Flagg* stuff.

Above: *We believe this might be Howard's version of The Spider but, hey, what do you think? Courtesy of Tim Barnes. The Spider ©2000 the respective copyright holder. Art ©2000 Howard Chaykin.*

CBA: *Were you inspired going into those projects for Byron?*

Howard: Yeah, and I was beaten down when I got out.

CBA: *Did you start conceiving yourself as not necessarily a comic book artist but a commercial artist at a certain point?*

Howard: I never really got good enough. I did paperbacks for a couple of years—Westerns and science-fiction. I did stuff for Jim Baen. The bottom fell out about the time Mike Gold and Rick Obadiah came to me with First Comics, with an opportunity to be in on the ground floor. The money was unbelievable—it was an opportunity to bring my income up to a serious level.

CBA: *Was it projected income?*

Howard: No, it was committed money.

CBA: *First Comics committed money to you?*

Howard: *American Flagg!* tripled my income and made it possible for me to pay off a lot of heavy credit card debt accrued from working for no money for Byron Preiss.

CBA: *Just to live?*

Howard: Yeah. It never paid off. Ultimately, the *Flagg* stuff paid off. I made serious dough in that.

CBA: *Were you conceiving of the character, Reuben Flagg, at all?*

Howard: No, they came to me and said, "Would you like to do something for us, and have you got any ideas?" A month later, I sent them a proposal.

CBA: *In a nutshell, who is American Flagg?*

Howard: It's James Garner as Maverick running around in a future that looks a lot like *Gunsmoke* with guys with guns and women with big tits.

CBA: *Right. Strong influx of humor, a la Maverick?*

Howard: I was a big fan of Jack Cole's Plastic Man when I was a little boy. It always had thrills, chills and laughs. Gil always said that one of the problems of comics is that they mistake gravity for enormity. I felt I could do more important, serious work by being funny than by striking adolescent misrepresentations of adulthood.

CBA: *You did it for quite a while, right?*

Howard: My run was a little over two years.

CBA: *It was a monthly book from the word go?*

Howard: Yeah. What an idiot.

CBA: *[laughs] That's a lot of pages!*

Howard: Yeah, well, I did the first 12 issues without an assistant, which is even shmuckier.

CBA: *How long before the series was released were you working on it?*

Howard: I have no idea.

CBA: *When did you meet Ken Bruzenak?*

Howard: I met Bruzenak in the early '70s. Ken was Steranko's guy, like I was Neal's. I never had to tell Bruzenak anything, he knew exactly what he was doing! He was amazing! He was an amazingly talented guy who has been superseded by technology.

CBA: *Did you start perceiving yourself as more and more of a designer?*

Howard: I was a comic book artist. I just happened to be applying stuff from other places to comics. Just like all of us did! Michael Kaluta had his own obsessions with illustration of the '20s and '30s. Simonson was applying all that graphic stuff. Wrightson was going through his Franklin Booth period. We were all just shoving the sh*t we'd learned elsewhere into comics.

CBA: *When you did American Flagg!, were you still on the East Coast?*

Howard: I moved to California in 1985. I did *Flagg!* between '82 and '84.

CBA: *Were you satisfied with the book after it was turned over to other people?*

Howard: I learned a long time ago that unless you do something, you don't complain about it.

CBA: *I would take it that with the success of American Flagg! that DC started courting you?*

Howard: I've always had a really good relationship with those guys.

CBA: *It seems a lot of the work you do for DC is the Elseworlds series.*

Howard: I like messing with these characters, and when I've tried to mess with them in the "real world," they get pissed. I'm working on one right now, as a matter of fact.

CBA: *So you like staying away from the continuity obsession?*

Howard: I respect people who can do it, but I also wonder why they spend that much time doing continuity.

CBA: *I read your Comics Journal interview from 1986, and it was a very hot year for comics, in that a lot of things changed. You came out with The Shadow, for instance, but you took him out and you put him into your own world.*

Howard: I pissed everybody off. Poor Harlan— like I give a sh*t.

CBA: *It's interesting that's when comic books started getting exciting, was with The Dark Knight Returns, The Shadow, Watchmen in these self-contained "universes," not concerned with continuity at all.*

Howard: Comics can be anything they want to be. I like the form, I'm not nuts for the content. It's as simple as that. I'm going to be doing a back-up feature for Walter Simonson's *New Gods* book, because he asked me to. I'm looking forward to that.

CBA: *Will this be a regular, or just a one-shot?*

Howard: Just a one-shot. I'm going to do one of those eight-page sequences in *Tom Strong*. It's an opportunity to stick my toe

Below: Line art detail from an American Flagg! cover by Howard Chaykin. Courtesy of Alex Wald. ©2000 Howard Chaykin.

back in without getting obsessed.

CBA: *Who's the character in* New Gods?

Howard: I told Walter when he asked me to do this, "I don't think I can write that kind of stuff in terms of plot. I'm not a fantasy guy, for me, it's guys with guns." He's sending me a plot—I'm going to do a breakdown.

CBA: *Have you been doing a lot of drawing?*

Howard: No. The last drawing I did—and that was the first in a long time—I penciled the covers for *Pulp Fantastic* for Rich Burchett.

CBA: *Was* Batman: Dark Allegiances *the last book?*

Howard: That was the last big-time book I did.

CBA: *Did you take some heat for* The Shadow, *with the infusion of real sexual elements?*

Howard: I don't recall. I did pretty much the same thing to The Shadow that Frank Miller did to Batman, but people seemed to feel that the Shadow deserved a different treatment. Come on! It's the Shadow. I'm always supposed to love the stuff more than I do.

CBA: *Back to* American Flagg!, *did you accomplish what you wanted to with that book?*

Howard: Yes. I worked my ass off, had a real good time, and did cool, weird sh*t!

CBA: *The success of the character obviously enabled you to do other things?*

Howard: It made it possible for me to come to California, because there were a lot of people out here reading my stuff. Some were ripping it off, some of them were liking it. Ultimately, it led me in a stumbling sort of zig-zag through a maze into film, then into television, where I make my living now.

CBA: *What are you doing in television?*

Howard: I just finished a season on *Earth: Final Conflict.* I'm a producer in television. I had dinner with this pal of mine last night, who said that one thing about comic books is, when you stop doing it, they think you've died.

CBA: *When did that start?*

Howard: In 1990. I started on *The Flash* as a story editor, and I finished off *Viper* a year-and-a-half ago as a supervising producer. Right now, I'm on a show on which my title is consultant, which is Writer's Guild code for, "It's a Canadian show, so we can't call you supervising producer, so we'll give you this and pay you the money." So yeah, I'm trying to figure out what I'm going to do next season. By the time this comes out, I will have figured that out—I hope.

CBA: *Is it much difference than doing comics? Obviously, comics is a very singular act, you worked with Ken on doing* American Flagg!, *but it's very collaborative to do television or film.*

Howard: The big difference is the audience. Comics is an audience of people talking to each other, and television is much more mass market.

CBA: *They're not talking. [laughs]*

Howard: You're also not speaking in a jargon that's so rarefied. I like television, when you're working the money's phenomenal. I like the process. It is a lot like comics, in the sense that you're turning out an episode in an extended picaresque idea.

CBA: *So, do you keep your foot in comics by writing?*

Howard: I have a writing partner that I work with who's also a television writer and producer. The two of us are doing a thing right now with Mike McKone, another Elseworlds book with the Justice League of America. We've just set up a monthly book at Vertigo called *American Century,* a left, liberal version of Steve Canyon, about an adventurer in the 1950s.

CBA: *Like going down to Guatemala and United Fruit?*

Howard: That's our first story arc.

CBA: *So, with television, would you like to do your own characters?*

Howard: That's the great wish of all television writers, to sell a pilot, become a god and make a lot of money and have other people working for them so they can retire.

CBA: *So you obviously have a pilot out there?*

Howard: I write a pilot every year. Nothing's been produced, but I've been paid. I wrote a spec pilot last season which didn't sell, which I'll do as a graphic novel. Hopefully, it'll sell on the back end, but that's a lot of the way comics get done.

CBA: *So, working in comics, is that like a co-career or a hobby?*

Howard: It doesn't pay enough alone. Comics is about ten percent of my income—but I take the work seriously.

CBA: *You obviously derive pleasure out of it, because…*

Howard: If I don't get a job in TV this season, I'll draw comics. The way the hiring season works, I have to stay available for work until June.

CBA: *Are you spontaneous? Like you said before, with the creation of* American Flagg!, *is it spontaneous with you? Somebody says, "Come up with something," and then it's just "Boom!"*

Howard: Sometimes. Different concepts emerge from different places. That sounds really banal, but it's true.

CBA: *Have you conceived of returning to* American Flagg!, *or is he a part of your past?*

Howard: There's always been talk. It's something I might do if I don't get a job this season. It'd be an interesting process. I'd rather have the old material reprinted. It's always a matter of trying to make money off the old stuff.

CBA: *What was the concept with* Black Kiss?

Howard: I wanted to do something utterly filthy—a book that pushed the bounds—a funny sex comic book. The book is pretty funny, if you read it closely. There're lots of laughs in it. I also wanted to do a book that reflected my feelings about Los Angeles. Back then, Los Angeles was a paranoia-creating world, and I wanted to convey that in a comic book.

CBA: *You did that for about a year?*

Howard: 12 issues.

Above: *Howard's cover painting for Marvel Comics Super Special #18 featuring the comics adaptation of* Raiders of the Lost Ark. *Courtesy of Tim Barnes. Indiana Jones ©2000 Lucasfilm, Inc.*

Right inset: *'80s picture of the artist. Photo by Todd Adams. Courtesy of Tim Barnes.*

CBA: *What was the response to that, do you remember? Was it...?*

Howard: I took a huge advance. I didn't expect it to sell. Comics fans tend to like pin-ups, not f*cking. It sold very well, and generated interest in other worlds and other realms.

CBA: *It was collected as a book, right?*

Howard: A lot of times. It was *Thick Black Kiss*, it was *Big Black Kiss*, and it's about to come back out under the Fantagraphics imprint.

CBA: *Did you ever conceive of self-publishing?*

Howard: I did. I had a book I was in prep on, but I got a job. I did *Power and Glory* at the same time I was staffing in television. It had so negative an effect on my personal life and my physical health that I finally realized I couldn't do both things at once. I could write, but I certainly can't draw. And especially not a labor-intensive book. As I said, staffing season this year is between now and June, and if I don't get a job, come July, I'll adapt this pilot that I wrote as a comic book.

CBA: *You said you give characters your personal sensibilities. Is that continuing? Do you still have characters you'd like to get out and is your world view changing as you get older?*

Howard: I don't think I could create a book like *American Flagg!* today. There was a book I was going to

self-publish, which was a reflection of a lot of how I'm feeling today, but again, in a far more abstract way, as opposed to the way *American Flagg!* was.

CBA: *Do you still maintain close contact with comic book professionals, your friends from the '70s?*

Howard: I do with Simonson, for example. I've recently remade the acquaintance of Bruce Jones.

CBA: *And how would you, overall, assess your career in comics?*

Howard: I don't know. I have no real interest in my own work, so it's a difficult question to answer. My walls are covered with pictures, and there's only two of my pieces on the wall—both at the behest of the woman I live with.

CBA: *Is that once it's done, you're not satisfied with it?*

Howard: I don't care. I once described the world's best comic book artist as the world's tallest midget… it's not much of a trick. I love the stuff, but I don't really think much about it anymore. I like *100 Bullets*, I love what Alan Moore's doing in the ABC books, but I don't care that much. I'm not the audience. I like the art and craft of making the stuff, but who gives a sh*t?

CBA: *It's funny, reading that* Comics Journal *interview, that was at the time that* Maus *was coming out, and* Secret Wars *was hot. You explicitly stated that you were kind of in the middle…*

Howard: The phrase was, "Democrats, Republicans and me." To a certain extent, that remains the case. I don't have the skills or the grasp or reach to produce work like *Maus,* I don't feel important enough to do that sort of work. At the same time, I get bored out of my mind doing guys running around in capes beating the sh*t out of each other. So I'm stuck in the middle, which is why I do television, the great middling medium. I'm happy with my life. I feel that comic books are going to go away in my lifetime. I don't think I have a masterpiece waiting to be done before I die.

CBA: *Is it that you live for the moment?*

Howard: I take the work I do seriously. I respect the work I've done before. I don't feel I ever transcended my influences. I don't think it's false modesty.

CBA: *You don't see television necessarily as an end-all, do you?*

Howard: At my age, if I have another ten years of career in television, I'll be perfectly happy. That's the bottom line. Most people out there think film is where the money is, but television is the big money. I have no problem with the idea of working commercially—I've always been a commercial artist.

CBA: *Do you look back on the '70s as a fond time?*

Howard: Absolutely! It was incredibly sexy. I've often said to guys younger than me, "You'll outlive me, but I had a much better time." I had a great time, the work was fun, but it was also a distraction from partying, and I partied out like a motherf*cker!

CBA: *With the '80s coming on, and your success with* American Flagg!… *?*

Howard: I was very married, I lived a very quiet life, but I had a good time. I have lived a charmed life. Unlike most men of my age, I've never had to do anything for a living I didn't want to do. I made a lot, I spent a lot, I had a really good time, and I got all the attention I'd ever want. I mean, what can you ask for? There're so many guys running around whining and complaining about their lives. I'm blessed.

CBA: *Do you see going into television as more of a segue into it, it wasn't that much of a change?*

Howard: When I started, I worked on *The Flash*. That was a really good scholarship to learn what I do for a living. I'm very happy working in television.

My high school career center instructor, Dan Welch, at a Michigan convention in '85 or 86.

This is me and Harold Cupec (r-l), a Pittsburgh cartoonist who took my workshop. He has since been published here and there. He was one of the older and more experienced cartoonists who took my class, most were teens.

This is me from about 1994, taken by student Tom Hall at my cartooning class.

Fiasco Foto Funfest!

Here's me and Gil Kane (l-r) circa 1994. I met him when many years before this, when he was robust if not strapping. By this time he looked pretty ill, and I'm one of those who probably couldn't hide my shock, as if I'd seen a ghost. Oh well...

I meet one of my heroes, Harvey Kurtzman (l), at a King Kon, a show put on by Gary Reed (who later went on to found Calibre Comics) in Michigan, 1985 or so. I guess being published by Kitchen Sink Publishing had certain advantages....

Here's me and indy stalwart Tim Truman (l-r) at a show in St. Paul, 1985. We were never close, it's just a good photo of me when I was skinny.

This is Mike Kazaleh and Denis Kitchen (l-r). Mike and I are meeting Denis for the first time at the Chicago Comicon 1984, after MM was accepted for publication, but before it came out. I snapped the photo.

Here's a photo I snapped of Keith Pollard at King Kon circa 1984.

Here's me, Larry Marder and his wife Cory (l-r), at Kim Howard Johnson's short-lived comic art gallery, circa 1994.

Don Simpson's Strange Saga
On *Megaton Man*, *Border Worlds* and Anton Drek

by Jon B. Cooke
Transcribed by Jon B. Knutson

Don Simpson's savagely satirical Megaton Man arrived just in time to poke fun at the increasingly un-fun Marvel Comics of the mid-'80s. While he has ventured to do other projects such as Border Worlds *and* Wastelands, *it is the Mighty Megaton Man whom the artist is always associated with, for better or worse. Currently drawing MM only for his Internet website, Don is also now working as an illustrator in advertising. This interview was conducted on January 12, 2000 and was copyedited by the artist.*

Comic Book Artist: *Where are you from?*
Don Simpson: I'm from Livonia, Michigan. That's a suburb of Detroit. I was born in 1961 and I grew up in a regular ranch house in the suburbs. We had a black-&-white TV that got UHF stations, and the first thing I remember were Saturday morning cartoons and the *Batman* TV show when it was new—the Adam West *Batman*—and the rerunning of George Reeves' *Superman* shows. I would've been about five or six years old. My mom is quite a seamstress, and she got a pattern that had all three costumes: Batman, Robin and Superman, and for three Halloweens I was one of each. [*laughter*] I was the only blonde Robin anyone had ever seen.
CBA: *When do you remember getting comics?*
Don: I remember them being around. The first one I remember reading was *Voyage to the Bottom of the Sea*, a Gold Key comic, and I read it, folding back the pages, which I saw other kids doing. You're not supposed to do that.
CBA: *To mark the pages?*
Don: No, just to fold back the spine, turn it around and read it. That would've been the late '60s, but I really didn't get the habit until third or fourth grade, at the age of ten. One of the teachers got a stack of comics and apparently somebody forgot to return them at a newsstand or drug store, because there were multiple copies of *Archie*, *Boris Karloff Tales of Mystery*, an issue of *Lois Lane*, a Jack Kirby *Jimmy Olsen* issue, and so on. This was 1972. Maybe the comics dated from late '71. So, we had multiple copies of half a dozen titles. There was a little bookshelf where we kept 'story time' materials, and at the end of the school year, I got a copy of each of these to take home. That Summer, I started reading comics, meaning that I bought new ones off the spinner myself. But I didn't care for the DC stuff. I read the Marvels. I can remember all the issue numbers that I started with—it was the September cover date of 1972, *Amazing Spider-Man* #112, *Avengers* #102….

I remember picking up a *Jimmy Olsen* after Kirby had left, when they'd gone to 20¢. I recall *Swamp Thing* on the stands and stuff like that, but after a little bit of experimenting, I just enjoyed Marvel comics from '72 to '73. I read comics voraciously. I started petering out around '77. Immediately, that first Summer, I decided I was going to draw comics, but by the late '70s, I was in high school, and more into music. I was playing in band, and the comics reading trailed off into studying how people were doing it, and studying page layouts. I was learning anatomy from Burne Hogarth's books, and teaching myself lettering and inking by the time I graduated high school in 1980. So, between 1972 and '80, it mutated from reading for entertainment, collecting and loving comics to more studying and thinking of them in terms of doing them professionally one day.
CBA: *When you were getting into comics, did you seek out back issues?*
Don: There were a few comic book conventions. In fact, I can remember the first convention I went to, and I ended up drawing flyers for this guy, his name was Stu Shapiro, and he's since become immortal in comics, because he was doing conventions in the Detroit area. He was doing a convention called "Fantasticon" up at the old San Souci Hall, which was a little Rotary type of venue, and I met my first couple of professional artists there. I started doing flyers for his shows, and he did a newsletter, and he started doing record conventions. I think he actually did a disco once, which just shows you the times. This would've been like '76, '77, when I was in junior high school. This was my first professional exposure. I'd get five bucks a shot doing these flyers, and in fact, the Howard the Duck craze was really huge at that point. Stu was one of the guys who had gone around and bought every *Howard The Duck* #1 that came out in a hundred square mile radius, one of the first speculators.
CBA: *A real wheeler-dealer, huh?*
Don: He had a whole bunch of these things (*Howard The Duck* #1s), and at a convention one month, he was giving away ten copies as door prizes. That same month, I had agreed to do a flyer in exchange for a *Howard the Duck* #1, which I couldn't afford at that time. It was $10! [*laughs*] He'd paid 25¢ a piece for them. Ten bucks was big money to me, so this was the most lucrative commercial art job I'd ever had up to that point.

I drew the flyer, and delivered it on the day of the convention. Stu was set up on a little tiny stage with a chalkboard and a microphone. This room was really tiny—maybe 40 tables or so—and from there, he had his cash box, and kept an eye on the con floor and made announcements. He had these 10 copies of *Howard the Duck* #1 taped to this freestanding chalkboard. So I came in, showed him the artwork, and I don't know what I'd drawn at that point—it could've been the Silver Surfer or something—and he said, "Oh,

Below: Woo! It's Megaton Man from a 1986 unfinished cover by Dandy Don Simpson! Don sent us so much unused artwork that we're ashamed to say we've only been able to use a fraction. But, muchas gracias, Don! ©2000 Don Simpson.

great, this is wonderful." I said, "You were going to pay me with a *Howard the Duck #1*." "Oh, yeah, right, right," so he turns around and one of the ten that was going to be a door prize, he pulls off and gives it to me! So there were only nine door prizes. And he had advertised ten, which I think shows something about his character. Anyway, this guy—you've probably read about him—disappeared from Detroit by the late '80s, and reappeared in San Diego, changing his name to Todd Loren.

Todd started Revolutionary Comics. Apparently, he was still exploiting teenagers, by the looks of the quality of his line. [*laughter*] Eventually, he was murdered and it's still unsolved. They were actually thinking this Andrew Cunanan guy (who murdered designer Gianni Versace) was involved. But that's my little brush with notoriety! [*laughter*] Stu was my first comic book publisher, as it were.

CBA: *Ah, comics! [laughs] Did you specifically want to do super-hero comics from an early age?*

Don: Oh, yeah. The thing about Marvel was that it went from the Silver Surfer to Howard the Duck, with a big chunk of imaginative territory in-between, where you had Spider-Man and other more-or-less conventional super-heroes. But you had this really Shakespearean melodrama of the Surfer—who was almost like Mr. Spock—an icon of the late '60s, the first New Age super-hero. Then you had Howard the Duck, almost a *National Lampoon/Saturday Night Live* irreverent satire at the other end of the spectrum. Between the two, it really offered quite an imaginary playground, and that was my idea of fun. To be a comic book artist meant drawing everything within those two frames of reference. [*laughter*] My heroes were guys like John Romita, Sr., Gil Kane, John Buscema, and Jack Kirby… all those guys had drawn a little bit of everything. Of course, Kirby had created everything.

To me, the idea of being a comic book artist meant drawing everything, doing a few issues on every series. That's why I have this enormous stable of characters I've created, which doesn't make a lot of sense for a so-called "independent" cartoonist, because if you're working for a company, you can draw *Fantastic Four* for five issues, and then you can move on, and it's not going to have to be canceled. Whereas if you're trying to sustain a solo career, you'll run into a lot of trouble. What I found was people wanted *Megaton Man* over and over again, and I wanted to draw a lot of different kinds of characters and ideas. So, that screwed me up, but that's typical of my career.

CBA: *One of the compelling things about* Megaton Man *is the Marvel "look" to the title. Did you study Artie Simek's lettering and his logo work, for instance? While you started reading Marvel in the '70s, it has a real '60s look to it.*

Don: Oh, yeah. Well, the thing about my neighborhood was, in about 1972, there were still a lot of late '60s comics floating around. There was a kid named Jim Barbee around the block who had *Thor*s dating back to around '66, and he had all the Steranko *Captain America*s, and he had some of the Barry Smith *Nick Fury* stuff. The trades would be pretty unfair, but I could trade five 1972 comics for an issue from '68 or something. There were no price guides then, so I

was pretty much at his mercy. But I did get my hands on the Steranko *Caps*, I recall, and I still have a *Thor* issue with the Wrecker. Kirby had the Wrecker with his crowbar and Thor using Loki's helmet… I mean, just these incredible things. And then I read Kirby's *Fantastic Four*s. Actually, I skipped over one thing, and that was that I do remember, before I started buying comics myself, we were on a newspaper drive—this would've been in the late '60s—and I did get a couple of *Fantastic Four*s from that. I remember the other kids found them and they were passing them around, and I ended up with them. But that didn't really prompt me to go out and buy comics on my own. Anyway, there was still enough of that stuff, and like I said, the first… even the *Jimmy Olsen*s introduced me to Jack Kirby, and then of course, *Origins of Marvel Comics* came out, and things like that in the '70s, and they were always reprinting the origins. In fact, the first *Fantastic Four* issue I bought featured a retelling of the origin, it had an homage to the first issue's cover. What was that, #126 or something? There's a dinosaur coming up from the earth.

CBA: *Right, by John Buscema.*

Don: So, it was still steeped in tradition, and you could still find so much of that stuff around. If I can digress for a moment: The thing about *Comic Book Artist,* and the particular issue that you sent me, #6, was that it just coincided with my time reading comics, and what's interesting about that time is that the Marvel formula had become a

Above: *Don writes: "This is as close to a photo as you're going to get! (I'm the guy wearing the tie.)"*
Below: *Faux* MM *cover from 1983. ©2000 Don Simpson.*

mean, Kirby would draw a hippie character over at DC, and it had no resemblance to anything, but then TV didn't have any resemblance to real life, either, so it wasn't all that remarkable. The comic book medium was just another medium that was getting it wrong. So, I don't know I perceived any nostalgia. I know that I started reading the *Doc Savage* paperbacks a couple of years later, which is set in the '30s, but I don't know that it was… I'm not really sure how it weighed in. I was conscious it was over, but….

CBA: *You obviously clued into it to some degree. What kind of art training did you have?*

Don: I'm self-taught, in terms of comics. The art schools I've attended… [*laughs*] I spent a lot of time in classrooms, but there was either a total absence of figure drawing, or a total absence of cartooning technique. I was completely on my own in terms of finding books and learning about brushes and pen points and Bristol board and things like that. I entered an art school in Detroit after high school. It had a commercial art curriculum and a fine arts curriculum. Cartooning was somewhere in between. The figure… the nude models were really ugly, and the advertising stuff was all client-oriented: Come up with six different ideas so the wrong one can be picked out, which I didn't care for. [*laughter*]

I found that I was learning more about cartooning on my own during the breaks, during Christmas vacation, so I just dropped out. Probably the best art training I had was in high school. There was a vocational program that was strictly commercial art, and for half a day in my senior year, I spent… outside of my high school, there was a magnet school that had various different vocational programs, and the commercial art program was really well-equipped, there were plenty of supplies, and the teacher—a guy by the name of Dan Welch—was really oriented to learning the tools and the procedures, and I got my hands on an airbrush, and ellipse templates, and Rapid-O-Graph pens, and pebble grain matte board, and rubber cement and wax and all that stuff. Pretty much, I was on my own in terms of… you could do a business card, or a logo, or a letterhead or a rubylith. The projects were… really, the emphasis was on the tools, and the materials, not necessarily on thinking like an advertiser, or thinking commercially or philosophizing about design. So, I walked out of there with quite a portfolio of pencil drawings, airbrush drawings, things that were more or less comic book oriented, because to a large degree, we were allowed to follow our own predilections.

CBA: *That was just a half a day?*

Don: Yeah. Like I said, then I went to art college, and it was "how to think like an art director," and I just wasn't prepared for that. I was interested in training in terms of the techniques and the materials and anatomy and storytelling. Not doing marker renderings based on a photograph you pulled out of a magazine. Like I said, the fine art stuff was all very alien… it was like pastels and still lifes and ugly models. So, you had to take some basic courses that involved fine art. Otherwise, in 1980, fine art meant abstraction. I'm still not sure where those two worlds are at. I know that cartooning really felt in-between them. The attitude of the school was, "We don't know anybody who makes a living in cartooning, so it must be incredibly difficult to break into that field, so we're not going to offer any courses in it." Of course, this was Detroit, and people they were turning out were going to airbrush automobile ads and retouch photographs and stuff like that. But at the same time, they were having people do sample *Time* magazine covers. I'm sure they didn't know anybody who had ever drawn a *Time* magazine cover. [*laughter*] That was the way it was. Like I said, I went for a year and then I just dropped out.

CBA: *You went back to the drawing board at home?*

Don: Oh, I washed dishes in a restaurant, and I went to the public library and looked at books, and I went to the museum, and I sat through a lot of art films. In my early 20s, I hung out with an animator by the name of Mike Kazaleh, who penciled *The Ren & Stimpy Show* comic for Marvel years later. He also did a book called *Cap'n Jack* for Fantagraphics.

We were roommates, a couple of undiscovered geniuses, and we had a third roommate who was a filmmaker… [*laughs*] I think he's still working on the same film. He introduced me to a lot of film theory and foreign movies. So the three of us lived the undiscovered genius lifestyle in Detroit, and I washed dishes and worked the odd job thing, at an office supply store, and various things like that.

textbook thing at that point. Kirby had laid down the ground rules, and what was interesting about that time period was that newer people were coming in and loosening it up a little bit. But there was still—even though Kirby wasn't there—it was still all his formulas in place. In a way, it's like *Mad* magazine.

That's really true of Marvel, even to this day. The templates were pretty much there, and it doesn't take much to get your hands on the original thing, or a reprint of it—in this case—the original Marvel comics with Artie Simek lettering.

CBA: *Did you perceive those '60s comics with a false nostalgia? Because you obviously weren't reading them at the time, other than those you got in the paper drive. You seemed to really clue into the Marvel method. I mean, the Stan Lee approach to soap opera.*

Don: John Romita, like I said, was my favorite artist, so I think issue #112 and 113 of *Amazing Spider-Man* probably had the most profound influence on me. I don't know who was lettering that (maybe Costanza, who is not my favorite letterer). I'm not sure I perceived nostalgia one way or another. I can tell, especially when Kirby was doing *Jimmy Olsen* and the Newsboy Legion, he was using these Brooklyn accents, and all these incredibly corny… I mean, I was always aware that comics were just out of it, that these old guys that were drawing this stuff just had no clue as to what was hip or happening in the real world, but that didn't seem to bother me. I

I did some freelance, I did a couple of flyers for Orchestra Hall. [laughs] Just really, strange odd things, business cards for people and stuff like that.

CBA: *What were your aspirations at the time?*

Don: [laughs] I was trying to break into *Heavy Metal*. Of course, by that point, I'd outgrown Marvel, and Jim Shooter had taken over, and John Byrne had taken over, and I remember buying a selection of Marvels off the newsstand in the early '80s—John Byrne's *FF*—and I looked at this stuff and I thought it was horrible, I thought it was just terrible. It didn't work for me at all as a reader anymore. I'd outgrown the whole genre, and it didn't seem like any kind of aspiration anymore, either. Actually, a book had come out called *The Masters of Comic Book Art.* I'd gotten that around the beginning of 1979. I think at that point, it had already been remaindered. But it introduced me to Corben, Wally Wood, Moebius, Crumb and Kurtzman, those in particular, and that extended my whole interest in comics. When I started seeing *Heavy Metal*—I don't think I was 18, but I looked old enough to buy this stuff. So, I started buying undergrounds and European comics. In fact, I was on a trip to France in 1980—a week after graduation I was off to France—I had 16 days in France and Belgium, and brought back a suitcase full of *Bandes Désinées* which is so *cliché* now, but to me it was all new. I remember there was this beautiful French edition of *Moscoso* that I later sold, it was oversized. Anyway, that extended my whole interest in comics. At the same time, the Marvel stuff just seemed to me to be reruns. The new stuff seemed to be just terrible. I remember there was a buzz in art school, when I was going down there, when I was still in it... [laughs] There was this one girl who was a real *X-Men* fanatic. She bought the reprints, and she'd been hoping her whole life they'd start doing new *X-Men* comics. She was really excited about the *X-Men*. So, I went out and I bought a copy, and it was... I don't remember the issue number, it was an issue... there was a two-part story where Kitty Pryde goes into the future...

CBA: *"Days of Future Past."*

Don: I thought it was *horrible*! [laughter] I thought it sucked and was miserable! Of course, that's considered the high point of the series! An absolute classic. You know, this just shows you how incredibly out of it I am. [laughter] This stuff had absolutely no effect on me. *X-Men*, to me, was a reprint book, it always will be a reprint book. I will never understand the *X-Men* phenomenon. So, I was completely out of it, and I was trying to break into *Heavy Metal*, [laughs] I did a couple of really pretentious strips with a naked woman in it, of course, and I sent them to *Heavy Metal* in '81. These were things I did on break from school. I still have the rejection letters from John Workman, saying, "This is nice stuff, but we're kind of filled up

right now. You keep at it, try to find a story." [laughter] I think the only story I had was, "There's a naked woman and a Patton tank." [laughter] And the two characters in the tank I later used in *Border Worlds,* they were the two guys that were driving around in this tank, and they didn't even know what battle they were in. They were lost in the fog, and it was this existential, theatrical black-out strip, and they come across this naked woman, and that's it, that's the whole thing. [laughter] I remember doing a lot of stippling. That was really big, I was doing a lot of stippling. I guess those were my aspirations in those early days.

CBA: *That was also the burgeoning alternative comic market was starting to open up with direct sales—Dave Sim was*

coming out with Cerebus, *and there was* Elfquest *and other books like that. Did you think of doing your own book?*

Don: No. Well, like I said, I bought a lot of undergrounds after high school, about '80, '81, '82. I was buying a lot of undergrounds that were floating around the used bookstores. There were a couple of little funky used bookstores in Detroit, by Wayne State University. So I remember John Pound and Peter Pontiac... who was the guy who did *Dealer McDope?*

CBA: *Dave Sheridan?*

Don: Dave Sheridan. Just anything. I was looking for layouts, looking for technique, looking for anything that had any remote connection to cartooning, and any new kind of influence at that point. I also started getting into modern art and fine art. I was watching a lot of European movies and going to museums and looking at strange photography exhibits, and going to beatnik poetry readings—the whole Bohemian routine! I did not read comics off the newsstand. Like I said, they just struck me as being really horrible. The only thing I do remember

Above: "Parsec," an early science-fiction concept from 1983. Don added, "A bit of Neal Adams in the pencils!" ©2000 Don Simpson.

Left inset: *1981 rejection letter from Jim "Straight" Shooter.*

Far left inset: *Don's scathing wraparound cover featuring Jim Shooter "under oath" for The Comics Journal #115. All characters ©2000 their respective copyright holder. ©2000 Fantagraphics, Inc.*

MARVEL COMICS GROUP
A DIVISION OF CADENCE INDUSTRIES CORPORATION

JAMES SHOOTER
EDITOR-IN-CHIEF

March 2, 1981

Donald Simpson
17416 Pershing
Livonia MI 48152

Dear Donald,

I don't know what to tell you. Your work is pretty far off the mark. It's pretty sketchy and crude -- the drawing is distorted and unconvincing, and the inking is heavy-handed and coarse. That's not what we're looking for.

There are things about your stuff that show me that you do have talent and skill, however. You move figures well, you have a sense of drama and a lot of power and presence in your stuff.

Look closely at some Byrne or Buscema comics and take it from the top. Do some more refined, more careful samples and let me see those.

Best,

J. Shooter

575 MADISON AVENUE
NEW YORK, NEW YORK 10022
212/754-0340
TELEX 23806J

CADENCE
PUBLISHING

reading was *The Comics Journal,* which I found a certain sympathy with because *The Journal* is all about readers who've outgrown super-hero comics and don't know what to do with themselves.

CBA: *[laughs] So they want to read a magazine about it.*

Don: So, they'd read the magazine, and it's got Frank Brunner's angry departure from Marvel, and Gil Kane's longwinded dissertations on how comics are a "virtuoso flea circus." [laughter] And all that stuff! Jan Strnad, "My Brilliant Career at Marvel." I remember that whole genre of articles, and basically, what underlied all of it was this feeling like, "We read Stan Lee when we were ten years old, and we thought we would always read comics, and we don't understand why it doesn't work anymore. We don't understand why the magic doesn't work anymore." That's exactly what I was going through, and it didn't quite rise to the level of film theory, or film criticism, like I was reading in other publications at the time, but it was the closest thing to it. So I read *The Comics Journal* for a few years.

CBA: *So you somewhat knew what was going on.*

Don: I became pretentious, I think.

CBA: *How did that lead to* Megaton Man?

Don: Well, how it leads directly to *Megaton Man* is… in a couple of ways: For one thing, I'd found that these… the Burne Hogarth anatomy and the whole Marvel method was ingrained in me by this point. And yet, I had no more ambitions towards Marvel and no real respect for their house style any more. I wanted to shed those influences, and attack and satirize them. More directly, my roommate Mike Kazaleh and I, we [laughs] had this funky apartment in Detroit, not far from the medical center, and used the kitchen as the art studio. We had two drawing boards set up. So, we had our refrigerator, a small kitchen table, and two drawing boards. One day we got into a really petty argument about what was harder to do, humor or drama. At that point, I was still—in fact, I still am—studying anatomy and different technical aspects of the craft, and we got into this bet, like "I can do comedy any time I want to." So I remember, for a couple of weeks, I was trying to do funny drawings, and I just couldn't do it, it was coming out like really dopey… I was doing little kids that were sappy looking, it looked like Scooby-Doo on Quaaludes or something, it just wasn't funny at all. The closest thing I came to anything that got a laugh was this over-muscled beach bum and with these girls in bikinis clinging around him, and it got a laugh, this was funny! It was this exaggerated muscula-ture, so I kept at that, I kept exaggerating… I found if I kept exaggerating all these super-hero conventions, so I added a costume, red yellow and blue, and the goggles, and tried to make it as over-the-top as I could, and so I had this character design for Megaton Man, and all I needed was a name. So, that's how it came into existence.

Once I had the name, and of course, you have to remember Ronald Reagan was in office, the Cold War was front-page news every day—there were phrases like "Minuteman

Above:
Referring to the panel featuring the drinking collegiates, Don notes, "This sums it all up: Young neurotic cartoonist can't get laid with the college gals!" From the pre-MM #1 experimental strip. ©2000 Don Simpson. **Below:** *MM and the gang from Kitchen Sink. House ad illo by Don. All characters ©2000 their respective copyright holders.*

missile" and "dense pack"; they were going to take missiles and put them on trains and move them around the Western states on rails, and "megaton" was a word right out of the news. Today, you have to explain what that means—a million tons of TNT, or the explosive force thereof. At first I was thinking of "Mighty Man" or something typical. But then when I thought of Megaton Man, that tied in the whole Cold War thing, so it became this hybrid of "What if our Cold War madness was embodied in a stereotypical super-hero character with all the *clichés* of the '60s?" and it was just irresistible at that point.

So, I finally succeeded in having something funny, and it also accomplished the fact that I could draw in any style. I could do Neal Adams inking and Artie Simek lettering, and I could just really have fun with all these influences that were clogging up my brain anyway. [laughter] With the hope and intent, in those days, of really trying to purge myself of these influences. Of course, I never managed to do that! [laughter] I just managed to purge myself of the need to purge myself. At some point, I realized—and I know I'm skipping ahead chronologically—it probably wasn't until the late '80s, maybe even 1990, when I realized I was making fun of comic books that didn't really exist anymore. I was making fun of Kirby and Buscema and Romita and Simek and Stan Lee, and by the late '80s, it was totally Todd McFarlane and Japanese comics and all these other trends, and I was attacking a tradition that was no more! There was nobody to get the jokes anymore. I realized, "Well, I'm a traditionalist at heart, I guess." So, if there's a real difference between early Megaton Man and late Megaton Man, it's that later Megaton Man is more like C.C. Beck's Captain Marvel, in that it's a humorous super-hero, more than a satire of super-hero conventions. But that's how it began, this desire to get these influences out of my system, and yet at the same time, have my cake and eat it, too. I could use all these influences, I could use Neal Adams' inking, and Tom Palmer inking and Steranko kinds of panel compositions and Jack Kirby dots and yet, I wasn't doing it "seriously." It was just a way to be yourself and not be yourself. [laughs]

CBA: *When did you start conceiving of it as an actual series?*

Don: I remember I came up with Megaton Man around November of '81, in terms of the design, this whole little bet I referred to about doing comedy. It would've been in the Fall of '81, and I came up with this character design, and once I had the name, I had the whole concept, because it was this Cold War madness embodied in a *cliché* super-hero who was not too bright, and the whole thing about the Manhattan Project, I needed the name of the newspaper he worked for… I had various other characters off the shelf, like Preston Percy and Rudy Mayo, who were, in fact, characters I'd developed for other ideas, but I brought them in instead of coming up with a parody name for Perry White or something. I just brought in these other characters to fill out these other roles. The concept was more or less complete right when I named the character. However, I didn't really tackle it, I still didn't really feel prepared to start telling stories or anything at that point. I'd done maybe five pages of actual comic artwork, which were really miserable.

CBA: *What was the story?*

Don: It was actually a "John Bradford" story, John Bradford being my *Kolchak: The Night Stalker* newspaper reporter character, who later appears in *Bizarre Heroes.* So I did a five-page story with him. All that time, since high school, I had been doing page layouts, working on my penciling, working on my inking, and it was all prac-tice, all samples. It wasn't anything tied together. It was some time after I had come up with Megaton Man that I really tackled a story, and did a little five-page stream of consciousness/Fellini-influenced little story. I did a little ashcan of it later, but it was really pretentious. After that, it was January of '83 before I started working on issue #1 of *Megaton Man,* and it took me 13 months to do it. I remember my job washing dishes and scrubbing toilets at nine o'clock in the morning, and then at night I'd be inking a panel for *Megaton Man* #1, and I'd do two or three pages at a time…. I'd do these little sequences and then I'd scrap half of it, and I would come back a week later and do five more pages, then I'd move everything around let it sit for a few weeks. Like I said, it was a 13-month process to do the first issue, and I was really obsessed with page turns, like, "Okay, the reader's eye will move across the page and they'll get to the last panel, and then they'll turn the page and there's a big surprise." I mean, I really put a lot of effort into all kinds of things like that, which after… now that I've done it a while, I'm not so keyed-up about those things. I think it's important when you're starting out, you want to consider all the aspects of it, the effect it's going to have on the reader.

So I was taking my time, I didn't have a publisher lined up, of course—I didn't have any contact with the comic book industry, I just had my friends look at it and critique it, and we'd discuss "should this be a close-up, or should this be a long shot?" or whatever. There was almost a film editing approach to it, where I would drop things, paste over panels or something, and finally, in early '84, I had a finished issue. I made Xerox copies of it. I'd only thought of this as a one-shot, but I had a list of 15 publishers, including Epic [laughs] and Heavy Metal and Mad magazine, and Marvel, DC, First Comics, Pacific Comics… Eclipse… all these publishers that are now no longer in existence. I mailed out… I remember I mailed out 15 separate copies to different publishers. In ten days I heard back from Kitchen Sink. Over the next eight months or so, I was still getting rejection letters back from other publishers.

CBA: *What did Kitchen Sink's letter say?*

Don: Well, I remember the moment it was slipped under the door. I was living in this little hovel of an apartment of my own at that point, and the landlady was delivering the mail on Sunday, for some reason. It all came to her place, so she was delivering it, and she shoved it under the door. I could see it was a blue envelope and it had the Kitchen Sink logo, the dripping faucet by Leslie Cabarga… it took up the whole left side of the front of the envelope. I'd sent a self-addressed stamped manila envelope for return, and I realized immediately if it had been a rejection, I'd have gotten my big manila envelope. When I saw the blue envelope, I realized I had someone who was interested.

CBA: *Was it from Denis Kitchen?*

Don: Oh, yeah. It said, "For 15 long years, I've been reading unsolicited submissions, *blah-blah-blah*, this is the first one that really made me laugh out loud, etc., etc., etc." He loved it, and wanted to do it as a regular series, which I had no conception of at that point. He also projected sales between 25,000 and 50,000… although we never made it to 25,000! [laughs] (We made it to 23,000, I think.) He also projected figures like I'd be paid $7000 an issue, and that never quite happened. In fact, the colorist made more money off the book than I did, generally. Kitchen Sink had this long-standing—well, I don't know if it was long-standing—they had this policy of paying the colorists $50 a page, which was something to brag about, I guess, but it was coming out of my money. [laughs] I think on most issues, I was making something like $43 a page for everything else. I would say, "Gee, Denis, I think it's great that we have the highest-paid colorists in the industry, but I'm only making 43 bucks for writing, drawing, lettering, inking, and designing a logo!" He said, "Well, Don, look at it this way: You own the copyrights, and you'll be able to reprint these books." At that point, the first two issues were sold out, so I said, "Well, okay, let's reprint those first two issues." And he said, "Hold on!" [laughs] "I've been a publisher for a number of years, and doing full-color reprint, I don't think would be feasible at this point. You can't expect the same level of sales." So consequently, we probably couldn't do any color, and if we did a black-&-white reprint, he didn't think that would do the work justice, and on and on and on. I had very little control over my destiny at this point.

CBA: *What frequency were you coming out with the magazine?*

Don: I ended up doing it bi-monthly. I did the first issue in 13 months, with a lot of learning and exploring, and trials and errors… I'd learned a lot about how to make a comic book, but I really didn't think of *Megaton Man* as more than a one-shot. I had science-fiction ideas, I had other kinds of ideas which, to some extent, I explored later on. But Denis said, "Well, you know, this ought to be in full color, because it parodies full-color comics," and he was doing *The Spirit* in full color at that point. The market, even into early '84, was still good for independent color comics. Eclipse had published *John Law*, which was an Eisner one-shot that sold 75,000 copies.

CBA: *Really?*

Don: Yeah. [laughs] It showed up at Eclipse, and Denis had passed on it, because he didn't think color would make money at that point.

So, he had passed up a chance to make a killing on Eisner in color that went to another publisher. So he started doing *The Spirit* in color. Of course, nobody ever sold 75,000 copies again. *The Spirit* in color maybe sold 18,000 copies or something like that. But he was still thinking, "I passed on this chance, I'm going to get in on this," so everything was going to be in color all of a sudden. I remember in those days, [laughs] we thought Baxter paper would make comics a household word, you know. "The public doesn't read comics, they think comics are for kids, if only we had Baxter paper, that's the solution!" [laughter] So, *Megaton Man* was going to be a Baxter color comic, but he didn't want to just do it as a one-shot, but as an ongoing thing. Psychologically, I'm just like Megaton Man: "Okay, as long as it's temporary, I'll give it a try." I can be talked into anything. So, [laughs] I endeavored to do a series, and I didn't really have a follow-up. But from the time the first issue was accepted in March of '84—it wasn't actually published until December—I don't know what was going on, there were a couple of different color printers he was looking at, and I think he was having trouble with some of them, so he finally found Quebecor in Montreal, which was known as Ronald's in those days. And so, there were several false starts with the first issue coming out, but that gave me some time, and all that Summer I was really sweating over the second issue.

I came up with 60 pages of material that didn't make any sense. [laughs] So, I put that aside, and one day I went for a walk and I got this inspiration for the second issue, which was that Megaton Man joins the Megalopolis Quartet for one issue. Since the See-Thru Girl leaves in the first issue to go to Ann Arbor, I thought, "Oh, yeah, there's the idea!" So, I did that in about six weeks, and that's really where I learned how to ink and how to draw, because if you would watch me ink a panel for *Megaton Man* #1, it would be very slow and painstaking, but I don't think I could do a curve more than half an inch long with a brush, I was just too insecure or

Above: *Page from the "lost" second issue of* Megaton Man *featuring material later reworked for subsequent issues of MM. Note the intense detail. ©2000 Don Simpson.*

something. But that second issue, I remember thinking, "I've got a deadline here!" So, I would actually whip that brush and really go to town! It really improved my efficiency a great deal, and after that, I had these 60 pages of material that was floating around, so I started breaking that off in chunks. The third issue, up through the sixth or seventh issue, I was still using pieces of this material, and I had little scenes and set pieces and stuff. So, that helped me out, but I was really going by the seat of my pants, and I didn't have any long-term ideas.

I didn't really think of *Megaton Man* at that point as being more than just a pastiche of clichés, and the characters were really just imitations of existing comic characters and so forth. I didn't really think of it in terms of this was a cast of characters that was of my own making, that I could really tell stories with. I don't think I really got the hang of it. Dave Schreiner, the editor, often would tell me—because I would complain, especially after I moved out to Wisconsin to be closer to Kitchen Sink (in fact, I lived on the property for a year)—I would complain, "I want to do other kinds of ideas, I don't want to just do this parody of the month, I don't want to be Weird Al Yankovic." Dave would say, "Well, you know, aside from the Marvel parody, you really have a nice little cast of characters here with nice personalities, and you're selling yourself short." But I couldn't see that, and I didn't really start to see that until *Return of*

Megaton Man, which was the miniseries I did later.

I was still thinking, "I have to make fun of Burne Hogarth and *Dynamic Anatomy,* and I have to make fun of Steranko, and Neal Adams and Marvel comics with every single panel." And if I wasn't making fun of it, if you weren't laughing, I was sinking to the level of just doing a commercial comic book, selling out or something. I really wanted those credentials of being an artiste, above this genre stuff. But I was just running out of material, because I was making fun of the comic books I read as a kid and cared about, and I loved, and after that, I really had no desire to make fun of whatever the latest thing was in the industry. Denis was coming up with these ideas like… I think the Punisher had a movie or something, so he said, "Why don't you do a *Punisher* movie parody." Oh, that would've made a lot of money, you know… [*laughs*] I don't think anyone ever saw that movie. I didn't really have any interest… *normalman* was going on at the same time, and Valentino was making fun of *Elfquest,* and he was making fun of *Cerebus,* and *Zot!* or whatever else was being published at that time. For me to read a book off the shelf and really try to get a sense of it, and try to make fun of it, was such an enormous labor. I mean, at least with the Marvel stuff, I had them in my memory bank, I could remember how the pages looked, literally!

The only time I had to do research, and there was a lot of money at stake, was when I was parodying Image comics, and Liefeld and Valentino called me up, and Larry Marder really facilitated this whole thing before he was officially on the payroll at Image. They called me up and they wanted me to do a parody of Image in 1992, and so I had to read a whole stack of Image comics [*laughter*] to try to find something to parody, and most of the comics at that point were nothing but press releases! In fact, even after they were published, they were still just press releases. They were just these very flimsy concepts, a couple of costume designs, I had to make fun of the title…. [*laughs*] It was really a lot of work! But, I made $45,000 off it, so [*laughter*] that was a different case. But, back in the early '80s, I was just in over my head! I was trying to do a bi-monthly series, storylines that were just barely out of control… I remember I took Yarn Man and I wrote him out of the strip, I thought I'd have him go off into the future and that was like a great idea, but then I couldn't remember what I was thinking when it came time to actually develop that concept [*laughter*], so I was just doing all kinds of things, and I didn't know what I was doing. I had too many characters—and like I said, my basic impulse was I wanted to try different things, I didn't just want to do one. I didn't want to do *Cerebus,* 300 issues of one title character. I didn't want to do 300 issues of *Megaton Man,* I didn't think all my ideas would fit into something called "Megaton Man." I had ideas for a *Star Wars* science-fiction saga, I had ideas for super-heroes that were not funny, I had sex comics ideas, as it turns out, that I didn't know I had at that point. But I had all kinds of different impulses and things I wanted to do in comics that I didn't want to try to shoehorn them all into one title.

As I say, I didn't quite realize—and of course, I didn't take anybody's word for it—that you couldn't be John Romita or Jack Kirby or Gil Kane when you were trying to do your own little one-comic career. I switched from *Megaton Man* to *Border Worlds* and just confused everybody. I thought, "Well, people will follow me." I follow artists, you know? If Robert Crumb does *Weirdo,* or if he does *Hup!,* or if he does *Best Buy Comics* or whatever he does, I'm always there. So, I figured that's just the way it would work for me, and of course, it didn't. [*laughs*] People were like, "I don't get this, I'm not going to buy this anymore." So, I was really struggling, and the first… the ten issues of *Megaton Man,* I was giving it the ol' college try, but it was a labor.

CBA: *When did you realize that it was going to be ten issues, that it wasn't going to continue? Were sales pretty steady, did they plateau?*

Don: The first issue, I think, initially sold 17,000. It sold out in a week, and the second issue sold 18,000. The third issue, I think, that was the highest-selling issue, that sold 22,500. Then, it leveled back to 19,000-18,000. At some point, I realized, "Well, I should really make this finite." *Amazing Heroes* did a preview issue—back in those days, Fantagraphics put out *Amazing Heroes* with these preview issues, which were like *TV Guide*'s fall previews. This was even before *Previews* became thick, and everybody would give them their press releases and draw covers and stuff. Everybody announced… 90% of this stuff never came out. I got together with Dave and Denis, and I said, "Look, I'll wrap up *Megaton Man* at #12." By that point, I was already doing *Border Worlds* as a back-up feature, that was in the back of my mind as the next thing. But then one day, Denis calls me into the office, and we sit down, and Dave and Pete Poplaski was there, and he says, "Look, the color comics are losing money. *Death Rattle*'s losing money, *The Spirit*'s losing money. *Megaton Man* is making money, but it's not enough to cover everything else. So, we're going to phase out the color comics." I was on issue #7 or 8 by then. So I said, "Look, we'll just make #10 the last issue. If we're going to do black-&-white comics, I'd rather do *Border Worlds*, because I think it's moody, it's s-f, it's more like a b-&-w movie."

Denis said, "Well, there's something to be said for continuing *Megaton Man* for the trademark, blah blah, you've established the character, etc. But I believe in artists, I believe you should do what you feel enthusiastic about, your stuff is great, etc.." So, it was decided. And there are still people out there that accuse me of breaking a promise. "Why didn't you go to #12 like you promised!?!" Well, it was an arbitrary number. But it's not like you were gypped out of anything, because those issues didn't exist, it was just a number. That was the demise of the color comic line at Kitchen Sink. It really hastened the end of *Megaton Man* for me, because I was eager to try other things.

CBA: *You actually lived at Kitchen Sink for a period?*

Don: Pete Poplaski and I both lived there. Let's see, the first couple of issues of *Megaton Man* had been published, the third issue was at press, and I remember working on the fourth issue and I was still living in Detroit. I took a trip to Chicago. I had lost my virginity with this girl [*laughs*] that had moved from Detroit to Chicago, so I went and visited her, and I was there for a week. I'd also told Denis I was going to be in Chicago, and he had come down… he was planning to come down to Chicago for a Capital Distributors' meeting because they had just opened a warehouse in Chicago. There was going to be an open house at this warehouse, so I went to Chicago, hung out with this girl, and we quickly realized that any prospect of a future relationship was just going nowhere. The minute I got off the elevator and knocked on her door, I thought, "What am I doing?" [*laughs*] So I hung around with her for a couple of days, and then this open house came and I went there. We'd already arranged that I was going to go back to Wisconsin with Denis and hang out there for a while. That was my plan, I was going to go to Chicago, hang out for a week, and then I was going to go to Wisconsin for a visit. So, I met up with Denis and his wife at the time, Holly Brooks, and we drove back to Princeton, Wisconsin that night, after this open house.

I also met Larry Marder that evening, which was probably even more fateful… it's interesting, because Larry Marder did a book called *Beanworld*, and my second issue of *Megaton Man* had come out, and there was a little signing at this store in Detroit, and we did the signing, we did some autographs, and I remember Bill Loebs was there, and a couple of other local artists were there. We had a nice little signing and we went out for pizza, but I remember that *Beanworld* #1 was on the racks, and I had picked that up, and it looked interesting, nice use of type and so on, and I was going to buy it, and the retailer said, "Oh, you can have it." So, I stuck it into my portfolio, and then I never thought anything more about it. Two months later, I'm in Chicago, and Larry appears… we're at this open house in the distributor's warehouse, and there's a little table set up, and there's all these retailers and they're all selling stuff 40% off, and they're going mad, and they're tearing apart boxes and stuff, and a few people were talking to me. I think there might've been a couple other artists there, and we were doing autographs and chatting and stuff, and Denis and Holly are there, and I think there was a little bit of wine and cheese, whatever… but it was mostly retailers tearing up the inventory, getting 40% off. Suddenly, this guy appears in front of me, a guy that looks like a beatnik or hippie… he had a goatee and the whole thing, and it was Larry Marder, and he says, "Hey man, you don't know me, but I do a book called *Beanworld*. I think *Megaton Man*'s great," and I said, "You're not going to believe this,

but… I think I still have it on me," I looked in my portfolio and I pull out *Beanworld* #1, and I said, "Is this what you mean?" [*laughs*]

CBA: *Nice entré.*

Don: [*laughs*] Larry goes, "Oh, wow!" It was like fate or whatever. So there we are, and he lived in Chicago at the time, so we really hit it off. Anyway, that night I drove back to Wisconsin, to this little farm house where Kitchen Sink was located in a barn. It was very rural, this was out in the cornfields, about two hours away from Milwaukee, about six hours away from Chicago. He had this farm property with a house and a cabin and a motor home and this barn which he converted into a warehouse and office space. So, I stayed out there, and I was only going to stay there for a week, and I thought, "You know what? I really don't have anything tying me to Detroit, so why don't I just move all my stuff?" So, a week later, me and Pete Poplaski took the Kitchen Sink van back to Detroit, loaded up, and so, I stayed at Kitchen Sink for a little over a year. I was out in the cornfield, a 20-minute drive just to get a hamburger, as I recall. [*laughter*] A very sparsely populated area, like a monastery for comic book artists.

CBA: *I think it was pretty early on, you teamed up with Alan Moore to do a wonderful job in* Anything Goes!, *"Pictopia"? How did that come about?*

Don: Gary Groth was doing this benefit book— he and Harlan Ellison were being sued by Mike Fleischer—and they had this Alan Moore script, and I guess somebody else was going to draw it,

Above: Don's unpublished ad for *Return of Megaton Man*. ©2000 *Don Simpson. Below: Page from Alan Moore & Don's "Pictopia," from* Anything Goes! #2. ©2000 *Alan Moore and Don Simpson.*

Above: Border Worlds #6 cover. **Below:** Jenny Woodlore, unemployed earthling, from Border Worlds, in a 1995 unpublished drawing. ©2000 Don Simpson.

but Gary ended up giving it to me. I remember I must've been working on *Megaton Man* #7 or 8, because I remember it was late in the day for *MM*. The Alan Moore thing was an eight-page script, but it was so dense I ended up expanding it to 13 pages. Since I was doing it for free, they couldn't control what I was doing. That came out very nice, in fact—up until that point, I'd only worked with my own ideas, I'd never collaborated with a writer, and Alan Moore, frankly, has spoiled me for anybody else, [*laughter*] because when you read an Alan Moore script, he just tells you everything on his mind. It's as if you're getting the idea yourself. I mean, "This is the idea, this is what we want to communicate to the reader, and now it's your problem. Draw it and interpret it whatever way you can." So, you're really, "Oh, gosh, this is a really great idea, how in the hell am I going to draw it?" I've never had a script like that from anybody else, where you feel like you've got a really great idea, and that you really have to live up to it. Most scripts are just a long shot, dialogue, dialogue, close up, dialogue. It's very cold.

CBA: *So, was this stream of consciousness? Was it an outpouring of information?*

Don: No, he'd be like, "Here's the idea of the story, and this is what's running through the characters' heads, and the mood, the time of day, the atmospheric conditions, the walls are sweating little beads of moisture.." He'd just paint this picture in words, and you'd think, "Oh, my God!" And then he would say, "Well, this is what I want in this shot," you could draw a 5,000 people crowd scene, or a close-up of a fly…. either way, you know, "That's what's on my mind." It's like that throughout the whole script, you'd get his whole idea, as if you'd thought of it yourself. If you'd read it, it'd just come alive in your mind, and then you had to figure out how to draw it.

CBA: *Did you ever talk to Alan about the finished product?*

Don: Oh, yeah, I think he was real happy with it. In fact, I actually changed the title. [*laughs*] It was originally called, "Fictopia," and I changed it to "Pictopia," because it just seemed to me that pictures are what comics are about, and again, Fantagraphics learned about it, and they called Alan, and they said, "I'm not going to bother fighting you, because you're doing it for free, so…" things like that. I met him in the Summer of '85 or '86, when he was in San Diego, and he thought it was great, and in fact, I remember we were at some banquet or something, and he leans over to me and says, "You know, I'm gonna rip-off *Megaton Man* , I thought I should tell you." I said, "Well, okay!" [*laughter*] He said, "I'm doing this thing called *Watchmen*,

and I've got Dr. Manhattan, and he's this radioactive hero, it's actually nothing like Megaton Man, but I just thought I'd tell you." Actually, there is a scene in *Watchmen* where Dr. Manhattan and his girlfriend are up on a rooftop, and they're "on patrol" and having an illegitimate rendezvous, and that's straight out off….

CBA: *"Stella by Starlight"?*

Don: Right, *Megaton Man* #4. And I'm like, "Hey, wait a minute! Don't I get any credit for this?" [*laughter*]

CBA: *So, he obviously liked your strip.*

Don: Yeah, I think so. And then, of course, we worked on… I wouldn't say collaborated, but there was a book called *1963* which I was lettering, and I inked one of the episodes. I got him on the phone in England, and I said, "I'm lettering this, and I think I have some questions." Everybody was going to have this funny name, like "Jaunty Jim Valentino," and "Roarin' Rick Veitch," and "Affable Al Moore"… everybody was coming up with a pseudo Marvel Bullpen name. I said… I think I was going to be "Dubious Don" [*laughter*] and I said to him, "Well, what do you think of Dandy Don?" He says, "Dandy Don? Oh, that's fine. You can do whatever you want, you're the letterer!" [*laughter*] So I was "Dandy Don" from that point on.

CBA: *The merchandising of Megaton Man started right off the bat with buttons?*

Don: Yeah, Kitchen Sink was big into buttons. They had a little button-maker, and they'd done a series of "World Famous Cartoonists," with Sergio Aragonés, Harvey Kurtzman and Hugh Hefner. [*laughs*] They had all these pin-back buttons they'd made, and so he naturally thought a set of Megaton Man buttons would be cool, and we did a T-shirt pretty quickly… I think that was about it. It wasn't so much licensing as it was in-house stuff that looked like licensing.

CBA: *You actually had the buttons made in-house, and an employee would actually work it all day?*

Don: Yeah, you had to print some paper, and then you had a little circular device that would cut it out, and you had a piece of plastic, then the paper, and the back metal pieces, and you'd put it into this little press thing, which looked like something you'd uncork a wine bottle with, and it was clamped down, and it would manufacture little buttons. It was in-house, made up as needed. They're pretty common, just about every political campaign can get ahold of that stuff.

CBA: *You were doing political satire within the realm of Megaton Man. Were you politically active at the time? Were you part of Nuclear Freeze movement?*

Don: Oh, no. [*laughs*] I was just making my commentary. In fact, Ronald Reagan was our President, but when it came to drawing the President, I couldn't imagine even caricaturing the guy, I just had no taste for him at all. Anybody that calls their wife "Mommy" is a little suspect. [*laughter*] I was big into movies, and the idea of Orson Welles playing the President struck me as very funny, combining different elements of his roles and the fact that he's the director… that appealed to me. It is Reagan to the extent it was an old Hollywood actor playing the President, but I thought Welles made it more universal.

CBA: *He made a better Hollywood actor, anyway.* [*laughter*]

Don: Certainly, we're still living with this potential nuclear nightmare. Back in the early '80s, I remember it just rising to a real level of palpable fear and paranoia that bombs were going to drop at any moment. In Detroit, the General Motors building was Ground Zero, and you could see that on the horizon.

CBA: *These are about the days of the mini-series* The Day After, *and* Threads, *that British film about post-nuclear war society.*

Don: Yeah, *Dr. Strangelove* seemed more appropriate in those days than ever, and that was playing in all the art houses. I think maybe my politics was more influenced by the satires like *Dr. Strangelove* than any real ideological commitment or anything. I think of *Megaton Man* mostly as a parody of super-heroes, but Detroit is a unique place. There were a lot of hard-core socially-active movements that I brushed up against, if nothing else. There used to be the newspaper called *The Fifth Estate* which preached a post-industrial radicalism. It was left of Communism, and was really out there. I remember articles in that, it's a free giveaway, and they ran a series of articles, one called "Words: The Enemies of Ideas." [*laughter*] An later, the same guy wrote an article called "Ideas: The Enemies of Thought." [laughter] I guess the functioning principle was that once you conceive something, and you crystallize it into a word, or into an idea, then you stop thinking about it. It stops being a living thing, it's just a packet of information or something. They were really out there, socialists, lesbian separatist groups… Detroit is really a hard-core place, it's not an easy town to survive comfortably in.

CBA: *Right, there's crime, but it's also a heavily union-influenced town.*

Don: It's a blue-collar town. I remember going to the art films and going to the museum and the library, but these were little oases that were separated by yards of concrete that were just really desolate. It sure wasn't Paris, where you'd have cafes and bookstores and movie houses all lined up, you know? In Detroit, it was really sporadic and it was a real harsh reality, this real Reagan America urban decay feeling that separated these little bits of culture. I'd go catch a 16mm movie over at the university, and I'd come back to the museum to catch a 35mm film, and in between, it was just this real desolate, arid wasteland of Detroit. And that was '80s America. Of course, it didn't help that I was completely broke and washing dishes for minimum wage. But I guess that was my outlook, and again, the people that I came in contact with in the art colony, and the people that were socially active, who were of this real independent strain, real die-hard breed that had really hardened, dogmatic thoughts about the way things should be, and….

CBA: *Up the proletariat, and all that?*

Don: Well, it varied, it was a little bit of everything. It would depend. I remember feminists, socialists, who had very strict theories about how things should work, and other people who were just drop-outs, you know, "f*ck everything!"

CBA: *Right. During the same time, while you were doing political satire, you were obviously satirizing Marvel comics. Did Marvel take any umbrage to your portrayal of the Fantastic Four, with the Megatropolis Quartet, Yarn Man as being The Thing, for instance?*

Don: Yeah. Like I said, I initially thought of *Megaton Man* as a one-shot, and when I introduced the Megatropolis Quartet in the first issue, I really wasn't planning on using them again. Then I had the idea of having Megaton Man join the Megatropolis Quartet in the second issue, and it stretched all the way through to the fifth issue, where I was still having flashbacks with the Megatropolis Quartet. So they inadvertently became a major component of the storyline. Not only that, but more particularly, we were selling a button that had Megaton Man saying, "Are you kidding? I eat X-Men for breakfast!" [laughter] So Marvel's lawyers finally sent us a little "cease-and-desist" note. I remember, I was at the Chicago Comi-Con, and Jim Shooter had mentioned this in passing. [laughs] "Oh, by the way, we're sending you a little cease-and-desist. It's nothing personal." When it finally came, it just really decimated me, I was depressed for six weeks. But I think now I can see it with a little more perspective. They just said, "You're selling this button, it's got our trademark on it, and you're making fun of our trademarks." It was really legal…

CBA: *There wasn't a drawing of X-Men, right? It was just him saying that?*

Don: Yeah. It's just the parody of their trademarks, and their concerns, *blah blah blah blah blah*…. so, Kitchen had his lawyer write back. We said, "Well, we're sold out of the button, and we're not producing any more…. fair use and satire, *blah blah blah*… in any event, we're moving on in our storyline, so we're not going to be doing those things any more." So, we basically just said, "We're not doing anything wrong, but as it turns out, we're not doing it anymore anyway." So that was how it was handled, and we never heard anything more from it. I think probably the worst thing about that whole incident was that we chose to publicize it, which I think was Denis saying, "Let's put out a press release, we're being picked on by Marvel." So we put out a press release, and frankly, like I said, it (Marvel's letter) had just been a run-of-the-mill legal document. It came right after issue #5, and it was one of the reasons I started doing the Border Worlds back-up feature, it prompted me to think about doing other things more seriously. But, it really never threatened… it's not like "Megaton Man looks like Cyclops" or something like that, or "We're going to shut you down," or anything like that.

SIMPSON 87

"You made fun of our characters for several issues, and now it's bordering on unfair use." And it was real run-of-the-mill. We should've just said, "Okay, we'll have our lawyers write back and that'll be the end of it," and not made anything more of it.

It should've just been the lawyers talking to each other and saying, "Okay, we're not going to do it anymore" and that's it. But instead, we chose to put out a press release, and the fall-out of that is, to this day, people come up to me and say, "Oh, it's too bad that Marvel made you stop doing *Megaton Man*." [laughs] Or, "It's too bad that you can't do *Megaton Man* any more, that you were interrupted, or you couldn't do it for five years." The public just can't follow the subtleties. They assume there was a cause-and-effect, when in fact my career just took some turns. It's assumed that it all happened within the space of one week, and that Marvel sued us, we lost, we had to pay untold amounts of damages, and I didn't draw *Megaton Man* for a period of time, or something. They just get it all confused. If we'd just never mentioned it… I stopped doing *Megaton Man* a couple years later because I didn't feel like doing *Megaton Man* any more at that point… but nobody can understand that. You get a lot of misunderstanding, and I think that's the one regret I have about it, is that we publicized it, just because subtleties escape people.

CBA: *Right, it was a very highly volatile time for relations with the*

Above: *Unpublished* Border Worlds *cover. Eghads!* Can it be the Megacontraptoid??? **Below:** *1996 unpublished sketch of Jenny Woodlore. ©2000 Don Simpson.*

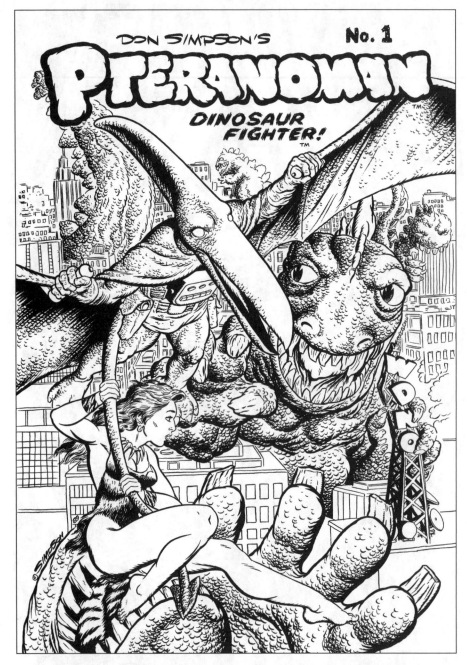

DON SIMPSON'S

PTERANOMAN
No. 1
DINOSAUR FIGHTER!™

fans, a hostile environment where even The Comics Journal *wasn't allowed within the Marvel offices, for instance.*

Don: Right.

CBA: *There was immediate sympathy for your cause, whatever it was, because it appeared anti-Marvel.*

Don: Yeah, those were the days. That's certainly the way we tried to play it. But I look at it now and it seems a lot more run-of-the-mill and unextraordinary. It only just confused people. Marvel's letter really had no effect, other that to get me thinking about eventually doing some of my other ideas besides *Megaton Man.*

CBA: *Then you moved over to do* Border Worlds *as its own book.*

Don: Yeah, that was my European, Wally Wood, and film influences, combined. I wanted to express those in this science-fiction epic, and again, I operated under the assumption that a comic book artist can pretty much do different kinds of material, and his audience would follow. Of course, I was in for a rude shock. [*laughs*]

CBA: *What happened?*

Don: Well, the sales just plummeted after the first issue. There was the b-&-w boom at the beginning, and the first issue we sold 20,000 of for a $1.95 b-&-w comic, so that was pretty good. Then, the second issue dropped to 14,000, then the next issue dropped to 8,000, something like that. The last issue solicited was something like 7,000.

CBA: *What do you attribute that to? The b-&-w implosion?*

Don: A lot of it to the b-&-w implosion, because they were selling

150,000 *Hamster* comics in those days. That all collapsed at the same time, and the fact that I'd switched from doing a full-color super-hero humorous title to a really depressing science-fiction story had a lot of people… it was also for mature readers, and people were just confused, and took this as a opportunity to drop it… drop me, I guess. [*laughs*]

CBA: *Were you single-minded in going as far as you could with the strip, continuing it? You must've had people, Denis among them, who were saying, "Well, do Megaton Man, at least that sells"?*

Don: Well, yeah. [*laughs*] Denis was the first one to say, "Just go back to *Megaton Man.*" It became apparent pretty quickly that he was not a big fan of *Border Worlds.* In fact, I can remember when we were talking about the color line folding, and he was saying, "Well, there's something to be said for continuing with a character you've established, but then, on the other hand, you've got to do what inspires you." Years later he virtually screamed at me in a fax—if you can scream in a fax. It was very strongly worded, to say the least, "You would never listen to anybody, and I told you to stick to *Megaton Man,* but you had to be mercurial, and you wouldn't listen!" and so forth.

CBA: *Were you mercurial?*

Don: [*laughs*] Well, I don't know. I clearly remember Denis being very dispassionate as we discussed the post-color options. The choice was left to me and I made the best one I could. I may be guilty of hearing only what I want to hear, but I did hear that doing *Border Worlds* was an option, if that was my choice. No, as far as *Megaton Man* is concerned, I think I finished what I started. I gave it the old college try. For *Megaton Man* being a one-shot, nobody's ever given me credit for trying to do it bi-monthly, least of all Denis. "You just wouldn't listen to anybody!" this thing. I'm like, "You're welcome, Denis, I tried my best." I tried doing *Border Worlds,* I was about halfway through the story when it ended. It was very painful for me to have to stop, and I said, "Look, Denis, at least offer me a mini-mum page rate or something." He said, "Oh, well, we can't do that." At that point, DC had come along with this thing called *Wasteland,* which I was doing, something like triple the page rate for half the work. And it was DC's worst beginner's page rate.

CBA: *You didn't write it, right?*

Don: Yeah, I was just hacking it out, which was kind of unfortunate and I got into some bad habits. I did 18 issues of *Wasteland.* Prior to that, I didn't have a lot of experience taking other people's scripts and ideas and trying to interpret them. But about halfway through those 18 issues, I developed a method which started to be successful where I could actually break down a script and do a thorough job with the artwork. Not great, but thorough, so at least I wasn't hating my time at the drawing board, which had become the case. It was a learning process.

I remember the moment when I had to pull the plug on *Border Worlds.* There was an issue of *Wasteland,* a new script that had come in the mail, and there was my plans for *Border Worlds #7,* versus this *Wasteland* script that would pay $1,200. I had to make a choice, and I did the *Wasteland* job, and we put *Border Worlds* on suspension, and it was very painful, and Denis was like, "Well, you couldn't even follow through and do 12 issues of *Megaton Man,* like you promised. Now this. You never finish what you start." [*laughs*] I killed a book he hated.

CBA: *I take it that relations with Denis were strained after this?*

Don: Well, you know…. [*laughs*] I became disillusioned almost the moment I moved out there, but definitely by September of '85. That would've been around the time we got the letter from Marvel, although that really had little to do with it. Familiarity breeds contempt, I guess. Living on your publisher's property isn't conducive to a long term partnership. I don't really even want to go into it, it's a lot of petty things.

But you'd just get disillusioned, you'd realize that the publisher has got more than one iron in the fire. Will Eisner would call, and we'd be like, "Shhh! Denis is on the phone with *Will Eisner!*" [*laughs*] At some point, you begin to resent that, and you'd say, "F*ck this." Denis was on the mountaintop talking to Moses… [*laughter*] And after he'd get off the phone with Eisner, he'd be radiating pure energy. [*laughter*] "I've just been speaking to *Will.*" And then, I felt, he'd lord it over the rest of us mortals.

It all sounds petty, but the point being familiarity breeds contempt, and I became disillusioned, I felt that my work should be promoted more, and things weren't being done, and sales were dropping, books weren't being reprinted, the colorist was making more off the book than I was. I actually started coloring half the book.

CBA: *Did you have Border Worlds completely mapped out?*

Don: *[laughs]* I don't have *anything* mapped out! These days if I can think six weeks in advance on the Internet, it's a lot further ahead than I did back in the '80s. The hardest thing to achieve for an artist is really gaining that overview, and I think it comes with experience. In the beginning it's enough to get a handle on doing a page layout. Covers are easy, pin-ups are easy in a certain sense. Although, I think my covers could probably be a lot stronger. But splash pages, and then… okay, now a six-panel page, where you have a progression of images, and then you turn the page, and there's another page… that piece-by-piece, step-by-step approach, it takes a long time to get the hang of that, and then, to think of a whole issue, or three issues, or ten issues—really plot out something and have that big picture in mind—it doesn't come naturally, I think it comes progressively the more you do it. I've been working on this storyline on the Internet now for three years, and I have a pretty clear idea of what scene follows what scene. But even now there are a lot of specific things that you don't really answer until you sit down and draw today's page or today's strip.

With *Border Worlds,* I had an idea of a plot, or so I thought. *[laughs]* The problem with doing a serialized comic book is you're doing a first draft that's being published as you go. You do issue after issue after issue, and you have six published issues, let's say. If I were to take that and then I could re-write it, and move things around… that's what Jeff Smith does with *Bone.* He actually redraws sequences and smooths things out a little bit when he publishes his collections. That's a real luxury, but it's obviously worth it in this case. I had an overall storyline for *Border Worlds,* but nothing like a real, clear conception like I might have now.

You can have an overarching structure to a strip or a series, but when it comes down to that blank piece of paper, and you're actually doing that page, it's got to come alive in some way, and sometimes in ways you didn't really plan. I think the best example I can think of is when I was doing *Yarn Man* #1. This is a book I thought I had a really solid plot for, and I had it all plotted out, I had page thumbnails and I went off and did a couple of comic book conventions, and I came back six weeks later, and this book was already on the schedule, I'd painted the cover, and this was already coming out, this was already announced. I looked at these thumbnails, and I looked at the plot, and I couldn't remember what the f*ck I was thinking! *[laughter]*

If you look at those first 10 issues of *Megaton Man,* there are about three brilliant pages per issue, and another six okay pages, and then 12 pages where I can't remember what the f*ck I had in mind when I plotted it out five weeks earlier! And it comes from the fact that I would thumbnail the whole book in a day. I would put stick figures on 30 pieces of Bristol board, and I would do these in a day or so, all these layouts, and the first three pages that I would finish would still be fresh in my mind. But after six weeks had elapsed, I'd get to page 23 and there would be these stick figures, and I wouldn't remember what I had been thinking! The inspiration had cooled. That is just inexperience. Now, I thumbnail things out quite extensively, and I actually sit at my word processor and type out a script. Back in those days, I'd be lucky if I scribbled something on the back of a napkin. *[laughter]*

Let me put it this way, since I write and draw my own stories, I've used every single approach you can think of… I've used the Marvel method, I've penciled and then I've scripted, I've done full scripts, I've done plots, I've written things… but even the most tightly-planned out thing, there's still room for improvisation, and even when I'm lettering, sometimes I'll change the dialogue as I'm lettering. It's been a progressive thing where, lately, I've become more of a stickler for planning things out, and especially doing the weekly strip, which only takes me a day out of the week of labor, to actually draw and color it and everything. If I didn't have some plan, I wouldn't know where I was from week to week. So, I've got an actual thumbnail, and I've got a script for, usually, 12 episodes ahead.

So, I can come back after a week of doing freelance jobs or commercial art or something, I can come back to my *Megaton Man* thumbnails and make something of them, pick up where I left off. Otherwise, I wouldn't have a clue what I was doing that week.

But in those days, I thought I had it really planned out, and now it's apparent I just had no sense of pacing from issue to issue. I remember alternating, depending on the issue. One issue I would really concentrate on the artwork, and the following issue, I'd concentrate on the writing. I remember at that point, the whole thing seemed so big to me, and so much to master that I was actually thinking in terms of, from issue to issue, setting goals for myself with narrow parameters. If you look at *Border Worlds,* I think issue #5 was more of a writerly issue, and issue #4 I was more into the artwork—not that I was trying to shortchange the other part, but I really focused on one or the other aspect of it. I think I probably would've developed faster as an artist… I often thought of Steve Rude, who was in Madison, Wisconsin at the time, and I'd get to see him every once in a while when I was living in Wisconsin. In fact, I helped him move apartments one time. *[laughs]* But, he was

Below: Blown-up thumbnail of Supergirl drawing becomes an unused Ms. Megaton Man #1 cover! Supergirl ©2000 DC Comics. Art ©2000 Don Simpson.

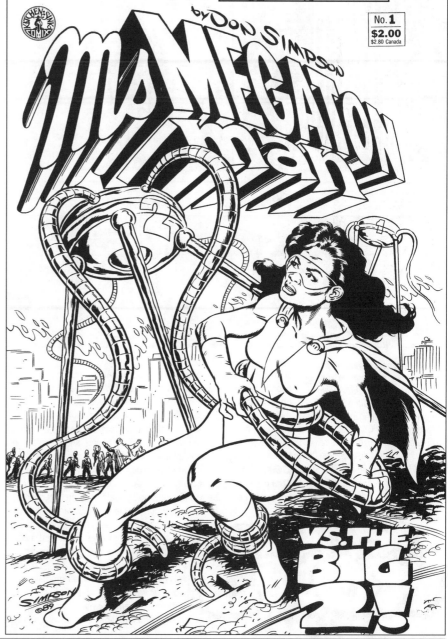

Above and next page: *Two pages cut from Don's adaptation of* King Kong *for Fantagraphics, deemed too bizarre by the editors. Ye ed's a longtime fan of Zepplins so it ain't too whack for CBA!* **Below:** *The original logo design for the same book, also rejected by Fantagraphics. Art ©2000 Don Simpson. King Kong © the respective copyright holder.*

strictly penciling, just concentrating on penciling and storytelling and anatomy and coloring and Andrew Loomis, Andrew Loomis, Andrew Loomis, and that was what his whole focus was. It made him develop much faster as an artist because he was concentrating on one thing. I was doing the lettering and the writing too. Sometimes, I'd ink rough pencils that would look like scribbles. Other times, I'd pencil more tightly. Because I wasn't really specializing, and it was all up to me, it was a lot more haphazard and a lot more experimental.

CBA: *That also made you more dependent upon yourself?*

Don: I'd say self-sufficient. Yeah, I don't have any regrets. I don't know that I'd do it any differently, or if I could. It's purely hypothetical, anyway, I don't think anybody can really rewind the clock. But, I was doing the best I could, and planning things out as best as I could. I really was trying to figure out what my audience was expecting, and I was trying to give them their money's worth. *Border Worlds* was just highly ambitious, in terms of the comic book market, and ambitious in terms of my own

abilities at the time. I look at all my old stuff, and there's certain things that I'm dumfounded I managed to pull off successfully. There's other things I just wince at, "Oh, that's just unacceptably bad." [*laughter*] So, I mean, it's always a mixed bag when you look at your old stuff. But I guess I would always opt for self-sufficiency. It's the only way I learn.

CBA: *At the end of* Border Worlds, *did you go back and do* Return of Megaton Man *right after that, or was that simultaneous?*

Don: Yeah, I was finishing off *Wasteland,* and I had gotten the idea to do *Return of Megaton Man,* and Kitchen Sink was amenable. I wanted to make sure it was in color, and I did do all the coloring myself, supervising a few assistants here in Pittsburgh. As I said, *Wasteland* was winding down, *Border Worlds* had been out of the picture for about a year, so I wanted to write and draw my own material and *Wasteland* wasn't affording me that, so I sold Kitchen Sink on it. One of the things I do remember [*laughs*] was I think the second issue. I wanted to get Mark Martin to ink it, and Kitchen Sink.. Denis threw such a sh*t-fit, it was unbelievable. I was going to art school, taking airbrush classes and this, that, and the other thing, so I had homework. I was doing *Wasteland,* and I was now committed to the *Return of Megaton Man* miniseries. I knew I was going to have people help me on the coloring, and so I thought, "Well, why don't I get somebody to ink this? I can write it, draw it, letter it, pencil it, and I'll get Mark Martin to ink it, this'll be a real coup." And this was great, and Mark was really into it.

Kitchen Sink was like, "Don, how can you do that? You're cheapening your product!" The auteur theory, you have to do everything yourself. "You're shortchanging the fans," and everything else. But I said, "This is *Mark Martin,* this guy's really talented! How can you have a problem with this? Besides, I'll make my deadline." They said "This is unheard of. We can't do it. This is the House of Will Eisner and Harvey Kurtzman, and everybody does their own stuff!" Denis just threw this ungodly sh*t-fit, and I'd already sent a few pages to Mark, and I said, "I'm really embarrassed, but can you send them back? I'm sorry, but my publisher's having a conniption fit that I'd use anybody to ink my stuff. I don't know why." Of course, only a few years later, Kitchen Sink was doing *Grateful Dead* work-for-hire comics, and *Crow* comics that weren't even drawn by J.L. Barr. So, Kitchen mellowed on that point. But that was another little incident, chalk that up. We also argued about should it be #1 or #11, and of course, I wanted to call it *Megaton Man* #11. Now I've got all these #1s and I can no longer keep count.

CBA: *You were also doing one-shots?*

Don: *Return of Megaton Man* was three issues, and I think they sold between 12,000 and 16,000, something like that. It wasn't as profitable as the first run of *Megaton Man,* but it was okay. Then, after that, it was just the simple b-&-w one-shots. Up to that point, still harbored the idea of something like *Zap Comix.* You know, *Zap* came out once every three years, and they still kept the numbering intact. They're up to #12 or something. Again, at that time, I'm thinking, "This is what my idea of comics should be, and I think this should apply to me," and of course, Denis is like, "No, you can't… we've got to put a #1 on this or we'll get killed." That really caused lot of consternation, but after the three issues, I just decided, "Well, you want number ones? I'll just do number ones. I'll do *Yarn Man* #1, I'll do *Pteranoman* #1." I did a book called *Bizarre Heroes* #1, which is an elaboration of my John Bradford story from high school.

CBA: *A serious super-hero strip?*

Don: Yeah. [*laughs*] Well, to think that Denis Kitchen got fired because he wouldn't do a super-hero comic. But that was years after I left. What else? I did another issue of *Border Worlds: Marooned #1* I also worked on *Wendy Whitebread* #1 at that time. I had about five different one-shots going at the same time, in five separate red tag folders as I worked on them, just because my imagination was going in five different directions.

CBA: *You had a continuing relationship with Gary and Kim at Fantagraphics? You did that memorable cover of* The Comics Journal *of Jim Shooter taking the witness stand.*

Don: Yeah, that was the first piece of artwork I did when I moved to Pittsburgh. It was a wraparound cover for *The Comics Journal* #115, with Shooter on the cover and the whole comic book industry attacking him.

CBA: *Even though you were doing work for DC, did you know you were just never going to work for Marvel? Was any fallout a consideration of doing that cover?*

Don: I didn't really think I had much of a future in mainstream comics. Even at DC, I was doing *Wasteland,* which was a fringe book, it was a pre-Vertigo book. I did a goofy *Flash Annual* story, which was a nine-page story, but I never really made any inroads into the main super-hero titles. I think a lot of it was just the association people had with my work, or… I don't know, I didn't have the political skills. I remember there were just editors I managed to piss off because I caught the flu or something, I couldn't turn in a job, and one thing led to another. But, it's all for the best, I don't have any regrets about it. There were other people even more off the beaten path than me who… Valentino had a miraculous transformation going from *normalman* to *Guardians of the Galaxy* and so forth. I mean, just sheer force of will, reinventing themselves. There are a lot of cartoonists I would've never imagined ending up… Sam Keith or even Bill Loebs, going from the fringes of small company comics to the mainstream, and I guess I just lacked the killer instinct or something. I just had a naked contempt for these people, or they just assumed I did, from my work.

In the early '90s, I tried getting work at Marvel, and I made Spider-Man samples, and I remember showing them to Tom DeFalco at a convention and getting a lot of blank stares, because I was doing 1968 John Romita. Or else, they'd look at me, and that blank stare you'd get from people, "Why are you asking me for work? We know who you are, and we don't want you." *[laughs]*

CBA: *[laughs] "We've got files on you, Don." [laughs]*

Don: "We can't even picture this." So, I ruled out working for them. I still do! *[laughter]* I'll probably never work for the New York assembly line, but that's just… of course, people will read that. 'New York assembly line'? F*ck this guy!" Maybe, I've often thought, in an alternate universe, if I had grown up in New York City or New Jersey, I might have broken into the biz as a teenager, had an entirely different career. Instead, I got corrupted into a pretentious independent nobody has any use for! *[laughter]*

CBA: *So, making a smooth transition here, how did the "Anton Drek" material start?*

Don: Well, that started as one of these one-shots. I had three pages of *Pteranoman,* and ten pages of *Bizarre Heroes,* and a few pages of *Marooned* #1—which was *Border Worlds*—and I remember working on these intermittently, jumping around from book to book, and I was doing a lot of Mirage stuff at the time—I was doing *Turtles* for Archie—occasionally something for DC, but nothing really prominent. I remember submitting the first half of *Wendy Whitebread* #1 to Kitchen Sink, and they didn't want to touch it.

They just thought it was too explicit, and just so over-the-top. This was a company that had been doing *Gay Comix,* and *Omaha,* and I thought… you know, I'm sure Denis had just this element of, "You're being difficult again, Don, you don't want to do *Megaton Man,*" so they just flat-out turned it down. The reason I went to Fantagraphics was I knew there was a kid named

Tom Powers from Detroit who was a fan, and he ended up doing an internship out at Fantagraphics, and happened to become the first Eros editor. I'd sent a copy out there, and it had been sitting in their files. Maybe they were beating off to it, I don't know. *[laughter]* But it was out there, and it was only in penciled form. This would've been '87.

So, Tom Powers calls me up one day, around 1990, and he said, "We've got the license to do *King Kong,* and we're going to get all these great cover artists, and we're wondering if you could hack out the interior." *[laughs]* Not in so many words, but that was their approach. It was like, "We've got these great cover artists, and we've got the King Kong license, and we just need a no-name or a semi-name to draw this." By that point, I was regarded as a comic book whore or something, *[laughter]* drawing whatever I could get my hands on, I guess. So, I was doing a six-issue *King Kong,* which was like the most poorly-marketed publication ever. You'd think with the household word status of King Kong, and the fact that the movie existed, and you could rent it for two bucks… Fantagraphics thought they could do a six-issue series, and keep everybody in suspense for

Inset: *King Kong being ye ed's favorite motion picture, you can be sure we'd sneak in this, the original splash page to Don Simpson's adaptation cut by Fantagraphics. Art ©2000 Don Simpson. King Kong ©2000 the respective copyright holder.*

Above: Don's Bizarre Heroes grace the cover of this 1995 newspaper insert. ©2000 Don Simpson.
Below: Episode #111 of Don's Megaton Man serial (ultimately rejected) makes a crack about a certain pornographic artist whose style is awfully similar to Don's! ©2000 Don Simpson!

a year! [*laughter*] Nobody would know how this story ended. [*laughter*] Instead of doing one king-sized annual or something. So, I was already roped into that, and then they said, "We're doing this Monster Comics line, but we're also going to do Eros Comix." He called me up a couple of weeks later, and he said, "Would you like to finish up *Wendy Whitebread* #1, and we'll publish it?" I said, "Oh, sure." That led to half a dozen Anton Drek comics for Fantagraphics.

CBA: *How were the sales on those books?*

Don: I think they were really strong. They certainly stayed in print. There was a paperback. The thing about Eros and the whole sex comic thing was, the market flooded really quickly. When I did *Wendy Whitebread,* my approach to it was, I wanted to show people how to do a sex comic. At that time, there was *Omaha,* and there was *Cherry….* *Omaha* was this politically correct thing, which I admired, and certainly liked reading Kate Worley. I knew her and Reed Waller, because I'd see them at conventions, and of course Kitchen Sink started publishing them at some point, so I knew them and I was aware of *Omaha,* but the sex seemed so… I don't know… so polite. [*laughter*] There was *Cherry,* which was very graphic, but it was also very, I thought, poorly drawn, or just not as illustrative as it could've been, it was more in that Archie style. Then there were things like Howard Chaykin's *Black Kiss,* which I totally had no respect for, because it was soft-core arty pretentious stuff. So, I endeavored to do *Wendy Whitebread,* which was like *Megaton Man* in the sense that it was overkill. [*laughs*]

CBA: *In your face, so to speak. [laughs]*

Don: Yeah, literally and figuratively. You know, Denis was certainly horrified at the prospect of publishing something like this, and even…. I showed it to Ron Turner, Last Gasp and he didn't think it was bad, but there were too many "wet shots," and they just weren't interested. Of course, Fantagraphics published it, and I remember Gilbert Hernandez was telling me that he'd done the first issue of *Birdland,* and then he saw the first issue of *Wendy Whitebread,* and he quadrupled the amount of sex in those issues as a result. [*laughter*] Frank Thorne, I guess, really liked *Wendy.* His work became a lot more hard-core. But then, there was just a flood of stuff, I mean, there were 90,000 sex comics all of a sudden. I was one of the first three on that whole trend.

CBA: *Do they still remain in print?*

Don: I think the paperback's still in print. I actually asked Fantagraphics to withdraw all the books. So, they haven't printed anything in the last year and a half. I'd reached the point where that was the only thing that was staying in print of my work, the only thing of mine in the comic book market, and I just thought, "What's the point this late in the game?" The last one I drew was in '92, and it's not due to any prudery on my part, but the fact that those six issues are the only thing I've done that seem to remain in print of their own volition really bothered me. I think the comic book market now is just completely hopeless, and if that's the only thing I'm going to have in it, I really don't want it to be there at all. I asked them about a year ago to stop printing them. I think they assumed that means they don't have to pay me any more royalties, because I know they were still selling off what they had and I haven't gotten a check for quite a while! [*laughter*] But I do know the paperback is still in their catalog, so they must have a boatload of those.

CBA: *Where did the name "Anton Drek" come from?*

Don: That's a good question, I don't really know. [*laughter*] Actually, one of the Partyers from Mars was named Anton Drek in *Megaton Man,* and I just used that name again. I think Anton… I was trying to be pretentiously phony. Anthony was a name I always thought was cool. Tony, I thought, was a cool name when I was a kid, "Wouldn't it be cool to be called Tony?" So Anton came from that, and Drek's just a satirical name. It was a name that was cleverly but openly, phony.

CBA: *So, you were doing one-shots. When did you start considering your own publishing gig, Fiasco? Was that always on your mind?*

Don: I didn't have the money to even consider self-publishing before I got involved with Image. Like I said, one day they called me up and they wanted to do a parody of Image, which I did a two-issue thing called *Splitting Image,* and then Erik Larsen wanted to do a Savage Dragon team-up with Megaton Man, and that and *1963* netted me about $150,000 in a year, for doing less than 40 pages of material.

CBA: *[laughs] The salad days, huh?*

Don: And that was by no means the record-setter. I was not even honorable mention. People were selling a million copies and then retiring. The guys from Tribe, Todd Johnson, Larry Stroman, and Dale Keown, would print a million copies, then they'd go build a recording studio. My little comics were considered failures! *The Savage Dragon vs. The Savage Megaton Man* only sold 300,000. [*laughter*] I netted

about $85,000 off of that, for doing my 12 1/2 pages of artwork. That's more than I got from Kitchen Sink entirely! [*laughter*] Splitting Image was somewhat more modest, I only made $45,000 off of that. It was completely unreal at the time, it certainly seems unreal now, because comic books sell in the hundreds of copies today, if at all.

CBA: *So, you took that kitty and…*

Don: Yeah, and I blew it! [*laughter*] Foolishly! Well, I bought a $15,000 Macintosh system in '93, which was fairly powerful at the time, but now a $900 iMac blows it away. My mom is basically using it for a doorstop now. I bought a Xerox machine, which I still use, and then I wasted my money on printing up comics, thinking that back issues were really going to move. I'd never seen numbers as small as when I started self-publishing. Like I said, *Megaton Man* sold in the teens, *Border Worlds* sold 10,000, or a little less, but *Bizarre Heroes*, the first issue sold 7,400 copies. I continued that title for 15 issues, and then I wised up and did *Megaton Man vs. Frankenstein #1*, and that sold about 3,000. Then, *Megaton Man #0* was the last book I published, which I think sold 2,300 or 2,700.

CBA: *2,700?!?*

Don: I mean, again, I don't regret it. I was using up that Image nest egg as I went along. I still have plenty of back issues, in case you want any. But it got me into computing, and it got me to put my money where my mouth is, and I really learned what it's like to publish. And it was a great experience. I don't regret a moment of it. That's what I did with my money, and that's why I didn't self-publish before then, was because…

CBA: *Money.*

Don: Of course, it didn't turn out to be nearly as frightful as I thought it would be. You have to find somebody to separate the colors on the cover, somebody to shoot the interior, and you have to talk to printers and distributors. You have to do a million things which are all vitally important, but you just never did them before. Of course, if you talk to a publisher, they'll go, "Oh, you're an artist, let me handle that, you don't want to bother with that stuff. You don't want to be corrupted by it." [*laughs*]

CBA: *So, when did you first go online?*

Don: That would've been 1996. I had an intern, I had a college intern by the name of Dave White, he went to Carnegie Mellon University here in Pittsburgh, which is a real computerized school. He was studying art, but he knows how to code and do everything. I started doing some workshops in the mid-90s around town. I had a following of students from class to class, maybe about a half-dozen people. Dave was one of these students, and he said, "Look, I'm looking for a college internship, and how would you like me to come out to Fiasco?" I had my own office space at the time, which was another foolish luxury, and he came out and filled mail orders, and that thing for a few days, and then he said, "Well, is there anything else?" I thought, "I always wanted to get online," so he said, "Well, give me your credit card, and I'll hook you up!" So, he got online, and hooked me up with an Internet service provider, and he wrote the first website, which was only a few pages. We started scanning covers, doing all that stuff, and I, of course, am a consummate do-it-yourself-er, and I've got to figure out how all this stuff works, and so I started learning HTML coding, and all that stuff, GIFs and JPEGs, and the Internet. Then his internship expired and Dave was gone, so I learned how to do all this stuff.

CBA: *Is it profitable?*

Don: Oh, no, not in itself! [*laughter*] But a lot of art directors and art studios are finding me on the web, and hiring me. Last year I got a freelance job that alone more than paid for my whole four years online, and then some. It's a client in Ohio who found my website… Brightnet, an Internet service provider in Cleveland, and they wanted to do a comic book with super-heroes on the Internet as the solution to everybody's problems, so we did an eight-page comic book, and it paid off quite nicely. There were a couple of other things along those lines. Having a website is like a portfolio. It's like a showcase, so I've gotten work from that. I sold a surprising amount of back issues, and I've sold original artwork. I sold a $500 piece of *Megaton Man* art to somebody over in Japan. It's different things, not like an everyday thing. I say, all told, it's been very profitable. It usually involves me having to do more work. It's not like I put up a website and I just make money, so I have to sit there and autograph some comics and

mail them out, or I have to actually do a commercial assignment, but hey, that's better than…. before, if you didn't have a comic book out on the stands for a couple of months, people would forget you completely, so it's a totally different animal.

CBA: *You recently came out with* Megaton Man: Hard Copy, *which reprinted strips that debuted on the Internet?*

Don: Here's what happened: I started this website, and I first thought of it as just selling back issues, and promoting the next thing. I just put out issue #15 of *Bizarre Heroes* about the time we started the website, so I was thinking of it as informational and promotional… forthcoming

Above: *Don explores the origin of Megaton Man in this sequence from the MM serial, ongoing at Don's website and in the pages of Savage Dragon. ©2000 Don Simpson.* **Below:** *Don makes a comment about his KSP experience. ©2000 Don Simpson.*

work, you know? Order through Diamond, order through your distributor, your local comic book store. The first thing we posted was

Above: Don's sketch of Megaton Man for collector Walt Parrish, 1998. ©2000 Don Simpson.

10 pages of a preview of *Megaton Man* #0, and we had it all linked, and at some point between then and when the book actually came out, I realized Capital Distribution was going of business. They owed me about $1,800, which was most of my cash flow at the time, and I realized I was not going to draw another comic book for the market. Even before Capital went out, they were very slow in paying. All the other distributors had folded, and there was just no point in playing this game. I couldn't imagine Diamond being my only distributor. I keep hearing stories and I'm sure it's just as horrible as everybody says, [*laughs*] but I just knew I wasn't going to be in on this.

I remember actually attending San Diego, Summer of '96, and I had copies of *Megaton Man* #0, and I was basically just giving them out to friends and fellow professionals, and I sold a few, I did a few sketch-es… I didn't even have a booth, I did-n't have… I think I set up in Artists' Alley a little bit. I was out there for free, by the way, because I was a judge in the Eisner retail of the year thing, so I had a free ticket out there, but the whole experi-ence seemed like, "This is the last, this is just it, I'm through with this." I remember sitting on the balcony of Larry Marder's hotel room Sunday night after the show's closing, and the Republican Convention was coming to town—that was the Bob Dole conven-tion—and you could see these red, white and blue elephant balloons dotting the landscape. They were putting together the National Republican Convention, and I remember sitting on the balcony and I said to Larry, "You know, I think my time in comics is over, it's just over. Barring some unforeseen…somebody hunting me down and

Right inset: Jack Davis-inspired Halloween illo by Don. ©2000 Don Simpson.

offering me a lot of money, or pulling me back in like Al Pacino or something—I just think it's over." That's pretty much been the case.

I came back to Pittsburgh, looked at my website, and I thought, "Why am I telling people that a book is coming out? Why not just let them read the book while I'm at it?" I figured at this point, I'm reaching real people out there in the real world, and I'm telling them, "Look, here's this thing called a comic book, and you have to go and find a comic book store, you have to go to this comic book store and you have to ask them for this thing called a distributor catalog, and you have to look at 600 pages of total horsesh*t to find maybe three things you want, then you have to order those, come back two months later, and maybe they'll get them, maybe they won't… maybe they were published, maybe not." This whole thing suddenly didn't make any sense to me, and I thought, "Well, I've got a computer."

By this point, I was actually teaching at this crappy art school [*laughs*] part-time, which was my main source of income, I was doing workshops and I was teaching at this art college. I still wanted to tell my stories, so I thought, "Why don't I just take my stories, scan them in, and color them—I can be in full-color now, and not have to worry about quadrupling my printing expenses, because s uddenly, there's no virtue of being in black-&-white, I can be in full-color. Why don't I just do a weekly serial over the Internet?" And that was it. So, I started doing this new material, which followed the storyline from *Bizarre Heroes* and from *Megaton Man Vs. Frankenstein,* and *Megaton Man* #0, and I just followed that story-line of the VW van and Megaton Man and his pals, and their odyssey through my little world. I posted these things weekly, just figuring, "If these are the tools at my disposal, I'm just going to use them." I mean, the comic book industry hasn't been supporting me anyway, so why should I even worry about it? So, I'm doing it for free, but I get work from other sources.

Erik Larsen was tuning in to my website, and he e-mailed, saying, "Why don't you let me run a couple of pages of Megaton Man in the back of *Savage Dragon* each month?" So, really beginning with week #80 of my serial… somewhere around there, it started appearing first on the website and then in the *Dragon,* and I've been there ever since. That's my only contact with the industry, just doing the back-up feature in the *Dragon.*

CBA: *You continue to get fan mail?*

Don: Yeah. It's an amazing thing. I mean, there are still some die-hard people out there. I don't know who the heck keeps going to the comic book stores, I really don't. It seems like so much work! There's never anything I want. And a lot of folks are just like me, not inspired enough to go through the hassles of the marketplace, but still loving comics— when they're convenient. And I guess my website is convenient.

CBA: *What does Megaton Man mean to you as a char-acter? As a presence in your life?*

Don: Well, the funny thing is, [*laughs*] when I was self-publishing, I decided to do *Bizarre Heroes* because I had a lot of characters from junior high school and high school, characters like The Meddler, and John Bradford, and B-50 the Hybrid Man—all these char-acters that I

wanted to do—and I thought it was a shame I was in the comic book business and yet, I hadn't really brought out these characters, and so I thought, "I want to do a regular series, but I don't want to be tied down to one title character, so I will make it open." Of course, the irony is that a lot of people have made quite a lot of success out of that concept, like *Astro City* or a couple of others… so Kurt Busiek has taken that concept of a universe as the title of the book, and var-ious different characters, but of course, me, I had no discipline, so I had 90 million characters in *Bizarre Heroes,* and people are writing me letters, "Why don't you do the Slick again?" or, "You showed this character for two panels, why don't you do that?" So all I do is frustrate the reader with so many. I thought I had it planned out, and again, it wrote itself, and people thought I went on with them for too long, or whatever. So, you just never please anybody when you're doing something that far-flung.

But I wanted to get all these characters into print, and I incorporated Megaton Man because I thought at that point he was really my ace in the hole. So I put Megaton Man in the opening issue, and then I was going to write him out of the strip. Of course, he came back in. Back during that 13 months when I was working on *Megaton Man* #1, before I had any contact with the comic book business, *Megaton Man* was something I was working on constantly, it was something I was thinking about, he was my only friend! [*laughter*] It was like me and this character, we're going to break into the comic book business together. I'll send out these samples and get a job doing lettering or something—I never really expected to get the issue published. But it seems as soon as I became involved in the comic book business, it began to become very sour, very frustrating and very disappointing in various ways. I never seemed to sell enough, never seemed to make enough money as I thought. I look at other people, and they seem to be having more success with their things than I am, or whatever.

Given my early history with *Megaton Man,* I was dying to do other projects. My publisher and my more vocal fans, they just wanted *Megaton Man* #1 over and over again. I was like, "Well, go and read that again, I don't want to keep doing that." I wanted to try other things. Everybody was saying, "*Megaton Man* is so popular, stick with that!" It's like, "Well, if it is so popular, why am I making so little money? Stop telling me this is a hit when it's not! It's a modest success, and I'm willing to trade that for what's behind door #2," so that's the way I approached it.

There was a time in the late '80s when I was doing *Border Worlds* or other things, and if you came up to me at a comic convention and found me sitting there autographing, and you said, "Oh, you're Don Simpson, I didn't expect to see you at this show! Hey, I would've brought all my comics! I love all your stuff, but I wish you'd do *Megaton Man* again!" At that point, I'd want to punch you. [*laughter*] I mean, it's like, "I don't want to draw Megaton Man! I'm doing other things now, can't you see?!" You'd have had me right up to the last sentence, I'd be very flattered and thrilled up to the point where you said, "*Megaton Man*'s my favorite," and I'd want to kill somebody or tear somebody's head off. It seems hard to believe now, but if somebody came up to me and complimented me on *Megaton Man* in 1987 or '88, I'd be furious!

How did I get to this point where I hated my own early work so much? I think there's a certain dynamic, and you can see it very vividly in a lot of rock 'n' roll stars: They break into the business with a band, say the Rolling Stones, and they make their success as a group, and then one day, Mick Jagger says, "I'm not the Rolling Stones, I'm Mick Jagger," and he puts out a solo album, because he wants an identity independent of The Rolling Stones. He wants recognition for being himself. Of course, the solo album tanks, and he realizes that The Rolling Stones is an unbeatable trademark which the public recognizes, and translates into bucks, he finally wises up. I think even John Lennon would have reached a point where he embraced The Beatles, instead of wanting to keep that part of his life at arm's length. It's a natural tendency, it seems to me.

It was not so much that I didn't like Megaton Man, but it evolved into the situation where I just hated to hear about him, I wanted some recognition on my own terms. I see that in other artists, actors and musicians, other kinds of people who have a first success, and they're tired of hearing people equate them only within the parameters of that first success. Pigeon-holing. Nobody wants to be pigeon-holed. And yet it's pretty unreasonable to blame the public for identifying you with your first success, since that was their first impression.

But it's changed now. I mean, when I chose to stop publishing paper comics in 1996 and draw my strip for the Internet, it was Megaton Man, of all things, that I chose to draw. I remember sitting there drawing the weekly strip a year-and-a-half ago (1998), and I'm thinking, "Gosh, I haven't had this much fun drawing Megaton Man since 1983. What's the similarity? Oh, yeah, I wasn't a professional then! I'm not professional now! This is bliss!" Maybe turning pro is over-rated. Somehow, something you love gets turned into something other people have expectations about, and it becomes like work, instead of doing what you love or choose to do. Hey, you liked the first thing I did, why not just trust me and look forward to my next thing with an open mind, okay?

The two successes I've really had were just like that. I made *Megaton Man* #1 without any contact with the industry, and I created *Wendy Whitebread* #1 completely in secret. It's not like the industry or the fans or publishers particularly requested those things—they had no idea about them. And that's the space you have to find in order to create, I feel. A space where you do what you like and spring it on the public later, when it's a *fait accompli.* That's what I like about the Internet, incidentally. It's very reminiscent of the old school room bulletin board, I can just post my latest strip and there hasn't been any mediation from the publisher, or an editor. You haven't read about it in a catalog three months ago—it's just there and you have no preconceptions about it.

But like I said, as far as at one point hating Megaton Man, I don't think I'm alone in handling that situation pretty poorly. I was just 23 when it all started—just look at all the musicians and TV actors who turn their back on their early success and only mellow when they get older.

CBA: *Was Megaton Man ever optioned for Hollywood?*
Don: Actually, there was a guy named Steven DeSouza, a screenwriter who wrote the *Die Hard* films, and he optioned it for a year back in '86, '87. Then there was the writer's strike in Hollywood, and we never heard from this guy again. Later, in 1994, when I was doing *Bizarre Heroes,* I had several issues out and I was at a convention. Kids are coming up and looking at the covers, and they see Megaton Man—there's a head shot of Megaton Man on the first issue of *Bizarre Heroes*—and they point and say, "Oh, I recognize this character!" At first I'm thrilled, but then he says, "Yeah, it's The Tick!" [*laughter*] I'm like, "Oh, $%&*@?!!"

There was one show I was at and there was a guy in his 30s, and he had his little daughter with him… he seemed like a fan who'd been away from the scene for awhile, and clearly had never heard of me. So he's looking at my comics for the first time, and he mutters, "Tsk! Tsk! Tsk!" I said, "What's the problem?" He says, "Well, this doesn't look very original." It's like the first eight issues of *Bizarre Heroes,* the covers. He says, "You're ripping off The Tick!" And I'm about to tell him as nice as I can that my character's a little bit older, and then he points to The Slick, and he says, "And this is definitely Spider-Man!" [*laughter*] I'm like, "Well, you've got me there!" I was just completely crushed… that was the worst, that was just the low point of my career. Worse than having to cancel *Border Worlds!* [*laughter*]
CBA: *"Go away!"* [*laughs*]
Don: Yeah. My one original contribution to the medium, and they think I've ripped it off. [*laughter*]

Above: Don's now actively doing advertising illustration work. Here's his work for a 1999 corporate pitch. ©2000 Don Simpson.

Right inset: Very recent figure drawing by Don for his art class. Done in black colored pencil. ©2000 Don Simpson.

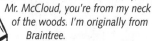

Zot! Inspection

Scott McCloud on his '80s comic series

Conducted by Chris Knowles
Transcribed by Jon B. Knutson

Does Scott McCloud, author of the seminal textbook (this side of Will Eisner) on the art of sequential storytelling, Understanding Comics, *really need an introduction? Well, maybe if you didn't know his credentials stretched back to the early 1980s, when Scott produced one of the truly delightful independent titles of that era,* Zot! *Part science-fiction strip, part romance comic, Scott's title is one of the most fondly-recalled books, and we're grateful he took time from his extremely hectic schedule (preparing the final proof for his forthcoming* Reinventing Comics*) to grant us an interview. Conducted by phone in January 2000, the transcript was copyedited by Scott. Much thanks to Kurt Busiek for supplying us with the artwork accompanying this piece.*

Comic Book Artist: *Okay, Mr. McCloud, you're from my neck of the woods. I'm originally from Braintree.*

Scott McCloud: That's right. I'm from, as you know, Lexington, Massachusetts.

CBA: *When did you first become aware of the fact that you were hopelessly addicted to comics? [laughter]*

Scott: Pretty late, actually. I was about 13, 14 years old, and a friend of mine in junior high school named Kurt Busiek was very heavily into comics, and he got me hooked. I was actually addicted to chess at the time, and we had a deal that Kurt would come over to my house to avoid being given chores by his dad, [laughs] and I would play him a game of pool—because he didn't care much about chess—and in exchange, he would play me a game of chess. During this time, he got me into comics after a lot of trying. I really didn't want to have anything to do with them.

CBA: *What kind of stuff was he trying to get you into? Just the standard-issue Marvel stuff?*

Scott: Yeah, he was into *Daredevil, X-Men, Avengers...* not much DC stuff, he felt the Marvel stuff was better, which in those days, it really was a little more adventurous. Eventually, he broke through my prejudices, because I really thought I was too old for comics at the time.

CBA: *What were you into besides chess?*

Scott: My childhood was a series of obsessions, I'd move from one obsession to another. I began with astronomy, mineralogy—this was in elementary school, around fourth grade! [laughs]—microbiology was a huge one.

CBA: *You went from all of these lofty, scien-*

tific ventures into something as lowbrow as comics. What was the appeal?

Scott: Well, the appeal wasn't lowbrow at all, in fact, it was the lowbrow image of comics that kept me away from them. If you asked me when I was twelve years old about comics, I would just tell you that I would have nothing to do with them, because they were lousy science-fiction, they were lousy writing, the art was crude, and I read real s-f, and I was interested in the surrealists and some fantasy art and whatnot... that was the good stuff, comics were the crappy stuff. It took an intelligent friend like Kurt, and a lot of determination and stubbornness, to break through that prejudice and convince me that, in fact, comics had the potential for loftier things, and it's always been that for me. I was never drawn to comics for their lowbrow appeal, but for their potential of comics to overcome that. Some of the first work that did it for me was some of the wilder stuff by Jim Steranko and Neal Adams.

CBA: *Yeah, they would be the fan favorites at that point in time.*

Scott: Right, and that appealed to me because I saw in it that there was potential to do something unusual and different in comics.

CBA: *In all your catalog of obsessions that you gave me, I didn't hear anything about drawing.*

Scott: I was always drawing. That was the funny part, is that drawing was always in the background, but I never considered drawing as a career, and by the time comics came in, drawing just sneaked up behind me, and I realized, "Oh, I've been doing this all my life, haven't I?" [laughs] I was drawing pictures of chess boards when I was into chess! I was drawing pictures of microbes when I was into microbiology.

CBA: *So it's always looming.*

Scott: Yeah, it was always there. But I never took it seriously because I wanted to build spaceships and change the world and invent things... art, to me, didn't seem to have that power to change the world.

CBA: *Did you and Kurt take any train trips to the Million-Year Picnic [comic shop in Cambridge] at the time?*

Scott: Yeah, but they were bus trips, actually. Indeed, we did. We used to get our comics from a local convenience store....

CBA: *Back in the "good old days"!*

Scott: Yeah, the good old days... well, they were the bad old days, because we were very frustrated by the selection on the spinner racks, so when we found out about the Million-Year Picnic—it was a Mecca, and Richard Howell was working at the Million-Year Picnic at the time, and we got to know Richard and Carol Kalish, who had an apartment in Cambridge. We would begin visiting with them, and learning sort of "at the feet of the masters," [laughs] because they had an incredible store of knowledge about comics storytelling, comics history, and even current comics gossip, and I think Kurt, in many ways, was the protégé of Carol and Richard at the time.. and me, too, to an extent. I was a protégé of all three of them. Kurt only got into comics a few months earlier than me, he told me this recently. I hadn't realized that, that it was a very short time from when he got into comics until when I did, but for us it seemed like a very long time. He was always sort of ahead of the game, and giving me tips, and making suggestions and whatnot.

CBA: *The Million-Year Picnic had this incredible mystique that I'd never experienced since in another store.*

Scott: It really is one of the great comics stores, and certainly one of the earliest... never one of the largest.

CBA: *Tucked away in the basement there.*

Above: Zot! by Scott McCloud. As best as we can ascertain, most of the images illustrating this interview have never been published. ©2000 Scott McCloud.

Below: Scott McCloud. Photo by Julian. Used with permission.

Scott: Yeah, [*laughs*] but a great selection and a great history, and it changed the way I looked at comics. I bought my very first comic here… I actually bought two, it was *Warlock* #7 or 8 by Jim Starlin, who was a favorite at the time… and *Avengers* #100, I think. I remember paging through them at the "infinite corridor" at MIT, where we were going for an open house. This was when I was still only 14, 15 years old, but they had that open house that day.

CBA: *Well, MIT was a haven for s-f fans as well, wasn't it?*

Scott: Yeah, it was. I didn't go there as a student, of course, I only went a couple of times. But the culture that surrounded geekdom and science-fiction fandom certainly bled over into our world. I had a friend who went to MIT, and I feel like it was always a presence there, computers were always in the background—just like drawing was always in the background when I was a kid—computers were always in the background when I was a teenager. Kurt and I, in fact, programmed a PDPA at our high school to generate random super-heroes and super-villains. [*laughter*]

CBA: *So you're in the middle of this, what I think is just a really unique flowering of fandom in the mid-'70s, when it was really starting to become an industry cross-over, when you had the direct market. When did you start to say, "All right, this is what I'm going to do." Did you say that at any point? Did you make plans to go to art school?*

Scott: I can tell you exactly when: It was the Summer between my sophomore and junior years at high school, and I was sitting at my desk and drawing and Kurt was sitting on the bed or something reading some comics, and I just turned to him and I said, "I've made a decision, I'm going to be a comic book artist." Kurt's attitude was, "Yeah, well, whatever." [*laughs*] It was a very conscious decision, and I just simply didn't turn back. For the rest of high school, I was going to be a comic book artist, I went to college and became an illustration major with the intent of being a comic book artist.

CBA: *Where did you go to college?*

Scott: Syracuse University. A lot of people from that area went to Syracuse if they weren't doing the Ivy League thing. Kurt, in fact, joined me in Syracuse after barely missing getting into Brown, I think it was.

CBA: *Were you and Kurt sort of a fandom universe unto yourselves, or did you guys have other friends involved?*

Scott: That's not a bad description, a fandom universe unto ourselves. We did form a comics club in Syracuse, and got to know some other like-minded people, but we were a writer/artist team all through the rest of high school and college. He would write the stories, I would draw them. We did a 60-page comic called "The Battle of Lexington," which we actually took on tour, just for fun, at conventions back in '94, because we thought some people would like to see this bizarre comic we did where we destroy our high school and a bunch of Marvel and DC super-heroes all fight each other. [*laughter*] Actually, they were all Marvel heroes, come to think of it.

CBA: *Did you guys get any stuff printed in the fanzines?*

Scott: Yeah, we did… *Rocket's Blast/ComicCollector*, I had a few spot illos in *The Comics Journal*, I think even Kurt had a couple of drawings published, because Kurt drew as well, just as I wrote. I pursued both things, he decided to pursue just writing in the end.

CBA: *Did you complete college?*

Scott: Oh yeah, we did the full four years, both of us. College was a pretty cool place… but I spent most of my time just drawing—drawing, and going to the library, and listening to music. I think I figured out pretty early on that an education for a comic book artist—especially when there is no such thing as a comics major—in many ways is just a general education. Everything played into my learning how to create comics. There was a course in Shakespeare that helps me to understand the uses that language can be put to, and understanding story structure. I got a lot of inspiration from various courses in music. I'll tell you, that's the one thing about college, though… as much as I enjoyed Syracuse, the one thing that I believe about college is that I think about 80% of what I know today, I've learned since leaving college. That's no knock on college, it's just that I believe that learning is a full-time job, and I think the purpose of school is to teach you how to learn.

CBA: *Yeah, how to think, not what to think.*

Scott: Right, exactly. Somewhere around my senior year, that

clicked for me, and ever since then, I've been self-taught, and am really enjoying it, and learning is one of my greatest pleasures in life.

CBA: *So, you graduated in '82, and when you got out of college, all of a sudden there was this incredible boom going on in the direct market. All of a sudden, after years of the New York companies monopolizing the comics industry, we started to have a number of publishers like Pacific, Eclipse, First, and Capital, all of a sudden. How did you… this may sound like a trite question, but how did you feel about this? Did you feel like since you knew you wanted to be a comic book artist, you would try to seek work with the big two, or did you feel this whole new world was really the place for you to be?*

Scott: You know, it's funny… one of the great gaps in my memory is I've never been able to figure out how my consciousness was raised regarding creators' rights. It just happened. My first task upon getting out of school was to find an actual job, [*laughs*] and that, fortunately, took care of itself, because three weeks before I left school, I sent a letter to DC's production department, asking if there was any work—and there was! Bob Rozakis called me up—he was the head of the production department at the time—called me up at about nine in the morning, woke me up from a nice, sound sleep,

Above: *Zot's Uncle Max, the inventor, by Scott McCloud.*
©2000 Scott McCloud.

here in my dorm room, right? [*laughs*] And he said, "Hi, may I speak to Scott McCloud?" I said, "This is Scott." "This is Bob Rozakis at DC Comics." "Oh! Oh! Uh…" [*laughter*] I sent out this letter, and it was the only letter I'd sent out so far, and I'd sent my resume along, and he said, "Would you like to come in for an interview?" I was like, "Uh, sure!" I took a train down to New York, and I did an interview at DC, and I got the job! So I came back to college, and three weeks before I finished college, I had a job waiting for me in New York City.

CBA: *Unusual in those days, it was the Recession.*

Scott: It was, I think it just came at the right time. I don't know, I guess somebody had just left or something.

CBA: *Well, DC was booming at the time, because they were really expanding into different formats, and the direct market, and the direct-only titles like* Thriller *and* Camelot 3000.

Scott: And *Amethyst*, I loved that one.

CBA: *Oh, I'm glad! I know, I'm glad I found somebody else who liked that book, because I'm a huge Ernie Colon fan, and I thought that was an amazing book.*

Scott: I like Ernie, I haven't talked to him in years, but he was around the office a lot, and there were several of us at the office that just liked to talk about comics. Ernie was one of them, and he is really great to talk to. So, I got the job at DC in the production department, and during that time, I always intended to make my own comics, but I had sort of given up on the "doing it quickly" stuff. The corporate mind-set was beginning to settle in as I was there in the office day after day, and seeing how slowly things worked. For instance, Bob Rozakis' own '*Mazing Man* had been pitched years and years before it actually went to the contract stage and he got to do it. So, I realized, "Oh, this may be just the way it's going to work," and just shortly after getting settled into New York City itself, my father died, and I sort of had a change of heart about that, and I decided to go for it, to do my own comic, and see if I could sell it, rather than waiting to get approval to do my own comic.

CBA: *Where were you living?*

Scott: I was living on East 82nd Street. I got an apartment in the city, after commuting for a little while from my relatives. It was a tiny little place. In fact, Kurt was my roommate for a little while, and then our friend Adam Phillips—who's now up at DC—took over his place when he moved back to Syracuse for a while, I think.

CBA: *So, at this time, the juices started flowing for* Zot!

Scott: You know what? When my dad died, *Zot!* was just the thing on top of my sketchbook at the time. It's the weirdest thing, it could've been anything… I had so many different ideas, *Zot!* just looked right, it seemed to be about right… he didn't even have that name yet, but I just liked it. I'd been looking at some old Dick Caulkins *Buck Rogers* at the time, and I'd worked out this sketch of an idea, just the germ of an idea, and I just decided, "Well, why don't I try this one?"

CBA: *Now, it obviously has the* Buck Rogers *influence, but one thing that always struck me about* Zot! *is it reminded me a lot of something like the* Wizard of Oz *material and some early newspaper strip material, things like* Little Nemo… *there was a lot of other influences there besides the straight-on adventure tale.*

Scott: Oh, sure.

CBA: *Were these things that were left over from your younger days? Were you into this kind of material, some of the fantasy newspaper strips and children's books from the early part of the century?*

Scott: You know what? Everything came late with me. That is, I was always discovering things after the time that I was supposed to have discovered them. I was always getting into childrens' work, after I was no longer a child! [*laughs*] Things like that. Kurt would make recommendations, I'd check them out. For instance, L. Frank Baum was not an influence, but the movie *The Wizard of Oz* was an influence. Even in issue #1, I was already thinking in terms of archetypes. In fact, the supporting cast was designed to mimic Jung's four sub-divisions of human thought, with Peabody being the intellectual side of things, Butch being sensation, Jenny being feeling, and then Zot being intuition. So, even at the very beginning, I was trying to think under the surface like that. The strip had a very kind of breezy sort of innocent feel to it; it wasn't nostalgia that was really pulling me forward, it was actually sort of post-modern emotional distance that lent itself to it. Though the book had a lot of emotion to it, I was very much behind-the-scenes manipulating things, trying to arrange everything. I was always a formalist, I was always trying to figure out the structure of the comic, and what the various symbols meant. I was playing it like a chess board. It doesn't mean the emotional content wasn't real—it was very real for me, I've always had a sentimental streak, and there was a lot of heartfelt stuff in it—but at the same time, there was also this inventor and scientist and tinkerer going about, arranging the pieces and seeing what happened.

CBA: *Well,* Zot! *definitely looked very different texturally than anything that was happening at the time. Those kind of almost art nouveau influences struck me, that very heavily European sense of design, it was one of the things that struck me in the book.*

Scott: Well, the storytelling, we should say, was very Japanese. The designs, the iconic design, simple faces and the more complicated backgrounds… I was already trying to deconstruct what Japanese comics were all about at the time.

CBA: *Let's get back to your relationship to the world outside. You were working at DC, and like I said before, "DC is on the move again" was the slogan, I believe. Dick Giordano was in as executive* editor. All sorts of new things were being tried. You were doing all these new things, and Bob Rozakis was very busy, because also Ronin was happening at the time. Were you there when Ronin was being worked on?

Scott: Sure, I remember Frank coming in with pages for *Ronin*, and carefully looking over the film as it came back, and making comments. This was very… that was a wonderful thing to see, for a young aspiring artist to have that as an example, to see the artist coming in and really being the boss on his own work. It was no secret that Frank had cut a deal that provided him a great deal of ownership and control over the work. Now, of course, in retrospect, that deal wasn't nearly as good as it sounded, but it didn't matter, it made an impression, you know?

CBA: *So at this point you're in New York City, at DC Comics, in the production department when the focus is on production, that DC is spending an enormous amount of money and time improving the look and feel of the books from the old World Color Press hand-separated letterpress, printed on toilet paper books that characterized the late '70s to Baxter and Mando.*

Scott: As a matter of fact, the very first Baxter books that came through the house was while I was there, things like *Camelot 3000* and *Thriller*. I remember how Tatjana Wood had been asked to do the colorings, I think if I remember correctly, for *Camelot 3000,* and I don't even know if they bothered telling her what kind of paper it would be on, so that it was the traditional CMYK palette with all the right primaries.

And when it came out on the white stock, it was just…

CBA: Blinding! *[laughs]*

Scott: It was *gouge-your-eyeballs-out* bright. Tatjana was a very talented colorist, and I don't know that she had any control over that. Like I said, I don't know if she even knew what kind of paper it would be on—but very quickly, we had to make adjustments. Not we, I wasn't really involved in the decision-making, but at DC Production in general, had to begin to use more muted tones to really take advantage of that. So, I got one of my first exposures to McLuhan's much-quoted idea of the new medium appropriating the language of the old; we were using the techniques of the old technology and it was no longer appropriate with the new technology.

CBA: *Let me ask you a question: All of a sudden, and I would say it happened almost overnight somewhere in the middle of 1981, all of a sudden there was a sense of mission, that kind of swept through all the smart people that were involved in fandom or in actually producing the work. Now, you being in the catbird seat with Bob Rozakis, I mean, did you feel that sense of mission, that, "We're on the cusp of a breakthrough," it seemed to be the dawn of a new age in the industry? Were you swept up with that fervor?*

Scott: Well, being in that particular spot didn't exactly give you the sense that the the the whole organization was headed in that direction. What it really was that there were a few of us who were kind of running under the radar, and had ideas of revolution and excitement, and had that fanaticism in our eyes that something great could be done, and then there was this sort of laid-back organization, just sort of getting along. On my end of it, DC was a company filled with people who, by and large, I liked very much, just doing their jobs, and a few of them, with these crazy ideas, making things happen—but it was still very much a corporation. But you know, it was just this quiet sense among some of the people up there that something much more exciting could be done, and let's see how long we can get away with it! *[laughs]* I was the kid who would corral these people and would talk to them, very presumptuously, as if I had anything to say, being a mere production guy, and some of the cool ones, like Ernie Colon, were only too happy to just talk about that stuff over coffee or the water cooler.

CBA: *Were you still conspiring with fandom? Kurt Busiek, from what I can gather, was still trying to find a niche somewhere.*

Scott: Well, Kurt actually started getting work as a writer before I did. I got the job in comics, at DC Production, before he did, and then he was the first one to get an actual creative assignment, writing some *Green Lantern Corps* or *Power Man and Iron Fist,* I forget which one came first. By now, of course, Carol Kalish, our friend and Kurt's mentor to a large extent—my own to a somewhat lesser extent—had herself gotten a pretty prominent gig at Marvel, and so

we were all kind of moving into the organization, infiltrating *[laughs]* the beast at that time.

CBA: *Let's take it up to about 1983. You've probably got a fairly healthy pitch together for* Zot!

Scott: This would be late '83, yeah, I had about 100 pages of material already.

CBA: *Let's talk about the process of getting* Zot! *on the stands. Let's talk about how you did that.*

Scott: Well, I created this monster proposal, and I had four packages which went out to the four independent publishers I was interested in, which were Eclipse Comics, Pacific, First, and WaRP. Then I had a larger proposal that colorist Tom Ziuko helped me put together. He was definitely one of the proletariat, revolutionary types running around. *[laughs]* He had done the colors for this wonderful, large-size presentation. The packages went out, it took a little while, but I got to show the presentation to Dick Giordano, and there was actually some discussion about the possibility of DC doing it. They were thinking in terms of starting a children's line at the time—that was sort of their idea for it—but Dick had asked me what I'd like in return, if they did decide to do it. Nothing was certain at the time; I don't want to make it sound as if it was right up at bat or anything; but I told him that ownership and control were really important to me, and he told me that DC couldn't really do it at the time, you know, "Sorry, we can't really offer that." I said I understood, it was all very cordial and all, but basically, what it came down to was that

Above: *Line art for the cover of* Zot! #1, April 1984, by Scott McCloud. ©2000 Scott McCloud.

DC couldn't give me what I needed, or what I felt I needed at the time, so I decided to go with a smaller company.

CBA: *So Cat Yronwode at Eclipse became enamored of it?*

Scott: In fact, all four of the companies I approached were interested, and I had nice talks with people at all four of those companies.

CBA: *What distinguished Eclipse from the others?*

Scott: Speed, and promises of real creative control and freedom. I had this bizarre obsession that there was going to be a nuclear war, and I just wanted to get a comic published before it happened.

CBA: *Well, that was part of the times. I don't think it's that unusual; I mean, I think that the nuclear anxiety was quite common. So, did you go out to California to deal with Eclipse, or did you do it all over the phone?*

Scott: All over the phone. I left DC shortly after to pursue drawing comics full-time.

CBA: *Was Eclipse paying you enough to supplant the income loss from quitting DC?*

Scott: I was losing money slowly. I had some money from when my dad died, my mom had given all four children some of the money that had come in, and that helped to offset this continual leakage of money from my bank account. I've always had financial problems, from then to this day.

CBA: *So, you find yourself, a young man of 23 years old, all of a sudden living a dream of a lot of guys in your shoes. A deluxe comic coming out, at a very exciting time, perhaps the most exciting time in the history of comics.*

Scott: Well, I don't necessarily agree with that, but we can get to that later.

CBA: *It was a time when most of the major titles at Marvel were running well over 100,000 copies in sales, and there was kind of what Alan Watts would refer to as a "turning of the Tao," where you have an old world and a new world colliding, and all of a sudden, you have the circulation to finance some of the exciting things that were being done, but you also had the steady sellers still doing relatively respectively, and the direct market was helping to cushion the blow of some of the falling circulations with greater profitability.*

Scott: There was also a sense of collegiality. In general, though there was plenty of fractious in-fighting and whatnot, the general sense was we had a common purpose, to move comics forward.

CBA: *So, at this time in comics history you were working in your apartment on East 82nd Street doing* Zot!

Scott: Shortly thereafter I moved to Tarrytown, a suburb, since I didn't need to come into the city as regularly.

CBA: *Were you doing the convention circuit to promote the title?*

Scott: Yes, I started doing conventions almost immediately, and I would go to maybe there or four conventions a year. Began San Diego in '86 and have gone to every one except one.

CBA: *So,* Zot! *comes out, and it gets noticed. You're not only doing a color book, but you're doing a color book that's noticed because it's just so different from everything else on the stands. Now, did you feel like a rock star?*

Scott: No, I always knew I was a medium-sized fish in a small pond, but I had the level of notoriety I felt comfortable with. I had at least some of the respect of my peers, and I was making sort of a living [*laughs*], and I was able to look to the future with some hope. So, that was good, and the reviews were consistently good when there were reviews. I was somewhat ignored by the *Journal*. By then of course, I was beginning to occupy that "no man's land" between the mainstream and the alternatives. I was coming about the same time as *Love and Rockets* and other books like it at Fantagraphics, and I really admired those books. They were some of the best stuff out there, and I knew I was doing a book that was neither fish nor fowl. People who were hard-core mainstream fans didn't really quite get the alternative aspects of the book, and people who were into the alternative black-&-white stuff looked at it as just, kind of "near beer." [laughs] I think there were people who would've enjoyed the book who never really quite knew what to make of it, and I thought it was kind of amusing that neither did the alternative artists I admired so much ever know quite what to do with me! [laughter] I would be the kind of wacky, smiling fanboy who kept telling them how great they were, but, you know, they had to politely excuse themselves if they wanted to go get dinner or something.

CBA: *Actually, at that time, when you think about it, at the time* Zot! *was running in color, you had* Love and Rockets, *but most of the other stuff Fantagraphics was doing wasn't really all that outré, you know what I'm saying? They seemed to be doing things similar in spirit, like* Dalgoda.

Scott: That's true, *Dalgoda* was very much the same type of thing. There was a crowd of us. There was *Zot!*, there was *Megaton Man*, there was *normalman*, *Dalgoda*, all of these books were alternatives to a degree, but they still were a kind of contiguous expansion out of that genre.

CBA: *What the Buddha would call "The path of tension."*

Scott: That sounds about right. So, we had not really broken free, I think we still measured ourselves as how far our particular pseudo-pod had expanded. But we knew we were not this completely self-sufficient external organism. In fact, I think much of what was going on—even at Fantagraphics, even a lot of the books I admired like *Hate* and *Eightball*—still….

CBA: *Which were much later.*

Scott: Yeah, that's right, that was late '80s, I think. They, though, still had that sense they were defining themselves in opposition to the mainstream, and it was only later that you had artists that really couldn't care less about the mainstream one way or the other.

CBA: *The Toronto school.*

Scott: Yeah, absolutely. That's part of it. In a lot of ways, I think they're my heroes, which is one of the reasons that I don't see necessarily the early and mid-'80s as the most exciting time, although it was certainly exciting for me, personally.

CBA: *Okay. Let's get back to* Zot! *in particular, because at the time* Zot! *came out, storm clouds were gathering on the horizon, because Marvel was reacting to the success of some of the larger independents by flooding the market with reprint titles. There was a panic—"the panic of late '83"—and it carried to late '84, where some of the more left-field... or I guess you'd be center field [laughs]...*

Scott: Yeah, right, definitely.

CBA: *...some of that material was starting to not do so well, and Pacific was beginning to show signs of imminent collapse. Were you aware of this? Were you starting to feel anxiety for the future of* Zot!, *at least with the way it started, with the full production color book?*

Scott: I was always worried. I worry by nature.

CBA: *It's a Massachusetts thing. [laughs]*

Scott: Yeah, right. But my worrying is always countered by my optimism, they're sort of the warring halves of my nature. I had plenty to worry about, of course; *Zot!'s* sales rarely, if ever, went up, they were always sort of eroding. It was always difficult to build an audience, it was always just sliding down. I didn't really understand at the time it was just part of the greater picture, what was happening in the market at the time due to things like the glut of reprints and various other factors—but I think I was able to scale down my expectations to a degree, and to just rejoice in the fact that in my own little corner of the world, I was still able to do what I did, and to reach X number of people. Even if it wasn't a big number, I knew that I was getting something done, and I….

CBA: *You were grateful to Eclipse for allowing you to finish the story.*

Scott: Yes. Getting to issue #10 was a real psychological barrier. I wanted to get to issue #10 and finish the story in the spirit I'd begun it in, and that was just so important to me, and I was just so grateful that they were able to keep it going through that adversity. Even losing money, I think, at the end in order to finish those first ten issues, and have a complete set.

CBA: *Were you aware of what the circulation levels were?*

Scott: Sure, I know the first issue sold around 28,000.

CBA: *Oh! [laughs] That's like what* Captain America *sells now!*

Scott: Right. It just slowly slid down, and I don't really know what it was at issue #10, but it was obviously much lower.

CBA: *It was probably respectable by today's standards.*

Scott: Yeah, I seem to know my first issues, how much things sell at the beginning, more than anything else. I know when it came back as a black-&-white the initial sales for issue #11, the "new #1," so to speak, was at about 13,000, 14,000.

CBA: *Sometime, and I assume it's after the end of* Zot!, *I'm never sure when exactly you did it,* Destroy! *shows up.*

Scott: That's right, after issue #10, and before I came back with issue #11, about a year-and-a-half later. So there's about a year-and-a-half where *Destroy!* was the only thing that I came out with, apart from some mini-comics.

CBA: *What were you doing to sustain yourself after the end of* Zot!?

Scott: I don't really remember. I know I worked moving office furniture for a fairly short period of time, maybe less than a month, so that's the only real, genuine job I had. Obviously, I exhausted what funds I had in the bank. *Destroy!* made a little money. There was some licensing from *Zot!*, a couple of foreign reprints at that time, I was doing a column on mini-comics... I became obsessed with mini-comics. As I said, everything is an obsession with me! [laughs] It's always one obsession or another. The small press became an obsession, I felt there was an enormous energy and promise in these self-published comics. Self-publishing was very exciting to me, even though I wasn't interested in doing it on the sort of scale like Dave Sim's. I really loved the minis and the creative freedom.

CBA: *I agree with you.*

Scott: I had enormous faith in the power of pure, creative freedom, and in a purely creative endeavor, which the minis frequently were. People like Chester Brown were starting back in the mid- to late-'80s, back when I was getting into it, starting out doing self-publishing stuff. There were lots and lots of just really exciting things that I was reviewing for *Amazing Heroes*, of all places; I'd do a one-page review strip of my own creation just for the purpose of spreading the word about these guys.

CBA: *So, the influence of some of this material was shown when* Zot! *came back. It came back with issue #11, as a black-&-white title, and the focus... not so much towards the beginning, but towards the end, the focus is much, much different.*

Scott: Shifts to everyday life, certainly.

CBA: *Yeah, and this is actually my favorite material.*

Scott: I think a lot of people feel that way.

CBA: *There was a depth there, that wasn't in the original color title. There was a sense of reality, and I would say that the mood of the book became much more melancholy. Eclipse was doing a number of b-&-w titles at the time, and I assume this is maybe a diminished expectations response.*

Scott: Well, maybe, as far as the black-&-white titles go, but remember, there was the b-&-w boom and bust, and Eclipse did their best to take advantage of that period to shore up their always troublesome bank accounts.

CBA: *That's right. I remember the boom was somewhere in '86, right?*

Scott: No, actually I think it was a little earlier. The funny part is that the boom and bust, the whole

Above: 9-Jack-9, probably the coolest (and most deadly) villain in the series. ©2000 Scott McCloud.

Below: Jenny. ©2000 Scott McCloud.

Above: Jenny, the real star of Zot! Even though the book is named after the blond-haired kid, it's largely about the trials and tribulations of an adolescent girl finding her way in the world. ©2000 Scott McCloud.

Teenage Mutant Ninja Turtles stuff, the obsession with #1 issues, the various knock-offs of the Turtles, from Eclipse's *Adolescent Radioactive Black-Belt Hamsters* [laughter]… that whole period, I believe, primarily took place between *Zot!*, so I came out with *Zot!* #10, I disappear for a year-and-a-half, we have the boom, and then we have the bust, and then I come back. So I missed the entire thing.

CBA: *I think that a lot is said about all the Turtles knock-offs, but there really was a lot of exciting, vital material that kind of got lost in the tide.*

Scott: Oh, sure, that's what I always gravitated towards, and during that period, I was saying that I would rather have two great books and 1000 bad ones than one great book and ten bad ones, you know? I believe we could find the good stuff. Of course, that doesn't necessarily work out in the marketplace, because how do you make a living? It was during that period I remember vividly a panel I was on—I showed up late, because it was San Diego, and my plane was late, and I showed up at the panel as it's already begun—and it's a panel about the b-&-w glut. On there are a whole lot of people—Gary Groth, Deni Loubert, a few other people, were all bemoaning the presence of all these crude "barbarians at the gate" publishing just anything. There were too many publishers. They were actually

talking about how there had to be some way of cutting back on the catalog, or getting distributors not to carry some of these crude, amateurish b-&-w books, and Will Eisner was on the panel, and I was just so impressed, because Will gave a little speech about how you never know which of these kids is going to change the world, and you really can't talk about restricting the flow of this stuff, and you just have to let it all come out, and sort it out later, and I was totally on his side. I thought it was totally interesting that he was taking a point of view that—to my mind—seemed a lot younger [laughs] and a lot more enlightened, and a lot less crusty and closed-minded than a lot of the other comments I was hearing on that panel.

CBA: *By that same token, Will wasn't taking the financial beating that the other people on the panel were taking, either.*

Scott: Maybe that's true, but still, who takes the beating if they actually did succeed in pushing those new artists out? These were kids, some of whom are some of our best artists today. I agreed with Will, and I have always agreed with Will.

CBA: *I'm not disagreeing with Will. The point I'm trying to make is the reason… I think the initial success of companies like Renegade and Fantagraphics and Aardvark-Vanaheim and some of the other companies that were doing the alternative material, they were an alternative, and all of a sudden, there was a new alternative, and they were taking a financial loss because all these new alternatives more closely mirrored the mentality of what fans were interested in.*

Scott: I do remember some of the comments Deni and Gary Groth made, was that basically they felt their revolution was being hijacked.

CBA: *Yeah, that's the point I was trying to make.*

Scott: I do think, actually, that may be true. Although I disagree with the solution, I don't disagree with their evaluation of the problem. Their revolution was being hijacked. It's more the proposed solution I think can lead to some very unpleasant things. That's why I feel as Will does, you can't restrict that flow.

CBA: *It would also be pretty much impossible to do so, unless you head a gun to the distributors' heads. The whole lesson of the Turtles was probably very fresh in a lot of peoples' minds.*

Scott: It was. As a matter of fact, it was so fresh that they hadn't figured out exactly what the lesson was. Some of them honestly thought the secret was to draw as badly as you could. [laughter] You would find people who thought that really was the secret, and that's what you had to do in order to sell.

CBA: *That reminds me of what Sol Harrison said about the secret to Marvel's success in the '60s. Are you familiar with that anecdote?*

Scott: No, but I can imagine from what you've said what it was.

CBA: *The story is Marvel was really starting to break through—this was about '67, '68, maybe a little earlier—and all the bigwigs at DC were sitting around a table looking at a stack of Marvel comics, scratching their heads, trying to figure out the appeal of them. Sol Harrison piped up, "I think it's the bad art." [laughter]*

Scott: This has been repeated over and over and over throughout comics history, that kind of evaluation. I think that Image, for all its real artistic problems, was the subject of a lot of that kind of speculation. I think people missed what fans were actually responding to in the art, which was a lot of visual excitement and a sense of wild compositional excess… things that, while they may have been bad storytelling by the standards of our generation, they were still very intoxicating and interesting art, compared to a lot of the staid, conservative linework of their contemporaries.

CBA: *I would say that helped more for the work they did while they were still at Marvel rather than the work they did at Image. I think they built up a mystique at Marvel because we were so used to the Shooter approach, the very solid, conservative approach, and then they came in and kind of trashed that, but they still were kind of tethered to some sense of storytelling. Like I said, there was that tension.*

Scott: Well, each of them has a different story, really. They had their own various tracks. It starts to get very complicated as soon as Image actually occurred… you had seven wild comics, all heading in different orbits! [laughter]

CBA: *So, you did quite a healthy run on the b-&-w version of Zot!*

Scott: Yeah, there were 36 issues altogether, the color for ten issues, and then 26 b-&-ws.

CBA: *So, was this your bread-and-butter? Were you able to support yourself with the proceeds from the work of* Zot!, *or were you supplementing it somehow?*

Scott: It was primarily that. Occasionally, some money from my mom [*laughs*] you know... bailing out her poor, starving artist, but for the most part, yeah, I was making a modest living from comics, and I was living modestly.

CBA: *One of the points I would like to make here—and I'm sure you'll have probably a differing viewpoint on it—my viewpoint on the time* Zot! *ended, say in '89, is the original impetus that was the spirit of '82, let's say, really had dissipated; the sense that the mainstream and the left field, the right field, and the center field could all sort of co-exist relatively comfortably was really starting to dissipate.*

Scott: There was more acrimony. The sense of collegiality eroded severely.

CBA: *The mainstream was becoming more extreme in its approach. Any of the kind of ideas that Frank Miller or Alan Moore or whomever that was doing mainstream work in a more intellectual capacity, these ideas were being flushed.*

Scott: I don't know that they were being flushed so much, I think they were being mindlessly imitated, actually. They were picking up on the surface elements of Moore and Miller, without understanding the core.

CBA: *That's what I'm talking about, the core. The core was being neglected. The center field material was really starting to surrender, and the left field was burgeoning at this time and the mainstream was going off in a totally different direction. What I'd liken it to is, say, the tension between Secular Humanism and the Religious Right, and the mainstream Protestant Church caught between a rock and a hard place.*

Scott: That's not a bad comparison, I know what you're talking about. Yeah, that middle ground certainly became less and less populous.

CBA: *How did you respond to this? It would seem that the ground you had occupied was really washing away in this schism.*

Scott: Yeah, but in a way, I was never renting with an option to buy that particular territory. [*laughter*] To me, I had no emotional stake in it, it's where I had chosen to be as just a creative decision, but there was always a part of me that would've been just as interested—if I thought it was viable—in doing some weird, surrealistic collage comic, or something more like Spiegelman was doing in his early work, like "Breakdowns," or some of the things in *Raw*. Or going off and doing mini-comics! In fact, I probably would've taken those different paths if my economic alternative had been less limiting. I had to find something that I thought would make me a living, but I always had these sidelines, these side projects that I hoped to do, these strange little things. I had whole file folders filled with other ideas that were not sought, and one of them, of course, was the book about comics done in comic book form. I never identified myself with the middle ground; in fact, in many ways, I felt sad that I wasn't part of that wild left field alternative stuff. Maybe I'm not really, by nature, not all that radical a personality, but those were the things I admired the most. My favorite books at that time were *Beanworld* and *Love and Rockets*, not *Nexus*, not *Camelot 3000* or *Watchmen*. So, the other thing you should know is personal life intruded, and I got married in '87, and as my world became that, it became our life together and moving from *Zot!* into *Understanding Comics*. It was during that period, too, I became obsessed with chess again for three years.

CBA: *So how were you supporting yourself after* Zot! *ended?*

Scott: After *Zot!*, we had just a little money in the bank, and I guess I managed to sell the idea of *Understanding Comics* to Kevin Eastman, just in the nick of time.

CBA: *Okay, so he gave you an advance?*

Scott: Actually, no. I had already done some work on the layouts, so I'd gotten paid for the work I'd done so far. I got a per-page... you could call it an advance, of course, it is technically an advance against royalties, but essentially what I wanted was to be paid as I turned in the work on a per-page basis, so my royalties were getting paid incrementally. I had an objection to getting paid for work I hadn't done, and even though, of course, the book—and this is how I've always worked, really, this is how I worked at Eclipse, this is how I'd worked on everything so far—where I'm getting a page rate, but really all the page rate amounts to at the end of the day is part of that lump sum advance against whatever the book actually earns. So, that way, I never felt like an indentured servant.

CBA: *So, I think enough has been written about* Understanding Comics. *[laughter] Needless to say, you did the book, and it became a huge hit, and established you as sort of the...*

Scott: The James Burke of comics, maybe?

CBA: *Something like that. So, let me just go back to the '80s for a bit. Comics, at some point in time, had this wonderful window of opportunity that was pretty quickly slammed shut a couple of years later, say around '86 with* Dark Knight, Watchmen *starting to get press, certainly* Love and Rockets, *I think that was the year* Love and Rockets *was on* Rolling Stone's *"Hot List." There was an immense amount of interest from other sectors of popular culture. In comics, and leading up to "Bat fever" in '89, at that time, did you see yourself creating something that could put you into that kind of realm, or were you not even interested in that? Were you just following your own vision?*

Scott: No, that one never bothered me. I wasn't hostile to the idea, the way that Sim was, that Sim still is. I had the example of the *Turtles,* as well, could happen. [*laughs*] It was always in the back of my mind. There had been a little bit of interest, by then, on the possibility of a movie deal, but I took the exact same attitude towards it that I did with the publishing, and that was fine, but I just wanted to continue making comics, I didn't want this to interfere with it, and I don't want to be embarrassed! [*laughs*] So, I wasn't going to sign off on anything, and I didn't pursue... I never pursued Hollywood to this day. I've been pursued by Hollywood from time to time, but I can always say no, I've always felt very comfortable saying no, I don't feel as if that's something I want. I'm a comics loyalist, it's always about the comics. If I ever signed a movie deal, it would be because I thought they would do a reasonably good job at it, not embarrass me, and I'd get more money so I could draw comics, I could just continue making comics. [*laughs*] I have no aspirations to do anything else at the moment. Maybe I never will, I don't know. We should probably touch on the Bill of Rights at some point here, because of course, that was about '88, '89. I don't want to overestimate its historical importance; I don't really know that too many career decisions were made on the basis of it, but the Creator's Bill of Rights, I think, summarizes a lot of people's feelings about where the important issues were at the time. The summit in Northampton, which was where it was put together by Eastman and Laird and Dave Sim, and included some people like Steve Bissette, Rick Veitch, and Larry Marder... people who had been pissed off by the majors, or—in the case of the Turtles—a couple of success stories that sort of felt like "Hey gang, let's put on a show," and a couple of purists like Sim's. And into this world, I just sort of waltzed in, and I proposed a Creator's Bill of Rights, as an alternative to something that had been done in an earlier meeting, which was something called "the creative manifesto," which you don't hear too much about these days. It was a little bit confusing, and not too focused. I proposed the Creator's Bill of Rights, as a clearer alternative to that, and it was adopted pretty quickly. We spent the two days that we were there... we spent about half of it just arguing about points in the bill. We put it out there, and there it hung, you know?

CBA: *There was some negative reaction from some of the freelancers?*

Scott: There was a cartoon in the *CBG* that showed a couple of industry executives just kind of laughing at the thing, which I thought was fair, because the higher-ups at Marvel and DC didn't feel particularly threatened by it [*laughs*]. It was kind of a goofy thing to run up the flagpole. But these were things that people were fighting to get at the time, like the return of their artwork, or the rights to creations they fully created, and many of those things have become standards. I don't think the bill necessarily was the catalyst for that, but I think it's an interesting reference point.

Above: *Of course, Scott McCloud is best known for authoring the renowned "text" book on sequential art,* Understanding Comics. *The tome cleverly uses the comic-book form to convey its content. ©2005 Scott McCloud.*

Mike Grell, Freelance

Jon Sable's creator on his days of independence

Conducted by Jon B. Cooke
Transcribed by Jon B. Knutson

Mike Grell arrived almost stealthlike onto the comics scene in the early '70s, and after working on numerous DC super-hero strips, the artist established a long-standing niche as creator/writer/artist of Warlord. *Though often critically unheralded, Mike went on to become a top-selling force in the direct sales market, notably with* Jon Sable, *his trademark character he is currently developing into novel form, and with the controversial* Green Arrow: The Longbow Hunters *mini-series for DC. Mike was interviewed via phone on February 4, 2000, and the artist copyedited the final transcript.*

Below: *DC's First Issue Special #8, featuring Mike Grell's first comics hit,* Warlord. *Check out the following pages for Mike's precursor syndicated strip pitch,* The Savage Empire. *©2000 DC Comics.*

Comic Book Artist: *Mike, where are you from?*
Mike Grell: Florence, Wisconsin, in the north woods, about 100 miles north of Green Bay.
CBA: *And when were you born?*
Mike: September 13, 1947.
CBA: *Did you have an early interest in comic books?*
Mike: I had an early interest in just about everything to do with comics or comic strips. My brothers and I used to buy comic books and swap them with the neighbors, usually a hot copy of *Sub-Mariner* or *Captain America* for a copy of *Donald Duck* or something like that. Interestingly enough, it probably provided our first interest in comics. I remember reading *The Human Torch* back in the days when it was The Human Torch and Toro, and that might've been a leftover from the Golden Age.
CBA: *Well, in '54, they revived the character for a year, so that might be the timing.*
Mike: That might be about right. Comic strips were always the evening get-together. Dad would come home and read us the comic strips (Well... read *me* the comic strips, my brothers were four and five years older than I was, so they were old enough to read them on their own). I remember Dad used to do a pretty fair impression of Alley Oop.
CBA: *What other strips do you recall?*
Mike: *Prince Valiant*, of course. *L'il Abner, Steve Canyon*, stuff like that. When I first started out to become a cartoonist, what I really wanted to do was the Al Capp style "bigfoot" stuff.
CBA: *Did you start picking up the pen at an early age?*
Mike: Oh, yes. I grew up in an area where we didn't have television until I was about eight years old, and I was 11 before we got a TV set, so I grew up with radio and comic books and comic strips, and actually learning to read books without pictures, too. My mother was a very good artist, and she always encouraged us to draw. Whenever a new movie would come out, my brothers and I would sit down and draw various scenes from the movie, and I suppose that's part of where that got started.
CBA: *Did your brothers subsequently become artists?*
Mike: Interestingly enough, both of my brothers were better artists than I was. Throughout high school, my middle brother Dick, espe-

cially, was just terrific, but both of them went on to other careers, never pursued art.
CBA: *At an early age, did you start considering that art might be a future for you?*
Mike: Actually, at an early age, I wanted to be a lumberjack, just like my old man.
CBA: *Oh, yeah?*
Mike: Just like the song says. [*laughter*] God bless him, one year when I was 16, he got me a job working in the woods, and I discovered how hard the old boy'd been working all these years. There had to be a better way of making a living! [*laughter*] I looked around, and my actual first thought was that I really wanted to be the next Frank Lloyd Wright. Unfortunately for me—or possibly fortunately for the rest of the world—I couldn't handle the math, and it was in the days long before computers or even calculators, so I never had any electronic help with it. I rapidly had to give that up, and decided on a career in commercial art. I went to the University of Wisconsin for about a year, dropped out and was going to switch to a private art school so I could get more direct training, and got caught up in the big draft, and faced the choice of either being drafted in the Army or enlisting in one of the other services. I decided four years in the Air Force was better than two years in a foxhole, and enlisted in the Air Force in 1967. While I was in basic training, I met a fellow by the name of Bailey Phelps—wherever he is today—I hope he's a cartoonist, so he knows how far of the mark he was. He told me I should forget about commercial art and become a cartoonist instead, because according to him, cartoonists only worked two to three days a week and earned a million dollars a year. [*laughter*] Apparently, he was talking about Charles Schulz, but I didn't realize it, I thought it was a generic thing for cartoonists in general. A while back, I did some quick math and decided that somebody owed me... let's see, 25 years in the business, they owe me about $25.5 million, and about 24 years vacation.
CBA: [*laughs*] *I always thought the syndicated life was the life to have, but I've learned through interviews that it's not necessarily what it's cracked up to be. You had an opportunity to work on the* Tarzan *strip in the early '80s. Was it grueling work?*
Mike: It was an absolute kick in the pants! It was the most fun I've ever had as a cartoonist. I found it to be so enjoyable and so exciting. When I was doing the color guide for my first Sunday strip, I started to hyperventilate, and laughed so hard, I had to go lie down. I was so excited, so thrilled by it, it was the answer to my dream, really. Of course, over the years, I switched my focus from the bigfoot style cartooning, the humorous stuff, to a more realistic illustration. As far as I was concerned, that was definitely the most fun I've had. Unfortunately, the financial rewards weren't there, I was earning about as much in 1982 and '83 as Hogarth was making 30 years before.
CBA: *Was it the dwindling circulation of the strip?*
Mike: Absolutely.
CBA: *On a Sunday page, how hard did you have to work? How many days did you work on it?*
Mike: It took me three and sometimes four days for a single Sunday page. It included the scripting time, lettering—at one point, was doing the lettering myself—all the pencils and inks and the color guide. It would take me somewhere between half a day and maybe full day to do the painting for the color guide.
CBA: *Were you exclusively on the strip, or were you also doing comic book work at the same time?*

Mike: I was also doing comic books at the same time. I was doing *Warslayer,* starting up *Jon Sable,* and I was continuing with covers on *Warlord,* despite the fact that I'd given over the writing to my then-wife Sharon Wright. She wrote under my byline with the editor's knowledge. It was quite a handful.

CBA: *Getting back to the chronology, were you stationed in Saigon?*

Mike: Yes, I was. From '70 to '71, I worked in the graphics shop there.

CBA: *Did you miss the Tet Offensive?*

Mike: Fortunately, yes. When I got in-country, they handed me a book, a "Welcome to Vietnam" sort of thing, and there was a photograph of a gunship in the air with a curtain of tracers coming down, and I looked out the window of my hootch, and there was the scene, right in front of me. Just two years earlier, the area I was had been overrun, it was very interesting. At that point, at the point I was in Vietnam, the Saigon area was particularly quiet.

CBA: *Were you exposed to action when you were in Vietnam?*

Mike: Not a lot. The occasional rocket attack—I went up-country once, did some projects up there that took me a little bit closer to the action, but I was non-combatant.

CBA: *While in the service, were you continuing to draw?*

Mike: Yes, as a matter of fact, I was an illustrator, I worked for a combined combat operations and intelligence unit. In Vietnam, I worked for the 377th Combat Support Group in the graphics shop, and ran the night shift for a while during that time. I produced drawings for pilots for escape and evasion tactics that are still being used in the survival schools today. I had a friend who went to the academy not long ago, and he spotted my signature on one of the posters that was hanging on the wall. These guys've really got to update that stuff! [*laughter*] The U.S. Government is either extremely happy with my work, or they're too cheap to spring for the new drawings.

CBA: *Was this every day you were drawing?*

Mike: Oh yes, definitely. Graphic arts, charts, graphs, briefings, illustrations, aircraft recognition photos, everything and anything you could name.

CBA: *When did you get out of the service?*

Mike: In 1971, I took my discharge and went to Chicago to go to school at the Chicago Academy of Fine Art, where I studied under an old fellow by the name of Art Huhta. Art was one of the animators who worked on *Fantasia,* in the dinosaur scene. Art was a vast body of knowledge. While I was going to school there, I was also working a couple of moonlight jobs, commercial art, one at an art studio doing illustration, and another for a printer, doing paste-up and flyers and stuff like that, little flyers. After a couple of years, both of them offered me full-time jobs. The paste-up job was paying about four times what the illustration job paid, but I took the illustration job, because I was learning more.

CBA: *You wanted to hone your chops?*

Mike: Absolutely.

CBA: *You'd gotten married previous to going into the Air Force?*

Mike: Yes, I was married for the first time in 1967.

CBA: *Did you start a family?*

Mike: No, I don't have any kids of my own. I am married now, and my third wife has presented me with a bouncing baby 17-year-old son! [*laughter*] Ready-made! Mostly grown! Lauri and I have been best friends for a long, long time. We've been together as a couple since 1993. We've been married three-and-a-half years.

CBA: *Did you start looking at comics again? Was there a point that you left comics behind, and then…?*

Mike: Yeah, I left comics behind at about the same time I got involved heavily in girls, at about puberty. It was pretty much normal, back then when I was a kid, that when you got into early high school years, you sort of stopped reading comics, although I was still involved enough to have had *Spider-Man #1, Fantastic Four,* all that other stuff, the great Marvel revolution. The New Age of DC was actually coming back, and things like that. Then I turned my back on comics for quite a while. Then, while I was in Saigon, I ran into a fellow who was quite a comics collector, and he brought a few of his favorites along with him! Among those was *Green Lantern/Green*

Arrow, by Denny O'Neil and illustrated by Neal Adams and Dick Giordano. It was eye-opening, I didn't realize that people were actually writing stories about the real world, with characters who were believable. I always thought the Green Arrow character was more interesting, because he had no special super-powers or anything like that, just his skill and his personal drive and determination, philosophical outlook on the world, that allowed him to do what he did. And right then and there I knew that was the kind of art I wanted to do. I had my eye on comic strips, and I worked towards that end. I took the Famous Artists' School's correspondence course in cartooning while I was in Saigon, and it was actually an extremely good course! It was written by guys like Milton Caniff and Rube Goldberg… One of my other friends who took this course 10 or 15 years before I did still had all of his old, graded lessons, and they were graded by Norman Rockwell, who would actually sit down and put a overlay over the work, and draw or paint over the top of his

SAVAGE EMPIRE

Above and opposite page: *Before freelancing for DC Comics, Mike tried to sell this syndicated strip idea,* The Savage Empire, *which was later modified to become* Warlord. *Here's a Sunday (above) and six dailies (opposite) worth of samples. ©2000 Mike Grell.*

work and send it back to him.

CBA: *I think that was a lucrative deal for those guys, too. It worked out quite successfully, I believe.*

Mike: It certainly worked out for me. When I got back to Chicago, I discovered it was extremely difficult to sell a comic strip having anything to do with action-adventure or continuity; everyone was interested in the next *Peanuts*. Gag strips were the way everything was going, and when I walked into the Chicago Tribune one day and presented my portfolio, the editor looked at me, shook his head, and said, "If you'd been here 15 years ago, you'd have had it made." What he did do was steer me towards Dale Messick, who was doing, of course, the *Brenda Starr* strip. She was in need of another assistant to take some of the workload off her, and so I went and showed her my portfolio, and went to work immediately. I used to do just about everything with the exception of the layouts; she had another assistant who did the layouts and the lettering, sort of blocking in future positions and things like that. I'd take those layouts and tighten them up, and draw in ink everything except Brenda's face, and Dale would do Brenda's face after that. When I write my autobiography, finally, I'm going to entitle it, *Doing Brenda's Body*. [*laughter*]

CBA: *Or a movie, for that matter.* [*laughs*]

Mike: I figure I've got a million-seller on the title alone!

CBA: *How was it, working for Dale?*

Mike: Oh, it was great. It was educational and inspirational at the same time. She's a wonderful lady, and truly, one of the great artists of the comic strips. She probably never got the recognition she deserved, but she's one of my all-time favorite people, ever, in the whole world.

CBA: *How long did you work with Dale?*

Mike: Just two years.

CBA: *What's the genesis of* The Savage Empire?

Mike: *The Savage Empire* was the comic strip I had drawn prior to going out to New York in 1973. They were my samples; I was trying to sell this fantasy comic strip in New York, and I thought the ideal spot to do that would be at the New York Comic Convention. I figured it would be swarming with people from all different walks of life in the comics industry, including comic strip editors… I didn't see how they could possibly turn me down. After New York, I discovered that not only were they not interested in adventure strips, I couldn't even get in the door. Fortunately for me, at the New York Comic Con in '73, I met Irv Novick and Allan Asherman. Allan was working for Joe Kubert at the time. They both took a look at my portfolio, and Irv told me in no uncertain terms I should get my carcass up to Julie Schwartz's office and show him my stuff. I was unable to do it on that trip, but I came back and marched into Julie's office with my portfolio in hand, and started my prepared encyclopedia salesman's speech, "Good afternoon, Mr. Schwartz, can I interest you in this deluxe 37-volume set of encyclopedias?" (If you get interrupted anywhere along the line, you have to go all the way back to, "Good afternoon, Mr. Schwartz.") [*laughter*] I got exactly as far as, "Good Afternoon, Mr. Schwartz," and he said, "What the hell makes you think you can draw comics?" [*laughter*] I unzipped my portfolio and dropped it on his desk, and I said, "Take a look, and you tell me." He flipped through the pages, and he called Joe Orlando in from next door, and I walked out half an hour later with a script in my hand. Joe managed to see something in those early drawings that led him to believe I was worth taking a shot on. He gave me the script to draw a back-up comic for "Aquaman."

CBA: *In your preparations in attempting to sell* The Savage Empire *to syndication, how much of a continuity did you prepare?*

Mike: I had six weeks of Sundays and dailies.

CBA: *Did that ever see print?*

Mike: It actually has in the *Chicago Star*, a very short-lived Sunday tabloid.

CBA: *Did you do the color on that, too?*

Mike: Yes.

CBA: *Is there a relationship between* The Savage Empire *and* Warlord?

Mike: Absolutely. After spending some time at DC, I still had this desire to do that story, and I found out there was another comic book company starting up, Atlas/Seaboard, and they were reportedly offering a rather munificent sum per page. (In fact, it was easily double what DC was paying at the time.) I wanted to cash in on that, but also didn't want to jeopardize my position at DC working on the books I had. I went over, spoke to the editor, and pitched them on *The Savage Empire*, and they liked it quite a lot. I said basically, what I wanted to do was keep this under our hats until I had the book handed in; I wanted to be able to demonstrate that I could still keep my commitment to DC at the same time. That lasted about the amount of time it took me to walk from Atlas' office to DC— Carmine had very quickly found out about it. He met me in the hallway, and explained he'd spoken with the editor over at Atlas, and had been informed they had me tied up for two books a month, and wanted to know why I hadn't come to him with this in the first place. I said, "DC doesn't really have a great track record for the fantasy type stuff, and I didn't think you'd be interested." He said, "Let me be the judge of that." So I followed him down the hall to his office, walked in and he had to take a call while I was sitting there. And in that brief period of time, I realized he wasn't going to buy it! There was something wrong with *The Savage Empire* as it stood, it just wasn't going to fly. So, in that minute-and-a-half he was talking to whomever on the telephone, I revamped and revised the story in my head and extemporized a pitch to him. And he bought it!

CBA: *On the fly, Mike, eh?*

Mike: He bought it. He said "Run it past Joe Orlando, and if Joe likes it, it's cleared."

CBA: *Do you remember what kind of changes you made?*

Mike: Oh, yeah. Basically, the original concept of *The Savage Empire* was the hero, an archaeologist named Jason Cord, stumbles on a time portal that transported him back to Atlantis. While there,

e's sort of the catalyst for all the advanced development… and disasters that occur in Atlantis.

CBA: *The time-travel thing.*

Mike: Yeah, the changes I made, of course, were
transporting him to a land at the center of the Earth, a
combination of… oh, lord, a lot of things, from Jules
Verne to Edgar Rice Burroughs' *Pellucidar.* There was a
book written called *The Smoky God,* and there were
stories about Admiral Byrd's expedition and having
found a land mass somewhere beyond the North Pole
and speculation that there was a world at the center of
the Earth. So I put that all together, kept a few of the
characters the same—the character Deimos is the
same—and changed the… actually, the character relationships are pretty much the same. A good deal of
plot direction is similar. Basically, I made it an Air Force
plot, drawing on some of my own knowledge and
background, brushed up the character and made him a
little bit more three-dimensional, and there it was.

CBA: *Backtracking a little bit, your first job was an
Aquaman story in* Adventure Comics?

Mike: Right.

CBA: *Was there any reaction to when you delivered
the job?*

Mike: Yeah, as a matter of fact, Joe Orlando took
one look at the first page and shook his head and said,
"You can't do this anymore." I said, "What anymore?" He said, "You've got Aquaman mooning the
reader."

CBA: *Oh, I remember that now! The swimming?*

Mike: Right. It never dawned on me. I'd done
another panel of Aquaman sitting on the throne, and it
made it look like he was sitting on a toilet. [*laughter*]

CBA: *You've got to learn these things!*

Mike: Between Joe and Julie, I became known as
the guy who drew Aquaman on the toilet. Joe became
my mentor. When I would bring an issue in-house,
and he spotted an error in drawing, he'd sit down and
give me a drawing lesson on the spot, show me where
I'd made mistakes, and help with a lot of corrections.

CBA: *Was that good advice?*

Mike: Oh, absolutely.

CBA: *So Joe was your first editor at DC, and then
Murray Boltinoff?*

Mike: Then Murray Boltinoff. I'd just turned in my
first Aquaman job, and picked up another story from
Joe, and Murray was on vacation. He came back and
discovered he was minus an artist; Dave Cockrum and
I had sort of passed each other in the hallway, him
walking out as I was walking in. Joe Orlando called me
up and said, "There's something coming up, and I was
wondering if you'd mind if I put your name up for it."
Mind? Lord, it would be a steady gig! I needed the
work, so I said, "Absolutely, I want it." Murray started
me inking over Dave on one story, and I took over
from then.

CBA: *Did you have any conversation with Dave,
that he left in anger?*

Mike: No. Not until years later, and in fact, the only
conversation at that point was the extent of congratu-
lating him on the hard work he'd done, and thanking
him for having created these elaborate character
sketchbooks that had served as a basic bible of how to
draw the characters. I was at a loss for some of the
costumes, it was very difficult to get them accurate.
When I told him that, he just laughed and said, "I had
the same problem myself, that's why I did the sketchbook, so I could remember them!" 26 characters and
56 costumes, a real army. The thing is, with the exception of the doodad on the front of the Shirking Violet
costume, I bet I can draw every one of them from
memory today. After two years of drawing them every

213

day, it tends to stick with you.

CBA: *The main reason Dave quit DC at the time was because he'd requested an exception to the rule that DC kept the art, and he said there was a couple-page spread of a wedding scene from "Legion" that he wanted, because he'd put so much work into it, and he was denied getting it, so he quit in anger. Did you ever have a problem getting your art back?*

Mike: Of course I wanted my art back. It was very interesting, because at the outset, I was told they'd just changed the policy, so possibly it was a reflection of Dave's move. Maybe that was the eye-opener that made them realize they had to do it. I know Marvel was giving the art back, or at least some of it, not necessarily all of the stuff. There were people who were getting their art back. I think that kind of attitude of the company keeping the art formed very early on, and of course continued on with *Mad* magazine, but no one seemed to mind because *Mad* always paid so much that nobody cared.

CBA: *So it obviously wasn't an issue with you, right?*

Mike: It didn't become an issue, because I got all my art back.

CBA: *Did you find inspiration in the work of Neal Adams when you were first starting out?*

Mike: What, am I going to lie and say no?!? [*laughter*] Of course, I was inspired by Neal. He was probably the strongest individual influence on my art, with the possible exception of Joseph Clement Coll and Paul Calle. I went through a couple of evolutions in my art style. (Art is a very much a growth process, and if you stop growing, and stop changing and developing, you stagnate, and the sound you hear is the footsteps of the next young hot-shot about to run you over.) I really admired Neal's pencil work and the realism he put into the characters, the feeling, the emotion that he could generate. Interestingly, I always thought that Dick Giordano was the better inker, and that was because of his style and technique for the medium we were working in. Neal's line tended to be a bit fine, and at times, reproduction in the medium didn't do it justice. Dick's was bolder, and I like that quite a lot. Then I started doing the *Tarzan*

comic strip, and I went back and re-introduced myself to Burne Hogarth and Hal Foster; Foster was my mother's favorite artist.

CBA: *On the* Tarzan *strip, did Gil Kane precede you, or did he come after you?*

Mike: He came before me. In fact, Archie Goodwin called me up to say he and Gil were leaving the strip, and would I mind if he recommended me for the job? It was the second time someone had done me a favor, the most incredible favor you could imagine, prefacing it by, "Would you mind…?".

CBA: *That's Archie.*

Mike: Yeah, that's Archie. We had met several years before. Arch and I used to have our standard greeting of shaking hands and then falling on our faces, because we could both stand up straight and f forward and catch ourselves in this sort of push-up fashion. For many, many years, that was our standard greeting. [*laughter*]

CBA: *At the time, you were born in '47, so you would've been 2 26 years old when you were at DC? Even though Neal was pretty much over at Continuity at the time, did you seek him out at all? A lot of young creators would seek out Neal for support, a place to find work… obviously, you were pretty steady with work, but did you go?*

Mike: In fact, I met Neal because I knew some folks who were sharing space over there. Cary Bates was in and out of that office quite a lot, and he was working on *Legion of Super-Heroes,* and he introduced me to Neal. I'd drop in from time to time to see what w going on, but that was pretty much the extent of it, other than wh I first… not exactly when I first hit town, but fairly early on, Neal offered very graciously to allow me to come into the studio if I wan ed and share a space there. But I thought I was better staying wher I was, which was working at home and not having to commute. I lived in Brewster, which is in Putnam County, about 50-odd miles north.

CBA: *So, you were obviously mailing your jobs in?*

Mike: No, I would actually go into the city a couple of times a week and deliver them. It was only an hour or so by rail.

BA: *Did you adapt pretty quickly to comics? How many pages could you do in a week, for example? Or any given day, what would be your schedule?*

Mike: Back then, my output of pencils was between three and five pages a day. If you ask me when I slept, the answer is, I didn't. I fell back on the Frank Lloyd Wright system of cat-napping, I would work for 20 hours straight and sleep for an hour, then I'd work for another eight or ten hours, until I couldn't work any more, then I'd sleep for two or three hours. Absolute minimums. I'd get up and work some more, until I dropped. Joe Orlando's wife had met me when I first hit town, and two months later, she took a look at me, and said, "My god, what happened to you?" I couldn't understand what she was referring to. I took a look at myself in the mirror, and realized I had aged quite considerably in that amount of time! [*laughs*] Almost as bad as being in the White House. [*laughter*] During that time, I never turned down any work. If someone said, "Can you do this?" the answer was always yes. I'd take the job, because you never know when the next one's coming. Sort of explained why, in a very short period of time, if you look at the books from '73, '74, '75, I seem to have done everything, been everywhere, and drawn just about every book there was. That's not really true, but my name appeared in a number of titles all at once.

BA: *You covered pretty much most of the major characters, it seems to me. Batman, Deadman, Phantom Stranger…*

Mike: Well, Deadman and Phantom Stranger was a story together, but yeah, at one time I think I've done covers at least for just about everyone, including *Superman* and *Batman, Wonder Woman*…. I even brutalized the inking on a story Doug Wildy penciled for *Our Army At War*, I think it was.

BA: *After Joe's wife said that to you, did you wake up, so to speak, and re-adapt your schedule to not killing yourself?*

Mike: No, I was a workaholic for seven years. I can't claim to be a workaholic any more, but there's a downside to that as well as an upside. The upside of course being the more prolific you are, the more rapidly your name and fame spreads. And the downside is it's very hard on relationships and marriages.

BA: *And yours suffered?*

Mike: [*laughs*] Yeah, I'd say so. I was married the first time for 13 years, and the second time for five, followed by ten years of bachelorhood. And then I finally found my soulmate.

BA: *Cool. So, the first appearance of Warlord was in* First Issue Special, *right? Was that cool with you, or did you hope they'd start the series at number one?*

Mike: The agreement I had with Carmine Infantino was that it would begin in *First Issue Special* because we were trying to show that *First Issue Special* was a springboard for new features, and that would guarantee me a six-issue run. Of course, after about the third issue of the book, I was surprised to find a little blurb on the bottom saying "The End"; Carmine had canceled the book without mentioning it to me. Fortunately for me, about a month later, the regime at DC Comics changed, and someone canceled Carmine. Jenette Kahn kept up on everything that was going on. She looked through the line-up of books and said, "Where's *The Warlord*?" They said, "Well, Carmine canceled it." She said, "Well, it's uncancelled," and she immediately put it back on the schedule. Shortly after that, there was the DC Implosion, and it went from being a bi-monthly book to a monthly book.

BA: *With the implosion?*

Mike: With the implosion.

BA: *So, to what do you attribute the success of Warlord? Was it that it fell into the* Conan *niche of readership that transcended comics fans per se, and you got to a male post-adolescent audience? The book lasted for quite a long time, didn't it?*

Mike: Ah, yes it did! I have to say that far from targeting a specific audience with that book, I wrote *Warlord* for me. I wrote the story I wanted to read, and yes, I like that kind of stuff. I like the *Tarzan* stuff, I like the high adventure/heroic action stuff, and I wanted to create a format where I could do any kind of story—you could get fantasy stories, you could get adventure stories, you could get romance, you could get comedy—to create a format where none of this would seem awkward or out of place, if I chose to do it. This is one of the reasons I fought for years and years against the concept

of ever doing a map of Skartaris, because that would instantly lock me into defining boundaries of the world that was a world of imagination, and I thought imagination was the most important part of it. So, whatever was "right" for the readers, it was because it was right for me first.

CBA: *It's one thing you ran counter to a lot of aspects of fandom that were going on at the time, the strict adherence to continuity; and yet you were blessed to have a book that wasn't a part of continuity, that you could create your own, so to speak.*

Mike: I was very fortunate, I had Joe Orlando's backing in that. There was a very strong cry for continuity; they wanted to know where this fit in the niche of the DC Universe, and I said, "It doesn't." They were upset by that because *everything* had to have its place.

CBA: [*laughs*] *Even Sugar and Spike!*

Mike: Julie Schwartz created a phrase, "Call it the Grellverse!" [*laughter*] It didn't fit into the niche, so in order to explain this, there was Earth-1, Earth-2, Earth-3, and Earth-Grell. [*laughter*]

CBA: *That must've felt good!*

Mike: Yeah, it was great as far as I was concerned. Again, it gave me the freedom to explore all of it, and did not bind me to any particular continuity. I was pretty alarmed after I left the series and found they'd almost immediately inserted DC super-heroes. Julie had a great argument for why they couldn't possibly put The Warlord into the standard universe, and why they had to leave it the hell alone, and that was, very simply, in the DC continuity, Superman had already drilled through the center of the Earth, straight through, and if Skartaris had been there, he'd have discovered it.

CBA: *Never mind Cave Carson! [laughs] So, did your star start to rise at DC? You had your own book, you were writing, you were drawing, you were inking.*

Mike: Yeah, as a matter of fact. At the time I took over *Legion of Super-Heroes*, sales were relatively marginal, but somewhere along the line—I'm not claiming credit for this, by any means, there were a number of really great writers and other people involved with the book—but sales on that book really escalated very quickly. For some reason, which I won't claim credit for, the book became DC's number one selling title, and shortly after I began doing *The Warlord, The Warlord* became DC's number one selling title.

CBA: *So did you see a commensurate raise in page rate?*

Mike: I saw a raise in page rate, I got the same raise that everyone else did, and I've always gotten DC's top rate with two exceptions: One was Curt Swanderson.

CBA: *Swanderson?*

Mike: God, I hate it when I get old. *[laughter]* Right, there you go, I'm thinking of both guys at the same time! Curt Swan and Murphy Anderson! I understand that Curt *Swan* had something of a sweetheart deal for a time, and I don't know how long that continued, but I may not have been getting the same rate he was, or perhaps anywhere near it, but I never really expected it. And I think Murphy Anderson possibly had that at the same time, but I can't say that with any certainty. There was one other time when Julie called me up and asked me to do a pin-up illustration for the Superman anniversary issue, and gave me a list of everybody who had worked on it. I knew that John Byrne's standard was, no matter where he went, he got the top rate or he got whatever the top guy got plus a dollar. That was perhaps a running joke, but when Julie said that, I said, "Okay, provided I get whatever John Byrne gets, plus a dollar!" *[laughter]* When the check arrived, it was for $251! *[laughter]* It had an annotation, "Per agreement, John Byrne's rate plus $1."

CBA: *Well, you're a hard negotiator, huh?*

Mike: Oh, yeah, the gun is on the table.

CBA: *So, were you delivering a complete package to DC, or did they do the lettering?*

Mike: They did the lettering and the coloring.

CBA: *Did they have to approve the story in pencil form before?*

Mike: Oh, yeah. I would always send the story in pencils first. In fact, I never trust myself to work without an editor, I've seen too many disasters from guys who thought they were their own best editors.

CBA: *Did many editorial changes take place working with Joe?*

Mike: There was the occasional Aquaman on the toilet… *[laughter]* a few minor things, as far as storylines, working with Joe, but overall, no. Working with Julie was another case altogether. Julie had a particular idea of what kind of stories he wanted to tell, and would occasionally run a bit roughshod over my stories. As a for instance, I wrote a plot for a Green Arrow story that was being done as a backup, and it was actually my first attempt at writing. Elliot Maggin was doing the scripts at that moment, and I wanted a shot at plotting a story. I submitted the plot, and Julie said, "No, no, no, this isn't what it is, this is what it is," and he told me my story, changing it pretty much completely. The story that was ultimately printed had to do with a young boy who was going around essentially tracking down and killing Nazi war criminals using a sling with rocks, and the young boy was actually the re-incarnation of King David. My version had to wait until *The Longbow Hunters*. I had created the character Shado, and Julie didn't like it, so I just put it on the shelf. But nothing is ever wasted, nothing is ever forgotten, until the time was right. Years later, when it was time to revise and revamp Green Arrow, I pulled up that character and

updated the story a bit.

CBA: *Were you involved at all in the lobbying for the revival of Green Lantern/Green Arrow?*

Mike: I happened to be in a hallway one day when I overheard a conversation where Denny O'Neil was talking about bringing back *Green Lantern/Green Arrow,* and I walked up to him and said, "W[ho] do I have to kill to get this job?" He said, "Are you interested?" I said, "Oh, yeah!" Thereby hangs fate! That as a real kick. I learne[d] more about storytelling from Denny O'Neil than anyone else in th[e] business. He's still the best storyteller there ever was.

CBA: *So, when you were doing* Warlord, *and you were obvious[ly] doing pretty much a complete package for them, were you disgru[n-] tled at all with the situation with creators, or did you have your e[ye] on the horizon for self-owned properties?*

Mike: Well, yeah, I was naturally disgruntled. I was disappointe[d] that the Atlas/Seaboard thing didn't pan out, and I thought I had been unfairly dealt with by the editor over there. I stayed with DC and I always resented the idea that, no matter what you created, i[t] was sort of like working for IBM and inventing a new computer, a[nd] after 20 years, getting a gold watch and a pat on the back. The sa[me] thing happened with Walt Disney and Oswald the Rabbit. Basically Disney and I did the same thing: We went to where the pastures were greener.

CBA: *So, you stayed with* Warlord *for 50 issues?*

Mike: I was with *Warlord* for about 50 issues, but for a year or s[o] after that, my then-wife Sharon and I plotted it together, and she would write the scripts and I'd do the covers.

CBA: *What was the genesis of* Starslayer?

Mike: I got the opportunity from Pacific Comics to create a proje[ct]. I was approached by the Schanes brothers, Bill and Steve, who ha[d] this concept for a new company that would allow people to create and own their own characters, and thereby sharing a larger portio[n] of the earnings on it. You'd keep the copyright, and things like tha[t] and it was exactly what I was looking for. I had *Starslayer* original[ly] planned as a DC project, and it was destined to be a direct counter point of *Warlord;* instead of a modern man in a primitive society, I decided to go the other way around and take a primitive man and put him into the middle of a very futuristic society, and watch wha[t] happened there. It was actually on the schedule at DC at the time [of] the Implosion, and it had been announced, but it fell by the waysi[de.] So Steve and Bill knew about *Starslayer,* and they said, "I understa[nd] you have a project, and we'd be very interested in having you com[e] over and do it." I was actually the first person to sign with them, [but] Jack Kirby signed a couple of weeks later. But because Jack was Ja[ck,] he'd draw half a book while we were speaking! *[laughter]* He deliv ered his first, and it was printed first, but I was actually the first pe[r-] son to sign.

CBA: *Were you nervous about that? This is the first real independent publisher.*

Mike: I wasn't the least bit nervous about it. This was another step. I was doing the *Tarzan* comic strip at the time, and *The Warl[ord]* was continuing… in fact, that was sort of the point where I decide[d] that my energy needed to be a bit more focused, and that was the reason I stepped back from doing the artwork and writing the scrip[t.] I sort of phased myself back, and had a lot more time to devote to what I knew was the coming wave.

CBA: *How long did you produce* Starslayer?

Mike: I did six issues with Pacific Comics, and then wrote the fir[st] few issues for First, when I made the switchover. Pacific had not su[c-] ceeded in doing what they had intended, at least not very well, I h[ad] thought, and there was some organizational difficulty, and some other problems they just couldn't surmount. So I finished out the r[un] I had intended, and while I was doing that, I got a call from Mike Gold, who was involved in a new start-up company called First Comics. (One of my friends said, "First comics, then drugs, then th[e] baby-sitter winds up in the freezer…".) *[laughter]*

CBA: *You knew Mike from DC, right?*

Mike: Yes. He wanted to know if I was interested in coming ove[r] and doing a project for them, and oh, by the way, there was also a[ ] spot in the line-up for *Starslayer,* if I wanted to bring *Starslayer* ov[er.] I jumped on the chance. In fact, I was the second person to sign w[ith] First Comics. I would've been first, except they already had Joe

...ton signed, and that was because Joe was their art director. It was ...tty much a natural thing, that he'd be first in line. I signed on to *Sable*, created the concept for *Sable*, and agreed that after that, ...stay with *Starslayer* and do the launch with them, write the first ...w issues for them, and turn it over to the able hands of John ...trander.

...BA: *You said that* Warlord *was put into the DC continuity. So, ...u didn't have any say on that character after you left the book?*
...ike: [laughs] I thought I was going to have a bit, but when the ...w editor came in (and I honestly don't recall the name of the first ...a), I had set up a scenario where Morgan and Tara had split up, ...cause basically he was a jerk. It had been my intent that they ...uld stay apart for at least a year—a full 12-issue arc of continu-...—before they came back together. But this fellow believed very ...ongly in the sanctity of marriage, and felt it was wrong for the ...ro to be separated from his ladylove, so, the very next issue, they ...re back together again. All that was followed by things like issues ...ere they dealt with such compelling storylines as "The Secret ...igin of Travis Morgan's Helmet." [laughter]
...BA: Ooo!
...ike: Ooo, *yeah!* [laughter] Apparently, they were a little desper-...for a story to tell.
...BA: *With* Starslayer, *did you talk with John about the approach ...the character, or did you just let it go?*
...ike: We spoke about it, and from our early conversation, I knew ...had a lock on the character, and I just let it go. I was interested ...ough in *Sable*, and confident enough in John that I was able to ...lk away and be satisfied with what he did. Perhaps it was philoso-...y that comes with age, or experience, or something, or maybe it ...s just a measure of the immense admiration I had for his talent. ...t I knew that what John was going to do with the character from ...e point I left it off was going to be perhaps different from what I ...uld have done, but certainly better than any idea I had in mind at ...t point. I had already taken the character where I wanted him to ...as far as I had planned for him to go, and I was quite content to ...ve him in John's care.
...BA: *What's the genesis of* Jon Sable?
...ike: *Jon Sable* is a reflection of all the great African adventure ...ries I'd read when I was a kid, and my dreams of going to Africa ...d hunting big game. And I suppose a combination of all those ...ngs plus the idea that people were—at least I was, at that ...ment—tired of drawing costumed super-heroes. I was tired of ...wing muscle-bound guys in skin-tight suits, and I wanted to do ...nething else that would allow me to do more stories that dealt ...h the real world. In order to do that, I needed a character that ...ke all the rules, so I did! I took the standard concept of a comic ...ok character, which is basically the Bruce Wayne/Batman formu-...—by day, the mild-mannered you-name-it, by night, the dark ...nger—and I reversed it! I said, "Here's the deal: Here is a guy ...om everyone knows is Mr. Blood 'N Guts, he's Mr. Action-...venture, go anywhere, do anything for hire," which is also break-...the mold of the standard comic book character, this guy is doing ...or money, or at least, he says he is. I decided that his big, deep, ...k secret was that he was also a closet nice guy who wrote chil-...n's books. Everyone who knew him in his day-to-day life knew he ...s Mr. Blood & Thunder, and only a few folks knew he wrote these ...y sweet children's books. I think that was probably the hook, the ...g that made *Sable* so unique. I fully expected that when I started ...t book, I'd lose anywhere from a third to even half of my reader-...p, and I was wrong. I had vastly underestimated my readers, and I ...covered that at the same time I was growing and changing and ...olving in my tastes, so were they! They were looking for some-...ng that would satisfy their changing taste, and I'm quite proud of ...fact that people used to walk up to me and say, "I don't read ...mic books, but a friend of mine showed me yours, and I'm ...oked." I'd just laugh, and say, "It might have been cheaper if ...y'd just bought you some cocaine." [laughter] It's a source of no ...all amount of pride to me that most of my *Sable* readers are older ...I won't say more intelligent, but they have a bit more refined ...e in their reading than other people. I met Walter Koenig, of *Star ...*, a number of years ago, and he said, "One of my friends rec-...mended your book to me, and I really like it." I said, "Oh, who's

your friend?" He said, "Harlan Ellison." [laughter] There's a compli-ment for you right there!
CBA: *You had a lot of long-running books.* Sable *lasted for how many issues?*
Mike: [laughs] I don't know… a lot… a bunch. [laughs]
CBA: *I'll look it up. [Jon Sable, Freelance lasted 56 issues at First Comics, from 1983-88… Then, it was Sable at First for 27 issues, from 1988-90, and finally Mike Grell's Sable at First lasted 10 issues in 1990, each time starting back at #1.—Jon Knutson.]*
Mike: I probably stayed on *Sable* for 50-odd issues.
CBA: *That was a monthly book?*
Mike: Yeah. At one point, I had to phase back and just do the writing. At that point, I was also involved with starting up *The Longbow Hunters*.
CBA: *Was there financial rewards in the direct market?*
Mike: Oh, of course, of course. My annual income tripled. It was nice to see that kind of financial payoff, but even more so, I think it was very heartening to discover we had done something right.
CBA: *You tmaintained an interest with Jon Sable; did it wane?*
Mike: To this day, Sable is still my favorite character I've ever creat-ed—to the extent that I've just completed my first novel, which is going to be published in July by Tom Doherty and Associates under their Forge imprint. I'm working on the second novel in the series now.

Above: *Mike's interest in wildlife conservation is evident in this poster design he contributed to the London group, Eye on the Wild. Art ©2000 Mike Grell.*

CBA: *Great. Are you doing the cover? [laughs]*

Mike: As a matter of fact, I did paint the cover for the novel.

CBA: *So, you're bringing Jon Sable into crime fiction?*

Mike: Yeah. Action-adventure, he's still what he is and what he was, but considerably more fleshed out. Anyone who reads the novel will find things that are familiar, and will find things that are different. Sable today is a reflection of my growth as well, a certain realization that the world today is not the world it was 18 years ago, when I first created the character. Sable lives in this world, or much of this world, and if anyone thinks they know the end of this story because they've read the comic book, they're in for a hell of a surprise! The story does not track the comic book strictly. The characters are not necessarily the same, although the characters who appear are basically the same characters, but there's a hell of a zinger in there that, every now and then, will take them by surprise.

CBA: *When did you say that book's going to be released?*

Mike: In July. It's coming out in hardcover first.

CBA: *So, during all this time, you were obviously having success within the direct sales only books, were you ever courted by Marvel?*

Mike: I was, as a matter of fact. A couple of years ago, I was approached by Marvel to do a version of Spider-Man. I worked on the concept, ran it past the editor, worked on it some more, ran it past the editor some more, and five variations later, after it had been tuned and refined to the absolute max, Marvel suffered their big implosion, and the project evaporated and will never see light of day.

CBA: *Was DC courting you through the '80s, while you were at First and Pacific? Obviously, they got you for a period of time.*

Mike: What happened was that Mike Gold had made the switch,

he'd gone back over to DC as an editor. He'd been with them as a publicist prior to that time. Mike phoned me up one day, and said, "What would it take to get you back to DC?" I said, "What do you mean?" He said, "Is there any one character you like well enough want to take a shot at it, come back and do a project?" I always fe my work on Batman was not up to snuff, and wouldn't mind gettin another shot at that character, except that I knew that Frank Miller had recently begun work on a project called *The Dark Knight.* I said "Well, when Frank is done with this, it's going to pretty well define that character for a lot of years." Mike said, "I was actually thinkin of Green Arrow." I said, "Oh, yeah!" He said, "Think about this: Green Arrow as an urban hunter." That was the hook. We based th entire *Longbow Hunters* and the whole revision/reversion of Green Arrow, the return and everything else, on that phrase. Green Arrow as an urban hunter.

CBA: *Didn't that book take some criticism for graphic violence?*

Mike: Yes, it did, as a matter of fact. It got mentioned in Time magazine and *The New York Times* in the same week! *The New Y Times* put it on the front page, but they didn't mention my name, the bastards! [*laughter*] In the same article, they did refer to Mindy Newell's rendition of *Catwoman.* Mindy's a friend. Her father's a major league stockbroker on Wall Street, and she received a royal summons from daddy to meet her for lunch that day. She was reall nervous. She thought, "Uh-oh, here it comes." When she stepped off the elevator, directly across from her, hanging on a wall, blown up, wall-sized, was that article with her name circled in yellow high lighter about 20 times. She got a standing ovation from the office. [*laughter*] Her dad said, "You know, I've been on Wall Street decades, and never got my name on the front page of *The New Y Times.*" [*laughter*] My single regret is they never mentioned my name. They did refer to *Green Arrow* and books like it at the time "pandering to the prurient interests of today's youth." Actually, the truth is, that was never my intent. I took my stories, by and large, from the headlines. I never did one single thing to any one of my characters that hadn't already been done to other human beings. There's a wildlife shelter nearby, and when a friend and I took in a injured crow, I was pretty shocked to see the sorry state of some of the animals that were there for rehabilitation. I said to the lady tha was running the place, "How can people do this?" She said, "Hon this is nothing compared to what they do to their own kids." She was right. I was always interested to see how people's imagination read more into what I did than I had ever written. For instance, a young artist who went on to do one of the more graphically-violen stories that DC printed during that time, and seemed to think noth ing of it, took me to task in front of a large crowd at the Chicago ComiCon for a scene in *Longbow Hunters* where Dinah Lance has been captured by the bad guys and strung up in a warehouse and tortured. His opening statement was something to the effect of, "Violence and brutality is not good storytelling, it's just an excuse. He walked away and I didn't get a chance to say anything to him, and his wife was sort of embarrassed at the moment. Later on, I sa him in the lobby, and I called him over, and I said, "Now, explain t me what this is about? Give me a sort of 'for instance'." He said, "Well, for instance, I resent the fact of you showing Dinah being raped." I said, "Whoa! Excuse me, whatever gave you the idea sh was raped?" If you take a look at that book, the guy who has her captive only touches her one time, and that's to lift her head up, so of by the hair, and nothing else is ever shown. In that particular sto nothing was even remotely implied that she was raped, and it was never my intent that someone should infer that from what I had written. So, later on, when I did the monthly book, I made a point raising that point. When Dinah's in therapy, she uses the phrase, "People say, 'well, at least you weren't raped,' as if that was the worst thing that could happen."

CBA: *Longbow Hunters was quite successful, wasn't it? Was it collected?*

Mike: Yes, it was. Several years later, it was collected in a volum did a new painted wraparound cover for it.

CBA: *I remember that as being the last really hot book I remem ber, number one was enormously popular, falling on the heels of Dark Knight Returns and The Shadow by Chaykin.*

Mike: The most interesting thing that occurred to me surroundin

at was when I went to Singapore to do a conven-
on over there, and I was wondering why the fans
ere so rabid. A ten-year-old kid walked up and had
e book signed, and he said, "Thank you, you've
st made this book worth $80!" Pretty alarming.

BA: *How would you assess your career?*

Mike: A blast.

BA: *You still drawing?*

Mike: I am, but not a hell of a lot of comics these
ays. My most recent comic project was *Tarzan,* for
ark Horse. I did a few issues for them, and prior to
at, I did a Batman project with DC, and am current-
 making plans for the return of *Jon Sable.*

BA: *In comic book form?*

Mike: In comic book form, yes.

BA: *Have you ever considered self-publishing?*

Mike: Actually, only briefly, and passed it over for a
uple of reasons—the same
ason I don't think anyone should edit their own
aterial, publishing your own material reaches down
e same path. It becomes very difficult to remain
jective enough about the work that you can tell
m one day to the next whether it's any good.

BA: *Was doing Shaman's Tears for Image as
crative as the legends have it?*

Mike: I don't know what the legends are, but…

BA: *Well, McFarlane being able to buy McGuire's
seball, for one. [laughter]*

Mike: Any book that came out from Image at that
e did well, and it's difficult to say. Unfortunately,
u're almost back to that question of, "Is it any
od, or was it selling just because it was an Image
ok?" There was no question that at the time
aman's Tears came out from Image that it was the
solutely best venue for it, because you would easily
l twice as many copies with the Image "I" in the
per left-hand corner as you could with any other
blisher.

BA: *Anything else you'd like to add?*

Mike: Gosharoonie. *[laughter]* Yeah, as a matter of
t, there are a couple of things. I'd like to mention
at I've been doing and where I've been directing
y energy. I made a concerted effort a couple of
ars ago to spend more time writing; I'm beginning
think that's where I have perhaps the greatest con-
ibution to give. If anything, I'd like to be remem-
red as a storyteller and that includes not just
mics, but in prose, as well. I have written this *Sable*
vel, and I'm at work on another story and I've also
gun the second novel in the *Sable* series. It's my
ent that this should be a continuing series, if I can
d the readership for it. I'm going to be doing
other *Sable* comic project. I'm also tackling screen-
ting; I've been working recently on closing an
tion for a screenplay, and hopefully, before this
s print, you can phone me back and I can actually
ke an announcement. At this point, I can't, other
n to say there is motion towards, and things are looking very posi-
e.

BA: *It's gratifying to hear you're a novelist now, and good luck
h that, because by gum, we have to look at alternatives as the
ustry dwindles!*

ke: Thank you. Yes, as far as the rest of it goes, I haven't surren-
ed art by any means. I've done quite a bit of commercial art over
 last year or so. To the extent of painting the cover of the *Sable*
vel, sort of part and parcel to making this transition. I also am
ociated with a wildlife conservancy based in London called Eye on
 Wild, and I'm their North American Trustee. It's dedicated to the
servation and preservation of endangered species, plants and ani-
s, you name it, all over the world. We have projects that are
ng extremely well, including the rhino conservancy in Zimbabwe
t we were involved in helping get started. I've just produced

another illustration that's ultimately going to be turned into a large-
sized painting and poster, and we hope to get it out to the school
systems for all the kids to sign on the bottom, on the dotted line. It
contains a pledge to the environment, where all the kids can sign and
promise to help take care of the world we live in. Things are changing so rapidly, in just my lifetime. I've seen hundreds of thousands of
acres of forest land chopped down, plowed under and paved over to
be built on; I've seem the environment polluted beyond the bounds
of anything we thought even possible, and for the first time, people
are aware that the earth has its limits. As a reflection of that, we're
trying to get people aware at as early an age as possible that it's our
responsibility. If there's anything we're going to achieve for
the next generation, we've got to start taking care of it
now; the Earth can't possibly maintain another century of
development.

Above: *Mike Grell movie poster
design for* Return of the Jedi.
©2005 Lucasfilm, Ltd.

Get in the Game!

Come on out to the Bullpen and be a part of the action

RetroHouse Press is pleased to offer the latest issues available of **COMIC BOOK ARTIST BULLPEN**, the mag featuring interviews and art (presented in a beautifully designed format, complete with lots of unpublished and rarely-seen material, all in the renowned *CBA* tradition!), all celebrating the careers of some of comic books most talented creators. **George Tuska,**

Frank Bolle, Jack Abel, and **Fred Hembeck** are the first four recepients of the *Bullpen* treatment, and we hope to feature many more such capable professionals over 2005. Upcoming issues will spotlight **Terry Beatty, Tony Tallarico, Jay Lynch, Arnold Drake, Bob Rozakis, Skip Williamson, Mike Netzer/Nasser,** and more!

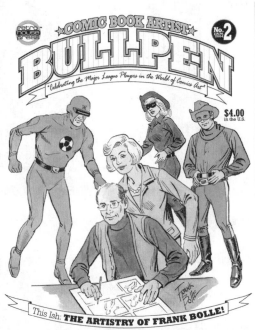

Comic Book Artist Bullpen #1: *The Tuska Technique!* Celebrating the artistry of Gentleman George Tuska in this 20-page issue featuring a career-spanning interview conducted by John D. Coates, with plenty of rarely-seen & unpublished art. New cover by G.T. depicts his most fondly-recalled character, Iron Man, doing battle with the gangsters of George's crime comics days! $4 postpaid.

CBA Bullpen #2: *Frank Bolle: Artist of Solar!* A life retrospective of the unforgettable Gold Key artist (who also drew *Tim Holt, Redmask, Winnie Winkle,* and for Warren, *Boys' Life* and Marvel) with a rare interview, plenty of art, and a new Bolle cover. Come learn the secrets behind the artist of *Doctor Solar, Man Of the Atom!* 20 pgs., $4 postpaid.

CBA Bullpen #3/4: *Jack Abel Remembered!* Special double-sized issue all-star tribute to the late renowned artist, Marvel Bullpenner & ranconteur, featuring comic-strip remembrances by **Joe Kubert, Marie Severin, Walter Simonson, Joe Sinnott, Terry Austin, Alan Weiss, Sergio Aragonés & Mark Evanier, Gray Morrow, Kyle Baker,** and many more. Compiled by **Rick Parker** (who contributes a new cover). $7.50 postpaid.

CBA Bullpen #5/6: *Fred Hembeck Forever!* The hilarity of Hembeck is on full display in this retrospective, featuring a long comprehensive interview, new cover, four-page unpublished *Li'l Freddy* strip, and more art than you imagine could fit in a 40-page ish! A must-have for any *Dateline: @*?!!* fan! $7.50 postpaid.

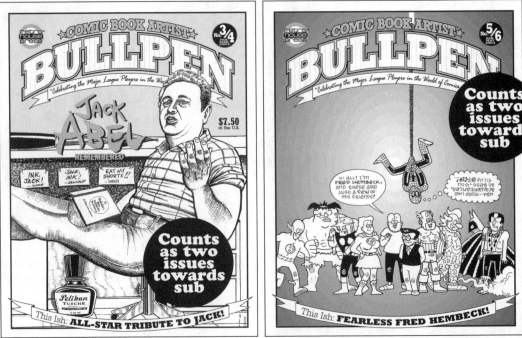

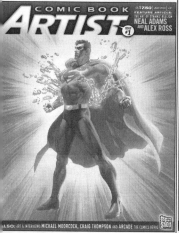

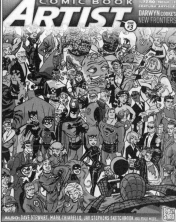

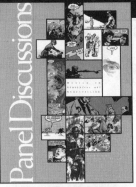

TRUE BRIT
CELEBRATING GREAT COMIC BOOK ARTISTS OF ENGLAND

A celebration of the rich history of British Comics Artists and their influence on the US with in-depth interviews and art by:

- BRIAN BOLLAND
- ALAN DAVIS
- DAVE GIBBONS
- BRYAN HITCH
- DAVID LLOYD
- DAVE MCKEAN
- KEVIN O'NEILL
- BARRY WINDSOR-SMITH

and other gents!

(204-page Trade Paperback with COLOR SECTION) **$26 US**

BEST OF DRAW! VOL. 1

Compiles material from the first two sold-out issues of DRAW!, the "How-To" magazine on comics and cartooning! Tutorials by, and interviews with: **DAVE GIBBONS** (layout and drawing on the computer), **BRET BLEVINS** (drawing lovely women, painting from life, and creating figures that "feel"), **JERRY ORDWAY** (detailing his working methods), **KLAUS JANSON** and **RICARDO VILLAGRAN** (inking techniques), **GENNDY TARTAKOVSKY** (on animation and Samurai Jack), **STEVE CONLEY** (creating web comics and cartoons), **PHIL HESTER** and **ANDE PARKS** (penciling and inking), and more!

(200-page trade paperback) **$26 US**

COMICS ABOVE GROUND
SEE HOW YOUR FAVORITE ARTISTS MAKE A LIVING OUTSIDE COMICS

COMICS ABOVE GROUND features top comics pros discussing their inspirations and training, and how they apply it in "Mainstream Media," including Conceptual Illustration, Video Game Development, Children's Books, Novels, Design, Illustration, Fine Art, Storyboards, Animation, Movies & more! Written by **DURWIN TALON** (author of the top-selling **PANEL DISCUSSIONS**), this book features creators sharing their perspectives and their work in comics and their "other professions," with career overviews, never-before-seen art, and interviews! Featuring:

- BRUCE TIMM
- BERNIE WRIGHTSON
- ADAM HUGHES
- LOUISE SIMONSON
- DAVE DORMAN
- GREG RUCKA & MORE!

(168-page Trade Paperback) **$24 US**

MR. MONSTER, HIS BOOKS OF FORBIDDEN KNOWLEDGE, VOLUME ZERO

- 12 Tales of Mr. Monster, with 30 ALL-NEW pages by **MICHAEL T. GILBERT!**
- Collects hard-to-find stories & the lost NEWSPAPER STRIP!
- New 8-page FULL-COLOR STORY by **KEITH GIFFEN** & **MICHAEL T. GILBERT!**

(136-pg. Paperback) **$14 US**

G-FORCE: ANIMATED
THE OFFICIAL BATTLE OF THE PLANETS GUIDEBOOK

The official compendium to the Japanese animated TV program that revolutionized anime across the globe! Featuring plenty of unseen artwork and designs from the wondrous world of G-FORCE (a.k.a. Science Ninja Team Gatchaman), it presents interviews and behind-the-scenes stories of the pop culture phenomenon that captured the hearts and imagination of Generation X, and spawned the new hit comic series! Co-written by **JASON HOFIUS** and **GEORGE KHOURY**, this FULL-COLOR account is highlighted by a NEW PAINTED COVER from master artist **ALEX ROSS!**

(96-Page Trade Paperback) **$20 US**

AGAINST THE GRAIN: MAD ARTIST WALLACE WOOD

The definitive biographical memoir on one of comics' finest artists, 20 years in the making! Former associate **BHOB STEWART** traces Wood's life and career, with contributions from many artists and writers who knew Wood personally, making this a remarkable compendium of art, insights and critical commentary! From childhood drawings & early samples to nearly endless comics pages (many unpublished), this is the most stunning display of Wood art ever assembled! **BILL PEARSON**, executor of the Wood Estate, contributed rare drawings from Wood's own files, while art collector **ROGER HILL** provides a wealth of obscure, previously unpublished Wood drawings and paintings.

(336-Page Trade Paperback) **$44 US**

WARREN COMPANION

The ultimate guide to Warren Publishing, the publisher of such mags as CREEPY, EERIE, VAMPIRELLA, BLAZING COMBAT, and others. Reprints COMIC BOOK ARTIST #4 (completely reformatted), plus nearly 200 new pages:

- New painted cover by **ALEX HORLEY!**
- A definitive WARREN CHECKLIST!
- Dozens of NEW FEATURES on CORBEN, FRAZETTA, DITKO, and others, and interviews with WRIGHTSON, WARREN, EISNER, ADAMS, COLAN & many more!

(288-page unsigned Hardcover) **$44 US**

FAWCETT COMPANION
THE BEST OF FCA

Presenting the best of the FAWCETT COLLECTORS OF AMERICA newsletter!

- New **JERRY ORDWAY** cover!
- Index of ALL FAWCETT COMICS!
- Looks inside the FAWCETT OFFICES!
- Interviews, features, and rare and previously unpublished artwork by **C.C. BECK, MARC SWAYZE, KURT SCHAFFENBERGER, MAC RABOY, DAVE BERG, ALEX TOTH, BOB OKSNER, GEORGE EVANS, ALEX ROSS**, Foreword by **MARC SWAYZE**, and more!

(160-page Trade Paperback) **$20 US**

CALL OR WRITE FOR OUR NEW CATALOG, OR DOWNLOAD IT NOW AT www.twomorrows.com

MODERN MASTERS SERIES
Edited by ERIC NOLEN-WEATHINGTON

WALLACE WOOD CHECKLIST

Lists Wood's PUBLISHED COMICS WORK in detail, plus FANZINE ART, ADVERTISING ILLUSTRATIONS, UNPUBLISHED WORK, and more. Illustrated with rare and unseen Wood work!

(68 Pages) **$7 US**

CRAZY HIP GROOVY GO-GO WAY-OUT MONSTERS #29 & #32

PETE VON SHOLLY's spoof of monster mags will have you laughing your pants off—right after you soil them from sheer terror!

(48 Pages) **$8 EACH US**

SPECIAL! GET BOTH ISSUES FOR $12 US POSTPAID

A new series of trade paperbacks devoted to the BEST OF TODAY'S COMICS ARTISTS! Each volume contains RARE AND UNSEEN ARTWORK direct from the artist's files, plus a COMPREHENSIVE INTERVIEW (including influences and their views on graphic storytelling), DELUXE SKETCHBOOK SECTIONS, and more!

VOL. 1: ALAN DAVIS
(128-Page Trade Paperback) **$17 US**

VOL. 2: GEORGE PÉREZ
(128-Page Trade Paperback) **$17 US**

VOL. 3: BRUCE TIMM
(120-Page TPB with COLOR) **$19 US**

VOL. 4: KEVIN NOWLAN
(120-Page TPB with COLOR) **$19 US**

Prices Include US Postage. Outside the US, Add $2 Per Item Canada, $3 Per Item Surface, $7 Per Item Airmail

TwoMorrows. Bringing New Life To Comics Fandom.

TwoMorrows Publishing • 10407 Bedfordtown Dr. • Raleigh, NC 27614 • 919/449-0344 • FAX 919/449-0327 • e-mail: twomorrow@aol.com • www.twomorrows.com